the ARAB–ISRAELI CONFLICT

the ARAB–ISRAELI CONFLICT

A History

DAVID W. LESCH
Trinity University

New York Oxford OXFORD UNIVERSITY PRESS *2008*

Oxford University Press, Inc., publishes works that further Oxford University's objective of excellence in research, scholarship, and education.

Oxford New York
Auckland Cape Town Dar es Salaam Hong Kong Karachi
Kuala Lumpur Madrid Melbourne Mexico City Nairobi
New Delhi Shanghai Taipei Toronto

With offices in
Argentina Austria Brazil Chile Czech Republic France Greece
Guatemala Hungary Italy Japan Poland Portugal Singapore
South Korea Switzerland Thailand Turkey Ukraine Vietnam

Published by Oxford University Press, Inc.
198 Madison Avenue, New York, New York 10016
http://www.oup.com

Library of Congress Cataloging-in-Publication Data

Lesch, David W.
The Arab–Israeli conflict: a history / David W. Lesch.
p. cm.
Includes bibliographical references and index.
ISBN 978-0-19-517230-0—ISBN 978-0-19-517229-4 1. Arab–Israeli conflict—History. I. Title.
DS119.7.L4667 2008
956.04—dc22 2007018280

Printing number: 9 8 7 6 5 4 3 2 1

Printed in the United States of America
on acid-free paper

CONTENTS

MAPS AND FIGURES

Maps

Figures

PREFACE

One would be hard-pressed to find a regional conflict as heated, prolonged, emotional, and with so much potential for catastrophic damage as the Arab–Israeli one. The Arab–Israeli conflict reached an acute stage, from which it has yet to recede, with the emergence of the State of Israel in 1948; however, the origins of the conflict can be traced back at least a century prior to this. Some would—mistakenly in my opinion—transport the beginnings of this seemingly intractable confrontation back over two thousand years, when religion and history intertwined to produce a volatile mix re-ignited by events in the twentieth century. Wherever one places the origins, the conflict, as it has developed since the end of World War II, has been a bloody one. By most counts, there have been seven Arab–Israeli wars, the first one producing the state of Israel and defining the parameters of the conflict, with the most recent one occurring in the summer of 2006. Each conflagration came perilously close to spiraling out of control in a way that often made world and/or nuclear war a distinct possibility. One particular Arab–Israeli war brought the global economy to a virtual halt. Regional powers, great powers, superpowers, and relatively small nonstate actors have been consistently drawn into the unpredictable Arab–Israeli cauldron, dealing with and against each other in incomprehensible ways. On the other hand, there have been innumerable attempts to construct peace processes and peace treaties between the combatants. Despite the tremendous courage of some leading figures on both sides of the equation, most of these attempts have failed, the result often leading to heightened tensions and a more volatile conflict environment. The dynamics of the Arab–Israeli conflict evolved and devolved into a seesaw of hopes for peace dashed by the reality of intransigence, hatred, narrowly defined interests, and violence.

It is a daunting task to try to describe, even unravel all of this in a way that is understandable, yet informative. When Oxford University Press contacted me about writing this book, I was actually hesitant to do so. But upon further deliberation, I decided to write it, mainly because I felt that while there are some very good texts on the history of the Arab–Israeli conflict, many of which I have successfully utilized in the classroom, there was still much left to explore on and different ways of looking at the subject matter. I wrote this book to create a vehicle through which college students can more readily learn about this immensely important topic, one that every day affects their lives in ways they do not even realize. It is a vehicle that hopefully offers a smoother and more comfortable ride than other ones in the literature. I wanted a text that was educational yet not overwhelming, accessible yet challenging, where a professor could assign a reasonable number of pages associated with a particular lesson in the syllabus and not deleteriously drown the student with pages of unnecessary minutia. It is a history that will hopefully offer the interested general public something significantly beyond an "idiot's guide" to the Arab–Israeli conflict, yet not smother them with the incomprehensible density that so often characterizes traditional scholarly works. Basically, the book reflects how I would introduce someone to this complex topic and, in fact, how I have done so in the college classroom for many years. This volume includes not only a narrative history but also an extensive selection of pertinent primary documents, bibliographies for each chapter, a glossary of selected terms, a chronology for quick reference, and a number of photos to provide some visual context. In addition to the book's combination of comprehensiveness and accessibility, another feature is the way in which the volume is organized in both a thematic and chronological manner. This will facilitate the learning process in terms of understanding dominant themes associated with the subject matter as well as their appropriate placement in terms of historical context and cause and effect relationships. Finally, in almost every chapter, I attempt to examine and delineate in a comprehensible fashion the complex multidimensional matrix surrounding each of the important episodes and periods in the history of the Arab–Israeli conflict: the domestic, regional, and international causal factors and implications of decision-making and concrete actions by individual, group, and state actors. Only then can one discern the obvious and oftentimes obscure rationale (if, indeed, one exists) for the onset of a series of events that forced their way into the annals of history—and into this book—collectively accumulating into what we call the Arab–Israeli conflict.

Objectivity is a funny thing, primarily because it is virtually impossible for anyone to be completely objective, especially on a controversial issue. We have all been fed various elements of the Arab–Israeli conflict filtered through the media, the classroom, film, and the written word. All of these things, despite best intentions, are subject to bias, even if ever so slightly, based on one's intellectual environment, upbringing, life experiences, and personality. I cannot emphatically say that this text is 100% objective, a difficult task to accomplish at best. With a subject as emotional as this one, people tend to see what they want to see, i.e., the degree of objectivity of those who read this book may color their impressions of it. I *can* emphatically state that I attempted to be as objective as possible, outlining a range of perspectives on a host of events the subject matter of which is replete with controversy, debate, and dispute.

As is always the case, there are many people who contributed in some way to the final product. Everyone (and there have been many) at Oxford University Press has been supportive, encouraging, and of great assistance to me during the entire process of writing this book, and I profusely thank each and every one of them. Robert O. Freedman carefully read a preliminary version of the manuscript and offered his usual insightful comments and suggestions. There are also a number of friends and colleagues who I am sure I have forgotten who offered helpful hints here and there. There was Denis Sullivan of Northeastern University, who I basically ran into on my way out of the hotel heading toward the airport at the closing stages of the 2005 annual Middle East Studies Association (MESA) meeting. He asked me what I was up to and I told him I was writing this book; he told me I really *had* to read Yoram Meital's just-then published book, *Peace in Tatters*. I rushed down to the MESA book fair where the publishers were all packing up their belongings, and I bought the last copy of Meital's book available; it turned out to be quite serendipitous because Meital's fine work turned out to be a boon for my research, especially in the last two chapters, which I just happened to be outlining at the time. Then there is my old friend James Gelvin, who had just published a (quite different) book of his own on the Israeli–Palestinian conflict; he unselfishly gave me some leads regarding finding photos and documents, as did my colleague Jeremy Pressman. I am sure there are more, and I apologize to those whose names should be included but are not due to my memory lapses—which is bad for a historian by the way!

The administration and organization of a work such as this are almost as daunting as writing the damn thing—they really aren't, but it just seems that way when you see the light at the end of the tunnel. For their diligent efforts and assistance, I thank Christopher Cornell, a student intern in the Department of History at Trinity University, and, as in most of my books, Eunice Herrington, the senior secretary in Trinity's History Department, who simply makes my professional life easier. Finally, of course, I thank my wife, Suzanne, who is always the first proofreader and barometer of anything I ever write (and has to put up with my compulsiveness to meet my self-imposed deadlines), and my incredible son, Michael, who at seventeen years of age has reached that confident stage in life when he thoroughly and fearlessly questions many of my assumptions and beliefs, thus compelling me to reexamine life in a way that has even led to some paradigmatic shifts in thought and interpretation, some of which no doubt made their way into this book.

NOTE ON THE TEXT

The transliteration of Arabic, Persian, Turkish, and Hebrew words into English varies quite a bit depending upon who or what publication is doing the translating. More often than not I selected the more recognizable version rather than a strict transliteration: for example, "Hussein" rather than "Husayn," "Nasser" rather than "Nasir" and "Faisal" rather than "Faysal." Sometimes the transliteration I utilize is different from that which appears in quotes from other sources in the text: for instance, I write "Hizbollah," whereas in newspapers it often is written as "Hezbollah." Also, I have selectively employed the important Arabic consonant ʻayn. I use it primarily for transliterated Arabic words whose pronunciation and spelling is enhanced by an indication of the diacritical mark; for other words, such as "Arab," the first letter of which in Arabic is actually the ʻayn consonant, I do not utilize the diacritical mark since its anglicized spelling is so commonly accepted in the English language. One hopes that few exceptions slipped through the cracks.

In addition, I have given a more neutral appellation to some of the Arab–Israeli wars over the years. The Arab–Israeli arena is still such a politically charged dynamic that oftentimes how a person designates a particular event says more about where he or she stands on the issue rather than being a reference to the event itself. As such, I simply refer to the war in 1967 as the "1967 Arab–Israeli war," rather than the "June War" or the "Six-Day War." Similarly, I refer to the 1973 conflict as the "1973 Arab–Israeli war," rather than the "Ramadan War," "Yom Kippur War," or "October War." Along these lines, since the international community, including the United States, still recognizes Tel Aviv as the official capital of Israel, I use this rather than Jerusalem in some references to Israeli policy even though the seat of government in Israel is clearly located in Jerusalem. The various sides to the conflict also give different names to bodies of water or tracts of land. I have attempted to be as neutral and objective in this regard as possible.

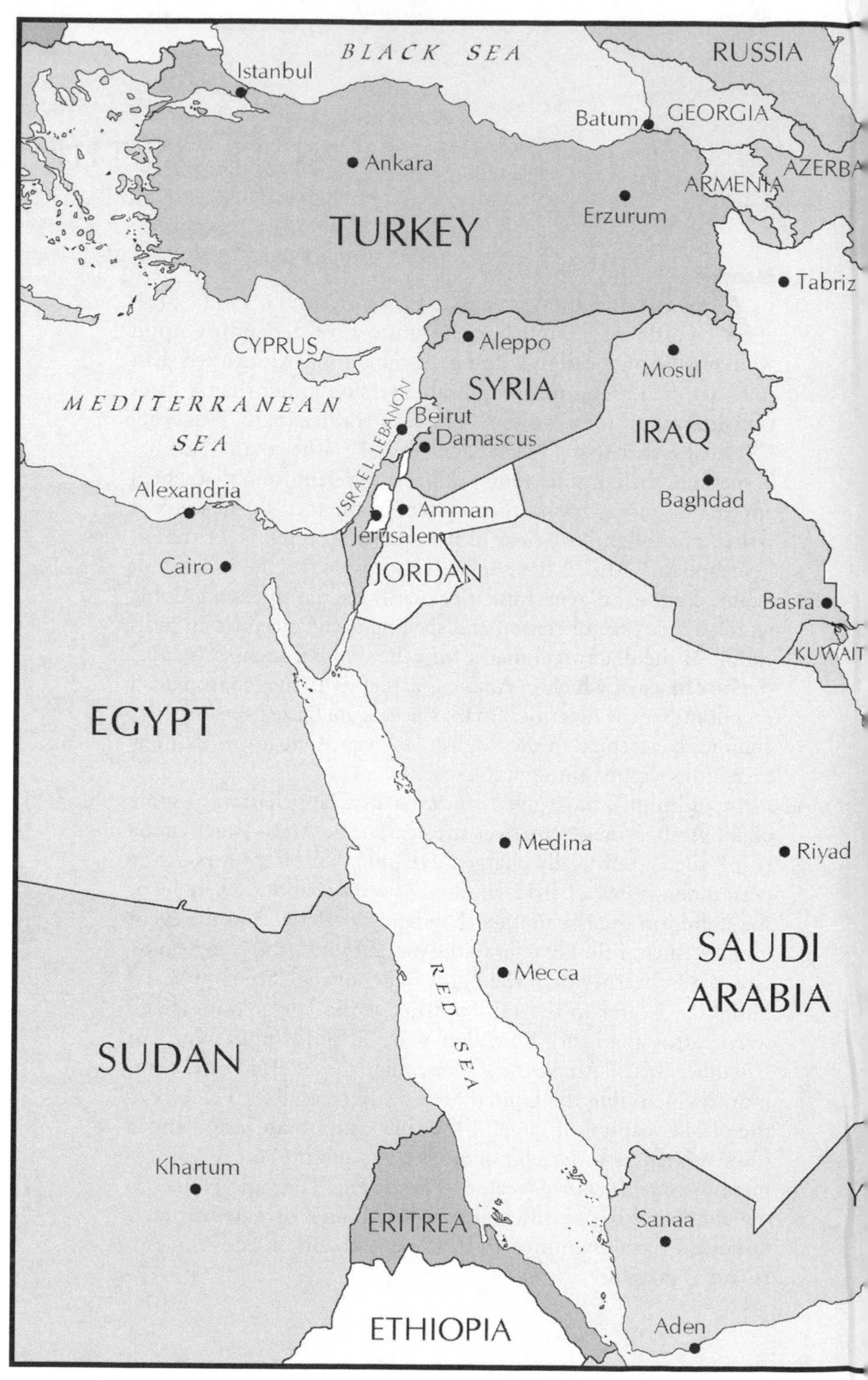

Present-day map of the Middle East and Central Asia. (Middle East Studies Association, Justin McCarthy, University of Louisville, © 2003.)

KAZAKHSTAN
UZBEKISTAN
Tashkent
KIRGYZSTAN
Samarkand
Bukhara
TAJIKISTAN
TURKMENISTAN
Ashkhabad
Mashhad
Tehran
Kabul
Islamabad
Herat
AFGHANISTAN
Esfahan
IRAN
PAKISTAN
Hyderabad
GULF
QATAR
Dubay
U.A.E.
Muscat
OMAN
ARABIAN
SEA
m. 100 200 300 400 500 600
k. 100 200 400 600 800

One

THE INTELLECTUAL AND PHYSICAL SETTING

In the lives of individuals, and of peoples, too, the worst conflicts are often those that break out between those who are persecuted.

Amos Oz[1]

Steven Spielberg directed and released a film in late 2005 called *Munich*. It was a critically acclaimed film that focused on the unofficially acknowledged efforts by the Israeli government to eliminate those Palestinian members of the group called Black September who planned and carried out the capture of eleven members of the Israeli Olympic delegation at the 1972 Summer Olympics in Munich, Germany. As is well known, all eleven Israelis were killed by the Palestinians during an attempted rescue by West German authorities. Reportedly, security surrounding the making of the film was unprecedented. In addition, it was released to the theaters with very little advance media hype, fanfare, or personal appearances by the actors hawking the film because of the controversial nature of the subject matter. Following some advance screenings to carefully selected groups, there were vociferous complaints from both sides of the Israeli–Palestinian equation that the film was too pro-Israeli or allowed too much time for a presentation of the Palestinian viewpoint. And this is a movie about an event that occurred thirty-five years ago.

I delivered a paper at a conference held at the State Department in early 2004. The conference, which was televised by C-SPAN, was composed of a number of panels focusing on various aspects of the 1967 Arab–Israeli war and was timed to coincide with the release of a *Foreign Relations of the United States* volume that contained official government documents and correspondence generated during the period surrounding this seminal conflict.[2] The first panel of the conference dealt with the tremendously controversial *USS Liberty* incident that occurred during the war. Briefly, the *USS Liberty* was an American electronic surveillance ship that was moored in the eastern Mediterranean to keep tabs on the progress of the war. On June 8, the ship was attacked by Israeli air and sea forces, which killed thirty-four and wounded more than seventy U.S. personnel—the ship barely remained afloat. The controversy surrounds whether or not the Israelis intentionally or accidentally attacked the naval vessel—and whether or not there has been a proper investigation that might definitively answer this question. Suffice it to say that the position that one adopts on this controversial issue often reflects more upon one's viewpoint on the Arab–Israeli conflict and U.S.–Israeli relations in general than on the specific incident itself. The audience was packed for this panel, which included some of the more well-known authors and commentators on both sides of the issue. Newspaper reporters and camerapersons from all over the United States and many from the Arab world were present to cover the proceedings. Moreover, there was a vociferous group of survivors of the *USS Liberty* and relatives of the deceased present at the panel. To say the least, it was an exciting start to the conference that made the succeeding panels, including my own, seem positively boring and anticlimactic. There was shouting, hard and driving questions, and expressions of disgust and shock from the audience, sometimes bordering on mayhem. And all this from an event that occurred forty years ago.

Actually, thirty to forty years ago is recent history when it comes to the Arab–Israeli conflict. Such shortened references as the Ottomans, Sykes-Picot, Balfour, White Paper, partition, Suez, refugees, Dayr Yassin, etc. resonate as clearly today to many in the region as they did in contemporary terms; indeed, many of these terms are referenced today, usually associated with someone who is trying to indicate that tragic history is again repeating itself. Americans sporadically are compelled by current events to search, rediscover, and reinterpret their own history. Involvement in a war often obligates us to do this. Certainly, the Iraq War in 2003 and its aftermath generated comparisons with a variety of past U.S. conflicts, from World War II to the Vietnam War. The hearings before the Senate Judiciary Committee of Judge Samuel Alito in early 2006 regarding his nomination to the Supreme Court focused national attention on the formation and interpretation of the U.S. Constitution. But this delving into history for Americans generally does not occur on anything close to a daily basis, which is not to say this is bad, for this historical lethargy is often brought about by stability and tranquility—even for a historian this is not a bad trade-off. But for many Arabs, Israelis, Jews, Christians, and Muslims who reside in the Middle East, historical reflection and comparison is often a daily occurrence. This is because almost on a daily basis there occur events that transport historical consciousness backward in time for comparative purposes, to locate a reference that provides context or meaning out of perceived chaos, to reinforce a particular argument, or even to offer a glimmer of hope. History is alive and well outside of the classroom in the Middle East precisely because the region is still so unsettled and burdened by so many volatile issues, not least of which is the Arab–Israeli conflict, maybe the most heated, controversial, and lethal of all of the disputes that still litter the world to this day. As such, one simply cannot understand the Arab–Israeli conflict, much less the passion emoted by its participants, without delving deeply into its history.

Having said this, however, I do not want to go back too far. It is at this point in many Arab–Israeli history books that a brief introduction to the three great Semitic religions of Judaism, Christianity, and Islam (and the theological relationship between them) is offered and/or an outline of the history of the land that now comprises Israel/Palestine going back to the Canaanites, Philistines, Babylonians, Assyrians, and Romans and/or an ethnographic explanation of the emergence of Arabs and Hebrews. I am not going to do this, however, and I am not doing so primarily for two reasons: (1) I believe it does a disservice to such rich histories and belief systems to offer a cursory examination of a few paragraphs or pages (to do them justice, one should consult the many fine works that treat the subject matter with the depth of explanation and delineation they deserve) and (2) to begin a book on the Arab–Israeli conflict with a brief survey of the religions and millennia-old histories of the region would, in my opinion, misrepresent the fundamentals of the dispute as it has come into being in modern history. Often, when I am at a cocktail party or some such gathering, during the course of which the inevitable mingling reveals my profession, someone who is lamenting the enduring nature of the Arab–Israeli conflict makes a comment along the lines of the following: "They've been at each other's throats forever!" Well, they haven't, and saying so, thus grounding the conflict into millennia of history, somehow rationalizes its endurance and cements the hopelessness of ever achieving a just and lasting peace. Just because the Israelite David fought the Philistine Goliath or because the Assyrians conquered the northern kingdom of Israel in the eighth century BCE does not make conflict between the Arabs and Jews of modern history inevitable. Neither does the assertion that, based on their respective traditions, since the Hebrews were descended from Abraham's son Isaac (by his wife Sarah) and the Arabs were descended from Ishmael, Abraham's son by his concubine wife Hagar, the fratricidal conflict of today was somehow fated.[3] The United States fought an intensely bloody war against the Japanese in World War II, yet within a generation the two countries were allies and economic partners. There were centuries of peaceful coexistence between Jew and Arab in the Middle East during the Persian, Greek, Roman, and Islamic eras. When a comprehensive peace finally does come to the Arab–Israeli arena, perhaps these long periods of tolerance will serve as the term of reference rather than the violent biblical and historical episodes that sporadically infiltrated their shared history.

Yes, religion at times fans the flames of the Arab–Israeli conflict. The city of Jerusalem (*al-Quds* to Muslims) is central to Jews, Christians, and Muslims; and it has witnessed more than its share of bloodshed over the centuries based on religious fervor. Certainly, there are today Islamic, Jewish, and Christian extremist groups that include the Arab–Israeli conflict in their skewed religious philosophies characterized by arrogant intolerance; they monopolize what they believe to be the truth (or the path), leaving very little, if any, room for compromise with such profound moral absolutism. They often utilize events and religious symbols from the remote past to sanction a particular ideology or plan of action. But there have been much more recent historical forces at work that have established the basis and parameters of the Arab–Israeli conflict, such as divergent nationalisms, imperialism, competition for the land, cold wars, socioeconomic development, nation-state building, demography, etc. It is into this multidimensional matrix that such cultural markers as religion and remote history have inserted themselves, complicating things even more so along the way, especially as they tend to be more relative and accessible at an emotional level.

Perhaps fifty years from now the Arab–Israeli conflict will have been peacefully settled; indeed, maybe the entire Middle East will be a model of stability. Historians a hundred years after that may then refer to the period between the end of World War II in 1945 and circa 2050 as simply the "100 Years' Middle East War." There will not be an "Arab–Israeli conflict" per se. It may be seen as simply one manifestation of the

The Ottoman Empire in 1795. (Middle East Studies Association, Justin McCarthy, University of Louisville, © 2003.)

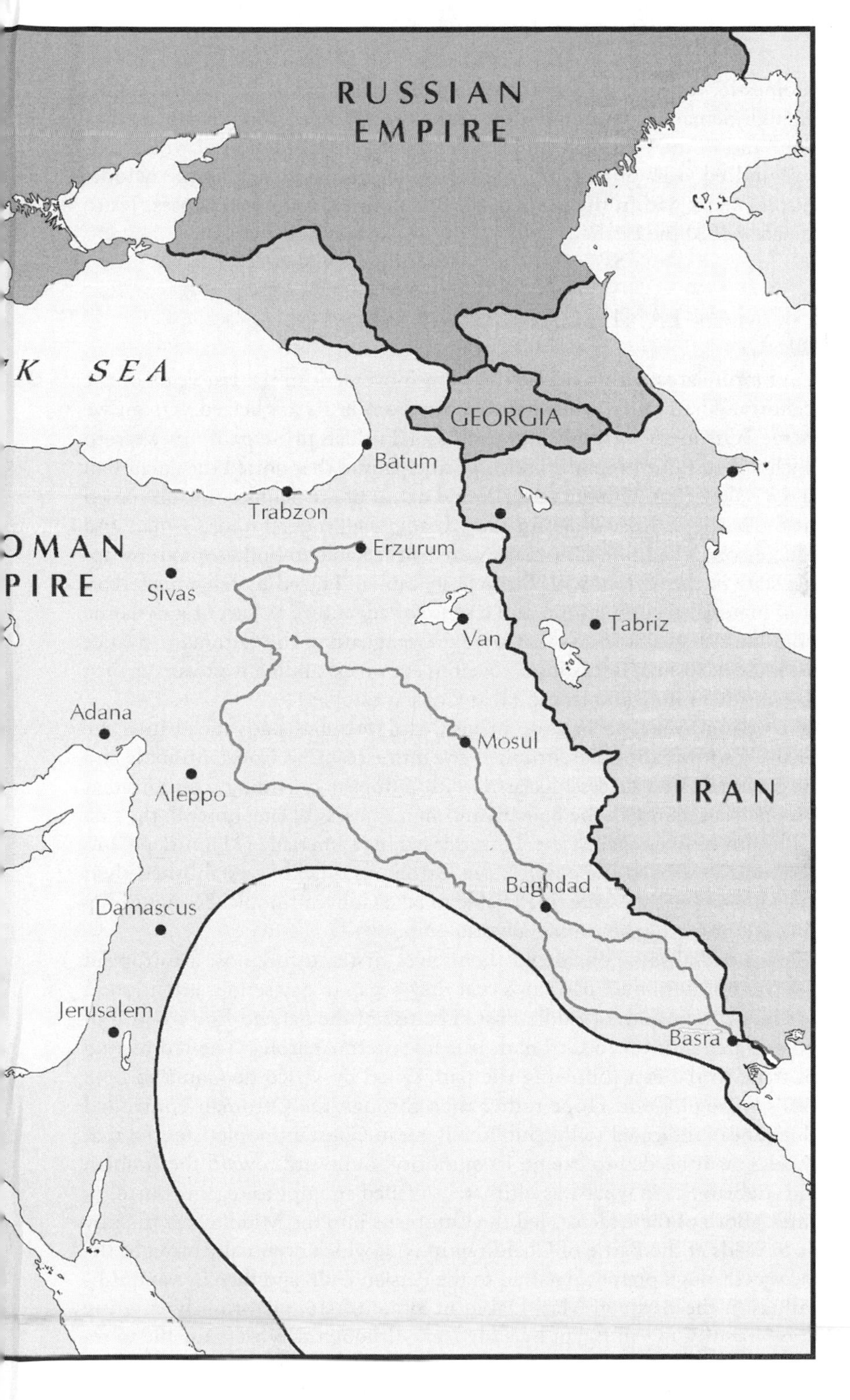
RUSSIAN
EMPIRE
K SEA
GEORGIA
Batum
Trabzon
OMAN
PIRE
Erzurum
Sivas
Van
Tabriz
Adana
Mosul
Aleppo
IRAN
Baghdad
Damascus
Jerusalem
Basra

deleterious domestic, regional, and international repercussions of the World War II era, which in itself demands an examination of the causal forces rising in nineteenth-century Europe and in the Ottoman Empire, the volatile combination of which culminated in a hundred years of instability and conflict in many parts of the Middle East. This history starts within the past couple of centuries, not when Moses, Jesus, and Muhammad walked the earth.

THE OTTOMAN LANDSCAPE

The Ottoman Empire arose as a Turkish–Muslim movement in the last years of the thirteenth century. The House of Osman (from whom in its anglicized version we derive the name "Ottoman") established itself as a Turkish principality in western Anatolia, which was just one of many Turkish principalities that dotted the Anatolian landscape in the wake of the Mongol advance and defeat of the Seljuks of Rum (based in Konya) at the battle of Kose Dagh in 1243. Under the leadership of Osman and his son and successor Orhan, the Ottomans were by 1326 able to build something approximating a state in the region, with Bursa as its capital. Fueled by religious fervor, the prospect of material accumulation, and a sense of adventure as part of a dynamic movement, the Turkish *gazi* warriors that were the vanguard of the Ottoman advance followed the House of Osman in casting a covetous eye on expanding westward against the weaker Byzantine Empire and its capital at Constantinople.

Officially crossing over into Europe in 1354, the Ottomans advanced into the Balkans, effectively surrounding the shrunken Byzantine realm of Constantinople and its immediate environs. After successful clashes with European crusading coalitions that expanded Ottoman suzerainty in the Balkans and an unsuccessful encounter in the first years of the fifteenth century against the Timurids led by Tamerlane ("Timurleng") to the east that almost destroyed the empire, the Ottomans quickly reestablished their control to the point where they were finally able to take Constantinople, extinguishing Byzantium in 1453, now truly becoming a world-empire.

The Ottomans had always considered themselves first and foremost a European empire, and it was not until the early 1500s that they began to pay serious attention to developments transpiring in the Middle East. The rise of the Safavid Empire in Iran in 1501 posed a strategic threat to Ottoman rule in eastern Anatolia. The redirecting of European trade to the east following the path sailed by Vasco de Gama in 1498 around Africa's Cape of Good Hope rather than through the Ottoman-controlled eastern Mediterranean indicated to the Sublime Porte in Constantinople/Istanbul that for economic reasons it needed to extend its authority southward toward the Arabian Peninsula and Arabian Sea in what was ultimately a failed attempt to regain control of the trade routes.[4] Both of these factors led the Ottomans into the Middle East, first by defeating the Safavids at the Battle of Chaldiran in 1514, which eventually brought the empire all the way through present-day Iraq to the Persian Gulf, and then by vanquishing the Mamluks in the Battle of Marj Dabiq in Syria in 1516, victoriously entering the Mamluk capital of Cairo in Egypt by early 1517. Although they were unable to recapture control of the new trade route from the Portuguese, the Ottomans were able to extend their dominion down both sides of the Red Sea coast, including the Islamic holy cities of Mecca and Medina in the Hijaz region of the Arabian peninsula. They also marched across North Africa all the way to Morocco, although their actual control over North Africa was more often than not quite nominal. Nevertheless, the Ottoman Empire was now Middle Eastern as well as European.

It was during the military campaign against the Mamluks that the Ottomans first entered and then established their rule over the area that became known as Palestine/Israel. Before the end of World War I and the institution of the British Mandate, however, there was never an official political entity known as Palestine during Ottoman rule. For most Arabs in the area, it was simply known as *al-Ard al-Muqadassa* (the Holy Land), and in administrative terms it was referred to as *Suriyya al-Janubiyya* (southern Syria, the southern part of *bilad al-sham* or Greater Syria) because it constituted the southern portion of geographical Syria, which at that time included the current countries of Syria, Lebanon, Jordan, and Israel.[5] The Ottoman Empire was at the broadest levels administratively divided into provinces (*wilayet,* singular *wilaya*) and districts (*sanajiq,* singular *sanjaq*—several of which usually made up a province). The borders of these provinces and especially the sanajiq shifted fairly often depending upon strategic, economic, political, and/or demographic circumstances. By the 1864 Wilayet Law passed by the Sublime Porte, Palestine was divided into several sanajiq, most of which belonged to the wilaya of Damascus. The sanajiq of Jerusalem, Hauran and Amman were administered by the wilaya of Damascus, although the Jerusalem sanjaq, which included the cities of Jerusalem, Jaffa, Gaza, Hebron, and Beersheba (Bir al-Sab), was made an independent administrative unit directly under the authority of the Ottoman sultan in Istanbul because of its religious importance. The sanjaq of Acre in northern Palestine, which included the cities of Acre, Haifa, Tiberias, and Safad as well as the sanjaq of al-Balqa, which consisted of the cities of Nablus, Jenin, and Tulkarm, came under the jurisdiction of the wilaya of Beirut in Lebanon.[6]

Population figures for the area that would come to comprise the Palestine mandate under British rule in the period between the first and second world wars vary and are grossly general. According to A. L. Avneri, by 1800 there were approximately 268,000 Arabs and 6,700 Jews in Palestine, which conforms with Donna Robinson Divine's "best guess" of between 250,000 and 300,000.[7] By 1880 there were 525,000 Arabs to 24,000 Jews, and by World War I around 85,000–90,000 Jews to 590,000 Arabs.[8] Muhammad Muslih, citing Janet L. Abu-Lughod's work, states that by the middle of the nineteenth century Palestine was comprised of about a half-million people, 80% of whom were Muslim, 10% Christian, and 5–7% Jewish. After the beginning of serious Jewish immigration to Palestine in the early 1880s, the population increased to about 690,000 by the outbreak of World War I in 1914, the Jews comprising nearly 85,000 or approximately 12% of the population.[9]

Until the early 1800s, political power in Palestine, as well as much of the rest of the Arab territories of the Ottoman Empire, was in the hands of local tribal *shaykhs* and Islamic religious leaders known as *ashraf* (singular *sharif*); indeed, Egypt would become virtually independent under the leadership of Muhammad Ali, who established a dynasty in Cairo by 1804 that would last until the Free Officers revolution in 1952 that brought Gamal 'Abd al-Nasser to power. Palestine and other areas of the Levant, however, remained under Ottoman control, save for a period in the 1830s when Muhammad Ali extended his dominion over Greater Syria at the expense of the Ottomans. For the most part, Palestinian Arabs throughout the nineteenth century defined themselves within the shifting parameters of Ottoman rule. Even in the early 1800s Palestine was of significant importance to the Ottoman leadership. Despite a certain level of instability characteristic of localized rule, agricultural production in Palestine and in Greater Syria as a whole continued to generate surpluses that were important in terms of tax collection and feeding the population. Local and imperial interests tended to clash over control of agricultural production, and oftentimes the Ottoman military contingents in the area behaved in a rapacious fashion; but the economy in Palestine, overwhelmingly agriculturally based as elsewhere in the empire, continued to grow. Palestine was also vital as an important transit route for Muslims performing the annual pilgrimage, or *hajj*, to Mecca, the security for which was a function the Ottomans took more and more seriously as the century wore on and as the sultans, especially Abdul Hamid II (1876–1908), emphasized the Islamic component of the empire. In addition, the maintenance of control over Jerusalem, the third holiest city in Islam and, of course, vitally important to both Christians and Jews, was essential in terms of padding the religious credentials of the Sublime Porte as well as proffering an alternative to Mecca and Medina, especially when the latter came under the control of Muhammad Ali.[10]

By the end of the eighteenth century, the Ottomans were compelled to begin an era of dramatic internal reform in order to stave off the increasing pressures of a predatory Europe, particularly Russia, as well as attend at the institutional level to the very real political, administrative, and economic problems that had beset the empire, particularly how to more efficiently collect taxes in order to raise the funds necessary for the reform efforts. Although haltingly started by Sultan Selim III (ruled 1789–1807) with his *Nizam-i Jedid* (New Order) launched in 1791, the nineteenth century was a period of dramatic reform in Ottoman lands, climaxing with the Tanzimat period begun officially in 1839. As such, in the first third of the nineteenth century, Ottoman officials had to negotiate good relations with local leaders in the Arab heartland in order to exert some level of authority in terms of tax collection. This began what would be a century-long process of altering the power relationships among the population of Palestine as power tended to shift from the traditional beacons of the various communities, the tribal shaykhs and ashraf, to those who were tied into the Ottoman system directly and indirectly as government officials and/or interlocutors. It was a slow and oftentimes disruptive process, but political power over the course of the century shifted from family, religious, and tribal elements to bureaucrats and increasingly a landed aristocracy, who by virtue of their wealth as expressed in landownership and economic advantage became the intermediaries for the Ottomans.

There were a variety of tax systems attempted by the Ottomans to replace the timar system (land grant in return for administrative service, including tax collection, and military service). The very existence of so many different types of tax systems was testament to the mounting problem of raising revenues. The military defeats at the hands of the Europeans at the same time the Ottoman military was adjusting to the new realities of modern warfare, and therefore in a weak position to exert the sultan's authority, ran counter to the Ottoman attempts at centralizing power first and foremost to raise revenues. This situation inevitably led to a clash between Ottoman authorities and local populations in the provinces, the former wishing to consolidate control without the means to do so and the latter stubbornly trying to hold onto their autonomy in the face of what was perceived to be the inability of the central government to effectively exert its authority. As Divine states,

Conquests of Muhammed Ali. (Middle East Studies Association, Justin McCarthy, University of Louisville, © 2003.)

> Commercial transactions and agricultural production expanded in ways that generated greater incentives and opportunities for the Ottoman state to intervene. Popular resistance, however, set limits to the exercise of imperial power. Effective resistance depended on political leadership and organization and, paradoxically, often contributed to strengthening the very process of political development that the local forces had set out to oppose.[11]

As such, it is not surprising that when Muhammad Ali sent his forces into Greater Syria in 1831 under the command of his son Ibrahim, for strategic and economic gain to offset his own domestic economic ills, the local population in Palestine and elsewhere, particularly those who had not been co-opted by the Ottoman bureaucracy, by and large tended to support the Egyptian expansion of power as a way to forestall the extension of Ottoman imperial authority, especially in the form of higher taxes without commensurate security and services. The first Ottoman attempt at centralization had simply rubbed the provincial populations the wrong way.

The Egyptians had raised expectations in Palestine that local autonomy would be respected and even expanded; however, within a few years the Egyptian authorities, ever in need of revenues, started to act suspiciously like the Ottomans. Palestinian Arabs therefore revolted in 1834 against Egyptian rule and locals who did its bidding, with 65,000 rebels in the Nablus region alone.[12] It was a tremendously chaotic period, one that belies the popular notion that modernity did not arrive in Palestine until the intervention of outside forces, first the Egyptians and then ultimately the Europeans. Some aspects of the Egyptian occupation were beneficial, especially in the economic sphere as Palestine became more embedded in the international economic system that was overtaking the Mediterranean region. But the Egyptian presence as well as the resulting revolt forever altered the relationship between the Arab elite in Palestine and the ruling element, whether it be Egyptian or Ottoman; i.e., political alliances became a necessity between the center and periphery in order to establish order and the efficient processing of government. By 1840–1841, elites in Palestine, what Muslih called the class of "officeholding urban notables," had for the most part been alienated by Egyptian rule and eased the way for the Ottoman Empire to reassert its control over *bilad al-sham*. As time would tell of the Ottoman provincial governor, "having no organized police force or armed forces, he could only rule with the help of local notables who knew the local population and had credit with it . . . and the local population sought the intervention of the notables in matters of conscription, taxes, and their other dealings with the government."[13]

At a more practical level, the Ottomans were able to push Egypt out of the Levant only with the assistance of the Europeans, who were all generally interested in maintaining the integrity of the Ottoman Empire to prevent a precipitous breakup that would, in turn, upset the balance of power among the European states. The European powers thus became much more heavily involved in the affairs of the Ottomans; indeed, the Tanzimat reforms launched in 1839 can largely be seen in this light; i.e., policies promoted by Constantinople, such as equality of all citizens, increasing government efficiency, and substantially reducing corruption embodied in such edicts as the Khatti Sharif of Gukhane in 1839 and the Khatti Humayun in 1856 (following European intervention to support the empire in the Crimean War), were meant in part to assuage European sensibilities in order to maintain the Ottoman lifeline of European economic, financial, and military assistance. This process certainly advanced the penetration of European commerce into Palestine and other provincial areas in the Arab world, especially after the opening of the Suez Canal in 1869. As a result, the process of economic growth and subsequent political changes and dislocations that started in Palestine at the opening of the century began to gather more steam, especially during the period of peace and relative stability that ensued in the 1880s following the accession of Sultan Abdul Hamid II in 1876, who also, because of the shrinking European holdings of the empire, paid more attention than any previous sultan to the Arab provinces. Ottoman lands, including Palestine, began to feel the twin pinch of European imperialism and internally driven reforms. This was a process bound to engender political, economic, sociological, and demographic change: "Increasingly, productive enterprise and political connection, not residence or relationship, emerged as the main measures and determinants of status and power in Palestine."[14]

The improvement in economic performance in Palestine during the post-Egyptian period was characterized primarily by the expansion of agricultural cultivation, especially in citrus and grain production. Combined with a growing population as a result of better security and health services, exacerbated by the 1880s with an influx of Jewish and Christian immigrants, land became the most valuable commodity in Palestine, and the prices for land skyrocketed as a result of the heightened demand for it. Two Tanzimat reforms had direct repercussions for Palestine in this regard. One was the 1858 Land Law, by which the Ottoman government could enlarge its ownership of state land while at the same time reducing the holdings, and thus the power, of large private landowners. The objective of the Land Law was to raise more revenues through more direct and efficient tax collection in order to fund the continuing reform efforts as well as repay debts owed to European powers from which Constantinople had borrowed to fund the Tanzimat efforts in the first place. The second reform policy was the Wilayet Law of 1864, mentioned previously, which was aimed at empowering the urban notables for tax collection purposes at the expense of the more traditional leadership classes, such as the tribal shaykhs. In Palestine, as well as other areas in the empire, the two laws yielded mixed results at best. The *fellahin* (peasants), who until then had largely situated themselves on the land in a sharecropping arrangement on state-held lands or as *musha* (tracts of land parceled out on a rotating basis among resident families of villages), accelerated the process of either escaping registration altogether or registering their meager holdings in the name of wealthy families, i.e. the landed aristocracy, the ashraf or local shaykhs. This was done in order to avoid heavy taxation as well as military conscription, especially as the Ottoman government was desperately trying to raise levies for their military forces in order to enforce the centralizing ethos of the Tanzimat and defend the empire against the Europeans. Many of the fellahin also simply outright sold their land to urban notables because they could not afford to pay taxes or pay off debts to local moneylenders, in most cases the same urban notables who were utilized in the first place to help them pay the heightened taxes—most of these tended to remain on what had been their land but now returning a percentage of their produce to the new landowners. In addition, corruption was not rooted out and efficiency did not increase due to a lack of trained personnel to carry out tax collection duties. What resulted was the concentration of wealth, i.e., land, in the hands of a small coterie of wealthy urban notables who frequently were absentee landlords—they resided in cities such as Beirut, Jerusalem, or Damascus while owning land in Palestine. Because of their wealth, and thus political power, they were able obtain for themselves and other members of their families important jobs in local administration and even in the central government. As Pamela Ann Smith states, these urban notables and other new landowners "were able to use their lands, position and kin to amass financial benefits and to expand their political influence in order to survive and compete in a society in which the accumulation and investment of capital was becoming increasingly important."[15] The Wilayet Law simply reinforced the trends that accumulated due to the Land Law, i.e., further shifting the loci of power from traditional elements to a new and growing landed aristocracy and commercial bourgeoisie. As it turned out, the Ottomans utilized these powerful urban families as intermediaries between the

Turkish (Ottoman) troops on David Street in Jerusalem in 1898. (Library of Congress, Prints & Photographs Division, LC-DIG-matpc-04769.)

government and the respective populations and as an instrument of control through whom the Ottoman government could do its bidding in what became something of a symbiotic relationship between the two sets of groups.[16]

Despite the changing nature of landownership, the overall economy of Palestine continued to grow and diversify, as it did throughout much of the Arab territories of the empire. The landowners generally were not engines of industrial ventures as they tended to plow their surplus capital back into land speculation or into an ostentatious lifestyle befitting their elite status.[17] Much of the commercial growth in Palestine as well as in many other locales in the Mediterranean zone fell into the hands of non-Muslim subjects, such as Greeks, Jews, Armenians, and Italians, who benefited from extraterritorial privileges granted by the Ottomans to European powers as part of the capitulation agreements over the years and the direct intervention by foreign consuls seeking protection and economic advantage (e.g., waiving taxes and import duties normally imposed on imported goods) for their nationals and for their respective governments.[18] Christian Arabs in Palestine and in Lebanon also benefited commercially from their more sympathetic relationship with the Christian Western powers. Although exports, especially in citrus products, continued to grow, Palestine always had a negative balance of trade.

This did not mean, however, that Arabs in Palestine were immune to commercial growth, but it was much more difficult for them to acquire the capital necessary for investment in industrial and commercial projects, especially foreign capital to which foreign immigrants had more direct access. Those Arabs who did prosper commercially tended to establish close links with the landowning class in order to enhance their access to decision making. Better transportation in Palestine, such as paved roads and, importantly, railroad lines linking Haifa, Jaffa, and Jerusalem with Syria and beyond, enhanced trade and commerce immeasurably and enriched the growing ports of Haifa and Jaffa as prime areas of ingress for European goods and services and Jerusalem as a major provincial center. One of the primary reasons for this industrial upswing in Palestine was the appearance of more Jewish settlers in the 1880s as part of what in Zionist lore is called the "first *aliyah*" (or ascent to the land). The rational and ideological foundation for Jewish immigration to Palestine and the beginnings of the Zionist movement in general will be elaborated in Chapter 2, but suffice it to say that Jewish settlers as well as other foreign immigrants, such as the German Templars and Protestant missionaries from the United States, on the whole had more capital available to them for investment (particularly from European-owned banks that were granted licenses in Palestine) as well as advantageous economic conditions secured through European pressure and Ottoman indulgence at a time when Palestine was experiencing an upsurge in economic growth, opportunity, security, basic services, and political concentration. Most of the land acquired by Jewish interests immigrating to Palestine had been purchased from the Ottoman state or the large Arab landholders, most of whom, as mentioned previously, were absentee landlords. The peasants who had been working the land either were employed by the Jewish settlements, left the land to reside elsewhere, or were evicted, the latter happening on a more frequent basis when the more self-sufficient, exclusive ethos of the second aliya began in 1904. Land prices rose more precipitously in Palestine than in other Arab territories of the empire due to the influx of Jewish immigrants and their demonstrated ability to successfully till the soil and engage in industrial projects due to their access to capital as well as more modern technologies and business practices imported from Europe.[19] For instance, land in the area of Jaffa by the last decades of the nineteenth century sold for 300–500 francs per hectare, whereas within two decades it was selling for 3,000–6,000 francs per hectare.[20]

As a result of this panoply of economic realities, Palestinian society became more stratified and differentiated, which was reflected in social and political divisions between rich and poor, urban areas and the countryside, and the coastal plains and the inland region—and increasingly between an indigenous population of Arabs and Jewish immigrants (whose population in Palestine doubled in 1904–1914, i.e., the second aliya, from 50,000 to almost 100,000), the former at first viewing the latter as economic competitors before competing ideologies and objectives raised the level of fear and animosity to a whole new level by World War I.

NOTES

1. Quoted in *Time*, December 12, 2005, 70.

2. *Foreign Relations of the United States*, vol. xix. (Washington, DC: Government Printing Office, 2004).

3. "Hebrew" is an ethnic and linguistic reference to the Jewish peoples, and it defines them within the Semitic ethnolinguistic group, which also includes Arabs and Aramaeans.

There are often groups, especially Christian ones, who employ the term "Hebrew" to refer to Jews of ancient times as opposed to those around the time of Jesus Christ and thereafter. The word "Jew" is a religious reference taken from the Hebrew term "Yehudi." "Jew" is the Middle English form of Yehudi (or Judah) through its Greek, Latin, and Old French versions. "Judah" refers to the southern kingdom of Judah (as opposed to the northern kingdom of Israel that was conquered by the Assyrians), which itself was conquered by the Babylonians in the sixth century BCE. After the fall of the northern kingdom of Israel, Israelites everywhere were referred to as "Yehudi" (Judah), i.e., "Jewish." For an excellent work on the relationship of Judaism, Christianity, and Islam with Abraham as the common patriarch (ergo, they are considered "Abrahamic" religions), see Bruce Feiler, *Abraham: A Journey to the Heart of Three Faiths* (New York: Perennial, 2004).

4. The "Sublime Porte" was mostly a Western reference to the Ottoman government or Ottoman court. It is a specific reference to the gate (porte) that was the entry into the Ottoman sultan's palace. Maintaining the tribal custom of consultation, the sultan would periodically meet with his subjects at or just inside of the gate in the courtyard, whereupon he would dispense justice and/or arbitrate disputes. The "Sublime" portion of the term in this regard is a reference to the wisdom of the sultan. There is still some mystery as to the etymological origins of the word "Istanbul." Most likely it is a corruption of the Greek colloquial reference to Constantinople of *eis stein polis* or "to the city," with there being no doubt that the "city" was a reference to Constantinople—there was no other city of note for travelers in the region. It is important to remember, however, that the word "Istanbul" did not come officially into use until after the fall of the Ottoman Empire and the abolishment of the sultanate and caliphate in the early 1920s by Mustafa Kemal Ataturk, the father of the modern Turkish republic. Before that time, even in official European and Ottoman correspondence as late as World War I, "Constantinople" was the name most often employed.

5. Muhammad Muslih, *The Origins of Palestinian Nationalism* (New York: Columbia University Press, 1989), 11.

6. Ibid.

7. Donna Robinson Divine, *Politics and Society in Ottoman Palestine: The Arab Struggle for Survival and Power* (Boulder: Lynne Rienner, 1994), 17. The Jews at the time lived primarily in Safad, Jerusalem, Tiberius, and Hebron.

8. A. L. Avneri, *Jewish Settlement and the Claim of Dispossession, 1878–1948* [in Hebrew] (ha-Kibbutz ha-Me'uhad, 1980), quoted in Yosef Gorny, *Zionism and the Arabs, 1882–1948: A Study of Ideology* (London: Oxford University Press, 1987), 5. Avneri continues the progression by stating that in 1931 there were 837,000 Arabs to 174,000 Jews and finally in 1947, just prior to the creation of the state of Israel in 1948, 1,310,000 Arabs to 630,000 Jews in Palestine. Using these figures, he calculates that the ratio of Jews to Arabs in Palestine since 1800 went from about 1:40 to approximately 1:2 by 1947.

9. Muslih, 13–14. Janet L. Abu-Lughod, "The Demographic Transformation of Palestine," in Ibrahim Abu-Lughod, ed., *The Transformation of Palestine: Essays on the Origin and Development of the Arab–Israeli Conflict* (Evanston, IL: Northwestern University Press, 1971), 140–141. Specifying further, by 1914 about 400,000 lived in the southern region of Palestine, including Jerusalem and Jaffa, 154,000 in the Nablus region, and 137,000 in the sanjaq of Acre. Among the Arabs, about 89% were Muslim, 10% were Christian, and 1% Druze. In Jerusalem, however, whereas half its population of 18,000 were Jewish in 1865, by 1884 two-thirds of its 35,000 were Jewish.

10. This would not be the first time such sentiments were expressed. There is sufficient evidence to suggest that in the early Umayyad dynasty based in Damascus, when Mecca and Medina were under the control of rebel forces, Umayyad caliphs attempted to develop Jerusalem as a viable religious alternative to the two holy cities. In fact, the construction of

the Dome of the Rock during this period has been offered as emblematic of the Umayyad attempts to establish a new center of Islam that was under their control.

11. Divine, *Politics and Society*, 39.

12. Ibid., 61.

13. Muslih, *The Origins of Palestinian Nationalism*, 23.

14. Divine, *Politics and Society*, 103.

15. Pamela Ann Smith, *Palestine and the Palestinians, 1876–1983* (New York: St. Martin's Press, 1984), 24.

16. Large landowners generally owned estates of over 5,000 Turkish dunums.

17. Smith, *Palestine and the Palestinians*, 24.

18. Ibid., 25.

19. By the start of World War I, the Jewish National Fund and other Zionist organizations owned approximately 420,700 dunums (about 94,000 acres or roughly 10% of available land) compared with 25,000 dunums in 1882, whereas the number of Jewish settlements increased from five in the early 1880s to forty-seven by 1914 (Ibid., 33).

20. Divine, *Politics and Society*, 127. According to James Reilly, "the area of cultivation expanded from 6,600 dunums in 1895 to 30,000 dunums in 1915" (quoted in Divine, 125).

Two
COMPETING PEOPLES AND IDEOLOGIES

ARABISM

Arab nationalism consists of the notion that the Arab peoples, loosely defined as sharing a cultural and linguistic heritage, should constitute a country, a nation-state, of their own. There has been a great deal of debate, however, over when Arab nationalism really came into being as something more than just idle thoughts by disaffected individual Arabs—in other words, when it actually became a movement worthy of notice and comprised of at least a rudimentary ideology. The various time periods given for the genesis of Arab nationalism often say more about the predilections of the person defining it rather than the validity of the argument. Most scholars who have analyzed the subject conclude that true Arab nationalism did not develop until the last phase of the Ottoman Empire's existence in the early twentieth century, particularly following the Young Turk revolution in 1908, World War I, and the imposition of the British- and French-dominated mandate system in the Arab world soon after the end of the war in 1918.[1]

But Arab nationalism did not suddenly appear in a vacuum. There had to exist general sentiments among certain groups of Arabs that fed into the development of a full-fledged nationalist movement when the circumstances dictated it and the opportunities presented themselves. What were the precursors to Arab nationalism? What were the impetuses for the evolution of Arab nationalist-type thoughts in the mid- to late nineteenth century? Were there any recognizable trends among the Arabs that can be labeled even in a general fashion? Most have described the period preceding the rise of Arab nationalism as one that contained the emergence of Arabism, a type of protonationalism that was comprised of the elements that informed nationalist movements but

Children in Nazareth in 1881. (The Otrakji Collection, www.mideastimage.com.)

did not yet define or appear broad enough to suggest clear-cut claims for nationhood, in this case, separation from the Ottoman Empire.

As outlined in the previous chapter, in the nineteenth century there occurred a great deal of change in Palestine due to the Ottoman reform efforts, which had political as well as social ramifications, particularly in education and the undermining of the traditional guild associations. Combined with the invasion by Muhammad Ali's Egypt and the increasing encroachment of the European powers and integration into the European-dominated economic system in the Mediterranean region, the whole political and socioeconomic structure of Palestinian society was transformed. This was no less the case in other parts of the Arab world that also experienced various levels of Ottoman reform during the Tanzimat era, European intrusion, and their own unique circumstances to produce similar domestic repercussions. Nowhere was this more apparent than in Greater Syria, including Palestine, which was the one region in the Arab world where the Ottoman Empire's control extended with the most depth all the way up to World War I.

Whenever there is change, there exist a variety of reactions to that change. It takes a reinforcing, supportive form among those whose political, economic, and/or social positions are enhanced as a result; it assumes a reformist and sometimes oppositional trend among those whose political, economic, and/or social positions are deleteriously affected. As the Ottoman Empire began to experience increasing military and economic pressure from the European powers through most of the nineteenth century and into the early twentieth century, a number of Ottoman citizens, among whom many were

Ottoman territorial losses between 1878 and the beginning of the Balkan wars in 1912. (Middle East Studies Association, Justin McCarthy, University of Louisville, © 2003.)

Arab Muslims, became concerned about the welfare of the Ottoman state, indeed, the Muslim world in general—could the empire, could Islam, survive the onslaught? The encroachment by Europe assumed many different shapes and sizes, but it became most noticeable with the extension of de facto European rule and the emergence of independence movements supported by European powers that plagued the empire and became more and more commonplace. France absorbed Algeria in 1830, the same year the Greeks, supported by a bevy of European powers, won their independence from the Ottomans. Serbia, Romania, and Bosnia-Herzegovina, following the Congress of Berlin, detached themselves from the empire in 1878. Tunisia fell to the French in 1881, and after bankruptcy, Egypt fell to the British in 1882; indeed, by this time the so-called Eastern Question became not how to best maintain the integrity of the empire but how best to oversee the orderly breakup of the once formidable Ottoman realm.[2] Bulgaria won its independence in 1908, Libya was taken by the Italians in 1911, and for good measure, although it was not a part of the Ottoman Empire, the French officially colonized Morocco in 1912. The Ottoman realm was contracting rapidly, to the point where, ethnically, the Arab element was roughly equal to the Turks in terms of population by the second half of the nineteenth century. This would be a reality that Ottoman Sultan Abdul-Hamid II would recognize by sanctioning more infrastructural improvement and reinforcing mutual cultural symbols in the Arab provinces. He also aligned with and appointed leading Arab elements, typically the traditional noble class, to official or quasi-official government positions. It was also this reality that emboldened many Arabs to question Constantinople's policies and raise demands befitting their real and perceived enhanced status within the empire.

Along with these changes there were also a number of other developments that influenced the rise of an Arabist impulse, i.e., a more widespread self-awareness of a common heritage, language, and culture. George Antonius, in his landmark book *The Arab Awakening*, described a literary renaissance in the Levant. In large measure this was engineered by the increased emphasis on secular education throughout the region compelled by the Tanzimat reforms and the building of private schools at all levels of education by American protestant missionaries: notably, the Syrian Protestant College opened in 1866, which later became the American University in Beirut.[3] This literary awakening, according to Antonius, was primarily carried forward by Lebanese Christian Arabs since the American missionaries' proselytizing and educational efforts were confined by Ottoman authorities to the non-Muslim population. While this theory has largely been abandoned as a causal factor of Arab nationalism, as put forth by Antonius, it is clear that it was one of a confluence of forces that shaped an Arabist impulse. More availability of printing presses and better modes of communication due to the Ottoman Empire's modernization efforts as well as European influence spread the written word through books and, importantly, a surge in the number of newspapers published in Arab cities. This tended to expose a growing educated stratum of Arab society to new ideas and ideologies emanating from Europe and beyond. It better allowed the transmission of these ideas to classes of Arabs hitherto confined to only the basic Islam-based education of the traditional *madrasa*; indeed, it "invited the masses into history."[4] Not only the transportation of goods and soldiers but also the global enlargement of the cross-cultural interaction of thought was facilitated by the international osmosis of the Industrial Revolution. In many ways, this was an early manifestation of globalization. And just as today's globalization has transnationalized politics, economy, and culture, so has it compelled a number of groups threatened by cultural diffusion to reinforce and solidify their identity when faced with what they perceive as an almost irreversible trend unless immediate measures of unity and action are implemented. The 1873 depression (which some economists contend lasted in effect into the 1890s), resulting from the dislocating socioeconomic repercussions of industrialization and subsequent globalization, produced a myriad of responses the world over. As James L. Gelvin writes,

> In every country hit by the depression, popular movements emerged. The ideologies expressed by these movements reflected local conditions and conventions: thus, communism, trade unionism, and anarchism in the cities and factories of Western Europe and North America; populism on the Great Plains of North America; and anti-Semitism in any place in Europe where Jews could be found. In the Middle East, discontent was often channeled into constitutionalism.[5]

In the Middle East, in addition to the liberal constitutionalists, there was an Islamist response, both of which in different ways would contribute to the later emergence of Arab nationalism.

Jamal al-Din al-Afghani (1838-1897), the peripatetic Islamist from Iran, is generally credited with having galvanized the pan-Islamist movement in the Middle East in the 1880s and 1890s in an attempt to protect Islamic lands from European imperialism. He was employed in the court of Abd al-Hamid II in the 1890s, who used al-Afghani to help promulgate his own pan-Islamist doctrine. With the Ottoman Empire much more Islamic by that time due to the loss of most of its Christian Balkan territories,

Jamal al-Din al-Afghani

The peripatetic Jamal al-Din al-Afghani was one of the most important figures in the Muslim Middle East in the nineteenth century. Almost single-handedly he shaped and developed a Muslim response to the heightened pressure applied by increasingly voracious European powers. As Sylvia Haim noted,

> The assault which Islam had to endure in the nineteenth century was twofold. It consisted, in the first place, of military attack on Muslim states or their political subjugation by different European powers, and, in the second place, of criticism of Islam as a system of beliefs and a way of life, a way of life that was belittled, ridiculed, and made to seem backward and barbaric in comparison with the achievements of Western learning, philosophy, and technical advance.*

Al-Afghani was born in 1838 as Jamal al-Din al-Asadabai in modern-day Iran, and he was most certainly a Shiite Muslim. He changed his surname to "al-Afghani," i.e., indicating that he was from Sunni-dominated Afghanistan, outside of Iran, probably to hide his Shiite and "Persian" origins in order to be more acceptable to the dominant Sunni Muslim population elsewhere in the Middle East.

Al-Afghani's basic call was for Muslim unity and solidarity (*asabiyya*) in order to ward off and defend the Islamic world from the predatory machinations of Europe.

It was not so much that he was a man devoted to Islam, but rather he saw the Islamic religion as the most efficient and readily available unifying element in the region. He believed that "the Islamic peoples... were in a deplorable situation; the states which ought to protect them and procure for them a good life were weak, misgoverned, and the prey of European ambitions. To remedy this... the Muslims had to take matters into their own hands; they had to force, even terrorize, their rulers into governing efficiently, and they had to band together in order to present a powerful and united front."** In this, al-Afghani gave rise to pan-Islamism in the late nineteenth century, a movement that was also exploited by the Ottoman Empire in its own attempts to defend its lands against European encroachment; indeed, the Ottoman Sultan Abdul Hamid II essentially employed al-Afghani for a time to organize pan-Islamist support for the Sublime Porte. In his travels to spread the word for his cause, al-Afghani spent time in Afghanistan, Egypt, Paris (where he edited the influential newspaper *al-'Urwa al-wuthqa* or *The Indissoluble Link*), Russia, India, Istanbul, and toward the end of his life back in Iran, where he helped arrange the assassination of the Qajar shah, Nasser al-Din, in 1896—al-Afghani was expelled and a year later died in exile.

Al-Afghani is so important because he laid the foundation for an activist Muslim response in the Middle East to their increasingly weak condition. In a way, he advocated a nationalistic ideological response not unlike that which was occurring contemporaneously in Europe, although rather than the unifying element of a "nation" being language, ethnicity, or a shared heritage, it was Islam. His response bridged several composite features of the Muslim Middle East at the time that would separate in coming decades under the leadership of such men as Muhammad Abduh, who was close to al-Afghani for fifteen years upon the latter's extended stay in Egypt. It was Abduh who was so pivotal, along with al-Afghani, to the rise of the *salafiyya* movement, taken from the term *salaf* or "ancestors," meant as an original reference by al-Afghani to a return to the greatness of the early Muslims. The salafiyya movement became synonymous with pan-Islamism, and under Abduh's influence it developed into an Islamic modernist response to European imperialism, i.e., a rationalist Islam that was less dogmatic and, as such, compatible with science and technology, even if emanating from the West. Another al-Afghani disciple, the Syrian Rashid Rida, was also a salafist; but he adopted a much more puritanical view of Islam than Abduh and became a supporter of Saudi Wahabism, which followed the rigid neo-Hanbalite legal school of Sunni Islam. In a way, Rida helped lay the foundation for the rise in the twentieth century of a much more virulently anti-Western form of Islamism (or Islamic fundamentalism) that in many ways rejected the more accommodationist paradigm of Abduh's school. With the intervening events of accumulated history as well as a myriad of more extreme interpretations along the way, one cannot discern the roots of someone such as Osama bin Laden and his al-Qa'ida transnational terrorist network without going back to the pan-Islamist movement begun by al-Afghani.

In addition, with the salafiyya movement's focus on early Islam, the predominant Arab role in its rise to greatness was emphasized—or rediscovered. Merging with al-Afghani's more activist and politicized response to European pressure, the salafiyya movement began to develop a more noticeable Arab consciousness in an Ottoman Turkish milieu in the late nineteenth and early twentieth centuries. None of these men mentioned could be considered Arab nationalists, but the movement they generated and perpetuated also directly contributed to the rise of Arab nationalist sentiments before World War I and the development of a distinct secular Arab nationalist ideology in the war's aftermath during the imposition of the European mandate system in the Middle East.

*Sylvia G. Haim, *Arab Nationalism: An Anthology* (Berkeley: University of California Press, 1962), 6.

**Haim, 9.

Abd al-Hamid II saw Islam as a kind of social cement to help unify the remaining Ottoman lands in a last-ditch effort to ward off further European pressure and encroachment.[6] Although it would turn out to be more fiction than fact, the sultan, who appropriately began to emphasize his role as caliph, hoped the universal appeal of his position and his potential call for a *jihad* would provide Constantinople with some leverage vis-à-vis the European powers, particularly Britain and France, who had sizeable Muslim populations within their respective colonial empires that could potentially be incited against them.

But the pan-Islamist movement also reflected a genuine desire among many Muslims in the Arab world to rediscover their own glorious past as a way to embolden the present in the midst of the Ottoman inability to protect the Islamic realm. As such, it has also been called the *salafiyya* (ancestors) movement, the definition betraying the gist of the ideology among Arab Muslims, i.e., not so much a literary reawakening as a religio-cultural one. By the simple act of recalling the heights of Islam in the days of the life of the prophet Muhammad, the Rashidun, and the Umayyad and Abbasid empires, the Arab element in terms of the origins of Islam in the Arabian Peninsula, Arabic as the sacred language of the Qur'an, and the scientific, military, philosophical, and cultural achievements of generations of Arabs was resuscitated and reinforced in a prideful way that had not existed for centuries. In fact, a number of cultural societies sprouted in Arab cities whose primary intent was simply to educate the Arab masses about their history and accomplishments; these were essentially precursors to the more politicized Arabist forums and societies that later developed as circumstances dictated during the Young Turk period. The true way of Islam had been abandoned when non-Arabs, such as the Ottoman Turks, had been at the forefront in Islamic lands. As Basheer M. Nafi stated, "...Arabic...was re-appropriated by the Arab–Islamic reformists and their students and employed to provide the psychological elevation of the Arabs over their political masters."[7]

Maybe the best way to reenergize the Islamic world was to take what was fitting and necessary from the modern world, i.e., Islamic modernism. After all, had not the Europeans grafted their modernity from the template delivered to them via the Renaissance from Islamic civilization? An Islamic unity of purpose could be an effective bulwark against European expansionism. The Egyptian Muhammad Abduh (1849–1905) and the Syrian (Muhammad) Rashid Rida (1865–1935) were the primary disciples of Jamal al-Afghani who gave ideological muscle to the efforts of al-Afghani, yet it was a discourse that generally was devoid of nationalist terminology and intent in the modern sense.[8] With official and unofficial support in Ottoman territories, Arabs generally began to develop a self-awareness of time, place, and space that invigorated, if not generated, the Arabist impulse.

Almost exclusively, however, the pan-Islamist movement saw itself as the most immediate way to strengthen the empire against the Europeans, not as a rebellious vanguard that would tear the empire apart. They were out to save the Ottoman Empire because, for better or worse, it was the last best hope for Islam, something that was seen to be its inherent right for the simple reason that it had been in power over a good portion of the Muslim world for four centuries—it deserved one last chance because there was no other viable alternative. So although Arabism became a potent by-product of the salafiyya movement, it was not framed in any serious way around the notion of separation from the Ottoman Empire—it called for reform from within, especially as the Tanzimat bureaucrats increasingly were seen as having failed in their mission. The Ottomanist–Islamist bond was much stronger than has been popularly perceived by those who place the beginnings of Arab nationalism squarely before the events during and after World War I.

Many believe that the bridge between the Arabist impulse and full-fledged Arab nationalism was the period surrounding the Young Turk revolution of 1908. The Young Turks were those Ottoman subjects (not all of whom were Turks, for there were a number of Arab and even some Jewish supporters) who coalesced around the idea that Abd al-Hamid II had perpetrated a crime by abolishing in 1878 the Ottoman constitution of 1876. A thoroughly secularized movement that tended to attract officers in the Ottoman military, it advocated a return to a representative parliamentary form of government that would curtail the arbitrary power of the sultan and his corrupt bureaucracy; the latter sentiments were shared by the Arab "salafists" who saw a more decentralized Ottoman system as the best way to strengthen the empire and thus the frontiers of Islam.[9] In this way, the declining fortunes of the empire could be reversed more efficiently and immediately, while at the same time expediting the overall modernization efforts that the Young Turks viewed as unevenly and inefficiently applied. The primary vehicle through which the Young Turks operated was the Committee of Union and Progress (CUP). Because of the pervasive nature of Abd al-Hamid II's security and spy network, the CUP was a secret society that had branches throughout the empire, including in a number of Arab cities.

It has often been remarked that the new Young Turk government, led at first in the background by the leading members of the CUP, implemented "turkification" policies that alienated the Arabs, thus compelling the latter to develop more fully the idea of separation from the Ottoman Empire. This is true to some extent, but it requires more explanation. Most of the Arab elites, with the exception of those traditional religious and notable elements who were co-opted by the Sublime Porte, supported the Young Turk revolution. The core of the CUP were certainly Turkish nationalists, but the "turkification" policies, such as the proscribed use of Turkish at educational levels above that of primary schooling, in commercial transactions, in government discourse and correspondence, and in the courts, had actually been on the boards for years prior to the Young Turks' ascension to power in 1908; indeed, they had been a product of the Tanzimat period as well as the sultanate of Abd al Hamid II. The difference was in more vigorous implementation and style, especially after the abortive counterrevolution of 1909 that led to the formal removal of Abd al-Hamid II. The new Young Turk regime, hardened by the real threat of oppositional forces, adopted a decidedly less liberal bent thereafter, including a more assertive tone of centralization and Turkish primacy at the very moment when Arabists were promulgating a decentralized structure with more political and cultural autonomy. The break between Arabism and Turkish nationalism in this regard became inevitable, especially as the Ottoman losses mounted due to the Tripolitan War (Libya) in 1911, the Balkan wars of 1912–1913 and, of course, World War I; the unrelenting pressure perforce compelled the CUP (officially a political party in power by 1913) to close ranks even further. It became more Turkish-exclusivist, dismissed many Arab participants in government, and adopted harsher policies against all forms of dissent, including what had been relatively innocuous calls by Arabists for various forms of autonomy only a few years earlier. The CUP also reduced the Islamic element in Ottoman government and society—the pan-Islamism of Abd al-Hamid II—in a process that had actually been under way since the *Nizam-i Jedid* of Selim III. In an ironic way, this may have created more political space for secular Arabism to rise to the fore of Arabist opposition to the CUP, foreshadowing the secularist nature of Arab nationalism that developed during the mandate period.

Even with these developments, however, most Arabists who were thoroughly opposed to the policies of the CUP still were not advocating clear separation. Their opposition to the CUP was framed more around the notion of bad governance and its failure to combat imperialist designs—it was also as much against the centralizing policies of the CUP regime as it was the turkification policies, the latter being more of a symptom of the former. Oftentimes it just depended on where a particular Arab was located that determined the nature of his opposition to the CUP.[10] Drastic change needed to take place in order to maintain the Ottoman Empire, but this required an almost total reordering of the Arab place within the empire. This would not only improve the lot of the Arabs generally speaking but also save the empire. This was a break with the CUP, not with the centuries-old Ottomanist bond that could not easily be extinguished or jettisoned. These sentiments were reflected during this period in the formation of various reformist parties, such as the Entente Liberal, al-Arabiyya al-Fatat (the Young Arabs); al-'Ahd (the Covenant), almost exclusively composed of Arab army officers in the Ottoman military; and, importantly, the Ottoman Administrative Decentralization party formed in Cairo in 1912, which was kind of a successor to the Entente Liberal and one of whose founders was Rashid Rida. All of these parties to varying degrees advocated more administrative and cultural (especially in terms of language) autonomy, but they still considered themselves to be Ottoman parties with a specific platform rather than opposition groups seeking political separation and/or the overthrow of Ottoman suzerainty. Defense of the empire was considered more important than nationalist objectives for the time being.

The parliamentary election in Istanbul in 1912, after the CUP had maneuvered to dissolve parliament earlier in the year, was a major turning point in Arab–Turkish relations as it "marked the culmination of the CUP's transformation into an authoritarian ruling power and its full embrace of the Ottoman regime with the whole package of its failings, shortcomings and traditional social base."[11] Despite the fact that there was a brief liberal, ententist interlude between periods of CUP dominance in Istanbul upon the outbreak of the war in the Balkans in October 1912, the political damage to Arab–Turkish relations had been done with the conscious exclusion of Arab elements in parliament. This also accelerated growing inter-Arab elite differences that partly resembled a generational gap, with the older, more established urban notables in Arab cities who had traditional ties with the Ottoman government as intermediaries and bureaucrats tending to remain pro-unionist, while the younger generation of Arab notables, with fewer ties to Ottoman authority, tended to be more energetic in their willingness and ability to oppose CUP policies.[12] Although research has shown this dichotomy to be less clear than originally conceived, it did reflect an intergenerational struggle that would come to characterize the Arab nationalist movement from the 1920s through the 1950s.

After the CUP returned to power in a military coup on January 23, 1913, where it would remain until the end of World War I, there was anticipation that its policies would be more exclusivist and centralizing than ever before. As such, the Arab societies, led by the Paris-based activists of al-Fatat, organized a conference comprised of leading Arabists, the First Arab Congress, that was held in Paris in June 1913. With war raging in the Balkans and world war about to break out, the CUP negotiated a settlement with Arab representatives and made some concessions, although most were never implemented. It seems as though Constantinople would be given at least one more chance to meet the demands of its multifarious subjects because, again, what alternative was there against the greater danger of European imperialism? In the April 1914 parliamentary elections, some Arab deputies were returned to office. It was definitely a period of reconciliation or, maybe more to the point, a burying of the mutual hatchets until better times prevailed. Even with the outbreak of World War I in August 1914, leading Arabists such as Rashid Rida attempted to rally Arabs around the flag of the Ottoman Empire against the enemy. But the exigencies of the war itself, particularly as the Ottomans began to lose ground in the Middle East, shifted the emphasis of Arabists more and more toward nationalist thought and opinion in reaction to certain events and opportunities presented by the conflagration. As Nafi concludes,

> ...Arabism evolved out of the complicated encounter of Arab–Islamic reformism with the dual impact of Ottoman modernization and the Western encroachment. It involved the revival of Arabic language and literature and the embrace of Western ideas of progress and renewal, turning thereby into a political movement amid repercussions amongst Arabs of the real or perceived Turkish exclusiveness of the CUP regime, the gradual demise of the empire and Jamal Pasha's [one of the CUP leaders] oppressive war order.[13]

ZIONISM

Zionism was never a monolithic movement. There were different strands of Zionism throughout its history. The term itself is taken from the word "Zion" (*Siyon* in Hebrew), which refers to the citadel constructed in Jerusalem during the biblical period; during the history of the Zionist movement, the term has simply been taken to mean the land of Israel or the homeland of the Jewish people. At its root, Zionism is a nationalist movement that seeks the creation of a homeland, in effect a nation-state, for the Jews. The impetuses for the emergence and growth of Zionism in the nineteenth century were the interrelated Jewish experiences of widespread official and unofficial repression throughout Europe, particularly in eastern Europe, combined with the desire among many Jews to carve a Jewish identity out of the diaspora in the face of the destructive cultural effects upon Judaism of modernization. Zionism, as it began to be formulated in the first half of the nineteenth century, was seen by a number of leading Jewish thinkers as a potential bridge that would create harmony between what was called "religion" and "life," i.e., between religious tradition and the demands of the modern world.[14]

As such, even though Zionism is often associated with the secular nationalism that eventually took control of the movement and formed the ideological basis of the state of Israel, it began primarily as a religiously based phenomenon. Even when Zionism evolved into a fiercely secularist movement, it could not completely divorce itself from Judaism or its religious history. As Ehud Luz states,

> Even those who rebelled against religion could not ignore the need to deal with it, for the simple reason that Jewish nationalism drew its legitimacy from the Jewish religion. Zionism was rooted in the Jewish past, and none denied that this past had a religious character. In this respect Jewish nationalism differed from other European nationalist movements, which did not have to contend with so broad an overlap between religious tradition and ethnic identity.[15]

This was especially the case with eastern European Jews, who were on the whole much more observant and accepted traditional religious authority to a greater degree than western European Jews, who under the influence of the Jewish Enlightenment (*haskalah*) were in large measure attempting to assimilate into the modern Christian world. Proponents of the haskalah (the *maskilim*) sought to, in the words of M. L. Lilienblum (1843–1910), give the Jews a "concrete view" of life by removing Judaism as the barrier between the eschatological world of religion and modern existence. As Luz comments,

> The nations of Europe had long since broken the religious fetters that hampered political action. For the Jews, however, these bonds persisted, both because of their practical weakness and because of their complete devotion to the religious ideal, which had lost its luster for other nations as part of their compromise with this world. The eschatological-messianic attitude, reinforced by the historical experience of the Jewish people, sapped any tendency to search for a realistic political solution to the problem of their national existence. The major concern was always to ensure survival in the present; the question of the future, and the direction it should take, was totally ignored. The Jewish people saw themselves as a nation living outside historical time; their continued existence did not depend on those historical and earthly factors that determined the existence of other nations.[16]

In essence, both the haskalah and Zionism in polar opposite ways reversed the nature of the response to the question of salvation in the face of persecution—now the Jews had to look to the future in order to save themselves, not the past. The maskilim, such as J. L. Gordon (1831–1892), who has been called one of the earliest prophets in the secular revolution in Judaism, saw a causal link between the destitute condition of the Jewish peoples and the "distorted spiritual nature" of Judaism itself.[17] The basic difference between western European and eastern European Jews along these lines is that the former tended to see Zionism as a "bridge" between Judaism and European culture, whereas the latter increasingly viewed Zionism as a rebellion against, if not a rejection of, traditional Judaism; therefore, eastern European Zionism was much less abstract than western European Zionism, and this is why it had a much more practical effect on the Yishuv, the Jewish community in Palestine.

The general response to the question of why the Zionist movement arose simply has to do with the consistent persecution of Jews at a variety of levels. People desire change because they are discontented with the existing environment. They want to move when all reasonable doors to better their situation from within are closed; therefore, they must go elsewhere to escape oppression and try to find better all-around living conditions, free of persecution and containing at least the seeds of opportunity. This being the case, it is not a surprise that the first inklings of Zionism in the nineteenth century as well as the bulk of the Jewish immigrants who arrived in Palestine beginning near the end of the 1800s emanated in eastern Europe, particularly in czarist Russia. The level of repression of Jews in Russia waxed and waned throughout the century depending upon who was czar. Even under a more benevolent ruler, Jews in Russia still experienced unofficial prejudice and restrictions; under openly anti-Semitic czars, life became utterly miserable as they were restricted in where they could live (the Pale of Settlement), in what occupations they could hold, and where they could travel. When a czarist government sanctioned such prejudice in the form of law, it was seen as a green light by anti-Semitic elements in Russian society to carry out pogroms against Jewish communities that resulted in frequent death and destruction; all the while, Russian military and constabulary forces would more often than not just cast a blind eye toward the perpetrators, if not participate in the pogroms themselves.

There had been calls by a number of Jewish thinkers for the Jews to return to Zion, to establish a homeland in Palestine, a number of years before Theodore Herzl, the generally acknowledged father of Zionism, began to commit his enormous energies to the task in the 1890s. Prussian Rabbi Zvi Kalischer (1795–1874), in his book *Derishat Siyon* (*The Search for Zion*), proposed the colonization of Palestine to be carried out by a corporation that would purchase land to be settled by Russian, German, and Polish Jews. In his book *Shivat Siyon* (*Return to Zion*), Rabbi Yehudah Hai Alkalai (1798–1878), from his home in Serbia, advocated a Jewish return to Palestine; and presaging the strategy of Herzl, it was to be accomplished through political and diplomatic bargaining and negotiations with the European powers and with the Ottoman sultan.

One of the most important early Zionists was Moses Hess (1812–1875), a German Jew who was heavily influenced by European nationalism; indeed, both Zionism and Arab nationalism are the children of the development of European nationalism. Hess was a socialist thinker, was a one-time associate of Karl Marx, and, more importantly, published the landmark book *Rome and Jerusalem* in 1862. Hess countered the dominant philosophy of assimilation embodied in the haskalah by purporting that the Jews throughout history had contributed so much to civilization in terms of ethics, law, religion, and science that it would be a tragedy for Jewish culture to dissolve itself, for Jews to totally lose their history and identity in the bowels of Christian society. This could be best accomplished by creating a community of Jews in Palestine, facilitated through negotiation with the rulers of Europe and the assistance of wealthy western European Jews such as the Rothschild family. Although not received very well by his religious cohorts in Germany, the book became quite popular among eastern European Zionists in its Hebrew translation.[18] In his influential book, Hess wrote the following:

> I am taking part in the spiritual and intellectual struggles of our day, both within the House of Israel and between our people and the gentile world. The Jews have lived and labored among the nations for almost two thousand years, but nonetheless they cannot become rooted organically within them.[19]

Hess also wrote that "despite enlightenment and emancipation, the Jew in exile who denies his nationality will never earn the respect of the nations among whom he dwells.

He may become a naturalized citizen, but he will never be able to convince the gentiles of his total separation from his own nationality."[20] He continued as follows:

> What we have to do at present for the regeneration of the Jewish nation is, first, to keep alive the hope of the political rebirth of our people, and, next, to reawaken that hope where it slumbers. When political conditions in the Orient shape themselves so as to permit the organization of a beginning of the restoration of a Jewish state, this beginning will express itself in the founding of Jewish colonies in the land of their ancestors…"[21]

As mentioned previously, the main reason Zionism, in both its religious and its secular forms, took hold more with Jews in eastern Europe than western Europe was the much more direct and overt nature in the former of discriminatory practices against the Jewish population. The turning point between individual voices calling for a return to Zion and the beginnings of a movement was the pogroms and the anti-Semitic laws enacted in Russia following the 1881 assassination of the relatively enlightened Czar Alexander II, who came to power in 1855, an incident that unleashed waves of latent anti-Semitism stemming from the mistaken claim that Jewish elements were responsible for the dastardly deed. Conditions in Russia prior to Alexander II, under Nicholas I, were quite repressive. Among other official discriminatory laws, in 1835 the Pale of Settlement was established, restricting Jewish inhabitants to specified areas in Lithuania, Poland, Little and White Russia, the Ukraine, and the Baltic provinces. On one occasion, while traveling through Russia, Czar Nicholas wrote the following about the Jews: "They drain the strength of the hapless White Russian people.… They are everything here: merchants, contractors, saloon-keepers, mill-owners, ferry-holders, artisans.… They are regular leeches."[22] In fact, the reinstitution of the more overt discriminatory practices in Russia following the assassination in 1881 were all the more dire because it followed a period of hope and a certain level of emancipation during the reign of Alexander II.

One of the first Zionist organizations formed was called BILU, the Hebrew acronym of the biblical phrase "O House of Jacob, come let us go." It was comprised of mainly students, often characterized as militant in their secular beliefs, first in the Ukraine and then in other cities in Russia, numbering about 500 by 1882.[23] The BILU called for a return to Zion by obtaining a permit (*firman*) from the Ottoman sultan to purchase land in Palestine and found a colony on a cooperative basis. Although the sultan did not comply, the BILU sent fourteen students to Palestine, arriving at what would become the primary port of entry for immigrant Jews, Jaffa, in 1882, thus inaugurating what would become in Zionist history the first *aliyah*, or "ascent" to the land.

A Russian physician who grew up in Odessa also was greatly affected by the pogroms—his name was Leo Pinsker (1821–1891). An avowed assimilationist until 1881, the harsher socioeconomic and political climate in Russia, climaxing with the 1881 pogroms, convinced Pinsker that emancipation and assimilation were going to be impossible to attain under current conditions. He authored a pamphlet that would be widely distributed in Zionist circles entitled *Auto-Emancipation*, which was actually published in Berlin in 1881 as an appeal to German Jews to act on behalf of their co-religionists in Russia. The gist of his argument lies in the title itself, that the Jews must undertake actions themselves in order to become free of repression and tyranny, or what Pinsker called "Judeophobia." He wrote that "for the living, the Jew is a dead man; for the natives an alien and a vagrant; for the property holders, a beggar; and for the poor, an exploiter and a millionaire; for the patriots, a man without a country; for all classes, a hated rival."[24] Although unclear at first on whether or not Palestine should be this Jewish sanctuary, Pinsker would soon focus upon *Eretz Yisrael* (the land of Israel) as the preferred choice. Now a leading voice in the embryonic Zionist movement, Pinsker became the acknowledged head of the *Hibbat Zion* (Love of Zion, whose members were called *Hovevei Zion* or Lovers of Zion), which held its first conference in Silesia in 1884, where participants from Russia, Germany, Romania, and France gathered. The Hibbat Zion, inspired by a series of articles written by Moses Lilienblum in 1881 that called for the colonization of Palestine, crystallized Pinsker's ideas; and it became the most recognized Zionist organization in eastern Europe and contributed to the implementation of the first aliyah. These were not the first calls among Jews for the migration to and/or colonization of Palestine, but they were the first that associated these calls with concrete action.[25] Most of these, however, including many of those in the Hibbat Zion, were Orthodox Jews who saw the return to Zion as a redemption of Israel and an inauguration of the messianic era; but with their religiohistorical connections to Eretz Yisrael was added the modern notion of nationalism, a component part of the Zionist movement that increasingly characterized it. In addition, observing European and American philanthropists and missionaries throughout the nineteenth century travel to the Holy Land only further encouraged some Jews to do the same.

Some 20,000–30,000 Jews immigrated to Palestine as part of the first aliyah (1882–1904), mostly from Russia and Romania. Most settled in areas that already contained Jewish communities dating back millennia as well as to the Sephardic Jewish emigration from Spain as a result of the Christian Reconquista and the Inquisition in the fifteenth and sixteenth centuries. At the turn of the nineteenth century, there were approximately 5,000 Jews living in Palestine out of a total population of some 275,000–300,000. Forty years later, the Jewish population in Palestine doubled to about 10,000, most of whom resided in and around Jerusalem as well as in the cities of Safed, Hebron, and Tiberias in the region of the Sea of Galilee to the north. By 1880, i.e., just before the first aliyah, it had risen to about 25,000 out of a total population of some 450,000. About two-thirds of this 25,000 lived in Jerusalem, where they constituted a majority.[26] So there were Jews in Palestine, and there would continue to be Jews who immigrated to Palestine, who were there for reasons quite different from that which was propagated by Zionism.[27]

Most of the Jews in the first aliyah were not around to greet the very different breed of Zionists who immigrated to Palestine by the time of the second aliyah (1904–1914). Most of those who came left after a short period of time and joined the bulk of other Jews who had emigrated from Russia and eastern Europe, destined for the most part toward greener pastures in the United States. A good number of Jews in the first aliyah left Palestine because of harsh conditions or died due primarily to disease, especially malaria and typhoid. The conditions were harsh not so much because Palestine as a whole was in some sort of decrepit state but because the areas that were available to incoming Jewish settlers were less than ideal. In fact, the Tanzimat reform efforts initiated officially by Sultan Abd al-Majid in 1839 went a long way toward improving certain conditions for Jewish immigration; importantly, they also made land transfers more feasible at the same time that a growing absentee landowning class in Palestine emerged—in other words, a market for land was created. As Stein states,

> These reforms paved the way for an improvement in the rule of law and for a general amelioration of burdens borne by non-Muslims and non-Turkish citizens. Furthermore, by virtue of the capitulations system, foreign citizens were granted immunity from Turkish courts and were afforded a measure of protection by their respective consuls. Consequently, Palestine as a destination for would-be Jewish migrants became somewhat less daunting.[28]

Many Jews at the time opined that had not the capitulations existed not a single settlement would have been founded. But all of this was mostly in the legal sense. The Tanzimat had pushed for more equal rights among the multitude of ethnicities and religions comprising the empire as well as for the end of administrative abuses and bureaucratic corruption, although these continued to be more realized in their abeyance rather than application as time went on. Many Jews acquired visas as religious pilgrims and simply stayed on. From the 1880s it seemed the Ottoman sultan waffled back and forth between restricting and allowing Jewish immigration depending upon the nature of pressure from European capitals or his Arab constituents starting to fear the impact, especially economic, of this new foreign element in Palestine. Even during the most restrictive periods, bribery of local officials for Jewish entry, purchasing land, and acquiring permits for construction was always a tried and true practice. This did not, however, mean that Jewish settlers had suddenly entered paradise—quite the contrary. As indicated above, disease was a constant companion, as was the insecurity that tended to bedevil all the inhabitants of Palestine, if not of the entire outlying areas of the empire, especially those who were devoid of the traditional clan and tribal affiliations that innately provided a level of security outside of the ineffective administrative apparatus. Ironically, they also encountered general hostility and uncooperativeness from the existing Jewish community in Palestine (the "old Yishuv" versus the "new Yishuv" embodied by the Zionists), for they saw them as comparatively irreligious and considered Zionist objectives as ill-formed and misguided (of course, this is not even to speak of the much more secularist nature of the second aliyah); indeed, first aliyah settlers often resided in harmony in Arab villages and in cooperation with Palestinian Arabs until they were able to set up functioning settlements.

Moreover, most of the Jews in the first aliyah were not experienced agriculturalists and laborers, to the point where some of the early settlements established agricultural training schools in order to adequately prepare new settlers for the rigors of Jewish life in Palestine. Although organizations such as the Hibbat Zion morphed first and foremost into funding mechanisms to help Jewish settlers in Palestine, they inevitably became inadequate for the task at hand. As such, Zionists in the first aliyah quickly turned to wealthy Jewish philanthropists in Europe, especially Baron Edmund de Rothschild, to fund the great experiment in Palestine. This the baron did; indeed, without his financial assistance, the first aliyah would have been a total failure and nary a settlement would have survived. The baron did, however, adopt a very authoritarian position, controlling through his staff almost every facet of finance and operations within the settlements he was now subsidizing.[29]

The first settlement established by the first aliyah immigrants in 1882 was called Rishon Letzion (First in Zion). As with the other embryonic settlements, at least until de Rothschild started to subsidize almost all of them, they were at the beginning supported at a pittance rate by organizations back in Russia and Romania, such as Hibbat Zion, the Association for the Colonization of Eretz Israel, or the Central Committee of the Society for the Colonization of Eretz Israel. Most of the first Zionist settlements were located fairly near the established Jewish enclaves of Safed, Tiberius, Jaffa, and Haifa. Hardly any were located near Jerusalem for the simple reason that that area, around the Judean Hills, was considered prime (more agriculturally fertile) land by the Arab owners, whereas the land along the coastal region was more easily acquired because it tended to consist of disease-ridden swamps, ill-drained or watered terrain, and was less fertile overall for traditional crops. By the end of the first aliyah in 1904, twenty-eight agricultural settlements had been established with a population of about 5,500, comprising 10% of the 55,000 total population of Jews in Palestine.[30]

Of course, it is Theodore Herzl who is considered the father of the Zionist movement. Born in Budapest in 1860, he was a thoroughly committed assimilationist, having attended the university and, despite experiencing anti-Semitic incidents during his youth, had all but shed his Jewish exterior in an attempt to integrate himself, like many European Jews, into the modern Western world—he had only a limited understanding of true Judaism. He became a journalist and a less than successful dramatist, but he represented his Vienna-based newspaper's (*Neue Freie Press*) interests in France, becoming its regular Paris correspondent in 1891. Like most Jews, the French Revolution in 1789, with the promise of the equal rights of man, had afforded European Jewry the qualified opportunity to finally be accepted in gentile society. The revolution, however, also unleashed the modern concept of nationalism, spawning the belief among groups of peoples commonly linked together through ethnicity, culture, heritage, and/or language—a nation—that they possessed an innate right to a nation-state, a country of their own. While the idea of nationalism provided the foundation upon which Zionism as well as Arabism crystallized their own conceptualizations of being and purpose, it also introduced over the course of the nineteenth century in Europe the propagation of racial purity as a basic building block for what was perceived to be the successful nation-state. As such, while the haskalah pushed many Jews toward the modern European way of life and into European society, the countervailing forces of the precursors of a fascist-based racism combined with latent anti-Semitism repelled just as many. It is often thought that the so-called Dreyfus affair in 1894–1895 was the incident that convinced Herzl to reject assimilation and organize Zionism. Alfred Dreyfus was a French military officer who happened to be Jewish. He was accused of treason, tried and found guilty, and then sent to the French penal colony of Devil's Island for four years before he was later, armed with incontrovertible evidence, acquitted of the crime (even then it was not a simple matter to overturn the original decision). The whole affair became a cause celebre in France, almost cathartically releasing anti-Semitic thought and action, much as the assassination of Czar Alexander II seemed to legitimize the darker side of anti-Semitism. As a correspondent in Paris during the Dreyfus affair, Herzl was a firsthand witness to all of this, including the chants of the crowds, "Death to the Jews."

In actuality, however, long before the Dreyfus affair, Herzl began to distrust the tenets of the haskalah based on his own observations of anti-Semitism.[31] If anything, the Dreyfus affair was the proverbial straw that broke the camel's back. It only convinced

Herzl of sentiments that had been in formation for years. He now came to the distinct conclusion that Jews would never be accepted as equals in Christian society; therefore, as early Zionists had advocated, the answer lay in finding a homeland for the Jews elsewhere, preferably in Palestine. It catalyzed Herzl to expend tremendous amounts of effort and energy toward this goal over the remaining years of his life. More importantly, it led to the publication in early 1896 of what would become his Zionist manifesto, *Der Judenstaat* (*The Jewish State*). In *The Jewish State*, Herzl expounds upon his analysis of why the Jews will never be able to truly assimilate into gentile society. Also referring to a kind of "Judeophobia," he concludes that only political action will bring about an independent state for the Jews. To do so, he believed that careful negotiation and bargaining with the European powers as well as the Ottoman sultan might create the desired result; political conditions for statehood must exist before mass immigration and the building of institutions that establishes the foundation of a state—this became the hallmark of political Zionism, i.e., the establishment of a nation-state must precede the formation of a Jewish nation—a common Jewish identity—out of the diaspora. As Stein wrote, "The appearance of *The Jewish State* represents a landmark in Zionist history. It issued the first modern call for the Jewish problem to be addressed by the international community at large."[32] As Herzl promulgated, the Zionist issue "is a national question, which can only be solved by making it a political world-question to be discussed and settled by the civilized nations of the world in council."[33]

Perhaps Herzl's greatest contribution to Zionism was his organizational ability. By the end of the 1890s, the Hibbat Zion as well as other Zionist institutions had shrunk to mere shells of their former selves, having become small-scale, uncoordinated charitable institutions. Herzl changed all this. He convened in August 1897 in Basle, Switzerland, the First Zionist Congress, which would give birth to the World Zionist Organization (WZO), the most functional of all the Zionist organizations to date and the progenitor and overseer of the worldwide Zionist movement that would eventually lead to the establishment of the state of Israel in 1948. He would be by far the dominant figure and the acknowledged leader of the Zionist movement until his death in 1904, which was symbolically anointed by his opening address at the meeting. Surprisingly to Herzl, his call to attend the congress found a much more receptive response among eastern European Jews, such as the members of Hibbat Zion, than western European Jews, most of whom still clung to the hope of assimilation and who believed that any calls rejecting it would only make things worse. Emerging out of the First Zionist Congress is what came to be called the Basle Program, in which "Zionism seeks to secure for the Jewish people a publicly recognized and legally secured home in Palestine." In his diary, upon returning to Vienna after the meeting, Herzl summed up the proceedings by saying that "in Basle I created the Jewish State" and that "five years hence, in any case, certainly fifty years hence, everyone will perceive it."[34] While the former prediction turned out to be wishful thinking, the latter was almost exact. In addition to and functioning within the parameters of the WZO, Herzl founded the Zionist weekly *Die Welt* (*The World*), and by the Fifth Zionist Congress in 1902, the Jewish National Fund had been established, geared toward raising funds for and coordinating the purchase of land in Palestine.

Herzl tirelessly, and for the most part fruitlessly, negotiated with countless intermediaries among the European powers and in the Ottoman Empire, often meeting with the respective heads of state, such as the Ottoman sultan and the German kaiser, in his attempts at obtaining political backing to legally establish out of Ottoman territory in Palestine a Jewish state. On one occasion in 1896 he even offered to pay the Ottoman Empire 20 million English pounds to rid itself of its international debt in return for Palestine. He was determined to obtain a charter for settlement in Palestine in order to acquire international legal sanction for continued immigration and avoid what he viewed to be the inevitable growing opposition of the native Arab population to the more incremental and uncoordinated Jewish entry that had to date characterized Zionist immigration to Palestine. At least in his own eyes, he came painstakingly close to achieving such international sanction on several occasions, only to be bitterly disappointed when what were perceived to be promises to do so flittered away in the winds of domestic and international politics beyond the reach of the peripatetic Hungarian Jew. Frustrated by these attempts, by the Fourth Zionist Congress in 1900 Herzl began to consider possible alternatives to Palestine, considering South Africa, the United States, and a host of locales that he hoped would be facilitated by the British, such as Cyprus and the Sinai Peninsula around al-Arish. For diplomatic and political reasons, these suggestions were ultimately rejected by London, but British Colonial Secretary Joseph Chamberlain in 1903 suggested to Herzl the possibility of Uganda in central Africa. It was not only frustration that led Herzl to consider a "new Palestine" that could act as a way station on the road toward claiming the original one someday but the news of a fresh wave of destructive pogroms throughout Russia. He saw an immediate need for a sanctuary in the face of such repression—thousands of Jews could wait no longer. Zion would be the ultimate goal, but Uganda could offer instant relief. He submitted the British proposal with his imprimatur at the Sixth Zionist Congress in 1903. Almost causing a major split with groups committed to Palestine, Herzl received only grudging approval to pursue the British plan; however, by the end of the year, due to opposition from Britain's East African colonies as well as continued concern within the Zionist movement, the Ugandan plan was formally abandoned. Exhausted by the years of endless efforts, Herzl died on July 3, 1904, at the age of forty-four; and despite his detractors, he was considered even at the time of his death a giant within the Jewish community worldwide.

In 1904–1905, events in Russia would have a significant impact on the evolution of the Zionist movement. The Russo–Japanese war and, especially, the 1905 Russian Revolution induced a new influx of Jewish immigrants to Palestine. The vast majority of Russian Jews, as they had before, emigrated to more inviting climes in western Europe and the United States, to the point that leading Zionists at the time would say that the relative attractiveness of America was the biggest threat to Zionism; i.e., it was siphoning off Jewish immigrants who otherwise might have fulfilled the Zionist program by settling in Palestine; indeed, between 1882 and 1914, 2.5 million Jews left Russia, with 2 million of these relocating to the United States. But those who did make it to Palestine (numbering anywhere between 20,000 and 40,000 depending upon the source) were primarily from Russia and Poland. Although most of the immigrants, as in the first aliyah, were non-Zionist orthodox, there was an important contingent that was imbued with a different ideology from those Jews who comprised the first aliyah; indeed, because of the disproportionate impact of this group, many consider this second aliyah (1904–1914) the most significant of them all. It was not so much the overall numbers of the second aliyah but the shift in direction they imposed on both the Zionist movement and the Yishuv, reshaping the very nature of the path toward statehood and the basic characteristics of the state of Israel; in addition, many of the early leaders of the Israeli state, first and foremost among them David Ben-Gurion, the first prime minister of Israel, arrived in Palestine during this period.[35]

The Zionists in the second aliyah tended to be younger, more activist, and more ideologically committed than the first aliyah settlers, to the point where there were distinct differences in the Yishuv that often separated the two sets of immigrants socially, culturally, and politically—the antagonisms between the two sets of groups cannot be overstated; the firebrand second aliyah immigrants were not at all welcomed by the first aliyah settlers, who were seen by the newcomers as having grown stale, lost whatever vision they had, and become too assimilated into a different environment—this time an Arab one. The newcomers were of a socialist political tinge, promoting the idea of a collective purpose and organization, particularly as expressed in their commitment to the land and tilling the soil as the most efficient way to establish a positive environment for the growth of the Jewish community in Palestine (or what was termed the "conquest of labor"). They tended to advocate the idea of a self-contained, self-sufficient, and all-Jewish entity, which conflicted with the more capitalist ethos of the first aliyah immigrants and particularly their practice of hiring Arab laborers to cultivate the land, more out of necessity than anything else because of the enormity of the task combined with dwindling numbers of Jewish settlers in the two decades that had passed since the beginning of the Zionist process in Palestine. Not only were these views based on a highly nationalistic mind-set born from generations of learning that they could not rely on non-Jews for assistance, but they also feared the creation of a colonial situation akin to what the French had established in North Africa, one that would ultimately erode the Jewish character of the Yishuv and dilute any political imperative they might obtain due to an inevitable minority status. Summarizing the differences between the two aliyahs is the following:

> The First Aliyah settlers had come to terms with an economic structure in which farm plantations were based on the exploitation of cheap, casual labor. Although socially undesirable, such a practice did not in itself threaten the Zionist enterprise. What did undermine it was the fact that while the farm owners were Jewish, virtually all their employees were Arabs. On average, each farmer employed the services of three Arab families, which meant that literally thousands of Arabs worked in the settlements. A situation was evolving, which to all intents and purposes, was a replica of the colonial settler societies that existed in Algeria, Kenya and in other European colonies. Had such a state of affairs persisted, the Arab natives would sooner or later have overthrown their alien taskmasters and a Jewish state in Palestine would have been no more than a pipe dream.[36]

The overall philosophy of the second aliyah has been termed "cultural" or "socialist Zionism." Whereas political Zionism considered the acquisition of territory the primary objective, socialist Zionists believed that the opposite should occur; i.e., the formation of a nation, a common identity, should precede the establishment of a nation-state because the latter could not survive, certainly not in the way envisioned, unless a shared culture could be carved out of the plethora of different backgrounds and languages that now comprised the Yishuv.[37] Territory was only important to the socialist Zionists to be utilized in order to build the nation from the ground up. Schools, publishing houses, farms, and other basic institutions that could create a Jewish community were more important than diplomacy with the great powers; indeed, they generally despised Herzlian Zionists, i.e., the political Zionists, for "their belief in capitalism, their admiration for the European aristocracy, and their connections to imperialist courts. In contrast, socialism would give Jews the opportunity to increase their political power, improve their economic lot, and raise their spiritual level."[38] Once a Hebrew nation was formed, including, importantly, the revivification and adoption of Hebrew as the national language (affirmed by the WZO at the Eighth Zionist Congress in 1906), political and military force could be employed when the opportunity arose to bring about official statehood. It was during this period that the concept of labor Zionism arose, which in essence was the implementation of socialist Zionism. It would be the labor Zionists, many coming from what would be the forerunners of the Labor party in Israel who formed in 1905 the Marxist Poale Zion (Workers of Zion, of which David Ben-Gurion was a leading member) and the non-Marxist party Ha'Poel Ha'Tzair (The Young Worker), one of whose leading lights was Aaron David Gordon, who would form the first model agricultural collectives in Palestine, the *kibbutzim* and *moshavim*, as well as construct a collective industrial base.[39]

By the Seventh Zionist Congress, any idea within the WZO of settling anywhere other than Palestine had been abandoned; and by 1911 at the Tenth Zionist Congress, the socialist Zionists, or what some have called the "practical" Zionists, had affirmed that the direction of Zionism would follow their prescription, i.e., a gradualist approach, constructing institutions from the ground up that would provide the necessary socio-cultural, economic, and political foundation for statehood.[40] It would be a program that ultimately proved to be successful when the time came in 1948, but its exclusivist and goal-oriented tendencies only heightened the nature of the Zionist threat as perceived by Palestinian Arabs as well as the level of animosity and confrontation. By 1914, there were 85,000–90,000 Jews in Palestine out of a total population of 700,000. Approximately 35,000 of these had come as part of the new Yishuv.

THE ARAB REACTION

Arab–Jewish relations before and during the early stages of the first aliyah were generally consistent with what existed between all groups, Arab and non-Arab, that resided in what became known as Palestine/Israel. There was tension and sporadic violence between Arabs and Jews, but it mostly reflected the overall lawlessness of the region that placed most residents in Palestine at a certain level of insecurity. As Jewish immigration continued during the first aliyah, disputes often took the form of economic competition, grazing rights, and/or territorial/boundary demarcation as locals began to see the newcomers as impinging upon their way of life. Sometimes disagreements occurred simply due to misunderstandings based on cultural differences. In other words, violent incidents based solely on an ethnic and/or religious basis were few and far between, and the region was for the most part devoid of any concerted anti-Jewish/Zionist or anti-Arab campaign or ideology on the part of either grouping. Quite to the contrary, more often than not Arab–Jewish relations were amicable; indeed, because of the employment opportunities offered the local Arab population by the first aliyah settlements, the general livelihood of the Palestinian Arabs living and working in and around the increasingly well-financed Jewish enclaves improved.

The first noticeable local political opposition to the Zionist presence occurred in 1891, when 500 Arab notables in Jerusalem signed a petition to the Ottoman sultan demanding that he end Jewish immigration. It is not surprising that this telegraphed appeal occurred in that year, for it was one of the high points of the first aliyah in terms of the number of immigrants, with more than 8,000 arriving in 1891—obviously from the local Arab point of view, it now seemed more than just a spasmodic phenomenon. By July, the sultan responded in favor of the appeal, prohibiting further Jewish immigration. Again, however, Jewish immigrants found ways to enter Palestine despite the ban; in any event, mostly due to European pressure, the edict was rescinded only a few years later, but it did foreshadow future hostile relations. A number of Zionists recognized the potentially diametrically opposed aims of Jews and Arabs in Palestine; of course, as mentioned already, this is one of the reasons Herzl was so intent on receiving international sanction for settlement in Palestine. Contrary to the perception that soon developed that painted a Palestine that was desolate and decadent only to be revived by the good efforts of Jewish settlers (embodied in the Zionist slogan regarding Palestine that it was "a land without a people for a people without a land"), Ahad Ha'Am wrote in 1891 in a report entitled "Truth from Eretz Israel" the following:

> We tend to believe abroad that Palestine is nowadays almost completely deserted, a non-cultivated wilderness, and anyone can come there and buy as much land as his heart desires. But in reality this is not the case. It is difficult to find anywhere in the country Arab land which lies fallow; the only areas which are not cultivated are sand dunes or stony mountains, which can only be planted with trees, and even so only after investing much labor and capital for land clearance and preparation.[41]

As one might expect, with the more exclusivist and committed ethos of the second aliyah immigrants, tensions between Arabs and Jews in Palestine increased after 1904. After an incident in Jaffa in 1908 that would become all too familiar in Palestine/Israel up to the present day, one characterized by retributive death and vigilante violence, the relationship began to become more antagonistic. The nature of foreign support for Jewish immigrants due to the capitulations and generally sympathetic attitudes of local foreign consuls that tended to provide Jewish settlers with political and economic advantages was increasingly rubbing the Arab population the wrong way, leading to more frequent calls for concerted and coordinated action to redress what they perceived to be a deteriorating situation. It was becoming a very serious competition, a competition first and foremost for land.

Echoing sentiments that were becoming more widespread in Palestine, if not the rest of the Arab world, Naguib Azoury prophetically wrote in his 1905 book *The Awakening of the Arab Nation in Turkish Asia* the following:

> Two important phenomena, with the same characteristics but which are diametrically opposed to each other, and which have so far not attracted notice, are appearing in Turkish Asia. They are the Arab national awakening and the latent efforts of Jews to re-establish, on a grand scale, their ancient kingdom of Israel. These two phenomena are destined to be locked in perpetual battle until one prevails over the other.[42]

There was a more open political atmosphere at first throughout much of the Ottoman Empire as a result of the Young Turk revolution in 1908. This manifested itself primarily in the proliferation of newspapers. In Palestine, the so-called Zionist problem became the leading topic of concern, with *Al-Karmel*, founded in Haifa in 1909, heading the anti-Zionist barrage. Other anti-Zionist organs included *Falestin*, which began publication in Jaffa in 1911, and *Al-Muntada*, founded in Jerusalem in 1912. Typically, anti-Zionist discourse revolved around calls for ending Jewish immigration and, most emphatically, prohibiting land sales to Jews. Soon, parliamentary elections, particularly during the early part of the Young Turk era before World War I, brought Palestinian delegates to Constantinople, where they attempted to make their case regarding the Zionist threat in Palestine. In this, they were joined by Arab parliamentarians from other parts of the empire as anti-Zionism became part and parcel of what in retrospect was an emerging Arab nationalism—it was, indeed, viewed as simply a function of the overall imperialist encroachment from Europe, and from the beginning the Zionists in Palestine were seen as a new "crusader" movement, i.e., a foreign element, even an instrument of European designs attempting to take over the Holy Land; as with the Crusades of history, it would inevitably be a temporary phenomenon that would ultimately fail. Interestingly, despite mounting differences, some leading Arabs in Istanbul in 1913, hoping to attach what they perceived to be global Jewish influence to their calls for more regional autonomy, approached some important Zionists to explore the possibilities of effecting a kind of reconciliation that could be mutually beneficial. A conference was scheduled with ten Arab and Jewish delegates, but world war broke out before it could commence, thus negating a potential breakthrough. Despite some rather outlandish conspiracy theories regarding some sort of an alliance between the Young Turks and Jews, some of which was propagated by European consuls and diplomats, the new Ottoman ruling elite generally adopted an unfavorable view toward Zionism, not only because it was alienating an increasingly significant element of their realm, i.e., the Arab population, but also because they did not want the situation in Palestine to set a precedent for other non-Turkish, non-Muslim groups within the empire to emulate.[43]

Slowly but surely the confrontation between Jews and Arabs in Palestine was taking shape, at first primarily an issue of local concern that only episodically drew the attention of Constantinople or other major cities in Arab lands. But the events of World War I would thrust the issue onto the world stage, from which it has yet to recede.

NOTES

1. See in particular the following: C. Ernest Dawn, *From Ottomanism to Arabism: Essays on the Origins of Arab Nationalism* (Urbana: University of Illinois Press, 1973); Rashid Khalidi, et al., eds., *The Origins of Arab Nationalism* (New York: Columbia University Press, 1991); and Israel Geshoni and James Jankowski, eds., *Rethinking Nationalism in the Arab Middle East* (New York: Columbia University Press, 1997).

2. M. E. Yapp, *The Making of the Modern Near East, 1792–1923* (London: Longman, 1990), 91.

3. George Antonius, *The Arab Awakening: The Story of the Arab National Movement* (New York: Capricorn Books, 1965). The book was originally published in 1938 by Hamish Hamilton out of London. For interesting discussions on the impact of Antonius' book, see Albert Hourani, "The Arab Awakening Forty Years After," in his *The Emergence of the Modern Middle East* (Berkeley: University of California Press, 1981), and William L. Cleveland, "The Arab Nationalism of George Antonius Reconsidered," in Geshoni and Jankowski, *Rethinking Nationalism.*

4. Basheer M. Nafi, *Arabism, Islamism and the Palestine Question, 1908–1941: A Political History* (Reading, UK: Ithaca Press, 1998), 8.

5. James L. Gelvin, *The Modern Middle East: A History* (New York: Oxford University Press, 2005), 142.

6. Yapp, *The Making of the Modern Near East,* 181.

7. Nafi, *Arabism, Islamism and the Palestine Question,* 7–8.

8. See Albert Hourani, *Arabic Thought in the Liberal Age, 1798–1939* (Cambridge: Cambridge University Press, 1983).

9. Shaykh Abd al-Rahman al-Kawakibi's (1849–1902) diatribe against Abd al-Hamid II is emblematic of the period. The book was titled *Tab'i' al-Istibdad* (*Traits of Despotism*) and that held the early Islamic state in Medina was the perfect form of government and that Islam began to decline when non-Arabs supplanted the Arabs as rulers and caliphs. The pristine form of Islam could only return via Arab enterprise and leadership. See Nafi, *Arabism, Islamism and the Palestine Question,* 19–20.

10. See Khalidi, et al., eds., *The Origins of Arab Nationalism,* for a series of essays outlining the varied responses to the Ottoman/CUP policies in the Arab world. Also see Hasan Kayali, *Arabs and Young Turks: Ottomanism, Arabism, and Islamism in the Ottoman Empire, 1908–1918* (Berkeley: University of California Press, 1997)—Kayali argues that the CUP was in fact committed to Ottomanism and did not forcefully push "turkification" policies, which only reinforces the notion that Arab dissidents were not necessarily looking to break away from the empire prior to World War I.

11. Kayali, *Arabs and Young Turks,* 39–40.

12. See Dawn, *From Ottomanism to Arabism,* as well as Philip S. Khoury, *Urban Notables and Arab Nationalism: The Politics of Damascus, 1860–1920* (Cambridge: Cambridge University Press, 1983).

13. Nafi, *Arabism, Islamism and the Palestine Question,* 55.

14. Ehud Luz, *Parallels Meet: Religion and Nationalism in the Early Zionist Movement (1882–1904)* (New York: Jewish Publication Society, 1988), x.

15. Ibid.

16. Ibid., xii.

17. Ibid.

18. Itshak Ivry, *Zionism: A Short History* (New York: Hadassah, 1976), 9.

19. Quoted in Arthur Hertzberg, *The Zionist Idea: Historical Analysis and Reader* (New York: Atheneum, 1979), 119.

20. Ibid., 121.

21. Ibid., 133.

22. Quoted in Leslie Stein, *The Hope Fulfilled: The Rise of Modern Israel* (Westport, CT: Praeger, 2003), 7.

23. Ivry, *Zionism,* 20.

24. Quoted in ibid., 26.

25. For instance, Judah Alkalai published in 1839 his book *Darhei Noam* (*Pleasant Paths*), which urged the establishment of Jewish colonies in Palestine in preparation for the coming of the Messiah.

26. By 1880, 60% of the Jews in Palestine were Ashkenazim, i.e., from central and eastern Europe, whereas the remainder were Sephardim, from the Arab countries as well as the Mediterranean basin—this gap would grow by leaps and bounds as Ashkenazis constituted the bulk of the Zionist movement.

27. Indeed, the first Jewish settlement in Zionist lore was set up by twelve male Jews from Jerusalem in 1878 about six miles outside of Jaffa; it was called Petah Tikva (Gate of Hope). It was abandoned in 1881 because of hardships, but it was later reconstituted.

28. Stein, *The Hope Fulfilled,* 2.

29. In 1900, the baron ended his subsidization and administration of the settlements, handing over control to the Jewish Colonial Association, which was founded in 1891 to help Russian Jews relocated to Argentina but turned its attentions to Palestine in 1895.

30. Stein, *The Hope Fulfilled,* 46.

31. See particularly his play *The New Ghetto,* written in 1894 before the Dreyfus affair.

32. Stein, *The Hope Fulfilled*, 58.

33. Theodore Herzl, *The Jewish State: An Attempt at a Modern Solution of the Jewish Question* (London: Henry Pordes, 1993), 15.

34. Quoted in Ivry, *Zionism*, 51.

35. Others included Yitzhak Ben-Zvi, the second president of Israel; Yosef Sprinzak, the first speaker of the Israeli Knesset (parliament); leading ideologist Aharon David Gordon; Yizhak Tabenkin, one of the founders of the Kibbutzim; and the two Israeli prime ministers following Ben-Gurion, Moshe Sharret and Levi Eshkol.

36. Stein, *The Hope Fulfilled*, 93.

37. See Bernard Avishai, *The Tragedy of Zionism: Revolution and Democracy in the Land of Israel* (New York: Farrar, Straus & Giroux, 1985), 45–50.

38. Ibid., 73.

39. Ibid., 72.

40. And even the military foundation as Hashomer (the Guard), a militia organization, was founded in 1909 to protect the Jewish settlements primarily from marauding bands of Arab Bedouin. It was the forerunner to the Haganah defense brigades formed during the Palestine mandate after World War I, which in turn was the precursor to the Israeli Defense Forces.

41. Quoted in Stein, *The Hope Fulfilled*, 45. Prophetically speaking, a Jewish revolutionary by the name of Ilia Rubanovich wrote in an 1886 anti-Zionist polemic that "the Arabs have exactly the same historical right and it will be unfortunate for you if—taking your stand under the protection of international plunderers, using the underhand dealings and intrigue of corrupt diplomacy—you make the peaceful Arabs defend their right. They will answer tears with blood and bury your diplomatic documents in the ashes of your own homes." Ibid.

42. Quoted in ibid., 110.

43. Yosef Gorny, *Zionism and the Arabs 1882–1948: A Study of Ideology* (Oxford: Clarendon Press, 1987), 15.

Theodor Herzl: *The Jewish State* (*Der Judenstaat*), 1896

The Idea which I have developed in this pamphlet is a very old one: it is the restoration of the Jewish State.

...The Jewish question still exists. It would be foolish to deny it. It is a remnant of the Middle Ages, which civilized nations do not even yet seem able to shake off, try as they will. They certainly showed a generous desire to do so when they emancipated us. The Jewish question exists wherever Jews live in perceptible numbers. Where it does not exist, it is carried by Jews in the course of their migrations. We naturally move to those places where we are not persecuted, and there our presence produces persecution. This is the case in every country, and will remain so, even in those highly civilized—for instance, France—until the Jewish question finds a solution on a political basis. The unfortunate Jews are now carrying the seeds of Anti-Semitism into England; they have already introduced it into America.

I believe that I understand Anti-Semitism, which is really a highly complex movement. I consider it from a Jewish standpoint, yet without fear or hatred. I believe that I can see what elements there are in it of vulgar sport, of common trade jealousy, of inherited prejudice, of religious intolerance, and also of pretended self-defence. I think the Jewish question is no more a social than a religious one, notwithstanding that it sometimes takes these and other forms. It is a national question, which can only be solved by making it a political world question, to be discussed and settled by the civilized nations of the world in council.

We are a people—one people.

We have honestly endeavored everywhere to merge ourselves in the social life of surrounding communities and to preserve the faith of our fathers. We are not permitted to do so. In vain are we loyal patriots, our loyalty in some places running to extremes; in vain do we make the same sacrifices of life and property as our fellow-citizens; in vain do we strive to increase the fame of our native land in science and art, or her wealth by trade and commerce. In countries where we have lived for centuries we are still cried down as strangers, and often by those whose ancestors were not yet domiciled in the land where Jews had already had experience of suffering. The majority may decide which are the strangers; for this, as indeed every point which arises in the relations between nations, is a question of might. I do not here surrender any portion of our prescriptive right, when I make this statement merely in my own name as an individual. In the world as it now is and for an indefinite period will probably remain, might precedes right. It is useless, therefore, for us to be loyal patriots, as were the Huguenots who were forced to emigrate. If we could only be left in peace....

But I think we shall not be left in peace.

Oppression and persecution cannot exterminate us. No nation on earth has survived such struggles and sufferings as we have gone through. Jew-baiting has merely stripped off our weaklings; the strong among us were invariably true to their race when persecution broke out against them. This attitude was most clearly apparent in the period immediately following the emancipation of the Jews. Those Jews who were advanced intellectually and materially entirely lost the feeling of belonging to their race. Wherever our political well-being has lasted for any length of time, we have assimilated with our surroundings. I think this is not discreditable. Hence, the statesman who would wish to see a Jewish strain in his nation would have to provide for the duration of our political well-being; and even a Bismarck could not do that.

For old prejudices against us still lie deep in the hearts of the people. He who would have proofs of this need only listen to the people where they speak with frankness and simplicity: proverb and fairy-tale are both Anti-Semitic. A nation is everywhere a great child, which can certainly be educated; but its education would, even in most favorable circumstances, occupy such a vast amount of time that we could, as already mentioned, remove our own difficulties by other means long before the process was accomplished.

Assimilation, by which I understood not only external conformity in dress, habits, customs, and language, but also identity of feeling and manner-assimilation of Jews, could be effected only by intermarriage. But the need for mixed marriages would have to be felt by the majority; their mere recognition by law would certainly not suffice....

No one can deny the gravity of the situation of the Jews. Wherever they live in perceptible numbers, they are more or less persecuted. Their equality before the law, granted by statute, has become practically a dead letter. They are debarred from filling even moderately high positions, either in the army, or in any public or private capacity. And attempts are made to thrust them out of business also: "Don't buy from Jews!"

Attacks in Parliaments, in assemblies, in the press, in the pulpit, in the street, on journeys—for example, their exclusion from certain hotels—even in places of recreation, become daily more numerous. The forms of persecutions vary according to the countries

and social circles in which they occur. In Russia, imposts are levied on Jewish villages; in Rumania, a few persons are put to death; in Germany, they get a good beating occasionally; in Austria, Anti-Semites exercise terrorism over all public life; in Algeria, there are travelling agitators; in Paris, the Jews are shut out of the so-called best social circles and excluded from clubs. Shades of anti-Jewish feeling are innumerable. But this is not to be an attempt to make out a doleful category of Jewish hardships.

I do not intend to arouse sympathetic emotions on our behalf. That would be a foolish, futile, and undignified proceeding. I shall content myself with putting the following questions to the Jews: Is it not true that, in countries where we live in perceptible numbers, the position of Jewish lawyers, doctors, technicians, teachers, and employees of all descriptions becomes daily more intolerable? Is it not true, that the Jewish middle classes are seriously threatened? Is it not true, that the passions of the mob are incited against our wealthy people? Is it not true, that our poor endure greater sufferings than any other proletariat? I think that this external pressure makes itself felt everywhere. In our economically upper classes it causes discomfort, in our middle classes continual and grave anxieties, in our lower classes absolute despair.

Everything tends, in fact, to one and the same conclusion, which is clearly enunciated in that classic Berlin phrase: *"Juden Raus!"* (Out with the Jews!).

I shall now put the Question in the briefest possible form: Are we to "get out" now and where to?

Or, may we yet remain? And, how long?

Let us first settle the point of staying where we are. Can we hope for better days, can we possess our souls in patience, can we wait in pious resignation till the princes and peoples of this earth are more mercifully disposed towards us? I say that we cannot hope for a change in the current of feeling. And why not? Even if we were as near to the hearts of princes as are their other subjects, they could not protect us. They would only feel popular hatred by showing us too much favor. By "too much," I really mean less than is claimed as a right by every ordinary citizen, or by every race. The nations in whose midst Jews live are all either covertly or openly Anti-Semitic.

The common people have not, and indeed cannot have, any historic comprehension. They do not know that the sins of the Middle Ages are now being visited on the nations of Europe. We are what the Ghetto made us. We have attained pre-eminence in finance, because mediaeval conditions drove us to it. The same process is now being repeated. We are again being forced into finance, now it is the stock exchange, by being kept out of other branches of economic activity. Being on the stock exchange, we are consequently exposed afresh to contempt. At the same time we continue to produce an abundance of mediocre intellects who find no outlet, and this endangers our social position as much as does our increasing wealth. Educated Jews without means are now rapidly becoming Socialists. Hence we are certain to suffer very severely in the struggle between classes, because we stand in the most exposed position in the camps of both Socialists and capitalists....

THE PLAN

The whole plan is in its essence perfectly simple, as it must necessarily be if it is to come within the comprehension of all.

Let the sovereignty be granted us over a portion of the globe large enough to satisfy the rightful requirements of a nation; the rest we shall manage for ourselves. The creation of a new State is neither ridiculous nor impossible. We have in our day witnessed the process in connection with nations which were not largely members of the middle class, but poorer, less educated, and consequently weaker than ourselves. The Governments of all countries scourged by Anti-Semitism will be keenly interested in assisting us to obtain the sovereignty we want.

The plan, simple in design, but complicated in execution, will be carried out by two agencies: The Society of Jews and the Jewish Company.

The Society of Jews will do the preparatory work in the domains of science and politics, which the Jewish Company will afterwards apply practically.

The Jewish Company will be the liquidating agent of the business interests of departing Jews, and will organize commerce and trade in the new country.

We must not imagine the departure of the Jews to be a sudden one. It will be gradual, continuous, and will cover many decades. The poorest will go first to cultivate the soil. In accordance with a preconceived plan, they will construct roads, bridges, railways and telegraph installations; regulate rivers; and build their own dwellings; their labor will create trade, trade will create markets and markets will attract new settlers, for every man will go voluntarily, at his own expense and his own risk. The labor expended on the land will enhance its value, and the Jews will soon perceive that a new and permanent sphere of operation is opening here for that spirit of enterprise which has heretofore met only with hatred and obloquy.

If we wish to found a State today, we shall not do it in the way which would have been the only possible one a thousand years ago. It is foolish to revert to old stages of civilization, as many Zionists would like to do. Supposing, for example, we were obliged to clear a country of wild beasts, we should not set about the task in the fashion of Europeans of the fifth century. We should not take spear and lance and go out singly in pursuit of bears; we would organize a large and active hunting party, drive the animals together, and throw a melinite bomb into their midst. If we wish to conduct building operations, we shall not plant a mass of stakes and piles on the shore of a lake, but we shall build as men build now. Indeed, we shall build in a bolder and more stately style than was ever adopted before, for we now possess means which men never yet possessed.

The emigrants standing lowest in the economic scale will be slowly followed by those of a higher grade. Those who at this moment are living in despair will go first. They will be led by the mediocre intellects which we produce so superabundantly and which are persecuted everywhere.

This pamphlet will open a general discussion on the Jewish Question, but that does not mean that there will be any voting on it. Such a result would ruin the cause from the outset, and dissidents must remember that allegiance or opposition is entirely voluntary. He who will not come with us should remain behind.

Let all who are willing to join us, fall in behind our banner and fight for our cause with voice and pen and deed.

Those Jews who agree with our idea of a State will attach themselves to the Society, which will thereby be authorized to confer and treat with Governments in the name of our people. The Society will thus be acknowledged in its relations with Governments as a State-creating power. This acknowledgment will practically create the State.

Should the Powers declare themselves willing to admit our sovereignty over a neutral piece of land, then the Society will enter into negotiations for the possession of this land. Here two territories come under consideration, Palestine and Argentine. In both countries important experiments in colonization have been made, though on the mistaken principle of a gradual infiltration of Jews. An infiltration is bound to end badly. It continues till the inevitable moment when the native population feels itself threatened, and forces the Government to stop a further influx of Jews. Immigration is consequently futile unless we have the sovereign right to continue such immigration.

The Society of Jews will treat with the present masters of the land, putting itself under the protectorate of the European Powers, if they prove friendly to the plan. We could offer the present possessors of the land enormous advantages, assume part of the public debt, build new roads for traffic, which our presence in the country would render necessary, and do many other things. The creation of our State would be beneficial to adjacent countries, because the cultivation of a strip of land increases the value of its surrounding districts in innumerable ways.

Walter Laqueur and Barry Rubin, eds., *The Israel–Arab Reader: A Documentary History of the Middle East Conflict* (New York: Penguin Books, 1984), 6–11.

Basle Program (August 23, 1897)

The aim of Zionism is to create for the Jewish people a home in Palestine secured by public law. The Congress contemplates the following means to the attainment of this end:

1. The promotion, on suitable lines, of the colonization of Palestine by Jewish agricultural and industrial workers.
2. The organization and binding together of the whole of Jewry by means of appropriate institutions, local and international, in accordance with the laws of each country.
3. The strengthening and fostering of Jewish national sentiment and consciousness.
4. Preparatory steps towards obtaining Government consent, where necessary, to the attainment of the aim of Zionism.

Bernard Reich, ed., *Arab–Israeli Conflict and Conciliation: A Documentary History* (Westport, CT: Praeger, 1995), 18–19.

Negib Azoury: Program of the League of the Arab Fatherland

THERE IS NOTHING more liberal than the league's program.

The league wants, before anything else, to separate the civil and the religious power, in the interest of Islam and the Arab nation, and to form an Arab empire stretching from the Tigris and the Euphrates to the Suez Isthmus, and from the Mediterranean to the Arabian Sea.

The mode of government will be a constitutional sultanate based on the freedom of all the religions and the equality of all the citizens before the law. It will respect the interests of Europe, all the concessions and all the privileges which had been granted to her up to now by the Turks. It will also respect the autonomy of the Lebanon, and the independence of the principalities of Yemen, Nejd, and Iraq.

The league offers the throne of the Arab Empire to that prince of the Khedivial family of Egypt who will openly declare himself in its favor and who will devote his energy and his resources to this end.

It rejects the idea of unifying Egypt and the Arab Empire under the same monarchy, because the Egyptians do not belong to the Arab race; they are of the African Berber family and the language which they spoke before Islam bears no similarity to Arabic. There exists, moreover, between Egypt and the Arab Empire a natural frontier which must be respected in order to avoid the introduction, in the new state, of the germs of discord and destruction. Never, as a matter of fact, have the ancient Arab caliphs succeeded for any length of time in controlling the two countries at the same time.

The Arab fatherland also offers the universal religious caliphate over the whole of Islam to that sherif (descendant of the Prophet) who will sincerely embrace its cause and devote himself to this work. The religious caliph will have as a completely independent political state the whole of the actual vilayet of Hijaz, with the town and the territory of Medina, as far as Aqaba. He will enjoy the honors of a sovereign and will hold a real moral authority over all the Muslims of the world.

One of the principal causes of the fall of the vast empire of the Arabs was the centralization in a single hand of the civil and the religious powers. It is also for this reason that the caliphate of Islam has become today so ridiculous and so contemptible in the hands of the Turks. The successor of the Prophet of Allah must enjoy an incontestable moral prestige; his whole life must be of unblemished honor, his authority suffering no diminution, his majesty independent [of anything other than itself]. His power also will be universal; from his residence he will rule morally over all the Muslims of the universe who will hurry in pilgrimage to the sanctuaries of Mohammed.

[About the position of the caliph, Azoury offers a word of explanation.]

The caliph of Islam must be either the sovereign of all the Muslims of the earth united in a single state, which has always proved impossible, even under the first caliphs, or, quite simply, the sovereign of a country entirely Islamic. There is indeed no country more Islamic than the Hijaz, and there are no towns more suitable than Medina and Mecca to receive the Supreme Head of the believers.

Negib Azoury, *Le Réveil de la Nation Arabe dans l'Asie Turque en Présence des Intérêts et des Rivalités des Puissance Étrangères, de la Curie Romaine et due Patriarcat Oecuménique* (Paris, 1905), 245–247, 248, as quoted in Sylvia G. Haim, *Arab Nationalism: An Anthology* (Berkeley: University of California Press, 1962), 81–82.

Three
THE CONVERGENCE

World War I is the most important period in the history of the modern Middle East, not least of all in the Arab–Israeli arena. Many, if not most, of the important issues in the Middle East during the twentieth century and into the twenty-first century, such as Arab nationalism, Islamic extremism, the Arab–Israeli conflict, and even Iraq's Saddam Hussein, can trace important links to the events that transpired in the region during and immediately after the "war to end all wars"; indeed, one could make the argument that World War I catalyzed, if not spawned, these and other important historical events and trends that have since occurred in the Middle East. This is the case even though the epicenter of the war was always in Europe and events in the Middle East were always of secondary concern to the course of the war on the continent to the primary European combatants; nonetheless, to the countries and peoples of the region, it had a direct and long-lasting effect.

World War I was a tremendously complex period in the Middle East, comprised of the establishment of new states; the end of the Ottoman Empire; the evincing of nationalist and territorial goals on the part of Arabs and Zionists; the intervention of European interests, designs, and intrigue; and crisscrossing, ambiguous, changing, and often contradictory promises, pledges, and declarations. As such, this is also a period in modern Middle East history that is quite difficult to comprehend for the relatively uninitiated. It has been my experience that the most efficient way to understand the complexities of the period is to first and foremost examine the British role. Britain was, by far, the prime mover of events in the Middle East during and immediately after the war. It was London that had the most influence in the region of all of the European powers before, during, and after the conflagration. It was London that largely initiated and engaged in the diplomatic machinations that resulted in such infamous documents as the Sykes-Picot Agreement, the Hussein–McMahon correspondence, and the Balfour Declaration, not to even mention the postwar negotiations that led to the redrawing of the map in the Middle East that has essentially remained geographically unaltered since that time.

If World War I is the most important period in modern Middle East history, the most important single decision may have been the Ottoman Empire's entrance into the war on the side of Germany and the Central powers. The Ottoman Empire had certainly shown some gumption that belied the "sick man of Europe" caricature in its unsuccessful efforts to prevent Libya from falling under Italian control (1911) and in the first and second Balkan wars in 1912–1913. Although they eventually lost in each of these, it did foreshadow that under certain conditions the Ottomans could still field a formidable fighting capability, something the entente powers, especially the British, would learn the hard way. Socioeconomically speaking, however, the Ottoman Empire could really ill afford to be drawn into an extended European conflict, although as in almost every other part of the world, when the "guns of August" sounded in 1914, it was thought the conflict would be of short duration, certainly not a largely static four years of unprecedented death and destruction. But the lure of reacquiring lands from and reordering the relationship with countries such as Russia, Britain, and France was ultimately too much to pass up. Germany had incrementally built up its economic and military position with the Ottomans, and certainly the choice was made that much easier when Russia, which had had its eye on Ottoman domains and had for over a century pressured the sultanate, positioned itself opposite the kaiser following the chain of events emanating from the assassination of Archduke Ferdinand of the Austro–Hungarian Empire in Serbia. And from the point of view of the Sublime Porte, particularly that of the acknowledged triumvirate of Committee of Union and Progress (CUP) leaders who held the reins of power—Talaat, Jamal, and Enver—the Central powers (Germany, Austria–Hungary, and Bulgaria) had at least as much chance to emerge victorious as the emerging coalition of Entente powers (Britain, France, Russia, Italy, and later Greece). The Ottoman Empire, already having experienced the reforms of the Tanzimat and on the precipice of a deeper reformation under the guidance of the Young Turks, could be on the cusp of launching a new era of dignity and power—provided they were on the winning side.

For Britain, the decision by Constantinople instantly transformed its age-old policy toward the Ottoman Empire. For over a century it had been British policy to maintain the integrity of the Ottoman Empire so as to ensure the lifeline to India and create a buffer to Russian expansionist designs toward the heartland of the Middle East. Although to many this stated policy may have seemed more like lip service when set against British actions in terms of its own territorial control over Ottoman lands and interference in Ottoman affairs, it often proved to be otherwise. Regardless, however, now the Ottomans were the enemy, and their defeat became official policy; indeed, recognizing the growing danger of imperial Germany, London buried the hatchet with St. Petersburg in the 1907 Anglo–Russian agreement (as they had with France earlier in 1904 with the Entente Cordiale), and Great Britain in World War I was now an ally of the Russian czar, whose friendship and interests were of the utmost importance upon the outbreak of the conflict. It was imperative that Russia stay in the

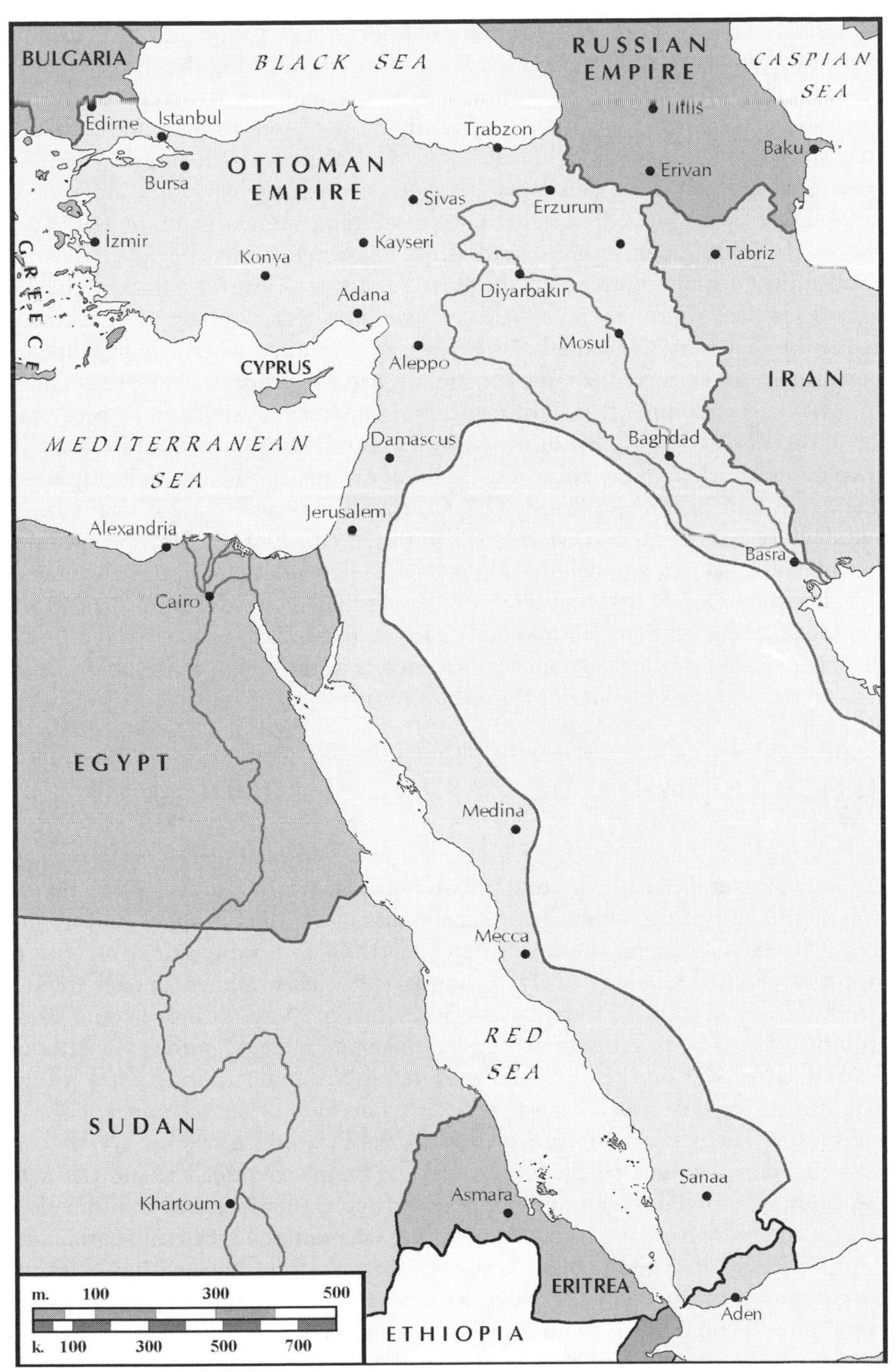

The Ottoman Empire in 1914. (Middle East Studies Association, Justin McCarthy, University of Louisville, © 2003.)

conflagration to force Germany to fight on multiple fronts. Despite the fact that many European diplomats envisioned the Ottoman Empire surviving the war, albeit most likely in a truncated fashion, plans began to emerge early in the war regarding the disposition of Ottoman territories, particularly those regions in the Middle East that were still under Ottoman control, such as Syria, Palestine, Iraq, and the Hijaz (the western strip of the Arabian Peninsula that contained Islam's two holiest cities, Mecca and Medina). In the immediate sense, once hostilities commenced in the war, British policy in the Middle East revolved around the following: (1) the strategic necessity of defeating the Ottoman Empire; (2) the creation of a pro-British bulwark in the Arab territories of the empire that most believed would be detached from Constantinople in some form or fashion (essentially, these new Arab entities, whether independent or protectorates, would serve the same function as had the Ottomans, i.e., maintain the lifeline to India and buffer British strategic interests in the region); and (3) accomplish both of these objectives while not upsetting London's allies, France and Russia, in a way that would deleteriously affect their abilities to carry on the war in Europe, especially as they were bearing the brunt of the German offensives. This was a tall task, and as we shall see, in order to achieve its goals in the Middle East, the British expediently constructed, amended, and reversed their policies depending upon the exigencies of the diplomatic and military situation at any given moment, producing in the end what on the surface seemed to be contradictory pledges to a variety of states and groups as well as setting up unrealistic parameters for success in the region that would in many ways shape the course of modern Middle East history.

BRITISH ENTRY IN THE WAR IN THE MIDDLE EAST

When the Sublime Porte formally allied itself with the Central powers in August 1914, there were distinct differences among British policymakers in London and in the field as to whether or not the Entente powers should engage the Ottoman Empire militarily. There was a general consensus that the Ottoman Empire was weak and that it could be defeated relatively easily, a complacency that would come back to haunt them; but there were initial fears that the war effort in western Europe could be deleteriously affected by diverting much needed men and materiel to the east. Although Britain declared war on the Ottoman Empire on November 5, 1914, scant military action directed against it had been considered. This view began to change, however, by early 1915. The main reason for this was that the war in Europe had clearly come to a virtual draw by then, characterized by static trench warfare. The war cabinet in the Asquith government began to listen to those (such as future prime minister David Lloyd George) who had long argued for opening up another front in the south and attacking Germany through the Balkans and the Austro–Hungarian empire—with little strategic movement in Europe, perhaps a quick strike through the underbelly of the Central powers could bring about a swift and conclusive end to the war. To do this, however, first necessitated a military confrontation with the Ottomans. Prime Minister Asquith, who had been particularly sympathetic to Russian interests, also saw an advantage to taking the strategically prized Turkish straits (Bosphorus and Dardanelles) and holding them as a carrot to ultimately award the czar for maintaining a zealous effort in the war.

Thus were the origins of what would become the disastrous Gallipoli campaign led by British, Australian, and New Zealander forces beginning in February 1915, intended to quickly move up the peninsula astride the Dardanelles toward Constantinople, swiftly knocking the Ottomans out of the war. It is not the purpose of this book to detail the nature of the campaign and the reasons for its failure, but suffice it to say that it was an extraordinary combination of military mismanagement, ill-timed and outright bad decision making on the part of a host of British civilian and military officials (for which Winston Churchill unwarrantedly received most of the blame), combined with the desperate effectiveness of outmanned and outgunned Turkish troops advised by their German allies. For our purposes, the Gallipoli campaign brought the Ottoman Empire front and center into the international war effort and international diplomacy. By doing so, its disposition, including the Arab Middle East, after its presumed defeat scaled the bureaucratic morass to become an item of increasing importance in London, Paris, and St. Petersburg as the war dragged on.

The British-led onslaught at Gallipoli, while on the one hand intended to acquire the carrot of the straits in exchange for the czar's continued involvement in diverting German resources on the eastern front (and, indeed, utilizing other Ottoman territories as inducement to countries such as Italy and the Balkan states to enter the fray on the side of the Entente powers), removing the Ottomans as a threat to Russian positions in eastern Anatolia (especially as the Ottomans actually went on the offensive there against Russia in September 1914), and maintaining a steady supply route to Russia through the Black Sea, on the other hand also raised fears in St. Petersburg, where a quick Ottoman collapse was expected, that Britain might just keep the straits. There were enough British officials (first and foremost Winston Churchill) who publicly cast Russia as London's primary foe following the conclusion of the war, essentially the "great game" taking up where it had left off a decade before. Therefore, Prime Minister Asquith felt the need to allay Russian concerns regarding the disposition of the Turkish prize. This manifested itself in the Constantinople agreement of March 1915, what Churchill termed a "convulsive gesture of self-preservation," as it essentially awarded the Turkish straits to Russia, something the British had ardently worked to deny to a succession of czars for over a century. But the expediency of war dictated a radical shift in traditional British policy. And with the Constantinople agreement, the Arab Middle East formally entered the diplomatic scene, and places such as Palestine suddenly became strategic ground to be bartered and negotiated for among a bevy of great powers and interested groups, the latter including Arabs and Zionists. As such, Asquith appointed career diplomat Sir Maurice de Bunsen to head an interdepartmental committee on April 8, 1915, to draw up recommendations on the question of the disposition of the Ottoman Empire following the war, formally beginning a process that would take many twists and turns before the postwar settlements actually came into being (the de Bunsen committee produced its report on June 30, 1915). The ultimate failure at Gallipoli, which became apparent by the fall of 1915, compelled the British to seek an alternative route toward defeating the Ottomans in the Middle East, a path that would ultimately lead to a campaign directed by British General Sir Edmund Allenby emanating out of Egypt up through Palestine toward Damascus. It also forced the British to recognize that they might need some assistance not only in this task but also in the postwar strategic map in the region, which would lead various British representatives to negotiate with groups of

Arabs and Zionists competing to convince London that they could serve its interests better than anyone else. Even if the British had been more successful at Gallipoli, there is no doubt that London would have had to deal with vexing issues regarding the Arab territories of the Ottoman Empire after the war once conflict on this front ended; but what failure meant was that Britain now had to deal with these complex issues during the military and diplomatic flux of wartime—for virtually the entire duration of the war itself. As such, a whole host of complicating factors entered the diplomatic equation that might otherwise have remained on the sidelines.

While the British certainly suspected the materialization of a Russian threat after the war, there were other British officials, especially those in the field in the Arab Middle East, who were convinced that France could be London's primary obstacle toward achieving its imperial objectives. These were certainly the views held by the legendary Lord Kitchener (although he also appreciated the Russian threat), who headed Britain's presence, as agent, in Egypt, which had been formally declared a British protectorate shortly after the war began; indeed, at about the same time, Kitchener vacated his post in Cairo (with Sir Henry McMahon replacing him in the newly created position of high commissioner) to assume the important position of minister of war in the Asquith cabinet. Well-positioned, the views of Kitchener's loyal lieutenants in Cairo found a strong voice representing them directly in the government, carrying far greater weight than they would have otherwise had and eventually outdistancing on a variety of issues the many other voices on Middle East affairs emanating from various corners in London as well as the British India Office, which had traditionally fashioned British policy toward the Persian Gulf region of the Middle East, including the area that would soon become the country of Iraq. While Kitchener at first thought the British should concentrate their military resources in Europe rather than the Middle East, a position he would change as exemplified by authorizing the Gallipoli campaign, he never wavered from his early conclusion that the Middle East would play a vital strategic role in the postwar environment; therefore, he and his diplomatic "groupies," even before Gallipoli, viewed the Middle East as part of the evolving international diplomatic game. Indeed, the importance that Kitchener and his people attached to the Middle East converged rather nicely with the shifting views in London in early 1915 regarding the fate of the Ottoman Empire and its Middle East holdings.

BRITISH AND FRENCH NEGOTIATIONS

France, for its part, was becoming a bit concerned that while it was bearing the brunt of the war on the western front, Great Britain was in the process of stealing away with the Middle East. The fact that the British were militarily engaged at both ends of the empire early in the war at Gallipoli as well as in Mesopotamia (Iraq), the latter guided by the British India Office and meeting with but little more success than what their compatriots experienced on the shores of the Dardanelles, informed Paris that it had best barter for its claims in the region before the British were in such a strong military position as to dictate the terms. As with Russia, British officialdom comprised two views: accommodation of the French in the Middle East for the sake of strategic cooperation in Europe and exclusion of the French from the region as much as possible in order to better advance British interests. Kitchener and his group, including Sir Mark

Sykes, who was the legendary general's representative on the de Bunsen committee, favored the latter position, anticipating that the prewar imperial game with France which many of them experienced firsthand in the 1898 Fashoda crisis in the Sudan would resume after the war. Whatever the case, they realized that it was a situation that must be delicately negotiated.

The British, however, began to listen more intently to French interests by late 1915, when it became clear that the Gallipoli campaign was a military disaster. The British, therefore, would not be able to impose at will their designs on the Middle East. The diplomatic battleground in the Middle East between the two European powers would revolve around Syria, including present-day Israel/Palestine and Lebanon. The French believed that Syria was practically their birthright, dating back to their involvement in this part of the region beginning with the Crusades. Paris also had a direct interest in the disposition of the Ottoman realm as it provided 45% of the private sector foreign capital in the empire and assumed 60% of the Ottoman public debt.[1] The British Arabists in the region, however, were not alone in entertaining some rather fanciful ideas about the region and the war itself. They tended to believe and propagate the fantastical idea that the CUP was controlled by pro-German Jews, a thought process that was part and parcel of and would reinforce their generally anti-Semitic and misguided notion of the extensive influence of world Jewry, which was ironically a significant contributing factor to the issuance of the Balfour Declaration in 1917 in order to win over the inflated power of the Zionist movement.[2]

There were some practical reasons beyond Gallipoli that compelled even Sykes to negotiate concessions to the French in the Middle East. If the British were to continue to militarily engage the Ottoman Empire, even via an alternative route, they would have to divert resources from the western front, something that would require French acquiescence, and Paris would only do so for a price—Sykes understood this. In addition, another plan that was being hatched to aid the British cause in the Middle East, one involving a possible Arab revolt led by the Sharif Hussein, the leader in the Hijaz and Guardian of the Two Holy Places (Mecca and Medina), might be scuttled because it was thought that if British and Arab military action was not taken quickly, the Ottomans might depose or otherwise get rid of Hussein before the rebellion could be launched. So, concurrently with British negotiations with representatives of the sharif (to be discussed shortly), the British hastened to meet with French diplomats to find mutual accord between London and Paris so that plans could move forward in the region.

The French sent François Georges Picot as their representative, and negotiations began in November 1915. After negotiations stalled by December, Sir Mark Sykes was designated as the lead British representative. Reflecting in many ways the de Bunsen committee report, what came to be called the Sykes-Picot Agreement, consummated in May 1916, consisted of dividing the heartland of the Arab world into spheres of influence. The French could assume direct control over the coast of Syria west of a line running north–south from Aleppo through Hama and Homs to Damascus (including modern-day Lebanon, which, at the time, consisted of a large and economically important Arab Christian population that had long had ties with France), while the interior of Syria would be a "sphere of influence" subject to some level of indirect control. The French also received the province of Mosul within their sphere of influence in what is now northern Iraq, while the British would retain the Ottoman provinces

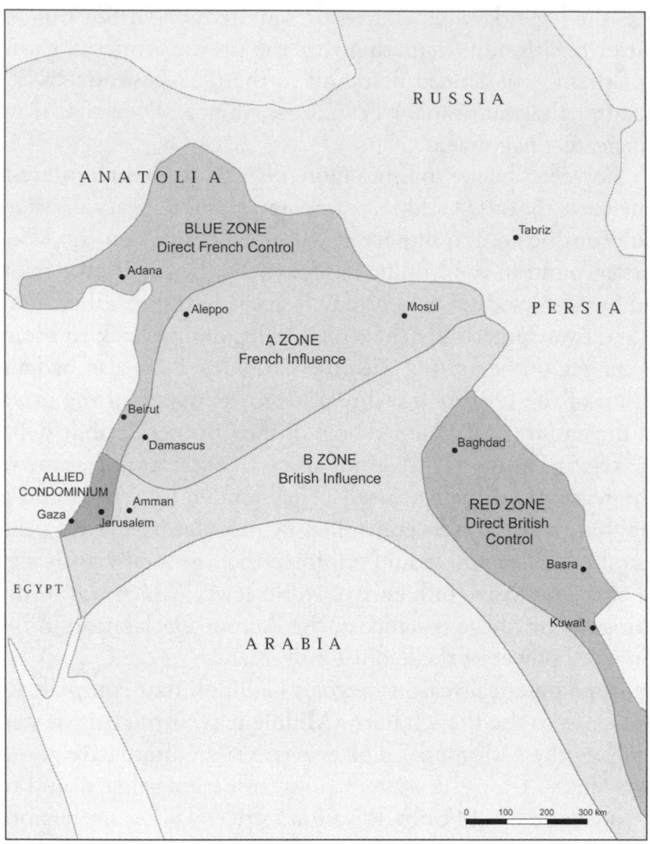

Sykes-Picot Agreement, 1916. (Palestinian Academic Society for the Study of International Affairs.)

of Baghdad and Basra to the south down to the Persian Gulf. From the British perspective, this would not only allay French concerns but also construct a French buffer between Russia and British-controlled territories in the Middle East. Palestine was a different story, however; both Britain and France wanted it within their respective spheres of influence. The intensity of the debate is revealed by the fact that no definitive agreement could be reached on the matter, and what was finally agreed to, more for the sake of expediency than anything else, was that neither the British nor the French would receive Palestine; instead, most of the territory, including Jerusalem, would fall under some sort of international administration that would presumably be delineated by an undetermined mechanism following the war. Otherwise in this part of the Arab world, the remaining territory would form some sort of Arab state or confederation of states that would be at least nominally independent, i.e., essentially Arabia minus the Persian Gulf shaykhdoms in which the British had established themselves and had held a dominant position since the early 1800s. The extent to which most British officials actually thought of Arab independence as a reality is a different question since many viewed the Arabs as incapable of statehood in the short term and as a vehicle through which Britain could exert its influence in the region, whether or not it would be through direct or indirect means. In addition, the British, especially those in Cairo, believed that it would just be a matter of time before they were able to establish facts on the ground through military action in order to secure Palestine,

ARAB INVOLVEMENT AND THE SHARIFIAN REVOLT

The Sharif Hussein was a Hashemite and therefore a direct descendant of the family of the prophet Muhammad. He was the Guardian of the Two Holy Places, Mecca and Medina, in the Hijaz region of Arabia, which did accord him with a certain amount of religious and political legitimacy, although not as much as one might think being a Hashemite would actually provide.[3] He was certainly an opportunist who had come to the conclusion in the years preceding World War I that he needed a patron in order to realize his ambitions of expanding his realm not only throughout Arabia against rival clans, such as the Saudis, but also across the Arab world in the Fertile Crescent region. He had not had the best of relations with Ottoman sultans; indeed, Abdul-Hamid II had placed him under house arrest in Constantinople for a number of years, and he was under constant fear that he would be removed. The entrance of the CUP into power in Constantinople was therefore welcomed by Hussein, and the CUP leaders in turn allowed him to return to the Hijaz with the hope of gaining a valuable ally among the Arabs. After Hussein returned to the Hijaz in 1908, he began to clash with the local Turkish governor sent by the Sublime Porte in a power game over who was actually in control of the area; again, he soon feared that he might be forcibly removed.[4] It is under these circumstances that he began his first halting steps toward establishing a relationship with the British, essentially at this point an attempt to keep all of his options open.

Before the outbreak of war in 1914, Abdullah, Hussein's eldest son, visited with British officials in Cairo on his way to and back from his visit to Constantinople. This seemed to be a "sounding out" type of visit, one in which Abdullah brought up for the first time the idea of British support for Hashemite objectives in return for rebelling against the Ottomans. While keeping the doors of communication open, the British responded unenthusiastically since there was still hope of maintaining the age-old policy of London toward Constantinople. By October, however, when it became apparent that Britain and the Ottoman Empire would be on opposite sides of the conflict, Kitchener, through his representative Ronald Storrs, communicated to Hussein that there existed the possibility of British support for an Arab caliphate (presumably with Hussein as caliph) in return for his efforts at launching an Arab rebellion. Thus began a period of each side trying to figure out exactly what the other wanted and whether or not they could deliver on any promises. For his part, Kitchener seems to have thought that the position of caliph was akin to that of the Catholic pope, i.e., a purely spiritual leader with little to no actual political power; on the other hand, as had been the case with many of the caliphs throughout Islamic history, Hussein understood this offer to mean both spiritual and political authority, which converged much more closely with his own political ambitions.

Hussein then began to explore if in fact he could indeed launch a genuine Arab revolt of the sort that the British anticipated. Another of the sharif's sons, Faisal, stopped in the hotbed of nascent Arab nationalism in Damascus in March 1915 on his way to Constantinople. There he met with representatives of Arab secret societies such as al-'Ahd and al-Fatat, who were bent on at least obtaining more autonomy from Ottoman rule, to discuss the possibilities of drawing up a program of action and cooperation with the Hijazis. To both the British and the Hashemites, the fact that most of the Ottoman military divisions in the Middle East were made up of Arabs, including many secret-society cohorts, was very appealing in terms of providing a tangible potentiality. While Faisal was in the Ottoman capital, members of the secret societies drew up what came to be called the Damascus Protocol, which outlined Arab demands to the British in return for rebelling against the Turks. It essentially called for British recognition of Arab independence in Syria (including present-day Lebanon, Israel, and Jordan), Iraq, and Arabia.[5] Faisal brought the Damascus Protocol to his father, whereupon it was adopted as the basis for Hashemite policy with the British. A number of leading members of the secret societies in Damascus, though certainly not all, agreed to accept Hussein as the Arab leader of any movement that might develop. Although still tentative regarding the British, it is under such conditions, armed with the apparent means to deliver a real rebellion, that the sharif initiated what came to be known as the Hussein–McMahon correspondence.

In July 1915, prior to the commencement of the Sykes-Picot negotiations, Hussein sent off the first salvo in the correspondence to the British high commissioner of Egypt demanding recognition of the territorial demands as outlined in the Damascus Protocol in addition to agreeing to an Arab caliphate—which, as many have pointed out, was quite ironic, i.e., a Muslim asking a representative of the Christian West to consecrate the caliphate. Sir Henry McMahon's response was lukewarm at best, believing as other British officials in Cairo did that the Arabs had little to offer, especially considering the fact that a good many of them had obviously chosen the German side and were at that very moment battling British forces at Gallipoli.[6] It was the troubles the British were encountering, however, in this very same Gallipoli campaign that soon compelled a dramatic change of policy in Cairo regarding the sharif's offer; indeed, British military commanders at Gallipoli were apparently appealing to McMahon to do something to dilute the Arab forces in the Ottoman army on the Dardanelles. Not only was a diversion desired, but it had also become clear with the failure of the Gallipoli campaign that an alternative route to defeating the Ottoman Empire in the Middle East would need to be taken; and for this, Arab compliance and assistance would be needed. Also important in this unfolding story was the role of a Kurdish soldier by the name of al-Faruqi, who had been fighting at Gallipoli but defected to the British side. He was brought to Cairo and wove a tail of intimate knowledge of the Arab secret societies, a widespread burgeoning Arab revolt if only it could be given the proper spark—and German inroads into the secret societies if the British did not act fast. Although his claim was greatly exaggerated as it turned out, it was a contributing factor in convincing British officials in Cairo that an Arab revolt that could debilitate the Ottomans was a very real possibility. This is certainly an instance when British policy was ill-informed; indeed, one could even say they were hoodwinked. The Arab secret societies and nascent Arab nationalist movement had already been crushed in Syria by Jamal Pasha, including scores of executions, and Arab units in Ottoman armies had already been scattered across the empire; so, in other words, the British decision to engage with Hussein was based on false pretenses and inadequate information—even misinformation. As we shall see, what the British eventually got in terms of an Arab revolt was considerably less than expected.

Sir Henry McMahon thus received sanction from London to negotiate with Hussein an Arab revolt. A letter from the Egyptian high commissioner dated October 24, 1915, was sent to the sharif. In it, McMahon, in return for a sharifian-led Arab revolt, offered independence to the Arabs along the lines of the Damascus Protocol with three reservations—notice the passive nature of the note as shown in the documents; i.e., it did not specify the borders of an independent Arab state but qualified a nebulous offer with restrictions. The Arabs would gain independence except in areas (1) which the British decided were not "purely Arab," which meant the eastern Mediterranean coast, or west of the line in Syria that goes from Aleppo in the north through Hama, Homs, and then Damascus in the south; (2) in which the special interests of France limited Britain—this pertained especially to the interior of Syria east of the aforementioned line as delineated in Sykes-Picot; and (3) in which Britain had already existing treaties, referring primarily to long-standing agreements between London and the Persian Gulf Arab shaykhdoms. The first two reservations would cause most of the consternation and bitter debate that has ensued ever since regarding what actually was included in an independent Arab state that might emerge out of the war. The different interpretations surrounding the first reservation would become particularly relevant with the onset of the Arab–Israeli conflict because it dealt with the disposition of Palestine. There have been volumes of dispute and discord over whether or not the west of the Aleppo to Damascus line meant the inclusion of Palestine. It all may come down to inadequate translations, but as in any diplomatic correspondence or agreement, individual words can cause decades of conflict. The dispute centers on the use of the term *vilayet* (*wilayat* in Arabic), which was an official Ottoman term meaning "province," the largest administrative unit below that of the empire itself, as it was translated into Arabic in the letter to Hussein. Usually a number of districts (singular *sanjaq*) constituted a province, the latter led by a provincial governor appointed by Constantinople. The confusion begins with the fact that oftentimes provinces, such as the Syrian province, were known more colloquially by the main city located there; therefore, the province of Syria was often simply called "Damascus." If this is the case, then the province of Syria/Damascus extended from around Hama just south of the vilayet of Aleppo all the way down to the Gulf of Aqaba. West of the *suriyya* vilayet was the special sanjaq of Jerusalem (which constituted about the southern half of present-day Israel) and the vilayet of Beirut (which was made up of the northern half of present-day Israel, Lebanon, and up to the northern coast of present-day Syria west of Aleppo). Under this interpretation, "west" of the Damascus/Syria province certainly included Palestine, and it therefore should be excluded from an independent Arab state. This tended to be the position adopted by the British, especially after the Balfour Declaration of November 1917 added a new group, the Zionist movement, to the list of claimants for the land of Palestine.

On the other hand, upon closer examination, this is clearly not what was meant. If "vilayet" does indeed refer to the province of Syria, then how could the same term be utilized to refer to Hama or Homs, both of which were districts within the Syrian province? It is more likely that the British, when referring to those four cities, meant west of the general region of those locales—more of a geographic designation. If this is the case, then the area they outlined as not being purely Arab consists of what is basically present-day Lebanon—definitely not Palestine. Under this interpretation, one that, for obvious reasons, has been championed by most Arabs ever since, Palestine, including the holy city of Jerusalem, should have been included in an independent Arab state under the apparent terms of the Hussein–McMahon correspondence. The reference to French interests has also come under intense scrutiny, especially when cast against the relief of the eighteen-month Arab kingdom in Syria headed by Faisal following the war that forcibly gave way to French control according to the loose strictures of Sykes-Picot. It seems as though Hussein was aware of British concern for French interests and the paramount position France had in British strategic calculations, as was made clear to him in McMahon's final letter in the correspondence of January 1916; but it is unclear how much the sharif knew (or was told) about the extent to which they were being met.

One of the problems with the Hussein–McMahon correspondence is that it was just that—a correspondence, not an officially recognized treaty. The letters were presumably the prelude to a negotiated settlement regarding an Arab revolt. But the Arab revolt launched by Faisal in June 1916 and assisted by the British liaison officer T. E. Lawrence came and went, yet no specific border discussions ensued during the war. McMahon's language in his letters has been variously described as flowery and ambiguous and purposely so since he knew of the simultaneous negotiations with the French over much of the same land. In strict diplomatic language, certainly along accepted Western standards of the day, there was no legal contradiction since there was no official document to stand up to Sykes-Picot, which itself did not survive the war unscathed and unaltered. And certainly the British were quite adept at always making sure, as good diplomats do, that there was an "out" if necessary regarding specific and legal commitments—something the Zionists would find out for themselves a few years after Balfour.

The moral obligation of the British, however, in terms of intent and deception may be quite another matter. It seems as though the British never really took the idea of true Arab independence seriously during the wartime negotiations. This was a combination, as mentioned previously, of the low regard British officials had for the capabilities of the Arabs to govern themselves and of the need to successfully maintain the strategic interests of London in the Middle East, something, it was soon realized, that would require some level of British influence and control in order to fill the vacuum created by the Ottoman retreat. The offer to Hussein appears to have been something of a convulsive reaction to the military disaster at Gallipoli, attempting to bait the Arabs into an arrangement that would augment in the immediate sense British strategic objectives vis-à-vis the Ottoman Empire. When responding to a British representative in India, who was becoming a bit concerned that what McMahon was offering the Arabs could infringe upon the British India Office's purview in Mesopotamia, the high commissioner of Egypt wrote the following:

> I do not for one moment go to the length of imagining that the present negotiations will go far to shape the future form of Arabia or to either establish our rights or to bind our hands in that country.... What we have to arrive at now is to tempt the Arab people into the right path, detach them from the enemy and bring them to our side.... This on our part is at present largely a matter of words and to succeed we must use persuasive terms and abstain from haggling over conditions—whether about Baghdad or elsewhere.[7]

On the other hand, there was certainly deception going in the other direction as well. Al-Faruqi's claims as well as Hussein's purported ability to rally the Arabs to

Lawrence of Arabia

Born Thomas Edward Lawrence in north Wales in 1888, "Lawrence of Arabia," as he came to be known, emerged out of World War I as one of the most celebrated, almost mythic, figures of the British military campaign in the Middle East and the Arab fight for independence. Lawrence wrote his thesis at Oxford University on Crusader castles in the Levant, and he traveled to the region a number of times on an archeological dig in northern Syria for the British Museum. While there, he became enamored with Arab culture, and he took to learning Arabic. When the war broke out in 1914, Lawrence was commissioned as a lieutenant in the British army and was assigned in 1915 to the Military Intelligence Department in Cairo.

Lawrence quickly impressed his superiors with his intellect, energy, and understanding of the region; and he was promoted to captain in early 1916. But he longed for more action and adventure, especially as his two brothers were killed on the western front in Europe. He was sent on a mission to Iraq to secure the release of British troops surrounded by Ottoman Turkish forces at Kut al-Amara. He was unsuccessful in this, but still his valiant efforts and his knowledge of indigenous elements won him praise. He seemed destined to become involved in bigger events. It was at this time that, per the Hussein–McMahon correspondence, the Sharif Hussein launched the Arab revolt in the Hijaz on June 5, 1916. Lawrence was assigned to report on the nature and development of the revolt.

While in Arabia, Lawrence met with all four sons of the Sharif Hussein, but he came to respect Faisal bin Hussein the most, describing him in his epic account of his Arabian exploits *Seven Pillars of Wisdom* as "the man I had come to Arabia to seek—the leader who would bring the Arab Revolt to full glory." For the next two years Lawrence would act as an adviser to and British liaison with Faisal. The initial object of the Arab revolt was to kick the Ottomans out of Medina and other cities in Arabia. Faisal and Lawrence, however, quickly altered the plan to that of bypassing, thus bottling up, the Turks in Arabia and setting out toward Damascus, in particular aiding General Allenby's Palestine campaign by raiding Ottoman trains, supplies, and depots associated with the 700-mile Hijaz railway from Medina to Damascus. The Arab revolt's most spectacular feat was the taking of the important coastal port of Aqaba on the Gulf of Aqaba. Surprise was the key element as the Arabs attacked from the direction of the desert behind the fortifications and guns of the Ottomans. Getting enough Bedouin Arab warriors was always an ongoing concern, and Faisal and Lawrence continuously struggled to acquire and maintain a minimum force level; in this, Lawrence's role was crucial in gaining the trust and participation of certain Bedouin shaykhs. Although the Arab warriors were hardy, they were also independent-minded and fickle. As one military colleague Colonel Pierce C. Joyce, who fought with him, commented on Lawrence, "It was not, as is often supposed, by his individual leadership of hordes of Bedouin that he achieved success, but by the wise selection of tribal leaders."* Lawrence wrote that "after the capture of Aqaba, things changed so much that I was no longer a witness of the Revolt, but a protagonist in the Revolt."** Indeed, the Ottomans actually offered a reward for his capture.

Lawrence continued to direct raids against Ottoman positions throughout 1917, although on one occasion while reconnoitering he was captured by Turkish forces. He apparently successfully convinced his captors that he was a light-skinned Circassian, but that did not prevent him from being beaten and, according to some speculation, sexually molested. It was an event that he obviously never forgot, the torment of it probably reaching depths of which even he was unaware. But he secured his release, rejoined the revolt, and pushed onward toward Damascus, which was captured by the Arabs under British auspices in 1918. Describing his entrance into the city on October 1 amid a jubilant population, Lawrence later wrote that "I drank as deeply as any man should do, when we took Damascus: and was sated with it."*** Two days later he returned to England.

Back in England, gladly away from it all, he began work on his memoirs. Celebrity, however, caught up with him as American journalist Lowell Thomas, who had spent some time with Lawrence during the war, began a series of popular lectures that focused upon—and embellished—Lawrence's role in the Arab revolt, labeling him at one point the "uncrowned king of Arabia." It was at this juncture that T. E. Lawrence became "Lawrence of Arabia." But Lawrence utilized this newfound celebrity to reengage in the complex politics surrounding the disposition of the Arab lands after the war. He traveled to Paris in 1919 as part of the British delegation to the postwar talks, meeting again with and interpreting for Faisal. On behalf of Arab postwar claims and offering cogent warnings to the British imperial position in the Middle East, Lawrence wrote a series of letters in *The Times*. He also joined the British Colonial Office headed by Winston Churchill in 1920 and was instrumental in the decision to bring Faisal to Iraq as king after the would-be Arab monarch was so unceremoniously ejected from Damascus by the French.

Lawrence spent the remainder of his life writing more books, corresponding with politicians and artists, and even joining up with the Royal Air Force under an alias for a time. He seemed to be haunted by his fame, however; and he remained a troubled soul until the end, which came as a result of a motorcycle accident in May 1935.

---

*O'Brien Browne, "The Enigmatic Lawrence of Arabia," *Military History* (October 2003): 29.

**O'Brien Browne, 30.

***O'Brien Browne, 32.

the British cause were greatly exaggerated. The sharifian revolt was primarily a ragtag conglomeration of Bedouin Arab Hijazis and some Arab allies they picked up along the way. It was not an all-Arab rebellion against the Ottomans—not even close—but rather more of a guerilla warfare outfit (contrary to the general depiction of the revolt in the award-winning film *Lawrence of Arabia*) that accompanied the British along the right flank of General Allenby's Palestine campaign. As we shall see, it became politically desirable for the British to trumpet the Arab role in the campaign in order to secure pro-British allies in the interior of Syria in the hopes of warding off the French by rewriting Sykes-Picot with facts on the ground. A number of leading Arabs in Syria, as became apparent in the June 1918 Declaration to the Seven, essentially disavowed Hashemite claims, marking the beginning of a process that would become manifest in the postwar years; indeed, the British themselves became progressively disenchanted with Hussein, viewing him as a bombastic, self-aggrandized would-be dynast; and they more and more turned to a rising force led by Abd al-Aziz ibn Abd al-Rahman Al Sa'ud in Arabia, allowing the latter to effectively jettison Hussein into exile soon after the war. From the British perspective, since the sharif did not deliver a revolt of the magnitude that they were led to believe and ignorantly assumed, any promises made to the Arabs, whether implicit or explicit, were essentially null and void—they did not deliver, so they do not necessarily deserve even what was inferred in the Hussein–McMahon correspondence. Only self-interest militated against further extortion with continued British support of the Arab cause in Syria for a brief spot of time during the Faisali period. This leaves us with possibly no single party to blame more than any other party for the serious disputes that would arise from the Sykes-Picot Agreement and the Hussein–McMahon correspondence, except that of the exigencies of war combined with human frailty.

THE BALFOUR DECLARATION

Under the Sykes-Picot plan, Palestine was to be administered after the war as an international "condominium" run by the British, French, and Russians, the latter having also been a signatory to the agreement. The port city of Haifa was excluded from this, and it was to be set aside for the British as a naval base. It had become clear to the British, especially after David Lloyd George assumed the position of prime minister from Asquith in December 1916, that Palestine had climbed up the ladder of strategic importance. Earlier Turkish incursions toward the Suez Canal had convinced British policymakers that this most prized possession in the Middle East required more of a land barrier to protect the east flank of the canal; indeed, by the end of 1915 there were over 300,000 British troops in the canal zone. When one speaks of British policy in the Middle East revolving around maintaining the lifeline to India, well, the Suez Canal *was* the lifeline. This was not atypical. The powers that be in Egypt ever since the pharaonic period had almost always concluded that a certain level of control over the land east of the Sinai Peninsula north to Syria was an essential security requisite in order to act as a buffer to invaders from the east. In this case, the British were concerned about the relative proximity of the French in the anticipated postwar atmosphere as they were expected to be in Syria and Lebanon.[8] They also wanted to prevent any possibility of German interests in the region being realized in an immediate sense (fending off purported rumors that Germany might issue its own "Balfour Declaration") or in the long-term sense following the war through their Ottoman alliance. As Sykes stated regarding Palestine, "I want to see a permanent Anglo–French entente allied to the Jews, Arabs, and Armenians which will render pan-Islamism innocuous and protect India and Africa from the Turco–German combine, which I believe may well survive the Hohenzollerns."[9] Palestine would be the final piece in the strategic puzzle that linked British dominions from the Mediterranean to India and on into Southeast Asia. The idea of an international administration for Palestine as articulated in Sykes-Picot had succeeded for the time being in keeping the French at bay; however, in essence, it put off any sort of decisive conclusion as to its disposition, yet it obviously indicated the sensitivity of the issue. If facts could be established on the ground, through Allenby's Palestine campaign as well as securing allies for the British position in Palestine, Sykes-Picot could be to all intents and purposes rewritten, something that Lloyd George was in favor of since he and a number of other British officials believed too much had been conceded to the French.

Negotiations between British officials and leading Zionists in England that would culminate in the Balfour Declaration actually began in February 1917. Initiated by the British, Sir Mark Sykes again played the lead role in the talks for London.[10] Ideas for using the Jews to advance British interests in Palestine had been put forth prior to this, but nothing came of them under the Asquith government.[11] By 1917, however, British officials were desperate to take any and every advantage they could in the war, a conflict whose outcome was still seriously in doubt despite the fact that the United States had declared war against Germany (however not against the Ottomans) on the side of the Entente powers (although officially as an "associate" and not as an ally) in April 1917. It would not be until early 1918 that the United States could mobilize and marshal its enormous resources onto the battlefield; indeed, in many ways, 1917 was a year full of serious reverses for Britain and France, especially when Russia withdrew from the war following the Bolshevik Revolution in November—Germany and its allies had hoped to end the war in terms favorable to them before the United States would inevitably turn the tide, and they almost succeeded in doing so. One almost gets the sense that the British were seeking any and all potential allies in the region, promising anything in order to win the war, and then worrying about the repercussions and possible contradictions later, particularly if they emerged from the war in such a position of power that what was agreed to or promised earlier did not matter. The Zionist movement was a potential ally that could not only help secure the British position in Palestine but also aid the British war effort globally, thus the attention it received from British policymakers by 1917. The Zionists, for their part, had been in search of a great power patron that could translate their desires for a national homeland into reality, and no country was better placed for this task than Great Britain, with the most powerful military in the world and with direct interests and influence in Palestine. The negotiations that resulted in the Balfour Declaration were a marriage of strategic necessity, timing, and opportunity.

One of the more interesting aspects of the Balfour Declaration is that the same kind of anti-Semitic myths surrounding the idea of the all-encompassing power of world Jewry that so affected British officials in their skewed vision of the CUP prior to the war now worked in favor of the Zionist movement. A pro-Zionist British policy was now viewed by enough British policymakers as essential to keep Russia in the war and to garner full and immediate support from the Americans, even though by 1913 only about 1% of the world's Jews were acknowledged Zionists. And in so doing, it would prevent world Jewry from siding with Germany, which was constantly rumored as being on the verge of enacting a similar pro-Zionist policy.[12] The Zionists had done an excellent job of convincing British officials that world Jewry was solidly behind the movement, when, in fact, it was not. Anti-Zionist Jews based their opposition upon religious reasons as well as the fear that support for a Jewish state could produce an anti-Jewish backlash in their home countries that could lead to an untenable situation toward effective expulsion. They were as vociferously against the Balfour Declaration as were those British officials in the Middle East who were concerned about the reaction of the Arabs and potential negative repercussions for British strategic interests in the region. Therefore, the knowledge that there were Jews (presumably pro-Zionist) in high places both in the Menshevik and Bolshevik revolutionary circles as well as among the closest advisers to President Woodrow Wilson (e.g., Felix Frankfurter and Louis Brandeis) had powerful policy repercussions regarding the fate of Palestine. Chaim Weizmann, one of the leaders of the Zionist movement in Britain, was quick to recognize the evolving British ideas regarding the importance of the Zionists and how that could be leveraged into British recognition of a Jewish position in Palestine.[13] He had railed against those Jews who remained on the sidelines or took a neutral position with regard to the combatants in the war—he clearly thought the future Jewish state would best be served by allying with the democracies rather than the Central powers. The platform of the Zionist Congress held in Britain in October 1916, which was subsequently delivered to the British government, outlined the following objectives: (1) the recognition of a separate Jewish nationality or national unit in Palestine; (2) the participation of the Jewish population of Palestine in local self-government; (3) autonomy in exclusively Jewish matters, such as Jewish education, religious, and communal organizations; (4) the Jewish colonization of Palestine; and (5) a Jewish company for the resettlement of Palestine by Jewish settlers. As we know from Chapter 2, the Zionist movement had since 1904 concentrated on Palestine for the creation of a Jewish state—the exigencies of the war now seemed to be close to making this a reality.

There were also other, more intangible reasons that some British officials supported the issuance of the Balfour Declaration. Anti-Semitic ideas of having "too many" Jews in England may have affected the thought processes of some British policymakers. For instance, Leo Amery, who was a secretary to the imperial war cabinet and who, along with Lord Alfred Milner, was one of the prime drafters of the Balfour Declaration, wrote the following in a letter to a fellow member of the war cabinet dated September 4, 1917:

> Once there is a national home for the Jewish persecuted majority, the English Jews will no longer have anything to trouble about. On the other hand, an anti-Semitism which is based partly on the fear of being swamped by hordes of undesirable aliens from Russia, etc., and partly by an instinctive suspicion against a community which has so many international ramifications, will be much diminished when the hordes in question have got another outlet, and when the motive for internationalism among the Jews is diminished.[14]

In addition, one cannot discount pro-Zionist sympathies based on humanitarian concerns regarding the centuries of persecution Jews have had to endure. This was often associated in the minds of those British policymakers who also had a religious basis for supporting the creation of a Jewish entity in Palestine. This is related to the strongly held Protestant belief in biblical prophecy, in that the Parousia, or second coming of Christ, cannot occur until the Holy Land is in the hands of the Jewish people. Support for the Jews in this sense is almost a religious obligation, and it continues to act as the basis for the strong support for present-day Israel by the so-called Christian right in the United States (often referred to as "Christian Zionists"). Certainly, Lloyd George and Balfour (who became foreign secretary in 1916) were devout Christians who tended to believe in the literal meaning of the Bible, so it is entirely possible this also influenced their pro-Zionist sympathies along with all of the other aforementioned factors.[15] It was also thought that President Wilson, known for his anti-imperialist and anticolonialist philosophy, might object at a critical moment in the war to any British move to exert direct control over Palestine. As such, the declaration was floated past Wilson, whose nonresponse was taken as tacit approval.[16]

As to the language of the document itself, the final product was the result of a series of negotiations between representatives of the Zionist movement in England, pro-Zionist British officials, and some British officials, such as former cabinet member Edwin Montagu (appointed secretary of state for India in July 1917 and a Jew himself) and Lord Curzon, who questioned whether or not Palestine could adequately absorb more Jewish immigration.[17] The Zionists, of course, had pressed for a statement advocating the establishment of a Jewish state in Palestine, but persistent opposition from Montagu forced a compromise in the Zionist position, amending the demand for a state to that of some sort of national home for the Jews in Palestine. The Zionist draft submitted in July had asked His Majesty's government to recognize "Palestine as the National Home for the Jewish People." Often, the most important words in diplomatic correspondence and agreements are the smallest; indeed, the most ardent diplomatic wrangling frequently revolves around the definite versus the indefinite article, the latter usually providing for more diplomatic wiggle room and/or a more liberal interpretation to suit all parties concerned. In this case, the discomfort expressed by Montagu and others eventually modified the declaration to say that "His Majesty's Government views with favor the establishment in Palestine of *a* National Home for the Jewish People" (italics mine). This certainly implied a more ambiguous commitment to an actual Jewish state in Palestine since it could be interpreted as some sort of Jewish autonomous presence in a Palestinian state. As an indirect reference to the Arabs already living in Palestine and to protect Jews living outside of Palestine, the following phrase was also included: "nothing being done which may prejudice the civil and religious rights of existing non-Jewish communities in Palestine, or the rights and political status enjoyed by Jews in any other country."

The Balfour Declaration was a tremendous boon to the Zionist movement. Despite the fact that the Zionists did not get everything they wanted in the note from Lord Balfour to Baron Edmund de Rothschild in terms of explicit denotation of a state with boundaries and a timetable, they did garner the support of the strongest military power in the world at the time. Finally, Herzl's dream of acquiring a strong international sponsor came to pass—or so it seemed at the time. Regardless of how much the British tended to backtrack from their commitment in Balfour in the interwar years, the declaration would receive international sanction through the League of Nations as well as official approval from the United States, therefore opening the door wider for continued Jewish immigration to and land acquisition in Palestine, the twin pillars of the Zionist movement.

WAR'S END AND THE MODERN MIDDLE EAST

The Balfour Declaration did not really achieve its objectives from the viewpoint of London; frankly, and this is something London would soon recognize, it only complicated British policy in the Middle East. It probably had little, if any, effect on the United States in terms of accelerating its mobilization in the war. Most importantly, it did not keep Russia in the war. By the end of 1917, the new Bolshevik regime had not only withdrawn from the conflict but also, even more embarrassingly to its erstwhile

British troops on parade at Jaffa Gate following the capture of Jerusalem, December 1917. (Library of Congress, Prints & Photographs Division, LC-DIG-matpc-11530.)

Entente allies, published the secret wartime agreements, the most damaging of which was Sykes-Picot. The apparent contradictions in the various pledges from Britain started to become manifest, but with approximately 1 million troops on the ground in the Middle East theater by war's end, the British appeared to care not. They had gone a long way toward establishing facts on the ground. General Sir Edmund Allenby's Palestine campaign, which, following some brilliant diversionary tactics, had taken Jerusalem by December 1917 and Damascus, Beirut, and Aleppo by October 1918, had effectively secured Palestine for the British and seemed to be on the verge of making good on most of what the sharif had demanded in the Hussein–McMahon correspondence, particularly concerning the interior of Syria (but, noticeably, not Palestine), all of which kept the French at bay.[18]

The sharifian revolt, launched in June 1916, had been something of a disappointment to British authorities during its first year. The fact that the ill-supplied Turkish garrison at Medina remained ensconced was ample evidence of the paucity of the Arab "rebellion." In July 1917, however, Faisal's forces surprised the small Turkish garrison at Aqaba, taking the city and finally alerting British officials in the midst of planning the Palestine campaign (Allenby had been appointed as its commander in June) that it could be of service to Britain's military designs vis-à-vis the Ottomans.[19] But with only an estimated 3,500 maximum at any one time in Faisal's army, there were built-in limitations as to what it could actually accomplish. By 1918, however, its main purpose had become more political than military anyway. It is interesting to note that a Jewish Legion was formed in Palestine in the summer of 1917 with about the same number of soldiers as that which comprised the Arab revolt. It became a unit in the British army, taking part in Allenby's campaign in Palestine. Vladimir Jabotinsky, the Russian-born Jewish extremist who later founded the Revisionist party in the Yishuv, helped form the Jewish Legion.

The lull of almost a year between the taking of Jerusalem and Damascus had more to do with the diversion of most of Allenby's troops to the European theater to meet a new spring German offensive rather than strategic circumstances in the Middle East. It was during this time that the various political ramifications of the division of the Arab lands of the Ottoman Empire became of immediate concern. The taking of Damascus became enmeshed in postwar diplomacy before the war was even over. Just how much should the British honor French interests as articulated in Sykes-Picot? Just how much should the British honor an apparent pledge to the Arabs as articulated in the Hussein–McMahon correspondence, and could this be an indirect way to keep the French boxed in along the Syrian coast rather than allow them to extend their influence into the interior of Syria? How much could the British dictate and, if necessary, reshape the terms of the postwar order in the Middle East with troops abounding across the region? And how would the commitment to the Zionists made in the Balfour Declaration fit into the mix? These were among the myriad of questions facing British politicians and military officers in the last year of the war and into the postwar diplomatic environment, and there was anything but a monolithic response, for there were definite divisions between British officials in London (who themselves did not speak with one voice) and British officials and military officers in the field. Gilbert Clayton, a brigadier general who served as chief political officer to Allenby but who was also quite close to the new British high commissioner in Egypt, Sir Reginald Wingate, proffered the following note to Sykes:

> I am not fully aware of the weight which Zionists carry, especially in America and Russia, and of the consequent necessity of giving them everything for which they may ask, but I must point out that, by pushing them as hard as we appear to be doing, we are risking the possibility of Arab unity becoming something like an accomplished fact and being ranged against us.[20]

This quote not only offers a snapshot of the different views held by various British officials but also foreshadows an increasing awareness, especially by British representatives and military officers in the field, of the potential torrent of Arab opposition as well as the potential utilization of the Arabs; indeed, Clayton agitated for a British protectorate in the Arab Middle East, a thought that betrayed a consistent British tendency to belittle Arab capabilities to run their own countries as well as the general insincerity of the offers initially made to Hussein. In fact, by early 1918 the British had moved away from Hussein, distrusting his intentions and lowering their estimation of his overall appeal—and they ex post facto downplayed the role they had envisioned for him at the beginning of the war. If anything, British officials attempted to build up Faisal as a viable alternative, to the distress of his father, who claimed the British were manipulating his son against him. The Declaration to the Seven made in June 1918, which was an attempt by the British to shore up their position with the Arabs and reinforce their commitment to Arab independence with seven Arab nationalist representatives from Syria following the Bolshevik publication of the secret agreements, clearly indicates an attempt to find an alternative to Hussein—in fact, the British India Office was already backing Abd al-Aziz ibn Sa'ud in the Najd region of Arabia as a viable replacement for the sharif. There then ensued a debate regarding the actual effectiveness of the sharifian revolt that revealed more about where one stood with regard to continued support of Hussein, pitting Faisal against Hussein, or turning to Syrian Arab leadership.

The British had actually been negotiating with Syrian Arabs in Cairo since early 1918 in an attempt to find an accommodation with the Balfour Declaration. Sykes was the one British official who tried to keep everyone happy; i.e., he believed that the agreement bearing his name could in fact be reconciled with Hussein–McMahon and Balfour—he was about the only one who did, although he remained a forceful voice in British policy that could not be entirely ignored. The most assertive attempt to find this accommodation with Zionism was represented by the creation of a Zionist commission led by Chaim Weizmann in early 1918, which was sent to Palestine under the supervision of British official William Ormsby-Gore. It is there that Weizmann met with Prince Faisal to discuss Palestine. Faisal was apparently willing to accommodate Zionist aspirations in Palestine in return for British support for his own aspirations in Syria, both of them, along with Ormsby-Gore, reiterating the long-held view that the inhabitants of Palestine were not "purely Arab." This accordance between Faisal and Weizmann would lead to Faisal's tacit support for the Zionist program at the Paris peace conference a year later in 1919. Regardless of the specious nature of Faisal having any authority to speak for Palestinian Arabs, it is interesting to posit that the later betrayal of Faisal by the British in lieu of French interests after he became king in Syria may not only have antagonized British–Arab relations that much more but also may have sounded the death knell to the last possibility for acceptance by at least one important Arab entity of Zionism in Palestine. If this is a legitimate hypothesis, then the British evacuation of Syria, leaving it to French designs, had an impact far beyond that which has been commonly accepted.[21]

The British, however, were attempting, as Sykes stated in 1917, to combine "Meccan Patriarchalism with Syrian Urban intelligentsia."[22] This was, in essence, the intent of the Declaration to the Seven. It declared as independent lands already under control of the Arabs and those lands liberated by the Arabs, while those areas under Entente control would be subject to negotiation.[23] This opened the door ever so slightly for the sharifian army, if the "conquest" of Syria could be arranged for them by the British. Faisal was the least objectionable of the Hijazis to the Syrians, especially since the latter began to realize that independence could not come without the former. In this way, Sykes could maintain some semblance of Hussein–McMahon while those British officials who had utter disdain for the concessions made to the French intimated in Sykes-Picot could utilize the Arabs to prevent Paris from extending its control beyond the Syrian coast. It is interesting that many of those British officials who had questioned the wisdom of the Balfour Declaration would support a policy of using indigenous and not so indigenous elements to secure strategic territory for them and keep it out of the hands of potential rivals—not unlike London's use of the Zionists.

Toward the end of World War I, on November 7, 1918, about one week after the Ottomans ended their participation in the war by signing the Armistice of Mudros on October 30, Britain and France jointly issued what came to be known as the Anglo–French Declaration. As with the Declaration to the Seven, it was intended to vitiate any potential opposition in the Arab world as well as mute the anti-imperialistic concerns of Woodrow Wilson on the eve of postwar diplomacy by stating the following:

> The aim of France and Great Britain in the Near East war ... is the complete and final liberation of the peoples so long oppressed by the Turks and the establishment of governments deriving authority from the free choice of the native population. France and Great Britain are agreed to encourage and help the establishment of native governments ... in Syria and Mesopotamia. Far from seeking to force upon the populations of these countries any particular institution, France and Great Britain have no other concern than to ensure by their support and their active assistance the normal working of the governments and institutions which the populations shall have freely adopted....

While on the surface the Arabs would seem to be very receptive to this declaration since it appears to promise true independence, it does not explicitly stipulate that; as usual, there is promise mixed with ambiguity, allowing the issuing parties enough latitude to move in either direction. Read from the hindsight of history, this declaration could easily be interpreted as an announcement of the mandate system soon to come.

It was only less than a month before the Anglo–French Declaration that Damascus was taken; indeed, as is well known, Faisal's forces were allowed to enter Damascus first by the British, even though the Turks had long evacuated the city in anticipation of Allenby's advance to the north from Palestine. Whether via Lawrence's and probably Faisal's interpretation of the Declaration to the Seven or British officialdom's conclusion that wherever Faisal's banners flew would constitute the independent Arab state, it was important that Arab forces entered Damascus first, therefore ameliorating French concerns that the British intended to take Syria while at the same time placing someone in Damascus through whom the British could extend their influence while keeping the French effectively locked up on the coast. These first months of Arab "rule" in Damascus were quite chaotic, amid British and French machinations to secure the interior of Syria through Arab surrogates, with the French hoping they could control Faisal as much as the British appeared to be doing.

Despite French efforts in the region itself, British policy, in fact, had a friend in this regard in Paris. French President Clemenceau was about as disinclined to extend French empire and foreign commitments as David Lloyd George was inclined to maintain British imperial interests and protect new acquisitions. Despite these complementary viewpoints, the fall of 1918 regarding the Middle East was a period of much diplomatic posturing and wrangling. Lloyd George was keen to jettison Sykes-Picot, an agreement for which he was never very enthusiastic and which he thought had been surpassed by intervening events; i.e., it was outdated. In addition, the British had done the lion's share of fighting and dying against the Ottoman Empire; there was thus a strong sense, despite agreements to the contrary, of a "to the victor go the spoils" attitude. Sykes himself seemed to realize by 1918 that the agreement bearing his name was no longer operative because of the changing regional and international landscape. Maurice Hankey, the secretary to the war cabinet, recorded the following in his diary dated October 6, 1918:

> Ll G [David Lloyd George] took a very intransigent attitude and wanted us to go back on the Sykes-Picot agreement, so as to get Palestine for us and to bring Mosul [promised to the French under Sykes-Picot] into the British zone, and even to keep the French out of Syria. He also had some subtle dodge for asking America to take Palestine and Syria, in order to render the French more anxious to give us Palestine, so that they might have an excuse of keeping Syria. He was also very contemptuous of President Wilson and anxious to arrange the division of Turkey between France, Italy, and G.B. [Great Britain] before speaking to America. He also thought it would attract less attention to our enormous gains in the war if we swallowed our share of Turkey now, and the German colonies later.[24]

To Lloyd George, obtaining his strategic objectives in the Middle East (and elsewhere) in the last stages of the war seemed to be a race against what he perceived would be Wilsonian pressure to abide by the American president's stated principles of self-determination and anticolonialism in the postwar diplomatic environment. While there were certainly those, such as Foreign Secretary Balfour, who sincerely hoped for direct American involvement in a Middle East settlement, even to the point of exploiting Wilson's principles of self-determination to secure an Arab veneer in the Middle East against French designs, the British prime minister saw the United States as a looming albatross.

On December 1, 1918, Lloyd George met with Clemenceau in London, and the British prime minister basically got what he wanted in a verbal agreement. Clemenceau gave him Mosul, an oil-rich Ottoman province in present-day northern Iraq, which had been previously ceded to the French under Sykes-Picot, and the French president acquiesced to British control of Palestine.[25] Adopting a policy position that would soon enough work in the opposite direction vis-à-vis Britain and France, Clemenceau was committed to making concessions to the British, especially in a way that conformed with his own philosophy regarding empire, because he was convinced that the French demanded British friendship and support on the European continent to contain Germany.

It is under these circumstances that the victorious powers met in Paris in January 1919 to begin to discuss the postwar environment. It was a venue in which the United States, particularly President Wilson, made a celebrated, albeit brief, appearance in the maelstrom of international diplomacy, dominating the direction of negotiations on the surface due to its putative economic power and newfound military strength but inexperienced, if not naive, in the ways of European diplomacy, which severely hampered the president's ability to implement his vision of a new world order set against the behind-the-scenes machinations of the allies attempting to implement their designs and achieve their diplomatic objectives underneath the veneer of Wilsonianism. Nowhere was this more apparent than in what became known as the King-Crane commission. Even the name of the commission itself reveals the reason for its failure; i.e., it is named only after the two Americans who led the mission rather than the Council of Four Entente powers in Paris (Britain, France, Italy, and the United States) that at first jointly indicated their support for the enterprise. Wilson's intent was to help resolve potential British and French differences over the disposition of the Arab territories of the Ottoman Empire by sending a commission to the region itself in order to ascertain the desires of the indigenous populations as well as report back on the overall state of affairs.

Although agreeing to it, Britain, France, and Italy did not appoint any delegates to the commission—it therefore became a solely American effort. Henry Churchill King, president of Oberlin College, and Charles R. Crane, a businessman from Chicago and Democratic party activist, led a group of Americans to Palestine, Syria, Lebanon, and Anatolia in the summer of 1919. In Syria, the commission found that public opinion preferred no mandate (and no separation of Syria and Palestine) and that, if a mandate was imposed on them, it would first be supervised by the United States or, if not, then by Britain—by no means did they indicate any desire for a French mandate. The King-Crane commission report, even in the best of circumstances, would be nonbinding—it was simply informational in an attempt to shore up Wilson's position. However, we know that Lloyd George and Clemenceau, while paying lip service to Wilson's tactics, had already gone a long way toward deciding who was going to get what in the Middle East, the French still holding out for some measure of supervision over the interior of Syria. If anything, Lloyd George was hoping to use Wilsonian anti-imperialism to grease the wheels for British influence in the Middle East through surrogates while minimizing the French position. The commission report was, in the end, essentially ignored by the Europeans; and having been chastened by European diplomacy as well as U.S. domestic politics in the interim and focused more on the great questions of the day with regard to Europe, such as the League of Nations, Wilson had by then lost interest in it. Indeed, at the peace talks, he was less concerned about Ottoman lands in general, especially since the United States had not formally declared war on the empire, which in strict terms meant that Wilson's Fourteen Points were not applicable there, despite the fact that one of the points dealt directly with the Ottomans.[26]

In the negotiations regarding the Middle East, Lloyd George was quick to point out that Britain had over 1 million troops stationed in Ottoman lands. Despite economic and political realities in Britain that would force upon the government a severe demobilization in due course, British military dominance in the region at the time gave London a very strong bargaining hand. If anything, the military overextension and post-war economic problems back home only doubled Lloyd George's negotiating pace before reality weakened his bargaining position. At the peace conference, Clemenceau would doggedly try to at least acquire the measure of supervision over the interior of Syria that had been mentioned in Sykes-Picot. Faisal also attended the conference, and he just as doggedly tried to hold onto Syria; indeed, he displayed a willingness to exclude Palestine from an independent Arab state, which, according to a number of officials at the time, he was never truly interested in to begin with—in any event, a concession on Palestine, which he suspected the British would keep anyhow in light of its dominant military position and commitment to the Zionists, might provide him more leverage vis-à-vis Syria. The French were not assuaged by Britain's support for Arab independence since they knew Faisal was beholden to the British financially, politically, and militarily. Syria was essentially the only bone of contention left to be negotiated out of the rump of the Ottoman Empire. The British had instituted direct rule in Mesopotamia (Iraq), first a military administration out of the British India Office and then a civilian administration soon thereafter; in fact, the King-Crane commission did not even bother venturing to Mesopotamia. Egypt had been declared a British protectorate in 1914, and Britain's position there after the war received continued international recognition. Britain's position in the Persian Gulf was not questioned, nor was its influence with the Saudi and Hashemite families reexamined. And as has been noted previously, Lloyd George and Clemenceau had already consummated a gentleman's agreement regarding Palestine. The problem is that even though much of the Arab provinces of the Ottoman Empire had already been allotted, final and official acknowledgment of such was the last element of the overall post-World War I negotiations to be settled; of course, this was especially the case in Syria. As such, events regionally and internationally began to negatively affect Britain's ability to achieve its initial objectives.

The regional and international environments were quite different by the fall of 1919 and into 1920 from what they were in 1916 and 1917. Russia had withdrawn from the war, and the specter of Bolshevism cast a shadow over the Paris negotiations; the United States had begun to adopt a more isolationist posture that would come to characterize its interwar diplomacy, especially as Wilson suffered a debilitating stroke in September 1919, thus removing the internationalist wing's most vocal and influential advocate amid a Republican-controlled Congress that was tired of the president's unilateral diplomacy and leery of entangling the country in European diplomatic perfidy and in international organizations that would usurp American sovereignty—Congress would not ratify the Treaty of Versailles or U.S. participation in the League of Nations. Britain itself, as economic problems mounted and the military remained overextended (as Churchill would continually iterate as secretary of war and air in 1919–1920 and as secretary for the colonies in 1921–1922), would be forced into retrenchment mode in the Middle East that would reduce it bargaining leverage; indeed, by 1920, British troop levels in the Middle East had been reduced to about 300,000.[27] Together these were compelling reasons for Lloyd George to make concessions to France regarding Syria. He could no longer count on the United States to play an active role in Europe and contain Germany—now, in an ironic twist of fate, he realized he had to rely more on the French for balance-of-power politics on the continent; indeed, the British prime minister would tellingly comment that "France is worth ten Syrias." In addition, his colleague in Paris, with whom he had been able to negotiate directly and with whom a trust had been built, fell from office in January 1920. Alexandre Millerand became the new French president, and he was someone who was much less inclined to make any concessions on Syria as well as more inclined to take advantage of Britain's decreasing leverage in the area.

It was these conditions that compelled the British to announce in September 1919 that they would withdraw their troops from the Syrian region, thus leaving Faisal to fend for himself against the French. If Clemenceau had remained in office, the new monarch of the Kingdom of Syria might have been able to work out a deal amenable to the French that would have kept him in power. But with Millerand as president and Faisal's supporters in Damascus defiant, the dye was cast—it would just be a matter of time. With the British out of the way in Syria, Paris and London could finally close the diplomatic book with regard to the disposition of the Ottoman Empire. On December 21, 1919, the British and French came to an agreement regarding the apportionment of oil rights in Mesopotamia: France would receive a 25% share of the British-controlled Turkish Petroleum Company, while Paris would allow Britain to traverse its Middle East holdings with oil pipelines from Iran and Mesopotamia to the Mediterranean. And at the Conference of London in February 1920, the borders of the Palestine mandate were delineated along British designs, while the French got in return their interpretation of the border between Turkey and Syria.

So by April 1920 British and French claims seemed to be settled, and in that month at San Remo, Italy, the Entente powers, among other things, apportioned the Arab world between Britain and France, assigning mandates that would later be formalized by the League of Nations in September 1922. Britain obtained Palestine (including present-day Jordan) and Mesopotamia, and its status in Egypt and in the Persian Gulf was confirmed. The French were assigned the Syrian mandate, including Lebanon. And Arabia remained independent, soon to be taken over by the Saudi family supported by Wahhabi fundamentalists, resulting in statehood by 1932 with the birth of Saudi Arabia. The Sharif Hussein would go into exile soon after the war to Cyprus, where he lived out his life watching his sons continue the Middle East game as the soon-to-be monarch of Iraq (Faisal, after being kicked out of Syria) and Transjordan (Abdullah). The term "mandate" was another bone thrown to Wilsonian sensitivities regarding imperialism. In other words, these were not protectorates or colonies in the Middle East; they were supposed to be more like international trusteeships. The mandates were to be supervised by the mandatory powers, ostensibly preparing them for eventual independence. While Britain and especially France only gave lip service to the intent of the mandate system, treating their mandates more as colonies than anything else, at least they were officially committed to granting independence, and as such, international oversight from the League of Nations and from the United States may have made the experience a bit less onerous from the point of view of the indigenous populations.[28]

By the summer of 1920, then, Faisal was living on borrowed time in Syria. The French, after quickly dispatching armed resistance outside of Damascus with their force of some 90,000 troops, ended the brief Hashemite Kingdom of Syria in July 1920, taking direct charge of what would become their Syrian mandate. It may have only *seemed* as if there was an air of inevitability about this course of events, but the British did indeed, for their own strategic reasons, fulfill most of what had been offered to the Hashemites in the Hussein–McMahon correspondence. It would be events in Europe and the United States that would transform the commitment to the Arabs into the French reading of Sykes-Picot. Faisal's withdrawal from Syria had important repercussions for Palestine. Up until that time, a number of Palestinians (primarily members of the Arab Club, a Palestinian-dominated Arab nationalist organization) worked in high-level positions in Faisal's administration, and for the most part, Palestinians in general supported a greater Syria under Faisal's rule, one obviously that would include Palestine.[29] This is despite the fact that most Palestinians were opposed to the sharifian revolt and Faisal himself throughout much of the war; certainly, Faisal's reported accommodations with Zionism could not have helped his popularity among Palestinian Arabs. But by war's end, Faisal seemed to be the horse on which to ride toward at least some semblance of independence. As evidence of this, the first two Palestinian national congresses were held in Damascus; the third, however, after Faisal's expulsion, was held in Haifa in December 1920.[30] In retrospect, as mentioned earlier, the British abandonment of Faisal in Syria may have had repercussions far beyond the issue of betraying Arab interests to the French. It may have crystallized the contentious issues developing in Palestine more quickly, particularly focusing Palestinian Arab opposition to not only the British presence but also growing Jewish influence and claims via continued immigration and land acquisition. It made "Palestine" Palestine.

Hashemite dreams would not be totally lost, however, following Faisal's exit from Syria and his father's exile a few years later from the Hijaz. The British feared that Transjordan, the roughly 75% of mandated Palestine that lay east of the Jordan River (and corresponding in the main to present-day Jordan), would be claimed by the French as a kind of inheritance after taking control of Damascus from Faisal. This was certainly an area within Greater Syria aspired to by Faisal and his Arab nationalist supporters as well as being wholly within the territory allotted to the Arabs under Hussein–McMahon. In addition, there were Arabs in Transjordan who were intent on returning Faisal to Damascus, something the French could utilize as an excuse to move troops into the arid region in order to quell potential counter-coup movements. If the British were not careful, they could fall into a military conflagration with the French in the Middle East and potentially lose the contiguous land corridor from the Mediterranean to the Persian Gulf that was of such strategic importance, especially as London envisioned oil pipelines rather than trade caravans traversing the route. This could then undermine Britain's position in Palestine (if not Mesopotamia) as there were elements (particularly anti-Zionist Catholics) in France who still hoped to extend French influence there. The British were unable to keep the French bottled up along the Syrian coast, but they certainly did not want French influence to extend beyond Syria itself. In order to meet this potential strategic threat at a time of British retrenchment in the region, it was decided at a conference in Cairo in March 1921, attended by Winston Churchill and T. E. Lawrence and dealing primarily with Transjordan and Iraq, to make Abdullah (Hussein's third son and the great-great-grandfather of the current King Abdullah of Jordan) the sovereign of Transjordan. Since Abdullah at that very moment had entered Amman with the apparent intent of liberating Syria for his brother, Faisal, it seemed like the proper thing to do at the time in order to ward off a potential conflict with the French that could draw in the British. Abdullah was officially recognized as emir of Transjordan by the British in December 1921. In this way, as the British typically did, London could work through a surrogate beholden to British interests and reliant upon British force to maintain its influence in the region, keep the French out, and hopefully assuage the Arabs. For good measure, and as much an attempt at restitution as political or strategic motivation, at the conference it was agreed that Faisal would be made the king of the newly stitched-together entity now called Iraq, supported by a number of former Arab nationalist Ottoman officers who had been with him in Damascus—he officially assumed his new position in August 1921. Thus, while one Hashemite "kingdom" was on its way out in the Hijaz (Hussein abdicated and went into exile in the face of Saudi pressure in 1924), two more were being created elsewhere in the Middle East.

In Palestine itself, the area had been under British military administration since Allenby's successful campaign took Jerusalem in December 1917. British officers on the ground during this time tended to oppose London's policy as announced in the Balfour Declaration. To them, Zionist aspirations in Palestine were inconsistent with British interests in securing overall Arab support in the postwar environment. In addition, the normal reaction to anyone in the field is to raise some concern over policies issued at home that only serve to complicate their tasks of stabilizing what would become the British Mandate in Palestine. As happened in other areas of the Middle East throughout 1920, there were riots in Palestine in April. Some of these riots in the

British Colonial Secretary Winston Churchill (*right*), T. E. Lawrence, Emir Abdullah, and other delegates at the Cairo Conference in 1921. (Library of Congress, Prints & Photographs Division, LC-DIG-matpc-04380.)

region, as in Palestine, revolved around protestations to the British or French presence; but they were also the result of indigenous societal fissures created by the interregnum between Ottoman rule and the mandate system. In Palestine, the emerging Arab–Jewish dynamic added fuel to the fire. A number of British military officers and officials saw the riots as confirmation of the utility of their anti-Zionist stance, especially during a period of military and economic retrenchment. Winston Churchill, who had been an avid pro-Zionist, even wrote to Lloyd George on June 13, 1920, that "Palestine is costing us 6 millions a year to hold. The Zionist movement will cause continued friction with the Arabs. The French . . . are opposed to the Zionist movement & will try to cushion the Arabs off on us as the real enemy. The Palestine venture . . . will never yield any profit of a material kind."[31] Lloyd George, however, reacted to the increased disturbances by reiterating his commitment to the Zionist cause as delineated in the Balfour Declaration. As a result, in July 1920, he replaced the military administration in Palestine with a civilian one, headed by Sir Herbert Samuel as high commissioner, who was Jewish and the first member of the British government to propose the establishment of a Jewish national home in Palestine in 1914.[32]

Samuel, however, turned out to be something of a disappointment to the Zionists. Additional riots in May 1921 compelled Samuel to temporarily suspend Jewish immigration, leading some radical Zionists to call for his removal. But even pro-Zionist British officials, such as Churchill as noted above, were beginning to question the wisdom of the decision to support the Zionist program in Palestine as delineated in the Balfour Declaration. This is certainly when the "a" rather than "the" in front of "national home" in the declaration began to seem like an act of diplomatic prescience to the British—in essence, the vagueness of Balfour allowed for some reinterpretation in order to fit existing circumstances. What resulted is what came to be called the "Churchill White Paper," issued in 1922, a document, for the most part, written by Samuel. This was an attempt to outline in more specific terms the nature of the British commitment to the Zionist program in line with realities that had shifted British strategic interests and capabilities since November 1917. Churchill was now in charge of colonial policy, and he would begin to put into practice what he had been preaching since the end of the war, i.e., the need for the British to curtail their commitments abroad during a period of economic distress at home. As he stated on one occasion, "everything else that happens in the Middle East is secondary to the reduction in expense."[33] In fact, he even advocated recreating the Ottoman Empire in the Arab world to relieve pressure on Britain and resuscitate the Ottoman barrier to Russian designs in the region—in essence, to go back to the nineteenth-century British policy of maintaining the integrity of the empire.[34]

The Churchill White Paper was essentially the official instrument through which Abdullah could be confirmed in Transjordan while redefining the British Mandate in Palestine before the League of Nations sanctioned the Balfour Declaration (which in its original intent had included Transjordan as part of Palestine). This was certainly a blow to the Zionist cause as 75% of mandatory Palestine (Transjordan) was now administratively separated from the rest of Palestine—but this was not viewed by the Zionists as a catastrophe as Jewish immigration had for the most part assembled on the western side of the Jordan River, including Jerusalem and, in any event, the separation was provisionally administrative and not necessarily permanent. This had been the position adopted by the Zionist leadership throughout much of the mandate period with Britain—i.e., accept British compromises, even if detrimental in the short term, with the hope that the policy could be reversed or made vestigial through prescient, active policies over the long term. The Palestinians, on the other hand, tended to wholeheartedly reject British compromise offers (or even olive branches from the Jews) for fear of de facto extending recognition to not only Zionist claims but also the British mandatory position; as such, they rejected the Churchill White Paper—this pattern on both sides of the Arab–Jewish equation in Palestine would continue during the interwar period, and although the Palestinians' dilemma is obvious, their nonaccommodationist policy might have deleteriously impaired their ability to elucidate their positions in regional and international forums as well as to develop a more definable claim to the land.[35] As we shall see in Chapter 4, however, and as was the case with the Sharif Hussein, Palestinian Arabs were hearing different policies from different British officials. As mentioned earlier, for a variety of reasons—possibly self-preservation in the main—British officials in Palestine gave the Palestinians, through word and action, cause to hope that the government in London would also see the situation similarly, soon implementing policies that would curtail the Zionist program; thus, obstreperousness could work to their advantage.

What was especially troubling for the Zionists with regard to the Churchill White Paper was that it also stated that Britain would not impose a Jewish state upon the inhabitants and that it would only be a center of Jewish culture—this was a definite whittling down of the Zionist view of the British commitment. It did state, however, that the Jews were in Palestine by right and not sufferance, therefore maintaining the legal framework for continued Jewish immigration. So despite the various strands of policy emanating from various strands of the British government, the Balfour Declaration remained the centerpiece of British policy in their Palestine mandate. By 1922 the seeds of the Arab–Israeli conflict had been laid.

NOTES

1. David Fromkin, *A Peace to End All Peace* (New York: Henry Holt and Company, 1989), 95.

2. To coordinate British policy in the Arab world and to assure British Cairo's predominant position in making it, Sykes moved to create by the end of 1915 the Arab Bureau in Cairo, composed of such venerable British representatives as Sir Reginald Wingate, Gilbert Clayton, and David Hogarth, the latter bringing into the bureau in due course a British junior officer by the name of Theodore Edward (T. E.) Lawrence, better known as "Lawrence of Arabia."

3. It is interesting that the United States under the Eisenhower administration in 1957 would make a similar mistake. It had anointed King Sa'ud of Saudi Arabia as a potential counterpoise to Egyptian President Gamal 'Abd al-Nasser, whose Arab nationalist policies were inimical to U.S. interests. Sa'ud was thought to be a good choice because of Saudi Arabia's role at the center of Islam (and Sa'ud's official role as Guardian of the Two Holy Places) and its growing influence in the oil market. As with Hussein, the book could not be judged by its cover and Sa'ud turned out to be a weak and ineffective leader who was much less than what the Eisenhower administration had hoped for.

4. Michael J. Cohen, *The Origins and Evolution of the Arab-Zionist Conflict* (Berkeley: University of California Press, 1987), 10.

5. Ibid., 13.

6. Indeed, many of the Arabs fighting at Gallipoli were the ones who made up the Ottoman divisions in Syria; the Porte, fearing that they may cause unrest in Syria, had the bulk of them transferred to the Gallipoli front, where they were needed much more urgently anyway.

7. Quoted in Cohen, *The Origins and Evolution,* 22–23.

8. Indeed, in 1923, Lord Curzon, who had been an opponent of the Balfour Declaration, now justified Britain's position in Palestine by saying, "We cannot now recede. If we did the French would step in and then be on the threshold of Egypt and on the outskirts of the [Suez] Canal. Besides Palestine needs ports, electricity, and the Jews of America were rich and would subsidise such development." Quoted in ibid., 63.

9. Quoted in Fromkin, *A Peace to End All Peace,* 290.

10. Cohen, *The Origins and Evolution,* 41.

11. A November 9, 1914, memo from Herbert Samuel, then a member of the British cabinet, stated the following: "British influence ought to play a considerable part in the formation of a [Jewish] state, because the geographical situation of Palestine, and especially its proximity to Egypt, would render its goodwill to England a matter of importance." Chaim Weizmann, the leader of the Zionist movement in Britain, recognized immediately that this strategic desire could work to the Zionists' advantage. In a letter from March 1915, Weizmann said that "a strong Jewish community on the Egyptian flank [in Palestine] is an efficient barrier for any danger likely to come from the north . . . England would have in the Jews the best possible friends. . . ."

12. As an example of this line of thought, a March 13, 1916, memo from the British embassy in Russia to the Russian foreign minister stated that "it is very clear that by utilizing the Zionist idea, important political results can be achieved. Among them will be the conversion, in favor of the Allies, of Jewish elements in the Orient, in the United States, and in other

places, elements whose attitude at the present time is to a considerable extent opposed to the Allies' cause. . . . "

13. Dr. Weizmann was a noted chemist. He discovered a way to extract acetone from maize, which is used in the manufacture of explosives. He was officially a member of the British Zionist Federation, elected as president of this organization in February 1917. Born in Russia, he became a naturalized British citizen.

14. Quoted in Cohen, *The Origins and Evolution,* 49.

15. Indeed, David Lloyd George was a legal representative on behalf of Herzl during negotiations between the Zionists and Britain over the various other venues that might be transformed into a Jewish state.

16. Wilson would publicly endorse the Balfour Declaration in a letter to the American Jewish community in September 1918. Congress would later formally endorse the Balfour Declaration in 1922 as defining U.S. policy on the matter.

17. Curzon remained a staunch opponent to the creation of a Jewish state in Palestine after the war. In March 1920, when he was foreign secretary, he objected to language being constructed regarding the terms of the British Mandate in Palestine in advance of San Remo by saying that the "development of a self-governing Commonwealth" was a "euphemism for a Jewish state. . . ." He went on, "Here is a country with 580,000 Arabs and 30,000 or is it 60,000 Jews (by no means all Zionists). Acting upon the noble principles of self-determination and ending with a splendid appeal to the League of Nations, we then proceed to draw up a document which reeks of Judaism in every paragraph and is an avowed constitution for a Jewish State. Even the poor Arabs are only allowed to look through the keyhole as a non-Jewish community. It is quite clear that this mandate has been drawn up by someone reeling under the fumes of Zionism. If we are all to submit to that intoxicant, this draft is all right." Quoted in Ritchie Ovendale, *The Origins of the Arab–Israeli Wars* (New York: Longman, 1999), 52.

18. The British had finally turned things around in the Mesopotamian campaign after some initial reverses, capturing Baghdad in March 1917.

19. Although in a variety of media Lawrence is credited with the planning of the attack on Aqaba, it is likely that indigenous forces attached to the sharifian revolt were at least as responsible for planning—and certainly carrying out—the attack.

20. Quoted in Fromkin, *A Peace to End All Peace,* 317–318.

21. There were British officials, especially those who were serving on the ground in Palestine with and among Arabs, such as British governor of Palestine Ronald Storrs, who continued to question the British commitment to the Zionists and the ignorance of the Arabs who lived there. He stated that, "Palestine, up to now a Moslem country, has fallen into the hands of a Christian Power which on the eve of its conquest announces that a considerable portion of its land is to be handed over for colonization purposes to a nowhere very popular people." Quoted in ibid., 325.

22. Quoted in ibid., 330.

23. The declaration clearly stated that comprising this independent state would be lands liberated by the Arabs as of the date of issuance, June 1918, which by then was essentially just most of Arabia, i.e., that which had already been taken for granted and thus not officially extending the offer to future lands liberated by the Arabs. Lawrence and possibly some other British officials seemed to interpret it differently and apparently relayed this to Faisal: that lands liberated by the Arabs throughout the war would comprise an independent Arab state. From Faisal and Lawrence's perspective this interpretation would come into play upon the entrance into Damascus (and elsewhere in Syria and Lebanon) of Faisal's forces in October 1918.

24. Quoted in Fromkin, *A Peace to End All Peace,* 374. From the extracts of a War Cabinet meeting on October 3, 1918, Lloyd George's position is described thusly: "The Prime Minister

said he had been refreshing his memory about the Sykes-Picot Agreement, and had come to the conclusion that it was quite inapplicable to present circumstances, and was altogether a most undesirable agreement from the British point of view. Having been concluded more than two years ago, it entirely overlooked the fact that our position in Turkey had been won by very large British forces, whereas our Allies had contributed but little to the result." Quoted in ibid., 365.

25. Mosul would be attached to the former Ottoman provinces of Baghdad and Basra, already under British control by war's end, to form what would become the country of Iraq.

26. For more on the King-Crane commission, see James Gelvin, "The Legacy of the King-Crane Commission," in David W. Lesch, ed., *The Middle East and the United States: A Historical and Political Reassessment,* 3rd ed. (Boulder: Westview Press, 2003), 13–29.

27. In fact, Churchill, as head of the Colonial Office, advocated returning the Arab lands to Ottoman control.

28. The Ottoman sultan would formally agree to the San Remo division of the Middle East in the Treaty of Sèvres (named after a town just outside of Paris) in August 1920, which also dealt with a variety of other important aspects of post-war Ottoman territories.

29. Cohen, *The Origins and Evolution,* 67. Two General Syrian Congresses, one held in mid-1919 and the other in March 1920, passed resolutions proclaiming an independent Syria that comprised present-day Syria, Lebanon, Jordan, and Israel, under the rule of Faisal. Traditional Syrian elites as well as Faisal were more willing to work with the French, especially when Clemenceau was in power; but with Millerand in Paris by January 1920, Faisal was caught between a more resistant French president and Arab nationalists in Damascus who refused to cave into French demands. Ultimately, Faisal was forced to join with his Arab cohorts against the French. The British had already made the decision to allow Faisal to fend for himself, but as Fromkin points out (*A Peace to End All Peace,* 438), Syrians' claims to British mandates in Palestine and Mesopotamia only helped isolate Syria that much more from the British. The British seemingly could not win with Faisal, as Fromkin states, "The French blamed them for putting Feisal up and the Arabs blamed them for letting Feisal down" (440).

30. Cohen, *The Origins and Evolution,* 68. Interestingly, as Cohen comments, the British military administration in Palestine, which had been in place since December 1918, recommended following Arab protests in Palestine in April 1920 due to the mandates agreed to at San Remo that Faisal be named as nominal ruler of Palestine (presumably in some sort of association with Syria) and the Balfour Declaration be nullified.

31. Quoted in Fromkin, *A Peace to End All Peace,* 448.

32. In a memo dated November 9, 1914, Samuel stated that "I spoke to Sir Edward Grey [British foreign minister] about the future of Palestine. . . . I said that now that Turkey had thrown herself into the European war and that it was probable that her empire would be broken up, the question of the future control of Palestine was likely to arise. Perhaps the opportunity might arise for the fulfillment of the ancient aspiration of the Jewish people and the restoration there of a Jewish state . . . British influence ought to play a considerable part in the formation of a Jewish state, because the geographical situation in Palestine, and especially its proximity to Egypt, would render its goodwill to England a matter of special importance."

33. Quoted in Fromkin, *A Peace to End All Peace,* 499. By September 1922, Churchill had eliminated 75% of the Middle East expenditures for Great Britain.

34. Churchill was behind the establishment in December 1920 of a Middle East department based in Cairo within the Colonial Office in order to coordinate Middle East policy. Churchill became head of the Colonial Office, replacing Lord Milner, in early 1921.

35. Fromkin, reflecting this view, states that "Palestine was and is an area of complex and competing claims, but the Arab delegation [that visited with Churchill in London in 1921] took account of no claims, fears, needs, or dreams other than its own. Unlike the Zionist leaders, who sought to compensate Arab nationalism by supporting Arab versus French claims to

Syria, who envisaged areas of Arab autonomy within Palestine, and who planned economic and other benefits for Arabs who chose to live within the confines of the Jewish homeland, the Arab leaders made no effort to accommodate Jewish aspirations or to take account of Jewish needs" (521). He goes on to say that "Arab opposition to Jewish settlement was rooted in emotion, in religion, in xenophobia, in the complex of feelings that tend to overcome people when newcomers flood in to change their neighborhood. The Arabs of Palestine were defending a threatened way of life. The Arab delegations that went to see Winston Churchill did not articulate this real basis for their objection to Zionism. Instead they argued that the country could not sustain more inhabitants; and Churchill took them at their word. He accepted their statement that they were objecting on economic grounds; and then he went ahead to prove that their economic fears were unjustified" (*A Peace to End All Peace,* 523). Churchill did so by showing the Palestinians British studies outlining how Palestine could sustain a much larger population than envisioned by the Arabs, thus safely allowing for significantly more Jewish immigration. A Palestinian might argue that even had they pursued a different tack in terms of presenting their argument to the British, London's commitment to implementing the Balfour Declaration, even as redefined by the Churchill White Paper, was a done deal; indeed, in June 1921 when Churchill met with the Palestinian delegation, the future prime minister stated "The British Government mean to carry out the Balfour Declaration. I have told you so again and again. I told you so at Jerusalem. I told you so at the House of Commons the other day. I tell you so now. They mean to carry out the Balfour Declaration. They do" (524).

Hussein–McMahon Correspondence (July 14, 1915–March 10, 1916)

LETTER FROM THE SHARIF HUSSEIN TO MCMAHON, JULY 14, 1915

Whereas the whole of the Arab nation without any exception have decided in these last years to live, and to accomplish their freedom, and grasp the reins of their administration both in theory and practice; and whereas they have found and felt that it is to the interest of the Government of Great Britain to support them and aid them to the attainment of their firm and lawful intentions (which are based upon the maintenance of the honour and dignity of their life) without any ulterior motives whatsoever unconnected with this object;

And whereas it is to their (the Arabs') interest also to prefer the assistance of the Government of Great Britain in consideration of their geographical position and economic interests, and also of the attitude of the above-mentioned Government, which is known to both nations and therefore need not be emphasized;

For these reasons the Arab nation see fit to limit themselves, as time is short, to asking the Government of Great Britain, if it should think fit, for the approval, through her deputy or representative, of the following fundamental propositions, leaving out all things considered secondary in comparison with these, so that it may prepare all means necessary for attaining this noble purpose, until such time as It finds occasion for making the actual negotiations:

Firstly.—England to acknowledge the independence of the Arab countries, bounded on the north by Mersina and Adana up to 37° of latitude, on which degree fall Birijik, Urfa, Mardin, Midiat, Jezirat (Ibn 'Umar), Amadia, up to the border of Persia; on the east by the borders of Persia up to the Gulf of Basra; on the south by the Indian Ocean, with the exception of the position of Aden to remain as it is; on the west by the Red Sea, the Mediterranean Sea up to Mersina. England to approve of the proclamation of an Arab Khalifate of Islam.

Secondly.—The Arab Government of the Sherif to acknowledge that England shall have the preference in all economic enterprises in the Arab countries whenever conditions of enterprises are otherwise equal.

Thirdly.—For the security of this Arab independence and the certainty of such preference of economic enterprises, both high contracting parties to offer mutual assistance, to the best ability of their military and naval forces, to face any foreign Power which may attack either party. Peace not to be decided without agreement of both parties.

Fourthly.—If one of the parties enters upon an aggressive conflict, the other party to assume a neutral attitude, and in case of such party wishing the other to join forces, both to meet and discuss the conditions.

Fifthly.—England to acknowledge the abolition of foreign privileges in the Arab countries, and to assist the Government of the Sherif in an international Convention for confirming such abolition.

Sixthly.—Articles 3 and 4 of this treaty to remain in vigour for fifteen years, and if either wishes it to be renewed, one year's notice before lapse of treaty to be given.

Consequently, and as the whole of the Arab nation have (praise be to God) agreed and united for the attainment, at all costs and finally, of this noble object, they beg the Government of Great Britain to answer them positively or negatively in a period of thirty days after receiving this intimation; and if this period should also lapse before they receive an answer, they reserve to themselves complete freedom of action. Moreover, we (the Sherif's family) will consider themselves free in word and deed from the bonds of our previous declaration which we made through Ali Effendi.

LETTER FROM MCMAHON TO THE SHARIF HUSSEIN, AUGUST 30, 1915

...We have the honour to thank you for your frank expressions of the sincerity of your feeling towards England. We rejoice, moreover, that your Highness and your people are of one opinion—that Arab interests are English interests and English Arab. To this intent we confirm to you the terms of Lord Kitchener's message, which reached you by the hand of Ali Effendi, and in which was stated clearly our desire for the independence of Arabia and its inhabitants, together with our approval of the Arab Khalifate when it should be proclaimed. We declare once more that His Majesty's Government would welcome the resumption of the Khalifate by an Arab of true race. With regard to the questions of limits and boundaries, it would appear to be premature to consume our time in discussing such details in the heat of war, and while, in many portions of them, the Turk is up to now in effective occupation: especially as we have learned, with surprise and regret, that some of the Arabs in those very parts, far from assisting us, are neglecting this their supreme opportunity and are lending their arms to the German and the Turk, to the new despoiler and the old oppressor....

LETTER FROM THE SHARIF HUSSEIN TO MCMAHON, SEPTEMBER 9, 1915

...With great cheerfulness and delight I received your letter dated the 19th Shawal, 1333 (the 30th August, 1915), and have given it great consideration and regard, in spite of the impression I received from it of ambiguity and its tone of coldness and hesitation with regard to our essential point....

Your Excellency will pardon me and permit me to say clearly that the coolness and hesitation which you have displayed in the question of the limits and boundaries by saying that the discussion of these at present is of no use and is a loss of time, and that they are still in the hands of the Government which is ruling them, &c., might be taken to infer an estrangement or something of the sort.

As the limits and boundaries demanded are not those of one person whom we should satisfy and with whom we should discuss them after the war is over, but our peoples have seen that the life of their new proposal is bound at least by these limits and their word is united on this.

Therefore, they have found it necessary first to discuss this point with the Power in whom they now have their confidence and trust as a final appeal, viz., the illustrious British Empire.

Their reason for this union and confidence is mutual interest, the necessity of regulating territorial divisions and the feelings of their inhabitants, so that they may know how to base their future and life, so not to meet her (England?) or any of her Allies in opposition to their resolution which would produce a contrary issue, which God forbid....

With reference to your remark in your letter above mentioned that some of our people are still doing their utmost in promoting the interests of Turkey, your goodness (lit. "perfectness") would not permit you to make this an excuse for the tone of coldness and hesitation with regard to our demands, demands which I cannot admit that you, as a man of sound opinion, will deny to be necessary for our existence; nay, they are the essential essence of our life, material and moral.

...In order to reassure your Excellency I can declare that the whole country, together with those who you say are submitting themselves to Turco–German orders, are all waiting the result of these negotiations, which are dependent only on your refusal or acceptance of the question of the limits and on your declaration of safeguarding their religion first and then the rest of rights from any harm or danger....

LETTER FROM MCMAHON TO THE SHARIF OF MECCA, OCTOBER 24, 1915

...I regret that you should have received from my last letter the impression that I regarded the question of the limits and boundaries with coldness and hesitation;

such was not the case, but it appeared to me that the time had not yet come when that question could be discussed in a conclusive manner.

I have realised, however, from your last letter that you regard this question as one of vital and urgent importance. I have, therefore, lost no time in informing the Government of Great Britain of the contents of your letter, and it is with great pleasure that I communicate to you on their behalf the following statement, which I am confident you will receive with satisfaction:—

The two districts of Mersina and Alexandretta and portions of Syria lying to the west of the districts of Damascus, Homs, Hama and Aleppo cannot be said to be purely Arab, and should be excluded from the limits demanded.

With the above modification, and without prejudice to our existing treaties with Arab chiefs, we accept those limits.

As for those regions lying within those frontiers wherein Great Britain is free to act without detriment to the interests of her ally, France, I am empowered in the name of the Government of Great Britain to give the following assurances and make the following reply to your letter:—

(1) Subject to the above modifications, Great Britain is prepared to recognise and support the independence of the Arabs in all the regions within the limits demanded by the Sherif of Mecca.

(2) Great Britain will guarantee the Holy Places against all external aggression and will recognise their inviolability.

(3) When the situation admits, Great Britain will give to the Arabs her advice and will assist them to establish what may appear to be the most suitable forms of government in those various territories.

(4) On the other hand, it is understood that the Arabs have decided to seek the advice and guidance of Great Britain only, and that such European advisers and officials as may be required for the formation of a sound form of administration will be British.

(5) With regard to the vilayets of Baghdad and Basra, the Arabs will recognise that established position and interests of Great Britain necessitate special administrative arrangements in order to secure these territories from foreign aggression, to promote the welfare of the local populations and to safeguard our mutual economic interests. . . .

LETTER FROM THE SHARIF HUSSEIN TO MCMAHON, NOVEMBER 5, 1915

. . . 1. In order to facilitate an agreement and to render a service to Islam, and at the same time to avoid all that may cause Islam troubles and hardships—seeing moreover that we have great consideration for the distinguished qualities and dispositions of the Government of Great Britain—we renounce our insistence on the inclusion of the vilayets of Mersina and Adana in the Arab Kingdom. But the two vilayets of Aleppo and Beirut and their seacoasts are purely Arab vilayets, and there is no difference between a Moslem and a Christian Arab: they are both descendants of one forefather. . . .

2. As the Iraqi vilayets are parts of the pure Arab Kingdom, and were in fact the seat of its Government in the time of Ali ibn Abu Talib, and in the time of all the

Khalifs who succeeded him; and as in them began the civilisation of the Arabs, and as their towns were the first towns built in Islam where the Arab power became so great; therefore they are greatly valued by all Arabs far and near, and their traditions cannot be forgotten by them. Consequently, we cannot satisfy the Arab nations or make them submit to give us such a title to nobility. But in order to render an accord easy, and taking into consideration the assurances mentioned in the fifth article of your letter to keep and guard our mutual interests in that country as they are one and the same, for all these reasons we might agree to leave under the British administration for a short time those districts now occupied by the British troops without the rights of either party being prejudiced thereby (especially those of the Arab nation: which interests are to it economic and vital), and against a suitable sum paid as compensation to the Arab Kingdom for the period of occupation, in order to meet the expenses which every new kingdom is bound to support; at the same time respecting your agreements with the Sheikhs of those districts, and especially those which are essential....

4. The Arab nation has a strong belief that after this war is over the Turks under German influence will direct their efforts to provoke the Arabs and violate their rights, both material and moral, to wipe out their mobility and honour and reduce them to utter submission as they are determined to ruin them entirely. The reasons for the slowness shown in our action have already been stated.

5. When the Arabs know the Government of Great Britain is their ally who will not leave them to themselves at the conclusion of peace in the face of Turkey and Germany, and that she will support and will effectively defend them, then to enter the war at once will, no doubt, be in conformity with the general interest of the Arabs.

6. Our letter dated the 29th Shawal, 1333 (the 9th September, 1915), saves us the trouble of repeating our opinions as to articles 3 and 4 of your honoured last letter regarding administration, Government advisers and officials, especially as you have declared, exalted Minister, that you will not interfere with internal affairs....

LETTER FROM MCMAHON TO THE SHARIF OF MECCA, DECEMBER 14, 1915

... I am gratified to observe that you agree to the exclusion of the districts of Mersina and Adana from Boundaries of the Arab territories.

I also note with great pleasure and satisfaction your assurances that the Arabs are determined to act in conformity with the precepts laid down by Omar Ibn Khattab and the early Khalifs, which secure the rights and privileges of all religions alike.

In stating that the Arabs are ready to recognise and respect all our treaties with Arab chiefs, it is, of course, understood that this will apply to all territories included in the Arab Kingdom, as the Government of Great Britain cannot repudiate engagements which already exist.

With regard to the vilayets of Aleppo and Beirut, the Government of Great Britain have fully understood and taken careful note of your observations, but, as the interests of our ally, France, are involved in them both, the question will require careful consideration and a further communication on the subject will be addressed to you in due course.

The Government of Great Britain, as I have already informed you, are ready to give all guarantees of assistance and support within their power to the Arab Kingdom, but their interests demand, as you yourself have recognised, a friendly and stable administration in the vilayet of Baghdad, and the adequate safeguarding of these interests calls for a much fuller and more detailed consideration than the present situation and the urgency of these negotiations permit.

We fully appreciate your desire for caution, and have no wish to urge you to hasty action, which might jeopardise the eventual success of your projects, but, in the meantime, it is most essential that you should spare no effort to attach all the Arab peoples to our united cause and urge them to afford no assistance to our enemies.

It is on the success of these efforts and on the more active measures which the Arabs may hereafter take in support of our cause, when the time for action comes, that the permanence and strength of our agreement must depend.

Under these circumstances I am further directed by the Government of Great Britain to inform you that you may rest assured that Great Britain has no intention of concluding any peace in terms of which the freedom of the Arab peoples from German and Turkish domination does not form an essential condition. . . .

LETTER FROM THE SHARIF HUSSEIN TO MCMAHON, JANUARY 1, 1916

. . . With regard to what had been stated in your honoured communication concerning El Iraq as to the matter of compensation for the period of occupation, we, in order to strengthen the confidence of Great Britain in our attitude and in our words and actions, really and veritably, and in order to give her evidence of our certainty and assurance in trusting her glorious Government, leave the determination of the amount to the perception of her wisdom and justice.

As regards the northern parts and their coasts, we have already stated in our previous letter what were the utmost possible modifications, and all this was only done so to fulfill those aspirations whose attainment is desired by the will of the Blessed and Supreme God. It is this same feeling and desire which impelled us to avoid what may possibly injure the alliance of Great Britain and France and the agreement made between them during the present wars and calamities; yet we find it our duty that the eminent minister should be sure that, at the first opportunity after this war is finished, we shall ask you (what we avert our eyes from today) for what we now leave to France in Beirut and its coasts.

I do not find it necessary to draw your attention to the fact that our plan is of greater security to the interests and protection of the rights of Great Britain than it is to us, and will necessarily be so whatever may happen, so that Great Britain may finally see her friends in that contentment and advancement which she is endeavouring to establish for them now, especially as her Allies being neighbours to us will be the germ of difficulties and discussion with which there will be no peaceful conditions. In addition to which the citizens of Beirut will decidedly never accept such dismemberment, and they may oblige us to undertake new measures which may exercise Great Britain, certainly not less than her present troubles, because of our belief and certainty in the reciprocity and indeed the identity of our interests, which is the only cause that caused us never to care to negotiate with any other Power but you. Consequently, it is impossible to allow any derogation that gives France, or any other Power, a span of land in those regions....

LETTER FROM MCMAHON TO THE SHARIF OF MECCA, JANUARY 25, 1916

...We take note of your remarks concerning the vilayet of Baghdad, and will take the question into careful consideration when the enemy has been defeated and the time for peaceful settlement arrives.

As regards the northern parts, we note with satisfaction your desire to avoid anything which might possibly injure the alliance of Great Britain and France. It is, as you know, our fixed determination that nothing shall be permitted to interfere in the slightest degree with our united prosecution of this war to a victorious conclusion. Moreover, when the victory has been won, the friendship of Great Britain and France will become yet more firm and enduring, cemented by the blood of Englishmen and Frenchmen who have died side by side fighting for the cause of right and liberty....

Bernard Reich, ed., *Arab–Israeli Conflict and Conciliation: A Documentary History* (Westport, CT: Praeger, 1995), 19–25.

The Sykes-Picot Agreement: 1916

It is accordingly understood between the French and British governments:

That France and Great Britain are prepared to recognize and protect an independent Arab state or a confederation of Arab states (a) and (b) marked on the annexed map, under the suzerainty of an Arab chief. That in area (a) France, and in area (b) Great Britain, shall have priority of right of enterprise and local loans. That in area (a) France, and in area (b) Great Britain, shall alone supply advisers or foreign functionaries at the request of the Arab state or confederation of Arab states.

That in the blue area France, and in the red area Great Britain, shall be allowed to establish such direct or indirect administration or control as they desire and as they may think fit to arrange with the Arab state or confederation of Arab states.

That in the brown area there shall be established an international administration, the form of which is to be decided upon after consultation with Russia, and subsequently in consultation with the other allies, and the representatives of the sherif of Mecca.

That Great Britain be accorded (1) the ports of Haifa and Acre, (2) guarantee of a given supply of water from the Tigres and Euphrates in area (a) for area (b). His majesty's government, on their part, undertake that they will at no time enter into negotiations for the cession of Cyprus to any third power without the previous consent of the French government.

That Alexandretta shall be a free port as regards the trade of the British empire, and that there shall be no discrimination in port charges or facilities as regards British shipping and British goods; that there shall be freedom of transit for British goods through Alexandretta and by railway through the blue area, or area (b), or area (a); and there shall be no discrimination, direct or indirect, against British goods on any railway or against British goods or ships at any port serving the areas mentioned.

That Haifa shall be a free port as regards the trade of France, her dominions and protectorates, and there shall be no discrimination in port charges or facilities as regards French shipping and French goods. There shall be freedom of transit for French goods through Haifa and by the British railway through the brown area, whether those goods are intended for or originate in the blue area, area (a), or area (b), and there shall be no discrimination, direct or indirect, against French goods on any railway, or against French goods or ships at any port serving the areas mentioned.

That in area (a) the Baghdad railway shall not be extended southwards beyond Mosul, and in area (b) northwards beyond Samarra, until a railway connecting Baghdad and Aleppo via the Euphrates valley has been completed, and then only with the concurrence of the two governments.

That Great Britain has the right to build, administer, and be sole owner of a railway connecting Haifa with area (b), and shall have a perpetual right to transport troops along such a line at all times. It is to be understood by both governments that this railway is to facilitate the connection of Baghdad with Haifa by rail, and it is further understood that, if the engineering difficulties and expense entailed by keeping this connecting line in the brown area only make the project unfeasible, that the French government shall be prepared to consider that the line in question may also traverse the Polgon Banias Keis Marib Salkhad tell Otsda Mesmie before reaching area (b).

For a period of twenty years the existing Turkish customs tariff shall remain in force throughout the whole of the blue and red areas, as well as in areas (a) and (b), and no increase in the rates of duty or conversions from ad valorem to specific rates shall be made except by agreement between the two powers.

There shall be no interior customs barriers between any of the above mentioned areas. The customs duties leviable on goods destined for the interior shall be collected at the port of entry and handed over to the administration of the area of destination.

It shall be agreed that the French government will at no time enter into any negotiations for the cession of their rights and will not cede such rights in the blue area to any third power, except the Arab state or confederation of Arab states, without the previous agreement of his majesty's government, who, on their part, will give a similar undertaking to the French government regarding the red area.

The British and French governments, as the protectors of the Arab state, shall agree that they will not themselves acquire and will not consent to a third power acquiring territorial possessions in the Arabian peninsula, nor consent to a third power installing a naval base either on the east coast, or on the islands, of the red sea. This, however, shall not prevent such adjustment of the Aden frontier as may be necessary in consequence of recent Turkish aggression.

The negotiations with the Arabs as to the boundaries of the Arab states shall be continued through the same channel as heretofore on behalf of the two powers.

It is agreed that measures to control the importation of arms into the Arab territories will be considered by the two governments.

I have further the honor to state that, in order to make the agreement complete, his majesty's government are proposing to the Russian government to exchange notes analogous to those exchanged by the latter and your excellency's government on the

26th April last. Copies of these notes will be communicated to your excellency as soon as exchanged. I would also venture to remind your excellency that the conclusion of the present agreement raises, for practical consideration, the question of claims of Italy to a share in any partition or rearrangement of Turkey in Asia, as formulated in article 9 of the agreement of the 26th April, 1915, between Italy and the allies.

His majesty's government further consider that the Japanese government should be informed of the arrangements now concluded.

---

http://www.yale.edu/lawweb/avalon/mideast/sykes.htm (accessed February 1, 2006).

The Balfour Declaration: 1917

November 2nd, 1917

Dear Lord Rothschild,
I have much pleasure in conveying to you, on behalf of His Majesty's Government, the following declaration of sympathy with Jewish Zionist aspirations which has been submitted to, and approved by, the Cabinet.

"His Majesty's Government view with favour the establishment in Palestine of a national home for the Jewish people, and will use their best endeavours to facilitate the achievement of this object, it being clearly understood that nothing shall be done which may prejudice the civil and religious rights of existing non-Jewish communities in Palestine, or the rights and political status enjoyed by Jews in any other country."

I should be grateful if you would bring this declaration to the knowledge of the Zionist Federation.

Yours sincerely,
Arthur James Balfour

---

http://www.yale.edu/lawweb/avalon/mideast/balfour.htm (accessed February 1, 2006).

British Declaration to Seven Arab Spokesmen

16 June 1918

His Majesty's Government have considered the memorial of the seven with the greatest care. His Majesty's Government fully appreciate the reasons why the memorialists desire to retain their anonymity, and the fact that the memorial is anonymous has not in any way detracted from the importance which His Majesty's Government attribute to the document.

The areas mentioned in the memorandum fall into four categories—

1. Areas in Arabia which were free and independent before the outbreak of war;

2. Areas emancipated from Turkish control by the action of the Arabs themselves during the present war;

3. Areas formerly under Ottoman dominion, occupied by the Allied forces during the present war;

4. Areas still under Turkish control.

In regard to the first two categories, His Majesty's Government recognise the complete and sovereign independence of the Arabs inhabiting these areas and support them in their struggle for freedom.

In regard to the areas occupied by Allied forces, His Majesty's Government draw the attention of the memorialists to the texts of the proclamation issued respectively by the General Officers Commanding in Chief on the taking of Baghdad and Jerusalem. These proclamations embody the policy of His Majesty's Government towards the inhabitants of those regions. It is the wish and desire of His Majesty's Government that the future government of these regions should be based upon the principle of the consent of the governed and this policy has and will continue to have the support of His Majesty's Government....

---

http://sitemaker.umich.edu/emes/sourcebook&mode=single&recordID=82633&nextMode=list (accessed February 1, 2006).

Anglo–French Declaration

7 November 1918

The goal envisaged by France and Great Britain in prosecuting in the East the War set in train by German ambition is the complete and final liberation of the peoples who have for so long been oppressed by the Turks, and the setting up of national governments and administrations that shall derive their authority from the free exercise of the initiative and choice of the indigenous populations.

In pursuit of those intentions, France and Great Britain agree to further and assist in the setting up of indigenous governments and administrations in Syria and Mesopotamia which have already been liberated by the Allies, as well as in those territories which they are endeavoring to liberate, and to recognize them as soon as they are actually set up.

Far from wishing to impose this or that system upon the populations of those regions, their only concern is to offer such support and efficacious help as will ensure the smooth working of the governments and administrations which those populations will have elected of their own free will to have; to secure impartial and equal justice for all; to facilitate the economic development of the country by promoting and encouraging local initiative; to foster the spread of education; and to put an end to the dissensions which Turkish policy has for so long exploited. Such is the task which the two Allied Powers wish to undertake in the liberated territories.

---

http://sitemaker.umich.edu/emes/sourcebook&mode=single&recordID=82633&nextMode=list (accessed February 1, 2006).

Resolutions of the General Syrian Congress (Damascus, July 2, 1919)

We, the undersigned, members of the General Syrian Congress assembled in Damascus on the 2nd of July 1919 and composed of delegates from the three zones, namely the southern, eastern and western, and furnished with credentials duly authorizing us to represent the Moslem, Christian and Jewish inhabitants of our respective districts, have resolved to submit the following as defining the aspirations of the people who have chosen us to place them before the American Section of the Inter-Allied Commission. With the exception of the fifth clause, which was passed by a large majority, the Resolutions which follow were all adopted unanimously:—

1. We desire full and absolute political independence for Syria within the following boundaries: on the north, the Taurus Range; on the south, a line running from Rafah to al-Jauf and following the Syria–Hejaz border below 'Aqaba; on the east, the boundary formed by the Euphrates and Khabur rivers and a line stretching from some distance east of Abu-Kamal to some distance east of al-Jauf; on the west, the Mediterranean Sea.

2. We desire the Government of Syria to be a constitutional monarchy based on principles of democratic and broadly decentralized rule which shall safeguard the rights of minorities, and we wish that the Amir Faisal who has striven so nobly for our liberation and enjoys our full confidence and trust be our King.

3. In view of the fact that the Arab inhabitants of Syria are not less fitted or gifted than were certain other nations (such as the Bulgarians, Serbs, Greeks and Rumanians) when granted independence, we protest against Article XXII of the Covenant of the League of Nations which relegates us to the standing of insufficiently developed races requiring the tutelage of a mandatory power.

4. If, for whatever reason that might remain undisclosed to us, the Peace Conference were to ignore this legitimate protest, we shall regard the mandate mentioned in the Covenant of the League of Nations as implying no more than the rendering of assistance in the technical and economic fields without impairment of our absolute independence. We rely on President Wilson's declarations that his object in entering the War was to put an end to acquisitive designs for imperialistic purposes. In our desire that our country should not be made a field for colonization, and in the belief that the American nation is devoid of colonial ambitions and has no political designs on our country, we resolve to seek assistance in the technical and economic fields from the United States of America on the understanding that the duration of such assistance shall not exceed twenty years.

5. In the event of the United States finding herself unable to accede to our request for assistance, we would seek it from Great Britain, provided always that it will not be allowed to impair the unity and absolute independence of our country and that its duration shall not exceed the period mentioned in the preceding clause.

6. We do not recognize to the French Government any right to any part of Syria, and we reject all proposals that France should give us assistance or exercise authority in any portion of the country.

7. We reject the claims of the Zionists for the establishment of a Jewish commonwealth in that part of southern Syria which is known as Palestine, and we are opposed to Jewish immigration into any part of the country. We do not acknowledge that they have a title, and we regard their claims as a grave menace to our national, political and economic life. Our Jewish fellow-citizens shall continue to enjoy the rights and to bear the responsibilities which are ours in common.

8. We desire that there should be no dismemberment of Syria, and no separation of Palestine or the coastal regions in the west or the Lebanon from the mother country; and we ask that the unity of the country be maintained under any circumstances.

9. We desire that Iraq should enjoy complete independence, and that no economic barriers be placed between the two countries.

10. The basic principles proclaimed by President Wilson in condemnation of secret treaties cause us to enter an emphatic protest against any agreement providing for the dismemberment of Syria and against any undertaking envisaging the recognition of Zionism in southern Syria; and we ask for the explicit annulment of all such agreements and undertakings.

The lofty principles proclaimed by President Wilson encourage us to believe that the determining consideration in the settlement of our own future will be the real desires of our people; and that we may look to President Wilson and the liberal American nation, who are known for their sincere and generous sympathy with the aspirations of weak nations, for help in the fulfillment of our hopes.

We also fully believe that the Peace Conference will recognize that we would not have risen against Turkish rule under which we enjoyed civic and political privileges, as well as rights of representation, had it not been that the Turks denied us our right to a national existence. We believe that the Peace Conference will meet our desires in full, if only to ensure that our political privileges may not be less, after the sacrifices of life which we have made in the cause of our freedom, than they were before the War.

We desire to be allowed to send a delegation to represent us at the Peace Conference, advocate our claims and secure the fulfillment of our aspirations.

---

http://sitemaker.umich.edu/emes/sourcebook&mode=single&recordID=82633&nextMode=list (accessed February 1, 2006).

Memorandum Presented to the King-Crane Commission by the General Syrian Congress

July 2, 1919

We the undersigned members of the General Syrian Congress, meeting in Damascus on Wednesday, July 2nd, 1919, made up of representatives from the three Zones, viz., the Southern, Eastern, and Western, provided with credentials and authorizations by the inhabitants of our various districts, Moslems, Christians, and Jews, have agreed upon the following statement of the desires of the people of the country who have elected us to present them to the American Section of the International

Commission; the fifth article was passed by a very large majority; all the other articles were accepted unanimously.

1. We ask absolutely complete political independence for Syria within these boundaries: the Taurus System on the North; Rafah and a line running from Al Jauf to the south of the Syrian and the Hejazian line to Akaba on the south; the Euphrates and Khabur Rivers and a line extending east of Abu Kamal to the east of Al Jauf on the east; and the Mediterranean on the west.

2. We ask that the Government of this Syrian country should be a democratic civil constitutional Monarchy on broad decentralization principles, safeguarding the rights of minorities, and that the King be the Emir Feisal, who carried on a glorious struggle in the cause of our liberation and merited our full confidence and entire reliance.

3. Considering the fact that the Arabs inhabiting the Syrian area are not naturally less gifted than other more advanced races and that they are by no means less developed than the Bulgarians, Serbians, Greeks, and Roumanians at the beginning of their independence, we protest against Article 22 of the Covenant of the League of Nations, placing us among the nations in their middle stage of development which stand in need of a mandatory power.

4. In the event of the rejection by the Peace Conference of this just protest for certain considerations that we may not understand, we, relying on the declarations of President Wilson that his object in waging war was to put an end to the ambition of conquest and colonization, can only regard the mandate mentioned in the Covenant of the League of Nations as equivalent to the rendering of economical and technical assistance that does not prejudice our complete independence. And desiring that our country should not fall a prey to colonization is farthest from any thought of colonization and has no political ambition in our country, we will seek the technical and economical assistance from the United States of America, provided that such assistance does not exceed 20 years.

5. In the event of America not finding herself in a position to accept our desire for assistance, we will seek this assistance from Great Britain, also provided that such assistance does not infringe the complete independence and unity of our country and that the duration of such assistance does not exceed that mentioned in the previous article.

6. We do not acknowledge any right claimed by the French Government in any part whatever of our Syrian country and refuse that she should assist us or have a hand in our country under any circumstances and in any place.

7. We oppose the pretensions of the Zionists to create a Jewish commonwealth in the southern part of Syria, known as Palestine, and oppose Zionist migration to any part of our country; for we do not acknowledge their title but consider them a grave peril to our people from the national, economical, and political points of view. Our Jewish compatriots shall enjoy our common rights and assume the common responsibilities.

8. We ask that there should be no separation of the southern part of Syria, known as Palestine, nor of the littoral western zone, which includes Lebanon, from the Syrian country. We desire that the unity of the country should be guaranteed against partition under whatever circumstances.

9. We ask complete independence for emancipated Mesopotamia and that there should be no economical barriers between the two countries.

10. The fundamental principles laid down by President Wilson in condemnation of secret treaties impel us to protest most emphatically against any treaty that stipulates the partition of our Syrian country and against any private engagement aiming at the establishment of Zionism in the southern part of Syria; therefore we ask the complete annulment of these conventions and agreements.

The noble principles enunciated by President Wilson strengthen our confidence that our desires emanating from the depths of our hearts, shall be the decisive factor in determining our future; and that President Wilson and the free American people will be our supporters for the realization of our hopes thereby proving their sincerity and noble sympathy with the aspiration of the weaker nations in general and our Arab people in particular.

We also have the fullest confidence that the Peace Conference will realize that we would not have risen against the Turks, with whom we had participated in all civil, political, and representative privileges, but for their violation of our national rights, and so will grant us our desires in full in order that our political rights may not be less after the war than they were before, since we have shed so much blood in the cause of our liberty and independence.

We request to be allowed to send a delegation to represent us at the Peace Conference to defend our rights and secure the realization of our aspirations.

Walter Laqueur and Barry Rubin, eds., *The Israel–Arab Reader: A Documentary History of the Middle East Conflict* (New York: Penguin, 1984), 31–33.

British White Paper of June 1922

The Secretary of State for the Colonies has given renewed consideration to the existing political situation in Palestine, with a very earnest desire to arrive at a settlement of the outstanding questions which have given rise to uncertainty and unrest among certain sections of the population. After consultation with the High Commissioner for Palestine [Sir Herbert Samuel] the following statement has been drawn up. It summarizes the essential parts of the correspondence that has already taken place between the Secretary of State and a delegation from the Moslem Christian Society of Palestine, which has been for some time in England, and it states the further conclusions which have since been reached.

The tension which has prevailed from time to time in Palestine is mainly due to apprehensions, which are entertained both by sections of the Arab and by sections of the Jewish population. These apprehensions, so far as the Arabs are concerned are partly based upon exaggerated interpretations of the meaning of the [Balfour] Declaration favouring the establishment of a Jewish National Home in Palestine, made on behalf of His Majesty's Government on 2nd November, 1917.

Unauthorized statements have been made to the effect that the purpose in view is to create a wholly Jewish Palestine. Phrases have been used such as that Palestine is to become "as Jewish as England is English." His Majesty's Government regard any such expectation as impracticable and have no such aim in view. Nor have they at any time contemplated, as appears to be feared by the Arab delegation, the disappearance or the subordination of the Arabic population, language, or culture in Palestine. They would draw attention to the fact that the terms of the Declaration referred to do not contemplate that Palestine as a whole should be converted into a Jewish National Home, but that such a Home should be founded "in Palestine." In this connection it has been observed with satisfaction that at a meeting of the Zionist Congress, the supreme governing body of the Zionist Organization, held at Carlsbad in September, 1921, a resolution was passed expressing as the official statement of Zionist aims "the determination of the Jewish people to live with the Arab people on terms of unity and mutual respect, and together with them to make the common home into a flourishing community, the upbuilding of which may assure to each of its peoples an undisturbed national development."

It is also necessary to point out that the Zionist Commission in Palestine, now termed the Palestine Zionist Executive, has not desired to possess, and does not possess, any share in the general administration of the country. Nor does the special position assigned to the Zionist Organization in Article IV of the Draft Mandate for Palestine imply any such functions. That special position relates to the measures to be taken in Palestine affecting the Jewish population, and contemplates that the organization may assist in the general development of the country, but does not entitle it to share in any degree in its government.

Further, it is contemplated that the status of all citizens of Palestine in the eyes of the law shall be Palestinian, and it has never been intended that they, or any section of them, should possess any other juridical status. So far as the Jewish population of Palestine are concerned it appears that some among them are apprehensive that His Majesty's Government may depart from the policy embodied in the Declaration of 1917. It is necessary, therefore, once more to affirm that these fears are unfounded, and that that Declaration, reaffirmed by the Conference of the Principle Allied Powers at San Remo and again in the Treaty of Sevres, is not susceptible of change.

During the last two or three generations the Jews have recreated in Palestine a community, now numbering 80,000, of whom about one fourth are farmers or workers upon the land. This community has its own political organs; an elected assembly for the direction of its domestic concerns; elected councils in the towns; and an organization for the control of its schools. It has its elected Chief Rabbinate and Rabbinical Council for the direction of its religious affairs. Its business is conducted in Hebrew as a vernacular language, and a Hebrew Press serves its needs. It has its distinctive intellectual life and displays considerable economic activity. This community, then, with its town and country population, its political, religious, and social organizations, its own language, its own customs, its own life, has in fact "national" characteristics. When it is asked what is meant by the development of the Jewish National Home in Palestine, it may be answered that it is not the imposition of a Jewish nationality upon the inhabitants of Palestine as a whole, but the further development of the existing Jewish community, with the assistance of Jews in other parts of the world, in order that it may become a centre in which the Jewish people as a whole may take, on grounds of religion and race, an interest and a pride. But in order that this community should have the best prospect of free development and provide a full opportunity for the Jewish people to display its capacities, it is essential that it should know that it is in Palestine as of right and not on the sufferance. That is the reason why it is necessary that the existence of a Jewish National Home in Palestine should be internationally guaranteed, and that it should be formally recognized to rest upon ancient historic connection.

This, then, is the interpretation which His Majesty's Government place upon the Declaration of 1917, and, so understood, the Secretary of State is of opinion that it does not contain or imply anything which need cause either alarm to the Arab population of Palestine or disappointment to the Jews.

For the fulfilment of this policy it is necessary that the Jewish community in Palestine should be able to increase its numbers by immigration. This immigration cannot be so great in volume as to exceed whatever may be the economic capacity of the country at the time to absorb new arrivals. It is essential to ensure that the immigrants should not be a burden upon the people of Palestine as a whole, and that they should not deprive any section of the present population of their employment. Hitherto the immigration has fulfilled these conditions. The number of immigrants since the British occupation has been about 25,000.

It is necessary also to ensure that persons who are politically undesirable be excluded from Palestine, and every precaution has been and will be taken by the Administration to that end.

It is intended that a special committee should be established in Palestine, consisting entirely of members of the new Legislative Council elected by the people, to confer with the administration upon matters relating to the regulation of immigration. Should any difference of opinion arise between this committee and the Administration, the matter will be referred to His Majesty's Government, who will give it special consideration. In addition, under Article 81 of the draft Palestine Order in Council, any religious community or considerable section of the population of Palestine will have a general right to appeal, through the High Commissioner and the Secretary of State, to the League of Nations on any matter on which they may consider that the terms of the Mandate are not being fulfilled by the Government of Palestine.

With reference to the Constitution which it is now intended to establish in Palestine, the draft of which has already been published, it is desirable to make certain points clear. In the first place, it is not the case, as has been represented by the Arab Delegation, that during the war His Majesty's Government gave an undertaking that an independent national government should be at once established in Palestine. This representation mainly rests upon a letter dated the 24th October, 1915, from Sir Henry McMahon, then His Majesty's High Commissioner in Egypt, to the Sharif of Mecca, now King Hussein of the Kingdom of the Hejaz. That letter is quoted as conveying the promise to the Sherif of Mecca to recognise and support the independence of the Arabs within the territories proposed by him. But this promise was given subject to a reservation made in the same letter, which excluded from its scope, among other territories, the portions of Syria lying to the west of the District of Damascus. This reservation has always been regarded by His Majesty's Government as covering the vilayet of Beirut and the independent Sanjaq of Jerusalem. The whole of Palestine west of the Jordan was thus excluded from Sir Henry McMahon's pledge.

Nevertheless, it is the intention of His Majesty's Government to foster the establishment of a full measure of self government in Palestine. But they are of the opinion that, in the special circumstances of that country, this should be accomplished by gradual stages and not suddenly. The first step was taken when, on the institution of a Civil Administration, the nominated Advisory Council, which now exists, was established. It was stated at the time by the High Commissioner that this was the first step in the development of self governing institutions, and it is now proposed to take a second step by the establishment of a Legislative Council containing a large proportion of members elected on a wide franchise. It was proposed in the published draft that three of the members of this Council should be non official persons nominated by the High Commissioner, but representations having been made in opposition to this provision, based on cogent considerations, the Secretary of State is prepared to omit it. The Legislative Council would then consist of the High Commissioner as President and twelve elected and ten official members. The Secretary of State is of the opinion that before a further measure of self government is extended to Palestine and the Assembly placed in control over the Executive, it would be wise to allow some time to elapse. During this period the institutions of the country will have become well established; its financial credit will be based on firm foundations, and the Palestinian officials will have been enabled to gain experience of sound methods of government. After a few years the situation will be again reviewed, and if the experience of the working of the constitution now to be established so warranted, a larger share of authority would then be extended to the elected representatives of the people.

The Secretary of State would point out that already the present administration has transferred to a Supreme Council elected by the Moslem community of Palestine the entire control of Moslem Religious endowments (Waqfs), and of the Moslem religious Courts. To this Council the Administration has also voluntarily restored considerable revenues derived from ancient endowments which have been sequestrated by the Turkish Government. The Education Department is also advised by a committee representative of all sections of the population, and the Department of Commerce and Industry has the benefit of the cooperation of the Chambers of Commerce which have been established in the principal centres. It is the intention of the Administration to associate in an increased degree similar representative committees with the various Departments of the Government.

The Secretary of State believes that a policy upon these lines, coupled with the maintenance of the fullest religious liberty in Palestine and with scrupulous regard for the rights of each community with reference to its Holy Places, cannot but commend itself to the various sections of the population, and that upon this basis may be built up that spirit of cooperation upon which the future progress and prosperity of the Holy Land must largely depend.

---

http://www.yale.edu/lawweb/avalon/mideast/brwh1922.htm (accessed February 1, 2006).

Four
THE PALESTINE MANDATE

The fault lines that would soon define the Arab–Israeli conflict and the Palestinian problem were for the most part drawn during the British Mandate period in Palestine between the two world wars, culminating with the first Arab–Israeli war in 1947–1949, from which the state of Israel emerged. The situation in the Palestine mandate was different from that which existed in the other British and French mandated territories in the Middle East. In Palestine there were two distinct groups, Zionists and Palestinian Arabs, attempting to put forward in a mutually exclusive fashion what they felt were their rightful claims to ownership of Palestine, i.e., statehood. All the while the British looked on in earnest bewilderment as to what policy would best achieve their imperial interests while maintaining at least a modest level of stability in the mandate, especially as the specter of World War II approached by the late 1930s. Commenting on London's swirling positions toward the Mandate, one British official stated that it was "nothing but fluctuations of policy, hesitations... no policy at all."[1] The numerous British investigative commissions sent to Palestine during the mandate period would seem to bear this out. All of this seems to suggest that there were three competing monolithic entities trying to sort out the increasingly complex and confusing situation in Palestine, yet that was not the case at all. Within each of the three main parties there existed different currents of opinion that tended to swing and sway policies constructed by each of the protagonists in a variety of directions, often retarding efforts to form unified positions on important issues. Competing claims to leadership—and the sometimes radically different approaches advocated by the competing groups—among the Zionists in the Yishuv as well as the Palestinian Arabs mixed with ambiguous and shifting British priorities to produce a very dynamic environment in Palestine in the interwar years, when the state of Israel and a Palestinian movement took shape and form. Essentially, in the end, one could say that the state of Israel emerged from the reality that the Zionists utilized this period of embryonic institution-building and national unification to much better effect than the Palestinians, or for that matter any of the other European-controlled mandated territories in the Arab world, a point driven home by the fact that the new Jewish state defeated not only the Palestinians in the quest for ownership of much of Palestine but also the five Arab states that tried to take it away in the first Arab–Israeli war.

BRITISH ADMINISTRATION

As noted in Chapter 3, most of Palestine had come under British military administration after the capture of Jerusalem in December 1917. Palestine had been ravaged by the war, both physically and economically, maybe more so than the other Arab territories involved in the conflict. This was particularly the case in the coastal areas, and loose estimates indicate that there was a 6% decline in the population due to the conflagration.[2] The region remained under military administration until 1920, when the San Remo Conference awarded Britain the mandate of Palestine; and shortly thereafter, the military administration was replaced by a civilian one under the leadership initially of High Commissioner Sir Herbert Samuel. In 1922, the League of Nations formally sanctioned the Palestine mandate, including the recognition of Hebrew as an official language and the British commitment in the Balfour Declaration as reinterpreted by the Churchill White Paper. Regardless of the latter, Zionists certainly interpreted the mandate and the British commitment to a national home for the Jews as the establishment of a Jewish state—Chaim Weizmann's remark at the time along the lines of making Palestine as Jewish as England is English reflected this expectation. But the British were ambiguous at best regarding the creation of a nation-state for the Jews, as was their intention. The Churchill White Paper was a prime example of the British predicament. Referring to the Balfour Declaration, William L. Cleveland remarks, "How could Britain facilitate the establishment of a Jewish national home on the one hand and ensure that the rights of the Arab majority (over 85% of the population of Palestine at the time—just under 670,000 Arabs) would not be threatened on the other?"[3] Ultimately, the British could never reconcile the two.

Upon assuming his position, Samuel genuinely believed that Arabs and Jews could be brought to work together to make the Palestine mandate work. He attempted to involve the Arab side in participating in the administration of the mandate, first through the creation in 1922 of a mixed legislative council comprised of a combination of elected and appointed Christian, Jewish, and Muslim representatives. As would become the norm, Arab leaders rejected participation in the council for fear that it would sanction the Zionist presence as well as the British Mandate, the latter of which was indeed one of Samuel's objectives. Certainly, among the Arabs the feeling persisted at the time that since they constituted 90% of the population, they should receive more than 50% of the benefits, economically and politically. Other mandates in the region were receiving the trappings of state that accrued to the dominant Arab populations, so why not in Palestine? As such, it was difficult for the Palestinian Arabs to identify leaders within the community, much less construct a leadership structure. The politics of notables was still being played out in Palestine, inhibiting the emergence of a clearly articulated political hierarchy. What resulted was policy paralysis born by political infighting and short-sightedness.

This and subsequent attempts by Samuel to form some sort of an advisory body failed to materialize by 1923. In retrospect, while one can understand the dilemma of the Palestinian Arabs, this may have been one of the most serious lapses in the formative stage of the mandate period, for as Cleveland states,

> The Arab rejection of Samuel's various proposals for unitary representation was of the utmost significance in determining the future course of the mandate. It meant that Palestine was governed by the high commissioner and his officials alone. Institutions representing the population as a whole were completely lacking: Palestine never had a constitution, a parliament, or mandate-wide elections. The Arab and Jewish communities, rather than jointly participating in the development of "national" institutions, became increasingly isolated from one another. Each community developed its own political apparatus and engaged in its own separate spheres of economic activity. These practices strengthened the communal solidarity within each community but widened the gap between them.[4]

This may have been the single most important development that led to the outbreak of civil war the moment the British effectively abandoned Palestine. While other Middle East mandated territories certainly had their share of problems in political and economic development; ethnic, religious, and class fissures; and European manipulation, perhaps nowhere was there less done to prepare for eventual statehood (the presumed goal of the mandate system to begin with) than in Palestine. Nowhere was there such a distinct and broad divide between two groups of inhabitants within a mandate that grew wider and wider with each passing year, marked by mutually exclusive development and internecine violence that reinforced separation and frustrated and confused the mandatory power.

As such, the Arabs and Jews in Palestine went about constructing, with differing degrees of success, institutions, leadership structures, and movements to fill the vacuum created by the absence of an integrated polity. Both sides realized, at least for a time, that they had to cooperate at least at some level with the British overlords in order to build their nascent structures, and each believed, although the Yishuv had much more of a right to do so than the Palestinian Arabs, that ultimately the British might indeed favor their own version of Palestine at the expense of the other. Interestingly, both the Jews and Arabs in Palestine eventually came to the conclusion that their national goals could only be achieved with the expulsion of Britain and an end to the mandate.

NATION-BUILDING IN PALESTINE

As was the case in the other mandates, the politics of urban notables prevailed amongst the Palestinians for most of the mandate period.[5] Or as C. Ernest Dawn observed in his analysis of the growth of Arab nationalism, those who had been Ottomanists had now become Arabists in the sense that the cooperation between the large landowning families and the Ottoman authorities had been replaced by that of the European mandate officials.[6] In other words, in order to secure their political, social, and economic status, the urban notables maintained a level of cooperation with the mandate power, even while at the same time often clamoring for more independence from it. The British, for their part, preferred to work with the existing social structure that they inherited, which was the best way to co-opt the only societal entities that could cause them long-term problems in terms of mass oppositional mobilization. This also facilitated their control of the apparatus of power and penetration of political and economic groupings. From the beginning, however, once the Balfour Declaration became enshrined in the official mandate, the Palestinians did not have, nor did they cultivate, as much access to Britain as the Zionists because, despite a level of cooperation with the British, the bottom line was that they *had* to oppose the mandate—the League of Nations confirmed a mandate that promoted a national home for the Jews, not the Palestinians. The Zionists, certainly until the 1939 White Paper, saw the mandate as a vehicle that would propel them toward a Jewish state—and the Arabs of Palestine, to their consternation, saw it exactly the same way.

The British administration in Palestine attempted to balance not only Jews with Arabs in a variety of proposed leadership councils but also power between rival Arab families, although some would say divide-and-rule tactics also played a role in the parceling out of positions. The Palestine Arab Executive was formed by the Third Palestinian Congress in December 1920 (the first two congresses had been held in Damascus during the Faisali period). This was intended to be a permanent representative body, and it was headed by Muza Kazam al-Husayni, who had been mayor of Jerusalem during the 1920 riots. At the 1923 congress in Jaffa, the term "southern Syria" was replaced by that of "Palestine," indicating the growth of a distinct Palestinian nationalism. The Palestine Arab Executive was ineffective at organizing a common Palestinian Arab policy, subject to the vicissitudes of intra-Arab divisions in Palestine, and it eventually was terminated in 1927. The two leading Muslim notable families in Jerusalem were the al-Husaynis and the Nashashibis. The mayoralty was rotated between members of the two families in the early 1920s, and when in 1921 a member of the Nashashibi family was appointed mayor of Jerusalem, it was arranged for a member of the al-Husayni family, Hajj Amin al-Husayni (1895–1974), to be the mufti of Jerusalem.[7] This major division at the top of the social spectrum in Palestinian Arab society was not the primary cause for the lack of a cohesive Palestinian movement during the mandate years, but it was certainly one of a confluence of obstacles inhibiting national unity. Hajj Amin al-Husayni's authority within the mandate continued to grow throughout the 1920s and 1930s. As mufti of Jerusalem, he was responsible for Islamic affairs in the district of Jerusalem, which was expanded by the British to include all of Palestine with his appointment as the president of the Supreme Muslim Council created by Samuel in 1921, according him a great deal of prestige and power within the Palestinian Arab community, especially as bodies such as the Palestine Arab Executive faded from the scene. From this elevated position, which was funded by the mandatory government, Hajj Amin al-Husayni was able to establish an extensive patronage system, exclude the rival Nashashibis from power, and translate this religious authority into essentially the only generally recognizable political authority in Arab Palestine.

The Jews in Palestine, however, were able to transfer and/or exploit to their advantage many of the existing Zionist organizational structures that had been in place for decades. The Yishuv had considerably more resources on which to draw, especially financial, than the Palestinian Arabs. The Yishuv had an economic, political, and diplomatic advantage from the very beginning, which was skillfully utilized over the course of the mandate to condition the Jewish community in Palestine for statehood when and if the opportunity arose. In addition, the Jewish presence in Palestine had been sanctified by the terms of the mandate itself, which, as we already know, incorporated the thrust of the Balfour Declaration. As such, there was regular contact and consultation between leading elements of the Yishuv, who saw the British Mandate as a necessary construction to achieve their ultimate goals, and the British Mandate authorities. There was also frequent contact with British officials in London, especially as the World Zionist Organization (WZO) relocated its headquarters to London in 1920 with Chaim Weizmann as its president. To many Zionists, the British Mandate was a means to an end, although they always suspected that in attempts to placate the Arab population in Palestine, the British could ultimately hinder progress toward an independent state; but for the time being, it was necessary to work with, rather than against, London. To this end, as an intermediary device between the Yishuv and the British, the WZO in 1921 created the Palestine Zionist Executive, which in 1929 was reorganized as the Jewish Agency, which became the closest thing to a government for the Jewish community in Palestine and was involved in a host of activities ranging from immigration to financial services to health care.[8] Weizmann was its titular president for most of the mandate period, although David Ben-Gurion as the chair of the executive really controlled its operations, especially as he was in-country, so to speak, reflecting the general trend of the Zionist movement as the Yishuv continued to construct an institutional capacity.[9] Also, in 1920 the Va'ad Leumi (National Committee) was established as an executive body representing the Jews in Palestine, responsible for a host of administrative tasks and decisions. Its members were chosen by a national assembly consisting of about 300 representatives, essentially the precursor to the Israeli Knesset, or parliament. Political parties, mostly representing various strains of labor Zionism, had also been formed. Ahdut Ha'Avodah (the Unity of Labor) was established in 1919 under the leadership of David Ben-Gurion. Along with the already existing Hapoel Hatzair (the Young Worker, founded in 1905), they were the two primary political parties in the Yishuv. They would merge in January 1930 into Mapai, the Hebrew acronym for Workers' Party of the Land of Israel. It was also led by Ben-Gurion, which would later morph into the Labor party in 1965, still today one of the most influential parties in Israel.

Reflecting the ideals of the second aliyah, particularly on issues relating to labor and self-sufficiency, and in an attempt to forge a working-class alliance, the General Federation of Jewish Labor in Eretz Israel, or Histadrut, was created in 1920 to organize and administer Jewish trade unions. Histadrut became a very powerful element in both the Yishuv and the future state of Israel, becoming the largest employer within the mandate. It involved itself not only in important activities such as public works projects, agriculture, and shipping but also in promoting the labor Zionist ideological foundation of the Jewish community in Palestine. As Stein states,

> The Histadrut was not comparable to the trade union federations that existed in Europe and North America. Above all, it regarded itself as an indispensable vehicle for realizing key Zionist objectives entailing the ingathering of the exiles and the creation of a democratic, worker-based Jewish state. Essentially, it was more like a state within a state, providing a comprehensive system of social welfare in the widest sense of the term.[10]

Membership in the Histadrut rose to approximately 25,000 by the end of the 1920s, about one-sixth of the entire population of the Yishuv.[11] Because of how deeply embedded the Histadrut was in the Yishuv, its leaders naturally exercised a great deal of power within the Jewish community. This is even more apparent by the fact that the Haganah, or Jewish defense forces, the precursor to the Israeli Defense Forces, was formed and organized by the Histadrut in 1920 in response to the riots that year. The Haganah turned out to be particularly effective because it was composed of a number of Jewish immigrants from central Europe in the third aliyah who had had considerable military experience in World War I; it also culled together the remnants of the Jewish Legion, who had fought with the British in the war. As one can readily observe, collectively these various Jewish organizations in and outside of the Palestine mandate provided a relatively streamlined, mutually reinforcing, and efficient organizational structure that provided the Yishuv with the trappings of statehood long before it actually materialized. In a sense, Jewish civil society in Palestine was highly developed and at a much more mature stage than its Palestinian Arab counterpart. Hebrew University in Jerusalem was even established in 1925. These organizations gave the Yishuv a certain institutional depth that facilitated the implementation of various policies as well as the resilience and pliancy to withstand and react to the pressures and disturbances that would soon arise as the opposition from both the Arabs and the British increased in due course. The Jews in Palestine made the decision to separate from the British much earlier than the Arabs did, a process that was facilitated not only by the very fact that they were ready to do so but also because they were encouraged by British authorities in order to reduce the financial burden on London.

This, however, is not meant to suggest that everything in the Yishuv was harmonious and worked like a well-oiled machine—the point is that the Jewish community, for reasons already outlined, was in a much better position on both counts than the Arab community in Palestine. Indeed, within the Yishuv there still existed the basic ideological division between cultural and political Zionism, which by this time could more accurately be called a division between socialist and revisionist Zionism. The primary alternative to the cultural or socialist Zionist approach in the Yishuv was directed by Russian Zionist Vladimir Jabotinsky (1880–1940), who in 1925 founded the Revisionist party in Paris, which propagated its message in Palestine through its protofascist "Betar" youth movement. He advocated an immediate proclamation of statehood, calling for massive Jewish immigration (at least 50,000 per year) to Palestine in order to create facts on the ground. Jabotinsky did not trust the British, a feeling he ironically shared with the Arabs in Palestine; and from the very beginning of the mandate he and his followers saw Britain as the biggest obstacle to attaining their national goals. The revisionists did not accept the separation of Transjordan from Palestine as outlined in the Churchill White Paper; indeed, in 1929, at the annual Zionist Congress, Jabotinsky stated "What does the word Palestine mean? Palestine is a territory whose chief geographical feature is this: that the River Jordan does not delineate its frontier, but flows through its center."[12]

The Revisionist party, because of the urgency with which it viewed the situation, also adopted a more militant approach toward their real and potential adversaries. Along these lines, in 1933 the party formally separated itself from mainstream Zionism (by withdrawing most Revisionists from the World Zionist Movement when it became apparent that their share of delegates in the Eighteenth Zionist Congress would drop

Lord Balfour opening the Hebrew University in Jerusalem in 1925. (Library of Congress, Prints & Photographs Division, LC-DIG-matpc-10366.)

commensurate with their electoral defeat in the polls from 25% the previous year to 14%). It essentially took over a military organization of its own, called the Irgun, a prominent member of which would be Menachem Begin, a protégé of Jabotinsky and a future prime minister of Israel. The Irgun (*Irgun Zvai Leumi,* or National Military Organization) was originally formed out of the Haganah in 1931 after the latter was found to be wanting in some respects during the 1929 riots; in fact, it was initially called the Haganah B. It was eventually taken over by the Revisionists by the late 1930s as an instrument to carry out a more active policy.[13] It would become known for carrying out acts of violence against both the British and the Arabs in the immediate post-World War II period in Palestine in order to achieve the Revisionist political program.

THE TWIN PILLARS OF ZIONISM

Whatever shade of opinion within Zionism both inside and outside of Palestine, on two things they all would agree: that the Zionist project could not succeed without people and land. As such, the twin pillars of Zionism, as it had been before the mandate, continued to be Jewish immigration and the acquisition/purchase of land. The accelerated efforts on both fronts required an impressive organizational and resource base. By the end of World War I, there were approximately 90,000 Jews and 800,000 Arabs in Palestine. About 30,000 Jewish immigrants entered Palestine, mostly from eastern Europe, between 1919 and 1923, a period considered the third aliyah in

Zionist history. It was generally envisioned by the Zionists that between 1922 and 1932 70,000–80,000 Jews would enter Palestine each year. In actuality, however, during this time span there was much less immigration than anticipated. An average of only 10,000 Jews immigrated per annum; in fact, in 1927 more Jews emigrated from Palestine than immigrated. One of the biggest problems facing Zionism was the attractiveness of other places where Jews could live as opposed to the relative difficulties and dangers of living in Palestine. As stated earlier, between 1881 and 1914, i.e., the period of the first two aliyahs, 2.5 million Jews emigrated from Russia—2 million of these went to the United States, with only about 30,000 going to Palestine. Only in 1925, for the first time, did Jewish immigration to Palestine exceed that to the United States (34,386 to 10,292, mostly because of stricter U.S. immigration quotas).[14] By the end of the decade, there were approximately 157,000 Jews in Palestine, constituting 17.7% of the entire population. Immigration did eventually increase, by leaps and bounds, in the 1930s for reasons that will be described shortly; but throughout the Zionist enterprise to this day immigration has been *the* foundation. As former Israeli prime minister Shimon Peres commented some eighty years later, "Zionism was built on geography, but it lives on demography."[15]

The Zionists encountered a bit more success on the land front. By the end of 1918, there were a total of fifty-one Jewish agricultural settlements in Palestine, most of which were either *moshovot* or *kibbutzim*. The Zionists had expected that large publicly owned tracts of land would be transferred to them for their use by the mandatory authorities. But this did not materialize, thus making it clear to them that if they were to acquire land it would have to be purchased. The Jewish National Fund had been set up to oversee the land purchase process in Palestine. It would negotiate the purchase of land and then, unless earmarked for some other purpose, would usually lease it at nominal rates to Jewish settlers—it also made sure that purchased land would not be subject to speculation or unauthorized resale. In addition, it provided funds for the purchase of agricultural equipment and other capital improvements that enabled Jewish immigrants to engage in agricultural pursuits in line with the labor Zionist ideology. This resource base certainly gave Jewish farmers an inherent advantage in terms of agricultural production over Arab farmers in Palestine. Most of the land acquired by Zionist interests was purchased from Arab absentee landowners, who owned more than 20% of the private land in the mandate. The largest tract of land purchased in this manner was 50,000 acres in the agriculturally rich Jezreel Valley from the Sursock family from Beirut in 1920; indeed, by 1939, Jews owned about 5% of the Palestine mandate, which made up some 10% of the arable land (the Arabs owned approximately 10%, with the remainder under state-owned British mandatory control). The fact that many of the Arab landowners in Palestine were of the absentee variety facilitated Jewish land penetration; they had little, if any, tie to the land through family heritage or history that might have created obstacles to Jewish land purchases, especially as Palestinian national awareness increased. Typically, the absentee landowners were informed mostly by profit motive, with the land considered merely an asset to be bought and sold. This became even more of a guiding principle after the harmful effects of the global depression in the 1930s infiltrated the region, with landowners of all types becoming more willing to liquidate remaining assets even at reduced prices and Jewish interests entering into land speculation as some of the only viable financial elements in Palestine interested in purchasing land, albeit for reasons that had little to do with market forces. The Arab peasants in Palestine often paid the stiffest price. Many Arab tenant farmers were evicted from the land they had been working, swelling the ranks of the unemployed and dissatisfied. Arabs who owned small plots of land in Palestine, small proprietors, were burdened by the changeover from Ottoman to British control. Under the Ottoman system, for centuries, small landowners could pay their taxes in kind. Upon the implementation of the mandate, however, British taxation policy required direct cash payments, which compelled many to either sell their plots (to either Jewish interests or Arab large landowners) or borrow money from moneylenders at high interest rates, many of whom were also the large landowners, who often simply took over the land when the small landowners could no longer pay their debt. As Cleveland notes,

> The cumulative effect of land transfers, British policy, and Arab notable attitudes was the increasing impoverishment and marginalization of the Palestinian Arab peasantry. Alienated from their own political elite, who seemed to profit from their plight; from the British, who appeared unwilling to prevent their expulsion from the land; and from the Zionists, who were perceived to be at the root of their problems, they expressed their discontent in outbreaks of violence against all three parties.[16]

For most of the 1920s, after the series of riots and disturbances in 1920 and 1921, Palestine was relatively quiescent. This can, in part, be attributed to the fact that there existed leadership struggles and developmental issues that focused much of the energy and efforts of the Jews and Arabs in Palestine in a more inward fashion rather than at each other or at the British. In addition, the fact that there was much less Jewish immigration than anticipated certainly lessened the pressure-cooker atmosphere in Palestine that might have otherwise existed had original immigration targets been reached. This relative calm, however, would soon dissipate in a dramatic fashion, ushering in a period of enhanced tension and conflict, a condition that would soon come to characterize both Palestine and Israel.

THE CYCLE OF VIOLENCE

The 1929 Western (or Wailing) Wall riots inaugurated a period of turbulence and conflict in Palestine that would continue almost unabated until the beginning of World War II in 1939 and the related issuance of the British White Paper that same year. For their part, the British constantly tried to discover the roots of the Palestine problem, thereby hoping to design a solution that could make the mandate work, or at least less volatile—and, therefore, less taxing on the exchequer and British citizenry. In essence, after a steady stream of investigative commissions and reports, British officials in London and in Palestine could not find a solution acceptable to all of the concerned parties, leading to the effective reversal of the British commitment made to the Jews in the Balfour Declaration as articulated in the 1939 White Paper, made necessary by the strategic situation on the eve of another world war.

The Western Wall is all that outwardly remains of the Jewish temple originally built by Solomon, destroyed by the Babylonians, reconstructed shortly thereafter, only to be destroyed once again by the Romans in the first century of the common era.

It is considered the holiest site in all of Judaism, making up part of one side of what is known among Jews as the Temple Mount (or what Muslims term the *Haram al-Sharif,* or Noble Sanctuary). For Muslims, the Haram al-Sharif is also sacred ground; indeed, for most it is the third holiest site in all of Islam after Mecca and Medina. On the plateau of the Haram al-Sharif, standing atop the Western Wall in the Old City of Jerusalem, sit two of Islam's holiest structures, the Dome of the Rock and

Dome of the Rock

The Dome of the Rock in Jerusalem is the most recognizable architectural feature in the fabled city. It has also over the years become a symbol of the competing claims for the city between Muslims and Jews and the focal point for Israeli–Palestinian rallies, protests, and violence. The Dome of the Rock commemorates the halfway point in the prophet Muhammad's miraculous night journey from Mecca before ascending through the seven heavens. During the course of this journey he met with and sought advice from preceding prophets, such as Moses, Jesus, Abraham, and John the Baptist, before entering into the presence of God (Allah) himself. The "Rock" contains Muhammad's footprint where he ascended into the heavens. It is located on the platform of the Temple Mount (or what Muslims refer to as the *Haram al-Sharif,* the Noble Sanctuary), the location of the Jewish temple built originally by Solomon around the year 950 BCE, situated on the site where Jews believe Abraham almost sacrificed his son Isaac. The First Temple was destroyed by Babylonian King Nebuchadnezzar in 586 BCE. Following the seventy-year Babylonian captivity of the Jews, the Second Temple was built in 515 BCE, only to be destroyed once again by the Roman legions in 70 CE following the Great Jewish Revolt that began in 66 CE. The Western Wall on one side of the Temple Mount is all that remains of the Second Temple, and it is considered the holiest site in all of Judaism. To many Jews, Israel itself is considered to be the Third Temple.

Some Muslims believe that Muhammad's night journey actually occurred, whereas others believe that it was more of a visionary experience rather than a physical one. Regardless, it displays the centrality of Jerusalem in Islam, making it the third holiest site for most Muslims (after Mecca and Medina). The night journey also positioned Islam in the pantheon of the Judeo-Christian experience and tradition, where Muhammad is seen by Muslims as the Seal of the Prophets, the last in the line of Old and New Testament prophets who received revelations from God. In fact, Jerusalem was the *qibla* or direction of prayer for Muslims in years immediately after Muhammad began receiving revelations from Allah through the archangel Gabriel; through revelation, the qibla was changed to the Ka'ba in Mecca later in Muhammad's life, and this has remained the direction of prayer for Muslims ever since.

Umar ibn al-Khattab, the second caliph or successor to the prophet Muhammad and one of the Prophet's closest companions, directed the initial wave of the great Islamic conquests. In 638 CE, after the defeat of Byzantine armies in the region, Umar entered the conquered city of Jerusalem. Since Jews and Christians are considered to be *ahl al-kitab,* or People of the Book, i.e., the Bible, and therefore are protected peoples, Umar ordered that all three Abrahamic faiths should coexist peacefully. According to Islamic tradition, Umar refused to pray in the Church of the Holy Sepulchre built by the Roman Emperor Constantine in the fourth century CE, which contains the site of Jesus Christ's crucifixion and tomb; if he had done so, Umar was afraid the Muslims would have wanted to transform the church into a mosque. Umar even invited a number of Jewish families to return to Jerusalem, for the Christian Byzantines did not allow Jews to establish a permanent residence in the city. The Caliph Umar apparently found the Temple Mount to be desecrated as a garbage dump, a place for refuse and ruins. He was sufficiently horrified and ordered it to be cleaned up. He reconsecrated the plateau at the top of the Temple Mount, building a relatively simple mosque that became the site of what today is called the al-Aqsa (Farthest) Mosque.

It was left to the Caliph Abd al-Malik (685–705 CE) during the Umayyad caliphate in Damascus to build the Dome of the Rock on the Temple Mount. Begun in 687 CE, it was completed together with its magnificent golden dome four years later. There is some speculation that Abd al-Malik built the Dome of the Rock as a possible alternative pilgrimage site and direction for prayer for Muslims since at the time of the decision to erect the structure both Mecca and Medina were under the control of a rival caliphate led by Ibn al-Zubayr, the son of Zubayr ibn al-Awwam, who was a companion of the Prophet and who himself rebelled against the caliphate of Ali ibn Abi Talib, the son-in-law and cousin of Muhammad. However, by the time the Dome of the Rock was completed, Mecca and Medina had been restored to Umayyad control.

Since that time the Dome of the Rock has been restored and embellished by a number of different rulers, the latest being the replacement of the rusting and worn gold dome in 1993 paid for by Jordan's King Hussein. It is a popular tourist site today, as are the other related structures on and around the Temple Mount/Haram al-Sharif, but it is also a source and symbol of the passion that nourishes the Arab–Israeli conflict.

the al-Aqsa (or Farthest) Mosque. The Dome of the Rock, built during the Umayyad caliphate in the late seventh century CE, is one of the defining features of the landscape of the Old City of Jerusalem with its blinding gold sheath covering the dome. It marks the place where, according to Islamic tradition, the prophet Muhammad made his nocturnal journey upward through the seven heavens, meeting the biblical prophets before coming upon Allah. In the Dome of the Rock is, indeed, a rock, where there is a foot imprint said to be Muhammad's upon leaving earthly ground on his journey. The al-Aqsa Mosque is one of the earliest mosques in Islam still in use, built as a commemoration soon after the Islamic conquest of this fabled city in 638 CE, only six years after Muhammad died (632). Even without the Prophet's night journey, Jerusalem would still be significant to Muslims simply because it has been associated over the centuries with such revered Qur'anic (as well as Old and New Testament) figures as Solomon, Mary, and Jesus. Throw in the fact that Jerusalem is, perhaps, the holiest site in Christianity, with the Church of the Holy Sepulchre (containing

Western and Egyptian tourists visiting the Dome of the Rock in 1890, before the Dome received its gold-plated makeover that is so recognizable today. (The Otrakji Collection, www.mideastimage.com.)

the sites of Jesus' crucifixion and tomb) and the Via Dolorosa (the path Jesus took carrying the cross toward his crucifixion) also located in the Old City close to the Haram al-Sharif/Temple Mount, and one has a prescription for tension and unrest irregardless of Zionist and Palestinian aspirations. If anything, though, the religious attachment to the city exhibited by followers of the three great Semitic religions only exacerbated the basic problem in Palestine, with Jerusalem often becoming a focal point of disturbances.

This happened in 1929. The Western Wall at this time during the mandate period was under the control of Muslim authorities as part of their administration of the Haram al-Sharif. They allowed the Jewish rite of passage of praying at the Western Wall, but they also invoked certain restrictions, such as the prohibition of screens to separate women and men, that aroused Jewish opprobrium for years. The British, in attempting to mediate such religious differences, more often than not sided with the Palestinian Muslims, fearing further alienation of the dominant population in Palestine. As the Mufti of Jerusalem, Hajj Amin al-Husayni exploited the tensions over the Western Wall to his own political advantage to reinforce his leadership position among the Palestinian Arabs and to warn that this dispute was but an inkling of the problems that would arise from continued Jewish immigration and Zionist control. It was in this heightened atmosphere, in August 1929, in response to Jewish demonstrations that Arab mobs in Jerusalem attacked the Jewish quarter in the city; in addition, Arabs in Hebron and Safad took to the streets, damaging Jewish property and killing a number of Jews. All in all, after the British finally quelled the riots, some 116 Arabs and

Following the 1929 riots in Palestine, an Arab "protest gathering" in the Rawdat al-Maaref hall in Jerusalem. (Library of Congress, Prints & Photographs Division, LC-DIG-matpc-03048.)

133 Jews were killed. As Ilan Pappe asserts, political despair and economic deprivation combined to produce "an uncontrollable protest movement. Amin al-Husayni was sucked into this maelstrom, at first watching, then approving, and finally inciting even more turmoil and action against Jewish settlers and settlements."[17] The mufti would form his own paramilitary youth movement to instigate violence in urban areas, especially in towns such as Hebron, Safad, and Jerusalem, where Jews and Arabs lived side by side. These youths represented the beginning of the formation of a cadre that was buffered by both urban and rural elements in the mid-1930s who were even more politically and economically desperate and would produce an even bigger and more violent protest movement, the Arab revolt.

The British understood that the apparent religiously based disturbances were but the tip of the iceberg (although there was a palpable fear among the Muslims that both the British and the Jews were out to "de-Islamicize" Palestine), so in the first of what seemed to be an endless stream of commissions, London sent an investigating group to Palestine to ascertain the root causes of the problem. Sir Walter Shaw (the Shaw Commission) headed this particular investigation in September 1929, concluding in its report that the primary source of tension was the growing fear in the Arab community of continued Jewish immigration and land purchases, especially how the latter contributed to a growing landless class of Arabs and how the combination of the two would lead to Jewish control of Palestine.[18] In responding to these complaints, the commission recommended that Britain place controls on Jewish immigration, end the eviction of Arab tenant farmers due to land transfers, and spell out much more clearly

Arabs and Jews working together nailing boxes in a factory in the Jewish village of Rehovoth in the mid-1930s. (Library of Congress, Prints & Photographs Division, LC-DIG-matpc-03667.)

the role of the Arab community in Palestine and British obligations to the Palestinian Arabs. The Va'ad Leumi called the Shaw Commission report "one of the most unjust documents which our people have had to face in the course of 2,000 years of persecution.... Every heinous Arab crime is presented in the Report as a mere error of judgment, whilst every Jewish merit is belittled into insignificance."[19] The findings of the Hope-Simpson Commission sent to Palestine in the summer of 1930 at the request of Lord Passfield to investigate the economic situation in Palestine reinforced much of what was found in the Shaw Commission report, both of whose recommendations were incorporated in the Passfield White Paper issued later in the year (named after the colonial secretary Lord Passfield, a.k.a. Sydney Webb).[20]

For London, the timing of the Passfield White Paper was certainly unwelcome. As the repercussions of the Great Depression were beginning to be felt on a global basis, economic concerns dictated to a large degree the British government's response. Even though the Jewish population in Palestine amounted only to a small portion of the total, the Jews there accounted for about 50% of the tax revenues that largely funded the mandate—in essence, the Jews paid twice as much as the Palestinians did. Prime Minister Ramsay MacDonald was clearly interested in making sure the British taxpayer, in such dire economic times, was not burdened any further by the demands of empire; therefore, from this vantage point, restricting Jewish immigration and land purchases (and Jewish settlements were usually, for reasons already mentioned, more productive than their Arab counterparts, thus also generating more tax revenue) would be cutting off one's nose to spite one's face. It was at about this time that the British acquiesced to the growing division of what had been (or at least intended to be) a unitary economic system in Palestine, encouraging what in essence was economic segregation based on financial reasons. This process coincided with the adoption of the Ben-Gurion, rather than the Weizmann, approach of the Yishuv in terms of seeking independence from the British and more actively pursuing institution-building and local control over the Zionist movement. Obviously as well, the Zionist movement, led by Chaim Weizmann in London, saw that the Passfield White Paper would undercut the twin pillars of the Zionist program in Palestine, so it launched an all-out offensive to defeat it, a campaign that proved to be ultimately successful. In what became known at the "Black Letter" among Palestinian Arabs, Prime Minister MacDonald in February 1931 read a letter before the House of Commons that he penned to Weizmann, effectively negating the Passfield White Paper, which then entered the dustbin of history containing a soon-to-be growing cadre of discarded and dismissed potential remedies to the Palestine problem.

Jewish immigration to Palestine grew by leaps and bounds in 1933 and the succeeding period thereafter, with more than 270,000 Jews entering during the decade, the largest immigration wave in Zionist history.[21] Of course, the primary reason for this was the victory of the Nazi party in Germany and rise to power of Adolph Hitler in 1933, whose anti-Semitic philosophy was already known and became immediately apparent; indeed, the number of Jewish immigrants to Palestine in 1932 was about 9,500, while in 1933 the figure jumped to over 30,000. With this, of course, the tensions in Palestine increased proportionately. Between 1933 and 1936, the Jewish population in Palestine doubled to just under 400,000 (the Arab population in Palestine was 983,000).[22] By 1941, the Arab population had grown to 1.2 million (68% of the population of Palestine), while the Jewish population had increased to 490,000 (30% of the Palestine population). Many of the Jews in what is considered the fifth aliyah (1933–1936) were, in fact, not Zionist, but because of more restrictive immigration policies in the United States and elsewhere, most were compelled to settle in Palestine. This aliyah was composed mostly of Jews from central Europe, particularly Germany, which contrasts with the mostly eastern European and Russian composition of earlier aliyahs.[23] As such, they were different in style, profession, and ideology from the rest of the Yishuv as many were scientists, doctors, architects, lawyers, etc. Less predisposed to labor Zionism and more professional in character, these new settlers tended to bring with them valuable new capital and skills, and they engaged less in agriculture and more in commercial and industrial enterprises.[24] This new entrepreneurial spirit certainly injected new life into the Yishuv as well as professional depth and diversity despite cultural and social differences. It is important to reiterate that the doors of Jewish immigration to Palestine were never fully opened by the British mandatory authorities. Many Jews found other ways of remaining in Palestine, such as arranging "fictitious marriages" with Arabs, staying in the area beyond the time allotted in tourist visas, or just entering the country illegally. In fact, the illegal transport and/or arrangement of Jewish immigration to Palestine came to be known as *Aliyah Bet,* or "B" immigration, as in Plan B methods. This would prove to be even more valuable during and after World War II. Of course, this increased immigration heightened the necessity for more land transfers, and in the 1930s almost half the funds spent by the Jewish Agency were earmarked for land purchases and three-quarters of overall investment was funneled toward this activity. Practically everything was subordinated to the national goals of Zionism, even if it was more expensive (such as Jewish labor versus

Arab labor) or of lesser quality (local versus imported goods)—it was more important to solidify the all-Jewish, self-sufficient nature of the Yishuv that had been implanted in Zionism since the second aliyah.

THE ARAB RESPONSE

The new influx of Jewish immigrants induced more than just heightened political and ideological pressure. It also created some practical problems, such as an increase in unemployment among both Jews and Arabs caught in the midst of the Depression. A younger generation of Arabs became more frustrated with the established Palestinian leadership of Hajj Amin al-Husayni and his cohorts, and as such, they also grew more militant in their desire for change in a more immediate fashion. They began to question what they perceived to be the moderate policies of the mufti of Jerusalem and they started to push for a more radical approach that met what they believed to be the urgency of the situation before it was too late. This paralleled a process that could also be observed in other Arab mandates and territories under effective European control. The older generation of large landowning families who wielded both political and economic power in the other Arab territories dominated by the British or French had waved the flag of Arab nationalism since the imposition of the mandate system, but instead of delivering on true independence, it was increasingly seen by a younger generation who had become politically aware and active under the mandate system that they were being consciously and unconsciously co-opted and/or marginalized by the mandate powers, too timid to aggressively agitate against the very authorities from whom they derived their leadership positions. In searching for an effective riposte to what seemed to be a simple replacement of Ottoman hegemony with European imperialism in the form of mandates, a variety of responses began to coalesce among certain groups of Arabs, usually younger, middle-class, urban, and educated, particularly in Egypt, Syria, and Iraq but with reverberations as well in Palestine and across the Arab world.

The various responses crossed the political and cultural spectrum, united only in their rejection of the capitalist and/or liberal constitutionalism that embodied the mandatory powers and, for the most part, inculcated by the older generation of landowners. As such, the reactions took the form of socialism/communism, fascism, and Islamic fundamentalism, all sharing the common goal of expelling the British and French and obtaining true independence. It is during this period that the Ba'th party was founded by two Syrians, Michel Aflaq and Salah al-Din al-Bitar, studying at the Sorbonne in Paris; the Free Officers movement began in Egypt; fascist youth movements in the form of the Brown Shirts arose in small but vocal numbers in several Arab countries; and Hassan al-Banna in Egypt founded in 1928 the Muslim Brethren (*Ikhwan al-Muslimun*). The *Ikhwan* was the first major Islamist party in the Middle East formed in the twentieth century, primarily as a reaction against the Islamic modernism of the late nineteenth-century *salafiyya* movement that advocated an accommodation with Westernization—the Islamism of the Muslim Brotherhood was much more anti-Western and antimodern than its predecessors, largely as a result of having been born out of European imperialism. This version of Islamic fundamentalism, as will be seen in later chapters, would morph into even more virulent and violent forms as events unfolded in the decades after World War II and the creation of the state of Israel. The fascist alternative would be discredited with the defeat of Nazi Germany and the revelation of its horrors. The Islamists would combine their efforts with the secular Arab nationalists as both fought to expel the British, but they would soon be overwhelmed and repressed by the single-party secular Arab nationalist regimes, most particularly by Gamal 'Abd al-Nasser in Egypt. It was during this formative period of Arab nationalism in the 1930s that the plight of the Palestinian Arabs started to become an important element in its ideology, especially as the growing Zionist presence was seen as yet another European intrusion, another cancer infecting the Arab body. Only the strength provided by collective Arab action could achieve the goals of unity and freedom. A clear indication of this emerging trend appeared in Syria in September 1937 when a pan-Arab conference was held in which over 400 delegates from across the Arab world participated. It was declared at the conference that "Palestine was an integral part of the Arabian homeland and no part of this territory would be alienated with Arab consent."[25] And Hajj Amin al-Husayni attempted with some success to broaden the issue beyond the Arab arena to the Muslim world in general. In 1931 he convened the World Islamic Congress in Jerusalem in which Muslim delegates from India, East and Southeast Asia, and Africa participated, appealing to them that Palestine, particularly the status of Jerusalem, was an important issue to all Muslims and not just the Arabs.

In Palestine, representing these news sentiments in the Arab world was the *Istiqlal* (Independence) party, formed in the early 1930s and comprised of younger Palestinian notables who countenanced a pan-Arab policy in support of their cause and more strident action against the British. Although the party did not present a serious danger to Hajj Amin al-Husayni, it was emblematic of the shifting trends within Palestinian society that would become manifest later in the decade. The pressures of increased Jewish immigration combined with enhanced fear and frustration among the Palestinian Arabs to produce a combustible atmosphere that needed only a spark to be ignited. The Palestinian economy continued to suffer, especially in the rural areas. British colonial policy continued to emphasize self-sufficiency in its commonwealth (which is what the Jews wanted, whereas the Arabs desperately needed colonial support). Jewish land purchases accumulated and a basic absence of much needed agrarian reform enacted by the Arabs themselves combined to "pauperize" rural Palestine and fatten the position of the notables. As would become commonplace in future Palestinian–Israeli confrontations, a particular incident would launch an uprising, in this case what came to be called the Arab revolt of 1936–1939, or what some Palestinians call the first *intifada* (preceding the uprisings that began in 1987 and 2000, respectively).

The anger had risen exponentially on the Arab side by late 1935, especially after a respected local shaykh and some of his men were killed by the British when the former refused to surrender his position in Jenin. Also in 1935, Izz al-Din al-Qassam was killed by the British. He was a Syrian who moved to Haifa in the 1920s and found a receptive audience for his firebrand preaching among the shantytown dwellers. In 1933 he initiated a guerilla campaign against the British and Jewish settlements in northern Palestine. Today, the military wing of Hamas, the Islamist element of the Palestinians in the Occupied Territories, is known as the Izz al-Din al-Qassam Brigades. On April 15, 1936, a Jewish passenger was killed on a bus by some Arab robbers, eliciting a response by elements of the Haganah the next evening that resulted in the deaths of two Arab farmers. The cauldron was lit, and what followed was a series of mass demonstrations and attacks going back and forth between Jewish and Arab communities. On April 19, local Arab leaders called for a general Arab strike to hit at both the Jews and the British, demanding a complete halt to Jewish immigration and land purchases before it would be lifted. In a case of the horse following the cart (and eerily foreshadowing the relationship of indigenous Palestinians with the Palestine Liberation Organization in the 1987–1993 intifada), the localized actions compelled and galvanized the Palestinian leadership to ride on the developing tidal wave of discontent or get swept aside. As such, the Arab Higher Committee was formed on April 25 in a belated attempt to unify the Palestinian movement. It was led by Hajj Amin al-Husayni, but it also included Nashashibis, Christians, Muslims, and members of Istiqlal. The strike would last into the fall of 1936 amid British attempts to quell the nascent rebellion. With eighty Jews and hundreds of Arabs killed in the revolt by October, the Arab Higher Committee, in the midst of and in response to a British attempt to, yet again, investigate the situation, called for an end to the strike.

This investigative commission was chaired by Lord Peel, and it became known as the Peel Commission. The commission report, produced in July 1937, concluded that the situation in Palestine, as defined under the terms of the mandate, was untenable and impossible to sustain because of the mutual hostility and recriminations between the Arabs and Jews. The report stated that

> It is manifest that the Mandate cannot be fully or honorably implemented unless by some means or other the antagonism between Arabs and Jews can be composed. But it is the Mandate which created that antagonism and keeps it alive and as long as the Mandate exists we cannot honestly hold out the expectation that Arabs or Jews will be able to set aside their national hopes or fears or sink their differences in the common service of Palestine.

With this in mind, the commission recommended the termination of the mandate and the partition of Palestine into separate Jewish and Arab enclaves, with a corridor under British control from Jaffa eastward toward Lod and Ramallah encircling Jerusalem and Bethlehem. The Zionist leaders' reaction to the Peel Commission recommendation was somewhat ambiguous. While they generally supported the idea of partition, based on the fact that this would at least guarantee some portion of the land earmarked for statehood (seeing it as a springboard for acquiring more land as time progressed; as Ben-Gurion noted at the time, the proposed Jewish enclave "would constitute a decisive stage on the road to the achievement of Greater Zionism"),[26] the territory allotted to the Jews was unacceptable, and there were demands that the borders be redefined. The Zionists were also well aware of the deteriorating conditions of Jews in central Europe, so there were sentiments in favor of the partition simply to provide a refuge for persecuted Jews desperate to find sanctuary. The Arab Higher Committee, on the other hand, was unambiguous in its rejection of the recommendation, emphasizing that the proposed partition gave the Jews most of the fertile land, even if most of the total land area was allotted to the Arabs; indeed, the British had in mind that the allotted Arab territory might come under the sovereignty of Transjordan rather than an independent Palestinian state, a concept that was also rejected by the Arab leadership in Palestine. Furthermore, they continued to reject the idea, and thus the acceptance of any plan embodying it, that the Jews had any claim or right to a Jewish enclave, much less a state, within Palestine.

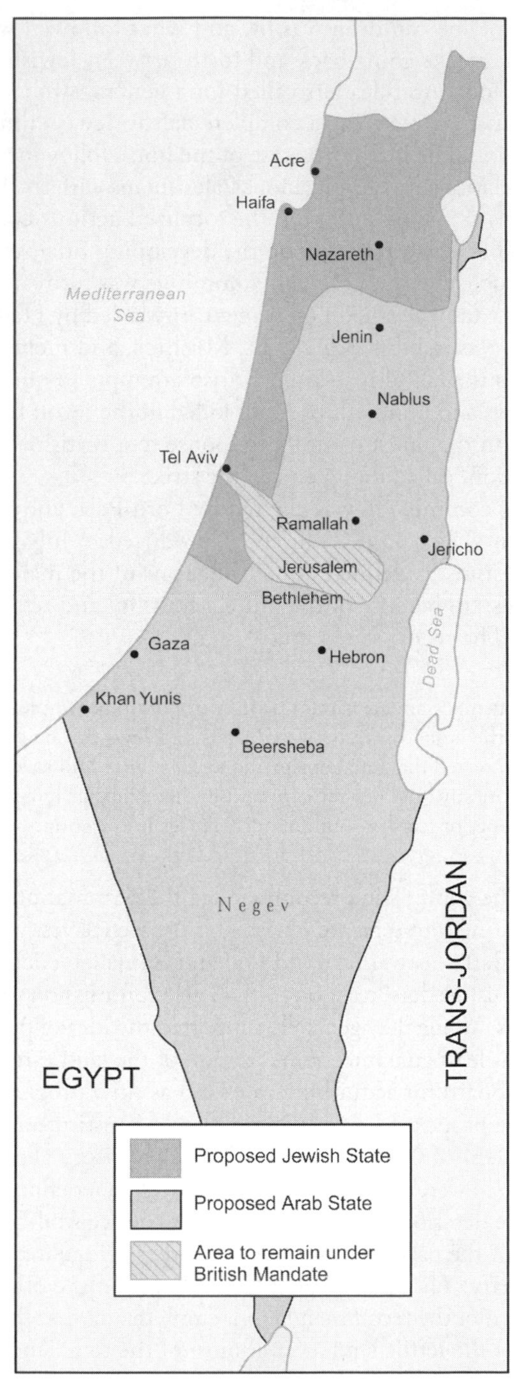

Peel Commission partition plan, 1937. (Palestinian Academic Society for the Study of International Affairs.)

The Arab revolt continued and, indeed, in many ways intensified following the publication of the Peel Commission report in the summer of 1937. In addition, Palestinian Arabs had observed events elsewhere in the Arab world as well as the increasingly vulnerable position of the British. Iraq had gained formal, if not real, independence in 1932, while both the French in Syria and the British in Egypt made important concessions to the respective local governments in 1936, with Egypt formally obtaining its independence, again in form if not reality. To the Arabs in Palestine the verdict was clear: resistance produces results. The British were back on their heels due to the rising tensions in Europe as well as the Italian takeover of Ethiopia (and Rome had already been in control of Libya since 1911). But they fought back ruthlessly, especially as some in London saw the disturbances as a regionwide conspiracy fomented by Germany and Italy. Following the murder of a high-level British Mandate official in October, the Arab Higher Committee was dissolved and its leaders were arrested or deported or went into exile. Hajj Amin al-Husayni went into exile in Damascus on a road that eventually led him to cooperate with Nazi Germany, attempting to lead the Palestinian Arab movement from abroad but confirming British fears of international conspiracy. But his days were probably numbered anyhow, and local identities and leaders among the Arabs in Palestine began to emerge. The intergenerational shifts became more apparent, especially as the British began to crack down even harder against the rebellion, which although never numbering more than 5,000, was able to control the countryside with the support of the rural population, tying down more than 20,000 British troops in Palestine by the end of 1938. As Cleveland comments,

> In addition to its anti-British, anti-Zionist thrust, the revolt contained elements of a peasant social revolution against the established notability. In villages under rebel control, rents were canceled, debt collectors were denied entry, and wealthy landlords were coerced into making "donations" to the rebel cause. Local resistance committees banned the tarbush, the headgear of the Ottoman administrative elite, and insisted that men should instead wear the *kaffiya*, the checkered headcloth that has become a symbol of Palestinian national identity.[27]

A Palestinian nationalism was emerging, in some ways reflecting and riding upon the crest of Arab nationalism arising throughout the region but in other ways, as in Egypt, Syria, Iraq, etc., a distinct local nationalism that represented a particular national experience within the borders defined by World War I; indeed, in some ways, the British removal and repression of the existing Palestinian Arab leadership, while lending itself to political shifts in the upper echelons of Arab society in Palestine, also created something of a vacuum that was increasingly filled by the pan-Arab aspirations of Arab figures outside of the mandate, thus further entangling the Palestine issue in a regional framework.

A semblance of order was finally restored by the British by early 1939, with some 3,000 Arabs, 2,000 Jews, and 600 British having been killed during the three-year revolt, with commensurate damage to the land and the economy of Palestine, disproportionately hurting the Arab population more than the relatively self-sufficient Jewish population.[28] What the Arab revolt did accomplish, however, was to make the British aware of the potential military and economic drain of an unsettled Palestine on the eve of World War II, when it became apparent by early 1939, after the failure of the Munich conference to quell Hitler's insatiable thirst for land and power, that British resources in its empire and commonwealth would need to be diverted elsewhere. As such, strategic concerns began to supercede moral and diplomatic ones in Palestine. Just as the British had done in World War I, so would they do in the next world war, i.e., attempt to placate the Arabs so that they would not rise up in support of the German side against British interests. If the Arabs could at least remain neutral, this would free up British resources to meet the threat of the Axis powers. As stated previously, the Palestine issue had by the late 1930s become an important element in the construction of Arab nationalist ideology and discourse. Certainly, it was thought in London that a policy that favored the Arab population in Palestine would not only help ameliorate conditions in the mandate, thus allowing Britain to reduce its military commitment there, but also sufficiently salve the wounds in the Arab world that had been inflicted during the interwar period in the Middle East.

THE 1939 WHITE PAPER AND ITS REPERCUSSIONS

A conference convened in London by the British in February 1939 (formally called the London Round Table Conference) in which Palestinian Arabs and Jews participated was aimed at constructing a joint disentanglement of the Palestine problem. Also invited were a number of notables from other Arab countries, such as Egypt, Saudi Arabia, Iraq, Yemen, and Transjordan—clearly recognition by the British of the pan-Arab nature of the Palestinian problem, although some might claim that London needlessly enlarged the issue beyond the borders of Palestine to the Arab world as a whole, thus helping to consign it for decades as an *Arab*–Israeli issue rather than just a Palestinian–Jewish concern. But the conference failed to produce a resolution, compelling the British to construct a policy unilaterally. What resulted was the White Paper of 1939, in which the British essentially reversed the commitment they had made to the Jews in the Balfour Declaration. In fact, the White Paper stated very bluntly that "His Majesty's Government therefore now declare unequivocally that it is not part of their policy that Palestine should become a Jewish State." Echoing the more liberal interpretation of Balfour, the White Paper called for the establishment of a Jewish national home in an independent Palestinian state within ten years. And most detrimental to Zionist interests, it restricted Jewish immigration and land purchases (75,000 over the next five years, thereafter subject to the consent of the Arabs, and that land transfers would be restricted to certain zones). The Zionist movement emphatically rejected the White Paper, especially as it came at a time when Jews were desperately seeking flight from Nazism combined with more restrictive immigration laws in the United States, Canada, and elsewhere in Europe. Ben-Gurion called it "the greatest betrayal perpetrated by the government of a civilized people."[29] They would marshal their considerable influence in London in an attempt to defeat the implementation of the White Paper. As it turned out, however, they did not have to since World War II broke out with the September 1939 German blitzkrieg of Poland, thus changing the rules of the game once again. What the White Paper did indicate to Zionists worldwide was that the British could no longer be the patron through which statehood could be achieved; indeed, they were in many ways the enemy, and while the

Jews would largely cooperate and fight with the British in the war against the greater evil of Hitlerian Germany, there was no doubt that Zionist objectives were on a collision course with the British in Palestine. It also compelled world Zionism to seek out a new patron that could help facilitate their national objectives, and this new direction would lead it eventually to the United States. In addition, the Arab revolt helped the Yishuv condition itself for statehood in terms of defense and military means. As Stein comments, "were it not for the Arab rebellion, which compelled the Yishuv to realign and reorganize its military resources, it is highly unlikely that the Jews would have prevailed in their War for Independence ten years later."[30]

The Palestinian Arabs, perhaps somewhat surprisingly, also rejected the 1939 White Paper. But one must remember that Arab confidence in British assurances was specious at best, and if they needed any more proof of British perfidy, London had now just turned its back on the Jews. Much could happen in ten years. Just what guarantee was there that an independent Palestinian state would actually be allowed to come into being? The strategic situation could shift again, compelling the British to retract the offer of statehood ten years hence. No, they wanted independence immediately and an immediate halt to Jewish immigration, and they felt that the international and regional circumstances gave them the necessary leverage to hold out for what they wanted. The Arab revolt had produced the desired results: if the pressure is maintained, then the British will cave in even more and the Palestinian Arabs will acquire the Palestine mandate in its entirety. In retrospect, one might judge the Palestinian response to the White Paper as an egregious error. But throughout the mandate period, the Palestinian Arabs, to the extent that there was a coordinated policy, believed that they should stand fast and not recognize either a Jewish or a British presence through negotiation and/or agreement that would accord legitimacy to either. One must not forget that the British had just brutally crushed the Arab rebellion, so it was naturally difficult for the Palestinian Arabs to turn right around and trust the British, much less cooperate with them. While the decision to reject the White Paper may have damaged the Palestinian cause in the long term, as events would indicate, this steadfastness, for better or worse, did help to forge a Palestinian national consciousness that defined the parameters of the emerging Palestinian movement as well as the Arab–Israeli conflict.

The British Mandate in Palestine obviously produced more, rather than less, tension. In effect, if the idea of the mandate was to produce a stable, independent entity, it obviously failed. In a way, however, it only failed for one element in Palestine, the Arab population. The Jews were actually able to produce a stable, independent entity, which was due as much to their own Zionist philosophy as it was to British policies.[31] As Israeli writer Tom Segev comments, "The British had found an underdeveloped country when they arrived, and they left behind much progress, especially among the Jews. But they also left behind much backwardness, especially among the Arabs."[32] What emerged in Palestine was, of course, of a completely different character from what was produced in the other mandates in the region that had dominant Arab populations. The British did contribute to a number of improvements in Palestine after World War I, especially in the areas of health care, hygiene, infrastructure, communications, and transportation. And despite the separate Jewish and Arab communities that would emerge, a development consciously and unconsciously encouraged by the British and galvanized by Jewish and Arab nationalisms, there was a higher level of interdependence and more cooperative ventures between Arabs and Jews in Palestine than most realize. It is a shame that this interaction became lost amid British colonial policy and Zionist/Palestinian elite-driven agendas. Indeed, the British had created an enclave for competing nationalisms. What began as a military administration in charge of a territory that had Jews, Muslims, and Christians, by the beginning of World War II had been transformed into a seething cauldron of vibrant Zionism and Palestinian angst as well as a receptacle for emerging Arab nationalism.

NOTES

1. Quoted in Tom Segev, *One Palestine Complete: Jews and Arabs Under the British Mandate* (New York: Henry Holt and Company, 2000), 9.

2. According to these estimates, out of about 800,000 inhabitants, 40,000 Muslims, 10,000 Christians, and 1,000 Jews died due to war, famine, and disease as a result of the war. The British at first classified the population in Palestine according to religious affiliation.

3. William L. Cleveland, *A History of the Modern Middle East* (Boulder: Westview Press, 1994), 229.

4. Ibid., 230.

5. In Syria, for instance, see Philip S. Khoury, *The Urban Notable and Arab Nationalism: The Politics of Damascus, 1860–1920* (Cambridge: Cambridge University Press, 1983).

6. *From Ottomanism to Arabism: Essays on the Origins of Arab Nationalism* (Urbana: University of Illinois Press, 1973).

7. On Hajj Amin al-Husayni, see Philip Mattar, *The Mufti of Jerusalem: Al-Hajj Amin al-Husayni and the Palestinian National Movement* (New York: Diane Publishing, 1988).

8. Cleveland, *A History,* 233.

9. Moshe Chertock (later Moshe Sharett) was named the head of the political department, essentially the foreign office of the agency—he would become Israel's first foreign minister and later prime minister. This is further indication of how these early institutions in the Yishuv provided a skilled and experienced cadre of leaders upon statehood.

10. Leslie Stein, *The Hope Fulfilled: The Rise of Modern Israel* (Westport, CT: Praeger, 2003), 167.

11. Ibid.

12. Ibid., 235.

13. The turning point seems to have come in June 1938, when a young Revisionist by the name of Shlomo Ben Yosef was executed by the British for attempting to blow up an Arab bus. The next month, the Irgun set off a bomb in an Arab market, killing fifty people; and shortly thereafter a bomb was thrown on an Arab bus, killing five people. These acts were roundly condemned by the main Zionist organizations. Stein, *The Hope Fulfilled,* 211.

14. Ibid., 179.

15. *Washington Post*, August 13, 2005.

16. Cleveland, *A History*, 237.

17. Ilan Pappe, *A History of Modern Israel: One Land, Two Peoples* (Cambridge: Cambridge University Press, 2004), 91.

18. There was actually an earlier British team sent to Palestine in 1920, the Palin Commission, to investigate the riots of 1920; and it recommended that the Balfour Declaration, in effect British policy, be revised to take into account the rising dissatisfaction among the Palestinian Arabs. The commission report was not implemented immediately, but it most likely affected the process that led to the 1922 Churchill White Paper.

19. Quoted in Stein, *The Hope Fulfilled,* 184–185.

20. The Zionist response to this was to point out that 93% of the land purchases had been from Arab landowners and the tenant farmers had been properly compensated. It was further admonished that Arab farmers, indeed the entire Arab economy, had actually benefited from Jewish agricultural investment and production, and it had provided a model that Arab farmers increasingly adopted.

21. This figure represents the number of authorized immigrants; there were also about 40,000 illegal Jewish migrants to Palestine.

22. Justin McCarthy, *The Population of Palestine: Population History and Statistics of the Late Ottoman Period and the Mandate* (New York: Columbia University Press, 1990), 36.

23. Only 2.5% of all Jewish immigrants between 1920 and 1932 were German, whereas between 1933 and 1938, 27.7% were German.

24. Between 1921 and 1931, it is estimated that the Jews brought in no more than about 20 million Palestine pounds into the mandate territory, whereas in the much shorter period between 1932 and 1935, about 30 million Palestine pounds were brought in. Stein, *The Hope Fulfilled*, 197.

25. Quoted in Ibid., 218.

26. Quoted in Ibid., 216.

27. Cleveland, *A History*, 241.

28. Although Stein puts the numbers at 545 Jewish and 2,176 Arab fatalities (*The Hope Fulfilled*, 209) based on A. Cohen's work *Israel and the Arab World* (Tel Aviv: Sifriat Hapoalim, 1964), 203–204. A leading Zionist at the time as well as a future prime minister of Israel, Moshe Sharett, commenting on the Arab revolt, stated that he "would rebel even more vigorously, bitterly, and desperately against the immigration that will one day turn Palestine and all its Arab residents over to Jewish rule" (quoted in Stein, 207).

29. Quoted in Stein, *The Hope Fulfilled*, 220.

30. Stein, *The Hope Fulfilled*, 209.

31. Some, such as Israeli writer Tom Segev, would go even further in crediting the British for the consolidation of the Yishuv. He states that "The British kept their promise to the Zionists. They opened up the country to mass Jewish immigration; by 1948, the Jewish population had increased by more than tenfold. The Jews were permitted to purchase land, develop agriculture, and establish industries and banks. The British allowed them to set up hundreds of new settlements, including several towns. They created a school system and an army; they had a political leadership and elected institutions; and with the help of all these they in the end defeated the Arabs, all under British sponsorship, all in the wake of that promise of 1917. Contrary to the widely held belief of Britain's pro-Arabism, British actions considerably favored the Zionist enterprise." Segev, *One Palestine, Complete*, 5.

32. Ibid., 9.

Peel White Paper (Peel Commission)

June 22, 1937

THE FORCE OF CIRCUMSTANCES . . .

2. Under the stress of the World War the British Government made promises to Arabs and Jews in order to obtain their support. On the strength of those promises both parties formed certain expectations.

3. The application to Palestine of the Mandate System in general and of the specific Mandate in particular implied the belief that the obligations thus undertaken towards the Arabs and the Jews respectively would prove in course of time to be mutually compatible owing to the conciliatory effect on the Palestinian Arabs of the material prosperity which Jewish immigration would bring to Palestine as a whole. That belief has not been justified, and we see no hope of its being justified in the future.

4. On that account it might conceivably be argued that Britain is now entitled to renounce its obligations. But we have no doubt that the British people would repudiate any such suggestion.... We are responsible for the welfare of the country. Its government is in our hands. We are bound to strive to the utmost to do justice and make peace.

5. What are the existing circumstances? An irrepressible conflict has arisen between two national communities within the narrow bounds of one small country. About 1,000,000 Arabs are in strife, open or latent, with some 400,000 Jews. There is no common ground between them. The Arab community is predominantly Asiatic in character, the Jewish community predominantly European. They differ in religion and in language. Their cultural and social life, their ways of thought and conduct, are as incompatible as their national aspirations.... The War and its sequel have inspired all Arabs with the hope of reviving in a free and united Arab world the traditions of the Arab golden age. The Jews similarly are inspired by their historic past. They mean to show what the Jewish nation can achieve when restored to the land of its birth....

6. This conflict was inherent in the situation from the outset....

7. The conflict has grown steadily more bitter. It has been marked by a series of five Arab outbreaks, culminating in the rebellion of last year....

8. This intensification of the conflict will continue....

9. The conflict is primarily political, though the fear of economic subjection to the Jews is also in Arab minds....

10. Meanwhile the "external factors" will continue to play the part they have played with steadily increasing force from the beginning. On the one hand, Saudi Arabia, the Yemen, Iraq and Egypt are already recognized as sovereign states, and Trans-Jordan as an "independent government." In less than three years' time Syria and the Lebanon will attain their national sovereignty. The claim of the Palestinian Arabs to share in the freedom of the Asiatic Arabia will thus be reinforced....

11. On the other hand, the hardships and anxieties of the Jews in Europe are not likely to grow less in the near future. The pressure on Palestine will continue and might at any time be accentuated.... The Mandatory will be urged unceasingly to admit as many Jews into Palestine as the National Home can provide with a livelihood and to protect them when admitted from Arab attacks.

12. Thus, for internal and external reasons, it seems probable that the situation, bad as it now is, will grow worse. The conflict will go on, the gulf between Arabs and Jews will widen....

14. In these circumstances, we are convinced that peace, order and good government can only be maintained in Palestine for any length of time by a rigorous system of repression.... The lesson is plain, and nobody, we think, will now venture to assert that the existing system offers any real prospect of reconciliation between the Arabs and the Jews....

17. . . . To put it in one sentence, we cannot—in Palestine as it now is—both concede the Arab claim to self-government and secure the establishment of the Jewish National Home. . . .

19. Manifestly the problem cannot be solved by giving either the Arabs or the Jews all they want. The answer to the question "Which of them in the end will govern Palestine?" must surely be "Neither". . . . But, while neither race can justly rule all Palestine, we see no reason why, if it were practicable, each race should not rule part of it.

20. No doubt the idea of Partition as a solution of the problem has often occurred to students of it, only to be discarded. There are many who would have felt an instinctive dislike to cutting up the Holy Land. The severance of Trans-Jordan, they would have thought, from historic Palestine was bad enough. . . .

CANTONISATION

1. The political division of Palestine could be effected in a less final and thoroughgoing manner than by Partition. It could be divided as federal States are divided into provinces or cantons; and this method has been so often mentioned and so ably advocated under the name of "Cantonisation" as a means of solving the Palestine problem that it is incumbent on us to discuss it before setting out the plan for Partition which we ourselves have to propose. . . .

A PLAN OF PARTITION

1. We return, then, to Partition as the only method we are able to propose for dealing with the root of the trouble.

2. . . . we feel justified in recommending that Your Majesty's Government should take the appropriate steps for the termination of the present Mandate on the basis of Partition.

3. . . . There seem to us to be three essential features of such a [partition] plan. It must be practicable. It must conform to our obligations. It must do justice to the Arabs and the Jews.

CONCLUSION

1. "Half a loaf is better than no bread" is a peculiarly English proverb; and, considering the attitude which both the Arab and the Jewish representatives adopted in giving evidence before us, we think it improbable that either party will be satisfied at first sight with the proposals we have submitted for the adjustment of their rival claims. For Partition means that neither will get all it wants. It means that the Arabs must acquiesce in the exclusion from their sovereignty of a piece of territory, long occupied and once ruled by them. It means that the Jews must be content with less than the Land of Israel they once ruled and have hoped to rule again. But it seems to us possible that on reflection both parties will come to realize that the drawbacks of

Partition are outweighed by its advantages. For, if it offers neither party all it wants, if offers each what it wants most, namely freedom and security.

2. The advantages to the Arabs of Partition on the lines we have proposed may be summarized as follows: (i) They obtain their national independence and can co-operate on an equal footing with the Arabs of the neighbouring countries in the cause of Arab unity and progress. (ii) They are finally delivered from the fear of being "swamped" by the Jews and from the possibility of ultimate subjection to Jewish rule. (iii) In particular, the final limitation of the Jewish National Home within a fixed frontier and the enactment of a new Mandate for the protection of the Holy Places, solemnly guaranteed by the League of Nations, removes all anxiety lest the Holy Places should ever come under Jewish control. (iv) As a set-off to the loss of territory the Arabs regard as theirs, the Arab State will receive a subvention from the Jewish State. It will also, in view of the backwardness of Trans-Jordan, obtain a grant of £2,000,000 from the British Treasury; and, if an arrangement can be made for the exchange of land and population, a further grant will be made for the conversion, as far as may prove possible, of uncultivable land in the Arab State into productive land from which the cultivators and the State alike will profit.

3. The advantages of Partition to the Jews may be summarized as follows: (i) Partition secures the establishment of the Jewish National Home and relieves it from the possibility of its being subjected in the future to Arab rule. (ii) Partition enables the Jews in the fullest sense to call their National Home their own: for it converts it into a Jewish State. Its citizens will be able to admit as many Jews into it as they themselves believe can be absorbed. They will attain the primary objective of Zionism—a Jewish nation, planted in Palestine, giving its nationals the same status in the world as other nations give theirs. They will cease at last to live a "minority life."

4. To both Arabs and Jews Partition offers a prospect—and we see no such prospect in any other policy—of obtaining the inestimable boon of peace. . . .

5. There was a time when Arab statesmen were willing to concede little Palestine to the Jews, provided that the rest of Arab Asia were free. That condition was not fulfilled then, but it is on the eve of fulfillment now. . . .

6. There is no need to stress the advantage to the British people of a settlement in Palestine. We are bound to honour to the utmost of our power the obligations we undertook in the exigencies of war towards the Arabs and the Jews. . . . Partition offers a possibility of finding a way through them, a possibility of obtaining a final solution of the problem which does justice to the rights and aspirations of both the Arabs and the Jews and discharges the obligations we undertook towards them twenty years ago to the fullest extent that is practicable in the circumstances of the present time.

7. Nor is it only the British people, nor only the nations which conferred the Mandate or approved it, who are troubled by what has happened and is happening in Palestine. Numberless men and women all over the world would feel a sense of deep relief if somehow an end could be put to strife and bloodshed in a thrice hallowed land.

ALL OF WHICH WE HUMBLY SUBMIT FOR YOUR MAJESTY'S GRACIOUS CONSIDERATION.

Bernard Reich, ed., *Arab–Israeli Conflict and Conciliation: A Documentary History* (Westport, CT: Praeger, 1995), 45–53.

British White Paper of 1939

In the light of these considerations His Majesty's Government make the following declaration of their intentions regarding the future government of Palestine:

The objective of His Majesty's Government is the establishment within 10 years of an independent Palestine State in such treaty relations with the United Kingdom as will provide satisfactorily for the commercial and strategic requirements of both countries in the future. The proposal for the establishment of the independent State would involve consultation with the Council of the League of Nations with a view to the termination of the Mandate.

The independent State should be one in which Arabs and Jews share government in such a way as to ensure that the essential interests of each community are safeguarded.

The establishment of the independent State will be preceded by a transitional period throughout which His Majesty's Government will retain responsibility for the country. During the transitional period the people of Palestine will be given an increasing part in the government of their country. Both sections of the population will have an opportunity to participate in the machinery of government, and the process will be carried on whether or not they both avail themselves of it.

As soon as peace and order have been sufficiently restored in Palestine steps will be taken to carry out this policy of giving the people of Palestine an increasing part in the government of their country, the objective being to place Palestinians in charge of all the Departments of Government, with the assistance of British advisers and subject to the control of the High Commissioner. Arab and Jewish representatives will be invited to serve as heads of Departments approximately in proportion to their respective populations. The number of Palestinians in charge of Departments will be increased as circumstances permit until all heads of Departments are Palestinians, exercising the administrative and advisory functions which are presently performed by British officials. When that stage is reached consideration will be given to the question of converting the Executive Council into a Council of Ministers with a consequential change in the status and functions of the Palestinian heads of Departments.

His Majesty's Government make no proposals at this stage regarding the establishment of an elective legislature. Nevertheless they would regard this as an appropriate constitutional development, and, should public opinion in Palestine hereafter show itself in favour of such a development, they will be prepared, provided that local conditions permit, to establish the necessary machinery.

At the end of five years from the restoration of peace and order, an appropriate body representative of the people of Palestine and of His Majesty's Government will be set up to review the working of the constitutional arrangements during the transitional period and to consider and make recommendations regarding the constitution of the independent Palestine State.

His Majesty's Government will require to be satisfied that in the treaty contemplated by sub-paragraph (6) adequate provision has been made for:

the security of, and freedom of access to the Holy Places, and protection of the interests and property of the various religious bodies.

the protection of the different communities in Palestine in accordance with the obligations of His Majesty's Government to both Arabs and Jews and for the special position in Palestine of the Jewish National Home.

such requirements to meet the strategic situation as may be regarded as necessary by His Majesty's Government in the light of the circumstances then existing. His Majesty's Government will also require to be satisfied that the interests of certain foreign countries in Palestine, for the preservation of which they are at present responsible, are adequately safeguarded.

His Majesty's Government will do everything in their power to create conditions which will enable the independent Palestine State to come into being within 10 years. If, at the end of 10 years, it appears to His Majesty's Government that, contrary to their hope, circumstances require the postponement of the establishment of the independent State, they will consult with representatives of the people of Palestine, the Council of the League of Nations and the neighbouring Arab States before deciding on such a postponement. If His Majesty's Government come to the conclusion that postponement is unavoidable, they will invite the co-operation of these parties in framing plans for the future with a view to achieving the desired objective at the earliest possible date.

During the transitional period steps will be taken to increase the powers and responsibilities of municipal corporations and local councils.

SECTION II. IMMIGRATION

Under Article 6 of the Mandate, the Administration of Palestine, "while ensuring that the rights and position of other sections of the population are not prejudiced," is required to "facilitate Jewish immigration under suitable conditions." Beyond this, the extent to which Jewish immigration into Palestine is to be permitted is nowhere defined in the Mandate. But in the Command Paper of 1922 it was laid down that for the fulfilment of the policy of establishing a Jewish National Home:

> "it is necessary that the Jewish community in Palestine should be able to increase its numbers by immigration. This immigration cannot be so great in volume as to exceed whatever may be the economic capacity of the country at the time to absorb new arrivals. It is essential to ensure that the immigrants should not be a burden upon the people of Palestine as a whole, and that they should not deprive any section of the present population of their employment."

In practice, from that date onwards until recent times, the economic absorptive capacity of the country has been treated as the sole limiting factor, and in the letter which Mr. Ramsay MacDonald, as Prime Minister, sent to Dr. Weizmann in February 1931 it was laid down as a matter of policy that economic absorptive capacity was the sole criterion. This interpretation has been supported by resolutions of the Permanent Mandates Commissioner. But His Majesty's Government do not read either the Statement of Policy of 1922 or the letter of 1931 as implying that the Mandate requires them, for all time and in all circumstances, to facilitate the immigration of Jews into

Palestine subject only to consideration of the country's economic absorptive capacity. Nor do they find anything in the Mandate or in subsequent Statements of Policy to support the view that the establishment of a Jewish National Home in Palestine cannot be effected unless immigration is allowed to continue indefinitely. If immigration has an adverse effect on the economic position in the country, it should clearly be restricted; and equally, if it has a seriously damaging effect on the political position in the country, that is a factor that should not be ignored. Although it is not difficult to contend that the large number of Jewish immigrants who have been admitted so far have been absorbed economically, the fear of the Arabs that this influx will continue indefinitely until the Jewish population is in a position to dominate them has produced consequences which are extremely grave for Jews and Arabs alike and for the peace and prosperity of Palestine. The lamentable disturbances of the past three years are only the latest and most sustained manifestation of this intense Arab apprehension. The methods employed by Arab terrorists against fellow Arabs and Jews alike must receive unqualified condemnation. But it cannot be denied that fear of indefinite Jewish immigration is widespread amongst the Arab population and that this fear has made possible disturbances which have given a serious setback to economic progress, depleted the Palestine exchequer, rendered life and property insecure, and produced a bitterness between the Arab and Jewish populations which is deplorable between citizens of the same country. If in these circumstances immigration is continued up to the economic absorptive capacity of the country, regardless of all other considerations, a fatal enmity between the two peoples will be perpetuated, and the situation in Palestine may become a permanent source of friction amongst all peoples in the Near and Middle East. His Majesty's Government cannot take the view that either their obligations under the Mandate, or considerations of common sense and justice, require that they should ignore these circumstances in framing immigration policy.

In the view of the Royal Commission the association of the policy of the Balfour Declaration with the Mandate system implied the belief that Arab hostility to the former would sooner or later be overcome. It has been the hope of British Governments ever since the Balfour Declaration was issued that in time the Arab population, recognizing the advantages to be derived from Jewish settlement and development in Palestine, would become reconciled to the further growth of the Jewish National Home. This hope has not been fulfilled. The alternatives before His Majesty's Government are either (i) to seek to expand the Jewish National Home indefinitely by immigration, against the strongly expressed will of the Arab people of the country; or (ii) to permit further expansion of the Jewish National Home by immigration only if the Arabs are prepared to acquiesce in it. The former policy means rule by force. Apart from other considerations, such a policy seems to His Majesty's Government to be contrary to the whole spirit of Article 22 of the Covenant of the League of Nations, as well as to their specific obligations to the Arabs in the Palestine Mandate. Moreover, the relations between the Arabs and the Jews in Palestine must be based sooner or later on mutual tolerance and goodwill; the peace, security and progress of the Jewish National Home itself requires this. Therefore His Majesty's Government, after earnest consideration, and taking into account the extent to which the growth of the Jewish National Home has been facilitated over the last twenty years, have decided that the time has come to adopt in principle the second of the alternatives referred to above.

It has been urged that all further Jewish immigration into Palestine should be stopped forthwith. His Majesty's Government cannot accept such a proposal. It would damage the whole of the financial and economic system of Palestine and thus affect adversely the interests of Arabs and Jews alike. Moreover, in the view of His Majesty's Government, abruptly to stop further immigration would be unjust to the Jewish National Home. But, above all, His Majesty's Government are conscious of the present unhappy plight of large numbers of Jews who seek refuge from certain European countries, and they believe that Palestine can and should make a further contribution to the solution of this pressing world problem. In all these circumstances, they believe that they will be acting consistently with their Mandatory obligations to both Arabs and Jews, and in the manner best calculated to serve the interests of the whole people of Palestine, by adopting the following proposals regarding immigration:

Jewish immigration during the next five years will be at a rate which, if economic absorptive capacity permits, will bring the Jewish population up to approximately one third of the total population of the country. Taking into account the expected natural increase of the Arab and Jewish populations, and the number of illegal Jewish immigrants now in the country, this would allow of the admission, as from the beginning of April this year, of some 75,000 immigrants over the next five years. These immigrants would, subject to the criterion of economic absorptive capacity, be admitted as follows:

For each of the next five years a quota of 10,000 Jewish immigrants will be allowed on the understanding that a shortage one year may be added to the quotas for subsequent years, within the five year period, if economic absorptive capacity permits.

In addition, as a contribution towards the solution of the Jewish refugee problem, 25,000 refugees will be admitted as soon as the High Commissioner is satisfied that adequate provision for their maintenance is ensured, special consideration being given to refugee children and dependents.

The existing machinery for ascertaining economic absorptive capacity will be retained, and the High Commissioner will have the ultimate responsibility for deciding the limits of economic capacity. Before each periodic decision is taken, Jewish and Arab representatives will be consulted.

After the period of five years, no further Jewish immigration will be permitted unless the Arabs of Palestine are prepared to acquiesce in it.

His Majesty's Government are determined to check illegal immigration, and further preventive measures are being adopted. The numbers of any Jewish illegal immigrants who, despite these measures, may succeed in coming into the country and cannot be deported will be deducted from the yearly quotas.

His Majesty's Government are satisfied that, when the immigration over five years which is now contemplated has taken place, they will not be justified in facilitating, nor will they be under any obligation to facilitate, the further development of the Jewish National Home by immigration regardless of the wishes of the Arab population.

SECTION III. LAND

The Administration of Palestine is required, under Article 6 of the Mandate, "while ensuring that the rights and position of other sections of the population are not prejudiced," to encourage "close settlement by Jews on the land," and no restriction has been imposed hitherto on the transfer of land from Arabs to Jews. The Reports of several expert Commissions have indicated that, owing to the natural growth of the Arab population and the steady sale in recent years of Arab land to Jews, there is now in certain areas no room for further transfers of Arab land, whilst in some other areas such transfers of land must be restricted if Arab cultivators are to maintain their existing standard of life and a considerable landless Arab population is not soon to be created. In these circumstances, the High Commissioner will be given general powers to prohibit and regulate transfers of land. These powers will date from the publication of this statement of policy and the High Commissioner will retain them throughout the transitional period.

The policy of the Government will be directed towards the development of the land and the improvement, where possible, of methods of cultivation. In the light of such development it will be open to the High Commissioner, should he be satisfied that the "rights and position" of the Arab population will be duly preserved, to review and modify any orders passed relating to the prohibition or restriction of the transfer of land.

In framing these proposals His Majesty's Government have sincerely endeavoured to act in strict accordance with their obligations under the Mandate to both the Arabs and the Jews. The vagueness of the phrases employed in some instances to describe these obligations has led to controversy and has made the task of interpretation difficult. His Majesty's Government cannot hope to satisfy the partisans of one party or the other in such controversy as the Mandate has aroused. Their purpose is to be just as between the two people in Palestine whose destinies in that country have been affected by the great events of recent years, and who, since they live side by side, must learn to practice mutual tolerance, goodwill and cooperation. In looking to the future, His Majesty's Government are not blind to the fact that some events of the past make the task of creating these relations difficult; but they are encouraged by the knowledge that as many times and in many places in Palestine during recent years the Arab and Jewish inhabitants have lived in friendship together. Each community has much to contribute to the welfare of their common land, and each must earnestly desire peace in which to assist in increasing the well being of the whole people of the country. The responsibility which falls on them, no less than upon His Majesty's Government, to cooperate together to ensure peace is all the more solemn because their country is revered by many millions of Moslems, Jews and Christians throughout the world who pray for peace in Palestine and for the happiness of her people.

---

http://www.yale.edu/lawweb/avalon/mideast/brwh1939.htm (accessed February 1, 2006).

Five
INDEPENDENCE AND *AL-NAKBA*

On the surface, World War II ironically provided something of a respite to the spiraling tension in the Palestine mandate that boiled over in the Arab revolt in 1936, culminating with the issuance of the 1939 White Paper. Underneath this veneer of relative calm, however, the Palestinian Arabs and the Yishuv seemed to sense that a day of reckoning over the disposition of Palestine lay in the near future. Again, it would be the Jews who would better prepare for the inevitable conflict for Palestine, while the Palestinian Arabs diplomatically blundered amid the wreckage of the Arab revolt and continuing divisions in their leadership. For the British, the war reinforced the importance of their position in Palestine astride the Suez Canal, even though, as opposed to World War I, there was no significant fighting in the area, most of that which did occur in the region taking place against German and Italian positions in North Africa. Palestine was a logistical center for London, teeming with British soldiers and administrators, generally pumping up the economy with the influx of spending and the creation of jobs. The British would vainly attempt to maintain their predominant position in the region following World War II; however, they would ultimately realize, as they did elsewhere in their colonial possessions—most notably in India in 1947—that their weakened condition following the war could not withstand the demands of empire, and they would begin a systematic withdrawal and paring down of their colonial commitments, including Palestine. In the British wake would emerge a new superpower, the United States, beginning to come to terms with its enhanced global military and economic status following the war and asserting positions in the international diplomatic arena that occasionally ran up against British interests, one of these being the fate of the Palestine mandate and the Jewish presence there.

ZIONISTS AND PALESTINIAN ARABS DURING WORLD WAR II

Ultimately for the Yishuv, even though London stood in the way of creating a Jewish state in Palestine, Great Britain was certainly the lesser of two evils when compared with Nazi Germany. As such, the Jews in Palestine generally supported the British war effort while utilizing the opportunity to not only surreptitiously acquire British armaments but also to gain the military experience and training that would prove to be so vital in the first Arab–Israeli war. As David Ben-Gurion exhorted, "We shall fight with Great Britain in this war as if there was no White Paper, and we shall fight the White Paper as if there was no war." During the war, especially as the atrocities of the genocidal Holocaust perpetrated by the Nazi regime that resulted in the deaths of almost 6 million Jews became known, immigration became a central feature of Yishuv efforts. Jews outside of the mandate were clamoring to immigrate to Palestine for the first time, but it came at a moment, following the Arab revolt, when Britain had severely curtailed Jewish immigration. This led to a proliferation of attempts to get Jews into Palestine legally or illegally simply to save lives. It was also intended to build up the Jewish population in the mandate territory in order to be in a better position demographically, militarily, and politically to put forth claims to statehood in the aftermath of the war. Restrictive immigration policies in the United States during the war, for which it received a healthy amount of criticism, made it that much more imperative to find a way to bring European Jews to Palestine during and immediately after the conflagration.

The Zionist movement at the beginning of World War II believed it once again had support in London with its old pro-Zionist friend Winston Churchill as British prime minister. Ben-Gurion had proposed the formation of a Jewish division to fight within the British army. Although Churchill favored a Jewish division in Palestine that may lessen the British burden there, he was convinced by a slew of British officials that it would cause an eruption in the Arab world at a time when Britain required Arab cooperation—or at least quiescence, particularly as Germany had made inroads in some Arab states, such as Iraq with the pro-German Rashid Ali al-Kaylani (Gailani) coup in 1941.[1] Ben-Gurion saw the failure to develop a Jewish division as a further sign of British perfidy in appeasing the Arabs as well as a discrediting of Chaim Weizmann's long-standing policy of diplomatic negotiations, if not cooperation, with London. In response, the Zionist movement convened a conference in New York City at the Biltmore Hotel in May 1942. In what came to be known as the "Biltmore Program," the Zionist movement for the first time called for the establishment of a Jewish commonwealth, in effect a state, in Palestine in addition to open immigration following the war.

The Biltmore Program signified a number of important transitions for Zionism and the fate of a Jewish state. First, it provided the forum for Ben-Gurion to wrest control of the World Zionist Organization from Weizmann, thereby giving sanction to Ben-Gurion's more aggressive and activist approach toward statehood, especially as reflected in policy on the ground in Palestine. Secondly, the convening of the conference in New York marked a symbolic shift in Zionist policy away from British patronage toward that of the United States, a shift that would prove to be decisive in the political run-up to the creation of the state of Israel and culminate in the "special relationship" between Tel Aviv and Washington established by the 1960s and 1970s. The connection would become and still is, by far, the most important single relationship for Israel. Finally, the conference marked the emergence of American Zionists as a force to be reckoned with in U.S. domestic politics and foreign policymaking. As William Cleveland states, "In the wake of the Biltmore gathering, the United States became the center of international Zionist activity, and American and Palestinian Zionists embarked on an intensive publicity campaign to involve the U.S. electorate and U.S. politicians in the issue of Palestine."[2]

The Palestinian Arabs during the war were in a state of flux following the British suppression of the Arab revolt. As such, as a group, they were not able to advance their position in Palestine to any measurable degree, resulting in a calm that belied the internal Palestinian turmoil and divisions that would irreparably harm their position diplomatically and militarily in the aftermath of World War II. Emblematic of this were the travails of Hajj Amin al-Husayni. After spending his exile in one Arab capital after another, he, along with other members of the Arab Higher Committee, found his way to Berlin and openly championed the Nazi regime, in what turned out to be the mistaken belief that he had chosen the winning side. Of course, all this did was discredit and damage Palestinian Arab demands and grievances in the eyes of the international community during and after the war, and more importantly, it alienated the British, with whom there may have been some common cause if he had not been identified with the Nazis. This exiled Palestinian leadership resulted in the atomization of the Arab elite in Palestine, with the Nashashibis establishing an alternative political structure supported externally by the Hashemites in Transjordan and Iraq; indeed, with the lack of an overall leadership structure for the Palestinian Arabs, increasingly other Arab regimes began to advance the cause to fill the void. Ultimately, however, these Arab regimes, particularly Egypt, Transjordan, and Iraq, would attempt to utilize the Palestinian issue to advance their own interests in Palestine and in the inter-Arab arena.

It was difficult during the war for the Jewish Agency and its military wing the Haganah to control the Irgun and Lehi (Lohamei Herut Yisrael, or Fighters for the Freedom of Israel, also known as the Stern Gang). The two organizations, of which Lehi was by far the smaller, had always seen Britain as the primary obstacle to statehood and were less inclined to put down their arms against British interests. Menachem Begin, a future prime minister of Israel, took over the Irgun in 1943 after recently immigrating from Poland. The goal was to inflict as much pain as possible on the British so as to compel London, pressured by a war-weary public, to disengage from the mandate. The Jewish Agency, while publicly disapproving of both groups in order to maintain a semblance of peace with Britain, often cast a blind eye toward their activities since ultimately they shared the same goal. The Irgun and Lehi were widely considered at the time in international circles—and certainly by the British—to be terrorists. A turning point in this regard was the assassination in November 1944 by Lehi of Lord Moyne, the British minister of state for the Middle East. Whatever sympathy was left in Britain toward the Zionists dissipated considerably after the incident. London adopted a more pro-Arab (although not necessarily pro-Palestinian Arab) position. In the House of Commons, Churchill himself stated the following in the aftermath of the assassination:

> If our dreams for Zionism are to end in the smoke of assassins' pistols and our labors for its future to produce only a new set of gangsters worthy of Nazi Germany, many like myself will have to reconsider the position we have maintained so consistently in the past.[3]

Following upon this, the Jewish Agency finally sent the Haganah out to round up members of Irgun and Lehi, imprisoning many of them in a process that was quite wrenching for the Yishuv at the time, some contemporary observers even commenting that the Jewish community in Palestine was on the verge of a civil war. But the Jewish Agency had to act before the British did to the Yishuv what they had done to the Palestinians in the Arab revolt. As a result, for the remainder of World War II, Jewish actions or "terrorism" against the British in Palestine dropped considerably, and the Jewish Agency won tacit cooperation from remaining members of Irgun and Lehi to suspend their attacks.[4] But this was too little, too late, for the British had already moved sufficiently away from their perceived commitment of establishing a Jewish state in Palestine, abandoning even earlier partition plans. As a clear indication of just how far the British had veered away from the Balfour Declaration, in referring to the Palestine mandate, Churchill stated the following in July 1945:

> I do not think that we should take the responsibility upon ourselves of managing this very difficult place while the Americans sit back and criticize. . . . I am not aware of the slightest advantage which has ever accrued to Great Britain from this painful and thankless task. Somebody else should have their turn now.[5]

Even though it emerged victorious after the war, Britain was nonetheless reeling following the conflict politically, economically, and, maybe most importantly, psychologically. This was not lost upon the Yishuv. Britain's foreign policy after the war tended to reflect the sentiments expressed in the 1939 White Paper, i.e., that good relations with the Arabs was a strategic necessity. The Yishuv, for its part, emerged from the war with a new cadre of experienced fighters, weapons, and ammunition taken from Allied supply depots. The time to push for statehood seemed at hand. As such, Zionist "terrorism" against British interests picked up again following the war, culminating with the Irgun-led attack against the King David Hotel in Jerusalem, a wing of which housed the British Mandate headquarters. Ninety-one British, Arab, and Jewish people lost their lives in the spectacular attack. It became a symbol of the increasingly precarious position of the British in Palestine. Even though Ben-Gurion condemned the act and the Haganah isolated Irgun and curtailed its own efforts against the British, the Yishuv was taking matters into its own hands. The British public, government officials, and soldiers and authorities in Palestine itself were becoming more and more disenchanted with the mandate despite the fact that it remained strategically significant.

THE UNITED STATES BECOMES A PLAYER

It was in this atmosphere that the United States began to play a more important role in the disposition of Palestine, at first in the face of some British displeasure and resistance but ultimately with the blessing of London. American Zionists had stepped up their propaganda and lobbying efforts since the Biltmore conference in 1942. The Zionist issue by 1944 had become a salient element in U.S. politics, something that would become a permanent feature of the American political scene. In that year, both houses of Congress introduced resolutions urging unrestricted Jewish immigration to

Palestine and called for the eventual establishment of a Jewish state there.[6] In the 1944 presidential election campaign, both parties for the first time adopted pro-Zionist positions in their respective platforms. Zionist organizations in the United States, especially after the war, tended to target groups such as Protestant evangelicals, who saw in the creation of a Jewish state the fulfillment of biblical prophecy. In addition, a Jewish state could be seen as a liberal, democratic entity existing precariously in a sea of tyranny and authoritarianism, something that Americans would—and should—support. Finally, as the extent of the Holocaust became known, American sympathies toward the Jews—and probably a significant amount of guilt—could be expressed in support for the creation of a Jewish state; and certainly Zionist interests in the United States, Europe, and Palestine were not immune to utilizing this global outrage and horror to their advantage.

Against this growing pro-Zionist position in the United States were arrayed those who were concerned that U.S. support for a Jewish state contradicted developing American interests in the Arab world, particularly, of course, with regard to oil. Although the United States was not dependent on Middle Eastern oil at that time, a rebuilding Europe (and Japan) was, and economic progress in Europe was key to the continuing expansion of the U.S. economy. A dynamic began to develop in Washington that would become characteristic in ensuing decades regarding the Arab–Israeli conflict: there would always be administration officials positioned on both sides of the issue, with the State Department, interested in pursuing policies that would, from its perspective, establish good relations with the vast majority of states in the Middle East, increasingly taking the lead in cautioning against too close of an attachment with Zionism (and then Israel) at the expense of growing U.S. strategic interests in the Arab world. In this vein, the State Department produced a general policy in 1943 that no decision regarding the "basic situation" in Palestine would be made without "full consultation with both Arabs and Jews."[7] Aware of this as well, a number of Arab states pressed the United States to articulate more clearly what on the surface seemed to be a balanced approach toward Palestine despite the intended ambiguity in the State Department policy. President Franklin D. Roosevelt reiterated the U.S. position when he met with Saudi Arabia's King ʻAbd al-Aziz ibn Saʻud (along with Egypt's King Farouk) on a ship in the Great Bitter Lake in Egypt in February 1945, stating (and later committing to written form) a promise not to do anything regarding Palestine without first consulting the Arabs.

Harry S. Truman became president upon Roosevelt's death in April 1945. Truman brought a much different style and personality to the Oval Office, and he was not someone known to have much interest or experience in foreign policy, which is ironic considering the fact that after the war the United States was about to embark upon an era of unprecedented involvement in international affairs; indeed, Roosevelt kept Truman largely in the dark as to his intricate diplomacy during the wartime years, which had important repercussions for a more antagonistic (certainly less subtle) U.S. relationship with the Soviet Union, adding fuel to the fire in the emerging superpower cold war. Among other things, Truman also inherited the problem of Palestine.

As is well known, Truman generally supported the twin ideas of Jewish immigration to Palestine and the creation of a Jewish state, in the latter case becoming the first to recognize the new state of Israel in May 1948. There has been a great deal of conjecture and debate over the decades about exactly what led Truman to adopt this position,

The Lobby

The so-called Jewish or pro-Israeli lobby is popularly perceived to be one of, if not the, most powerful political lobbies in Washington. It has certainly become an influential political force in American politics and foreign policymaking, but it is not the monolithic, invincible bloc that it is sometimes made out to be. Certainly, the extent of its influence over the years has been exaggerated, especially in the Arab world, which tends to see the Jewish lobby in the United States as an informal arm of the Israeli government, where practically every presidential policy is enacted at the behest of or to curry favor with pro-Israeli elements. It is not unlike the embellished global power ascribed to Jews by a variety of governments and groups before and during World War I, which had its roots in overt and latent anti-Semitism dating back centuries. Capturing these sentiments, there is a widely told joke in the Arab world that goes as follows: "Why doesn't Israel want to become the fifty-first state of the United States? Because then it would have to be satisfied with being represented by only two senators whereas now it has one hundred."

But make no mistake: the Jewish lobby has worked very hard over the decades since the creation of the state of Israel to position itself as a very influential force in Washington, particularly in Congress but also in the White House. The group that has become synonymous with the Israeli lobby is the American–Israeli Public Affairs Committee (AIPAC), headquartered in Washington, DC. It was formed in 1954 as the American Zionist Council of Public Affairs, changing its name five years later to AIPAC. It is the only Jewish pro-Israeli lobbying organization officially registered under the 1946 Federal Registration of Lobbying Act. There are, however, a number of other influential Jewish-based groups, such as the Conference of Presidents of Major American Jewish Organizations, the Anti-Defamation League of B'nai B'rith, and the American Jewish Committee. These groups do not always agree with each other regarding the actions of the Israeli government (particularly evident with the Israeli invasion of Lebanon in 1982) or at times the methodology toward achieving an objective, but they are all generally united in the ultimate goal of improving U.S.–Israeli relations (including the continuance of military and economic support) and opposing threats to Israeli security. Although chalking up a number of successes over the years, AIPAC has also had some notable setbacks, especially when the weight of the White House is placed behind a particular policy in opposition. In 1978, for instance, over the strenuous objections of pro-Israeli elements in and outside of Congress, the Carter administration carried through with the sale of F-15 fighters to Saudi Arabia, as did the Reagan administration with its sale of the Airborne Warning and Control System (AWACS) planes to Saudi Arabia in 1981.

Today, there are approximately 5–6 million Jews in the United States, depending upon the source, in which case Israel may or may not be the only country in the world with more Jews than the United States. Regardless of this, the concentration of Jews in a number of states, particularly in New York, has made them a valuable political constituency to both political parties, although the vast majority of Jews matriculated to the Democratic party. When the electorate in the United States in presidential elections is so evenly divided, such as in 1960 or 2000, winning the

"Jewish vote" in certain states (or reducing the margin of the Jewish vote toward one party) can mean the difference between winning and losing the presidency, especially as 90% of eligible Jewish voters regularly turn out at the polls on election day. Individual Jews and Jewish groups also contribute substantial sums of money to political campaigns and political action committees in order to influence the policies and votes of congresspersons (although AIPAC, which is not a political action committee, does not do so directly because it would be illegal).

There are also lobbies that are considered to be pro-Arab, most importantly the powerful oil lobby representing U.S. oil corporations, most of which have substantial interests and investment in oil produced by Arab countries. Defense corporations have also been influential lobbyists on behalf of arms sales to Arab states such as Egypt, Jordan, and Saudi Arabia. Finally, in 1972, the Arab American community established the National Association of Arab Americans to counter the pro-Israeli lobby. There exists as well the American Arab Anti-Discrimination Committee, which describes itself as a grassroots civil rights organization working to empower and defend the civil rights of the 3 million Arab Americans in the United States while also striving to promote a more balanced U.S. foreign policy toward the Arab world. Despite the efforts of these pro-Arab groups, they have thus far fallen far short of the pro-Israeli lobby in terms of organizational capability, fund-raising, and overall political influence, especially as the divisions in the Arab world itself are often reflected in the divergent agendas of different groups of Arab Americans.

especially since there were powerful figures in his administration, such as Secretary of State George Marshall, who strongly advised against it. Many have tried to identify the primary rationale behind Truman's decisions, pointing to his humanitarian concerns for the Jews in the wake of the Holocaust, his bending to the influence of Zionist pressure in and outside of his administration, his concern for the Jewish vote in key electorates in the 1946 congressional elections and the 1948 presidential election, his biblical background and evangelical leanings, and, finally, his strategic concerns, particularly vis-à-vis the Soviet Union as Moscow was keen to gain a foothold in the Middle East in supporting the Zionist cause. It is well-nigh impossible to identify exactly what was foremost in Truman's mind. It is probably more realistic to suggest that it was a confluence of all of the above that moved Truman to ultimately support the establishment of a Jewish state in Palestine. It is clear, however, that during the crucial period between 1945 and 1948, it was the White House that took the lead in decision making regarding the Palestine mandate. It is also true that Truman believed the Arab–Israeli issue would be resolved in the near future—and as we shall see in upcoming chapters, maybe it should have been. He certainly did not expect it to be a conflict that would span well over half a century, consisting of seven wars and associated death and destruction. It is seductive to speculate, if Truman had a crystal ball and could see into the future, whether or not he would have been so supportive of the creation of the state of Israel. Then again, he was so doggedly strong-willed he probably would have thought he could have changed an already foretold future anyhow.

As early as August 1945, Truman had written British Prime Minister Clement Attlee, urging the immediate admittance of 100,000 displaced Jews from Europe to Palestine. Attlee, realizing the negative impact this would have upon the British position in the Arab world yet not wanting to summarily reject the country that was underwriting Britain's recovery, advanced the notion of a joint commission to investigate the problem. This would be the British dilemma for the next couple of years: London generally resented U.S. interference in the Palestine problem and disagreed with Truman's approach, but it could not alienate its powerful friend amid economic disaster at home and the need for a superpower ally to confront the Soviet Union. The November 1945 Anglo–American Committee of Inquiry was the first of many Anglo–American attempts to paper over the differences regarding Palestine and construct a workable policy. In April 1946, the committee issued a unanimous report containing a series of recommendations regarding the disposition of Palestine, including the admission of 100,000 Jewish displaced persons from Europe along with the rather nebulous admonition that Palestine should neither be a Palestinian Arab state nor a Jewish state but should remain under trusteeship (essentially a continuance of the mandate). The Jews and Arabs rejected the committee report, as did the British; however, Truman, while remaining silent on other parts of the report, did say he welcomed the recommendation regarding the admittance to Palestine of 100,000 displaced Jews.

While the British were very concerned about admitting another 100,000 Jews, still very mindful of the turmoil caused by increased immigration in the 1930s that led to the Arab revolt, it seems as if London was prepared to take this step as long as it did not presage a flood of further Jewish immigration and the United States was prepared to provide the economic, political, and military support that would accompany it. As such, British and American officials again met during the summer of 1946, ostensibly to work out details of the Anglo–American Committee report, particularly the logistics of transporting 100,000 Jews. What resulted is what has been called the "Morrison-Grady plan," constructed in July 1946, which also provided for the immigration of the 100,000 refugees. What drew attention, however, was the idea of establishing provincial autonomy for Arabs and Jews in Palestine. It was, as Michael Cohen states, a British scheme that consisted, in essence, of "a compromise designed to give each community some outlet for its national aspirations, while reserving British federal control."[8]

The British government, as expected, announced its support for the Morrison-Grady plan; however, Jews and Arabs both rejected it, and the Truman administration continued to adopt an ambiguous position, neither endorsing nor rejecting the plan. Zionist pressure in the United States on Truman was intense, to the point that even the American president was reportedly becoming frustrated with the Zionist lobby by the end of the summer for its part in foiling potential opportunities to resolve the issue.[9] With Arab opposition as well, the plan was probably destined to fail anyhow; but Truman was certainly getting wind of how influential the Zionist lobby could be entering a two-year period in the fall of 1946 that would consist of congressional midterm elections and then a presidential election campaign.

With the midterm elections on the horizon, compounded by the fact that in the important state of New York it was anticipated that Governor Thomas Dewey, the likely Republican challenger in the next presidential election, was about to make a pro Zionist speech, Truman gave an important speech on October 4, 1946, one day before Yom Kippur, the Jewish Day of Atonement. In the speech, Truman called for the immediate admission of 100,000 displaced Jews to Palestine, essentially bringing an end to Anglo–American discussion that attempted to diplomatically handle the volatile issue. Dewey came out on October 6 with a speech calling on the immediate admission of several hundred thousand Jews—the game of one-upmanship was on. Ironically, despite Truman's efforts, the Republicans actually won a majority in both houses in the November congressional elections, the first time they had done so since 1928.

The British government had, by now, begun to lose hope for a diplomatic resolution to the Palestine issue that would protect its strategic interests while maintaining good relations with the United States. Palestine was also becoming more of an economic, military, and domestic political burden, especially as there were about 100,000 British troops in the mandate by 1947. British politicians were wondering aloud why the British were relinquishing India but not yet, as Winston Churchill put it, "tiny Palestine." One must remember that by 1947, the British were seemingly in full retreat from empire, realizing the debilitating economic effects of World War II. Not only India, but it was also in February 1947 that London informed Washington that it could not continue to maintain its position in Greece and Turkey, which elicited the Truman Doctrine in March, one of the first official shots in the superpower cold war and designed to prevent further communist expansion in the Mediterranean. The United States was slowly replacing (and displacing) the British.

As a result, British Foreign Secretary Ernest Bevin announced on February 18, 1947, that Great Britain was turning over the problem of Palestine to the United Nations (UN). This would relieve the British of the problem of unilaterally resolving the issue while placing it in the lap of a multilateral organization that would obviate the possibility of allowing it to fester and sour U.S.–British relations and cooperation. The General Assembly subsequently established the United Nations Special Committee on Palestine, otherwise known as UNSCOP, to come up with a viable plan, including boundaries, for a binational solution to the problem, i.e., partition. Contiguity for either the Jewish or Palestinian Arab state would be a difficult problem to overcome because of the already intermixed nature of Jewish settlements among the Arab population, in addition to the fact that at the time the latter still outnumbered the former in Palestine almost two-to-one (1.2 million Arabs to 650,000 Jews).

In September, UNSCOP produced a majority report and a minority report. The former called for the partition of Palestine into separate Jewish and Arab states with Jerusalem to come under international administration, a recommendation that the Zionists supported but the Arabs wholeheartedly rejected. The minority report recommended an independent federal state. Between this moment and late November, when a formal UN vote would decide the fate of Palestine, there was intense lobbying by Zionist groups in the United States and in other countries that would be voting at the General Assembly. The Departments of State and Defense strongly recommended against the partition plan for fear of upsetting the Arab states too much, on whom U.S. cold war strategy more obviously depended as well as growing oil interests—especially as there was the expectation that the Soviet Union would vote against partition, thus winning points in the Arab world and potentially leading to a Soviet–Arab rapprochement. The British, per their dwindling commitment to Palestine, had already announced in September that they would withdraw their troops and end the mandate by May 15, 1948, creating a certain level of tension and an atmosphere of finality to the situation as it developed in the fall of 1947. The outcome of the vote was anything but assured only two days before the final tally on November 29. Indeed, pro-Zionist groups, members of Congress, and business interests threatened and cajoled various countries in economic terms if they were to vote against partition.[10] Finally, on November 29, the roll call was taken, with thirty-three votes in favor (including the Soviet Union), thirteen against, and ten abstentions, barely the two-thirds majority vote needed for passage of General Assembly Resolution 181. Palestine was to be partitioned into separate Jewish and Arab states, along the lines of the majority report, with Jerusalem being designated an international zone. This is also the point at which the first Arab–Israeli conflict (or Israeli War of Independence) essentially began.

PALESTINE CIVIL WAR

The war can be divided into two overall stages: an intercommunal conflict between Jews and Arabs in Palestine (or what some have called a Palestine civil war) in the first stage that transformed itself into an interstate conflict in the second. The dividing point was May 15, 1948, just after Israel declared its independence and at the official end to the British Mandate, whereupon five Arab armies invaded the new Jewish state. The inter-communal stage was characterized by its haphazardness, with little to no traditional battle lines—in a way, it was an intensification of the Arab revolt of 1936, only this time the British were on their way out and progressively doing less of the fighting while the Yishuv was struggling for statehood and doing more of the fighting.

The Yishuv had about 35,000 forces, mostly in the Haganah (including about 3,000 in the elite Palmach—Plugot Mahatz, or shock platoons—formed in 1941) as well as about 2,000–4,000 in the Irgun and about 800–1,000 in Lehi. There were also thousands more in reserve for home guard and local defense that could be called upon if necessary. The Yishuv was very lightly armed, with mortars constituting its "heaviest" weaponry—there were no heavy machine guns, artillery, armored vehicles, or antitank and anti-aircraft weapons. And the air force consisted of about eleven single-engine light civilian aircraft, while the navy was little more than a few motorboats.[11] The vaunted Israel Defense Forces (IDF) would develop over time such a technological advantage as to negate the larger numbers of their enemies. This was not the case in this particular conflict, so being worn down by attrition was a very real concern for the Jewish leadership.

The Palestinians, on the other hand, were from the beginning operating with no single command structure or strategy and, as with the Yishuv, had no heavy weapons. Palestinian society had still yet to recover fully from the effects of the Arab revolt and, in this sense, were at a clear disadvantage to the better-trained, -led, and -organized Yishuv. The factionalized leadership within the Palestinian community before World War II had been exacerbated with the exile (and discrediting for hanging out with the Nazis) of Hajj Amin al-Husayni.[12] Further making matters worse, the ablest Palestinian military leader, ʻAbd al-Qadir al-Husayni (Hajj Amin's cousin), was killed in combat on April 9, 1948, in a battle just outside of Jerusalem. As Rashid Khalidi states,

> The Palestinians entered the fighting which followed the passage of the UN Partition resolution with a deeply divided leadership, exceedingly limited finances, no centrally organized military forces or centralized administrative organs, and no reliable allies. They faced a Jewish society in Palestine which, although small relative to theirs, was politically

> unified, had centralized para-state institutions, and was exceedingly well led and extremely highly motivated [especially in light of the horrors of the Holocaust].[13]

Indeed, in lieu of any cohesive leadership that could provide a coherent and organized response to the Biltmore Program, the newly formed League of Arab States (the Arab League), formalized with seven founding Arab state members in 1945, by default directed the Arab response to the problem of Palestine.[14] Because of this, however, the collective Arab response represented the often divergent and self-aggrandizing interests of its constituent members that did not coincide with what Palestinian Arabs actually desired; this dynamic would prove to be particularly harmful in the first Arab–Israeli war itself. The Palestinians were suspicious of the Arab League and, in turn, Arab League members were at times contemptuous of what they viewed as feeble Palestinian efforts. The Palestinian issue early on also became a lightning rod upon which Arab governments focused public attention (by adopting popular anti-imperialist positions) away from their inability (and unwillingness) to satisfactorily detach themselves from British and French de facto colonial rule—it could also come in handy to divert attention away from socioeconomic problems domestically. On the other side of the spectrum, Transjordan's King Abdullah held discussions with Zionist leaders hoping to arrange for the partition of Palestine between his kingdom and a Jewish state. It was this prospect as much as the concern for the Palestinians that galvanized several Arab states, most particularly Egypt and Syria, to eventually intervene in the burgeoning conflict in an attempt to prevent or restrict Abdullah's land grab in Palestine to the detriment of their own standing in the region.

Despite the advantage in training and organization, the Yishuv in the earlier months of the conflict was forced on the defensive by the scattered Palestinian response as well as surreptitious assistance supplied to them as material and volunteers from other Arab states. This reflected not only the vehemence with which the Palestinians fought for what they certainly viewed as their right to the land but also the conscious decision by the Jewish leadership to protect as many settlements as possible throughout the mandate. Orthodox military doctrine would probably have dictated confining and consolidating their forces to coastal areas or zones that contained a substantial Jewish presence instead of extending the lines of defense and dispersing forces; in addition, it was seen as essential to gain control of Jerusalem for religious and political reasons, which also dictated military strategy.[15] The city was isolated and situated in difficult, hilly terrain; but with over 100,000 Jews, it also constituted about one-sixth of the entire Jewish population in Palestine.[16] The Jews feared, probably correctly, that facts on the ground would do more to determine the final borders of a Jewish state whether partitioned or not—after all, UN General Assembly Resolution 181 was only a recommendation, not a written-in-stone dictum. If they retreated from even some of the territory allotted them in the partition plan, they may never be able to retrieve it due to political considerations that may emanate out of New York, Washington, and London, much less the battlefields of Palestine.

This dynamic was demonstrably brought home to the Yishuv leadership in March 1948. The U.S. State Department, which had never really supported the partition plan, determined that the difficulties in Palestine afforded the United States an opportunity to abandon partition. Indeed, from the State Department point of view, the communist coup in Czechoslovakia in February 1948, ominous signs already appearing in Berlin that would soon evolve into the Soviet blockade of the Allied-controlled portion of the city, and continued Soviet activities in Greece and Turkey dictated a different course of action in Palestine that would put the issue to rest for the time being. The State Department and its supporters still held to the idea that the European recovery could ill-afford a disruption in oil supplies from the Middle East that might be caused by the deteriorating situation in Palestine. As such, the United States announced in the UN Security Council on March 19, 1948, that it was withdrawing its support for the partition plan and now advocating that Palestine be placed under some sort of temporary international trusteeship. It would never come into being, however, as the UN would not be able to implement whatever was meant by the trusteeship before the British vacated the mandate in mid-May.

The floating of the trusteeship idea, especially as it came from the United States, did, however, galvanize the Jews in Palestine into more assertive action and reinforce the notion that facts on the ground would ultimately determine the outcome. It is at this point that the Haganah implemented a new and what would become a very controversial strategic operation, called Plan D (following upon Plans A, B, and C earlier). The plan was aimed at "gaining control over the territory assigned to the Jewish state and defending its borders, as well as the blocs of Jewish settlement and such Jewish population as were outside those borders, against regular, para-regular, and guerilla forces operating from bases outside or inside the nascent Jewish state."[17] To its critics, especially in the Arab world, Plan D was nothing short of a conscious attempt at ethnic cleansing, i.e., compelling as many Palestinian Arabs as possible through force or fear to flee Palestine so that the new Jewish state could maintain contiguity, acquire more land, and rid itself of a potential fifth column within the country. Many scholars who have examined this delicate issue have essentially concluded that Plan D was not intended to expel the Arabs entirely from Palestine but that it did create an operative framework and possibly a mind-set among some Jewish commanders and paramilitary groups taking matters into their own hands that led to unfortunate and tragic excesses. As noted Israeli scholar Benny Morris stated, the plan "provided for the conquest and permanent occupation, or leveling, of Arab villages and towns."[18] In other words, regardless of intent, the plan seemed in the end to serve this purpose. Because of the confused nature of this stage of the conflict, without hardened battle lines or in many cases recognizable forces taking up military positions and/or refuge in villages and settlements, some level of tragedy to the civilian population on both sides was inevitable. The aggressive implementation of Plan D certainly enhanced the fear among Palestinian Arabs that contributed to their mass exodus from the mandated territory, thus creating what would become the Palestinian refugee problem that exists to this day. One of those tragic excesses was the incident at the village of Deir (Dayr) Yasin on April 9, when elements from the Irgun and Lehi, led by Menachem Begin, killed (critics would say "massacred") over 200 men, women, and children in response to what they claimed to be enemy fire. It was also an attempt to break the Arab blockade of Jerusalem by opening up another road into the city and its beleaguered Jewish population. But instilling fear in the Arab population may well have also been Begin's and his followers' objective, and either as an intended or an unintended by-product, it seemed to work to a certain degree as word spread to other Arab villages, compelling many Palestinians to leave. It is also important to note that many Palestinians left their homes of their own accord to simply get out of the way of the fighting, especially as the conflict broadened with the entrance of the Arab armies in mid-May. There is also some evidence to suggest that Palestinians heeded the call of Arab leaders to vacate certain areas so as not to impede their progression into Palestine. Again, however, regardless of the cause, it is clear that those Palestinians who either left or were forced out intended to return to their homes once the fighting was over. The Arabs retaliated for Deir Yasin on April 13, ambushing a column of primarily Jewish doctors and nurses on their way to Jerusalem—seventy-seven were killed. These incidents are only two of the more notorious, but no less violent, episodes during this intercommunal stage of the war, the mutual enmity generated from which still sours relations between the two populations.

ARAB–ISRAELI WAR

On May 14, 1948, the last British High Commissioner in Palestine, General Alan Cunningham, departed from Haifa—the British Mandate had come to an end. As William Cleveland astutely observed, however, "There had been no formal transfer of powers from the mandate authority to a new local government for the simple reason that there was no government of Palestine. Britain had failed to create politi-

Israel's first prime minister, David Ben-Gurion, present at the Haifa docks as the last contingent of British troops leaves Israel on July 4, 1948. (Bettmann/CORBIS, BE034772.)

cal institutions in its mandate, instead leaving the Arab and Jewish communities to struggle for supremacy."[19] As opposed to the other British and French mandates in the Arab world, the one in Palestine was an abject failure—the British supervisory role as ordained by the mandate did not lead toward a relatively seamless transition to independence for the majority of the population. And the minority group in Palestine that eventually did gain independence did so despite, and more often than not in opposition to, the British. The Haganah significantly improved its strategic position in Palestine with the implementation of Plan D as well as the effort born by having its back against the wall in what was seen to be a life-or-death struggle. Its operational mobility was also facilitated by the fact that British troops were withdrawing with alacrity in the spring, more concerned with an orderly departure than with maintaining any semblance of stability. As such, David Ben-Gurion announced Israel's independence at 4:00 p.m. local time on May 14, and he became the country's first prime minister. Both the United States and the Soviet Union immediately recognized the new state of Israel.

On May 15, elements of five Arab armies invaded Israel, now that the British were safely out of the way, thus escalating the intercommunal conflict to an interstate war with international implications. Jewish leaders had overtly indicated that an Arab invasion would release Israel from any obligations to the UN partition plan.[20] Although sources differ, the combined Arab armies committed to the battlefield a total of only about 25,000 soldiers, which was actually less than what Israel had been able to field (35,000), even though the populations of the Arab combatant states outnumbered the population of Israel forty to one. There were about 10,000 from Egypt, 4,500 in the Jordanian Arab Legion trained and led by British officer John Bagot Glubb, 3,000 Syrians, and 3,000–4,000 Lebanese, including the Arab Liberation Army (ALA), a hodgepodge of Arab fighters who had actually been engaged in battle well before May 15.

There are several reasons for the discrepancy on the Arab side of the equation. There was a certain level of complacency in Arab commands regarding the fighting capacity of the Israelis that may have led to a downgrading of their overall assessment on how many troops would be necessary for victory. Since many of the Arab regimes were tenuously holding onto power at that point in the chaotic aftermath of World War II and as history would soon show were for the most part on their last legs, portions of the military were kept at home in order to safeguard the ruling regimes against any potential domestic foes; in addition, the armies often were purposely kept small because the ruling regime could not trust them—this was particularly the case with Syria. Primarily, however, aside from the British-trained Arab Legion in Transjordan, which was, by far, the best fighting force the Arabs could put in the field, the militaries in most of the Arab states were dreadfully ill-trained, undermanned, poorly led, and ill-equipped. For the most part, the conscripts were not the best and the brightest, and the armies became sinecures for minorities (as in Syria with the Alawites) and other bastions of outcasts who saw it as the only avenue of upward social mobility even though they were discredited to some extent for working in apparent cooperation with the mandate powers. Where there was some military reform, as in Egypt in the 1930s, the army soon became sinews for discontented and ideologically driven opposition movements, such as the Egyptian Free Officers, a situation that exacerbated the mistrust already existing within and between Arab commands. Regardless of why, the bottom line is this: on the battlefield, the Israelis outmanned and outclassed their

Arab counterparts. While their eventual victory was a tremendous achievement by any measure, considering the condition of the Yishuv as late as the early 1930s, it was close to being a foregone conclusion when the numbers are examined. This is not to even speak of the disunity and uncoordinated battle plan on the Arab side; indeed, saying there was a plan at all is rather generous. The invasion of Israel was officially an Arab League–mandated action, but it was a pathetic failure. The Arab League itself displayed disunity, in that the only form of unity the Arabs could achieve at that time despite the growing ideological prominence of pan-Arabism was a loosely bound coalition of individual states that were ultimately not subject to any Arab League decision. This "individuality," if you will, became manifest on the battlefield as the Arab combatant states pursued their own strategic objectives vis-à-vis each other as much as against Israel. Collectively, as Israeli scholar Avi Shlaim put it, "The Arab coalition was one of the most divided, disorganized, and ramshackle coalitions in the entire history of warfare."[21]

Despite this apparent inept and disorganized attack, the Arab armies in some areas fared quite well, particularly an Egyptian thrust (with only about half the troops it committed to Palestine) up the coast toward Tel Aviv. This leads one to conclude that had the Arab armies, as corrupt and inefficient as they were, coordinated their assault, the outcome might have been different. A most welcome cease-fire was arrived at on June 11, particularly from the Israeli perspective, many of whose fighters had been on the front lines for months; indeed, as a sign of the desperate situation the Jews in Palestine were in during those frantic first months of 1948 and during the early stages of the next phase of the conflict in May–June, Jewish refugees just off the boat were being given rifles and brought to the front. The cease-fire was negotiated by UN mediator Count Folke Bernadotte of Sweden, but it lasted only until July 9. The Israelis, however, made much better use of the brief respite to reinforce and build up their forces than the Arabs did. While a Western arms embargo implemented in late 1947 initially hampered both sides to the conflict, it now began to hurt the Arab side more. This is because Israel was able to secure military hardware, including tanks, armored cars, artillery, and aircraft, from the Soviet Union—through Czechoslovakia—and other sources that decisively tipped the scales in favor of the Jewish state in arms as well. In addition, the IDF, by the end of the cease-fire, had enlarged its numbers to 65,000 and, by December 1948, had reached about 100,000; while the Arab side also built up its force capacity to about 35,000–45,000 troops, it still was nowhere near what Israel had accomplished. On the battlefield by the end of 1948, Israel had an almost three to one advantage. In the end, Israel outmanned and outgunned its opponents.[22]

The Arab coalition was terribly divided. Transjordan's Abdullah, as noted earlier, had clear ambitions to control the West Bank. He engaged in negotiations with Jewish leaders in November 1947 (meeting future Israeli prime minister Golda Meir) and in May 1948, trying to peacefully split up between them the spoils of the abandoned British Mandate. From the Israelis' perspective, this was a godsend, for it could negate the possibility of an independent Palestinian state coming into being as well as sow dissent among the Arab states. The Egyptians, Saudis, and Syrians were very suspicious of Abdullah's motives, especially when the latter bombastically pronounced himself commander-in-chief of the Arab coalition in May. Certainly, the Saudis and Egypt's King Farouk had long been wary of Hashemite designs for enlarging their territorial

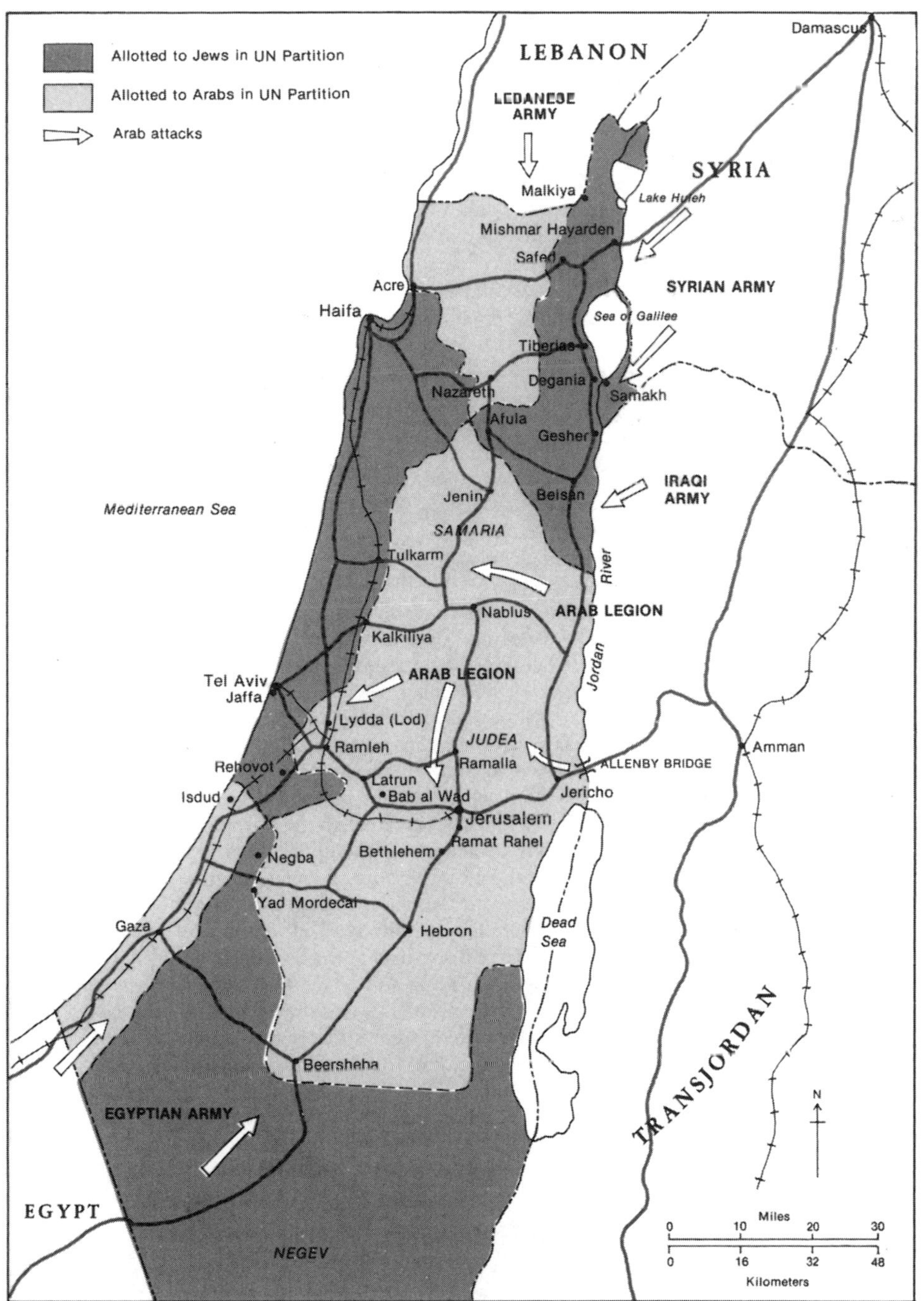

U.N. partition boundaries and initial Arab invasion, May 15–June 11, 1948. (Reprinted by permission of the publisher from *Israel, the Embattled Ally: The United States and Israel* by Nadav Safran. Cambridge, MA.: Belknap Press of Harvard University Press, 51. Copyright © 1978 by the president and fellows of Harvard College.)

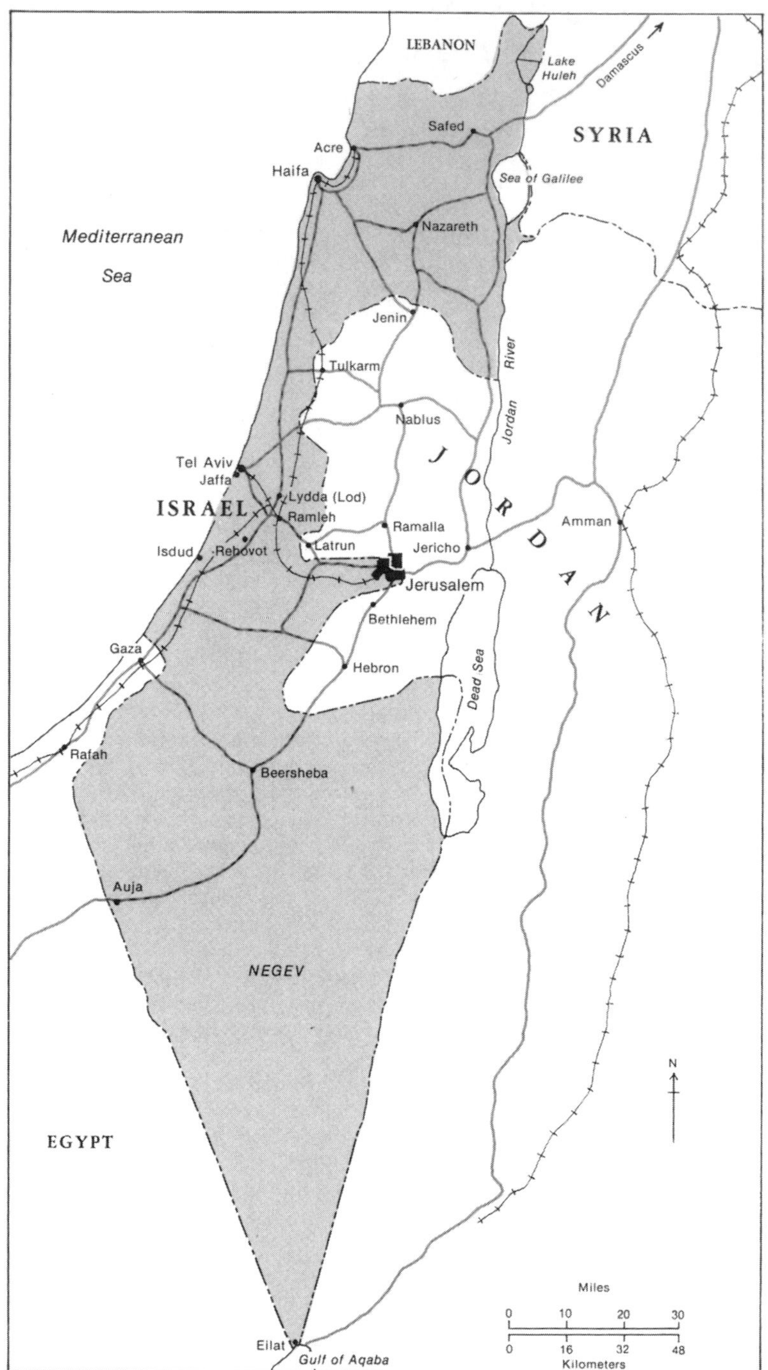

The 1949 armistice demarcation lines. (Reprinted by permission of the publisher from *Israel, the Embattled Ally: The United States and Israel* by Nadav Safran. Cambridge, MA.: Belknap Press of Harvard University Press, 61. Copyright © 1978 by the president and fellows of Harvard College.)

hold in the region beyond Transjordan and Iraq. Although some Syrians were supportive of such Hashemite designs, the Syrian leadership, particularly President Shukri al-Quwwatli, understood that if Abdullah gained control of a healthy portion of Palestine, this might whet his appetite for Syria as well, creating his long-sought-after control over Greater Syria with his throne situated in Damascus. Arab military operations were carried out with these considerations in mind as much as concern about what the Israelis were doing. The Arab Legion basically maintained a defensive posture in Jerusalem and areas of the West Bank, betraying the fact that it was not out to defeat Israel but just to claim some territory and prevent the establishment of an independent Palestinian state, something which the British were encouraging Amman to do as the enhancement of Hashemite influence naturally propped up London's dwindling position in the region. The Egyptians, with the largest Arab contingent in the war, split their forces in two, one heading up the coast of Israel toward Tel Aviv (and experiencing some success until it reached the outskirts of the city) and the other heading toward the West Bank in order to make sure the Arab Legion did not gobble it all up. Syria had wanted Arab League action first and foremost to protect itself from a rapacious Transjordan. Syria's creation of the ALA was an attempt to secure its credentials in the Arab world and with its own public clamoring for action, but it was also intended as a vehicle through which to enter the conflagration before the British withdrew so as to preemptively strike at Abdullah's Greater Syria plan; in addition, it was an admission of the ineptitude of the Syrian army itself.[23] Indeed, Quwwatli's decision to delay full engagement in the war and to carry out only limited operations once he did—leading some Arab critics to portray him as treasonous—resulted from the accurate recognition that his forces would easily be defeated and the fear that Abdullah could then have the way paved for him into Damascus by virtue of the Israelis. Emblematic of Arab disarray and half-heartedness on behalf of the Palestinians is the following quote from Syrian Prime Minister Jamil Mardam:

> The popular movement in Palestine is responsible for saving the situation, with the help of the Arab governments. This is because I doubt in the unity of the Arab armies and their ability to fight together.... If the Arab armies, not least of all the Syrian army, are hit with an overwhelming surprise attack by the Jewish Haganah, it would lead to such a loss of reputation that the Arab governments would never be able to recover. The best thing is to leave the work to the Palestinians and to supply them with the help of the Arab governments.[24]

On the other hand, there were those such as 'Abd–Rahman Hassan Azzam (known also as Azzam Pasha), the first secretary-general (1945–1952) of the Arab League who on May 14 bombastically commented, "This will be a war of extermination and a momentous massacre which will be spoken of like the Mongol massacres and the Crusades."[25] While this was certainly misplaced bravado, it only made the Jews in the Yishuv, coming so soon after the Holocaust, understand that this would be a fight for their own survival.

Israel fully exploited the disunity in Arab ranks, allowing it to essentially pick and choose on what front to concentrate its forces rather than having to disperse vital elements to multiple fronts at the same time. Egypt and Jordan actually attempted to set up rival Palestinian governments in the fall of 1948, more aimed at each other and

Arab public opinion rather than truly trying to improve the chances of success for the Palestinians. As Josh Landis comments, "From the beginning, the fight was over the balance of power in the region and the future of the Arab world; this was not a war waged to destroy the Jewish state."[26]

Fighting again broke out on July 9 in what some have called the "Ten Days' War," with a second UN-brokered truce coming into being on July 18. Diplomatic activity intensified during this more lengthy cease-fire. Bernadotte had suggested modifying the original UN partition plan with a new one, which he submitted to the UN on September 16, 1948. According to this version, Jerusalem would come under UN control as an international city, the Negev (along with Lydda and Ramle) would be allotted to the Arabs, and the Galilee would go to Israel. In addition, Bernadotte emphasized that Palestinian refugees would have the right to return to their homes.[27] On September 17, Bernadotte was assassinated by elements of Lehi, an action sanctioned by one of its leading members, Yitzhak Shamir, a future prime minister of Israel. The assassination was not condoned by the Israeli government, and Ben-Gurion ordered the dissolution of both Irgun and the Stern Gang soon thereafter. It is interesting to note that Syria and Egypt both rejected Bernadotte's plan, for although it would have limited the size of Israel, ended the fighting without total defeat, and provided for Palestinian repatriation, it also would have "gratified Abdullah and the British by allowing Jordan to annex the non-Jewish parts of Palestine."[28]

Realizing there was obviously some international sentiment to redraw the original UN partition plan, Ben-Gurion saw the need to once again create facts on the ground. The Negev would be important to the future of the Jewish state as an area for further Jewish settlement. It was also of strategic and economic importance because it provided another outlet to the open seas through the Gulf of Aqaba, and the port of Eilat would soon fulfill this role. As such, Israeli forces initiated hostilities in mid-October with Operation Yoav, which attempted to secure the Negev by driving out Egyptian forces. Interestingly, the Arab Legion, which was in a position to help Egypt, chose not to do so; indeed, Transjordan was not at all that unhappy to see the Egyptians pushed back. As Glubb exclaimed, "If the Jews are going to have a private war with the Egyptians and the Gaza government [the Egyptian-created government of All-Palestine], we do not want to get involved. The gyppies and the Gaza government are almost as hostile to us as the Jews."[29] On October 29, Operation Hiram began, which further solidified Israeli control of the Galilee, in what Ben-Gurion in September called the "cleaning" and "emptying" of Arabs from the area, a clear indication that certain "cleansing" operations took their cue from the government.[30] Another cease-fire was arranged on October 31, but in the last stage of fighting, Israel launched Operation Horev on December 22 to drive Egyptian forces completely out of Palestine and force Cairo to negotiate an end to the conflict by actually taking the battle into Egypt proper in the Sinai Peninsula. In this, the operation was a success. A final UN-brokered cease-fire came into being on January 7, 1949, bringing an end to the first Arab–Israeli war. Subsequently, Dr. Ralph Bunche from the United States, the new UN mediator replacing Bernadotte, met with the combatant parties in a series of negotiations on the Greek island of Rhodes. Egypt agreed to an armistice on February 24. With the most populous and powerful Arab state agreeing to an armistice, Lebanon, Transjordan, and Syria followed in line in March, April, and July, respectively. It is important to note that these armistice agreements were not peace treaties nor did they include Arab recognition of Israel or the borders as they stood at the time. In essence, it was little more than a new internationally sanctioned and monitored cease-fire. The Arab states were still in a formal state of war with Israel. They could not lose face at home by formally relenting through the vehicle of a treaty. The Arabs had not put forth their best effort by any means; all they needed, it was thought, was time to reform and build up their militaries to put forth a better effort in the near future. The Arab public did not buy it, however—the leaders of four of the five Arab states that invaded Israel were either exiled or assassinated within the next three years, and the fifth (Iraq), with British support and a bit more distance from the Arab–Israeli front lines, hung on for another nine years until the 1958 revolution violently swept him away as well. For its part in the war, Israel had gained 21% more territory than had been allotted to it in the original UN partition plan and by early 1949 had control of about 80% of what had been the Palestine mandate, including West Jerusalem.[31] The remainder of the mandate was taken mostly by Transjordan (the West Bank and Arab East Jerusalem, which were annexed in 1950, although only Britain and Pakistan recognized the annexation) and Egypt (the Gaza Strip), with Syria gaining a sliver of disputed territory along the southern portion of the Golan Heights.

For the Israelis, the first Arab–Israeli war was a tremendous victory that bore their long-sought-after statehood, and their success clearly displayed how effective the Zionist movement and the Yishuv marshaled their resources toward achieving a singular goal. It is easy to understand the mythology that was erected around the conflict and Israel's "founding fathers," most prominently the image of the Israeli "David" versus the Arab "Goliath," i.e., the underdog, ragtag group of Jews defeating the behemoth of the combined Arab armies. Even though these mythical images have been questioned and countered in recent years—most effectively by Israeli scholars themselves, who have mined the archives and memoirs—the founding of Israel dramatically changed the face of the Middle East and launched the new Jewish state into a largely successful experiment of state-building in a hostile environment.

For the Palestinians, the first Arab–Israeli conflict was an unmitigated disaster; indeed, following upon Constantine Zurayq's widely read book *The Meaning of the Disaster*, Palestinians came to call the war simply *al-Nakba,* the Disaster or Catastrophe. The UN partition plan was smashed into oblivion, so there would be no independent Palestinian Arab state emerging from international diplomacy. For average Palestinians, the international community had failed them, the Arab states had failed them, and their own divided, weak leadership had failed them. In such conditions, they had absolutely no chance against the Israeli juggernaut. And the enduring legacy to this day of this failure was the creation of the Palestinian refugee problem. According to most sources, 700,000–750,000 Palestinians either were forced out of their homes or left of their own accord, leaving the dream of a Palestine behind them. Only about 160,000 Palestinians would remain within the borders of the new state of Israel, most of whom would come to be known as Israeli Arabs, i.e., Palestinian Arabs who remained in Israel following the 1947–1949 war and became Israeli citizens. Of the 700,000–750,000, about 60% went to Transjordan/Jordan (which, of course, after the war included the West Bank and Arab East Jerusalem), 20% found themselves under Egyptian control in the Gaza Strip, and about 20% went to Syria and Lebanon. General Assembly Resolution 194 of December 1948 created a UN Conciliation Commission for Palestine and affirmed the right of return to the Palestinian refugees. The resolution states that "the refugees wishing to return to their homes and live at peace with their neighbors should be permitted to do so at the earliest practicable date, and that compensation should be paid for the property of those not choosing to return." The Truman administration supported this policy, admonishing Ben-Gurion for not making more progress on this issue by mid-1949.[32] The consistent Israeli response to this, however, has been that the refugee problem derived from the fact that the Palestinians and the Arabs rejected the UN partition plan and initiated hostilities to begin with; therefore, they should not expect Israel to deal with this burden willy-nilly and certainly not before the Arab states recognize the Jewish state and sign peace treaties. It remains one of the most vexing issues in the Arab–Israeli dynamic to this day, currently with some 4 million refugees (the original Palestinian refugees and their descendants) registered with the UN. As for Israeli responsibility, I will let Benny Morris, the Israeli scholar who has delved into this delicate, controversial issue more deeply than anyone else, have the final word:

> Nothing that I have seen in Israeli archives . . . indicates the existence before 1948 of a Zionist master plan to expel the Arabs of Palestine. Nor, in looking at the materials from 1948, is there anything to show that such a plan existed and was systematically unleashed and implemented in the course of the war, or that any overall expulsory policy decision was taken by the Yishuv's executive bodies . . . in the course of the 1948 War (apart from the June–July 1948 Cabinet decision to bar a refugee return). None the less, expulsion was in the air in the war of 1948. From April [1948] on, Palestinian Arabs were the target of a series of concrete expulsions from individual villages, clusters of villages, and towns. The readiness among the Israeli commanders and officials to expel fluctuated in relation to the local conditions and to the national military situation (certainly there was a greater willingness to expel after the Arab states invaded . . . putting the Yishuv's very existence temporarily in question), the character and outlook of the Israeli commanders, and the nature of the Arab villagers and townspeople involved (traditional anti-Zionists or "friendly" Arabs, Muslims, Christians, Druse, etc.), topographical conditions, and so on. Clearly, the readiness to resort to compulsory transfer grew . . . as the fighting became more desperate, bloody and widespread, with Ben-Gurion himself setting the tone and indicating direction, usually resorting to a nod and a wink if not actually issuing explicit orders.[33]

NOTES

1. Britain did allow the formation of a Jewish brigade in 1944 that fought in Italy, but it was one-third the size of the proposed Jewish division. It did, however, provide invaluable military experience to a number of Jews.

2. William L. Cleveland, *A History of the Modern Middle East* (Boulder: Westview Press, 1994), 243.

3. Quoted in Michael J. Cohen, *The Origins and Evolution of the Arab–Zionist Conflict* (Berkeley: University of California Press, 1987), 104.

4. The definition of "terrorism" is not universally accepted. One man's terrorist is another man's freedom fighter or resistance movement. Some define "terrorism" as the use of violence in any form for political gain, while others more narrowly define it as violence against civilians within the rubric of unconventional warfare. On the other hand, even if civilians were not the intended target, they often were killed collaterally. This author does not make a judgment on who is or who is not a terrorist, but the term is used in the text to reflect the general view toward a particular group or action at the time, whether or not that perspective stands the test of time.

5. Cohen, *The Origins and Evolution,* 105.

6. Evan M. Wilson, "The American Interest in the Palestine Question and the Establishment of Israel," in *Annals of the American Academy of Political and Social Science,* vol. 401, *America and the Middle East* (May 1972): 66.

7. Ibid.

8. Cohen, *The Origins and Evolution,* 111.

9. As a result, the Jewish Agency voted to at least temporarily abandon the Biltmore Program and tentatively accept the idea of partition, and it communicated this new position to Truman. Influencing the Jewish Agency was also the worrisome prospect of the Jewish displaced persons in Europe suffering another cold winter without any hope of being transferred.

10. For instance, upon the threat of a Jewish boycott of products from Firestone, Harvey Firestone informed the Liberian government that plans for the expansion of a Firestone plant located there would be placed on hold unless Liberia voted for partition.

11. Efraim Karsh, *The Arab–Israeli Conflict: The Palestine War 1948* (Oxford: Osprey Publishing, 2002), 25.

12. As Rashid Khalidi points out, "For all his dominance of Palestinian politics for nearly two decades, Hajj Amin al-Husayni did not approach the stature of a Sa'd Zaghlul [in Egypt] or even a Shukri al-Quwwatli [in Syria], perhaps most notably because no nationalist political party remotely resembling the Wafd Party [Zaghlul's party in Egypt] or even the Syrian National Bloc (Kutla Wataniyya), existed in Palestine." Rashid Khalidi, "The Palestinians and 1948: The Underlying Causes of Failure," in Eugene L. Rogan and Avi Shlaim, eds., *The War for Palestine: Rewriting the History of 1948* (Cambridge: Cambridge University Press, 2001), 31.

13. Ibid.

14. The seven founding members were Egypt, Iraq, Syria, Saudi Arabia, Yemen, Jordan (then Transjordan), and Lebanon.

15. There were thirty-three Jewish settlements outside of the territory allotted to the Jews in the partition plan. In addition, most of the sparsely populated Negev desert, with its twenty-seven isolated Jewish villages, made up the vast majority of the land allotted to the Jews; and Ben-Gurion and the Haganah leadership believed they had to secure it or the Arabs would take it for good. Ben-Gurion stated that, "If we fail to defend the Negev, Tel Aviv will not stand either. If we will not be in the Negev, the [Arabs] will occupy it, and it is an illusion to think that they will subsequently return it to us" (quoted in Karsh, *The Arab–Israeli Conflict,* 34).

16. More Jews were killed trying to secure the road to Jerusalem—the Latrun corridor—than any other campaign in the war.

17. Quoted in Karsh, *The Arab–Israeli Conflict,* 42.

18. Benny Morris, *The Birth of the Palestinian Refugee Problem, 1947–1949* (Cambridge: Cambridge University Press, 1988), 63.

19. Cleveland, *A History,* 247–248.

20. Mark Tessler, *A History of the Israeli–Palestinian Conflict* (Bloomington: Indiana University Press, 1994), 264.

21. Avi Shlaim, "Israel and the Arab Coalition in 1948," in Eugene L. Rogan and Avi Shlaim, eds., *The War for Palestine: Rewriting the History of 1948* (Cambridge: Cambridge University Press, 2001), 82. Shlaim further points out that "All these states... only sent an expeditionary force to Palestine, keeping the bulk of their army at home. The expeditionary forces were hampered by long lines of communication, the absence of reliable intelligence about their enemy, poor leadership, poor coordination, and very poor planning for the campaign that lay ahead of them" (p. 81).

22. Ibid., 81.

23. Joshua Landis, "Syria and the Palestine War: Fighting King 'Abdullah's Greater Syria Plan," in Rogan and Shlaim, *The War for Palestine,* 193–196.

24. Quoted in Landis, "Syria and the Palestine War," 194.

25. Quoted in Howard Sachar, *A History of Israel* (New York: Knopf, 1979), 333; also see Benny Morris, *Righteous Victims: A History of the Zionist–Arab Conflict, 1881–2001* (New York: Vintage Books, 2001), 219. Azzam Pasha stated a week before to a British official that, "It does not matter how many [Jews] there are. We will sweep them into the sea" (quoted in Sachar, 333).

26. Landis, "Syria and the Palestine War," 178. He even later suggests that maybe the war could more accurately be characterized as an inter-Arab conflict rather than an Arab–Israeli one (p. 200).

27. Ritchie Ovendale, *The Arab–Israeli Wars* (New York: Longman, 1999), 136.

28. Landis, "Syria and the Palestine War," 180.

29. Quoted in Shlaim, "Israel and the Arab Coalition of 1948," 99. As Shlaim points out, in one of the besieged pockets—at Faluja—was an Egyptian brigade that included a Major Gamal 'Abd al-Nasser (98).

30. Ibid., 99.

31. Ovendale, *The Arab–Israli Wars*, 138.

32. Tessler, *A History of the Israeli–Palestinian Conflict*, 311.

33. Benny Morris, "Revisiting the Palestinian Exodus of 1948," in Rogan and Shlaim, *The War for Palestine*, 48–49.

Biltmore Program (May 11, 1942)

1. American Zionists assembled in this Extraordinary Conference reaffirm their unequivocal devotion to the cause of democratic freedom and international justice to which the people of the United States, allied with the other United Nations, have dedicated themselves, and give expression to their faith in the ultimate victory of humanity and justice over lawlessness and brute force.

2. This Conference offers a message of hope and encouragement to their fellow Jews in the Ghettos and concentration camps of Hitler-dominated Europe and prays that their hour of liberation may not be far distant.

3. The Conference sends its warmest greetings to the Jewish Agency Executive in Jerusalem, to the Va'ad Leumi, and to the whole Yishuv in Palestine, and expresses its profound admiration for their steadfastness and achievements in the face of peril and great difficulties. The Jewish men and women in field and factory, and the thousands of Jewish soldiers of Palestine in the Near East who have acquitted themselves with honor and distinction in Greece, Ethiopia, Syria, Libya and on other battlefields, have shown themselves worthy of their people and ready to assume the rights and responsibilities of nationhood.

4. In our generation, and in particular in the course of the past twenty years, the Jewish people have awakened and transformed their ancient homeland; from 50,000 at the end of the last war their numbers have increased to more then 500,000. They have made the waste places to bear fruit and the desert to blossom. Their pioneering achievements in agriculture and in industry, embodying new patterns of cooperative endeavor, have written a notable page in the history of colonization.

5. In the new values thus created, their Arab neighbors in Palestine have shared. The Jewish people in its own work of national redemption welcomes the economic,

agricultural and national development of the Arab peoples and states. The Conference reaffirms the stand previously adopted at Congresses of the World Zionist Organization, expressing the readiness and the desire of the Jewish people for full cooperation with their Arab neighbors.

6. The Conference calls for the fulfillment of the original purpose of the Balfour Declaration and the Mandate which "recognizing the historical connection of the Jewish people with Palestine" was to afford them the opportunity, as stated by President Wilson, to found there a Jewish Commonwealth. The Conference affirms its unalterable rejection of the White Paper of May 1939 and denies its moral or legal validity. The White Paper seeks to limit, and in fact to nullify Jewish rights to immigration and settlement in Palestine, and, as stated by Mr. Winston Churchill in the House of Commons in May 1939, constitutes "a breach and repudiation of the Balfour Declaration." The policy of the White Paper is cruel and indefensible in its denial of sanctuary to Jews fleeing from Nazi persecution; and at a time when Palestine has become a focal point in the war front of the United Nations, and Palestine Jewry must provide all available manpower for farm and factory and camp, it is in direct conflict with the interests of the allied war effort.

7. In the struggle against the forces or aggression and tyranny, of which Jews were the earliest victims, and which now menace the Jewish National Home, recognition must be given to the right of the Jews of Palestine to play their full part in the war effort and in the defense of their country, through a Jewish military force fighting under its own flag and under the high command of the United Nations.

8. The Conference declares that the new world order that will follow victory cannot be established on foundations of peace, justice and equality, less the problem of Jewish homelessness is finally solved. The Conference urges that the gates of Palestine be opened; that the Jewish Agency be vested with control of immigration into Palestine and with the necessary authority for upbuilding the country, including the development of its unoccupied and uncultivated lands; and that Palestine be established as a Jewish Commonwealth integrated in the structure of the new democratic world. Then and only then will the age-old wrong to the Jewish people be righted.

Bernard Reich, ed., *Arab–Israeli Conflict and Conciliation: A Documentary History* (Westport, CT: Praeger, 1995), 53–54.

United Nations General Assembly Resolution 181

November 29, 1947

The General Assembly, Having met in special session at the request of the mandatory Power to constitute and instruct a Special Committee to prepare for the consideration of the question of the future Government of Palestine at the second regular session;

Having constituted a Special Committee and instructed it to investigate all questions and issues relevant to the problem of Palestine, and to prepare proposals for the solution of the problem, and

Having received and examined the report of the Special Committee (document A/364)(1) including a number of unanimous recommendations and a plan of partition with economic union approved by the majority of the Special Committee,

Considers that the present situation in Palestine is one which is likely to impair the general welfare and friendly relations among nations;

Takes note of the declaration by the mandatory Power that it plans to complete its evacuation of Palestine by 1 August 1948;

Recommends to the United Kingdom, as the mandatory Power for Palestine, and to all other Members of the United Nations the adoption and implementation, with regard to the future Government of Palestine, of the Plan of Partition with Economic Union set out below;

PLAN OF PARTITION WITH ECONOMIC UNION

Part I. Future Constitution and Government of Palestine

A. Termination of Mandate, Partition and Independence

The Mandate for Palestine shall terminate as soon as possible but in any case not later than 1 August 1948.

The armed forces of the mandatory Power shall be progressively withdrawn from Palestine, the withdrawal to be completed as soon as possible but in any case not later than 1 August 1948.

The mandatory Power shall advise the Commission, as far in advance as possible, of its intention to terminate the mandate and to evacuate each area. The mandatory Power shall use its best endeavours to ensure that an area situated in the territory of the Jewish State, including a seaport and hinterland adequate to provide facilities for a substantial immigration, shall be evacuated at the earliest possible date and in any event not later than 1 February 1948.

Independent Arab and Jewish States and the Special International Regime for the City of Jerusalem, set forth in Part III of this Plan, shall come into existence in Palestine two months after the evacuation of the armed forces of the mandatory Power has been completed but in any case not later than 1 October 1948. The boundaries of the Arab State, the Jewish State, and the City of Jerusalem shall be as described in Parts II and III below.

The period between the adoption by the General Assembly of its recommendation on the question of Palestine and the establishment of the independence of the Arab and Jewish States shall be a transitional period.

F. Admission to Membership in the United Nations

When the independence of either the Arab or the Jewish State as envisaged in this plan has become effective and the declaration and undertaking, as envisaged in this plan, have been signed by either of them, sympathetic consideration should be given to its application for admission to membership in the United Nations in accordance with article 4 of the Charter of the United Nations.

Part II. Boundaries

A. The Arab State

The area of the Arab State in Western Galilee is bounded on the west by the Mediterranean and on the north by the frontier of the Lebanon from Ras en Naqura to a point north of Saliha. From there the boundary proceeds southwards, leaving the built-up area of Saliha in the Arab State, to join the southernmost point of this village. There it follows the western boundary line of the villages of 'Alma, Rihaniya and Teitaba, thence following the northern boundary line of Meirun village to join the Acre-Safad Sub-District boundary line. It follows this line to a point west of Es Sammu'i village and joins it again at the northernmost point of Farradiya. Thence it follows the sub-district boundary line to the Acre-Safad main road. From here it follows the western boundary of Kafr-Inan village until it reaches the Tiberias-Acre Sub-District boundary line, passing to the west of the junction of the Acre-Safad and Lubiya-Kafr-I'nan roads. From the south-west corner of Kafr-I'nan village the boundary line follows the western boundary of the Tiberias Sub-District to a point close to the boundary line between the villages of Maghar and 'Eilabun, thence bulging out to the west to include as much of the eastern part of the plain of Battuf as is necessary for the reservoir proposed by the Jewish Agency for the irrigation of lands to the south and east.

The boundary rejoins the Tiberias Sub-District boundary at a point on the Nazareth-Tiberias road south-east of the built-up area of Tur'an; thence it runs southwards, at first following the Sub-District boundary and then passing between the Kadoorie Agricultural School and Mount Tabor, to a point due south at the base of Mount Tabor. From here it runs due west, parallel to the horizontal grid line 230, to the north-east corner of the village lands of Tel Adashim. It then runs to the northwest corner of these lands, whence it turns south and west so as to include in the Arab State the sources of the Nazareth water supply in Yafa village. On reaching Ginnciger It follows the eastern, northern and western boundaries of the lands of this village to their south-west corner, whence it proceeds in a straight line to a point on the Haifa-Afula railway on the boundary between the villages of Sarid and El-Mujeidil. This is the point of intersection. The south-western boundary of the area of the Arab State in Galilee takes a line from this point, passing northwards along the eastern boundaries of Sarid and Gevat to the north-eastern corner of Nahalal, proceeding thence across the land of Kefar ha Horesh to a central point on the southern boundary of the village of 'Ilut, thence westwards along that village boundary to the eastern boundary of Beit Lahm, thence northwards and north-eastwards along its western boundary to the north-eastern corner of Waldheim and thence north-westwards across the village lands of Shafa 'Amr to the southeastern corner of Ramat Yohanan. From here it runs due north-north-east to a point on the Shafa 'Amr-Haifa road, west of its junction with the road of Ibillin. From there it proceeds north-east to a point on the southern boundary of I'billin situated to the west of the I'billin-Birwa road. Thence along that boundary to its westernmost point, whence it turns to the north, follows across the village land of Tamra to the north-westernmost corner and along the western boundary of Julis until it reaches the Acre-Safad road. It then runs westwards along the southern side of the Safad-Acre road to the Galilee-Haifa District boundary, from which point it follows that boundary to the sea.

The boundary of the hill country of Samaria and Judea starts on the Jordan River at the Wadi Malih south-east of Beisan and runs due west to meet the Beisan-Jericho road and then follows the western side of that road in a north-westerly direction to the junction of the boundaries of the Sub-Districts of Beisan, Nablus, and Jenin. From that point it follows the Nablus-Jenin Sub-District boundary westwards for a distance of about three kilometres and then turns north-westwards, passing to the east of the built-up areas of the villages of Jalbun and Faqqu'a, to the boundary of the Sub-Districts of Jenin and Beisan at a point northeast of Nuris. Thence it proceeds first northwestwards to a point due north of the built-up area of Zie'in and then westwards to the Afula-Jenin railway, thence north-westwards along the District boundary line to the point of intersection on the Hejaz railway. From here the boundary runs southwestwards, including the built-up area and some of the land of the village of Kh. Lid in the Arab State to cross the Haifa-Jenin road at a point on the district boundary between Haifa and Samaria west of El-Mansi. It follows this boundary to the southernmost point of the village of El-Buteimat. From here it follows the northern and eastern boundaries of the village of Arara rejoining the Haifa-Samaria district boundary at Wadi 'Ara, and thence proceeding south-south-westwards in an approximately straight line joining up with the western boundary of Qaqun to a point east of the railway line on the eastern boundary of Qaqun village. From here it runs along the railway line some distance to the east of it to a point just east of the Tulkarm railway station. Thence the boundary follows a line half-way between the railway and the Tulkarm-Qalqiliya-Jaljuliya and Ras El-Ein road to a point just east of Ras El-Ein station, whence it proceeds along the railway some distance to the east of it to the point on the railway line south of the junction of the Haifa-Lydda and Beit Nabala lines, whence it proceeds along the southern border of Lydda airport to its south-west corner, thence in a south-westerly direction to a point just west of the built-up area of Sarafand El 'Amar, whence it turns south, passing just to the west of the built-up area of Abu El-Fadil to the north-east corner of the lands of Beer Ya'aqov. (The boundary line should be so demarcated as to allow direct access from the Arab State to the airport.) Thence the boundary line follows the western and southern boundaries of Ramle village, to the north-east corner of El Na'ana village, thence in a straight line to the southernmost point of El Barriya, along the eastern boundary of that village and the southern boundary of Innaba village. Thence it turns north to follow the southern side of the Jaffa-Jerusalem road until El-Qubab, whence it follows the road to the boundary of Abu-Shusha. It runs along the eastern boundaries of Abu Shusha, Seidun, Hulda to the southernmost point of Hulda, thence westwards in a straight line to the north-eastern corner of Umm Kalkha, thence following the northern boundaries of Umm Kalkha, Qazaza and the northern and western boundaries of Mukhezin to the Gaza District boundary and thence runs across the village lands of El-Mismiya El-Kabira, and Yasur to the southern point of intersection, which is midway between the built-up areas of Yasur and Batani Sharqi.

From the southern point of intersection the boundary lines run north-westwards between the villages of Gan Yavne and Barqa to the sea at a point half-way between Nabi Yunis and Minat El-Qila, and south-eastwards to a point west of Qastina, whence it turns in a south-westerly direction, passing to the east of the built-up areas of Es Sawafir Esh Sharqiya and Ibdis. From the south-east corner of 'Ibdis village it runs to a point southwest of the built-up area of Beit 'Affa, crossing the Hebron-El-Majdal road just to the west of the built-up area of Iraq Suweidan. Thence it proceeds southward along the western village boundary of El-Faluja to the Beersheba Sub-District boundary. It then runs across the tribal lands of 'Arab El-Jubarat to a point on the boundary between the Sub-Districts of Beersheba and Hebron north of Kh. Khuweilifa, whence it proceeds in a south-westerly direction to a point on the Beersheba-Gaza main road two kilometres to the north-west of the town. It then turns south-eastwards to reach Wadi Sab' at a point situated one kilometer to the west of it. From here it turns north-eastwards and proceeds along Wadi Sab' and along the Beersheba-Hebron road for a distance of one kilometer, whence it turns eastwards and runs in a straight line to Kh. Kuseifa to join the Beersheba-Hebron Sub-District boundary. It then follows the Beersheba-Hebron boundary eastwards to a point north of Ras Ez-Zuweira, only departing from it so as to cut across the base of the indentation between vertical grid lines 150 and 160.

About five kilometres north-east of Ras Ez-Zuweira it turns north, excluding from the Arab State a strip along the coast of the Dead Sea not more than seven kilometres in depth, as far as 'Ein Geddi, whence it turns due east to join the Transjordan frontier in the Dead Sea.

The northern boundary of the Arab section of the coastal plain runs from a point between Minat El-Qila and Nabi Yunis, passing between the built-up areas of Gan Yavne and Barqa to the point of intersection. From here it turns south-westwards, running across the lands of Batani Sharqi, along the eastern boundary of the lands of Beit Daras and across the lands of Julis, leaving the built-up areas of Batani Sharqi and Julis to the westwards, as far as the north-west corner of the lands of Beit-Tima. Thence it runs east of El-Jiya across the village lands of El-Barbara along the eastern boundaries of the villages of Beit Jirja, Deir Suneid and Dimra. From the south-east corner of Dimra the boundary passes across the lands of Beit Hanun, leaving the Jewish lands of Nir-Am to the eastwards. From the south-east corner of Beit Hanun the line runs south-west to a point south of the parallel grid line 100, then turns north-west for two kilometres, turning again in a southwesterly direction and continuing in an almost straight line to the north-west corner of the village lands of Kirbet Ikhza'a. From there it follows the boundary line of this village to its southernmost point. It then runs in a southerly direction along the vertical grid line 90 to its junction with the horizontal grid line 70. It then turns south-eastwards to Kh. El-Ruheiba and then proceeds in a southerly direction to a point known as El-Baha, beyond which it crosses the Beersheba-El 'Auja main road to the west of Kh. El-Mushrifa. From there it joins Wadi El-Zaiyatin just to the west of El-Subeita. From there it turns to the north-east and then to the south-east following this Wadi and passes to the east of 'Abda to join Wadi Nafkh. It then bulges to the south-west along Wadi Nafkh, Wadi 'Ajrim and Wadi Lassan to the point where Wadi Lassan crosses the Egyptian frontier.

The area of the Arab enclave of Jaffa consists of that part of the town-planning area of Jaffa which lies to the west of the Jewish quarters lying south of Tel-Aviv, to the west of the continuation of Herzl street up to its junction with the Jaffa-Jerusalem road, to the south-west of the section of the Jaffa-Jerusalem road lying south-east of that junction, to the west of Miqve Yisrael lands, to the northwest of Holon local council area, to the north of the line linking up the north-west corner of Holon with the northeast corner of Bat Yam local council area and to the north of Bat Yam local council area. The question of Karton quarter will be decided by the Boundary Commission, bearing in mind among other considerations the desirability of including the smallest possible number of its Arab inhabitants and the largest possible number of its Jewish inhabitants in the Jewish State.

B. The Jewish State

The north-eastern sector of the Jewish State (Eastern Galilee) is bounded on the north and west by the Lebanese frontier and on the east by the frontiers of Syria and Trans-jordan. It includes the whole of the Huleh Basin, Lake Tiberias, the whole of the Beisan Sub-District, the boundary line being extended to the crest of the Gilboa mountains and the Wadi Malih. From there the Jewish State extends north-west, following the boundary described in respect of the Arab State. The Jewish section of the coastal plain extends from a point between Minat El-Qila and Nabi Yunis in the Gaza Sub-District and includes the towns of Haifa and Tel-Aviv, leaving Jaffa as an enclave of the Arab State. The eastern frontier of the Jewish State follows the boundary described in respect of the Arab State.

The Beersheba area comprises the whole of the Beersheba Sub-District, including the Negeb and the eastern part of the Gaza Sub-District, but excluding the town of Beersheba and those areas described in respect of the Arab State. It includes also a strip of land along the Dead Sea stretching from the Beersheba-Hebron Sub-District boundary line to 'Ein Geddi, as described in respect of the Arab State.

C. The City of Jerusalem

The boundaries of the City of Jerusalem are as defined in the recommendations on the City of Jerusalem. (See Part III, section B, below.)

Part III. City of Jerusalem (5)

A. Special Regime

The City of Jerusalem shall be established as a corpus separatum under a special international regime and shall be administered by the United Nations. The Trusteeship Council shall be designated to discharge the responsibilities of the Administering Authority on behalf of the United Nations.

B. Boundaries of the City

The City of Jerusalem shall include the present municipality of Jerusalem plus the surrounding villages and towns, the most eastern of which shall be Abu Dis; the most southern, Bethlehem; the most western, 'Ein Karim (including also the built-up area of Motsa); and the most northern Shu'fat, as indicated on the attached sketch-map (annex B).

ADOPTED AT THE 128TH PLENARY MEETING:

In favour: 33

Australia, Belgium, Bolivia, Brazil, Byelorussian S.S.R., Canada, Costa Rica, Czechoslovakia, Denmark, Dominican Republic, Ecuador, France, Guatemala, Haiti, Iceland, Liberia, Luxemburg, Netherlands, New Zealand, Nicaragua, Norway, Panama, Paraguay, Peru, Philippines, Poland, Sweden, Ukrainian S.S.R., Union of South Africa, U.S.A., U.S.S.R., Uruguay, Venezuela.

Against: 13

Afghanistan, Cuba, Egypt, Greece, India, Iran, Iraq, Lebanon, Pakistan, Saudi Arabia, Syria, Turkey, Yemen.

Abstained: 10

Argentina, Chile, China, Colombia, El Salvador, Ethiopia, Honduras, Mexico, United Kingdom, Yugoslavia.

---

http://www.yale.edu/lawweb/avalon/un/res181.htm (accessed February 1, 2006).

United Nations General Assembly Resolution 194 (111) (December 11, 1948)

The General Assembly, Having considered further the situation in Palestine, 1. Expresses its deep appreciation of the progress achieved through the good offices of the late United Nations Mediator in promoting a peaceful adjustment of the future situation of Palestine, for which cause he sacrificed his life; and Extends its thanks to the Acting Mediator and his staff for their continued efforts and devotion to duty in Palestine; 2. Establishes a Conciliation Commission consisting of three States Members of the United Nations which shall have the following functions: (a) To assume, in so far as it considers necessary in existing circumstances, the functions given to the United Nations Mediator on Palestine by the resolution of the General Assembly of 14 May 1948; (b) To carry out the specific functions and directives given to it by the present resolution and such additional functions and directives as may be given to it by the General Assembly or by the Security Council; (c) To undertake, upon the request of the Security Council, any of the functions now assigned to the United Nations Mediator on Palestine or to the United Nations Truce Commission by resolutions of the Security Council; upon such request to the Conciliation Commission by the Security Council with respect to all the remaining functions of the United Nations Mediator on Palestine under Security Council resolutions, the office of the Mediator shall be terminated; 3. Decides that a Committee of the Assembly, consisting of China, France, the Union of Soviet Socialist Republics, the United Kingdom and the United States of America, shall present, before the end of the first part of the present session of the General Assembly, for the approval of the Assembly a proposal concerning the names of the three States which will constitute the Conciliation Commission; 4. Requests the Commission to begin its functions at once, with a view to the establishment of contact between the parties themselves and the Commission at the earliest possible date; 5. Calls upon the Governments and authorities concerned to extend the scope of the negotiations provided for in the Security Council's resolution of 16 November 1948 and to seek agreement by negotiations conducted either with the Conciliation Commission or directly with a view to the final settlement of all questions outstanding between them; 6. Instructs the Conciliation Commission to take steps to assist the Governments and authorities concerned to achieve a final settlement of all questions outstanding between them; 7. Resolves that the Holy Places—including Nazareth—religious buildings and sites in Palestine should be protected and free access to them assured, in accordance with existing rights and historical practice; that arrangements to this end should be under effective United Nations supervision; that the United Nations Conciliation Commission, in presenting to the fourth regular session of the General Assembly its detailed proposal for a permanent international regime for the territory of Jerusalem, should include recommendations concerning the Holy Places in that territory; that with regard to the Holy Places in the rest of Palestine the Commission should call upon the political authorities of the areas concerned to give appropriate formal guarantees as to the protection of the Holy Places and access to them; and that these undertakings should be presented to the General Assembly for approval; 8. Resolves that, in view of its association with three world religions, the Jerusalem area, including the present municipality of Jerusalem plus the surrounding villages and towns, the most Eastern of which shall be Abu Dis the most Southern, Bethlehem; the most Western, Ein Karim (including also the built-up area of Motsa); and the most Northern Shu'fat, should be accorded special and separate treatment from the rest of Palestine and should be placed under effective United Nations control; Requests the Security Council to take further steps to ensure the demilitarization of Jerusalem at the earliest possible date; Instructs the Conciliation Commission to present to the fourth regular session of the General Assembly detailed proposals for a permanent international regime for the Jerusalem area which will provide for the maximum local autonomy for distinctive groups consistent with the special international status of the Jerusalem area; The Conciliation Commission is authorized to appoint a United Nations representative who shall cooperate with the local authorities with respect to the interim administration of the Jerusalem area; 9. Resolves that, pending agreement on more detailed arrangements among the Governments and authorities concerned, the freest possible access to Jerusalem by road, rail or air should be accorded to all inhabitants of Palestine; Instructs the Conciliation Commission to report immediately to the Security Council, for appropriate action by that organ, any attempt by any party to impede such access; 10. Instructs the Conciliation Commission to seek arrangements among the Governments and authorities concerned which will facilitate the economic development of the area, including arrangements for access to ports and airfields and the use of transportation and communication facilities; 11. Resolves that the refugees wishing to return to their homes and live at peace with their neighbours should be permitted to do so at the earliest practicable date, and that compensation should be paid for the property of those choosing not to return and for loss of or damage to property which, under principles of international law or in equity, should be made good by the Governments or authorities responsible; Instructs the Conciliation Commission to facilitate the repatriation, resettlement and economic and social rehabilitation of the refugees and the payment of compensation, and to maintain close relations with the Director of the United Nations Relief for Palestine Refugees and, through him, with the appropriate organs and agencies of the United Nations; 12. Authorizes the Conciliation Commission to appoint such subsidiary bodies and to employ such technical experts, acting under its authority, as it may find necessary for the effective discharge of its functions and responsibilities under the present resolution; The Conciliation Commission will have its official headquarters at Jerusalem. The authorities responsible for maintaining order in Jerusalem will be responsible for taking all measures necessary to ensure the security of the Commission. The Secretary-General will provide a limited number of guards for the protection of the staff and premises of the Commission; 13. Instructs the Conciliation Commission to render progress reports periodically to the Secretary-General for transmission to the Security Council and to the Members of the United Nations; 14. Calls Upon all Governments and authorities concerned to cooperate with the Conciliation Commission and to take all possible steps to assist in the implementation of the present resolution; 15. Requests the Secretary-General to provide the necessary staff and facilities and to make appropriate arrangements to provide the necessary funds required in carrying out the terms of the present resolution.

Bernard Reich, ed., *Arab–Israeli Conflict and Conciliation: A Documentary History* (Westport, CT: Praeger, 1995), 79–81.

Testimony on Palestinian Arab Reaction to the UNSCOP Proposals to the UN Ad Hoc Committee on the Palestinian Question

Jamal al-Husseini, Head of Arab Higher Committee

September 29, 1947

The case of the Arabs of Palestine was based on the principles of international justice; it was that of a people which desired to live in undisturbed possession of the country where Providence and history had placed it. The Arabs of Palestine could not understand why their right to live in freedom and peace, and to develop their country in accordance with their traditions, should be questioned and constantly submitted to investigation.

One thing was clear: it was the sacred duty of the Arabs of Palestine to defend their country against all aggression. The Zionists were conducting an aggressive campaign with the object of securing by force a country which was not theirs by birthright. Thus there was self-defence on one side and, on the other, aggression. The raison d'etre of the United Nations was to assist self-defence against aggression.

The rights and patrimony of the Arabs in Palestine had been the subject of no less than eighteen investigations within twenty-five years, and all to no purpose. Such commissions of inquiry had made recommendations that had either reduced the national and legal rights of the Palestine Arabs or glossed them over. The few recommendations favourable to the Arabs had been ignored by the Mandatory Power. It was hardly strange, therefore, that they should have been unwilling to take part in a nineteenth investigation. . . .

The struggle of the Arabs in Palestine had nothing in common with anti-Semitism. The Arab world had been one of the rare havens of refuge for the Jews until the atmosphere of neighbourliness had been poisoned by the Balfour Declaration and the aggressive spirit the latter had engendered in the Jewish community. . . .

Mr. Husseini disputed three claims of world Jewry. The claim to Palestine based on historical association was a movement on the part of the Ashkenazim, whose forefathers had no connexion with Palestine. The Sephardim, the main descendants of Israel, had mostly denounced Zionism. Secondly, the religious connexion of the Zionists with Palestine, which he noted was shared by Moslems and Christians, gave them no secular claim to the country. Freedom of access to the Holy Places was universally accepted. Thirdly, the Zionists claimed the establishment of a Jewish National Home by virtue of the Balfour Declaration. But the British Government had had no right to dispose of Palestine which it had occupied in the name of the Allies as a liberator and not as a conqueror. The Balfour Declaration was in contradiction with the Covenant of the League of Nations and was an immoral, unjust and illegal promise.

The solution lay in the Charter of the United Nations, in accordance with which the Arabs of Palestine, who constituted the majority, were entitled to a free and independent State. . . .

Once Palestine was found to be entitled to independence, the United Nations was not legally competent to decide or to impose the constitutional organization of Palestine, since such action would amount to interference with an internal matter of an independent nation. . . .

In conclusion, Mr. Husseini said that he had not commented on the Special Committee's report because the Arab Higher Committee considered that it could not be a basis for discussion. Both schemes proposed in the report were inconsistent with the United Nations Charter and with the Covenant [sic] League of Nations. The Arabs of Palestine were solidly determined to oppose with all the means at their command any scheme which provided for the dissection, segregation or partition of their country or which gave to a minority special and preferential rights or status. Although they fully realised that big Powers could crush such opposition by brute force, the Arabs nevertheless would not be deterred, but would lawfully defend with their life-blood every inch of the soil of their beloved country.

UNO Ad Hoc Committee on the
Palestinian Question, third meeting

T. G. Fraser, *The Middle East, 1914–1979* (London: Edward Arnold, 1980), 49–51.

Declaration of Israel's Independence 1948

Issued at Tel Aviv on May 14, 1948 (5th of Iyar, 5708)

ERETZ-ISRAEL [(Hebrew)—The Land of Israel] was the birthplace of the Jewish people. Here their spiritual, religious and political identity was shaped. Here they first attained to statehood, created cultural values of national and universal significance and gave to the world the eternal Book of Books.

After being forcibly exiled from their land, the people remained faithful to it throughout their Dispersion and never ceased to pray and hope for their return to it and for the restoration in it of their political freedom.

Impelled by this historic and traditional attachment, Jews strove in every successive generation to re-establish themselves in their ancient homeland. In recent decades they returned in their masses. Pioneers, ma'pilim [(Hebrew)—immigrants coming to Eretz-Israel in defiance of restrictive legislation] and defenders, they made deserts bloom, revived the Hebrew language, built villages and towns, and created a thriving community controlling its own economy and culture, loving peace but knowing how to defend itself, bringing the blessings of progress to all the country's inhabitants, and aspiring towards independent nationhood.

In the year 5657 (1897), at the summons of the spiritual father of the Jewish State, Theodore Herzl, the First Zionist Congress convened and proclaimed the right of the Jewish people to national rebirth in its own country.

This right was recognized in the Balfour Declaration of the 2nd November, 1917, and re-affirmed in the Mandate of the League of Nations which, in particular, gave international sanction to the historic connection between the Jewish people and Eretz-Israel and to the right of the Jewish people to rebuild its National Home.

The catastrophe which recently befell the Jewish people—the massacre of millions of Jews in Europe—was another clear demonstration of the urgency of solving the problem of its homelessness by re-establishing in Eretz-Israel the Jewish State, which would open the gates of the homeland wide to every Jew and confer upon the Jewish people the status of a fully privileged member of the comity of nations.

Survivors of the Nazi holocaust in Europe, as well as Jews from other parts of the world, continued to migrate to Eretz-Israel, undaunted by difficulties, restrictions and dangers, and never ceased to assert their right to a life of dignity, freedom and honest toil in their national homeland.

In the Second World War, the Jewish community of this country contributed its full share to the struggle of the freedom- and peace-loving nations against the forces of Nazi wickedness and, by the blood of its soldiers and its war effort, gained the right to be reckoned among the peoples who founded the United Nations.

On the 29th November, 1947, the United Nations General Assembly passed a resolution calling for the establishment of a Jewish State in Eretz-Israel; the General Assembly required the inhabitants of Eretz-Israel to take such steps as were necessary on their part for the implementation of that resolution. This recognition by the United Nations of the right of the Jewish people to establish their State is irrevocable.

This right is the natural right of the Jewish people to be masters of their own fate, like all other nations, in their own sovereign State.

ACCORDINGLY WE, MEMBERS OF THE PEOPLE'S COUNCIL, REPRESENTATIVES OF THE JEWISH COMMUNITY OF ERETZ-ISRAEL AND OF THE ZIONIST MOVEMENT, ARE HERE ASSEMBLED ON THE DAY OF THE TERMINATION OF THE BRITISH MANDATE OVER ERETZ-ISRAEL AND, BY VIRTUE OF OUR NATURAL AND HISTORIC RIGHT AND ON THE STRENGTH OF THE RESOLUTION OF THE UNITED NATIONS GENERAL ASSEMBLY, HEREBY DECLARE THE ESTABLISHMENT OF A JEWISH STATE IN ERETZ-ISRAEL, TO BE KNOWN AS THE STATE OF ISRAEL.

WE DECLARE that, with effect from the moment of the termination of the Mandate being tonight, the eve of Sabbath, the 6th Iyar, 5708 (15th May, 1948), until the establishment of the elected, regular authorities of the State in accordance with the Constitution which shall be adopted by the Elected Constituent Assembly not later than the 1st October 1948, the People's Council shall act as a Provisional Council of State, and its executive organ, the People's Administration, shall be the Provisional Government of the Jewish State, to be called "Israel".

THE STATE OF ISRAEL will be open for Jewish immigration and for the Ingathering of the Exiles; it will foster the development of the country for the benefit of all its inhabitants; it will be based on freedom, justice and peace as envisaged by the prophets of Israel; it will ensure complete equality of social and political rights to all its inhabitants irrespective of religion, race or sex; it will guarantee freedom of religion, conscience, language, education and culture; it will safeguard the Holy Places of all religions; and it will be faithful to the principles of the Charter of the United Nations.

THE STATE OF ISRAEL is prepared to cooperate with the agencies and representatives of the United Nations in implementing the resolution of the General Assembly of the 29th November, 1947, and will take steps to bring about the economic union of the whole of Eretz-Israel.

WE APPEAL to the United Nations to assist the Jewish people in the building-up of its State and to receive the State of Israel into the comity of nations.

WE APPEAL—in the very midst of the onslaught launched against us now for months—to the Arab inhabitants of the State of Israel to preserve peace and participate in the upbuilding of the State on the basis of full and equal citizenship and due representation in all its provisional and permanent institutions.

WE EXTEND our hand to all neighboring states and their peoples in an offer of peace and good neighborliness, and appeal to them to establish bonds of cooperation and mutual help with the sovereign Jewish people settled in its own land. The State of Israel is prepared to do its share in a common effort for the advancement of the entire Middle East.

WE APPEAL to the Jewish people throughout the Diaspora to rally round the Jews of Eretz-Israel in the tasks of immigration and upbuilding and to stand by them in the great struggle for the realization of the age-old dream—the redemption of Israel.

PLACING OUR TRUST IN THE ALMIGHTY, WE AFFIX OUR SIGNATURES TO THIS PROCLAMATION AT THIS SESSION OF THE PROVISIONAL COUNCIL OF STATE, ON THE SOIL OF THE HOMELAND, IN THE CITY OF TEL-AVIV, ON THIS SABBATH EVE, THE 5TH DAY OF IYAR, 5708 (14TH MAY, 1948).

David Ben-Gurion
Daniel Auster
Mordekhai Bentov

Yitzchak Ben Zvi
Eliyahu Berligne
Fritz Bernstein
Rabbi Wolf Gold
Meir Grabovsky
Yitzchak Gruenbaum
Dr. Abraham Granovsky
Eliyahu Dobkin
Meir Wilner-Kovner
Zerach Wahrhaftig
Herzl Vardi Rachel Cohen
Rabbi Kalman Kahana
Saadia Kobashi
Rabbi Yitzchak Meir Levin
Meir David Loewenstein
Zvi Luria
Golda Myerson
Nachum Nir
Zvi Segal
Rabbi Yehuda Leib Hacohen Fishman
David Zvi Pinkas
Aharon Zisling
Moshe Kolodny
Eliezer Kaplan
Abraham Katznelson
Felix Rosenblueth
David Remez
Berl Repetur
Mordekhai Shattner
Ben Zion Sternberg
Bekhor Shitreet
Moshe Shapira
Moshe Shertok

---

http://www.yale.edu/lawweb/avalon/mideast/israel.htm (accessed February 1, 2006).

Six
COLD WARS AND THE MIDDLE EAST MATRIX

Given the fact that the first Arab–Israeli war ended with the signing of armistice agreements and not peace treaties, the unleashing of Arab–Israel enmity as a result of the conflagration, and the existence of a burgeoning Palestinian refugee problem, it would not have been difficult to find those who believed that there would be an early resumption of the conflict, i.e., another war within the next few years. The "next" Arab–Israeli war, in fact, would not occur until the 1956 Suez episode, and even this war was precipitated as much by external machination (British and French) and regional politics as by the Arab–Israeli dynamic. But there were a number of intervening processes at work at the domestic, regional, and international levels in the Middle East that tended to focus the potential Arab–Israeli combatants' attentions away from each other toward more immediate goals, tasks, and concerns.

In general, the 1950s might be the most complex decade in modern Middle East history, with compelling forces at the domestic, regional, and international levels coming into play in the region, creating an almost incomprehensible multidimensional matrix that is almost as difficult to decipher in retrospect as it was at the time. In the immediate post-World War II period, there was the European decolonization movement combined with the rise of Third World nationalisms. A number of Arab states—and Israel—had recently escaped or were in the process of escaping from the shackles of imperial control and had embarked on what became for the most part a painful journey toward true independence and state-building. Focusing more international attention on the region was the increasing share of world oil production coming from the Middle East as well as its share of estimated world oil reserves. From 16.7%

of world oil production in 1950, the Middle East's share rose to 21.2% by 1955; in addition, its estimated oil reserves rose from 45% of the world total in 1950 to 75% in 1956.[1] Finally, superimposed on all of this was the emerging superpower cold war between the United States and the Soviet Union, a battle that increasingly began to be fought by proxy in the Third World. And winding its way into the jetties created by these turbulent waters was the Arab–Israeli conflict, quickly becoming a legitimate dimension in and of itself, affecting in a direct way the other levels of the Middle East matrix.

ISRAELIS AND PALESTINIANS IN THE AFTERMATH OF WAR

In essence, both sides to this new Arab–Israeli conflict were regrouping and dealing with the myriad of consequences that resulted from the 1947–1949 war. On the Arab side there existed, as one might expect, a great deal of turmoil. The respective governments' abject failure in the war was the last straw for a restive population and a plethora of ideologically driven groups such as the Ba'th party in Syria and the Free Officers movement in Egypt. The ineptitude of the corrupt regimes was finally revealed in all its ingloriousness, and they could no longer get away with any more excuses for the maldistribution of wealth, the political disenfranchisement of broad swaths of the population, and the perceived servitude to the Western powers. Political change was the order of the day. There were three military coups in Syria in 1949 alone. Prime ministers in Lebanon and in Egypt were assassinated in 1949; the latter case served as a foreshadowing of the coup in July 1952 that would overthrow the monarchy. King Abdullah, perhaps, was seen as the most self-serving and opportunist of Arab leaders in the aftermath of the first Arab–Israeli war. As a further blow to the Palestinians, in April 1950 Transjordan annexed the West Bank and East Jerusalem, and its name was thenceforth changed to the Hashemite Kingdom of Jordan. An independent Palestinian state was thus out of the question for the foreseeable future. Abdullah actually issued a royal decree in March 1950 outlawing the use of the word "Palestine" in official documents, thus giving more unofficial sanction to the use of the terms "East Bank" and "West Bank" to describe the territory in question.[2] He had also begun secret talks with Israeli officials in November 1949, discussing an Israeli–Jordanian peace treaty and, barring that, at least a nonaggression pact. Before things could get too far, however, word of the talks leaked out, with the Arab League threatening to expel Jordan—the talks then broke off.[3] While publicly maintaining that he remained committed to a just settlement of the Palestine question, the criticism continued to mount. Finally, on July 20, 1951, on the steps of the al-Aqsa Mosque in Jerusalem, he was shot dead by a Palestinian who apparently was connected with Hajj Amin al-Husayni and other Palestinians who had opposed the Jordanian monarch.[4] Early on it became evident that veering away from supporting what had become the Palestinian cause in the Arab world could be very damaging politically and potentially lethal. Abdullah was briefly succeeded by his son Talal, but because of a mental illness that some have described as schizophrenia, he was soon deposed by parliament, with his son Prince Hussein ibn Talal becoming king on August 11, 1952, at the age of sixteen. King Hussein would rule until his death from cancer in February 1999.

For Israel, it was a triumphant period in the immediate aftermath of the 1947–1949 war: the dream of a Jewish state had come to pass. This sense of accomplishment, however, soon gave way to the very real challenges that faced the young state, one that was bred out of violence and now had to face these challenges in a very hostile environment. Given the nature of the Zionist movement and its leadership, it was to be expected that the new state would be patterned along the lines of a secular democracy. As such, a parliamentary system was established, with the unicameral Knesset as the legislative body, with its first meeting in West Jerusalem in December 1949.[5] The Knesset consisted of 120 elected representatives, but these representatives ran on political party slates rather than individually from certain districts, states, or provinces, the membership of each party being determined by an intraparty selection system. Coalition-building thus became a sine qua non of Israeli political life because no single party has ever been able to acquire a majority of the 120 seats on its own. The political institutions of the state revolved around a centralized cabinet with a strong prime minister, and certainly David Ben-Gurion, as the founding father of the Israeli state and the first prime minister, was a very strong and active leader of state; indeed, he was essentially the most powerful political figure in Israel through the early 1960s regardless of whether or not he was in office as prime minister. An office of the president was created as well, but it was largely ceremonial, the first occupant being none other than Chaim Weizmann. The Israeli political scene was dominated by Ben-Gurion's Mapai party (later the Labor party in 1965) until the mid-1970s. This does not mean, however, that there were no other influential parties. Spanning the spectrum from the religious orthodox to leftist Arab, political parties took many shapes and sizes, adopting disparate and often very narrow political agendas. But the nature of Israel's political system necessitated coalition-building in order for the largest parties to achieve a majority in the Knesset. This gave smaller parties disproportionate influence upon political platforms of a ruling government because their support was needed to build this majority. This occurred most often with the Jewish orthodox parties in Israel, which on the surface would seem to be the complete polar opposite of the secular, socialist Mapai party. But with certain compromises, especially in the areas of personal and family law, observance, and defining who is and who is not a Jew, the religious parties were able to wrestle away a number of concessions while giving in on (or not getting in the way of) larger economic, political, and foreign policy issues important to Mapai/Labor or later to the secular right-of-center party Likud, which emerged from the Herut party (itself largely composed of former members of Irgun, led by Menachem Begin in the Knesset).[6] This usually meant the assignment of portfolios to these smaller parties in the cabinet, usually in the sociocultural arena such as education. Thus, the duality of the Israeli state, the secular versus the religious, has never been far from the surface and, indeed, has really not been settled in its entirety. Was this really a Jewish state in practice as well as faith, or was it simply a state for the Jews? Regardless of where one stood on this question, there was virtual unanimity in the belief that Israel was a home for Jews worldwide if they chose to immigrate, especially in light of the Holocaust. As a result, the Law of Return was promulgated in 1950, which established the right of any Jew across the globe to immigrate to Israel. The Jewish population in Israel subsequently increased from about 650,000 to over 1.3 million from 1948 to 1951 as over 680,000 immigrants poured into the country.[7] About half of these immigrants were of Eastern European origin (Ashkenazi or European Jews), many of whom were displaced persons/refugees from World War II, and the other half immigrated from Arab countries (the Oriental or Sephardic Jews).[8] The Sephardic Jews immigrated en masse to Israel following the first Arab–Israeli war in response to real and expected pressure from the majority Arab populations in their countries of origin as well as a very active and effective Israeli campaign to attract them to the country. As such, however, Sephardic and Ashkenazi Jews often differed quite dramatically linguistically, ethnically, economically, and socioculturally. They tended to drift toward different political blocs that better represented their own interests: the Ashkenazi more identified as time went on with the European Jewish–dominated Labor party, while the Sephardic Jews tended to gravitate toward Likud, which actively courted them as well as other more economically disadvantaged Jews in Israel in order to better compete with Labor in the electoral process.

What is interesting is that despite the varied origins of the Israeli population and the relatively recent attempts at constructing a Hebrew identity, the country was able to forge out of all of this a national purpose and cohesiveness missing from many Arab countries that had considerably more history and ethnolinguistic homogeneity behind them. Part of the reason for this may be, in fact, the threatening environment in which Israel came into being, which persisted for well over thirty years, i.e., until its existence was no longer in question following the spectacular military victory in 1967 and the 1979 Egyptian–Israeli peace treaty, which removed the Jewish state's primary threat from the equation. The perceived constant threat to their survival, coming on the heels of the Holocaust, and existing in an isolated island in a sea of hostility forged a unity and common purpose that may have been much more difficult to construct had Israel emerged in a more peaceful environment. It may be no surprise, then, that the fissures in Israeli society have, in part, manifested themselves more in recent years just as the country has solidified its place and the existential threats have receded from view.

For the Palestinians, the vast majority of refugees were settled in camps that were designed to be temporary abodes while waiting for a solution to the problem, one that centered around Palestinian repatriation to what was now Israel. But with a massive influx of Jewish immigrants of its own (many of whom settled in the very homes and villages that Palestinians had evacuated), the continued fear of an Arab fifth column in the country, and the persistent ethos of socialist Zionism that demanded the Jewish character of the state, Israel was not about to consent to a repatriation of Palestinian refugees of any appreciable number. Indeed, this became one of the main obstacles to a resolution of the Arab–Israeli conflict before other intractable issues were added to the mix after 1967, i.e., the inability to bridge the vast gap in the number of Palestinian refugees that Israel would allow to be repatriated (usually in the neighborhood of 10,000–25,000) versus the amount sought by a variety of other parties (usually in the hundreds of thousands).

Most of the Arab states in which the refugee camps were located did the very least they could do to assist in the everyday lives of the Palestinians. The camps, initially aided by the Red Cross and Red Crescent societies, were soon run by the United Nations Relief and Works Agency (UNRWA), established in December 1949; but it was underbudgeted at first as it was never intended to last more than a short period of time—again, anticipating a resolution in the near future. UNRWA is still the overseeing organization for the refugee camps today. The camps quickly became hosts to squalor, poverty, and hopelessness. Some of the camps as time went on began to resemble villages, with utilities and a small semblance of an economy; but they never rose far above the dilapidated conditions under which they were formed. Other Palestinians who were better off financially, primarily because they were from prominent families in Palestine, were able to travel to other countries in the Arab world as well as to Europe and North America, where they obtained a solid education and carved out a middle- to upper-class existence. This Palestinian diaspora would soon take on a life of its own, consisting of varied classes, ideologies, and domesticities that would significantly affect the shape and nature of the Palestinian movement as it grew in the 1960s. It was only in Jordan that Palestinians were granted citizenship and integrated to a noticeable degree into society. In Egypt (Gaza Strip) and Lebanon, for instance, Palestinians were restricted in terms of employment and travel. The Arab states that received the bulk of the refugees tended to be wary of the Palestinians inciting conflict with Israel before they were ready for a confrontation; therefore, they had to be watched and controlled in their activities. In addition, many of these states had employment problems of their own and could ill-afford to absorb tens of thousands of Palestinians into the workforce. The land available for cultivation for their own growing populations was scarce to begin with, so as long as the United Nations (through donor countries, with the United States traditionally making the largest donation) was footing the bill, there was very little incentive to invest time and capital into the situation. Finally, particularly as the Palestinian problem became a political football regionally and often a useful device through which countries could express anti-Israeli sentiments, assimilating Palestinians into their societies might undermine the utility of the movement itself. As such, the Palestinians became completely dependent on the Arab states in which they resided, hoping that their new overlords could return them to Palestine now that they were publicly advocating the Palestinian cause. This dependent alienation, however, helped to preserve, reinforce, and expand a Palestinian identity. As Cleveland states, "Their lack of integration into their host societies and their confinement to the camps served to keep alive their identity as Palestinians and to nurture the idea that their refugee status could be terminated only by returning to Palestine."[9]

THE GREAT POWERS AND THE REGIONAL MATRIX

While Israel and the Arab states were dealing with the aftermath of their first war, the international community began to recognize that the simmering volatility of the situation could lead to another conflagration, something that no one wanted so soon upon the end of a world war. Toward this end, Great Britain, France, and the United States issued the Tripartite Declaration in May 1950, which opposed the use of force or threat to settle the Arab–Israeli dispute and offered immediate action independently or through the UN if any state sought to violate the armistice agreements; in essence, the declaration guaranteed the borders of Israel as demarcated under the 1949 armistice arrangements. Although it is difficult to assess how vigorously the three powers would have applied the principles of the declaration if there were attempts to violate it, it certainly dampened the possibility of an early resumption of an Arab–Israeli war simply for the fact that the Arab states had very little war-making capacity of their own and still relied heavily on British and French military supplies and training. One wonders, even in the midst of growing Soviet influence, how long the Tripartite Declaration would have helped to prevent an Arab–Israeli war if not for the fact that two of its signatories, Britain and France, violated it themselves in the 1956 Suez war. For the time being, however, the fact that following the 1947–1949 Arab–Israeli war there was a buildup of some 80,000 British troops stationed at the British Suez Canal Zone base acted as a powerful deterrent to Egyptian–Israeli hostilities; indeed, the Israelis viewed the British presence in Egypt, in an ironic twist, as a desirable and necessary buffer. Since Egypt was the most powerful and populous Arab state, as long as it was deterred, dormant, or turning its attentions elsewhere, an Arab war coalition arrayed against Israel was highly unlikely.

The instability in Egypt following the 1947–1949 war burst into flames in 1952 with the July 23 Egyptian Revolution that brought Gamal 'Abd al-Nasser and the Free Officers to power, sending King Farouk into exile. While this coup d'etat compelled Egypt to turn its attentions inward rather than toward Israel for the time being, it also brought to power a man and a movement that would soon become the biggest threat to the Jewish state.

The Free Officers formed the Revolutionary Command Council (RCC) as the ruling authority of the state, ostensibly led by popular General Muhammad Naguib as president; but Nasser was the orchestrating voice behind the scenes. Outside of Naguib, this was a group of mostly junior officers who had entered the military academy in Egypt in the 1930s following the lifting of certain entry restrictions. Until then, the academy had closed off a military career to all but the rich and landed; this created a military that was anything but professional. The Free Officers railed against corruption, which had so characterized the Farouk monarchy and the feudalist-controlled party structure embodied by the Wafd party.

The United States was not at all displeased with the July Revolution, and depending on which source one consults, Washington may have played a role in at least encouraging, if not sanctioning, the Free Officers' coup.[10] In addition to getting military people into the government in a decision-making capacity, thus gaining a better understanding of the military dimensions of the Soviet threat, it continued to nudge aside the British in Egypt by removing their assets and replacing them with leaders with whom Washington could more readily engage. The new Egyptian leaders were intent on implementing the type of reform that the United States believed was necessary in order to redirect capital away from the landed interests and toward more productive utilization in the industrial and commercial sectors. Washington felt that the dilapidated nature of the Farouk regime was more of a threat to Egyptian stability (and thus regional stability) in the long run. The change of regime, it was thought, might also allow for a fresh start in Anglo–Egyptian negotiations over the removal of British forces from Egypt. In any event, for the sake of regional stability, the United States was more than willing to put up with a military dictatorship, or what was called a "transitional authoritarian regime," until conditions evolved whereby the installation of democratic institutions could be attempted. Indeed, this was the rationalization of the Free Officers themselves for not immediately reinstituting a parliamentary system—Egypt simply was not ready for it, and any premature return could jeopardize the revolution itself.[11] The RCC believed that with political and economic stability, long-term objectives could be achieved: removing the British from Egyptian soil, reducing the power of the landed aristocracy, eliminating detrimental foreign interests and their local cohorts, and attaining regional stature. Notice there is no direct mention of Israel in this list. Indeed, the RCC, since it was not responsible for the 1948 debacle, did not feel compelled to immediately redress the issue, although its commitment to reform the military and make it an efficient fighting force was at least implicitly made in order to more successfully confront Israel in the future. In other words, the Free Officers regime in Egypt was taking care of its own house for the time being, trying to consolidate its hold on power and institute internal reforms that facilitated this objective.

Indeed, much of the Arab world was experiencing profound change, some of it from the tremendous increase in oil production in the 1950s that fed the economic boom in the United States and a reconstructed post-war Europe and some of it from the socialist-tinted ideological foundation that accompanied the transformation in the ruling structures from the old generation of rulers to the new. In many Arab states, the state apparatus (state capitalism) was seen as necessary to intervene in the making of national economic policy to combat the inequalities of the preexisting capitalist market–oriented economies.[12]

Because of the mandate system, when the British and French seemed just to trade places with the Ottomans with respect to economic decision making, many Arab states would have to wait until after World War II before they could actually begin to chart a new economic course and promote the state apparatus to a dominant position. This, however, did not preclude change from occurring in other spheres. The older generation of Arab leaders, primarily the monarchical families and landed aristocracy, had been discredited by World War II in the eyes of the younger generation of Arabs. These younger activists had become politically aware during the mandate period and saw their elders as corrupt and failing to deliver on their promise of true independence. The older generation of leaders were also seen to have been co-opted by the British and French and to be leading their countries economically toward what was termed "capitalist exhaustion."

What was rejected by this new generation, symbolized by such movements as the Ba'th and the Free Officers, was not only the ancien regimes in and of themselves but also, in many cases, their ideologies based on such western European imports as liberal constitutionalism and free-market capitalism. As someone once remarked, the leaders of the ancien regimes grew up quoting Voltaire, Locke, and Mill while their sons and daughters quoted Marx and Lenin (as well as Hegel and Nietzche on the other end of the political spectrum until fascism was discredited with the fall of Nazi Germany—or even the Qu'ran by some, such as Hassan al-Banna, the founder of the Muslim Brethren in Egypt in 1928). In a way, the Arab world is still searching for ideological constructs that will establish stable, relatively free political systems that are characterized by good governance and economic well-being. In the wake of the failure of socialist and capitalist paradigms (however imperfectly applied) have risen alternative ideologies to fill the void, particularly that of Islamic extremism, which in itself is simply a descendant of the Islamist response of the 1930s that has been transformed into a much more virulent strain with the accumulation of grievances and history.

The final straw for the ancien regimes was the humiliating defeat at the hands of Israel in 1948. It is this wave that many Arab leaders, such as Nasser, rode into the heart of Arab politics in the 1950s and 1960s. As Charles Issawi wrote in the early 1960s,

> In the last forty years, and more particularly in the last ten, three main shifts of power have taken place in the Middle East: from foreigners to nationals; from the landed interest to the industrial, financial, commercial and managerial interests; and from the private sector to the state.[13]

It was, of course, a well-intentioned process aimed at redistributing wealth and political power more equitably, ending reliance on outside powers, eliminating corruption, and restoring justice. This path of state capitalism was chosen by a number of countries in the developing world, not just in the Middle East. One of the first official acts of these new regimes after they came to power was land reform in order to undercut the influence and wealth of the landed aristocracy. As part of their social contract with the people (driven either by ideology in states such as Syria, Egypt, and Algeria or by oil in countries such as Saudi Arabia and Kuwait), these regimes promised to establish adequate safety nets; provide employment, education, and social services; and ensure political and economic equality.

As typically happened in many countries, what instead developed were bloated and inefficient public sectors that have for over four decades provided the support base for the ruling regimes. In the process, what was established was the classic "Bonapartist" state, where economic policy has been driven by regime survival, especially in a regional environment that was anything but a benevolent capitalist world order, producing inefficient and shrinking economies in the non-oil states at the same time there was a population explosion.[14] As time went on, the wealth funneled to the state as the capital accumulator became the source of patronage in erecting a pervasive and corrupt clientelist network, primarily in the military, bureaucracy, and other elements of society tied into the state apparatus. This is the structural and ideological paradigm from which many of these Arab countries are still trying to emerge today, with very little success.

Ironically, this period of relative calm through 1954 may have been the most propitious time for a comprehensive resolution of the Arab–Israeli conflict up to the flurry of diplomatic activity in the 1990s. Abdullah was not the only Arab leader considering peace with Israel. Husni al-Za'im, who led the first of three military coups in Syria in 1949, gave indications of seriously considering a peace treaty with Israel through his enhanced contacts with the United States. Za'im's overthrow less than five months later essentially squashed for the time being attempts to draw him into a peace agreement with Israel, one that would have been based on healthy amounts of U.S. economic and military aid to Syria, reflecting what would become a paradigm in U.S.–Arab relations, i.e., military and financial assistance in return for concessions on the Arab–Israeli front.[15] Nasser himself engaged in serious discussions with U.S. officials regarding peace with Israel in 1954 and early 1955, again usually predicated on unconditional military and economic aid from the United States and, in Egypt's case, a prior agreement with London that removed British troops from Egyptian soil.[16] All of this was before the accumulation of hostilities born from multiple wars, before vexing issues such as the Occupied Territories came into being, before the Palestinian question became cemented in Arab political psychology and exploited by Arab regional dynamics, before Nasser became Nasserism, before the Soviet Union started playing the anti-Israeli card to enhance its position in the Arab world, before the United States established its "special relationship" with Israel, and before the superpowers collectively entrapped the Middle East in its global zero sum cold war competition. This is possibly what Truman saw when making the decision to support the creation of the state of Israel, i.e., that the situation was not nearly as complicated as it would become and, thus, the possibility of resolving the dispute almost as soon as it started seemed viable.

TENSIONS RISE TOWARD WAR

When I wrote that there was relative quiescence on the Arab–Israeli front in the years 1949–1954, it was not to say that there was no Arab–Israeli violence. On the contrary, there was sustained low-level conflict all along the borders of Israel, but the overall regional atmosphere was not conducive to an eruption of an Arab–Israeli war along traditional lines during this span of time. Palestinians living in the refugee camps periodically carried out *fedayeen* (self-sacrificer) raids against Israeli villages and settlements across the border from the Arab countries in which they lived. They were often independently organized and arranged and took on a haphazard quality, but they were also from time to time encouraged and supported by Arab governments in an attempt to maintain the pressure on Israel, shore up their pro-Palestinian credentials to their own domestic audiences, and even help in extending control over disputed territory along the 1949 armistice lines. The UN established Mixed Armistice Committees (MACs) in 1949 for each of the Arab–Israeli frontiers to resolve the border disputes, although they only investigated problems and reported back to the UN with no enforcement capability. As such, Israel felt compelled to respond to these raids with reprisals of their own. Usually, the reprisal was far out of proportion to the act that precipitated it, primarily aimed at sending a strong message to the fedayeen as well as to the Arab host state, hoping to compel the host government to take action on its own to prevent the raids. This certainly fit in with what has been called "Ben-Gurionism," i.e., an activist, militaristic response to Arab hostility and intransigence, making it very clear that Israel was here to stay and could not be defeated; this being the case, the Arab states would have no choice but to come to terms with Israel along lines favorable to Tel Aviv.

An example of this type of Ben-Gurionism (even though Ben-Gurion himself had gone into self-imposed retirement in July 1953) was the Israeli response in October 1953 to a fedayeen raid that killed an Israeli mother and her two children. It was a response that, from the Israeli point of view, was necessary in order not to bleed a thousand wounds from the continuous pinpricks of fedayeen raids—Israel had to hit back and hit back hard. Led by Colonel Ariel Sharon, Unit 101, a special Israeli force, hit the Palestinian village of Qibya in Jordan on October 14–15, killing over fifty of the inhabitants and blowing up houses and other facilities. The timing of the Qibya incident was unfortunate in several ways. The United States was in serious discussions at that moment with Syrian President Adib al-Shishakli, who came to power in December 1949 in the third military coup in Damascus that year. In addition, Eric Johnston, a U.S. presidential envoy, was in the region to promote what was called the "Johnston plan." The Johnston plan, based on the Tennessee Valley Authority, was a project to irrigate the Jordan Valley through the redistribution of the Jordan River waters, which would allow for refugee resettlement, thus removing one of the main obstacles to an Arab–Israeli peace. Israel was at best lukewarm about the project. The Qibya raid elicited outrage throughout the Arab world and in the UN, thus severely complicating the efforts of Washington to secure an agreement with Syria as well as acquire Arab support for the Johnston plan. In fact, the United States, France, and Great Britain led the condemnation of Israel in the UN Security Council and agreed to express their "strong censure." The United States actually suspended all economic aid to Israel on October 20 as an expression of U.S. dissatisfaction with Israeli behavior, especially in the demilitarized zones delineated by the armistice agreements along the Jordanian and Syrian borders; however, Washington resumed economic aid a little over a week later after sufficient pressure from supporters of Israel in Congress.[17] Again, while these pinpricks against Israel and the Israeli reprisals were fairly consistent, they were not an existential threat to the Jewish state and actually were emblematic of the Arab states' unwillingness and inability to directly confront Israel. They did, however, maintain a level of tension in the Arab–Israeli arena as well as the attention of the international community to the problem. In addition, this raid–reprisal environment could quickly escalate into something much more dangerous.

Heightening tensions at a number of different levels in the Middle East far beyond the fedayeen raids was a series of related events that occurred from 1954 through 1956, culminating in the October–November 1956 Suez war. The first was an Anglo–Egyptian accord agreed to in the summer of 1954 (signed the following October) on the evacuation of British troops from the Suez Canal base by 1955. This was a victory for Nasser (who had sacked Naguib and formally assumed the presidency in 1954) as the legitimacy of the Free Officers and the RCC rested in large measure on removing the British. The accord was actually criticized by the Egyptian Muslim Brethren (MB), who had supported the Free Officers coup at first due to the shared anti-imperialist and antimonarchical interests. However, they also believed it was inadequate because the British retained a measure of influence in the country, particularly in reserving the right to militarily intervene in Egypt under certain circumstances. The MB actually attempted to assassinate Nasser in October 1954, after which the Egyptian regime ruthlessly cracked down on the Islamist group, imprisoning hundreds of members and executing those who were behind the assassination attempt. Israel also vehemently opposed the accord because it would remove the buffer of 80,000 British troops between itself and its primary threat in the Arab world. In addition, the Israelis knew the United States had been pressuring the British to negotiate an accord with Nasser so that Egypt would more likely participate in U.S. plans to construct a pro-West defense alliance in the Middle East to ward off Soviet encroachment. Even though Egypt's inclusion was the key to Washington's cold war containment defense schemes in the Middle East, Tel Aviv was adamantly opposed to any Arab state being in a position to acquire advanced military technology and aid from the West for fear that it might someday be used against Israel. The United States also believed that an Anglo–Egyptian accord had to precede any renewed attempts at an Arab–Israeli peace; in fact, Nasser had made this very clear. The Israelis were thus also concerned that a peace agreement might be imposed upon them by the United States and the combined weight of the international community. Indeed, within a few months after the accord was signed, the United States put forth the ill-fated Alpha plan, which attempted to resolve the Arab–Israeli conflict by pledging American assistance to three principal problems left unresolved at the end of the 1947–1949 war: the "tragic plight" of the Palestinian refugees; "the pall of fear that hangs over the Arab and Israel people alike"; and "the lack of fixed permanent boundaries between Israel and her neighbors."[18] To address these three issues, the Eisenhower administration proposed the creation of an international fund to enable Israel to pay compensation to the refugees, American assistance to adjust the armistice lines to acceptable boundaries, and a formal treaty engagement between the United States and the pertinent states in the area ensuring that neither side can "alter by force" the defined boundaries.[19]

The Israelis were so concerned about the developing situation that elements in the government attempted to sabotage the Anglo–Egyptian accord as well as torpedo any developing U.S.–Egyptian relationship in what became known as the "Lavon affair." Moshe Sharett, who had been foreign minister, became acting prime minister in July 1953 when Ben-Gurion entered into semiretirement on his desert kibbutz. He formally resigned the following December. This did not mean, however, that he did not have his hand in government policies, especially as Ben-Gurion acolytes such as military Chief of Staff Moshe Dayan and Defense Minister Pinhas Lavon both regarded Sharett with disdain. They believed Sharett was too accommodating and a weak prime minister, particularly as he advocated negotiations with Nasser—definitely not "Ben-Gurionism." In fact, the Qibya raid was a Dayan–Lavon enterprise with the approval of Ben-Gurion—Sharett was virtually shut out of the planning, and his objections to this type of reprisal in general were ignored. Lavon took this apparent leeway one step further. As stated earlier, the 1954 Anglo–Egyptian accord was looked upon with great consternation in Israel. Lavon was determined to scuttle the agreement before it was signed. He and the head of Israeli intelligence, again with the tacit approval of Ben-Gurion, assembled during the summer of 1954 an Israeli spy ring in Egypt made up of Egyptian-born Jews. They were tasked to carry out bombings of British and American embassy buildings as well as other facilities frequented by Westerners. The plan was to foment discord and chaos in Egypt, thus compelling the British to nix the accord and keep their troops in Egypt to maintain order. As an added bonus to Lavon, all of this might also stop in their tracks any momentum toward Egyptian–Israeli negotiations. A number of the conspirators were apprehended fairly quickly after the bombings and held for trial in December. Two were summarily executed in January 1955 despite pleas from the international community to commute the sentence. Nasser, though, having just survived an assassination attempt and having executed the MB perpetrators, believed he could not but follow through with the execution of the Israeli spies.

Since the truth was unknown to the Israeli public until 1960, outrage permeated the country, which demanded the government take action. They believed that Nasser had fabricated the charges just to redirect domestic pressures he was encountering in the wake of the accord with Britain as well as his tussles with the MB.[20] Calls for Ben-Gurion to return to the government intensified, and he complied by assuming the post of defense minister (in the wake of Lavon's resignation after a suspiciously incomplete investigation) on February 17, 1955. Less than two weeks later, on February 28, Ben-Gurion, in keeping with his own Ben-Gurionist policy prescription, launched the infamous Gaza raid.

In an attack against an Egyptian outpost, ostensibly in retaliation for fedayeen raids, two platoons of Israelis killed over forty Egyptian soldiers—the Israelis lost eight. This was definitely Ben-Gurionism at its finest (or worst depending upon one's perspective), especially since the Egyptian–Israeli border had been quite calm for at least two months preceding the raid. The effect of the raid was, however, profound. Nasser was humiliated by it, and it propelled him in a direction that he had been hesitant to travel until that point. This was the leader of a regime that had told the Egyptian population that it had reformed the military into a capable fighting instrument—the Gaza raid made it appear as if it was not. He had to do something to respond, or he risked being overthrown; remember, this is not yet the Nasser that became a virtual "god" in the inter-Arab arena—that would occur later, after Suez. This was still a Nasser that was tenuously in power, having just recently removed the popular Muhammad Naguib and survived an assassination attempt by elements of his own population. As such, Nasser began to sanction and support more actively fedayeen attacks into Israel from the Gaza Strip; in addition, he started to search for arms without the conditions the Americans were always trying to impose that would provide him with at least the appearance of the wherewithal to combat Israel. It would be a search that would lead him to the Soviet Union.

While tensions were rising between Israel and Egypt at the bilateral level, virtually simultaneously great power policies in the Middle East regarding pro-West defense pacts in the cold war began to reverberate regionally, heightening tensions even further. The idea for a pro-West defense pact in the Middle East had gone through several permutations, cutting across the Truman and Eisenhower administrations. Anglo–American ideas such as the Middle East Command and the Middle East Defense Organization, both of which envisioned Egypt as a key component, were basically still-born due to Egypt's understandable refusal to sign onto a defense pact that included the country (Britain) from which it was trying to completely break away. One finally did come into being, however, that did not include Egypt: the Baghdad Pact (officially CENTO, the Central Treaty Organization) that was culled together in February and March of 1955. To understand the origins of the Baghdad Pact, one must understand the strategic background of the emerging superpower cold war that would trickle down to the Middle East.

The Eisenhower administration came to power in January 1953 with the intention of implementing its New Look foreign policy in an attempt to correct what it viewed were the deficiencies inherent in the approach of the Truman administration as defined in the April 1950 policy paper commonly referred to as "NSC-68" (National Security Council Resolution 68). Containing the Soviet Union (and the People's Republic of China after the communist revolution in 1949) from expanding its influence beyond that which already existed was the paramount foreign policy objective in both administrations; however, the means by which this was to be accomplished changed when Dwight D. Eisenhower became president. This change had an important impact upon the Middle East, affecting the political dynamics that had already produced tensions in the area at the regional and domestic levels.

NSC-68 was loosely based on George F. Kennan's theory of containment of the Soviet Union and postulated that the United States should meet any communist advances anywhere in the world with a direct reciprocal response. U.S. entrance into the Korean War in June 1950 can be seen in this light. The Republican party, however, in the runup to the 1952 presidential elections castigated the Truman administration for "losing China" as well as what had become a stalemate in Korea. It accused Truman's strategic conception of giving the communists the initiative in fomenting trouble, requiring a costly American military posture in order to symmetrically respond to these advances in a timely fashion. The budget-conscious and economically conservative Republican platform in 1952 preached a foreign policy that would more effectively meet the communist threat at less cost. As former commander of the allied forces in the European theater in World War II, Eisenhower was one of the few people who could get away with such policy admonitions; i.e., the public trusted that he would not sacrifice security for the sake of cost.

To meet the combined need of global defense against communist expansion and a more economically efficient foreign policy, Eisenhower and his secretary of state, John Foster Dulles, formulated the New Look. It was based on the proposition that the American people should not and would not suffer the debilitating effects of a lower standard of living just to maintain the high military profile ordained under NSC-68. To address this problem, the idea of asymmetrical strategic deterrence was adopted, or as it is more popularly termed, "massive retaliation." This portended a reliance on nuclear weapons to retaliate directly against the perpetrator of communist aggression in order to deter such aggression a priori rather than be placed in a defensive position by being forced to react via the much more costly means of conventional forces sent halfway across the globe (as in Korea) to meet communist advances *after* they had been initiated. In this fashion, conventional force levels could be reduced at the same time since the focus was on maintaining, at much cheaper cost ("more bang for the buck"), an adequate nuclear deterrent that would enable the administration to balance the federal budget and allow Americans to maintain the high standard of living to which they had become accustomed. This was a fundamental difference and departure from the path chosen by the Soviet Union, which continued to commit a much higher percentage of its gross national product to both its nuclear and its conventional forces.

The focus on nuclear weapons tended to overlook two other legs of the New Look: establishing strategic alliances (or military pacts) to share the burden of containment and covert operations to fill the gaps in the strategic design of the New Look, i.e., countering indirect aggression or subversion engineered through nonmilitary means. Both of these aspects of the New Look would be directly applied to the Middle East. The North Atlantic Treaty Organization (NATO) had been formed in 1949 under Truman, an alliance that Turkey joined in 1952. The Southeast Asian Treaty Organization was constructed in 1954, in which Pakistan was a member, so the fringes of the Middle East were part of pro-West defense pacts. But there was a strategic gap in the belt surrounding the two communist behemoths, the Soviet Union and China—the heartland of the Middle East, which happened to border the underbelly of the Soviet Union and to contain about 75% of the world's proven oil reserves. The Middle East Command and Middle East Defence Organization were attempts to fill this gap and tighten the belt of containment, one that needed forward bases to launch the B-52s carrying nuclear warheads to the cold war enemies—this was before the era of intercontinental ballistic missiles (ICBMs), which would obviate the necessity of having these forward bases. Soon after coming to power, Dulles traveled to the Middle East and South Asia to sound out the leaders of various countries as to their willingness to join a pro-West defense pact. The U.S. secretary of state found in the Arab world a distinct unwillingness to

U.S. Secretary of State John Foster Dulles leaving the defense ministry in Damascus, Syria, in May 1953 as part of his tour of Middle East states to assess the viability of constructing a pro-West, anti-Soviet defense alliance in the region. (The Otrakji Collection, www.mideastimage.com.)

become members of an organization that would include the two European states from which most of them had just achieved independence. Dulles prudently concluded that a Middle East defense pact would best be achieved without the inclusion of any Arab states. This would also allow Washington to not be drawn into Arab–Israeli or inter-Arab disputes related to the pact. As such, Dulles proposed in 1954 the Northern Tier approach, i.e., a military alliance composed of states along the northern and eastern periphery of the Middle East that were non-Arab: Turkey, Iran, and Pakistan.

Britain, however, was not at all pleased to see the United States further expand its influence in the region at London's expense. This was driven home to the British in April 1954 when Washington brokered a Turko–Pakistani security pact—and London found out about it only after the fact. Later in April, Washington and Baghdad exchanged notes regarding military aid. Already out of Palestine and on their way out of Egypt by the end of 1954, the British were concerned lest they lose their influence in Iraq, one of their last remaining significant areas of ingress in the Arab world, for the British-installed Hashemite monarchy was still clinging to power. If Dulles' Northern Tier approach could be attached to Iraq in the formation of a military pact, London could maintain or even enhance its level of influence in the region. Nuri al-Sa'id, the pro-West powerful prime minister of Iraq, was also not shy about trying to achieve his ambitions, and the British were his stepladder for doing so. If Iraq could become the linchpin to a defense pact, with corresponding access to advanced Western weaponry, it could become the dominant player in the inter-Arab arena, eclipsing Egypt's natural spot at the top of the pecking order. Turkey and Iraq concluded a security pact in February 1955, establishing the foundation for the Baghdad Pact when Britain announced its adherence about a month later.[21] Iran would soon join Britain, Pakistan, Iraq, and Turkey in the Baghdad Pact, or what was officially known as CENTO. Iran's accession to the pact was not surprising given the fact that the United States, in its first spectacular application of the covert action leg of the New Look foreign policy, employed the Central Intelligence Agency (CIA) to overthrow the popularly elected prime minister of Iran, Muhammad Musaddiq, in August 1953, re-installing the pro-West shah of Iran, Muhammad Reza Pahlavi.[22]

The inclusion of an Arab state went against the Northern Tier approach. Dulles, however, was by this time becoming more and more disenchanted with Nasser. The secretary of state began to see the Egyptian president as more of an enemy than a potential friend, whose regional interests were in conflict with U.S. global interests.[23] As such, Dulles would acquiesce in the formation of the Baghdad Pact; however, trying to maintain a certain aloofness from the European element in it as well as a detachment from the Arab–Israeli and inter-Arab arenas, the United States assumed an observer status in the defense alliance.[24] The hope in London and Washington was that other Arab states, namely Jordan, Syria, and Lebanon, would soon join the pact, thus isolating Egypt and compelling it to come to terms with the West. Dulles' worst fears came to pass however. With the inclusion of Iraq, Nasser correctly felt his position threatened at the inter-Arab level, and he launched a heated propaganda campaign against Baghdad for becoming a lackey of Western imperialism. An Arab cold war began, and the soul of the Arab world was at stake. As a result of this new threat, coming on top of the Gaza raid, Nasser was desperate for a countermove. After an agreement on arms from the United States failed to come to fruition in the summer of 1955, Nasser went to the Soviet Union. For Moscow, this was a godsend. Not only could it leapfrog the containment belt that had been drawn around it in the Middle East, but it also would do so with the most powerful and populous Arab state. The Soviets grabbed at the opportunity, and an arms deal—with no such conditions as were demanded by the United States—was consummated in September 1955 through its eastern bloc client Czechoslovakia. The Baghdad Pact had totally backfired: instead of containing the Soviets, it helped facilitate their first significant entry into the Arab world.

Nasser was an all-Arab hero overnight. Finally, it seemed an Arab state had acquired the wherewithal to confront Israel. The Egyptian president would utilize this momentum to turn the tables on Iraq, isolating Baghdad in the inter-Arab arena rather than the other way around. Iraq was the only Arab state to join the Baghdad Pact, and it seemed more and more out of tune with the rest of the Arab landscape. Nasser had won this inter-Arab contest.

The Eisenhower administration was certainly taken aback by this development. Although instead of trying to punish Nasser, in December 1955 it offered, along with the British and the International Bank for Reconstruction and Development, to fund a large portion of the Aswan High Dam project in Egypt.[25] This was a very important project for Nasser. Not only would it control the flooding of the Nile River in Egypt that periodically caused agricultural havoc, but it would also increase the area of cultivable land and provide hydroelectric power for a rapidly growing population. Dulles also reactivated the Alpha plan along with the funding offer, implicitly making the latter contingent on Egyptian cooperation in the former. He sent Robert Anderson as a secret emissary to negotiate with both Nasser and Ben-Gurion from January to March 1956. But while Nasser displayed some interest in the ideas offered by the Alpha plan for an Arab–Israeli peace, depending as it was on Israeli–Egyptian progress, Ben-Gurion showed very little interest in it. Conditions demanded by each side, however, led to the collapse of the talks, which were soon overtaken by events in any case.[26] But with an end to the Anderson mission, linked in Washington's mind to the funding of the Aswan High Dam, there was less incentive in trying to woo Nasser.

Nasser's use of the popularity that he absorbed from the Soviet arms deal was not, however, endearing to the British, French, or Israelis. Now he was a bigger threat or problem, depending on one's viewpoint, than he was before. For Israel, one of its biggest fears had become reality: Egypt had access to arms from one of the superpowers. Remember, this is well before the United States became the primary supplier of military aid to Israel. In fact, Israel had been receiving arms from France by 1954, in contravention of the tripartite agreement. With the Algerian revolution beginning in 1954 as well as the defeat at Dien Bien Phu in Vietnam that same year, Paris was concerned lest its colonial position be eliminated entirely, so it was seeking out any and all potential allies, especially if it was one arrayed against Arab nationalism, the same type of nationalism that it saw behind the Algerian uprising.[27] France opposed the Baghdad Pact because of concerns that it enhanced the British position in the Middle East, which again placed French and Israeli interests on the same wavelength. A major arms delivery from France to Israel was agreed to in late 1955 following the Soviet–Egyptian arms deal, but the Egyptian threat persisted from Israel's point of view, especially as Cairo negotiated a defense pact with Syria in October (and Damascus signed an arms deal of its own with the Soviets—through Czechoslovakia—in February 1956). Given the opportunity to cut Nasser down to size, especially if it could be done before Egypt assimilated Soviet weaponry into its military, Israel would jump at the chance.

Nasser, however, continued to pursue his regional interests vis-à-vis Iraq, making sure Egypt won the battle over the Baghdad Pact. He built up his assets in Jordan, Syria, and Lebanon, successfully preventing any of these countries from joining the pact. He was also acting more boldly in the Arab–Israeli arena, supporting more fedayeen attacks and blockading the Strait of Tiran, thus preventing Israeli shipping through the Gulf of Aqaba. The strategic interests of Britain and France vis-à-vis their waning positions in the Middle East, and even the United States vis-à-vis the cold war, could not be reconciled with Egyptian nationalist interests and Nasser's own regional objectives. As evidence of this from the perspective of London, in March 1956, Jordan's King Hussein dismissed Glubb Pasha, who had led the Arab Legion for twenty-five years, an act heartily applauded by Nasser. The Egyptian president also offered to substitute the British subsidy to Jordan with joint Arab funds. And the French believed that Egypt's obsolete arms, made so by the Soviet arms deal, were being sent to the rebels in Algeria. While Nasser's popularity and influence were reaching greater heights in the Arab world, he was becoming more and more isolated from the great powers and antagonistic toward Israel. It is no surprise, then, that exhortations from London and Paris increasingly began to paint Nasser as an obstruction to peace in the Middle East. Even worse, he was beginning to be compared to Hitler in European circles, which, if generally accepted, meant that he must be removed from power—after all, following World War II, no Hitler-like figure could be allowed to remain in power. British Prime Minister Anthony Eden insisted that "Nasser was the incarnation of all the evils of Arabia who would destroy every British interest in the Middle East unless he himself were speedily destroyed."[28]

Although Dulles was frustrated with Nasser as well, he did not quite feel the same way toward him as Eden—at least not yet. But after the failure of the Anderson mission, there was less incentive to fund the Aswan High Dam project. Additionally, the Eisenhower administration was bombarded by ministrations from opponents of the funding, ranging from pro-Israeli activists to congresspersons from the southern states who were fearful the dam would increase Egypt's cotton production at the expense of the American market share. The final straw for Dulles probably occurred in May, when Nasser recognized communist China, which the secretary of state saw as a direct slap in the face of the United States given the known position of Washington toward Beijing at the height of the cold war struggle against communism. This also added the so-called China lobby of mostly Republican congresspersons who were adamantly opposed to Beijing to the growing list of those who pressured Dulles to rescind the offer to fund the dam. While Nasser must have certainly known that recognition of China would have severe repercussions in Washington, many have also speculated that his action was simply the culmination of his growing role in the nonaligned movement. Nasser attended the Bandung meeting in Indonesia in April 1955 that sparked the nonaligned movement, i.e., allied with neither the West nor the Eastern bloc. Apparently, Nasser established a cordial relationship with Chinese Premier Chou En-lai. Since China was a leading element in the nonaligned movement, in order for Egypt to acquire a similar standing it must first establish formal diplomatic relations with Beijing. In addition, Nasser was never completely sanguine about his reliance on the Soviet Union for arms; this could also have been an early indication of an attempt to diversify his great power contacts, for he may have seen, well before the United States recognized it later in the decade, that China and the Soviet Union were more often at odds with each other than cooperating to spread communism.

In reaction to this, Dulles did, indeed, withdraw the offer to fund the Aswan High Dam on July 19, 1956. From this point on, events would move swiftly, leading almost inexorably to the Suez war.

SUEZ CRISIS AND WAR

Nasser responded to Dulles' action by nationalizing the Suez Canal Company on July 25, whose toll revenues would now go into Egyptian coffers. The company maintained the Suez Canal and provided the pilots to guide ships through the waterway. Britain and France were the primary shareholders in the company; however, the last of the British troops had departed Egypt on June 13 per the 1954 Anglo–Egyptian accord. Britain and France were determined to use the Suez crisis to teach Nasser a lesson, to cut him down to size, if not get rid of him altogether. Both London and Paris saw him as the root of their troubles in the Arab world. Nationalization is legal as long as the shareholders are appropriately compensated, the amount of which is either set out in prior agreements or established by independent arbitration, usually in a third-party country. This is one of the main reasons corporations engaged in foreign investment carry overseas private investment insurance. For Eden, Nasser's action confirmed his characterization of Nasser as the new Hitler. The British prime minister was adamantly opposed to appeasement, having been vociferously against Neville Chamberlain's policy at Munich in 1938 that gave rise to the so-called Munich mentality, i.e., no appeasement of aggression because it will only lead to more of the same, as happened with Hitler's Germany after the Munich conference. Some have said that Eden's obsession with Nasser can also be partly explained by some narcotics he was taking to deal with the pain of several, and largely unsuccessful, bile duct operations.

The British and, especially, the French tried to manufacture a situation that would necessitate their interference to keep the vital waterway open. First, they said that the Egyptians would not be able to handle the operation of the canal or pilot the ships through it—they did just fine. Finally, they stated that Cairo was being obstructionist during attempts to diplomatically resolve the crisis, but Egypt had actually agreed to engage in several negotiations and plans to deal with the situation through diplomacy. The United States tried to take the lead in resolving the crisis without resorting to force, Dulles brainstorming an idea called the Suez Canal Users Association composed of maritime nations to manage the canal and distribute revenues; however, it really went nowhere with the British and the French more determined to use force. The UN also attempted to mediate the crisis. In all of these cases, Cairo maintained a cooperative stance, and comments by Eisenhower during the presidential election campaign that the diplomatic efforts had appeared to put the crisis behind them did not sit well with London and Paris. The British were concerned that all of these delays would make it more difficult to use military force, especially as the weather would not be ideal after October. They also believed that Dulles was purposely delaying things so that military force, if used, would not occur until after the November presidential election, for the American public did not appear to have an appetite for war just then and Eisenhower had been running on a peace platform. In other words, the British and the French were running out of excuses to intervene. In essence, they felt compelled to make one up.

This allowed for the entrance of Israel into the equation. Israel had been preparing for a preemptive strike against Egypt for over a year. The joint British and French hostility toward Nasser provided Tel Aviv with an opportunity it could not pass up. Together they concocted a plan whereby Israel would launch a war against Egypt independently. The British and the French could not be seen to be fighting in coordination with Israel for fear of losing their remaining positions in the Arab world. For Israel, the battle for Suez was simply a device to take the Strait of Tiran in order to open Israeli shipping through the Gulf of Aqaba. In response to the Israeli "attack," Britain and France would issue an ultimatum to both sides to withdraw from the Suez Canal area, at which time the British and French would militarily intervene to take over the canal at both ends (Port Sa'id in the north and Suez City in the south), ostensibly to restore order and maintain canal operations. In gaining control over the canal, it was hoped that the loss of face might be enough to force the overthrow of Nasser; but further military action was contemplated, if necessary, to ensure such an outcome. For Britain, military intervention could be rationalized as "protecting" its ally, Egypt, from attack by a third party, a condition (or "reservation" as it was often called) reinforced by successive Anglo–Egyptian agreements dating back to 1922. If all went according to plan, Nasser would be gone, Israel would have the straits, and the British and French would be in a position to reexert their influence in the region. They did not, however, count on U.S. opposition.

The Eisenhower administration was not entirely against the ultimate objective of the tripartite invasion, i.e., getting rid of Nasser. It had grown quite weary of the Egyptian leader by that time. It was, however, the timing and the means with which it was attempted that drew the ire of Eisenhower. There were different opinions among the tripartite invaders over when to launch the attack: before or after the U.S. presidential elections in early November. There is some evidence to suggest that Eisenhower would have been more supportive of the invasion if it had just been delayed until after the election. Probably because the preponderance of British, French, and Israeli officials involved in the planning believed that Eisenhower would not come out against U.S. allies and friends right before an election, the attack proceeded on October 29 with an Israeli two-pronged attack in the Sinai Peninsula, one ostensibly toward the Suez Canal with a paratroop drop at the Mitla Pass, some thirty miles east of the canal, and an armored column moving down the east coast of the Sinai toward the Strait of Tiran near the peninsula's southernmost tip. These arrangements only came together in French–British–Israeli meetings outside of Paris at Sèvres less than a week before the war began, although French and Israeli officials had been meeting to discuss joint military action since early September.

As planned, the next day, October 30, the British and French issued an incredible ultimatum to the combatants, Egypt and Israel. It demanded that Israeli and Egyptian forces withdraw ten miles away from the canal on both sides. The folly of the whole episode is embodied in the fact that the Israelis would actually have to *advance* twenty some miles from the Mitla Pass to just get to ten miles away from the canal, while the Egyptians were being asked to evacuate their own territory. Egypt, as expected, refused the ultimatum on November 1, while the Israelis gladly accepted, having already achieved their strategic objective—indeed, by the end of the fighting, Israel would control almost the entire Sinai. The Egyptian refusal was the pretext for the British and French to militarily intervene. On November 5, an Anglo–French bombing campaign and amphibious landing operation commenced, the largest since D-Day; and after unexpectedly tough resistance from the Egyptians, they took Port Sa'id. The Americans were taken aback at least by the timing of the operation a week before the presidential election. Although they suspected military action was in the offing, they were not apprised as to the specific plans. Both Eisenhower and Dulles (who would soon enter the hospital for a cancer operation) were irked that at the same time the Russians were ruthlessly stamping out a Hungarian uprising; its erstwhile allies were off on their own brand of neoimperialism. This meant that on front pages of newspapers across the globe the story would be the Suez war and not the Hungarian uprising—the West lost some valuable propaganda points in the Third World and a poignant opportunity to cast the communist bloc as rapacious aggressors. The United States had stayed somewhat aloof of any vestiges of European colonialism, as was evident in U.S. observer status in the Baghdad Pact; and Eisenhower was determined to maintain this posture. The Suez war was such a blatant and obvious display of perfidy that it spurred the unlikely event at the height of the cold war of bringing the United States and Soviet Union together in the UN to pass a cease-fire resolution on November 6, which all parties to the conflict accepted by November 8. The United States had threatened Britain with stiff economic measures if it proceeded to take control of both ends of the canal. While this was

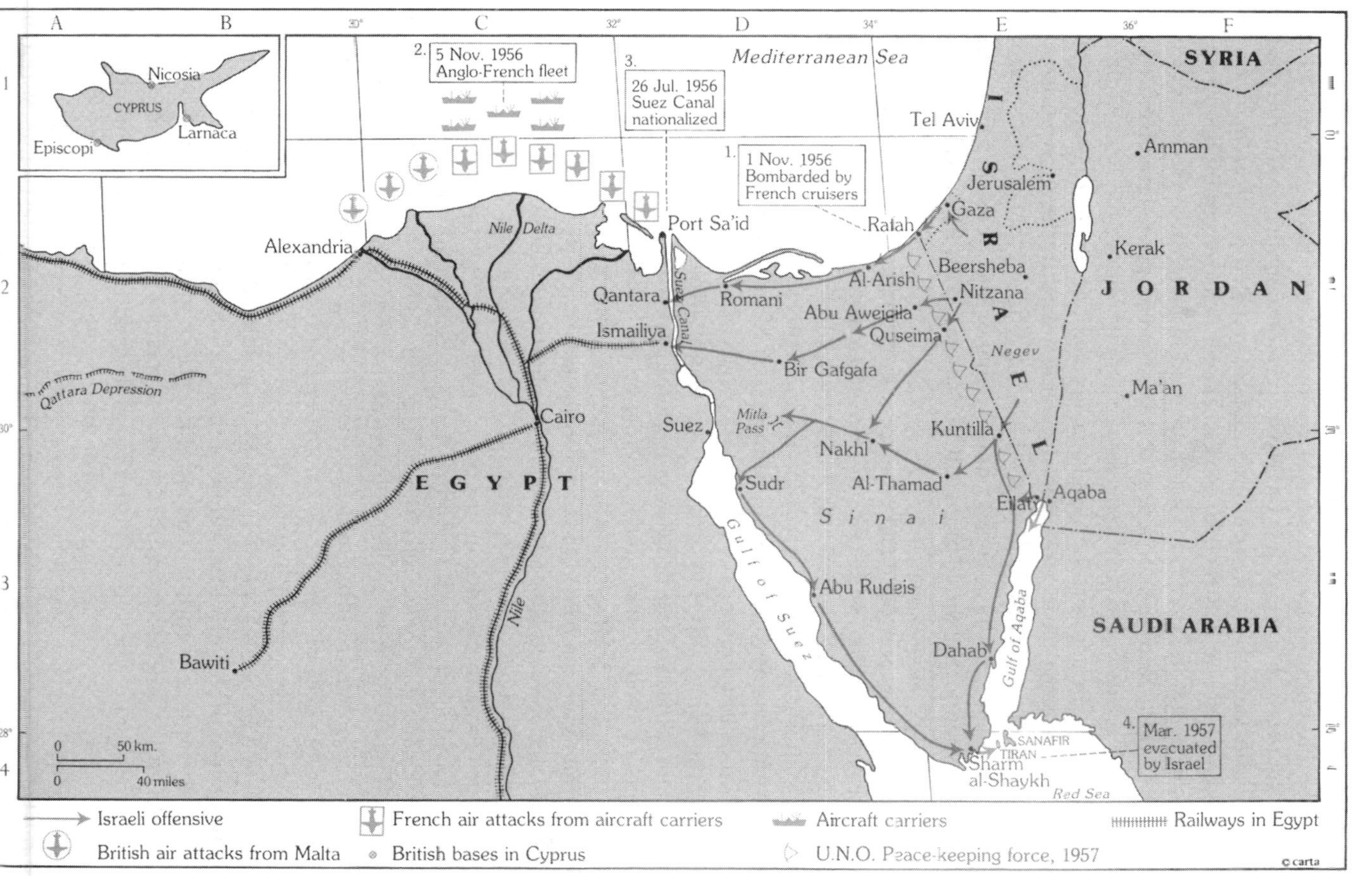

The Suez War, 1956. (G.S.P. Freeman-Grenville, *Historical Atlas of the Middle East.* New York: Simon & Schuster, 1993, p. 123.)

happening, the Soviets were literally making bombastic remarks, implicitly threatening London, Paris, and Tel Aviv if they did not cease and desist; although the latter had little impact on the British and French decision, to the rest of the world the Soviet Union looked equally as responsible as the United States for thwarting the tripartite invasion.

The war was a tremendous success for Nasser, even though he was in the process of being militarily defeated. One could say that he snatched political victory from the jaws of military defeat. His popularity skyrocketed to astronomical heights as he engaged two great powers, the traditional European imperialist countries as well as mortal enemy Israel—and he survived. It was no longer Arab nationalism or pan-Arabism. It was Nasserism. He became by far the guiding light in the Arab world and every Arab's hero. If Britain, France, and Israel deemed him a threat before Suez, he was ten times more lethal in its aftermath. Nasser appeared in the Arab world to be the conduit through which real Arab integral unity could be achieved. It also created expectations for Nasser that he was never quite willing or able to reach, a situation in the inter-Arab dynamic that would ultimately pit Nasser against Israel again nine years later, with drastically different results.

For Israel, the Suez war was a qualified success. It had, indeed, opened up the Gulf of Aqaba to Israeli shipping, which was its primary strategic objective. Tel Aviv also claimed that it received a commitment from the Eisenhower administration that guaranteed Israel's internationally sanctioned maritime rights to use the waterway. After stubbornly withdrawing from the Sinai Peninsula by March 1957 and only after direct pressure from Eisenhower, the UN Emergency Force (UNEF) was stationed in the Sinai and the Gaza Strip. The area was also demilitarized. Although it certainly was not the buffer that 80,000 British troops supplied, it was an important international trip wire and monitor that would, considering the fact that Egypt invaded Israel in 1948, hopefully keep the Egyptians at bay (although the Egyptians were probably thinking it would keep the Israelis at bay given the fact that it was Israel that invaded Egypt in 1956). Israel would later take home a lesson from this: do not withdraw from Arab territory unless a peace treaty is agreed to first because Egypt would remilitarize the Sinai by marching forces back in just prior to the 1967 war. On the negative side of the ledger for Israel, it tended to confirm Arab suspicions that the Jewish state was nothing more than a tool to Western imperialism, especially as it owed its creation to the support of the West. A great deal of international opprobrium also fell on Israel for its actions, again contributing to its isolation not only in the Middle East but in the Third World in general—and at the same time that Nasser's stature and influence multiplied.

For Britain and France the Suez war was an unqualified disaster. Both were already on their way out of the Middle East, but this almost ludicrous episode put a final stamp on it. Their attempts at restoring some lost influence completely backfired, which in a way, by default, compelled the United States to increase its attentions toward and presence in the region. The actions of the Eisenhower administration reinforced the distrust that Paris had for Washington. The British came to a completely different conclusion (and to a certain extent the Israelis) from the war: never be on the opposite side of the United States in such situations and always keep whatever administration is in Washington informed. Ironically, it ultimately led to much more cooperation between London and Washington in the area of foreign policy in ensuing years and decades as Britain became as much, or even more so, Atlanticist as Europeanist.

THE UNITED STATES INTENSIFIES ITS INVOLVEMENT

Following the British and French debacle at Suez, there was a strong perception in Washington that a vacuum of power had been created in the region. The United States, it was thought, had best adopt a more forward and active posture in the Middle East in order to fill the vacuum before the Soviets did. What resulted was the Eisenhower Doctrine, announced by the administration in January 1957 and passed by Congress the following March. The Eisenhower Doctrine offered U.S. military and economic aid to any country in the Middle East that requested it in order to fend off the advances of "international communism." Its primary objective was to prevent any further expansion of Soviet influence. Its regional interpretation was to "roll back" Nasserism, which was seen at the time to be favorable to the Kremlin. Attempts were made by the White House to build up other leaders in the Arab world who might possibly rival the Egyptian president and become the long-sought-after strategic partner in the Middle East.[29] The United States began to realize what the British had long feared: that Nasser's policies, whether generated by regional objectives or not, were at least indirectly aimed at undermining Western interests in the area to the intended and unintended benefit of the Soviets. Even though the Arab nationalists and the communists in the Middle East were distinguishable in Washington, their goals were not; and their apparent collusion in eliminating any remaining vestiges of European imperialism was therefore all the more sinister and potentially dangerous. For the Eisenhower administration, a resolution addressing the perceived vacuum in the Middle East, similar to the Formosa resolution issued in 1955 during the Taiwan straits crisis over the islands of Quemoy and Matsu, was preferable to becoming a full member of the Baghdad Pact, which, in essence, damned the latter to irrelevance regardless of the Iraq Revolution in 1958.

The Eisenhower Doctrine was not received particularly well in the Arab world. The United States sent emissaries to Arab states to gain approval for the doctrine but found very few takers. The doctrine came under a great deal of criticism in Arab newspapers as the United States simply appeared to be trying to fill the shoes of the British and French. Many Arab officials were scratching their heads regarding the meaning of the new policy. The doctrine obviously targeted communism as the primary threat to the Arab states, yet it was only a few months earlier that the standard-bearer of the Arab world (Egypt) was attacked not by the Soviet Union or communism but by the West (Britain and France) and Israel. To the Arabs, Zionism and Western imperialism were the main threats. The Eisenhower Doctrine was one of only many instances when the United States and many of the Arab states were on totally different wavelengths, the one operating at the international level with the Soviet Union as the primary antagonist and the other operating at the regional and domestic levels with Israel and imperialism as the enemies to be confronted. It is no surprise, then, that only tiny Lebanon, a country with a pro-Western Christian president, was the only Arab state to officially endorse the Eisenhower Doctrine.

Now that the lines in the Middle East seemed to be (re)drawn, with the United States rather than Europe assuming the burden of responsibility, the years 1957 and 1958 were replete with a series of crises that pitted the Eisenhower administration against various manifestations of Nasserism. In 1953 it was the CIA in Iran; in April 1957 it was the Eisenhower Doctrine that was employed in Jordan to restore authority to a monarch—in this case, King Hussein—against a rebellious, nationalist government. Then there was the American–Syrian crisis that began in August, an event that actually brought about a change of attitude in the Eisenhower administration toward Nasser and Arab nationalism in general.

The crisis itself was launched by the Syrian discovery of a U.S.-backed plot to overthrow what Washington believed to be a regime that was becoming too closely tied to the Soviet Union.[30] Rather than act as if it were caught red-handed, the Eisenhower administration saw this development as further proof of Syria's leap toward Moscow. From Washington's point of view, the crisis created an opportunity to rally pro-West Arab allies to precipitate action against the leftist, Arab regime in Damascus. The problem was that Washington's Arab friends were not particularly interested in aggressive action against their Arab brethren. So soon after Suez and with Nasser at the height of his popularity, such pro-West countries as Iraq, Jordan, and Saudi Arabia could only instigate virtually worthless diplomatic initiatives, lest they be accused of kowtowing to the United States. Nasser had set the bar high for pan-Arab nationalism, and any regime perceived to be doing the bidding of the West would indeed be on shaky ground domestically.

Bereft of its Arab allies, Washington looked to its fellow NATO member on Syria's northern border, Turkey. With the Soviet Union already bordering on the north, Ankara was not terribly anxious to see a Soviet client-state possibly come into being on its southern border. But when Turkey started mobilizing its troops on the Syrian border, the Soviet Union began to make some threatening noises toward Ankara. Suddenly, a regional crisis had turned into an international one, with the Soviets and Americans facing off against one another. Nasser, however, took advantage of the superpower standoff by sending what was really only a symbolic number of troops to Syria to ostensibly help fight off the Turks. In short order, Nasser had won the day by fending off any Arab pretenders to his mantle of leadership (especially those pushed by Washington), and he had "saved" the Syrian regime from falling further into the embrace of the Soviet Union. Nasser had worked long and hard to keep Syria from joining the Baghdad Pact and building up pro-Nasserist assets within the country—he was not about to lose all of this to the Soviets or Syrian communists.

Taking stock of these developments was the Eisenhower administration, which had essentially failed at the domestic, regional, and international levels to correct the situation in Syria. Therefore, why not entrust the job to Nasser, the only man who could prevent the Soviets from gobbling up Syria? He had kept the Soviets at arm's length in Egypt, despite his reliance on Moscow for military arms; and he had repressed communist movements within his own country. Maybe he could do the same in Syria. It certainly seemed in Washington to be the lesser evil. Indeed, there was some communication between Egyptian and American officials, recognizing the shared interests in Syria, at the UN in October and November 1957 during the latter stages of the crisis. Washington's knowledge of and acquiescence to Cairo's actions in Syria, and ultimately even the merger of Syria and Egypt into the United Arab Republic in February 1958, reduced the danger of misinterpreting events that could spin out of control.

In fact, the Eisenhower administration had come full circle. At the beginning of the year, with the introduction of the Eisenhower Doctrine, Nasser was the enemy. By the end of the year, the administration was tacitly working with Nasser.[31] In other words, considering the failures of U.S. policy to contain Soviet influence in the Middle East to date, it finally dawned on pertinent policymakers that Arab nationalism in the form of Nasserism could be something of an ally in the area against Soviet expansionism. This new line of thinking would be formalized in 1958 and carried out in earnest under the Kennedy administration, but its seeds were sown at the end of the American–Syrian crisis.

NSC Resolution 5820 of October 1958 (signed by Eisenhower on November 4, 1958), while adhering to the same objective that had been delineated in previous policy dictates regarding containing Soviet influence and protecting oil supplies, outlined the new approach to Arab nationalism.[32] Of course, it was the Iraqi revolution in July 1958, violently overthrowing the pro-British monarchy, which helped to nudge things in this direction. The new regime in Baghdad seemed to welcome, and even embrace, communists into the government—a development that, not unlike the situation in Syria in late 1957, brought about a convergence of interests between Cairo and Washington. The NSC planning board now believed that working with Nasserist pan-Arabism was an "essential element in the prevention of the extension of Soviet influence in the area."[33] Although there was some disagreement within the administration over how close the United States should associate itself with Nasser, it was clear that Washington would improve relations with him in at least the short term. As such, the United States would try to work with, rather than against, nonaligned nations. This new policy emphasized the economic aspects of a relationship much more than in the recent past, which heretofore had generally relied more on strategic and diplomatic relations relative to the cold war.[34]

Nasser also desired a better working relationship with the United States. Iraq, ironically, was as much, or even more, of a threat to his stature in the region now than it had been prior to the revolution. As the Iraqi president, 'Abd al-Karim Qassim, drew closer to the communists in his own country and as Moscow subsequently drew closer to Baghdad, clearly relieved to find someone in the Arab world who welcomed communist participation in government, Nasser began to distance Egypt from the USSR. In terms of the zero-sum cold war game, this almost automatically triggered an improvement in relations by December 1958 with the other superpower. The Egyptian president had also seen the United States send the marines into Beirut, Lebanon, upon hearing the news of the Iraqi revolution concurrent with British troops landing in Jordan, both of which were designed to protect two of the few remaining outwardly pro-Western regimes. The U.S. action in Lebanon came as Maronite Christian President Camille Chamoun attempted to extraconstitutionally extend his mandate in office, something that the United States supported. Chamoun was pitted against pro-Nasserist elements in the country, although the fissures in Lebanon that gave rise to such political disputes were certainly home-grown. In essence, however, Lebanon became another minibattleground between the United States and Nasser, especially as the new regime in Baghdad expressed allegiance to Nasser at first. The United States certainly seemed to be losing ground, a development that helped influence the passage of NSC 5820; i.e., a different tactic need be formulated. But the Iraqi revolution heated up the Arab cold war as Qassim proved to be more of an Iraqi than Arab nationalist who marched to the beat of a different drummer from Nasser, someone to whom the Iraqi president was not going to play second fiddle in the inter-Arab arena. Ironically, this was an Arab cold war within an Arab cold war. On the surface, Egypt,

Syria, and Iraq after July 1958 embodied the progressive, Arab nationalist future, while countries such as Jordan, Saudi Arabia, and Kuwait, which happened to be pro-West, were the conservative, reactionary Arab monarchies that should be consigned to the past. But beneath this division within the Arab world lay actually a more dangerous rivalry between Egypt, Iraq, and Syria for leadership in the Arab arena and the direction of Arab nationalism and Arab development. It would be this latter rivalry that would heighten tensions in the early to mid-1960s that spilled over into the Arab–Israeli arena, creating an environment out of which the 1967 war broke.[35]

The simultaneous multiple Arab cold wars allowed the Soviets and the Americans to dabble more deeply into Middle East affairs, attempting to take advantage of rivalries to establish relationships with states in the region against states that had established a relationship with the other superpower. On the other hand, it also allowed Middle Eastern leaders to play one superpower off against the other in an attempt to acquire as much economic, military, and political assistance as possible, a game that Nasser played extremely well throughout his tenure in power. It is, therefore, not a surprise that the Soviets assumed the bulk of the funding for the Aswan High Dam project after the United States and Britain withdrew their offer. For now, Arab regional dynamics dictated that Washington try to work with Nasser in order to curtail Soviet influence and safeguard oil supplies, which really meant protecting Saudi Arabia (after all, U.S.–Egyptian ties were less confrontational and Egypt became more dependent on PL-480 surplus wheat and other commodities bought from the United States—Egypt would therefore have little incentive to pressure the Saudis).[36] However, with the death of John Foster Dulles in May 1959, a lame-duck presidency, and the sobering experience of the Middle East in recent years, the Eisenhower administration adopted a low-key approach toward the region for the remainder of its time in office. Since there seemed to be no pressing matters and since the Arab states seemed content to bicker among themselves, the White House was all too happy to remain on the sidelines. In fact, there was probably a certain amount of sadistic satisfaction in the Eisenhower administration to see the Soviets experience the pitfalls of inter-Arab politics for a change as the Egyptian–Iraqi–Syrian cold war triangle compelled Moscow to make difficult choices between friends and presumed friends in the region. Not only did Egypt send troops to supposedly reactionary, monarchical Kuwait upon its independence in June 1961 to help protect it from a rapacious Iraq, but Syria had seceded from the United Arab Republic in September 1961 amid mutual recriminations on why this much ballyhooed attempt at integral Arab unity had been such a pathetic failure. The Arab world was divided and Nasserism had certainly lost some of its luster by the end of 1961.

Israel, on the other hand, was with satisfaction observing all of this. As long as the Arab states were politically divided and fighting among themselves, they would have less time and energy to spend on Israel. In addition, Tel Aviv did not at all mind seeing the more antagonistic attitude that the United States adopted toward Nasser in early 1957. Even though NSC-5820 was certainly not to Israel's liking, as mentioned earlier, it was not really until the Kennedy administration (1961–1963) that the new policy would be applied in a meaningful way. In the interim, Israel continued to develop the country, welcome more immigrants, and break out from its diplomatic isolation by establishing important relationships with countries as diverse as Germany and Iran. Maybe most importantly along these lines, especially considering the effect it would have on the Arab–Israeli dynamic in the not too distant future, was the development of the national water carrier, a project that would be completed in 1964. The objective of this project was to take water from the Sea of Galilee (Lake Kinneret), into which the Jordan River flowed, to replenish the water table along the Mediterranean coast and to irrigate the northern Negev desert; accordingly, it was claimed by the Israelis not to exceed the prescriptions as set out in the Johnston plan, which divided the Jordan River irrigation schemes equally between Israel and Jordan, but it was rejected by the Arabs.[37] In order to absorb the continuing stream of immigrants, the Israelis had to make "the desert bloom" so that it could sustain itself agriculturally, especially with the production of fruits and vegetables. Irrigation is vital to the Israeli economy, so the national water carrier project was as important to Tel Aviv as the Aswan High Dam was to Cairo. And just as in the Egyptian case, it would be a project that would become entangled in regional and international politics, during the course of which it would generate a series of events in the mid-1960s that would, again, focus regional attentions on the Arab–Israeli arena.

NOTES

1. Ritchie Ovendale, *The Arab–Israeli Wars* (New York: Longman, 1999), 146. Europe received 79% of its oil needs from the Middle East in 1955, thus was much more dependent on this region than the United States.
2. Mark Tessler, *The History of the Israeli–Palestinian Conflict* (Bloomington: Indiana University Press, 1994), 276.
3. Ibid., 278.
4. Ibid.
5. In January 1950, the Knesset approved legislation that Jerusalem was the capital of the state, an action not recognized by the international community, including the United States, which formally maintain their embassies in Tel Aviv as of this writing. Despite this, Israel was accepted as an independent, sovereign state by most of the international community within a year of its formation. Obviously, the Arab states were not among these.
6. Since non-Jewish communities in Israel were given the right to follow their own laws on personal status matters, in essence Israel reestablished the Ottoman millet system. William L. Cleveland, *A History of the Modern Middle East* (Boulder: Westview Press, 1994), 253.
7. Ibid.
8. "Sephardim" refers to the so-called Oriental or Eastern Jews who originated from the Iberian Peninsula (Spain and Portugal) following their forced expulsion due to the Spanish and Portuguese inquisitions in the late 1400s and into the 1500s. Most of these Jews immigrated to Arab or Berber territories, primarily in North Africa, mainly because in Muslim lands, while they were certainly second-class citizens, for the most part they enjoyed protected status as *ahl al-kitab,* or People of the Book, i.e., the Old Testament. They were able to practice their religion openly and lived a much better life in Muslim lands than they would have in Christian Europe at the time.
9. Cleveland, *A History,* 327.
10. On this question of the extent of U.S. prior knowledge of the coup, see Miles Copeland, *The Game of Nations: The Amorality of Power Politics* (New York: Simon and Schuster, 1969), and Wilbur Crane Eveland, *Ropes of Sand: America's Failure in the Middle East* (New York: W. W. Norton, 1980). Both Copeland and Eveland were CIA officials in the Middle East during this period and had intimate knowledge of a number of

American-sponsored covert activities, although they disagree on the extent of U.S. knowledge of or involvement in the 1952 coup. It seems logical, however, as Copeland argues, that at the very least elements of Nasser's cabal were in touch with American embassy officials in Cairo to gauge the U.S. response and to help make sure that the British, with their 80,000 troops at the Suez Canal base, did not intervene militarily to restore the monarchy. The failure of the 'Urabi revolt in the 1880s due to British intervention weighed heavily on the minds of the Free Officers. In fact, the Soviets believed that the coup was orchestrated by the United States and initially adopted a very negative view toward the new regime. See also, David W. Lesch, "'Abd al-Nasser and the United States: Enemy or Friend?" in Elie Podeh and Onn Winckler, eds., *Rethinking Nasserism: Revolution and Historical Memory in Modern Egypt* (Gainesville: University Press of Florida, 2004), 205–229.

11. Kirk J. Beattie, *Egypt During the Nasser Years: Ideology, Politics, and Civil Society* (Boulder: Westview Press, 1994), 70, 79.

12. Roger Owen, *The Middle East in the World Economy 1800–1914* ((New York: Methuen, 1981), 293.

13. Charles Issawi, *The Economic History of the Middle East 1800–1914* (Chicago: University of Chicago Press, 1966), 505.

14. The socialist regimes, adopting anti-Malthusian theories of expanding production, and the oil states, usually because of their conservative religious nature, actually promoted larger family sizes, producing perennially some of the highest birth rates in the world.

15. See David W. Lesch, *Syria and the United States: Eisenhower's Cold War in the Middle East* (Boulder: Westview Press, 1992), 18–24. Also see Douglas Little, "Cold War and Covert Action: The United States and Syria, 1945–1958," *Middle East Journal* 44, no. 1 (1990): 45–65.

16. Washington was, in fact, pressuring the British to come to an agreement with Cairo that would then facilitate an Arab–Israeli agreement as well as the inclusion of Egypt into pro-West defense alliance schemes that were being considered at the time.

17. Lesch, *Syria and the United States,* 36–37.

18. Ibid., 70.

19. Gulshan Dietl, *The Dulles Era: America Enters West Asia* (New Delhi: Lancer International, 1986), 67–68.

20. This coming on top of the *Bat Galim* incident. The *Bat Galim* was an Israeli-owned ship that attempted to pass through the Suez Canal, the first since 1949. It was seized by Egypt on September 28, 1954, in the Gulf of Suez for allegedly firing on Egyptian fishermen. The crew was released on January 1, 1955.

21. On the formation of the Baghdad Pact, see Elie Podeh, "The Perils of Ambiguity: The United States and the Baghdad Pact," in David W. Lesch, ed., *The Middle East and the United States: A Historical and Political Reassessment* (Boulder: Westview Press, 2003), 100–119. Also see his book-length treatment of the topic: *The Quest for Hegemony in the Arab World: The Stuggle over the Baghdad Pact* (Leiden: E. J. Brill, 1995).

22. On differing opinions on the need for and efficacy of the coup, see the chapters "U.S. Foreign Policy Toward Iran During the Mussadiq Era" by Mark Gaziorowski and "The Mussadiq Era in Iran; 1951–1953: A Contemporary Diplomat's View" by Sir Sam Falle in David W. Lesch, ed., *The Middle East and the United States,* 51–65, 78–86.

23. See Lesch, "'Abd al-Nasser and the United States."

24. Israel also vociferously opposed the formation of the Baghdad Pact, for the same reason it opposed Egypt's inclusion in any pro-West military alliance. The United States deepened its involvement in the pact after the 1958 Iraqi revolution, becoming a full member in several important committees; but it was still not a full member in the pact itself. Baghdad withdrew from the pact in March 1959; it was renamed formally to CENTO, and the headquarters was moved from Baghdad to Ankara, Turkey. When Iran withdrew from CENTO following the 1979 Iranian Revolution, CENTO ceased to exist.

25. The United States would provide $56 million to the construction in the first stage of the project, with Britain committing $14 million, with possibly more to come in later stages. The International Bank for Reconstruction and Development (World Bank) would provide $200 million.

26. The Alpha plan (or project) was originally crafted in October 1954. It entailed a resolution of the Palestinian refugee problem with the settling of most of the refugees in the Arab states, with some returning to Israel—the United States was to finance the resettlement operation. In addition, the plan called for a land link across the Negev between Jordan and Egypt, while most of the Negev would remain in Israeli hands. This rapprochement between Israel and Egypt, it was hoped, would lead to a peace agreement that would soon be followed by other Arab states.

27. Although there is some debate as to whether Nasser supported the Algerian rebels because France was supplying arms to Israel or France supported Israel because Nasser was backing the Algerian revolution.

28. Anthony Nutting, *Nasser* (London: Constable, 1972), 123.

29. The Eisenhower administration attempted to build up the inept King Sa'ud of Saudi Arabia as this potential rival to Nasser, an ill-conceived plan that, for the most part, backfired by the summer of 1957. See David W. Lesch, "The Role of Saudi Arabia in the 1957 American–Syrian Crisis," *Middle East Policy* 1, no. 3 (1992): 33–48.

30. See Lesch, *Syria and the United States.* For a shorter version, see David W. Lesch, "The 1957 American–Syrian Crisis: Globalist Policy in a Regional Reality," in Lesch, *The Middle East and the United States,* 133–148.

31. On Nasser's role, see David W. Lesch, "Gamal 'Abd al-Nasser and an Example of Diplomatic Acumen," *Middle Eastern Studies* 31, no. 2 (1995): 362–374.

32. See a point–counterpoint debate on the value of NSC 5820 by Paolo Olimpo and Daniele De Luca in David W. Lesch, ed., *History in Dispute: The Middle East Since 1945,* 2nd series, vol. 15 (New York: St. James Press, 2004), 165–171.

33. Operations Coordinating Board, U.S. Policy Toward the Near East, NSC 5820, *Foreign Relations of the United States, 1958–1960*, vol. 11 (October 20, 1958): 3.

34. Fawaz A. Gerges, *The Superpowers and the Middle East: Regional and International Politics, 1955–1967* (Boulder: Westview Press, 1994), 130.

35. See Malcolm H. Kerr's classic work *The Arab Cold War: Gamal 'Abd al-Nasir and His Rivals, 1958–1970* (New York: Oxford University Press, 1971).

36. By the early 1960s, the United States supplied $150 million per year in surplus wheat, which accounted for more than half of Egyptian grain consumption. Ian J. Bickerton and Carla L. Klausner, *A Concise History of the Arab–Israeli Conflict* (Upper Saddle River, NJ: Prentice Hall, 1998), 144.

37. Ibid., 140.

Speech by President Nasser on Nationalization of the Suez Canal

September 15, 1956

In these decisive days in the history of mankind, these days in which truth struggles to have itself recognized in international chaos where powers of evil domination and imperialism have prevailed, Egypt stands firmly to preserve her sovereignty.

Your country stands solidly and staunchly to preserve her dignity against imperialistic schemes of a number of nations who have uncovered their desires for domination and supremacy.

In these days and in such circumstances Egypt has resolved to show the world that when small nations decide to preserve their sovereignty, they will do that all right and that when these small nations are fully determined to defend their rights and maintain their dignity, they will undoubtedly succeed in achieving their ends....

I am speaking in the name of every Egyptian Arab and in the name of all free countries and of all those who believe in liberty and are ready to defend it. I am speaking in the name of principles proclaimed by these countries in the Atlantic Charter. But they are now violating these principles and it has become our lot to shoulder the responsibility of reaffirming and establishing them anew....

We have tried by all possible means to cooperate with those countries which claim to assist smaller nations and which promised to collaborate with us but they demanded their fees in advance. This we refused so they started to fight with us. They said they will pay toward building the High Dam and then they withdrew their offer and cast doubts on the Egyptian economy. Are we to declaim [*sic,* disclaim?] our sovereign right? Egypt insists her sovereignty must remain intact and refuses to give up any part of that sovereignty for the sake of money.

Egypt nationalized the Egyptian Suez Canal company. When Egypt granted the concession to de Lesseps it was stated in the concession between the Egyptian Government and the Egyptian company that the company of the Suez Canal is an Egyptian company subject to Egyptian authority. Egypt nationalized this Egyptian company and declared freedom of navigation will be preserved.

But the imperialists became angry. Britain and France said Egypt grabbed the Suez Canal as if it were part of France or Britain. The British Foreign Secretary forgot that only two years ago he signed an agreement stating the Suez Canal is an integral part of Egypt.

Egypt declared she was ready to negotiate. But as soon as negotiations began threats and intimidations started....

Eden stated in the House of Commons there shall be no discrimination between states using the canal. We on our part reaffirm that and declare there is no discrimination between canal users. He also said Egypt shall not be allowed to succeed because that would spell success for Arab nationalism and would be against their policy, which aims at the protection of Israel.

Today they are speaking of a new association whose main objective would be to rob Egypt of the canal and deprive her of rightful canal dues. Suggestions made by Eden in the House of Commons which have been backed by France and the United States are a clear violation of the 1888 convention, since it is impossible to have two bodies organizing navigation in the canal....

By stating that by succeeding, Abdel Nasser would weaken Britain's stand against Arab nationalism, Eden is in fact admitting his real objective is not Abdel Nasser as such but rather to defeat Arab nationalism and crush its cause. Eden speaks and finds his own answer. A month ago he let out the cry that be was after Abdel Nasser. Today the Egyptian people are fully conscious of their sovereign rights and Arab nationalism is fully awakened to its new destiny....

Those who attack Egypt will never leave Egypt alive. We shall fight a regular war, a total war, a guerrilla war. Those who attack Egypt will soon realize they brought disaster upon themselves. He who attacks Egypt attacks the whole Arab world. They say in their papers the whole thing will be over in forty-eight hours. They do not know how strong we really are.

We believe in international law. But we will never submit. We shall show the world how a small country can stand in the face of great powers threatening with armed might. Egypt might be a small power but she is great inasmuch as she has faith in her power and convictions. I feel quite certain every Egyptian shares the same convictions as I do and believes in everything I am stressing now.

We shall defend our freedom and independence to the last drop of our blood. This is the staunch feeling of every Egyptian. The whole Arab nation will stand by us in our common fight against aggression and domination. Free peoples, too, people who are really free will stand by us and support us against the forces of tyranny....

---

http://www.fordham.edu/halsall/mod/1956Nasser-suez1.html (accessed February 2, 2006).

Statement to the General Assembly by Foreign Minister Golda Meir

1 March 1957

The Government of Israel is now in a position to announce its plans for full and prompt withdrawal from the Sharm el-Sheikh area and the Gaza Strip, in compliance with resolution I of 2 February 1957.

We have repeatedly stated that Israel has no interest in the strip of land overlooking the western coast of the Gulf of Aqaba. Our sole purpose has been to ensure that, on the withdrawal of Israeli forces, continued freedom of navigation will exist for Israeli and international shipping in the Gulf of Aqaba and the Straits of Tiran. Such freedom of navigation is a vital national interest for Israel, but it is also of importance and legitimate concern to the maritime Powers and to many States whose economies depend upon trade and navigation between the Red Sea and the Mediterranean Sea.

There has recently been an increasingly wide recognition that the Gulf of Aqaba comprehends international waters in which the right of free and innocent passage exists.

On 11 February 1957, the Secretary of State of the United States of America handed to the Ambassador of Israel in Washington a memorandum dealing, among other things, with the subject of the Gulf of Aqaba and the Straits of Tiran.

This statement discusses the rights of nations in the Gulf of Aqaba and declares the readiness of the United States to exercise those rights on its own behalf and to join with others in securing general recognition of those rights.

My Government has subsequently learnt with gratification that other leading maritime Powers are prepared to subscribe to the doctrine set out in the United States memorandum of 11 February and have a similar intention to exercise their rights of free and innocent passage in the Gulf and the Straits.

The General Assembly's resolution (II) of 2 February 1957 contemplates that units of the United Nations Emergency Force will move into the Straits of Tiran area on Israel's withdrawal. It is generally recognized that the function of the United Nations Emergency Force in the Straits of Tiran area includes the prevention of belligerent acts.

In this connection, my Government recalls the statements by the representative of the United States in the General Assembly on 28 January and 2 February 1957, with reference to the function of the United Nations Emergency Force units which are to move into the Straits of Tiran area on Israel's withdrawal. The statement of 28 January, repeated on 2 February, said:

> *"It is essential that units of the United Nations Emergency Force be stationed at the Straits of Tiran in order to achieve there the separation of Egyptian and Israeli land and sea forces. This separation is essential until it is clear that the non existence of any claimed belligerent rights has established in practice the peaceful conditions which must govern navigation in waters having such an international interest." (AIPV. 645, pages 3–5)*

My Government has been concerned with the situation which would arise if the United Nations Emergency Force, having taken up its position in the Straits of Tiran area for the purpose of assuring non-belligerency, were to be withdrawn, in conditions which might give rise to interference with free and innocent navigation and, therefore, to the renewal of hostilities. Such a premature cessation of the precautionary measures taken by the United Nations for the prevention of belligerent acts would prejudice important international interests and threaten peace and security. My Government has noted the assurance embodied in the Secretary-General's report of 26 February 1957 that any proposal for the withdrawal of the United Nations Emergency Force from the Gulf of Aqaba area would first come to the Advisory Committee, which represents the General Assembly in the implementation of its resolution of 2 November 1956. This procedure will give the General Assembly an opportunity to ensure that no precipitate changes are made which would have the effect of increasing the possibility of belligerent acts We have reason to believe that in such a discussion many members of the United Nations would be guided by the view expressed by Ambassador Lodge on 2 February in favour of maintaining the United Nations Emergency Force in the Straits of Tiran until peaceful conditions were in practice assured.

In the light of these doctrines, policies and arrangements by the United Nations and the maritime Powers, my Government is confident that free and innocent passage for international and Israeli shipping will continue to be fully maintained after Israel's withdrawal.

It remains for me now to formulate the policy of Israel both as a littoral State and as a country which intends to exercise its full rights of free passage in the Gulf of Aqaba and through the Straits of Tiran.

The Government of Israel believes that the Gulf of Aqaba comprehends international waters and that no nation has the right to prevent free and innocent passage in the Gulf and through the Straits giving access thereto, in accordance with the generally accepted definition of those terms in the law of the sea.

In its capacity as a littoral State, Israel will gladly offer port facilities to the ships of all nations and all flags exercising free passage in the Gulf of Aqaba. We have received with gratification the assurances of leading maritime Powers that they foresee a normal and regular flow of traffic of all cargoes in the Gulf of Aqaba.

Israel will do nothing to impede free and innocent passage by ships of Arab countries bound to Arab ports or to any other destination.

Israel is resolved, on behalf of vessels of Israeli registry, to exercise the right of free and innocent passage and is prepared to join with others to secure universal respect of this right.

Israel will protect ships of its own flag exercising the right of free and innocent passage on the high seas and in international waters.

Interference, by armed force, with ships of Israeli flag exercising free and innocent passage in the Gulf of Aqaba and through the Straits of Tiran will be regarded by Israel as an attack entitling it to exercise its inherent right of self-defence under Article 51 of the Charter and to take all such measures as are necessary to ensure the free and innocent passage of its ships in the Gulf and in the Straits.

We make this announcement in accordance with the accepted principles of international law under which all States have an inherent right to use their forces to protect their ships and their rights against interference by armed force. My Government naturally hopes that this contingency will not occur.

In a public address on 20 February, President Eisenhower stated:

"We should not assume that if Israel withdraws, Egypt will prevent Israeli shipping from using the Suez Canal or the Gulf of Aqaba."

This declaration has weighed heavily with my Government in determining its action today.

Israel is now prepared to withdraw its forces from the Gulf of Aqaba and the Straits of Tiran in the confidence that there will be continued freedom of navigation for international and Israeli shipping in the Gulf of Aqaba and through the Straits of Tiran.

We propose that a meeting be held immediately between the Chief of Staff of the Israel Defence Forces and the Commander of the United Nations Emergency Force in order to arrange for the United Nations to take over its responsibilities in the Sharm el-Sheikh area

The Government of Israel announces that it is making a complete withdrawal from the Gaza Strip in accordance with General Assembly resolution (I) of 2 February 1957 (A/RES/460). It makes this announcement on the following assumptions:

(a) That on its withdrawal the United Nations Forces will be deployed in Gaza and that the takeover of Gaza from the military and civilian control of Israel will be exclusively by the United Nations Emergency Force.

(b) It is further Israel's expectation that the United Nations will be the agency to be utilized for carrying out the functions enumerated by the Secretary-General, namely: *"safeguarding life and property in the area by providing efficient and effective police protection as will guarantee good civilian administration; as will assure maximum assistance to the United Nations refugee programme; and as will protect and foster the economic development of the territory and its people." (AIPV. 659, page 17)*

(c) It is further Israel's expectation that the aforementioned responsibility of the United Nations in the administration of Gaza will be maintained for a transitory period from the takeover until there is a peace settlement, to be sought as rapidly as possible, or a definitive agreement on the future of the Gaza Strip.

It is the position of Israel that if conditions are created in the Gaza Strip which indicate a return to the conditions of deterioration that existed previously, Israel would reserve its freedom to act to defend its rights.

Accordingly, we propose that a meeting be held immediately between the Chief of Staff of the Israel Defence Forces and the Commander of the United Nations Emergency Force in order to arrange for the United Nations to take over its responsibilities in the Gaza area.

For many weeks, amidst great difficulty, my Government has sought to ensure that, on the withdrawal from the Sharm el-Sheikh and the Gaza areas, circumstances would prevail which would prevent the likelihood of belligerent acts.

We record with gratitude the sympathetic efforts of many Governments and delegations to help bring about a situation which would end the insecurity prevailing in Israel and among its neighbours these many years. In addition to the considerations to which I have referred, we place our trust in the vigilant resolve of the international community that Israel, equally with all member-States, enjoy its basic rights of freedom from fear of attack; freedom to sail the high seas and international waterways in peace; freedom to pursue its national destiny in tranquillity without the constant peril which has surrounded it in recent years.

In this reliance we are embarking upon the course which I have announced today.

May I now add these few words to the States in the Middle East area and, more specifically, to the neighbours of Israel:

We all come from an area which is a very ancient one. The hills and the valleys of the region have been witnesses to many wars and many conflicts. But that is not the only thing which characterizes that part of the world from which we come. It is also a part of the world which is of an ancient culture. It is that part of the world which has given to humanity three great religions. It is also that part of the world which has given a code of ethics to all humanity. In our countries, in the entire region, all our peoples are anxious for and in need of a higher standard of living, of great programmes of development and progress.

Can we, from now on, all of us turn a new leaf and, instead of fighting with each other, can we all, united, fight poverty and disease and illiteracy? Is it possible for us to put all our efforts and all our energy into one single purpose, the betterment and progress and development of all our lands and all our peoples?

I can here pledge the Government and the people of Israel to do their part in this united effort. There is no limit to what we are prepared to contribute so that all of us, together, can live to see a day of happiness for our peoples and see again from that region a great contribution to peace and happiness for all humanity.

---

http://mfa.gov.il/mfa/go.asp?MFAH01bw0 (accessed February 2, 2006).

Seven
THE EARTHQUAKE

The relative quiescence in the Arab–Israeli dimension in the period between the late 1950s and the mid-1960s belied the shifting tectonics below the surface, appearing to lie dormant from the outside but underneath it all gathering kinetic energy and combustible heat, waiting to burst forth with shattering fury in the form of the 1967 Arab–Israeli war, sometimes known as the June war or the Six Day War. This war would change the Middle East forever. It is without a doubt the single most important event in the modern history of the Middle East after the creation of the state of Israel. Its effects reached far beyond the Arab–Israeli arena; indeed, it traversed the political, economic, and military spectrums to directly affect in a profound way the sociocultural milieu—religion, media, film, literature, and music—in Israel, in the Arab states, and in the Muslim and Jewish communities beyond the Middle East. A simple listing of the more noticeable repercussions of the war reveals the depth and breadth of the change it wrought at the domestic, regional, and international levels: (1) the Occupied Territories situation came into being after Israel captured the Sinai Peninsula and Gaza Strip from Egypt, the Golan Heights from Syria, and the West Bank, including Arab East Jerusalem, from Jordan; (2) the land-for-peace framework was established with United Nations (UN) Security Council Resolution 242 (passed in November 1967) as a direct result of the war, i.e., creating a bargaining situation, although it was asymmetrical because Israel held all of the land; (3) the war sounded the death-knell to Nasserism and, in effect, Arab nationalism; (4) in the latter's wake, Islamism, in a much more virulent form, began to resuscitate as an alternative to secular pan-Arabism—indeed, one can draw a direct line, through the permutations of history, to the creation of al-Qa'ida and the tragedy of September 11, 2001; (5) divisions in Israel began to manifest themselves following the war over the question of how much, if any, land to return to the Arabs in exchange for peace and recognition, a question that has still yet to be definitively answered in Israel; and, finally, (6) the conflagration compelled the superpowers to become more intimately involved in the Arab–Israeli conflict, with all of the associated dangers of a possible direct superpower confrontation, a situation that almost became manifest in the latter stages of the 1973 Arab–Israeli war.

In the following comment from Gideon Aran, one can clearly see the symbolic, cultural, and even eschatological significance of the 1967 war for Israelis:

> The war reconnected the State with the Land. The rediscovery of the ancient Promised Land was perhaps no less significant than the rediscovery of Jewishness. The return to the Land of Israel, or, more specifically, to the territories severed from the state at its establishment in 1948 and considered to be the cradle of religion and nationhood, brought secular Zionism closer to Judaism. In the land of the Bible the Israelis met the Israelites. The return to cherished landmarks and longed-for vistas, pregnant with rich cultural associations, reawakened a long-dormant impulse associated with the mystique of the land. The famous photograph of a weeping paratrooper kissing the stones of the Western Wall is a symbol of the unforeseen emergence of religious motifs in contemporary Israel.[1]

For the Arabs, there was obviously quite a different reaction, one of utter shock, despair, and introspection. Emblematic of Arab sentiments following the war is the writing of noted Arab author Halim Barakat, in which, as with the Israelis, there were distinct religious overtones. In his novel *Days of Dust*, Barakat writes the following in part one (entitled), "The Threshold: June 11–June 20, 1967," i.e., from the day the war ended on June 11:

> The world changed into water, and darkness covered all. The sun was extinguished, and the moon did not yet exist.... it seemed that all was taking form anew; the biblical legend was repeating itself. Earth was a desolate wasteland and there was darkness over the face of the deep; but the spirit of God did not move upon the waters. The Arab was not made in the likeness of God, so the fish of the sea, the birds of the air, and the creatures of the land had dominion over him. And the Arab saw all he had done and, behold, it was very bad. A bitter silence overwhelmed all. The world was water, and darkness covered everything. A dove descended from the skies in the form of a napalm bomb on a magus searching for peace on earth.[2]

The origins of this seminal event, as in most wars, can be traced back a number of years. They reside in large measure in the developing multidimensional inter-Arab rivalries in the years preceding the conflict, a rising tension at one level that focused more and more on the Arab–Israeli arena.

ARAB COLD WAR INTO ARAB–ISRAELI CONFLICT

Gamal 'Abd al-Nasser had had a bad year in 1961: the Kuwaiti crisis in June and the Syrian secession from the United Arab Republic (UAR) in September had certainly tarnished some of the Egyptian president's luster. In addition, Nasser announced a series of socialist decrees in July 1961, injecting a heavy dose of what was called "revolutionary socialism" into the Arab cold war mix. In essence, Egypt adopted socialism and the principles of a planned economy that required nationalization on a large scale on the path to state capitalism as the basis of its economy.[3] In a way, this was the final straw for elements in Syria that had become weary of Egyptian domination of the UAR, eliciting a coup d'etat in Damascus and subsequent withdrawal from the union.

The following year Nasser would attempt to recoup his lost standing in the Arab world. Ironically, this included for a time an improved relationship with the United States during the Kennedy administration. While other issues (Berlin, Cuba, and Vietnam, e.g.) were certainly higher on the foreign policy priority list during the abbreviated Kennedy administration, the Middle East did receive some serious attention. Kennedy brought a whole new ideological conception of the Third World to the White House. Especially coming on the heels of Soviet Premier Nikita Khrushchev's speech in January 1961, promoting wars of liberation in the Third World, Kennedy also saw these areas as opportunities to combat the Soviet Union and expand U.S. influence. Popular nationalists were not to be feared but embraced, and in the Middle East this meant a different attitude toward Nasserism—National Security Council (NSC) 5820 was finally being applied. In addition, after the Syrian secession from the UAR, Nasser was seen in Washington to be in a weakened position and, therefore, less able to stir up trouble in the region while possibly being more amenable to American demarches. The traditional concern in Washington about the Hashemite monarchies in Jordan and Iraq pressuring the Saudis was no longer much of one after the Iraqi revolution. Keeping Nasser closer to the United States was seen as an efficient way to protect Saudi Arabia, which might otherwise have been a natural target for Nasser's progressive Arab nationalism.

Soon after taking office, Kennedy circulated a letter to five Arab leaders, promising his support for the UN Conciliation Commission to resolve the Palestinian refugee problem on the basis of repatriation and compensation for lost property.[4] The United States had also voted against Israel in the UN regarding a resolution condemning Tel Aviv for a retaliatory raid against Syria. Recognizing the potential for shifting winds in Washington, Nasser also sent out some positive signals. After his visit to Cairo, Chester Bowles, Kennedy's ambassador-at-large to the Third World (itself an indication of the new policy direction), commented that "the leaders of the UAR are pragmatists searching for techniques that will enable them to expand their economy rapidly and to maintain their political grip.... If Nasser can gradually be led to forsake the microphone for the bulldozer, he may assume a key role in bringing the Middle East peacefully into our modern world."[5] The Kennedy team was composed of policymakers convinced that state-to-state relations could be scientifically managed, even though Kennedy's actual relationship with Nasser was carried out through the highly personal diplomacy of letters exchanged between them. There existed the belief that the relatively quiescent state of the Middle East—of course, only looking at it through the prism of the superpower cold war and the Arab–Israeli dimension—could be used to U.S. advantage to sway Egypt, and possibly others, onto the path of socioeconomic development and modernization.

As such, the Arab–Israeli conflict could be, as one Egyptian official put it, placed in the "icebox" in order to allow time for the new relationship to develop. Under these favorable regional conditions, seemingly uncomplicated by a multitude of forces as they had been in the 1950s—and would be again in the not-too-distant future—it was thought that an Arab–Israeli peace might be possible, without its conclusion having to first await a crisis situation. Thus, Kennedy approved increased grain shipments to Egypt under the already existing PL-480 program. The policy seemed to work and, on the whole, was able to withstand small bumps in the road. Nasser appreciated Washington's cautiousness following the embarrassing and politically damaging breakup of the UAR (after initial accusations that the Central Intelligence Agency [CIA] played a prominent role in causing it). It also weathered Nasser's severe criticism of the United States for its policies in such areas as the Congo and Cuba.

Despite sporadic clashes between Israeli troops and Palestinian guerillas in late 1961 and skirmishes on the Israeli–Syrian border in early 1962, the Middle East seemed to be free of an impending major crisis for the time being. Seeing that this relative calm was an opportune moment to begin building bridges between Israel and the Arab states on substantive issues, Kennedy pushed forward a new plan in mid-1962, making good on that earlier promise to Arab leaders to deal directly with the Palestinian refugee problem. During the process, it was hoped that a new dialogue could be established between Israel and Egypt that might lead to a comprehensive settlement of the Arab–Israeli conflict. It was called the Johnson Plan, named after Dr. Joseph Johnson, who was head of the Carnegie Endowment. Essentially, the plan allowed Palestinian refugees the choice of returning to Israel or resettling in neighboring Arab states, with compensation for lost properties and relocation costs. While Johnson was convinced that only a small portion of the refugees (perhaps fewer than 10% of the 1.2 million at the time) would actually choose to return to Israeli territory, the Israeli leadership determined that even 10% would, in their view, amount to an unacceptable fifth column inside the country. The most Israel would be willing to accept was 20,000 refugees, a number that was likewise unacceptable to many Arab leaders—who were still negotiating on behalf of the Palestinians. Remember, there was no Palestine Liberation Organization (PLO) yet, i.e., an organization composed of Palestinians and representing Palestinian interests.

Sensing the reluctance of the Israeli government for the plan, the Kennedy administration began to link military aid as an additional enticement to sweeten the pot. Particularly in demand by the Israelis were the Hawk surface-to-air missiles, for which a sale was approved in September 1962. Administration officials also saw the military aid as a way to influence Israeli policy and to curtail the development of any Israeli nuclear option that appeared to be well under way with the assistance of the French. Little did Kennedy officials know that they were establishing a paradigm for peace negotiations between Israel and Egypt that would be more rigorously pursued in the 1970s, namely, military and economic aid to relieve mutual anxieties and induce the parties to the negotiating table.

Administration officials believed that both sides indicated a willingness to make concessions, and they engaged in relatively intense diplomatic negotiations during the summer of 1962. Israeli opposition to the Johnson Plan was more real than Washington realized, however; and along with an increasingly negative stance from domestic Jewish groups, Kennedy's advisors began to recommend his disengagement from the plan as quickly as possible.[6] Also dismembering the plan was the fact that news of the impending sale of Hawks to Israel had begun to leak to the Arabs, who were not at all pleased.[7] Kennedy had obviously misjudged his position, whereby he thought that he could successfully play both sides of the fence.

Whatever hope the Johnson Plan had was finally dashed in September 1962, when a pro-Nasserist republican coup d'etat in Yemen overthrew the monarchy of Iman Muhammad al-Badr. The event divided the Arab world along the more traditional progressive Arab nationalist state versus reactionary monarchy Arab cold war lines, which placed the United States in a very difficult position between Egypt and the pro-U.S. Arab monarchies, namely Saudi Arabia and Jordan. While Nasser saw an opportunity to assist the so-called progressive forces on the republican side with 40,000 Egyptian troops (a number that would grow to about 80,000 into 1967), in part to rebuild the status that had been so diminished by the Syrian secession from the UAR and the continuing diatribes from Baghdad, the Saudi and Jordanian regimes were obliged to support countercoup attempts by royalist forces regrouping along the Saudi–Yemeni border. The situation created a dilemma for Kennedy. On the one hand, he had to support Riyadh in order to maintain the important U.S.–Saudi relationship, especially when Egypt launched aerial forays into Saudi territory in an attempt to strike at royalist forces. On the other hand, in doing so he risked alienating Nasser, someone with whom the president had established a level of confidence and trust.[8]

Israeli Nuclear Capability

Israel has never officially announced that it possesses nuclear weapons, preferring to adopt a position of strategic ambiguity on the subject, or what some call nuclear "opacity." As Israeli Foreign Minister Shimon Peres stated in a speech in 1995, "ambiguity regarding the nuclear issue is part of Israel's national security concept. There is no reason for us to hurry in removing this ambiguity. This is particularly the case as neighboring countries, like Iran and Iraq, are calling for Israel's destruction."* Despite the apparent contradiction, Israel has also often pledged that it will not be the first to introduce nuclear weapons—in terms of actually using them—into the Middle East. The question also exists as to whether Israel maintains a nuclear option, i.e., nuclear weapons that can be assembled on short notice, or actually possesses nuclear weapons. As part of its deliberate strategy of ambiguity, Israel has not signed the Nuclear Nonproliferation Treaty (NPT), which was opened for signature in 1968 and entered into force in 1970. The NPT was indefinitely extended in 1995 and requires that states other than the charter members of the nuclear club (Britain, China, France, Soviet Union/Russia, and United States) submit their facilities to inspections by the International Atomic Energy Agency (IAEA) and limit their use of nuclear power to civilian purposes. Various estimates place Israel's nuclear capability at anywhere between fifty and three hundred warheads, depending upon the source.

Israel's first prime minister, David Ben-Gurion, made the decision in the 1950s to pursue a nuclear deterrent program, deeming it a last-resort defense option against a presumed alliance of Arab countries arrayed against the Jewish state. Through the combination of clandestine activities as well as crucial assistance from the French government in the mid-1950s (at a time when France began to provide military aid to Israel), the Israeli nuclear program accelerated dramatically. French–Israeli cooperation came to fruition with the signing of the Franco–Israeli nuclear treaty of 1957, which laid the foundation for France's transfer of nuclear technology to Israel and the construction of a nuclear reactor at Dimona, located in the Negev desert, by 1963. The French reportedly gave up on this project before the reactor was completed, but in short order Israel was able to produce weapons-grade plutonium, construct a separation plant, assemble the bombs, and by the late 1960s and early 1970s produce a reliable delivery system. Israel's nuclear strategic plan was modeled along the lines of the U.S. strategic triad, i.e., the ability to deliver nuclear weapons by air (fighter bombers), land (ballistic missiles), and sea (submarines).

To date, no other Middle Eastern state officially possesses nuclear weapons, although Iraq, Libya, and Iran have attempted (or perhaps are currently attempting in the case of Iran) to acquire or develop a nuclear capability. Many Arab states, however, do have other weapons of mass destruction (WMD), the "poor man's nuclear bomb" in the form of chemical and biological weapons, including the ability to deliver them to Israel and other potential targets on the back of short-range and long-range missiles. Critics of Israel's nuclear posture contend that it feeds into an arms race in the Middle East, especially into the area of WMD. Proponents point out, however, that Arab acquisition of chemical and biological weapons has often been done for reasons other than the Israeli threat and is not due to Israel's nuclear capability. Israel also generally does not trust the NPT regime or IAEA inspections, especially as it has failed to prevent North Korea from developing nuclear weapons or Iran from placing itself in a position to develop a nuclear capability in the near future. This is why Israel will not acquiesce to Arab demands for a nuclear-free zone or even consider signing the NPT until there is a comprehensive peace. As Israeli scholar Gerald Steinberg states,

> ... the undeclared nuclear option is seen to provide the fundamental deterrence capacity that is seen as vital to national survival in a hostile and dangerous environment, while at the same time leaving the option open for eventual negotiation of a viable regional nuclear-weapons-free zone. However, until the establishment of mutual recognition, peaceful relations, and regional stability, Israel's nuclear deterrent policy will remain a core element of its strategic posture and national security doctrine.**

---

*Quoted in David W. Lesch, "Israel: Nuclear Capability," in David W. Lesch, ed., *History in Dispute: Israel Since 1945*, 1st series, vol. 14 (New York: James Press, 2004), 143.

**Gerald M. Steinberg, "Israeli Nuclear Capability," in Lesch, *History in Dispute: The Middle East Since 1945*, 1, 144.

Ultimately, Kennedy, wanting to stem the downward slide in U.S.–Saudi relations and responding to pleas by oil lobbyists, authorized a token level of American military forces to be sent to the kingdom (Operation Hard Surface). Although purely symbolic, the move angered Nasser and pushed Egypt and the United States further apart. It was a no-win situation, and the longer the conflict continued, the deeper the wedge that was driven between Washington and Cairo. As often happens in the Middle East, events would alter diplomatic conditions that placed the United States in an untenable situation. By the end of Kennedy's abbreviated presidency, the policy focus relative to the Middle East surrounded the question of a security guarantee for and increased military aid to Israel. Washington was no longer interested in the Johnson Plan. Nasser's ambitions, which he articulated in his 1959 book *The Philosophy of the Revolution*, positioned Egypt at the center of three concentric circles: the Arab states, Africa, and the Islamic world. Egypt's long history as a central focus in each of these circles made it a natural choice to lead all three, and certainly after the boost provided by the Suez war, Nasser believed he was at a pivotal moment in history; however, ultimately his pursuit of the leadership position in any of these circles, much less all three, ran him afoul of the European powers and eventually even the United States under Kennedy. If the Yemen civil war had been resolved in a relatively short time, then Kennedy's Middle East balancing act might have been preserved. But the conflict continued into 1967, costing Egypt about $1 million per day, and persistently weakened Nasser's position from another angle, which eventually influenced his fateful decisions leading up to the June war. For the Kennedy administration there existed the inherent paradox of the globalist nature of U.S. foreign policy vis-à-vis the Middle East at the time: the relative calm that compelled the Kennedy administration to adopt an active posture toward the Arab–Israeli equation also pre-determined that it would not be at or near the top of the foreign policy priority list; thus, it would be without the presidential and bureaucratic commitment necessary for creative implementation.

But Nasser had more immediate problems to deal with, ones that would require his attention, his leadership, and a forceful response. In fact, a number of things started to converge that placed Nasser in a position in which he felt compelled to react in uncharacteristic ways, all the while heightening the tensions in the Arab–Israeli arena. First, Israel by 1963 began to implement in earnest its water diversion plan of the Jordan River, to be used to expand Israeli industry and agriculture. The Arab world naturally looked to Nasser to engineer an appropriate response to the Israeli action, which had been long known but was now near completion. The Egyptian president gathered thirteen Arab heads of state in Cairo in January 1964 in an emergency Arab League summit meeting to craft a collective Arab riposte. The inter-Arab recriminations characteristic of the Arab cold war, some of them quite personal, suddenly disappeared for a brief moment, as the subject of Israel seemed to be the only major issue on which the normally divergent Arab states could agree or cooperate even to a limited extent.

While some Arab leaders came to the summit meeting with the intent of galvanizing a strong response to Israel, Nasser was actually trying to carve out something that would make it appear as if he were actively leading the charge, short of going to war with Israel. While jingoistic statements against Israel abounded at the summit, Nasser's true position was enunciated a week before in a speech at Port Sa'id. He stated the following somewhat prophetically:

> We cannot use force today because our circumstances will not allow us; be patient with us, the battle of Palestine can continue and the battle of the Jordan is part of the battle of Palestine. For I would lead you to disaster if I were to proclaim that I would fight at a time when I was unable to do so. I would not lead my country to disaster and would not gamble with its destiny.[9]

Nasser had long felt, certainly since Israel's convincing military performance at Suez, that the Arabs were still far from adequately prepared to take on Israel. This was especially the case when the Arab world's most powerful country had almost half its forces ensconced in a civil war in Yemen, one that would continue to drain Egyptian resources and become known as Egypt's "Vietnam," i.e., a military quagmire from which it was increasingly difficult to extricate itself. In effect, he had to restrain those countries, such as Syria, from implicating Egypt in a war for which it was thoroughly unprepared to fight, a stance he reiterated to his Arab brethren at an Arab League summit meeting in Casablanca in 1965. What was discussed at the Cairo summit meeting in January 1964 were ways to interdict Israel's attempt to complete the diversion of the Jordan River by, in turn, diverting the tributaries in Syria, Lebanon, and Jordan that fed into it. This was a haphazard, somewhat spontaneous reaction, however, as the Arab states in question would not be able to divert the tributaries in a timely fashion, in addition to the fact that Israel would, and did, prevent any Arab attempt to do so. But the key for Nasser was to divert attention away from an immediate military response, not so much water from the Jordan River.

The key element that emerged from the Cairo meeting was a decision to provide for Palestinian representation, an idea that evolved by May 1964 into the creation of the PLO. The PLO was designed to be a government in exile for the Palestinian people with the Palestine National Council as the central political body, together with a Palestine Liberation Army (PLA) recruited from Palestinian refugees. This was touted as an important step toward the liberation of Palestine, but in essence it was a vehicle through which Nasser hoped to control the Palestinian movement, shift some of the burden of confronting Israel directly away from the Arab states onto the PLO, and be seen as having adopted a forward policy vis-à-vis the Israelis. Ahmad Shuqayri, a rather nondescript Palestinian lawyer from Lebanon, was elected as the first PLO chair; and he and the PLO were dependent upon the Arab states for political and financial support, especially Egypt. The PLO as a whole is made up of a myriad of factions that often reflect the different agendas of the Palestinian exiles that compose them; in addition, these factions just as often reflected the agendas of the host Arab countries in which they were based—if they did not, then they might not be welcome in that country for long. Even early in the Palestinian movement in the 1950s, the main faction of the PLO (as it remains to this day) was al-Fatah ("conquest"), which is also the reverse acronym of *Harakat al-Tahrir al-Falastin*, the "Movement for the Liberation of Palestine." Yasser Arafat, a member of the prominent Husayni family, was one of the group of Palestinian students in Cairo who later founded al-Fatah in Kuwait. The PLO and the factions that composed it often became political footballs in the Arab cold war, usually in the early to mid-1960s between Egypt and Syria. Oftentimes the intra-PLO factional infighting mirrored the interstate contests at the regional level, making it very difficult for the PLO to adopt anything but watered-down policies that the majority of factions could agree upon. Its nebulous composition was something of a strength in terms of being varied and spread out enough not to be defeated in one fell swoop, but it was also a perpetual weakness in terms of generating cohesive policies. By 1965–1966, al-Fatah and other PLO factions tended to launch *fedayeen* raids more and more from Syria or receive Syrian support to operate through Jordan against Israeli targets, especially as the presence of the UN Emergency Force (UNEF) in the Gaza Strip as well as Nasser's fear of unwarrantedly eliciting an Israeli reprisal greatly inhibited Palestinian actions along the Egyptian–Israeli border. Intensified PLO raids outside of the control of Cairo exacerbated inter-Arab and Arab–Israeli tensions.

Also, Nasser started to become even more captive to the Arab nationalist rhetoric he did so much to activate and promote through words but so little to cultivate in deeds. Nasser only reluctantly agreed to the formation of the UAR after his popularity skyrocketed following the Suez war and in response to events on the ground in Syria. By 1963 Nasser was proclaiming that before integral Arab unity could be seriously attempted again there must be "unity of purpose" before "unity of ranks"; in essence, he was calling for change from within the Arab states, i.e., look more like Egypt before he would go down that road again. Two coups that finally brought the Baʿth party to power occurred in Iraq in February and Syria in March 1963. It seemed as though "unity of purpose" had been achieved, at least in the other two major Arab political players. The leaderships in both countries immediately began calling for union with Egypt, something to which Nasser again was reluctant to acquiesce; but he could not be seen to be against a movement that he himself led. The unity talks in Cairo failed, probably just as Nasser had wanted. But the recriminations between Cairo, Damascus, and Baghdad—and between these and the capitals of the reactionary monarchies—resumed in earnest, only to subside by early 1964 when the focus of attention shifted to Israel. It was clear, however, that despite the Arab nationalist pronouncements of support and solidarity, the Arab cold war was still in force, and the contest for Arab leadership between Syria and Egypt would emerge as possibly the single most important long-term dynamic that would lead to the outbreak of the 1967 Arab–Israeli war. In fact, Syria was playing a very dangerous game. The Baʿthist regimes in Damascus, especially the more radical one led by Salah Jadid that came to power in an intra-Baʿth coup in 1966, were driving this contest with Nasser of "more anti-Israeli than thou." This revealed Nasser's hesitancy to do anything precipitous against Israel while promoting Syria as the Arab state that matched words with deeds, ergo its more active sponsorship of PLO raids. But while the regime in Damascus was reinforcing its Arab nationalist credentials and undercutting Nasser in the continuing Arab cold war, at the same time it raised the level of tension in the Arab–Israeli arena and forced the Egyptian president to take the type of aggressive steps against Israel that he had long cautioned against. If this continued, it could create so much concern in Tel Aviv that it might opt to launch a preemptive strike against its Arab neighbors before things got too out of hand. In a nutshell, this is the origin of the June war.[10]

The Soviet Union was playing a dangerous game as well, which, if anything, only added more fuel to the growing fire. Moscow soon discovered after 1958 the travails of trying to establish a dominant position in the Middle East. It soon became trapped in the Arab cold war, having to lean toward one particular Arab state and away from another. At the same time, the Soviets were coming under increasing criticism from China for supporting regimes, such as that which existed under Nasser, which persecuted local communists. The first Marxist–Leninist state was behaving in an entirely nondoctrinaire, yet pragmatic fashion befitting the zero-sum superpower cold war game. The Soviets, through their propaganda machine and diplomacy, began to feed the Arabs a full plate of Zionist and American imperialism and conspiracies, which only reinforced growing anti-Israeli trends by the end of 1963. For Moscow, this seemed to be the only way to craft a unified pro-Soviet Arab position that would relieve the Kremlin of the headaches of the Arab cold war. Again, however, the danger would be that in its attempts to solidify its position in the Arab world by playing the Israeli card, the Soviet Union could also enhance the danger felt by Tel Aviv by raising overall Arab–Israeli tensions. In fact, it would be Moscow's diplomatic indelicacy in this regard that most believe was an immediate cause of the series of events initiated by Nasser in May 1967 that led to the outbreak of war the following month.

Finally, the Arab world saw in the United States after the assassination of Kennedy in November 1963 the assumption of power by a president whose sympathies toward Israel and antipathies toward Nasser were well known even prior to coming to office. President Lyndon B. Johnson's foreign policy lacked the subtle distinctions between communists and nationalists that Kennedy had made. It was a globalist foreign policy, one that saw the Soviet Union lurking behind every trouble spot seeking to enhance its power and influence, and nationalist leaders were either willing or unwilling dupes to Kremlin designs. But whereas the Eisenhower administration often viewed Israel as something of an obstacle to achieve its objectives in the region, Johnson was sympathetic and even empathetic toward the Jewish state. Indeed, Levi Eshkol became the first Israeli prime minister to officially visit the White House in June 1964.[11] Egypt's continuing presence in Yemen, its backing of the Congo rebels, and such actions as the burning of the U.S. Information Agency library in Cairo in November 1964 and the shooting down of an American plane owned by one of Johnson's friends tended to confirm for Johnson that Kennedy's wooing of Nasser had been ill-conceived. The Johnson administration increased U.S. support for the conservative Arab regimes threatened by radical Nasserism and built upon Kennedy's military aid commitments to Israel, the latter made that much more necessary by the former. From Nasser's perspective, the United States and Egypt were on a collision course, which, of course, only reinforced Soviet propaganda at the time. One gets the sense that Nasser believed he was becoming a trapped animal and needed something dramatic in order to break out of his perceived predicament. But he had escaped from such a position once before at Suez—maybe he could do so again. Indeed, the 1956 conflagration in important ways established the parameters of the war in 1967. Whereas Nasser was confident he could successfully play a game of brinksmanship and at least come away with a political, if not a military, victory, the Israelis were just as determined to make sure he did not. For this to happen, Israel wanted a short, decisive war so that its objectives could be achieved before the international community intervened, and it would make sure that the United States was apprised of the situation and would not get in the way this time. It also became a long-held axiom in Israel that any land it gained in the war would not be returned outside of the consummation of a peace treaty with the pertinent Arab state(s)—not repeat what happened after Suez, when Israel withdrew from the Sinai Peninsula outside of the framework of a peace treaty, only to see it become a battleground again nine years later.

THE STEPS TOWARD WAR

On November 4, 1966, the Soviet Union encouraged a mutual defense pact between Egypt and Syria. Moscow was interested in protecting the regime in Damascus; it was one of the few bright spots in recent years for Moscow in the region in terms of its international ideological position as the Syrian regime openly welcomed communists into the government, even though its stepped-up activities and rhetoric against Israel made the Kremlin nervous. Although the Soviets enjoyed their enhanced position in

Damascus, they did not want this more radical Ba'thist regime initiating a war with Israel that could quickly spiral out of control into a superpower confrontation. This was not all that long after the Soviet Union was forced to back down to the United States in the 1962 Cuban Missile Crisis, primarily because of the seventeen to one nuclear advantage the United States had at the time—even though Moscow engaged in a massive nuclear buildup of its own in response, it was still in no position to confront its superpower opponent directly. As such, the defense pact between the Arab cold war rivals might help restrain the Syrians and/or act as something of a deterrent against Israel, which was getting much the better of the cross-border skirmishes that the Kremlin believed were undermining the Salah Jadid regime. Israel, it was thought, would now have to think twice about escalating the border conflict with Syria for fear of activating an Egyptian response—and a multifront war—per the defense treaty. But Egypt was in no mood to fight Israel. The allure of being drawn into a pact, however, that was ostensibly designed to bail out Syria was an opportunity Nasser could not pass up in his attempt to regain the initiative in the inter–Arab arena.

The Egyptian president was aware of Israeli industrial, agricultural, and military advances since the Suez war. The Israeli population by the early 1960s had grown by a factor of three, and it was enjoying yearly annual economic growth of 10%, a figure matched only by the Japanese economic juggernaut.[12] During this time, Israel also developed a comprehensive military strategy that was based on preemptive strikes, taking the war to the territories of its enemies, and rapid, mobile warfare that would end any conflict quickly.[13] Because of the preponderance of men and materiel that the Arabs had over Israel, the latter did not want to find itself in a long, protracted war in which attrition became a mitigating factor. As such, the Israeli air force, mechanized divisions, and paratrooper corps (especially for commando operations) were sufficiently expanded to carry out Israel's military doctrine. Nasser was well aware of the fact that the Arabs still had very little, if any, coordinated strategic plan against Israel and that Egypt still had about half of its troops mired in Yemen.

Only nine days after the signing of the Egyptian–Syrian pact, Israel struck the village of Samu, just over the border in Jordan. Eighteen Jordanians died in the attack, and well over one hundred buildings were destroyed by Israeli forces. It was in response to repeated fedayeen attacks emanating from Jordan in previous months. The Israeli raid was roundly condemned by the international community, including the United States in a UN Security Council resolution. From Washington's point of view, the raid not only raised the level of tension in the area but also undercut the authority of its Arab ally, King Hussein, who had been slowly watching the PLO establish a state within a state right in front of him. Tel Aviv may have also been sending a message to its Arab foes following the Egyptian–Syrian agreement that it would not be deterred; the fact that it hit Jordan rather than Syria directly, however, may suggest otherwise.

Tensions along the Syrian–Israeli border continued, culminating on April 7, 1967, with an Israeli–Syrian air battle that resulted in six Syrian MiGs being shot down and Israeli jets buzzing Damascus. From Moscow, the Jadid regime seemed to be teetering on the edge, especially as Nasser did nothing in response, for which the Egyptian president received a healthy amount of criticism in the Arab world. This concern by the Soviets possibly led to a fateful decision by the Kremlin to launch a disinformation campaign on May 13 that focused on purported massive Israeli troop movements (ten to thirteen brigades) along the Syrian border, possibly gearing up for an invasion or, at the very least, a major military reprisal on a scale heretofore not seen in the over-a-decade-long cycle of raids and reprisals between Israel and its Arab neighbors. There is still some mystery surrounding this disinformation. It is possible the Russians misinterpreted Israeli troop movements, and there are some who claim there was no Soviet disinformation. The reason for doing so, if it in fact happened according to most historical analyses, was to compel Nasser to do something in reaction that might take some heat off of the Syrian regime, allowing this pro-Soviet ally to remain in power by deterring Israel. Nasser did react, but instead of deterring Israel, his progression of escalatory moves in May only created a more propitious environment for the Jewish state to test its new military doctrine.

Regardless of the source or intent of the disinformation regarding Israeli troop movements, Nasser acted as if the information was true, even though he probably understood it was false. Multiple sources, including the UN Truce Supervision Organization and Egyptian officials sent to the Syrian–Israeli border, indicated that the Soviets must have been hallucinating—there was no buildup of Israeli forces. On May 14, Nasser mobilized his forces and marched combat units into the demilitarized Sinai Peninsula, thus beginning the train of events that would lead to the outbreak of war on June 5. The question to ask at this point is why did Nasser, knowing the information was false, take an initial step that indicated that, indeed, Syria was being threatened?[14] And make no mistake: Nasser took the situation by mid-May into his own hands and drove it invariably into conflict with Israel, whether he intended to go all the way to war or not. As with most important decisions, there is probably a confluence of reasons. First and foremost, again he could be seen as matching words with deeds while bailing out a rival in the inter-Arab arena—it was an opportunity too attractive to pass up, one that might vault him back into the position of unquestioned leadership in the Arab world. Second, Egypt—in fact, all the Arab states that depended primarily upon Moscow for military arms—believed that the Soviets always fell short of really committing themselves to providing the Arabs the military and political wherewithal to defeat Israel. They were correct, of course, as the Kremlin was indeed wary of fomenting a regional conflict that might lead to a superpower confrontation. The Soviet disinformation was an uncharacteristically risky move that might indicate the Russian leadership had finally made the decision to offer its Arab friends unqualified support—Nasser did not want to miss this opportunity to possibly entangle the Soviet Union more deeply into the Arab–Israeli arena. In addition, because of the continuing hostility emanating from Washington under the Johnson administration, Nasser also may have felt that the United States was out to get him anyway—if not now, it would do so in the near future. As such, it would be advisable to play along and improve Egypt's relationship with the other superpower for protection. Finally, Egypt was still stuck in the Yemeni quagmire, which only exacerbated the already difficult economic problems the country had been experiencing. A dramatic move into the Sinai might distract Egyptian attentions away from domestic problems and place Nasser back on his pedestal. In any event, it was a relatively low-risk investment with a potentially high return.

But Nasser was still being criticized in some circles in the Arab world because he was seen to be still hiding behind UNEF—if he was really serious, he would demand their removal, which was his prerogative. Nasser had actually only requested a partial withdrawal by UNEF from certain zones in the Sinai—not in the Gaza Strip or Sharm al-Shaykh however. But in a decision that would be heavily criticized in the aftermath of the war, the UN secretary-general, U Thant, informed Egypt that a partial withdrawal was not possible, leaving Nasser with the choice of leaving UNEF in place and continuing to endure the taunts from his Arab critics or demanding total withdrawal. He opted for the latter on May 18, still considering it to be a relatively safe maneuver, one that would silence the doubters. U Thant was also criticized for acceding to the request too easily and not referring it to the Security Council or General Assembly for discussion. Interestingly, Nasser did not order Egyptian troops to move into Sharm al-Shaykh until May 21, knowing that this might dangerously arouse Israel as the city near the tip of the Sinai Peninsula sat astride the Strait of Tiran through which ships to and from the Israeli port of Eilat passed. All the while, however, Israel was caught somewhat off guard by Nasser's moves and becoming increasingly nervous about how far the Egyptian president might push this. It had begun mobilizing some reserve units and calling in reserves for active duty. Israeli Prime Minister Levi Eshkol, known in Israeli circles along the lines of Moshe Sharett—i.e., not the aggressive, hawkish type of prime minister such as Ben-Gurion—gave a speech on May 22 that was uncharacteristically mild coming from an Israeli leader. He essentially disavowed any aggressive intentions on the part of Israel and called for the withdrawal of Israeli and Egyptian forces to their positions held before May 14.

Despite these moves, however, Nasser was still hearing criticism from his Arab critics, particularly in Jordan and Syria, for not doing enough. He had not moved troops to Sharm al-Shaykh until May 21, and in any event, he was still allowing ships bound to and from Israel to pass right by his nose, so to speak. In response, in a move that exponentially escalated the crisis, in a speech at an Egyptian air base on May 22 (following Eshkol's speech), Nasser announced the closure of the Gulf of Aqaba to Israeli ships and any other ships carrying strategic material to the Jewish state. This may have been the point where Nasser crossed the Rubicon in terms of the inevitability of war with Israel. Tel Aviv, ever since the Suez war, had made it very clear that any blockade of the Strait of Tiran would be a casus belli. Israel also felt it was on firm international ground since it believed it had received an American guarantee under Eisenhower to keep the Gulf of Aqaba, as an international waterway, open. Nasser took this significant step primarily because he believed he had seized the diplomatic advantage over Israel based on the latter's rather tepid response thus far, exemplified by Eshkol's May 22 speech. This relates to a difference in perception that hampered Nasser throughout the crisis. Authoritarian regimes such as Egypt's often have difficulty interpreting the actions emanating from democracies such as Israel's, where a free and open press reveals, to all who care to observe, political infighting, differences of opinion, and societal fears—and certainly the Israeli hierarchy was scrambling to put together a coherent response while various political factions aired their disagreements. Nasser probably saw this as a weakness that led him to possibly downgrade in his own mind the strength of Israel and its ability to respond to his bold moves. He estimated that the chances of war after the closure of the Gulf of Aqaba were about fifty–fifty. To Nasser, the gamble for a fabulous payoff was thus worth the risk. He had definitely re-established his stature in the Arab world, Arab states from across the region were steadfastly announcing their support for him, and he might be able to leverage this diplomatic advantage he thought he had vis-à-vis Israel into some meaningful Israeli concessions. Besides, Nasser was confident that if war did break out, Egypt could survive an initial onslaught by Israel and wait for the intervention of the international community to save him, as happened in 1956. And he would be able again to steal political victory from the jaws of military defeat.

Israel responded more forcefully on May 23. Eshkol, in a speech to the Knesset, stated that "any interference with freedom of shipping in the Gulf and in the Strait constitutes a gross violation of international law, a blow at the sovereign rights of other nations, and an act of aggression against Israel."[15] In close consultation with Israel this time around, as opposed to the Suez war, the Johnson administration the same day in a television address stated that "the United States considers the Gulf to be an international waterway and feels that a blockade of Israeli shipping is illegal and potentially disastrous to the cause of peace. The right of free, innocent passage of the international waterway is a vital interest of the international community."[16] The Soviets, not to be outdone since their prestige was on the line in the proxy superpower battleground of the Third World, chimed in on the same day as well, proclaiming that "should anyone try to unleash aggression in the Near East, he would be met not only with the united strength of Arab countries but also with strong opposition to aggression from the Soviet Union and all peace-loving nations."[17] Moscow also vetoed attempts led by the United States in the UN Security Council to pass a resolution condemning Egypt for blockading the Gulf of Aqaba. These iterations from the Kremlin could only have emboldened Nasser to believe that the Soviet Union was, indeed, fully behind him. This was important to Nasser because he knew that if he had any chance against Israel, the United States must not be allowed to intervene in the war on the Israeli side. Soviet warnings just might deter the Americans from any thoughts about military intervention in any impending conflict. They also might compel the United States and the Soviet Union to cooperate in imposing a cease-fire if war did break out, both mutually fearing any conflict that could escalate to the superpower level. This could be used to Nasser's advantage, as happened in 1956. Of course, the Israelis, as mentioned previously, were determined not to let Nasser off the hook this time.

Nasser continued the onslaught. In public speeches on May 26 to the Arab Trade Union Congress and on May 29 in front of the Egyptian National Assembly, Nasser essentially called for the destruction of Israel. In the latter speech, Nasser stated "the issue today is not the question of Aqaba or the Strait of Tiran, or UNEF. The issue is the rights of the people of Palestine.... We say: We want the rights of the people of Palestine—complete."[18] In the course of the following week, Nasser informed his subordinates that the chance of war with Israel had escalated to 80%. Why did Nasser maintain the pressure on Israel, practically ensuring that war would break out? Nadav Safran writes that Nasser had convinced himself that his moves had created a unique opportunity for dealing Israel at least a decisive diplomatic, and possibly even military, blow.[19] Obviously, Nasser felt he had to have Arab unity and superior military power, the former contributing to the latter. Yet, as late as one month prior to the crisis, Nasser was cautioning against war with Israel because the Arabs were not adequately prepared. But such was the course of events in the succeeding month that Nasser became convinced—or he convinced himself—that his conditions had been met. This could very well be a case of a leader seeing what he wants to see and hearing what he wants to hear despite evidence to the contrary, and sycophantic associates unwilling to counter the momentum toward war with anything as risky as the truth. Maybe he was psychologically intoxicated by the concentration of troops and weaponry, the apparent support of the Soviet Union, and the collective Arab voice supporting him as military contingents from across the Arab world, as far away as Morocco, made their way to Egypt as a tangible sign of support. Somehow he believed he had engineered the impossible. Again, he apparently had downgraded Israeli capabilities by misinterpreting Israeli responses. The day before Nasser's speech to the Egyptian National Assembly, Levi Eshkol declared in a speech to the nation that the Israeli Cabinet had decided on "the continuation of political action in the world arena ... to obviate the necessity of Israel having to use armed forces for her defense."[20] Eshkol was actually ill at the time of the speech, worn down by the crisis and the associated political battles in Israel, and he came across in a very weak and almost incoherent fashion. The waffling by Israeli leaders only fed into Nasser's re-evaluation of the Jewish state. Of course, Nasser was wrong on all counts.

Maybe most importantly, Nasser also believed that for the Arabs to be successful in any sort of conflict, the United States had to be diplomatically isolated from Israel; i.e., he had to be relatively certain the Americans would not enter the fight on the Israeli side—there would be no hope of victory then, either diplomatically or militarily. After all, he was depending on superpower intervention to stop the war if events on the battlefield started to turn against him, not to fight in it. Ironically, in this case Nasser turned out to be correct. The Johnson administration decided well into the crisis that it should not—and could not—intervene militarily. Of course, part of the reason for this decision was the fact that both Israeli and American intelligence were certain that Israel could fairly easily defeat any combination of Arab states.

The Johnson administration was taken by surprise by the course of events in May 1967 as much as the Israelis were. As first, as with the Israelis, U.S. officials believed Nasser was probably bluffing, mobilizing troops just to distract attention away from other problems and score some points in the inter-Arab arena. He did something quite similar in February 1960, sending troops into the Sinai, claiming he deterred impending Israeli aggression. With the United States ensconced in Vietnam, Johnson was determined not to go too far out in front of Congress, the American people, or the international community with his response to the crisis.[21] American forces were committed to Vietnam, so the last thing Johnson or Congress wanted to see was the eruption of a war that could ensnare U.S. participation and/or spiral out of control into a superpower confrontation.[22] The Soviet Union was foremost on the mind of Johnson throughout the crisis. As such, Johnson wanted to restrain Israel while the United States attempted to construct a multilateral diplomatic solution, especially after Nasser closed the Gulf of Aqaba. He wanted the Israelis to give him time, two to three weeks, to work on a multilateral process to resolve the crisis, possibly even some sort of international maritime fleet that would reopen the Gulf of Aqaba. Johnson met with Israeli ambassador to the United States, Abba Eban, on May 26. At the meeting, Johnson told Eban, in what would become an oft-repeated expression by U.S. officials to the Israelis, that "Israel will not be alone unless it decides to go alone." Johnson hoped that this would send a signal to the Israelis to stay with administration efforts to arrange a multilateral solution. And when Eshkol came out with his rather conciliatory speech on May 28 after Eban returned to Israel to consult with his prime minister on his meeting with Johnson, the administration believed the peak of the crisis had passed—Israel was going to wait.[23] This is the burden of being a superpower; i.e., there are a great many important policy items on the plate at any given moment, and the leadership in the White House is compelled to attend to one item, spend a certain amount of delegated time on it, then turn the page and move on. In contrast, Nasser, Eshkol, and their cohorts were essentially eating, sleeping, and breathing the crisis to the point of becoming ill, with every word and action emanating from Washington dissected and analyzed over and over.[24] When events in the Middle East continued to escalate the tension and as the hawks in the Israeli government began to gain the upper hand over Eshkol, the Israelis tended to view Johnson's position as advocating caution; but in the end he was not saying "do not go to war." William Quandt called it a "yellow light" response from the United States rather than a "green light," but "as for most motorists, the yellow light was tantamount to a green one."[25] Even if the Israelis acted alone, Johnson administration officials believed this would be better for U.S.–Arab relations, although this did not stop the Arabs after the war from blaming the United States for colluding with Israel.

War seemed all but inevitable when King Hussein of Jordan visited Cairo on May 30 and concluded a treaty of joint defense with Egypt that placed the Jordanian armed forces at Egypt's disposal. Jordan also allowed contingents of Iraqi troops to enter into the country for use in case of war.[26] Israel was now effectively surrounded. Israel responded to this development by forming a national unity government on June 1, including former Irgun leader Menachem Begin and bringing in Moshe Dayan, who was military chief of staff during the Suez war, as minister of defense (Eshkol was both prime minister and minister of defense until this time). The decision to go to war by launching a pre-emptive strike now seemed to be a fait accompli. There was some urgency among the Israeli hawks, who dominated the Cabinet by this time, because it was announced on June 4 that Egypt was sending its vice president, Zakaria Muhieddin, to Washington to hold talks with U.S. officials. The last thing they wanted to see was Egypt backing out of the situation under the cover of U.S. diplomacy, thus giving Nasser a chance to claim a diplomatic victory—Israel needed to strike first before this had an opportunity to develop. According to some, this is the way Nasser wanted it anyhow because he feared U.S. intervention if Egypt struck first, and one of the keys to any hope of success lay in the United States staying out of it. The problem was that he expected Egypt to be able to absorb an Israeli first strike (with about only 20% at most of its combat jet fleet destroyed) and then successfully launch a counterattack in coordination with Jordanian and Syrian forces. It did not exactly go according to his plan.

WAR ERUPTS

The 1967 Arab–Israeli war is often referred to as the "Six Day War," usually by Israeli sources since it was Yitzhak Rabin who purportedly named the war based on the biblical account of how long it took God to create the earth and everything on it. The appellation is also a bit of a boast on how little time it took to defeat the combined Arab armies. In actuality, however, the war was effectively over in a few hours. The Arab side in the war has often been cited with incompetence for being defeated so quickly. However, as Safran writes, "the Egyptians thought and acted according to accepted military doctrine and practice; their misfortune was that the Israelis thought and acted in thoroughly unorthodox, almost inconceivable, ways."[27]

The war began on June 5 at approximately 8:00 a.m. Tel Aviv time, with a massive Israeli air strike against Egyptian airfields and other targets as well as armored columns moving against Egyptian positions in Gaza and Sinai. Contrary to what Nasser and his high command expected, the Israelis threw almost their entire fighter-bomber fleet against

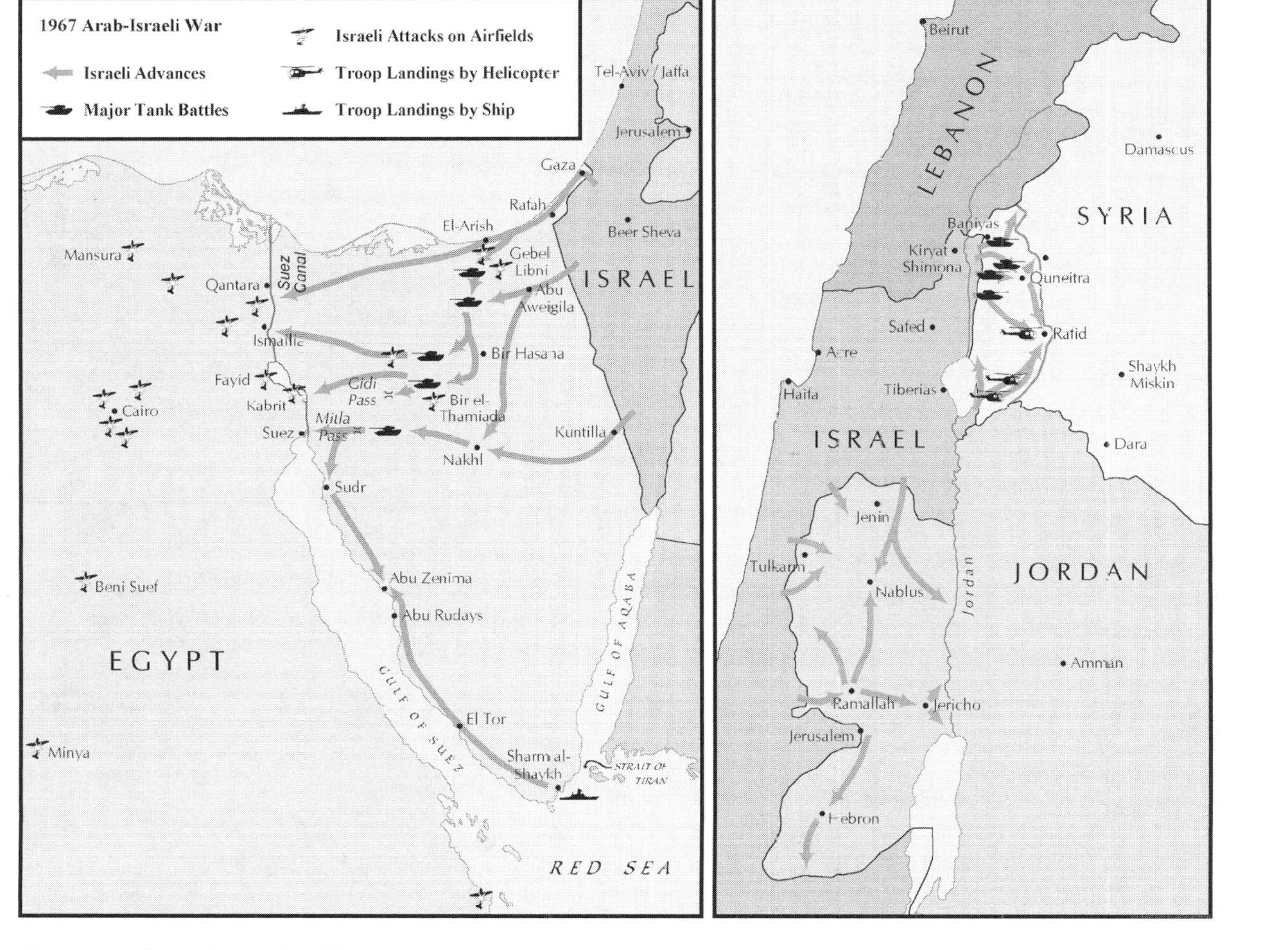

The 1967 Arab–Israeli War. (Middle East Studies Association, Justin McCarthy, University of Louisville, © 2003.)

the Egyptians, leaving the Jordanian and Syrian fronts virtually exposed in the air. And the Israelis did not come at Egypt as the crow flies or all in one thrust. They hit Egypt from a variety of directions and in waves, à la British volley fire, which kept the Egyptians from regrouping or launching their own planes—two and one-half hours of constant bombardment. The idea was to sow so much confusion in the Egyptian command-and-control structure with the audacious strike that the Israeli air combat fleet would be able to return in time to take on Jordan and Syria before the Arab allies of Egypt could assess exactly what had happened. It worked almost to perfection as Israel destroyed 80% of Egypt's bomber fleet and 55% of its fighters. With little to no air support, Egyptian columns in the Sinai were practically defenseless against the Israeli armored incursions and air superiority. With Egypt essentially knocked to its knees within hours, it was just a matter of time before Israel defeated the Jordanians and Syrians. In four days, Israel captured the Gaza Strip and the entire Sinai Peninsula from Egypt. All the captured territories in the war together made Israel three times larger than it was in 1949.

There would still be fierce fighting on both the remaining fronts, but by June 11, when the last cease-fire was agreed to by Israel and Syria, the Jewish state had also captured the West Bank, including East Jerusalem, from Jordan and the Golan Heights from Syria. With the inclusion of the West Bank, Israel now had strategic depth, more control of water aquifers, and possession of much of biblical Israel (Judea and Samaria), including a united Jerusalem as its capital. The capture of the Golan Heights eliminated Syria's strategic advantage of looking down upon the Huleh Valley in

Egyptian prisoners in a truck taken by Israeli soldiers near al-Arish, Egypt, during the 1967 Arab–Israeli war, June 8, 1967. (Bettmann/CORBIS, BE023179.)

northern Israel and, importantly, more control over the tributaries that fed into the Jordan River. Taking the Sinai reestablished the buffer that Israel enjoyed during the days of the stationing of British troops and UNEF in Egypt—only now, Israel itself was the buffer. Although Israel would have to extend its defenses to the limit to guard the newly won territory, it did buy itself time if Egypt ever again launched an invasion of Israel proper—it would have to cross the Israeli-held mountainous, barren Sinai first.

A very controversial incident took place on June 8 during the course of the war. The USS *Liberty*, an American intelligence-gathering ship, had been sent to the eastern Mediterranean off the coasts of Israel and Egypt to ascertain the course of the war. The Johnson administration was particularly concerned about possible Soviet intervention. The ship was attacked by Israeli fighter jets and patrol boats in broad daylight, killing thirty-four U.S. crewmen and wounding 164. The ship itself was barely able to limp back to port. The Israelis admitted that they had, in fact, mistakenly attacked the ship. The Johnson administration, greatly relieved that it was not the Soviets that attacked the ship, accepted the Israeli explanation, an Israeli apology, and $3 million of compensation for the families of the victims. The incident is still an emotional one to this day, kept alive by many of the family members of the victims and the surviving crewmen of the *Liberty*. This episode has become something of a lightning rod in assessing the value of the close U.S.–Israeli relationship. Is Israel really a cooperative ally and friend of the United States, or is its relationship with the United States solely based on need, where Israel acts according to its own national interests even if they are contrary to U.S. objectives? The issue revolves around the question of whether or not the Israelis intentionally attacked the U.S. ship. In fact, where one stands on this question often says more about one's position on the value of the U.S–Israeli "special relationship." There is some evidence to suggest that Israel attacked the ship because it did not want the Johnson administration to know that it was planning to take the Golan Heights in the last phase of the conflict. If Washington knew about these plans a priori, it might work to prevent the Israelis from doing so for fear of eliciting a Soviet response. There are also indications that the Johnson administration was informed of the Israeli intention to strike against Syria—after all, Damascus, in Israeli eyes, was primarily responsible for the tensions leading up to the war but had to date gotten off scot-free—and, therefore, there was no need for the Israelis to attack the ship based on this rationale. Another theory postulated that the Israelis were trying to keep the United States from finding out about a massacre of Egyptian prisoners in the Sinai. There is scant evidence to support this, however. The counterargument by Israel and its supporters is simply that it was due to the fog of war. In fact, the whole incident has taken on the air of a capital murder case. As such, one has to examine the motive of the suspected perpetrator, and this is where many claim the case against Israel breaks down. What possible motive could Israel have had to knowingly attack a U.S. ship, thus threatening its most important state-to-state relationship? Even though the weaponry utilized by the Israelis in the war was mostly European, the United States under Johnson had become a major supplier of military and economic aid to the Jewish state, and this aid would increase exponentially in the 1970s. One of the problems has been the lack of a satisfactory independent investigation that could shed more light on the incident. Because of this, there is still plenty of room for alternative explanations and conjecture.[28]

THE AFTERMATH

Regardless of the attack on the USS *Liberty*, the overwhelming victory by Israel was an astonishing military achievement. The country itself was exultant after the war—it appeared that Israel's existence was, at long last, assured since it was clear no Arab coalition could hope to eliminate the Jewish state. Israel acquired land and, with it, more security. But now there was the delicate and potentially divisive question of what to do with what would become known as the Occupied Territories: should the land be settled by Jews and kept in perpetuity, or should some or all of the land be given back to the Arabs in return for peace? It is a question still bedeviling the Israeli polity today. With the new territories Israel also inherited 1.3 million more Palestinians, while approximately 300,000 more Palestinians joined the ranks of refugees, fleeing to neighboring camps much as the original set of Palestinian refugees had done in 1947–1949. The Palestinian population was a demographic time bomb for Israel as their higher birth rates would make them the majority within forty to fifty years in Israel if it held onto the Occupied Territories. If that happened, the democratic nature of Israel would be in question with minority rule, the fear being the development of an apartheid situation not unlike that which existed in South Africa. Since the 1967 war sparked these concerns, ones that have grown and multiplied in the ensuing decades, the initial assessment of the conflict as an unmitigated success has been somewhat diminished in recent years. And as we will see, Israel's own embellished view of its power would create a complacency and stubbornness that would help lay the foundation for the next major Arab–Israeli war in 1973.

For the Arabs, the decisive loss in 1967 was utterly devastating—maybe even more so than the 1948 *al-Nakba* because expectations were so much higher this time, with the almost god-like figure of Nasser leading the way. The fall, therefore, was greater and the long-term repercussions deeper. Nasserism had come to an effective end as its standard-bearer was forever tarnished and discredited in the eyes of many. With it went the dominant paradigm of secular Arab nationalism, which, although always more façade than reality, would never again reach the ideological pitch it had attained in the 1950s and early 1960s. Many Islamists began to vocalize their belief that the Arabs had lost so badly because they had veered away from Islam under the secular, socialist doctrines of the "progressive" Arab states. They even paid a backhanded compliment to Israel by claiming the Jewish state was victorious because the Israelis had stayed true to their religion. This loss, the Islamist explanation for it, and the Islamist remedy to correct it established a foundation for a resurgence of Islamic "fundamentalism," albeit in a much more virulent form that would grow more lethal with the passage of time.

Nasser himself was bitterly distraught. There were trials and purges in Egypt following the war in an attempt to assign appropriate blame for the debacle. He even resigned as Egyptian president, only to be coaxed back into office after the spontaneous and arranged appearance of hundreds of thousands of Egyptians in the streets calling for him to return. But he would never be the same nor would he command as much authority in the Arab world. His dilemma was almost immediately revealed when he was compelled to mend fences with Saudi Arabia, Jordan, and the other Arab "reactionary" states in order to finally escape the Yemeni quagmire as well as acquire much needed economic aid for his ailing economy, made all the more necessary since the Suez Canal was closed (until 1975) and the oil fields in and astride the Sinai Peninsula in the Gulf of Suez and Red Sea were now in Israeli possession. Seeking support in numbers, Nasser joined hands with many of his former Arab rivals at the Arab League summit meeting in Khartoum, Sudan, in August 1967. The collective Arab policy that emerged from the summit on the Arab–Israeli issue resulted in the famous three no's: no peace, no recognition of, and no negotiations with Israel. The hope was that the international community would pressure Israel into returning the territories.

This international pressure would eventually take the form of perhaps the most famous of all UN resolutions: Security Council Resolution 242. The Johnson administration initially engaged in steps that might defuse the crisis atmosphere following the war and create parameters for a peaceful resolution of the conflict. Arab–Israeli hostilities were still acute, and Johnson did not want a second barrier erected in addition to the one he had in Vietnam to the "woman he really loved," i.e., the Great Society domestic programs. In general, there was a great deal of resentment in the Arab world toward the United States for, in their eyes, aiding and abetting Israel's victory.[29] While this viewpoint confused the Johnson administration's relative passivity and aloofness during the crisis and war with intent, it would still be a difficult obstacle to overcome for Washington to establish itself as an even-handed broker. Indeed, Algeria, Egypt, Iraq, Sudan, Syria, and Yemen severed diplomatic relations with the United States, while the Soviet Union and some of its Eastern bloc client-states broke relations with Israel during and after the war (except for Romania). The problem now, however, was that the war, if anything, greatly complicated the Arab–Israeli situation, especially as Israel had all of the captured territory and was clearly far stronger than the Arab states militarily—not exactly the parity one would like in order to advance negotiations. Johnson himself doubted Israel's willingness to return the occupied lands for peace, and the Arab states were in no position to negotiate from such a clear position of weakness.

Presaging Resolution 242, Johnson outlined his "five principles for peace" program soon after the war, linking an Israeli withdrawal with "respect for the political independence and territorial integrity of all the states in the area" and calling for "progress in solving the refugee problem, freedom of innocent maritime passage, [and] limitation of the arms race." While constructing what in essence was a land-for-peace formula, the Johnson administration, as Kaufman states, "largely ignored the overwhelming sentiment in Israel in favor of keeping at least some of the lands and wrongly assumed that, at some point, the Arab states would be willing to bargain with the Israelis."[30] After the Egyptian sinking of the Israeli destroyer *Elath* in October 1967 along with the Israeli response against Egypt's oil refineries in Suez City, it became clear that tensions were still high. It was thought in Washington that an international forum, the UN, should take the lead in addressing the issue—whether this was a case of passing the buck (à la the British in February 1948) or recognizing that international attention to the problem might bring pressure to bear on both parties to make the necessary concessions is a matter of debate. But one thing is definite: by involving the Soviet Union in the process and collecting its vote for a peaceful resolution on record in the Security Council, the Johnson administration believed it had insulated the conflict from direct superpower confrontation, which greatly simplified the issue of pursuing détente with Moscow in direct relation to the U.S. position in Vietnam. Moscow was just as much interested in insulating the conflict, especially if it meant being welcomed on board as essentially an equal partner with Washington regarding Middle East frameworks for peace and negotiations. The result is what many have called a masterpiece of ambiguity, Resolution 242, which established the land-for-peace formula; but it did not specifically delineate how much land Israel would return in exchange for peace and secure and recognized borders. The ambiguity, as in the case of the Balfour Declaration, has to do, again, with the definite versus the indefinite article. While the resolution talks of "the inadmissibility of the acquisition of territory by war and the need to work for a just and lasting peace in which every state in the area can live in security," in operative clause number one it calls for the "withdrawal of Israeli armed forces from territories occupied in the recent conflict." Not *the* territories, which strongly implies *all* of the occupied land. The use of the indefinite has been interpreted by Israel as *some* but not necessarily *all* of the territories, and certainly the nature of any withdrawal must be negotiated. The resolution also does not directly mention the Palestinians, only calling for a "just settlement of the refugee problem." Egypt, Jordan, and Israel accepted Resolution 242, which was passed by the Security Council on November 22, 1967. While adopting vastly different interpretations of the resolution, this acceptance at least indicated a willingness on the part of the erstwhile combatants to consider compromise.

The United States, however, was not willing, and possibly not even able, to insert itself into the mix; and the forces in the region were not, at least on the surface, predisposed toward a negotiated settlement—and certainly not without sufficient superpower pressure. The Johnson administration, after the passage of 242, lost much of its interest in the region.[31] Rather than viewing the UN resolution as an initial salvo toward a settlement, it seemed to be satisfied that it had put the Arab–Israeli issue back into the icebox. In any event, with the Tet offensive in Vietnam in early 1968 and the subsequent decision by Johnson not to run for reelection, the Middle East lost its brief period of salience. There would be no more concerted efforts from a lame-duck administration primarily interested in leaving as soon as it could with as little damage as possible.[32]

With little progress in sight, Nasser chose to develop a different strategy. He could not sue for peace from such a weakened negotiating position. He also could not just live with the status quo, for the longer Israel held onto the territories, the more difficult it would be to get them back, especially as Tel Aviv started to construct Jewish settlements in the occupied lands. Because of his reduced credibility and legitimacy in the Arab world, Nasser was also under pressure to do *something*. Ironically, considering the breadth of his loss in 1967, Nasser chose to prepare for an early resumption of war with Israel. This portended a repair of his relationship with the Soviet Union, which was ruptured somewhat because of Moscow's inability to "save" its Arab allies in the war. The Kremlin was very concerned that some of the Arab states might "go over" to the West if it did not adequately resupply the weapons and material lost in the war. However, the Soviets were also worried that by doing so they could provide the wherewithal for the Arabs to engage in another conflagration with Israel that could, indeed, lead to the dreaded superpower confrontation. It was quite the dilemma for Moscow because it felt it could not lose ground to the United States in the Third World by not supporting its friends. And Nasser would play the superpower card to the maximum in order to acquire arms from Russia. The Soviets attempted to bridge the dilemma by emphasizing in arms deliveries more defensive rather than offensive weapons in order to inhibit the Arab states' abilities to initiate a conflict. This would become a perennial bone of contention between Moscow and its Arab allies.

But Nasser would fight this war differently. He would engage in low-intensity warfare, trying to wear down Israel by utilizing Egypt's advantage in overall men and materiel, especially when the latter was being readily resupplied by the Soviets. This would not be the mobile, blitzkrieg type of war at which Israel excelled. This conflict, which formally began in March 1969 and ended with a cease-fire in August 1970, appropriately came to be called the War of Attrition. Nasser's objective was not to defeat Israel but to improve his bargaining position by inflicting some pain on the Jewish state, possibly even establishing a bridgehead across the Suez Canal in the Sinai and garnering international attention toward the issue so as to generate more international pressure on Israel to return the territories—this would be a strategy much more successfully pursued by Nasser's successor, Anwar Sadat, in the 1973 Arab–Israeli war.

The War of Attrition ebbed and flowed over its seventeen months. It was characterized by artillery exchanges across the Suez Canal and aerial dogfights and bombings, essentially just an intensification of what had been going on ever since the end of the 1967 war. At certain times, it got fairly intense, especially when during a particularly difficult time for Egypt in early 1970 the Soviets started massively resupplying the Egyptian armed forces and providing sophisticated surface-to-air missiles to protect Egypt from Israeli air raids. More alarmingly, Soviet pilots actually began flying Egyptian Soviet-supplied MiGs wearing Egyptian insignia in order to better combat Israeli fighter jets. Once Washington received news of this, it started to look much more closely at bringing about a cease-fire in the War of Attrition before it transformed itself into an all-out conventional war.

The new Nixon administration came to office in January 1969, paying more attention to the Middle East, especially with William Rogers as secretary of state, someone who was a regionalist and known to be fairly even-handed on the Arab–Israeli issue. Rogers saw the War of Attrition as an opportunity to advance a comprehensive Arab–Israeli peace plan in December 1969, aptly named the "Rogers plan." It was based on Resolution 242 and envisioned a binding peace agreement with Israeli withdrawal to the June 4, 1967, borders, i.e., the day before the war began (including the redivision of Jerusalem), with a repatriation of Palestinian refugees or resettlement outside of Israel with compensation. As one might expect, the Israelis adamantly opposed the Rogers plan. Tel Aviv launched a concerted campaign to undermine it through its domestic allies in the United States as well as engaging in deeper raids in Egypt, hoping to humiliate, if not overthrow, Nasser, which would render the Rogers plan null and void. As mentioned earlier, all it did was to provoke the Soviets to intervene more directly, which in turn led to heavier Israeli losses. The Rogers plan also suffered from internecine conflict within the Nixon administration, particularly between Rogers himself and Nixon's national security adviser, Henry Kissinger. Kissinger disagreed with Rogers' regionalist approach to foreign policy, preferring a more globalist policy that focused more on excluding the Soviets entirely from the area and any peace process therein. If the Soviet Union was shown to be vestigial, the Arab states would have no choice but to approach the United States regarding Arab–Israeli issues, thus cementing Moscow's exclusion. The Rogers plan, based as it was on Resolution 242, envisioned Soviet participation at some level. Kissinger also resented the fact that he did not have complete control over U.S. foreign policy, and in his attempts to gain complete control, he established lines of communication with foreign leaders, including Israel's, that went around Rogers, thus undercutting the secretary of state's authority. In short, the combination of these factors killed the Rogers plan.

But with the War of Attrition in danger of spiraling out of control, in addition to the fact that the combatants were indeed being worn down, Rogers, through the guise of what was called the "Rogers initiative," worked assiduously during the summer of 1970 to arrange a cease-fire. After initial rejection of it by Israel and Egypt, both parties finally agreed to it in August. The initiative called for a cease-fire with a resumption of negotiations based on Resolution 242. Israel was quite wary that the Rogers initiative might inevitably lead to the Rogers plan, and it was only after personal assurances by President Nixon that it would not—with promises of more arms shipments to boot—that Tel Aviv signed on. Even though the cease-fire would be repeatedly broken, it did show that an Arab state and Israel could agree to *something*. This was of particular interest to Kissinger, who began to think that maybe limited agreements—small steps—instead of a comprehensive one made more sense. These smaller diplomatic victories would build confidence and trust and lead eventually to the much more complicated task of a comprehensive accord that dealt with a plethora of seemingly intractable issues, such as the Palestinian problem.

Excluded again from the bargaining, it would, in fact, turn out that some Palestinian factions would see the cease-fire to the War of Attrition as very dangerous to their cause. Any sort of an agreement that could lead to peace between Israel and an Arab state was vociferously opposed at the time by the PLO. It needed the combined support of the Arab states, especially Egypt, if it ever hoped to establish Palestine—the state of war between the Arabs and Israelis must continue unabated. In an attempt to disrupt any hint of progress toward peace negotiations, a reinvigorated PLO became embroiled in a civil war in Jordan, what the Palestinians call "Black September." While it was an episode of relatively isolated regional importance in and of itself, the repercussions of Black September would reverberate throughout the region in an immediate and profound manner, dramatically changing the course of the Arab–Israeli conflict.

NOTES

1. Quoted in Robert H. Mnookin and Ehud Eiran, "Discord Behind the Table: The Internal Conflict Among Israeli Jews Concerning the Future of Settlements in the West Bank and Gaza," *Journal of Dispute Resolution* 1 (2005): 26.

2. Halim Barakat, *Days of Dust* (Washington, DC: Three Continents Press, 1983), 5, 9.

3. See John Waterbury and Alan Richards, *A Political Economy of the Middle East* (Boulder: Westview Press, 1996).

4. Burton I. Kaufmann, *The Arab Middle East and the United States: Inter-Arab Rivalry and Superpower Diplomacy* (New York: Twayne, 1996), 32.

5. Quoted in Douglas Little, "From Even-Handed to Empty-Handed: Seeking Order in the Middle East," in Thomas G. Paterson, ed., *Kennedy's Quest for Victory: American Foreign Policy, 1961-1963* (London: Oxford University Press, 1989), 162.

6. Little, "From Even-Handed to Empty-Handed," 166.

7. Nasser was notified of the Hawks sale ahead of time by U.S. officials, and he reportedly appreciated being so informed; but once news spread across the Arab world, Nasser was compelled to adopt at least a prima facie negative posture.

8. The relationship between Washington and Riyadh had cooled noticeably since early 1961, when Crown Prince Faisal (Faysal) refused to renew the U.S. lease on the airbase at Dhahran, possibly in part due to Kennedy's new approach to Nasser. Kennedy's rapprochement with Nasser had been viewed by the Saudi regime with derision. The Kennedy view contended that improving the relationship with Nasser actually helped protect Saudi Arabia. The Saudis countered that such an approach only gave Nasser the wherewithal and perceived flexibility to cause more problems in the area.

9. Quoted from Michael B. Oren, *Six Days of War: June 1967 and the Making of the Modern Middle East* (New York: Ballantine Books, 2003), 19.

10. Oren writes that Israel and Egypt shared a mutual concern regarding restraining Syria. In June 1966 Egypt and Israel actually established a secret line of communication discussing possible concessions: Israel would support international aid for Egypt in return for a lessening of the Suez Canal blockade and a reduction of the vehemently anti-Israeli propaganda emanating from Cairo. Oren reports that Egypt even invited the Israeli head of Mossad to Cairo for direct talks. The meeting never occurred, and the secret communications ended as Eshkol did not want to send his intelligence chief to Egypt and Nasser became concerned that news of the communication might leak out in the Arab world. Oren, *Six Days of War*, 30. This episode certainly points to Nasser's unwillingness to confront Israel as well as the fact that, despite the vitriolic rhetoric and fears, both sides showed a willingness to entertain compromise—if only there was a more concerted international and/or superpower push toward a potential breakthrough. With the Arab cold war it may not have resulted in a peace accord, but it might have staved off the 1967 war.

11. Johnson reportedly told an Israeli diplomat following Kennedy's assassination "You have lost a very great friend. But you have found a better one."

12. Oren, *Six Days of War*, 17.

13. In Israel, women were required to serve eighteen months and men two years of active duty in the military. Both served in the reserves until age fifty-two. As Oren states, ". . . Israeli civilians were more like permanent soldiers on temporary leave." Ibid.

14. Most of the information in this section detailing the events of May–June, unless otherwise indicated, is drawn from Nadav Safran's classes and his excellent analysis contained in his landmark book *Israel, the Embattled Ally* (Cambridge, MA: Harvard University Press, 1981). Nadav was a teacher, mentor, and friend, and he is missed. I am privileged to be able to pass on some of his teachings and scholarship.

15. Quoted in Safran, *Israel, the Embattled Ally,* 388.

16. On the demand for consultation this time around, Johnson sent a note to Eshkol on May 17 that said "I am sure you will understand that I cannot accept any responsibilities on behalf of the United States for situations which arise as a result of actions on which we are not consulted." Quoted in William B. Quandt, *Peace Process: American Diplomacy and the Arab–Israeli Conflict Since 1967* (Berkeley: University of California Press, 2001), 25.

17. Quoted in Safran, *Israel, the Embattled Ally,* 389.

18. Quoted in ibid, 389.

19. Ibid. 234.

20. Quoted in ibid, 389.

21. For a more specific discussion of the Johnson administration's actions during the crisis and war, see Quandt, *Peace Process,* 23–52.

22. In addition, with the Gulf of Tonkin incident in the recent past (1964), when Johnson used an incident in the Gulf of Tonkin in Vietnam to broaden his powers regarding U.S. military involvement in Southeast Asia, the U.S. president was not about to act unilaterally and without full consultation with Congress in this instance.

23. Although immediately after the meeting with Abba Eban on May 26, Johnson said "I've failed. They'll go." In the end, he was proven correct.

24. David W. Lesch, "From Eisenhower to Johnson: Shifts in US Policy Toward the Arab–Israeli Conflict," in Elie Podeh and Asher Kaufman, eds., *Arab–Jewish Relations: From Conflict to Reconciliation* (London: Sussex Academic Press, 2005), 88.

25. Quandt, *Peace Process,* 41.

26. Hussein was in a difficult position. The Israelis actually urged him not to enter the conflict, but he was under tremendous pressure in the Arab world to join the war coalition. Ultimately, Hussein decided that not participating was more perilous than entering the war, even though the latter probably would—and did—result in the loss of the West Bank and East Jerusalem.

27. Safran, *Israel, the Embattled Ally*, 240.

28. For opposing views on this incident, see James Bamford, *Puzzle Palace* (Boston: Houghton Mifflin, 1982 (he claims the Israelis might have knowingly carried out the attack, and at the very least there has not been a proper investigation of the incident); on the other side of the argument, see Jay A. Cristol, *The* Liberty *Incident: The 1967 Israeli Attack on the U.S. Navy Spy Ship* (Washington, DC: Brassey's, 2002). Also see James M. Ennes, Jr., *Assault on the* Liberty (New York: Reintree Press, 2002) and the website www.ussliberty.org.

29. On Arab perceptions of the war, see Fawaz A. Gerges, "The 1967 Arab–Israeli War: U.S. Actions and Arab Perceptions," in David W. Lesch, ed., *The Middle East and the United States: A Historical and Political Reassessment* (Boulder: Westview Press, 2003), 191–210.

30. Kaufman, *The Arab Middle East*, 61.

31. See Moshe Ma'oz, "From Conflict to Peace? Israel's Relations with Syria and the Palestinians," *Middle East Journal* 53, no. 2 (1999): 399.

32. See Lesch, "From Eisenhower to Johnson," 86; also see David W. Lesch, "The Reluctant Interlocutor: The United States in the Middle East, 1963–1975," in Malcolm Muir, Jr., and Mark F. Wilkinson, eds., *The Most Dangerous Years: The Cold War, 1953–1975* (Lexington: Virginia Military Institute, 2005), 360.

Nasser's Speech to National Assembly Members on May 29, 1967

Brothers, when Brother Anwar as Sadat informed me of your decision to meet me I told him that I myself was prepared to call on you at the National Assembly, but he said you were determined to come. I therefore responded to this and I thank you heartily for your consideration.

I was naturally not surprised by the law which Brother Anwar as Sadat read because I was notified of it before I came here. However, I wish to thank you very much for your feelings and for the powers given me. I did not ask for such powers because I felt that you and I were as one, that we could co-operate and work for the sublime interest of this country giving a great example of unselfishness and of work for the welfare of all. Thanks be to God, for four years now the National Assembly has been working and has given great examples. We have given great examples in co-operation and unselfishness and in placing before us the sublime and highest objective—the interest of this nation.

I am proud of this resolution and law. I promise you that I will use it only when necessary. I will, however, send all the laws to you. Thank you once again. The great gesture of moral support represented by this law is very valuable to my spirit and heart. I heartily thank you for this feeling and this initiative.

The circumstances through which we are now passing are in fact difficult ones because we are not only confronting Israel but also those who created Israel and who are behind Israel. We are confronting Israel and the West as well—the West, which created Israel and which despised us Arabs and which ignored us before and since 1948. They had no regard whatsoever for our feelings, our hopes in life, or our rights. The West completely ignored us, and the Arab nation was unable to check the West's course.

Then came the events of 1956—the Suez battle. We all know what happened in 1956. When we rose to demand our rights. Britain, France and Israel opposed us, and we were faced with the tripartite aggression. We resisted, however, and proclaimed that we would fight to the last drop of our blood. God gave us success and God's victory was great.

Subsequently we were able to rise and to build. Now, 11 years after 1956, we are restoring things to what they were in 1956. This is from the material aspect. In my opinion this material aspect is only a small part, whereas the spiritual aspect is the great side of the issue. The spiritual aspect involves the renaissance of the Arab nation, the revival of the Palestine question, and the restoration of confidence to every Arab and to every Palestinian. This is on the basis that if we are able to restore conditions to what they were before 1956 God will surely help and urge us to restore the situation to what it was in 1948 [prolonged applause].

Brothers, the revolt, upheaval and commotion which we now see taking place in every Arab country are not only because we have returned to the Gulf of Aqabah or rid ourselves of the UNEF, but because we have restored Arab honour and renewed Arab hopes.

Israel used to boast a great deal, and the Western powers, headed by the United States and Britain, used to ignore and even despise us and consider us of no value. But now that the time has come—and I have already said in the past that we will decide the time and place and not allow them to decide—we must be ready for triumph and not for a recurrence of the 1948 comedies. We shall triumph, God willing.

Preparations have already been made. We are now ready to confront Israel. They have claimed many things about the 1956 Suez war, but no one believed them after the secrets of the 1956 collusion were uncovered—that mean collusion in which Israel took part. Now we are ready for the confrontation. We are now ready to deal with the entire Palestine question.

The issue now at hand is not the Gulf of Aqabah, the Straits of Tiran, or the withdrawal of the UNEF, but the rights of the Palestine people. It is the aggression which took place in Palestine in 1948 with the collaboration of Britain and the United States. It is the expulsion of the Arabs from Palestine, the usurpation of their rights, and the plunder of their property. It is the disavowal of all the UN resolutions in favour of the Palestinian people.

The issue today is far more serious than they say. They want to confine the issue to the Straits of Tiran, the UNEF and the right of passage. We demand the full rights of the Palestinian people. We say this out of our belief that Arab rights cannot be squandered because the Arabs throughout the Arab world are demanding these Arab rights.

We are not afraid of the United States and its threats, of Britain and her threats, or of the entire Western world and its partiality to Israel. The United States and Britain are partial to Israel and give no consideration to the Arabs, to the entire Arab nation. Why? Because we have made them believe that we cannot distinguish between friend and foe. We must make them know that we know who our foes are and who our friends are and treat them accordingly.

If the United States and Britain are partial to Israel, we must say that our enemy is not only Israel but also the United States and Britain and treat them as such. If the Western Powers disavow our rights and ridicule and despise us, we Arabs must teach them to respect us and take us seriously. Otherwise all our talk about Palestine, the Palestine people, and Palestinian rights will be null and void and of no consequence. We must treat enemies as enemies and friends as friends.

I said yesterday that the States that champion freedom and peace have supported us. I spoke of the support given us by India, Pakistan, Afghanistan, Yugoslavia, Malaysia, the Chinese People's Republic and the Asian and African States.

After my statements yesterday I met the War Minister Shams Badran and learned from him what took place in Moscow. I wish to tell you today that the Soviet Union is a friendly Power and stands by us as a friend. In all our dealings with the Soviet Union—and I have been dealing with the USSR since 1955—it has not made a single request of us. The USSR has never interfered in our policy or internal affairs. This is the USSR as we have always known it. In fact, it is we who have made urgent requests of the USSR. Last year we asked for wheat and they sent it to us. When I also asked for all kinds of arms they gave them to us. When I met Shams Badran yesterday he handed me a message from the Soviet Premier Kosygin saying that the USSR supported us in this battle and would not allow any Power to intervene until matters were restored to what they were in 1956.

Brothers, we must distinguish between friend and foe, friend and hypocrite. We must be able to tell who is making requests, who has ulterior motives, and who is applying economic pressure. We must also know those who offer their friendship to us for no other reason than a desire for freedom and peace.

In the name of the UAR people, I thank the people of the USSR for their great attitude, which is the attitude of a real friend. This is the kind of attitude we expect. I said yesterday that we had not requested the USSR or any other state to intervene, because we really want to avoid any confrontation which might lead to a world war and also because we really work for peace and advocate world peace. When we voiced the policy of non-alignment, our chief aim was world peace.

Brothers, we will work for world peace with all the power at our disposal, but we will also hold tenaciously to our rights with all the power at our disposal. This is our course. On this occasion, I address myself to our brothers in Aden and say: Although occupied with this battle, we have not forgotten you. We are with you. We have not forgotten the struggle of Aden and the occupied South for liberation. Aden and the occupied South must be liberated and colonialism must end. We are with them; present matters have not taken our minds from Aden.

I thank you for taking the trouble to pay this visit. Moreover, your presence is an honour to the Qubbah Palace, and I am pleased to have met you. Peace be with you.

Walter Laqueur and Barry Rubin, eds., *The Israel–Arab Reader: A Documentary History of the Middle East Conflict* (New York: Penguin, 1984), 185–189.

United Nations Security Council Resolution 242

November 22, 1967

The Security Council,

Expressing its continuing concern with the grave situation in the Middle East,
Emphasizing the inadmissibility of the acquisition of territory by war and the need to work for a just and lasting peace in which every State in the area can live in security,

Emphasizing further that all Member States in their acceptance of the Charter of the United Nations have undertaken a commitment to act in accordance with Article 2 of the Charter,

Affirms that the fulfillment of Charter principles requires the establishment of a just and lasting peace in the Middle East which should include the application of both the following principles:

Withdrawal of Israeli armed forces from territories occupied in the recent conflict;

Termination of all claims or states of belligerency and respect for and acknowledgement of the sovereignty, territorial integrity and political independence of every State in the area and their right to live in peace within secure and recognized boundaries free from threats or acts of force;

Affirms further the necessity

For guaranteeing freedom of navigation through international waterways in the area;

For achieving a just settlement of the refugee problem;

For guaranteeing the territorial inviolability and political independence of every State in the area, through measures including the establishment of demilitarized zones;

Requests the Secretary-General to designate a Special Representative to proceed to the Middle East to establish and maintain contacts with the States concerned in order to promote agreement and assist efforts to achieve a peaceful and accepted settlement in accordance with the provisions and principles in this resolution;

Requests the Secretary-General to report to the Security Council on the progress of the efforts of the Special Representative as soon as possible.

---

http://www.yale.edu/lawweb/avalon/un/un242.htm (accessed February 1, 2006).

The Khartoum Resolutions

September 1, 1967

1. The conference has affirmed the unity of Arab ranks, the unity of joint action and the need for coordination and for the elimination of all differences. The Kings, Presidents and representatives of the other Arab Heads of State at the conference have affirmed their countries' stand by and implementation of the Arab Solidarity Charter which was signed at the third Arab summit conference in Casablanca.

2. The conference has agreed on the need to consolidate all efforts to eliminate the effects of the aggression on the basis that the occupied lands are Arab lands and that the burden of regaining these lands falls on all the Arab States.

3. The Arab Heads of State have agreed to unite their political efforts at the international and diplomatic level to eliminate the effects of the aggression and to ensure the withdrawal of the aggressive Israeli forces from the Arab lands which have been occupied since the aggression of June 5. This will be done within the framework of the main principles by which the Arab States abide, namely, no peace with Israel, no recognition of Israel, no negotiations with it, and insistence on the rights of the Palestinian people in their own country.

4. The conference of Arab Ministers of Finance, Economy and Oil recommended that suspension of oil pumping be used as a weapon in the battle. However, after

thoroughly studying the matter, the summit conference has come to the conclusion that the oil pumping can itself be used as a positive weapon, since oil is an Arab resource which can be used to strengthen the economy of the Arab States directly affected by the aggression, so that these States will be able to stand firm in the battle. The conference has, therefore, decided to resume the pumping of oil, since oil is a positive Arab resource that can be used in the service of Arab goals. It can contribute to the efforts to enable those Arab States which were exposed to the aggression and thereby lost economic resources to stand firm and eliminate the effects of the aggression. The oil-producing States have, in fact, participated in the efforts to enable the States affected by the aggression to stand firm in the face of any economic pressure.

5. The participants in the conference have approved the plan proposed by Kuwait to set up an Arab Economic and Social Development Fund on the basis of the recommendation of the Baghdad conference of Arab Ministers of Finance, Economy and Oil.

6. The participants have agreed on the need to adopt the necessary measures to strengthen military preparation to face all eventualities.

7. The conference has decided to expedite the elimination of foreign bases in the Arab States.

---

http://www.yale.edu/lawweb/avalon/mideast/khartoum.htm (accessed February 1, 2006).

The Palestinian National Charter: Resolutions of the Palestine National Council

July 1–17, 1968

Text of the Charter:

Article 1:

Palestine is the homeland of the Arab Palestinian people; it is an indivisible part of the Arab homeland, and the Palestinian people are an integral part of the Arab nation.

Article 2:

Palestine, with the boundaries it had during the British Mandate, is an indivisible territorial unit.

Article 3:

The Palestinian Arab people possess the legal right to their homeland and have the right to determine their destiny after achieving the liberation of their country in accordance with their wishes and entirely of their own accord and will.

Article 4:

The Palestinian identity is a genuine, essential, and inherent characteristic; it is transmitted from parents to children. The Zionist occupation and the dispersal of the Palestinian Arab people, through the disasters which befell them, do not make them lose their Palestinian identity and their membership in the Palestinian community, nor do they negate them.

Article 5:

The Palestinians are those Arab nationals who, until 1947, normally resided in Palestine regardless of whether they were evicted from it or have stayed there. Anyone born, after that date, of a Palestinian father—whether inside Palestine or outside it—is also a Palestinian.

Article 6:

The Jews who had normally resided in Palestine until the beginning of the Zionist invasion will be considered Palestinians.

Article 7:

That there is a Palestinian community and that it has material, spiritual, and historical connection with Palestine are indisputable facts. It is a national duty to bring up individual Palestinians in an Arab revolutionary manner. All means of information and education must be adopted in order to acquaint the Palestinian with his country in the most profound manner, both spiritual and material, that is possible. He must be prepared for the armed struggle and ready to sacrifice his wealth and his life in order to win back his homeland and bring about its liberation.

Article 8:

The phase in their history, through which the Palestinian people are now living, is that of national (watani) struggle for the liberation of Palestine. Thus the conflicts among the Palestinian national forces are secondary, and should be ended for the sake of the basic conflict that exists between the forces of Zionism and of imperialism on the one hand, and the Palestinian Arab people on the other. On this basis the Palestinian masses, regardless of whether they are residing in the national homeland or in diaspora (mahajir) constitute-both their organizations and the individuals—one national front working for the retrieval of Palestine and its liberation through armed struggle.

Article 9:

Armed struggle is the only way to liberate Palestine. This is the overall strategy, not merely a tactical phase. The Palestinian Arab people assert their absolute determination and firm resolution to continue their armed struggle and to work for an armed popular revolution for the liberation of their country and their return to it. They also assert their right to normal life in Palestine and to exercise their right to self-determination and sovereignty over it.

Article 10:

Commando action constitutes the nucleus of the Palestinian popular liberation war. This requires its escalation, comprehensiveness, and the mobilization of all the Palestinian popular and educational efforts and their organization and involvement in the armed Palestinian revolution. It also requires the achieving of unity for the national (watani) struggle among the different groupings of the Palestinian people, and between the Palestinian people and the Arab masses, so as to secure the continuation of the revolution, its escalation, and victory.

Article 11:

The Palestinians will have three mottoes: national (wataniyya) unity, national (qawmiyya) mobilization, and liberation.

Article 12:

The Palestinian people believe in Arab unity. In order to contribute their share toward the attainment of that objective, however, they must, at the present stage of their struggle, safeguard their Palestinian identity and develop their consciousness of that identity, and oppose any plan that may dissolve or impair it.

Article 13:

Arab unity and the liberation of Palestine are two complementary objectives, the attainment of either of which facilitates the attainment of the other. Thus, Arab unity leads to the liberation of Palestine, the liberation of Palestine leads to Arab unity; and work toward the realization of one objective proceeds side by side with work toward the realization of the other.

Article 14:

The destiny of the Arab nation, and indeed Arab existence itself, depend upon the destiny of the Palestine cause. From this interdependence springs the Arab nation's pursuit of, and striving for, the liberation of Palestine. The people of Palestine play the role of the vanguard in the realization of this sacred (qawmi) goal.

Article 15:

The liberation of Palestine, from an Arab viewpoint, is a national (qawmi) duty and it attempts to repel the Zionist and imperialist aggression against the Arab homeland, and aims at the elimination of Zionism in Palestine. Absolute responsibility for this falls upon the Arab nation—peoples and governments—with the Arab people of Palestine in the vanguard. Accordingly, the Arab nation must mobilize all its military, human, moral, and spiritual capabilities to participate actively with the Palestinian people in the liberation of Palestine. It must, particularly in the phase of the armed Palestinian revolution, offer and furnish the Palestinian people with all possible help, and material and human support, and make available to them the means and opportunities that will enable them to continue to carry out their leading role in the armed revolution, until they liberate their homeland.

Article 16:

The liberation of Palestine, from a spiritual point of view, will provide the Holy Land with an atmosphere of safety and tranquility, which in turn will safeguard the country's religious sanctuaries and guarantee freedom of worship and of visit to all, without discrimination of race, color, language, or religion. Accordingly, the people of Palestine look to all spiritual forces in the world for support.

Article 17:

The liberation of Palestine, from a human point of view, will restore to the Palestinian individual his dignity, pride, and freedom. Accordingly the Palestinian Arab people look forward to the support of all those who believe in the dignity of man and his freedom in the world.

Article 18:

The liberation of Palestine, from an international point of view, is a defensive action necessitated by the demands of self-defense. Accordingly the Palestinian people, desirous as they are of the friendship of all people, look to freedom-loving, and peace-loving states for support in order to restore their legitimate rights in Palestine, to re-establish peace and security in the country, and to enable its people to exercise national sovereignty and freedom.

Article 19:

The partition of Palestine in 1947 and the establishment of the state of Israel are entirely illegal, regardless of the passage of time, because they were contrary to the will of the Palestinian people and to their natural right in their homeland, and inconsistent with the principles embodied in the Charter of the United Nations; particularly the right to self-determination.

Article 20:

The Balfour Declaration, the Mandate for Palestine, and everything that has been based upon them, are deemed null and void. Claims of historical or religious ties of Jews with Palestine are incompatible with the facts of history and the true conception of what constitutes statehood. Judaism, being a religion, is not an independent nationality. Nor do Jews constitute a single nation with an identity of its own; they are citizens of the states to which they belong.

Article 21:

The Arab Palestinian people, expressing themselves by the armed Palestinian revolution, reject all solutions which are substitutes for the total liberation of Palestine and reject all proposals aiming at the liquidation of the Palestinian problem, or its internationalization.

Article 22:

Zionism is a political movement organically associated with international imperialism and antagonistic to all action for liberation and to progressive movements in the world. It is racist and fanatic in its nature, aggressive, expansionist, and colonial in its aims, and fascist in its methods. Israel is the instrument of the Zionist movement, and geographical base for world imperialism placed strategically in the midst of the Arab homeland to combat the hopes of the Arab nation for liberation, unity, and progress. Israel is a constant source of threat vis-à-vis peace in the Middle East and the whole world. Since the liberation of Palestine will destroy the Zionist and imperialist presence and will contribute to the establishment of peace in the Middle East, the Palestinian people look for the support of all the progressive and peaceful forces and urge them all, irrespective of their affiliations and beliefs, to offer the Palestinian people all aid and support in their just struggle for the liberation of their homeland.

Article 23:

The demand of security and peace, as well as the demand of right and justice, require all states to consider Zionism an illegitimate movement, to outlaw its existence, and to ban its operations, in order that friendly relations among peoples may be preserved, and the loyalty of citizens to their respective homelands safeguarded.

Article 24:

The Palestinian people believe in the principles of justice, freedom, sovereignty, self-determination, human dignity, and in the right of all peoples to exercise them.

Article 25:

For the realization of the goals of this Charter and its principles, the Palestine Liberation Organization will perform its role in the liberation of Palestine in accordance with the Constitution of this Organization.

Article 26:

The Palestine Liberation Organization, representative of the Palestinian revolutionary forces, is responsible for the Palestinian Arab people's movement in its struggle—to retrieve its homeland, liberate and return to it and exercise the right to self-determination in it—in all military, political, and financial fields and also for whatever may be required by the Palestine case on the inter-Arab and international levels.

Article 27:

The Palestine Liberation Organization shall cooperate with all Arab states, each according to its potentialities; and will adopt a neutral policy among them in the light of the requirements of the war of liberation; and on this basis it shall not interfere in the internal affairs of any Arab state.

Article 28:

The Palestinian Arab people assert the genuineness and independence of their national (wataniyya) revolution and reject all forms of intervention, trusteeship, and subordination.

Article 29:

The Palestinian people possess the fundamental and genuine legal right to liberate and retrieve their homeland. The Palestinian people determine their attitude toward all states and forces on the basis of the stands they adopt vis-à-vis to the Palestinian revolution to fulfill the aims of the Palestinian people.

Article 30:

Fighters and carriers of arms in the war of liberation are the nucleus of the popular army which will be the protective force for the gains of the Palestinian Arab people.

Article 31:

The Organization shall have a flag, an oath of allegiance, and an anthem. All this shall be decided upon in accordance with a special regulation.

Article 32:

Regulations, which shall be known as the Constitution of the Palestine Liberation Organization, shall be annexed to this Charter. It will lay down the manner in which the Organization, and its organs and institutions, shall be constituted; the respective competence of each; and the requirements of its obligation under the Charter.

Article 33:

This Charter shall not be amended save by [vote of] a majority of two-thirds of the total membership of the National Congress of the Palestine Liberation Organization [taken] at a special session convened for that purpose.

---

http://www.yale.edu/lawweb/avalon/mideast/plocov.htm (accessed February 1, 2006).

Rogers Plan (December 9, 1969)

I am going to speak tonight about the situation in the Middle East. I want to refer to the policy of the United States as it relates to that situation in the hope that there may be a better understanding of that policy and the reasons for it.

Following the third Arab–Israeli war in 20 years, there was an upsurge of hope that a lasting peace could be achieved. That hope has unfortunately not been realized. There is no area of the world today that is more important, because it could easily again be the source of another serious conflagration.

When this administration took office, one of our first actions in foreign affairs was to examine carefully the entire situation in the Middle East. It was obvious that a continuation of the unresolved conflict there would be extremely dangerous, that the parties to the conflict alone would not be able to overcome their legacy of suspicion to achieve a political settlement, and that international efforts to help needed support.

The United States decided it had a responsibility to play a direct role in seeking a solution.

Thus, we accepted a suggestion put forward both by the French Government and the Secretary-General of the United Nations. We agreed that the major powers—the United States, the Soviet Union, the United Kingdom, and France—should cooperate to assist the Secretary-General's representative, Ambassador Jarring, in working out a settlement in accordance with the resolution of the Security Council of the United Nations of November 1967. We also decided to consult directly with the Soviet Union, hoping to achieve as wide an area of agreement as possible between us.

These decisions were made in full recognition of the following important factors:

First, we knew that nations not directly involved could not make a durable peace for the peoples and governments involved. Peace rests with the parties to the conflict. The efforts of major powers can help, they can provide a catalyst, they can stimulate the parties to talk, they can encourage, they can help define a realistic framework for agreement; but an agreement among other powers cannot be a substitute for agreement among the parties themselves.

Second, we know that a durable peace must meet the legitimate concerns of both sides.

Third, we were clear that the only framework for a negotiated settlement was one in accordance with the entire text of the U.N. Security Council resolution. That resolution was agreed upon after long and arduous negotiations; it is carefully balanced; it provides the basis for a just and lasting peace—a final settlement—not merely an interlude between wars.

Fourth, we believe that a protracted period of no war, no peace, recurrent violence, and spreading chaos would serve the interests of no nation, in or out of the Middle East.

For 8 months we have pursued these consultations in four-power talks at the United Nations and in bilateral discussions with the Soviet Union....

The substance of the talks that we have had with the Soviet Union has been conveyed to the interested parties through diplomatic channels. This process has served to highlight the main roadblocks to the initiation of useful negotiations among the parties.

On the one hand, the Arab leaders fear that Israel is not in fact prepared to withdraw from Arab territory occupied in the 1967 war.

On the other hand, Israeli leaders fear that the Arab states are not in fact prepared to live in peace with Israel.

Each side can cite from its viewpoint considerable evidence to support its fears. Each side has permitted its attention to be focused solidly and to some extent solely on these fears.

What can the United States do to help to overcome these roadblocks?

We have friendly ties with both Arabs and Israelis. To call for Israeli withdrawal as envisaged in the U.N. resolution without achieving agreement on peace would be partisan toward the Arabs. To call on the Arabs to accept peace without Israeli withdrawal would be partisan toward Israel. Therefore, our policy is to encourage the Arabs to accept a permanent peace based on a binding agreement and to urge the Israelis to withdraw from occupied territory when their territorial integrity is assured as envisaged by the Security Council resolution.

In an effort to broaden the scope of discussion we have recently resumed four-power negotiations at the United Nations.

Let me outline our policy on various elements of the Security Council resolution. The basic and related issues might be described as peace, security, withdrawal, and territory.

PEACE BETWEEN THE PARTIES

The resolution of the Security Council makes clear that the goal is the establishment of a state of peace between the parties instead of the state of belligerency which has characterized relations for over 20 years. We believe the conditions and obligations of peace must be defined in specific terms. For example, navigation rights in the Suez Canal and in the Strait of Tiran should be spelled out. Respect for sovereignty and obligations of the parties to each other must be made specific.

But peace, of course, involves much more than this. It is also a matter of the attitudes and intentions of the parties. Are they ready to coexist with one another? Can a live-and-let-live attitude replace suspicion, mistrust, and hate? A peace agreement between the parties must be based on clear and stated intentions and a willingness to bring about basic changes in the attitudes and conditions which are characteristic of the Middle East today.

SECURITY

A lasting peace must be sustained by a sense of security on both sides. To this end, as envisaged in the Security Council resolution, there should be demilitarized zones and related security arrangements more reliable than those which existed in the area in the past. The parties themselves, with Ambassador Jarring's help, are in the best position to work out the nature and the details of such security arrangements. It is, after all, their interests which are at stake and their territory which is involved. They must live with the results.

WITHDRAWAL AND TERRITORY

The Security Council resolution endorses the principle of the non-acquisition of territory by war and calls for withdrawal of Israeli armed forces from territories occupied in the 1967 war. We support this part of the resolution, including withdrawal, just as we do its other elements.

The boundaries from which the 1967 war began were established in the 1949 armistice agreements and have defined the areas of national jurisdiction in the Middle East for 20 years. Those boundaries were armistice lines, not final political borders. The rights, claims, and positions of the parties in an ultimate peaceful settlement were reserved by the armistice agreements.

The Security Council resolution neither endorses nor precludes these armistice lines as the definitive political boundaries. However, it calls for withdrawal from occupied territories, the non-acquisition of territory by war, and the establishment of secure and recognized boundaries.

We believe that while recognized political boundaries must be established and agreed upon by the parties, any changes in the preexisting lines should not reflect the weight of conquest and should be confined to insubstantial alterations required for mutual security. We do not support expansionism. We believe troops must be withdrawn as the resolution provides. We support Israel's security and the security of the Arab states as well. We are for a lasting peace that requires security for both.

By emphasizing the key issues of peace, security, withdrawal, and territory, I do not want to leave the impression that other issues are not equally important. Two in particular deserve special mention: the questions of refugees and of Jerusalem.

There can be no lasting peace without a just settlement of the problem of those Palestinians whom the wars of 1948 and 1967 have made homeless. This human dimension of the Arab–Israeli conflict has been of special concern to the United States for over 20 years. During this period the United States has contributed about $500 million for the support and education of the Palestinian refugees. We are prepared to contribute generously along with others to solve this problem. We believe its just settlement must take into account the desires and aspirations of the refugees and the legitimate concerns of the governments in the area.

The problem posed by the refugees will become increasingly serious if their future is not resolved. There is a new consciousness among the young Palestinians who have grown up since 1948 which needs to be channeled away from bitterness and frustration toward hope and justice.

The question of the future status of Jerusalem, because it touches deep emotional, historical, and religious wellsprings, is particularly complicated. We have made clear repeatedly in the past two and a half years that we cannot accept unilateral actions by any party to decide the final status of the city. We believe its status can be determined only through the agreement of the parties concerned, which in practical terms means primarily the Governments of Israel and Jordan, taking into account the interests of other countries in the area and the international community. We do, however, support certain principles which we believe would provide an equitable framework for a Jerusalem settlement.

Specifically, we believe Jerusalem should be a unified city within which there would no longer be restrictions on the movement of persons and goods.

There should be open access to the unified city for persons of all faiths and nationalities. Arrangements for the administration of the unified city should take into account the interests of all its inhabitants and of the Jewish, Islamic, and Christian communities. And there should be roles for both Israel and Jordan in the civic, economic, and religious life of the city.

It is our hope that agreement on the key issues of peace, security, withdrawal, and territory will create a climate in which these questions of refugees and of Jerusalem, as well as other aspects of the conflict, can be resolved as part of the overall settlement.

During the first weeks of the current United Nations General Assembly the efforts to move matters toward a settlement entered a particularly intensive phase. Those efforts continue today.

I have already referred to our talks with the Soviet Union. In connection with those talks there have been allegations that we have been seeking to divide the Arab states by urging the U.A.R. to make a separate peace. These allegations are false. It is a fact that we and the Soviets have been concentrating on the questions of a settlement between Israel and the United Arab Republic. We have been doing this in the full understanding on both our parts that, before there can be a settlement of the Arab–Israeli conflict, there must be agreement between the parties on other aspects of the settlement—not only those related to the United Arab Republic but also those related to Jordan and other states which accept the Security Council resolution of November 1967.

We started with the Israeli–United Arab Republic aspect because of its inherent importance for future stability in the area and because one must start somewhere.

We are also ready to pursue the Jordanian aspect of a settlement; in fact the four powers in New York have begun such discussions. Let me make it perfectly clear that the U.S. position is that implementation of the overall settlement would begin only after complete agreement had been reached on related aspects of the problem.

In our recent meetings with the Soviets we have discussed some new formulas in an attempt to find common positions. They consist of three principal elements:

First, there should be a binding commitment by Israel and the United Arab Republic to peace with each other, with all the specific obligations of peace spelled out, including the obligation to prevent hostile acts originating from their respective territories.

Second, the detailed provisions of peace relating to security safeguards on the ground should be worked out between the parties, under Ambassador Jarring's auspices, utilizing the procedures followed in negotiating the armistice agreements under Ralph Bunche in 1949 at Rhodes. This formula has been previously used with success in negotiations between the parties on Middle Eastern problems. A principal objective of the four-power talks, we believe, should be to help Ambassador Jarring engage the parties in a negotiating process under the Rhodes formula.

So far as a settlement between Israel and the United Arab Republic goes, these safeguards relate primarily to the area of Sharm al-Shaykh controlling access to the Gulf of Aqaba, the need for demilitarized zones as foreseen in the Security Council resolution, and final arrangements in the Gaza Strip.

Third, in the context of peace and agreement on specific security safeguards, withdrawal of Israeli forces from Egyptian territory would be required.

Such an approach directly addresses the principal national concerns of both Israel and the U.A.R. It would require the U.A.R. to agree to a binding and specific commitment to peace. It would require withdrawal of Israeli armed forces from U.A.R. territory to the international border between Israel [or Mandated Palestine] and Egypt which has been in existence for over a half century. It would also require the parties themselves to negotiate the practical security arrangements to safeguard the peace.

We believe that this approach is balanced and fair....

Bernard Reich, ed., *Arab–Israeli Conflict and Conciliation: A Documentary History* (Westport, CT: Praeger, 1995), 102–107.

Eight
THE ROAD TO 1979

The Palestine Liberation Organization (PLO) had markedly evolved since being created in 1964 as a pawn in the Arab cold war and Arab–Israeli conflict. The 1967 war had dramatically changed the situation from the Palestinian perspective. The Arab states were largely discredited, as was the leadership of Ahmad Shuqayri as PLO chair and his cohorts who had emphasized too much dependence upon Arab regimes. Following the war, Yasser Arafat, the Fatah leader, wanted to launch a war of liberation in the occupied territories, namely the West Bank. While an uprising in the territories themselves did not emerge, especially as the Israelis now had control of the lands from which *fedayeen* attacks had been launched, Arafat ordered a series of raids from Jordanian territory against Israel. Jordan's King Hussein still had his eye on regaining the West Bank through negotiation, but he realized he could not rein in the PLO for fear of appearing too nonconfrontational vis-à-vis the Israelis to what was now a Palestinian population in Jordan that comprised over half its total. In addition, he figured that the raids might compel the Israelis to return the West Bank for security concerns if nothing else. In July 1968, the PLO issued a revised charter, itself a sign of the organization's emerging presence and change in direction. It stated that "armed struggle was the only means to liberate Palestine." With this declaration, the commando groups that had been haphazardly launching raids from various directions against Israel in prior years immediately moved front and center in the Palestinian movement. As Yezid Sayigh points out, the change in the title of the charter from *Mithaq al-Qawmi* (nationalism) to *Mithaq al-Watani* (nation) signified an important shift from an ideology drawn from and based on pan-Arab nationalism to one focused more upon Palestinian nationalism, i.e., Palestinian statehood.[1] On the other hand, the secular nationalism of the PLO focused on "armed struggle" at the expense of social reform programs, with no serious religious orientation. This gave the PLO broad appeal, especially when it was in guerilla warfare mode; but it also opened the doors for a group, such as Hamas, to appropriate PLO ground decades later by focusing on social programs, and, of course, it had a distinct religious orientation.

Despite the apparent solidarity on the surface, however, the PLO remained factionalized, especially now that it was engaged in a war of liberation against Israel. Fatah was by far the most numerous of all the PLO factions, but others began to assert themselves in directions that were intended to compel Arafat to adopt a more aggressive posture and/or represented the interests of Arab states in which they resided and upon which they were dependent. A Marxist-leaning Christian Palestinian Arab, Dr. George Habash, who received his medical degree from the American University of Beirut, founded the Popular Front for the Liberation of Palestine (PFLP) in late 1967. Habash had formerly led the Arab National Movement (ANM) during much of the 1960s, which was an Arab nationalist organization composed mainly of Palestinians. The PFLP itself spawned several factions over the next year or so, while Habash languished in a Syrian jail over his disagreements with Damascus regarding raids into Israel. Ahmad Jibril, one of the founding members of the PFLP, went off and formed the Popular Front for the Liberation of Palestine—General Command (PFLP-GC), which received support from Syria. In early 1969, Nayef Hawatmah, another Palestinian Christian who helped found the PFLP, formed the Democratic Front for the Liberation of Palestine (DFLP), which on the whole tended to be less ideological and radical than the other PLO offshoots. These various factions vied for influence in the PLO over the years, each believing it represented the truest and most efficient path toward the liberation of Palestine. Although Fatah tended to remain more independent from Arab regimes than the smaller factions, all of them often forged alliances with various Arab states when necessary, reflecting the inter-Arab rivalries that had come to characterize the region and the shifting winds of regional politics. Regardless of this, however, Palestinian attacks inside Israel and against Israeli interests abroad became popularized, even mythologized, in the Arab world as a whole, particularly as they were in stark contrast to the inability of Arab governments to act.

Because of al-Fatah's dominant representation, Yasser Arafat was elected by the Palestine National Congress as the head of the PLO (formally, the chair of the Palestine National Congress executive committee) in February 1969 (Shuqayri had resigned by the end of 1967). The hostilities between the PLO factions curtailed Arafat's ability to carve out a coherent, unified policy, the result of which was an intensified guerilla campaign against Israel initiated by factions that sought to assert themselves within the Palestinian movement. This obviously led to Israeli reprisals, particularly in Jordan and increasingly in Lebanon, as PLO groups sought to establish a presence in the southern part of Israel's neighbor to the north—it would be the beginning of a cycle of violence in Lebanon that would deepen that country's involvement in the Arab–Israeli arena and would eventually result in a devastating sixteen-year civil war. PLO activities in Lebanon were facilitated by the so-called Cairo Agreement negotiated by Nasser in 1969. This was obviously an attempt by the Egyptian president to increase the pressure on Israel and buttress his pro-Palestinian credentials while in reality shifting some of the burden away from Egypt. While the PLO recognized Lebanese sovereignty in the agreement, it gained control of the Palestinian refugee camps, found primarily in and around Beirut, that had previously been under the watchful eye of Lebanese security forces. The agreement also arranged for PLO access in a specific corridor in south Lebanon in order to carry out raids against northern Israel. This was meant to restrict PLO operations to a confined area, but it did not stop them. Indeed, Syria was allowed to supply the PLO, bringing Lebanon that much closer to being a proxy battleground between Israel and Syria. It also led to more intimate involvement in Lebanese affairs by Damascus. With Lebanon's armed forces so clearly circumscribed in their ability to control their own land, paramilitary groups, especially Christian ones opposed to the PLO presence, began to emerge and take matters into their own hands—and oftentimes with support from Israel. The fractured nature of the PLO was beginning to have disruptive effects in the Arab world, particularly in countries that were fractured themselves and/or led by regimes of questionable legitimacy. Nowhere was all of this more apparent than in Jordan in September 1970.

BLACK SEPTEMBER

Jordanian–PLO relations had been severely strained by the summer of 1970, to the point where there was an outbreak of violence in June between PLO units and the Arab Legion. To most Jordanians, the PLO had become a state within a state, and PLO officials and guerillas seemed as if they were above the law, could intimidate the populace, and could carry out actions inimical to Jordanian interests with impunity. They had differences over the disposition of the West Bank as well as the nature of PLO guerilla activities against Israel that often led to Israeli reprisals against Jordanian villages. The Israeli strategy, which would also be applied to Lebanon later on, was to punish not only the guerillas directly but also the government that allowed them to operate out of its territory. The objective was to compel the host government to weigh the benefits versus the costs, ultimately determining that the latter exceeded the former, and subsequently to exert more effort to limit and restrain anti-Israeli raids—or better yet, from the Israeli perspective, eliminate or expel them. From the perspective of many Palestinian groups, King Hussein was a hopeless pro-Western lackey who was willing to negotiate away Palestinian rights and land to Israel. He should, therefore, be removed if possible. In this environment, the cease-fire to the War of Attrition was an opportune moment to act. Not only was it imperative to disrupt any momentum toward Arab–Israeli peace negotiations created by the cease-fire, but by doing so in Jordan, the most fertile ground in which to try, a second bird—the removal of Hussein—could be killed with the same stone.

The PFLP hijacked four passenger airliners between September 6 and 9, landing all of them at an airport only about twenty miles from King Hussein's palace. Hijacking airliners in and of itself was a quantum leap in terrorist strategy, one that unfortunately became more frequent, widespread, and deadly with a variety of groups in coming decades. After some negotiations, the hostages were released, but the planes were blown up on live television for the world to see. This was an affront to Hussein's authority and standing that he could not let pass, so he moved against the PLO militarily, launching on September 16 the Jordanian civil war, or what the Palestinians refer to as "Black September."

With a name like Black September, one can hazard to guess who lost in this conflagration. Indeed, over 3,000 were killed, mostly Palestinians; but the conflict did not end without the existence of the Jordanian regime coming into question. This was the case because the Syrians became involved in the civil war. The radical Ba'thist regime of Salah Jadid, which had done so much to heighten the tensions leading up to the 1967 conflict, was still in power; and it had apparently not lost its enthusiasm to bring about the fall of the conservative, reactionary regimes in the Arab world, especially the one to its south in Amman. This seemed to be a golden opportunity to get rid of the pro-Western Jordanian monarch, gain more control over the PLO, and enhance its credentials for leadership in the Arab world now that Nasser had lost a considerable amount of his luster. Damascus sent armored tank columns into Jordan to assist the PLO. Getting wind of this, Washington then ordered the Sixth Fleet to the eastern Mediterranean as a warning to the Syrians. Threatening to spiral out of control, the Soviets then issued their own warnings against the United States in order to protect their ally in Damascus. The Nixon administration's bluff, then, was about to be called because the Syrians did not cease and desist. At this point, the Israelis became concerned about the fate of Hussein. Although Israel reluctantly fought Jordan in 1967 and the Hashemite Kingdom was still officially at war with the Jewish state, Tel Aviv had had relatively cordial relations with King Hussein as well as his grandfather. Israel did not want to see him fall from power and a more radical regime along the lines of that which existed in Damascus take its place. As a result, Israel began to mobilize its forces against Syria. Tel Aviv was not operating at the same level as the United States, so it did not concern itself as much with the notion of a Soviet deterrent or superpower confrontation—it was operating underneath the superpower standoff; however, it did receive assurances from Washington that the United States would protect its back from an Egyptian attack if Israel engaged Syria. Sitting in Damascus, the commander of the Syrian air force, Hafiz al-Asad, also realized the reality and seriousness of Israeli intentions. As such, he disobeyed orders from Jadid to launch air strikes in Jordan because he believed—and he was probably correct—that Israel would then intervene against Syria, and that would lead to more Syrian losses. In effect, it was the initial thrust in what would become an intra-Ba'th coup d'etat that Asad would initiate against Jadid soon after the civil war.

With Israel deterring the Syrians and Washington professing its support, King Hussein's forces became more emboldened in their efforts to defeat the PLO, which it decisively accomplished by the end of the conflict on September 25. Although the vast majority of Palestinian refugees would remain in Jordan, the PLO infrastructure was evicted in total by the middle of 1971. Hussein had reasserted his authority, fending off yet another attempt to unseat him.

The repercussions of the Jordanian civil war, however, far exceeded the actual material impact of the conflict. Gamal 'Abd al-Nasser had engaged in his own form of shuttle diplomacy in an attempt to end the civil war, which he was eventually able to accomplish. The strain of the negotiations on a body already suffering from several ailments, however, was too much; and he died on September 28. Although his time had already passed him by, it still marked the end of an era of extraordinary hope coupled with grave disappointment. In his stead in Egypt was a fairly nondescript original member of the Free Officers by the name of Anwar al-Sadat, who would counter initial low expectations to carve out his own unique legacy. In Syria, Hafiz al-Asad pushed aside the Jadid regime in an intra-Ba'th coup in November, formally assuming the office of president in Damascus in March 1971. He would rule for thirty years,

(*left* to *right*) Libyan leader Muammar al-Qadhafi, PLO Chairman Yasser Arafat, Egyptian President Gamal 'Abd al-Nasser, and Jordan's King Hussein meeting at the Nile Hilton in Cairo, attempting to mediate the Jordanian civil war, or Black September, September 27, 1970. Nasser died the next day of a heart attack at the conclusion of these meetings. (Bettmann/CORBIS, BE026465.)

becoming in the process an icon in the Middle East; and he would also lead Syria in a different direction from his predecessors.

For the United States, the Jordanian civil war provided an education. The Nixon administration, so concerned with preventing the expansion of Soviet influence, especially as the United States was ensconced in Vietnam, began to view Israel in a different light. The U.S. bluff against Syria was in the process of being called by the Soviets when Israel took up the mantle of deterrence by threatening Damascus. Successive U.S. administrations since World War II had been searching for a surrogate in the Middle East to protect and promote U.S. interests in the region. They naturally focused on the Arab states, looking toward Egypt, Iraq, and even Saudi Arabia at various different junctures to fulfill this role. In the end, the role was not filled by an Arab state but by Israel, and it was the Jordanian episode that convinced Nixon and Kissinger that Tel Aviv could act as the U.S. regional deterrent against Soviet expansionism. After all, by deterring a Soviet client-state, Israel was, in effect, deterring the Soviet Union itself. This resulted in substantially increased U.S. military and economic support for Israel as well as adoption of Israel's more intransigent position regarding the Occupied Territories and the peace negotiations associated with them. Israel had shown it was vastly superior militarily than the Arab states in 1967. Now it had the almost unqualified support of the strongest nation on earth—Israel was virtually impregnable. Surely, the Arabs would have to be the ones to make any significant concessions for peace. Thus, the foundation for a protracted stalemate on the Arab–Israeli front ensued; but for Tel Aviv and Washington, time was on their side—or so it was thought. The so-called special relationship between the United States and Israel now, indeed, became quite special.[2]

The PLO was expelled from Jordan, but it quickly took up shop again in Lebanon, whose government, fractured and under pressure from other Arab states, reluctantly agreed to house the PLO. Soon enough, the PLO would establish a state within a state in Lebanon, a situation that would disrupt the delicate balance between various Christian and Muslim factions that had been successfully papered over for decades, contributing to the eruption of the sixteen-year civil war in 1975. It would also bring Lebanon directly into the Arab–Israeli conflict, something it had been desperately trying to avoid—it could no longer be the Switzerland of the Middle East. A wing of Fatah, taking the name Black September, also formed as a result of the dislocation. It engaged in a series of terrorist actions in order to publicize the Palestinian problem as well as prove to anyone who cared to take notice that the Jordanian civil war did not impair the ability of the PLO to act. But the PLO was much more on its own now, and thus the sporadic and nonconventional means of terrorism were, from its perspective, adopted as a necessary tactic. This was most spectacularly displayed at the 1972 summer Olympic Games held in Munich. Black September commandos took eleven Israeli athletes hostage. During an attempt by West German special units to free the hostages, all eleven Israelis were killed, as were several of their captors. As the saying goes, there is no such thing as bad publicity. The key was to get the Palestinian problem in the public consciousness of the international community. The PLO could no longer rely on the Arab states—it was no more accepted by them than by Israel. Ironically, this alienation helped to solidify a Palestinian identity, indeed a Palestinian nationalism, whether or not one believes it existed beforehand. The Arab–Israeli conflict was subtly being transformed into a Palestinian–Israeli conflict, a shift that

Munich 1972

September 5, 1972, was a terrible day. At the Summer Olympic Games in Munich, Germany, eleven members of the Israeli Olympic delegation were captured and eventually killed by a Palestinian group calling itself Black September, named after the Palestinian term for the Jordanian civil war of September 1970. For twenty-three hours the world tuned in to a live terrorist act. I remember being glued to the television myself, although I did not understand much of what was going on, who the terrorists were, or why they were holding the Israelis hostage. For many of my generation, it was our first introduction to modern terrorism as well as to the Arab–Israeli conflict in general, with the gas lines caused by the 1973 Arab–Israeli war bringing many of the issues home to us even more intimately.

A little after 4:00 a.m. on September 5, eight Palestinians simply climbed over the six-foot fence of the lightly guarded Olympic Village housing athletes from all of the participating countries. They headed toward the dorm where the Israeli delegation was residing, armed with AK-47s. They captured eleven of the Israelis, athletes competing at the games, coaches, and one referee. Two of the eleven were shot early on, probably during an initial struggle. The Palestinians demanded the release of 234 of their comrades held in Israeli jails before they would release the hostages, but the Israeli government of Prime Minister Golda Meir refused to negotiate, as was its standing policy. In order to buy some time, the West German government conducted fake negotiations with the leader of the terrorists, named Issa, who is indelibly etched in the viewing public's memory as he appeared several times in his sunglasses and white fedora hat.

The Palestinians demanded that they be flown to Cairo, and the West German ruse began. From the Olympic Village, the Palestinians and Israelis were choppered out to Furstenfeldbruck military air base. When Issa and a comrade inspected the plane sitting on the tarmac that was supposed to take them to Cairo, they found that there were no pilots on board—sensing a trap, they instantly started to run back to the helicopters holding the hostages. German snipers on the roof of a nearby building opened fire, killing and wounding several of the Palestinians, and a firefight broke out over the next hour. When four German armored police vehicles appeared, one Palestinian tossed a grenade into one helicopter, killing everyone onboard, while another shot the remaining Israelis in the other chopper—all eleven had died, or as ABC sportscaster Jim McKay immortally stated, "They're all gone."

Three of the Palestinians survived the melee and were taken into German custody, only to be released by the Germans two months later in return for the release of passengers on a hijacked Lufthansa airplane. Much of the rest of the world had no idea who the Palestinians were before this tragedy. After all, in UN Security Council Resolution 242 following the 1967 Arab–Israeli war, they are not referred to by name but only as "refugees." Abu Iyad, a deputy to PLO chair Yasser Arafat—and Black September was an unacknowledged offshoot of Arafat's dominant Fatah faction—stated that the reason for the taking of the Israelis at Munich was "to use the unprecedented number of media outlets in one city to display the Palestinian struggle—for better or worse."* To the Palestinians, the loss of eleven Israelis was nothing compared to the suffering of thousands for decades in refugee camps and living under Israeli (and Arab) oppression. Their situation had to be publicized. In this, they were successful, but the image of terrorism associated with the Palestinians has proven to be an enduring one—and difficult to overcome. The incident also launched an escalation in Israeli–Palestinian violence all over the world that over time only complicated the search for peace. Yet it is also a world in which former Zionist terrorists such as Menachem Begin and Yitzhak Shamir can become prime ministers, the former signing the first peace treaty between Israel and an Arab state, and one of the three Black September terrorists who survived Munich, Abu Da'ud, was allowed to enter Israel in 1996 in order to attend a PLO meeting in the Gaza Strip that convened to rescind an article in the PLO charter calling for Israel's elimination.

*Quoted in Lisa Beyer, "The Myths and Reality of Munich," *Time* 166, no. 24 (2005): 68.

would become more apparent as certain Arab states began to pursue war and peace more for their own national interests than pan-Arab interests and/or the Palestinians.

PRELUDE TO WAR

Anwar al-Sadat was a close confidante of Nasser and an integral part of the Revolutionary Command Council that came to power in Egypt in the July 1952 coup. At the time of his formal accession to the presidency in October 1970, most analysts in the West believed he was something of an interim, safe choice who would not last particularly long in power—and they certainly believed he was not the type of leader who was prone to do something dramatic. They were wrong on both counts.

Sadat knew that the legitimacy of his regime rested on his ability to return the Sinai Peninsula to Egyptian control, through either peace or war. Not only was there the political and psychological necessity to reacquire the Sinai, but there were also a number of practical reasons. Three of the four pillars of the Egyptian economy in terms of generating foreign exchange were directly or indirectly related to the level of tension in the Arab–Israeli arena. First, since most of the oil reserves in Egypt were located in or astride the Sinai Peninsula, this revenue-producing activity was obviously in abeyance while Israel held the territory. Second, Egypt relies heavily on Suez Canal tolls; but the canal had been blocked since 1967, and in any event, Israel held the east bank of the canal in the Sinai and could easily impede passing ships. Third, because of its unique pharaonic and Islamic history, Egypt counts on tourism to generate revenues. However, tourism declined sharply after the 1967 war and the War of Attrition, and it remained depressed when Arab–Israeli tensions were high, which was certainly the case in the early 1970s.[3] In addition, if a settlement could be reached with Israel, Egypt could, at least in theory, redirect a significant portion of its defense expenditures toward more productive purposes. Sadat anticipated that this would be augmented by tremendous amounts of U.S. military and economic assistance since he expected that Washington would help broker and guarantee any sort of arrangement regarding the Sinai. It would also lead to the integration of the Egyptian economy into the more lucrative economies of the West—and the only way to tap into Western investment and economic assistance was through Israel. For all of these reasons, Sadat felt compelled to focus almost the entirety of his efforts on regaining the Sinai.

Sadat, at first, attempted to do so through diplomatic measures. The Egyptian president announced his acceptance of a Middle East peace plan put forward by United Nations (UN) envoy Gunnar Jarring of Sweden upon his visit to Cairo in February 1971. Jarring's version was not dissimilar to the Rogers plan, based as it was on UN Security Council (UNSC) Resolution 242. Israel, however, rejected the plan, refusing to withdraw to pre-1967 war lines and insisting on direct negotiations without prior conditions. With this diplomatic stalemate, Sadat believed he needed to do something to break it. This became manifest in July 1972 when Egypt expelled some 15,000–20,000 Soviet military advisers and technicians from the country, only a year after Sadat had signed the Treaty of Friendship and Cooperation with the Soviet Union, which at the time seemed to portend a tightening of the relationship between Cairo and Moscow. However, Sadat swallowed his pride and signed the agreement with Russia because he needed the military assistance to go to war with Israel if necessary—this had to remain an option if diplomacy failed. To the West, the expulsion seemed to indicate that Egypt had soured on the Soviet Union and that the intransigent diplomatic posture exhibited toward Cairo was working—it was compelling Egypt to move toward the West, so why change the policy that had thus far been successful? Sadat was, indeed, looking for some sort of a positive response from the United States that could be parlayed into negotiations with Israel. But none would be forthcoming. There were a number of factors working against a U.S. countergesture. First, it was a presidential election year, so the Nixon administration, as with most presidencies, was hesitant to engage in risky foreign policy initiatives that might blow up in their face and/or alienate important segments of the electorate. In addition, the Watergate scandal and the continuing difficulties regarding Vietnam tended to deflect the attention of the administration from areas of the world that seemed to be crisis-free for the time being. Related to this, after the failure of the Rogers plan, U.S. administrations tended to become more interested in brokering deals and acting as a mediator to the relevant parties in the Arab–Israeli arena. This was a more passive posture that relied on the parties themselves establishing the conditions and timing for negotiations. Finally, the single most important foreign policy initiative at the time for both the United States and the Soviet Union revolved around détente, i.e., lessening the tensions at the superpower level through economic deals and negotiations to reduce the rate of growth of nuclear weapons. Nixon and Kissinger believed détente would have positive run-off effects for the U.S. position in Vietnam and possibly even the Middle East—this was the linkage promoted by Kissinger, who by 1972 had also added the position of secretary of state to his duties as national security adviser. As such, Moscow and Washington were interested in maintaining the status quo in the Middle East. At the superpower summit meeting in May 1972, when Nixon visited with Soviet Premier Leonid Brezhnev in Moscow, the two leaders also agreed to not take advantage of each other's position in the Third World, which might force a reaction and counter-reaction that could potentially lead to a superpower conflict. With this in mind, even without any other considerations, the Nixon administration would have been reluctant to react aggressively—and favorably from Sadat's perspective—to Egypt's expulsion of Soviet personnel. Neither the United States nor the Soviet Union wanted to do anything that could jeopardize détente.

For Sadat, expelling the Soviets was a clear sign that he had concluded that Moscow was not going to provide him with the wherewithal to go to war if necessary. Indeed, both the United States and Israel believed that with the Soviets essentially out of Egypt there was no way Sadat could or would choose the war option—it would now be impossible to defeat Israel. But the Egyptian president had other motives for his bold move. With Soviet advisers and technicians out of the way, it was actually much easier for Egypt to go to war with Israel if it chose to do so. There would be no Soviets on the ground who could hinder military operations or warn the Kremlin with enough advance time to take measures to prevent Egypt from going to war. It was also a gesture that appeased the Egyptian military, which had long disliked the heavy-handed and high-handed Soviet presence in the country. Sadat could now act with more independence if need be in order to reactivate diplomacy through military action. Since his diplomatic measures had not elicited the type of response he had hoped for, he would choose the war option to break the diplomatic stalemate. The result would be the 1973 Arab–Israeli war, variably called the "October War," the "Yom Kippur War" (primarily by Israeli sources because it was initiated during the Jewish Day of Atonement), and the "Ramadan War" (primarily by Arab sources because it occurred during the Muslim holy month of fasting).

In a way, the 1973 Arab–Israeli war was a completion of the paradigm that came into being between the Arab states and Israel following the war in 1967. As noted in the previous chapter, a bargaining situation had been created by the earlier conflagration, but it was an asymmetrical one. The pertinent Arab states were not going to negotiate from such a position of weakness, a posture enshrined in the August 1967

Khartoum summit. The relative bargaining positions had to become more symmetrical before real negotiations could begin. Nasser attempted, but failed, to achieve this via the War of Attrition. Sadat would be more successful this time in a war that shook the global economy to its knees with the near quadrupling of the price per barrel of oil from US $3.01 prior to the conflict to $11.65 by the end of the year, brought the superpowers toward the closing stages of the war to their closest nuclear confrontation since the 1962 Cuban Missile Crisis, and, per Sadat's strategy, inserted a bit more symmetry into the bargaining situation. Even though Israel decisively turned the war in its favor after initial setbacks, it had been bloodied; and maybe more important to the Arabs than taking a sliver of Israeli land for a change was the psychological boost of experiencing victory at any level against the vaunted Israeli military juggernaut after the humiliating defeats in 1948 and 1967. A new paradigm would be established that would lead directly to the 1979 Egyptian–Israeli peace treaty.

One of the biggest questions surrounding the success of the Arab combatants, Egypt and Syria, at the outset of the war is how Israel was caught so off-guard. This occurred primarily because Israeli officials were convinced that the Arabs would not initiate an all-out war unless they knew they could win. Every intelligence estimate concluded that any combination of Arab states could not defeat Israel. The Israeli military had grown considerably in strength since 1967. It had twice as many tanks and warplanes, with division-size armor formations with 300 tanks rather than brigade size with 100 tanks.[4] The ratio of total force numbers between Arabs and Israelis remained three to one, but the technological and tactical superiority gap had, if anything, grown. In August 1973, Defense Minister Moshe Dayan, commenting on Israel's military advantage as well as what he viewed as the Arabs' inherent weakness, stated "It is a weakness that derives from factors that I don't believe will change quickly: the low level of their soldiers in education, technology, and integrity; and inter-Arab divisiveness which is papered over from time to time but superficially and for short spans."[5] Abraham Rabinovich, however, describes the observations of a Mossad official who, after returning home from being posted abroad for five years since the 1967 war, commented on how the Israeli military had become too "self-satisfied" and "self-assured," especially as the enemy was much farther away than they had been in the past:

> The army had grown tremendously and so had its prominence in national life. There was a layer of brigadier generals, a newly created rank required by the expanding army. The Mossad official sensed arrogance in high places. Some generals had their offices redone to reflect their new status; some gave parties with army entertainment troupes singing in the background. All of this was foreign to the Spartan ways the official had known as distinguishing features of Israeli public life only five years before. An attitude of disdain for Arab military capability had etched itself insidiously into the national psyche.[6]

Prime Minister Golda Meir, who succeeded Eshkol upon the latter's death in March 1969, felt much the same way. The hardline position that Israel adopted regarding the territories was reflected in the fact that Jewish settlements were established in militarily strategic spots in the Gaza Strip, Sinai, West Bank, and Golan Heights for defensive purposes and to "create facts on the ground," i.e., essentially redraw the borders of Israel, which Tel Aviv believed it had every right to do considering the hostility of its Arab neighbors. There were plans, such as the so-called Allon plan, named after

Deputy Prime Minister Yigal Allon, that portended a series of settlements strategically located in the territories for defense; but it called for the return of the rest of the land to its former owners. This, however, began to succumb to calls by leading officials, Moshe Dayan first and foremost, to integrate the occupied territories into Israel to provide maximum security, i.e., strategic depth. This confident attitude toward the territories and the scant prospect of returning them any time soon to the Arabs also bred complacency, which would come back to haunt Israel in October 1973. Ebullient in its strength, any politicians who talked about a return of territory to the Arabs were vehemently attacked politically; and with elections scheduled for November, the Labor party talked more and more of annexation of the territories rather than returning them for peace.

Sadat, however, did not launch the war on October 6, 1973, to defeat Israel or even to regain the territory lost in 1967. He did it to achieve the more limited objectives of reactivating diplomacy by awakening the superpowers from their slumber and improving, if possible, Egypt's bargaining position with Israel by at least establishing a bridgehead on the east bank of the Suez Canal. Even though he did not receive the long-range bombers and Scud missiles from the Soviets that he had wanted (which also contributed to the Israeli conclusion that Egypt would not initiate a war), by October 1972 Sadat had made the decision that Egypt would go to war with what it had. But the war's objectives would fit the armaments and strategy and not go beyond it. This is where the Israelis failed: they lacked the political imagination to even conceive that Sadat would go to war with only limited objectives in mind. The Israeli defense strategy against a war to regain the territories remained the same; the Egyptian strategy changed. Sadat even stated "in fact, I believe the gap between our air force and the enemy's will tend to widen rather than narrow. We therefore have no choice but to prepare for a battle under conditions of enemy air superiority. We can do it by challenging that superiority with SAMs."[7] "SAMs" were sophisticated surface-to-air anti-aircraft missile defense systems provided by the Soviets. Egypt, in a way, would use a defensive weapon for an offensive thrust: to provide air cover for a crossing of the Suez Canal and the establishment and maintenance of a bridgehead on the east side of it. The Egyptian forces could advance no farther than five or six miles before they were out from under the SAM air cover, but, if successful, they could gain and hold some Israeli territory.

The Arab side was also more coordinated this time around. Sadat made sure that Syria was involved and that it would attack at the same time in order to force Israel to fight on multiple fronts. Syrian and Egyptian officials met in August 1973 in order to draw up plans for the time, date, and methodology of the joint operation. This was not the same regime in Damascus that had been at loggerheads with Cairo throughout much of the preceding decade. Contrary to popular belief, Hafiz al-Asad's assumption of power in Syria signaled the departure of an ideologically based foreign policy to a more pragmatic one prepared to diplomatically resolve the Arab–Israeli conflict but wholeheartedly committed to a full return of the Golan Heights. Asad was minister of defense during the 1967 war, so he had always felt a personal responsibility to secure its return since it was lost during his watch, so to speak. Asad wanted to bring Syria back within accepted parameters inside the Arab fold, mainly by establishing a working relationship with Egypt and Saudi Arabia in order to coordinate policy toward Israel, which would become manifest in 1973.

Domestically, the rise of Asad and his more moderate wing of the Ba'th party signaled a retreat from the radical economic policies of Salah Jadid's regime and the opening up of the economy to the private sector. Indeed, Asad's political program upon his ascension to power was called the Corrective Movement (*al-Harakat al-Tashihiyya*). This opening, or *infitah*, paralleled a similar process in Egypt under Sadat, one that especially gained steam after the October 1973 war. The expulsion of Soviet advisers from Egypt actually had a salutary effect on Syria. Asad was in an enviable position vis-à-vis the Soviets because he knew they were desperate to recoup their loss in Egypt and shore up their position in the Arab world; therefore, he could and did extract a high price from Moscow. In fact, there were rumors of Egyptian pressure on Syria to also expel Soviet advisers in order to provide extra leeway to choose if and when to go to war.[8] Knowing Asad preferred to keep the Soviets at arm's length, the Kremlin was quick to shower the Syrian president with economic and military aid—for instance, a $700 million arms deal upon Asad's visit to Moscow in July 1972 following Sadat's move, whereupon the number of Soviet advisers in Syria rose from about 400–700 at the end of July to about 3,000 by the end of the summer.[9]

The Saudis were also brought on board as Saudi officials had access to the command center in Cairo throughout the 1973 war. The mending of fences with Riyadh had actually begun with Nasser following the 1967 debacle, primarily to escape from the Yemeni quagmire and acquire much needed economic aid. The only way that oil-rich countries such as Saudi Arabia and Kuwait, whose populations—and therefore their militaries—are relatively small, could fight the Arab–Israeli conflict and maintain their "Arab" credentials was to provide healthy amounts of financial aid and grants to the so-called confrontation states such as Egypt and Syria. The international oil market had also changed drastically from the time of the 1956 and 1967 wars. By 1971, the oil-producing countries had acquired most of the production decisions and pricing away from the multinational oil companies, particularly the so-called Seven Sisters that had dominated every rung of the oil production system for four decades. This, in combination with the fact that demand was higher and supply tighter, provided the Arab oil-producing states with much more leverage to employ the "oil weapon" politically with much more bite than in previous years. The Organization of Petroleum Exporting Countries (OPEC), which had been created in September 1960 to counter the power and influence of the large multinational oil companies, was now in a position it had longed to be in, and the Arab members of OPEC (often referred to as the Organization of Arab Petroleum Exporting Countries, or OAPEC) would utilize this advantage effectively for the first time during the 1973 war by initiating a partial embargo of oil exports toward those countries (first and foremost the United States) which supported Israel. The results of this led to a fourfold increase in the price per barrel of oil, a global recession, and the largest transfer of wealth in world history from the oil-consuming nations to the oil-producing ones, allowing many of the oil producers, especially those Arab shaykhdoms in the Persian Gulf, to build up modern infrastructures and become influential financial and economic determinants in the international marketplace.

Sadat would utilize the newly developed Cairo–Riyadh–Damascus axis to launch a simultaneous invasion of Israel. On October 6, Egypt attacked across the Suez Canal in the south and Syria moved through the Golan Heights in the north, all of which was backed up by a Saudi pledge, as the swing producer in OPEC, to utilize, if necessary, the oil weapon: an oil embargo that would force the United States to intervene either to save the Arabs from total destruction if things turned for the worse or to enter the fray as an active mediator ready to pressure Israel to make the necessary concessions for peace—or both.

Every year since Sadat came to power he had proclaimed it to be the "year of decision" regarding Israel and reacquisition of the Sinai Peninsula. In the process of these proclamations, Egyptian forces mobilized from time to time to the point of routine, the plan, of course, being that when the real mobilization for war came the Israelis would conclude that it was just another exercise. All of these mobilizations and military-oriented constructions, such as a rampart on the west bank of the Suez Canal that effectively hid Egyptian intentions, were seen by the Israelis as an attempt to keep the Egyptian army busy so that it would not fall into idleness and contemplate such nefarious plans as removing the powers that be.

On one occasion, however, in May 1973, Israeli intelligence informed the Israeli high command and government that Egypt was preparing to attack across the canal. It turned out to be a false warning, but the damage had been done. Mobilization in Israel is no small affair. Practically the whole country mobilizes as reservists because of its small population base. The process is very disruptive to normal societal operations and quite expensive. When the warning turned out to be a red herring, Israeli intelligence took a beating for it. So when there were signs again in October that Egypt was preparing to invade, Israeli intelligence was somewhat hesitant to place itself too far out in front; in addition, any warnings coming from a branch of the government that had fallen into some disrepute might have landed on deaf ears anyway. This, combined with the complacency produced by 1967, certainly hampered Israeli responsiveness. It was this series of failures in intelligence and political imagination that led to the following in Israel: Golda Meir and Moshe Dayan leaving the government in 1974, with Yitzhak Rabin, the chief of staff during the 1967 war and former ambassador to the United States, beccoming prime minister; an official investigation examining the question of why Israel was caught so off-guard, the results of which led to the removal of a number of intelligence and military officials and the revamping of military intelligence overall; the weakening of the Labor party with its reduced plurality in the Knesset resulting from the December 1973 elections; and the related rise of Menachem Begin's Likud party to power in 1977.[10]

WAR AND ITS AFTERMATH

The day before the war began, there were five Egyptian divisions—100,000 men—stacked in full battle gear with over 1,300 tanks and 2,000 artillery pieces on the west bank of the Suez Canal. On the Golan Heights, Syria had five divisions with an eight to one advantage in tanks over the Israelis on the northern front; the Syrians had secondary lines arrayed all the way back to Damascus, forty miles to the northeast. In the Sinai, the Israelis had 290 tanks and forty-four artillery pieces along a one hundred–mile front protected by the Bar-Lev line, a huge manmade sand dune on the east bank of the canal containing strategically placed artillery and tanks that were intended to impede any cross-canal invasion long enough for the reserves to mobilize. On the Israeli side of the Golan Heights, there was no increase in Israeli forces and

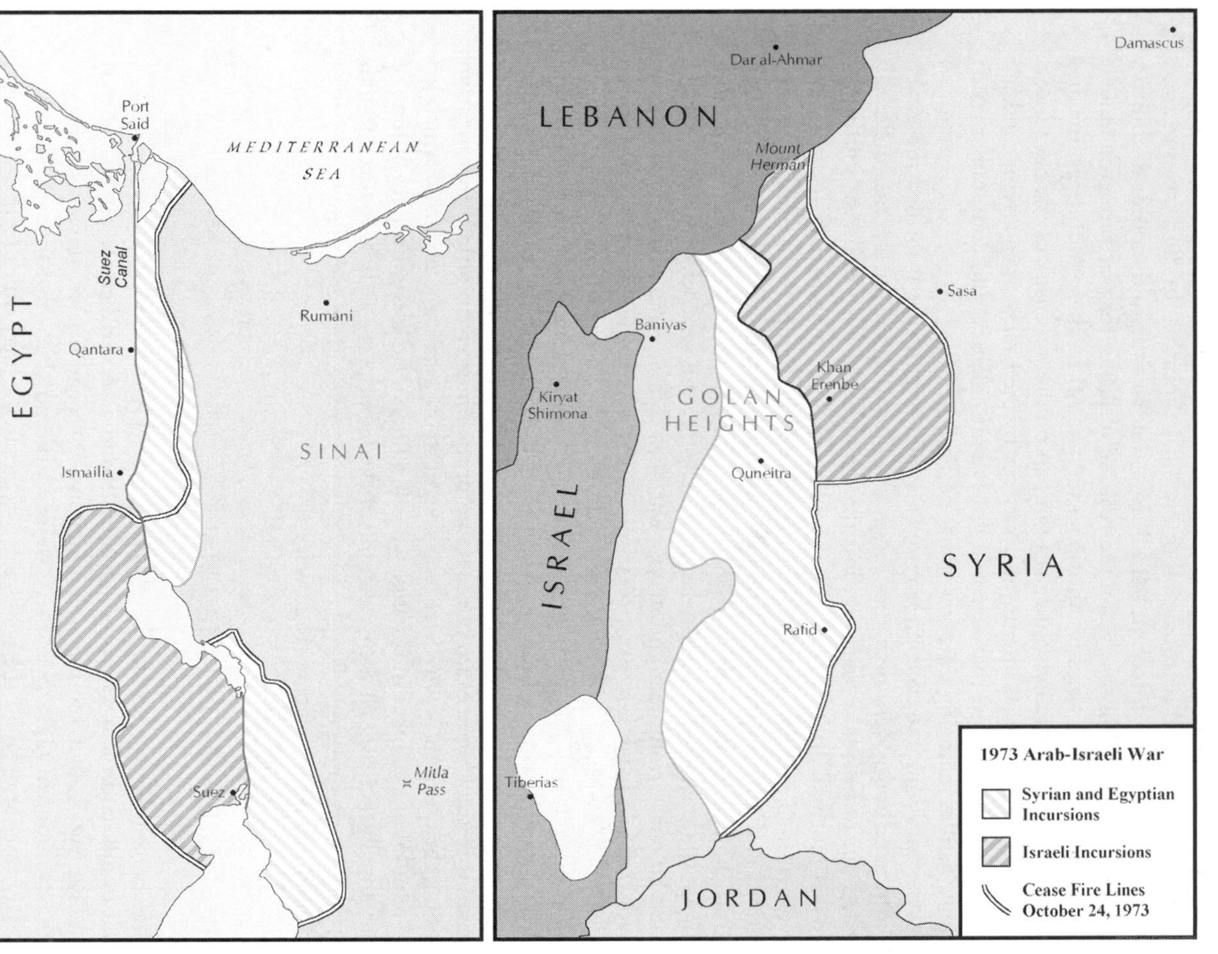

The 1973 Arab–Israeli War. (Middle East Studies Association, Justin McCarthy, University of Louisville, © 2003.)

secondary defense lines were non-existent.[11] The Soviets even evacuated nonessential personnel from Egypt on October 5; in fact, the demonstrative way in which they did so, obviously noticed by Israeli and U.S. intelligence, has led some to speculate that Moscow did so purposefully as a way to alert Tel Aviv and Washington of the impending attack—this seems the opposite of what a supposed ally would do, but one must remember that the Soviets were most interested in preventing an all-out regional conflagration that might escalate into a superpower confrontation. By giving notice, the Israelis would mobilize more quickly, possibly deterring the Egyptians and Syrians from launching their attacks; however, it was probably too late anyhow since it was estimated that it would take about a week for Israel to fully mobilize. Israeli officials did take notice of the Russian evacuation, with one even suggesting to Defense Minister Dayan a preemptive strike against Syrian forces; but there was a decision to undertake only a limited mobilization, with a Cabinet meeting to discuss the issue the next day at 2:00 p.m., the exact same time the attack commenced.[12] The country itself was in a very calm state, almost totally oblivious to what lay ahead. The Arab feint had worked. As Nadav Safran wrote:

> The Yom Kippur War was an effort by an Arab coalition to defeat Israel by breaking through a gap in its security concept. It was an attempt by the vast standing armies of Egypt and Syria to overcome the inferior standing forces of Israel before its reserves could be brought into play, and thus gain a decisively favorable position from which to defeat those reserves as they came into play. The attempt depended critically on surprise so that Israel should be unable to mobilize and deploy its reserves before the Arab forces attacked.[13]

The Egyptians and the Syrians launched a simultaneous invasion across the Suez Canal and Golan Heights, respectively, on October 6.[14] Both were successful in their initial stages. This was especially so for the Egyptians as they had to cross a natural barrier under withering fire. It took meticulous planning and imagination to launch such an audacious assault. With bridging equipment, rubber boats, and powerful water cannons that were used to blow holes through the Bar-Lev sand dunes, the Egyptians were able to establish a bridgehead on the east bank of the canal in the Sinai. Operation Badr, as the Egyptians called it, named after the prophet Muhammad's first military victory in 624 C.E. in his quest to take Mecca, was a stunning success, particularly when compared with past military disasters against Israel—so much so that it is celebrated as National Day each year in Egypt.

The United States and the Soviet Union were concerned lest this regional conflict escalate into a superpower one. In keeping with their summit pledges, they agreed to work for a cease-fire through the UN. The problem was that, despite their mutual commitment to détente, they still could not help but attempt to do so in a way that worked to their own cold war interests. Both Soviet and American officials calculated that it would take about three days for Israeli forces to regroup, go on the offensive, and rout the Arab combatants. As such, the Kremlin was pushing for a cease-fire to be in place no later than October 9, while Washington was working for one no earlier than the tenth. This fundamental reluctance to allow their respective client-states in the region to be caught in a disadvantageous position would lead to a diplomatic standoff at the superpower level that would escalate to a military one toward the end of the war. Neither superpower wanted to be seen in the Third World battleground as anything less than supportive of its presumed allies. For the Soviet Union this was particularly important given the black eye it had received in the 1967 war. It has been suggested that this almost intuitive disagreement in this war between the superpowers was the actual beginning of the unraveling of détente almost before it began, a process that would lead to a so-called second cold war later in the decade, made so apparently obvious with the Soviet invasion of Afghanistan in 1979 and the U.S. response.[15]

As expected, an Israeli counteroffensive began on October 8 on both fronts that lasted until the tenth. It was successful in the north against Syria, but it stalled in the south against Egypt. The only problem for Syrian President Hafiz al-Asad was that, according to him, Sadat never informed him that he entered the war with only limited objectives in mind. Asad held no illusions about completely defeating Israel, but at the very least he wanted to gain the Golan Heights back in its entirety, a military objective he thought Sadat shared with regard to the Sinai. Syria and Egypt were thus fighting with two different strategic designs after the initial assault, which caught Asad by surprise and undermined his own efforts to engage in a successful offensive in the Golan. In other words, after Egypt established the bridgehead on the east bank of the Suez Canal, it essentially stopped and assumed a defensive posture, which was strategically sound in terms of not fighting the mobile type of war at which Israel excels out in the open away from the SAM cover; but it also enabled the Israel Defense Forces (IDF) to concentrate more to the north to stall the more immediate Syrian threat. This infuriated Asad, and he would never forgive Sadat for it.[16] Even the name Syria has given the war—the October War of Liberation (*Harb Tishreen al-Tahririyya*)—suggests the clear objective of Asad to "liberate" the Golan Heights. The different war objectives precipitated a conflict of interests at various times during the war between Syria and Egypt and complicated Soviet efforts to arrange for a cease-fire acceptable to both.

The initial Syrian offensive that pushed the Israelis back across parts of the Golan Heights had come to a halt by October 8, brought to a standstill by the full fury of the Israeli air force. By October 9 and 10, Israeli jets were bombing economic and military targets deep in Syria and the IDF was able to push Syrian forces back to the so-called Purple Line that separated the Israeli-occupied Golan Heights from Syria proper. The Israelis focused most of their attention on the Syrian front since there was no buffer between the enemy and Israel proper, which the Sinai provided on the southern front; in any event, it appeared the Egyptians were not particularly interested in advancing beyond their bridgehead. This prompted the Soviets to begin a massive airlift of arms and ammunition to Syria by October 9 or 10. Moscow was very fearful that the Israelis could focus their attention on Syria since Sadat had dug in along the Suez and the Syrians had lost an enormous amount of material during the Israeli counteroffensive—as had the Israelis. The Soviets, however, always trying to balance need versus wherewithal, were careful to provide the Syrians only with that which was necessary to preserve their position and not try to initiate further hostilities against Israel that might bring the United States directly into the game. Despite this, the Israelis by October 13 had pushed on to created a salient toward Damascus beyond the Purple Line up to the village of Sasa on the road to the Syrian capital. By this time, Asad was fully aware of Sadat's more limited objectives, and he later even learned that the Egyptian president had entered into diplomatic contact with U.S. Secretary of State Henry Kissinger from a very early stage in the conflict. To put it mildly, Asad was furious, and the tone of communication between Damascus and Cairo quickly deteriorated as he demanded that Egypt do something to take the pressure off Syria.

From Cairo's point of view, however, things were going rather well militarily. The Israeli counteroffensive in the south had failed; indeed, Moshe Dayan made the comment at this point that "the third temple is about to fall."[17] Although somewhat overly alarmist, Dayan feared that Israel was in danger of losing by attrition, especially when it became apparent that the Soviets were rearming the Arab combatants. Prime Minister Golda Meir was pleading with the United States for arms, but none would be forthcoming in an immediate sense. This was because Kissinger stalled on the requests, believing that Israel would still be victorious but that it would just take a few more days. It also dawned on him that he did not want a decisive Israeli victory that would again humiliate the Egyptians, possibly compelling Cairo to embrace the Soviet Union for protection. From Kissinger's perspective, the optimal result would be a partial victory for both sides that would bring about more symmetry in the bargaining situation created in 1967. He also wanted Egypt to come directly to the United States to broker a new arrangement and/or at least keep the Israelis at bay if the latter regained the initiative, all of this devoid of Soviet participation. He did not want to provide the Israelis with the wherewithal to beat up on the Arabs again, thus producing the same asymmetrical bargaining situation that had been in place since the last Arab–Israeli war. Kissinger had learned that the immovable policy adopted by the United States prior to the outbreak of the October War had actually helped create conditions favorable for conflict. A negotiated settlement was necessary, and he saw how he could establish conditions for this process while also excluding the Soviet Union from it. Certainly, Sadat's behind-the-scenes diplomatic contacts with Kissinger in the early stages of the war did nothing to dispel this notion.

The problem for Israel was that while Kissinger stalled on the arms requests, it was falling into a precarious military situation, especially with the Soviet airlift. When Washington got wind of the Soviet arms arriving in Damascus and Cairo, combined with Israeli hints that it may have to use nuclear weapons if the situation appreciably worsened and its request for a cease-fire to be in place linked to Resolution 242, i.e., with Israeli territory held by the Arabs at that juncture—something that was unheard of up to this point—the Nixon administration all of sudden gave the green light for its own massive arms airlift to Israel on October 14. Both superpowers were now intimately—and dangerously—involved in the war, totally contrary to the intent of their summit pledges.

In the meantime, Sadat came under tremendous pressure from both Damascus and Moscow to launch another offensive into the Sinai to take some of the heat off of Syria. Against his better judgment, Sadat finally relented and launched an offensive in the south on October 14, fatefully abandoning the air defense umbrella that had hitherto protected Egypt's defensive position on the east bank of the canal. The timing could not have been worse, for Israel launched its own second counteroffensive on October 15, emboldened by the U.S. airlift that commenced the day before. While the front in the north remained relatively static, with Israel perched to move on Damascus itself if necessary, the south turned into something close to a replay of 1967 in the Sinai. Israeli forces decisively turned back the Egyptian offensive and approached the Suez Canal south of the Egyptian bridgehead. On October 16, an Israeli column led by Ariel Sharon crossed the Suez Canal onto the west bank and began a rearguard operation that would soon turn into an encirclement of the Egyptian Third Army

Israeli Defense Minister Moshe Dayan (*left*) and Major General Ariel Sharon on the west bank of the Suez Canal on October 18, 1973, following the Israeli push across the canal into Egypt. (Reuters/CORBIS, 42-16306057.)

encamped at Suez City near the southern portion of the canal. The Egyptian position, and all of its hard-earned success to this point, was teetering on the brink.

The Soviets began to involve themselves even more directly in the ensuing course of events. Only satellite photos personally delivered to Sadat in Cairo by Soviet Premier Alexsei Kosygin on October 18 convinced the Egyptian president of the precariousness of his position. He immediately gave Moscow the go-ahead to work for a cease-fire at the UN to preserve what was still in Egyptian possession in the Sinai and, indeed, even the entire Egyptian military position because the Israelis were in no mood to cease and desist at this point, wanting to punish Egypt in a way that would render any small victory on the east bank completely meaningless.

It is at this point, on October 19, that the Arab members of OPEC announced an oil embargo against any nation (read "United States") that was supplying Israel. At first glance, this seems to have been an immediate response to the Nixon administration's request to Congress on the same day for $2.3 billion in military aid to Israel. Upon further examination, however, it also seems to have been an attempt by the Saudis to save Sadat. As noted earlier, Saudi officials were present in the Egyptian high command in Cairo, so they were fully aware of the precarious military situation Egypt was in at the time. The Saudis had established a cooperative relationship with Sadat, contrary to what had been the case with Nasser for most of his tenure in power. They did not want to see Sadat fall, much less Israel go on to inflict another humiliating defeat. If Sadat was forced from power due to a decisive Israeli victory, his successor may, in fact, be someone from the opposite end of the political spectrum: a radical in the mode of Nasser or worse from the perspective of Riyadh, and that could only lead to another long-term antagonistic relationship with the most powerful and influential Arab state, possibly dividing the Arab world even more deeply than during the Arab cold war and complicating the Saudi relationship with the United States. The only way to stop the Israelis—and save Sadat—was for it to be in the interest of Washington to do so. The Saudis had actually been a moderate influence within OPEC, and they had fought off attempts by some of the Arab OPEC hawks who were pressing Riyadh to launch an embargo at the beginning of the war. But by October 19, it became clear that it was time for the Saudis to make good on their prewar pledge to Sadat. The result would dramatically shake the global economy.

While the oil embargo certainly raised the stakes for Washington, it was something else that really served as a wake-up call: the Soviet Union. The Kremlin could envision its whole position in the Middle East going up in flames if the Israelis continued their military actions on the east bank in Egypt and destroyed the Egyptian Third Army. As such, Moscow became directly engaged, working hard with the United States to pass UNSC Resolution 338 on October 22, which called for an immediate cease-fire, a withdrawal to prewar lines, and a resumption of negotiations based on Resolution 242. The problem was that Israel did not cease. The Soviets knew they had to come through for Sadat to stop the Israelis lest he go to the Americans for a security guarantee. Soviet leader Leonid Brezhnev sent an ominous letter to Nixon threatening to intervene directly if the Israelis did not stop. For good measure, Soviet strategic forces were placed on high alert. At this point, Sadat communicated with Washington, asking for an American guarantee before agreeing to another cease-fire. This is what Kissinger had hoped for to begin with, and he did everything he could to deliver on it, telling the Israelis that the United States was not prepared to go to a third world war just so they could have the Egyptian Third Army. He also had tremendous leverage since Israel was, if anything, now much more dependent on U.S. largesse. In addition, Kissinger placed the U.S. strategic air command, containing the nuclear strike forces, on its highest alert since the Cuban Missile Crisis to face down the Soviets. Finally, on October 24, Resolution 339 was passed, calling for the application of Resolution 338. With intense U.S. pressure, the Israelis finally ceased fire on October 25, thus ending the 1973 Arab–Israeli war. Syria and Egypt lost considerably more men and materiel; but Israel was bloodied, and the Arabs could claim at least a psychological victory.[18]

Kissinger had to move quickly to take diplomatic advantage of the postwar environment. After all, it was only a cease-fire, one that could be easily broken, especially as the opposing forces were still faced off against one another. In addition, the price per barrel of oil was rising fast with the oil embargo, and the Saudis had set stiff conditions for it to be lifted: that Israel should return to the June 4, 1967, borders and Palestinian rights should be specifically discussed. The U.S. secretary of state thus began his odyssey of shuttle diplomacy to secure the cease-fire and build upon it. On November 11, in a tent in the Sinai at kilometer 101 from Cairo, Kissinger negotiated an agreement between Israel and Egypt for a return to the October 22 cease-fire lines (when Resolution 338 was passed) and relief was arranged in the form of medical supplies and food for the Egyptian Third Army at Suez City. Even though relatively small-scale, the "kilometer 101" agreement was officially the first between Israel and an Arab state since the armistice talks in 1949.

But this still was not enough. It was not enough to lift the oil embargo, and it was not enough to ensure that Israeli and Egyptian forces would not resume fighting at any moment. Kissinger proposed a UN-sponsored conference to be held in Geneva in December. Egypt and Jordan agreed to negotiate directly with the Israelis at such a meeting based on the provisions of Resolution 338; however, Syria refused to attend. The meeting was held on December 21, with the United States and the Soviet Union in attendance; but it broke down after only a day, although Egypt and Israel agreed to negotiate a further separation of forces. This was not a terribly bad outcome for Kissinger since he could now pursue separate talks between Egypt and Israel without the involvement of the UN or the Soviet Union. His focus was on Egypt since the cease-fire was most vulnerable to breaking down on this front, with the still-intimate deployment of forces. But beyond this, plucking Egypt away from the Soviet camp would be a major diplomatic and strategic coup in the cold war zero-sum game; in addition, and maybe more importantly over the long haul, placing Egypt on the road to peace with Israel would effectively remove the most populous and powerful Arab state from the Arab–Israeli belligerency equation. The destructiveness of the 1973 Arab–Israeli war was starkly apparent, and the danger of a superpower confrontation was all too real. Without Egypt, no Arab coalition could even hope to take on Israel; thus, there would not be an occasion for another all-out Arab–Israeli war. The grim reality and repercussions of the 1973 war portended regional and possibly even global catastrophe for the next war—negotiations that held out the hope of putting the Arab–Israeli conflict to rest therefore had to commence, and to at least some extent, all sides of the conflict realized this. Of course, for reasons based more on national interest and survival, this had also been one of Israel's primary foreign policy objectives: to separate Egypt from the rest of the Arab fold.

Kissinger then began his famous shuttle diplomacy between the capitals of Israel and Egypt. He needed another agreement beyond kilometer 101 because the longer Israeli forces remained on the east bank, the more hollow were Sadat's claims of victory. One of the main objectives of the war for Sadat was to reactivate diplomacy—it worked, and now was the time for it. The Israelis were also overextended militarily, and their position would become more vulnerable with each passing day as the Egyptians rearmed and reinforced their positions. There was, therefore, a bargain to be struck that Kissinger exploited. He also began to employ what he learned in 1970 upon the conclusion of the War of Attrition: that progress on the Arab–Israeli front would have to come in steps—a comprehensive Arab–Israeli accord was too complicated and fraught with obstacles to even be considered at this point; therefore, it is no surprise that Kissinger's negotiating strategy has often been referred to as the "step-by-step" approach. The result was a disengagement agreement brokered by Kissinger between Egypt and Israel in January 1974. The agreement, often called "Sinai I," arranged for, most importantly, the removal of Israeli troops from the west bank of the Suez Canal and some twenty miles inland from the east bank into the Sinai. In between Egyptian and Israeli forces was placed a UN-monitored and -patrolled buffer zone. Egypt also agreed to a significant reduction of its forces in the Sinai. And for good measure, U.S.–Egyptian diplomatic relations were restored in February 1974.

Kissinger was no less a frequent visitor to Damascus in an attempt to arrange a similar disengagement agreement between Syria and Israel. The secretary of state traveled to and from Damascus no less than twenty-six times and met with Hafiz al-Asad

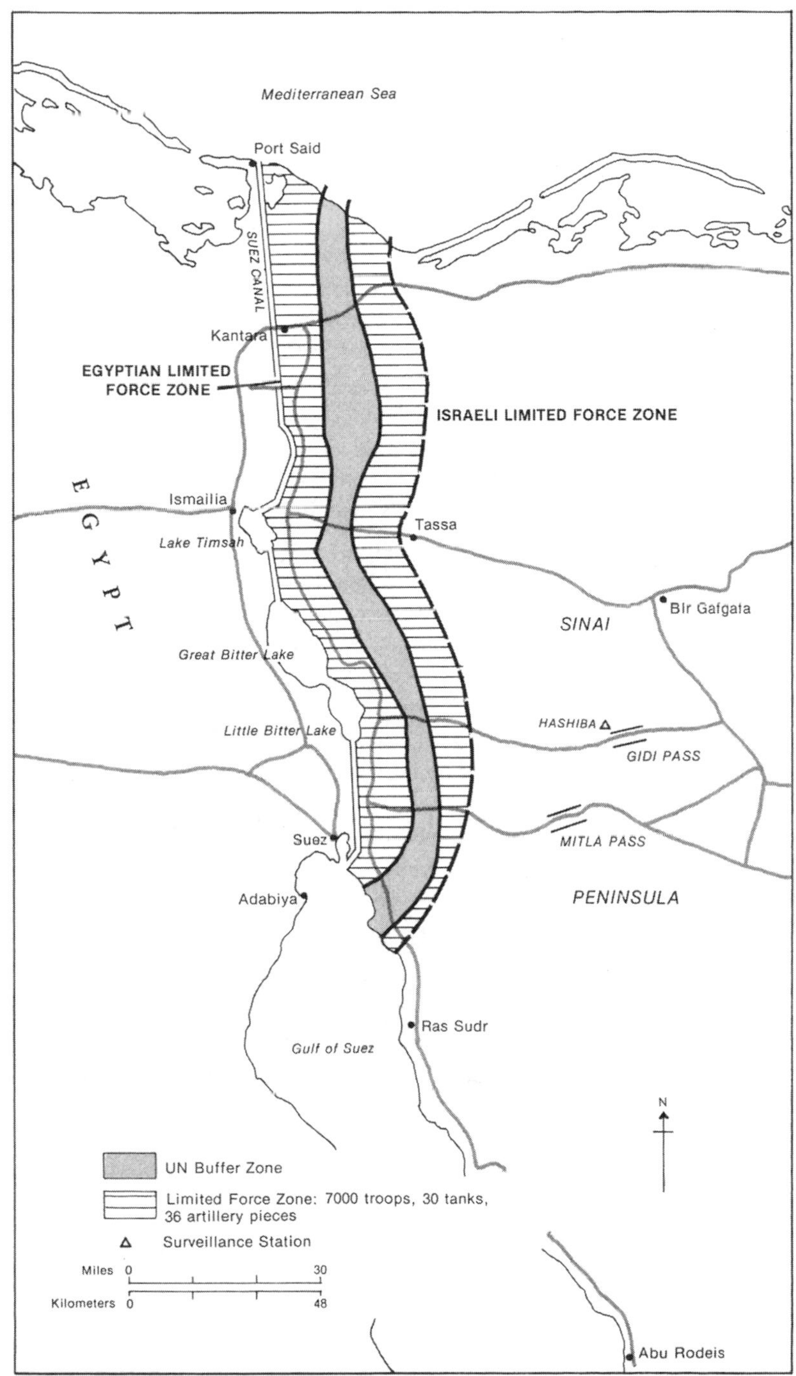

First Israeli–Egyptian Sinai agreement, January 18, 1974. (Reprinted by permission of the publisher from *Israel, the Embattled Ally: The United States and Israel* by Nadav Safran. Cambridge, MA.: Belknap Press of Harvard University Press, 526. Copyright © 1978 by the president and fellows of Harvard College.)

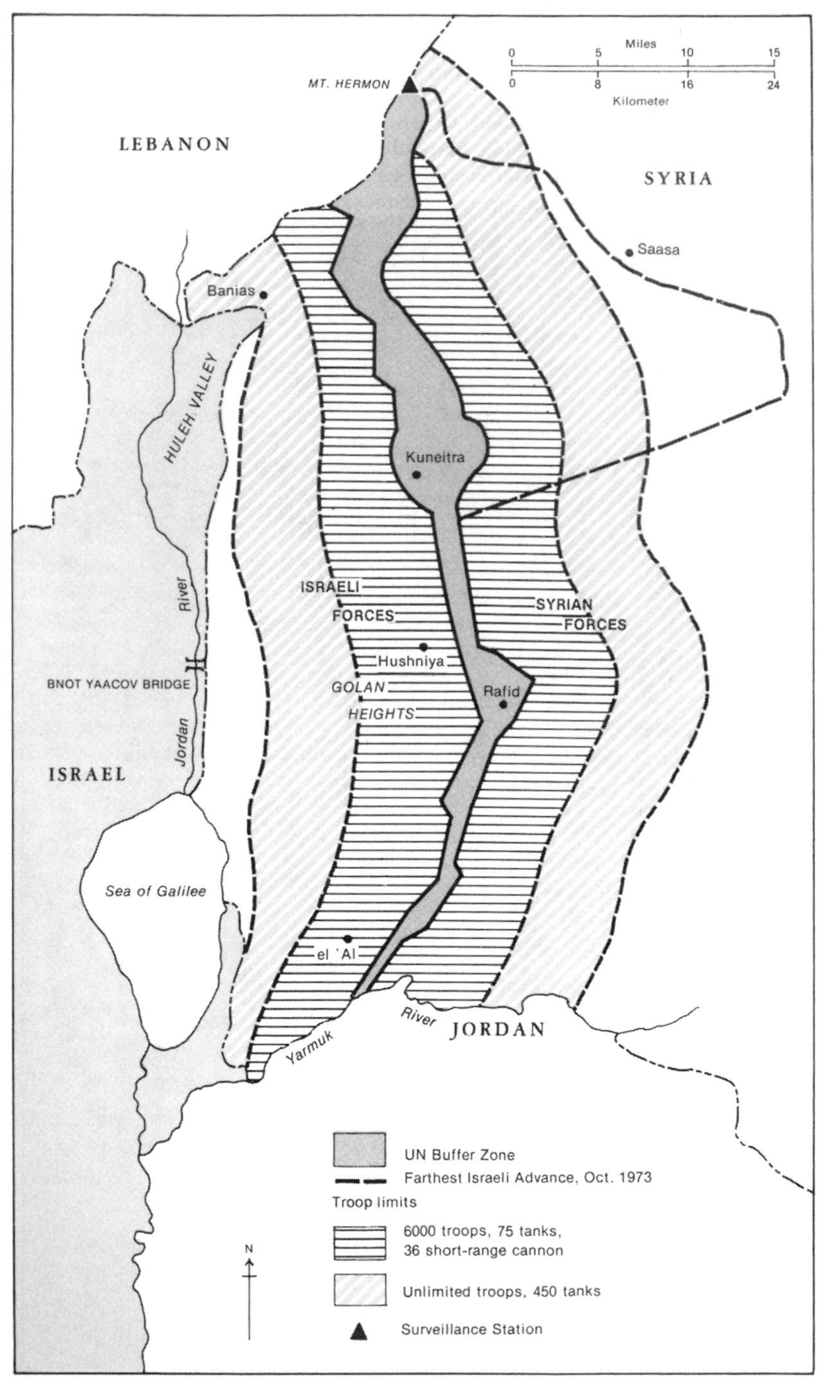

Israeli–Syrian Golan agreement, May 31, 1974. (Reprinted by permission of the publisher from *Israel, the Embattled Ally: The United States and Israel* by Nadav Safran. Cambridge, MA.: Belknap Press of Harvard University Press, 533. Copyright © 1978 by the president and fellows of Harvard College.)

for approximately 130 hours of face-to-face discussions.[19] A disengagement agreement was reached in May 1974. It took quite a bit longer because the oil embargo, the hoped-for lifting of which had been one of Kissinger's primary objectives of his shuttle diplomacy in the first place, ended in March—it seems as though, with the fourfold increase in the price per barrel of oil, the stiff conditions for the lifting of the embargo outlined by Saudi Arabia had been conveniently forgotten. From Riyadh's point of view, there was some progress in negotiations. In any event, it was time to make money, and to maintain the embargo against the world's largest oil consumer was akin to cutting one's nose off to spite one's face. Also, the array of forces in the Golan was less combustible than that which existed along the Suez, so there was a touch less urgency to the negotiations. Finally, Hafiz al-Asad would become famous for his deliberate, if not stubborn, negotiating style—it was on public display for the first time in this episode. Kissinger, however, kept working at it because he wanted to make sure Egypt was not portrayed in the Arab world as leaping out on its own and abandoning the Palestinians and a coordinated Arab stance. It was important at this stage to get another Arab state to sign along the dotted line in order to allow Egypt more flexibility to move forward even further. The Syrian–Israeli disengagement agreement was just such a vehicle for Kissinger—it was an end to another means, while Asad considered it a first step toward the return of the entire Golan Heights. The Syrian president was wrong, and it would be a lesson he learned early in his tenure in power. He would be careful not to make this mistake again in the future; maybe, then, Kissinger should share the blame for Asad's deliberate, suspicious, and incremental negotiating style that for better or worse would come to define his approach to diplomacy in the future. Per the agreement, the Israelis withdrew from their salient toward Damascus, and they even relinquished part of the Golan Heights captured in 1967 to allow UN Disengagement Observer Forces (UNDOF) to establish their position as a buffer between Israeli and Syrian forces. Asad also agreed to end Palestinian fedayeen raids into Israel through the Golan Heights. This disengagement agreement has held up remarkably well to this day, and it is one of the success stories in UN peace monitoring and troop deployment.

Gerald Ford succeeded Richard Nixon as president in August 1974 upon the latter's resignation due to the repercussions of the Watergate scandal. Ford and Kissinger (who remained as secretary of state) considered the two disengagement agreements a stepping stone toward the convening of an international conference in Geneva that could take that one huge last step: a comprehensive Arab–Israeli peace agreement. For a variety of reasons, however, an international peace conference, much less a comprehensive peace accord, was not feasible at this time. There were a number of obstacles from the perspective of Washington: (1) differences among the Arab states in trying to formulate a unified position, which would only be exacerbated by the outbreak of the Lebanese civil war in April 1975 (to be discussed more fully in Chapter 9); (2) disagreements within the administration about what role, if any, the Soviets would play; (3) traditional Israeli opposition to any international peace conference that would increase the pressure for Israeli concessions and negate Israel's advantage in one-on-one negotiations with individual Arab states; and (4) maybe the biggest obstacle, the nature of representation of the PLO. Israel considered the PLO a terrorist organization and would not recognize it or negotiate with it. The problem was that at the Arab League summit meeting held at Rabat, Morocco, in October 1974, it was unanimously decided that the PLO was "the sole legitimate representative of the Palestinian people," with authorization to establish an independent national authority in "liberated Palestinian territory." This was a blow to Jordan's King Hussein, who still held out hope of reacquiring the West Bank and East Jerusalem. It was also something of a blow to Israel and the United States, both of which saw Jordan as a much more viable negotiating partner than the PLO regarding the disposition of the West Bank. For Yasser Arafat and the PLO as a whole, it was a diplomatic triumph as the organization more and more took center stage as the heartbeat of the Palestinian movement and Palestinian rights. Arafat even addressed the UN General Assembly in November 1974, telling the assembled delegates "I have come bearing an olive branch and a freedom fighter's gun. Do not let the olive branch fall from my hand." The moderates in the PLO, including Arafat as well as most of the Palestinians still living in the Occupied Territories, tended to lean more toward a two-state solution, with a Palestinian state in the West Bank and Gaza Strip and East Jerusalem as its capital. Not all factions in the PLO agreed with Arafat. The PFLP, PFLP-GC, and DFLP were still committed to regaining all of Palestine; and they continued to engage in terrorist operations aimed at disrupting progress toward peace, just as they had in September 1970. Most Israelis did not accept the two-state solution implicitly offered by Palestinian moderates, either because they believed that a Palestinian state already existed, called Jordan (since the majority of the population was Palestinian) or that it was really an attempt at subterfuge, i.e., that the Palestinians would play the moderate, victimized people until they got their state in the West Bank and Gaza Strip, which they would then use as a base of operations to carry on the struggle and try to regain the rest of Israel. These views are still held to this day by a number of Israelis who are perpetually suspicious of PLO motives—and the PLO over the years, since it is indeed an amorphous jumble of different factions adhering to a wide variety of positions, has done little to instill confidence in the Israeli public.

As a result of this impasse, the United States, Israel, and Egypt worked on another limited disengagement agreement similar to Sinai I—in essence, another step. Even this was not easy to come by. Rabin was very reluctant to withdraw any further across the Sinai or give up the oil fields. Progress was very slow during the summer of 1975, with Ford even calling for a "reassessment" of the U.S.–Israeli relationship, including a suspension of aid, because of what he perceived to be Israeli intransigence. Israel could not afford to alienate its primary external patron however. And Israeli leaders realized that their country's position in the region had been weakened as a result of the 1973 war. They also were aware of the growing power of OPEC, which compelled many European and East Asian countries to distance themselves from Israel in order to curry favor with the Arab oil-exporting states. Israel was becoming increasingly isolated internationally—and not just in the Middle East, a fact driven home later in the year on November 10, 1975, when the UN passed UNGA 3379 that equated Zionism with racism.[20] Israel had to be more forthcoming. The result was another disengagement agreement with Egypt in September 1975, often referred to as "Sinai II."

In this disengagement accord, it was agreed that Israeli forces in the Sinai would pull back beyond the strategically important Giddi and Mitla passes (about halfway across the upper Sinai) in return for the establishment of a more formal demilitarized buffer between Egypt and Israel, supervised by the UN and monitored by American-controlled and manned sophisticated electronic early warning stations. The oil fields at Abu Rudeis were also returned to Egypt, which was very important for the Egyptian economy, while nonmilitary Israeli cargo could pass through the Suez Canal. Egypt also

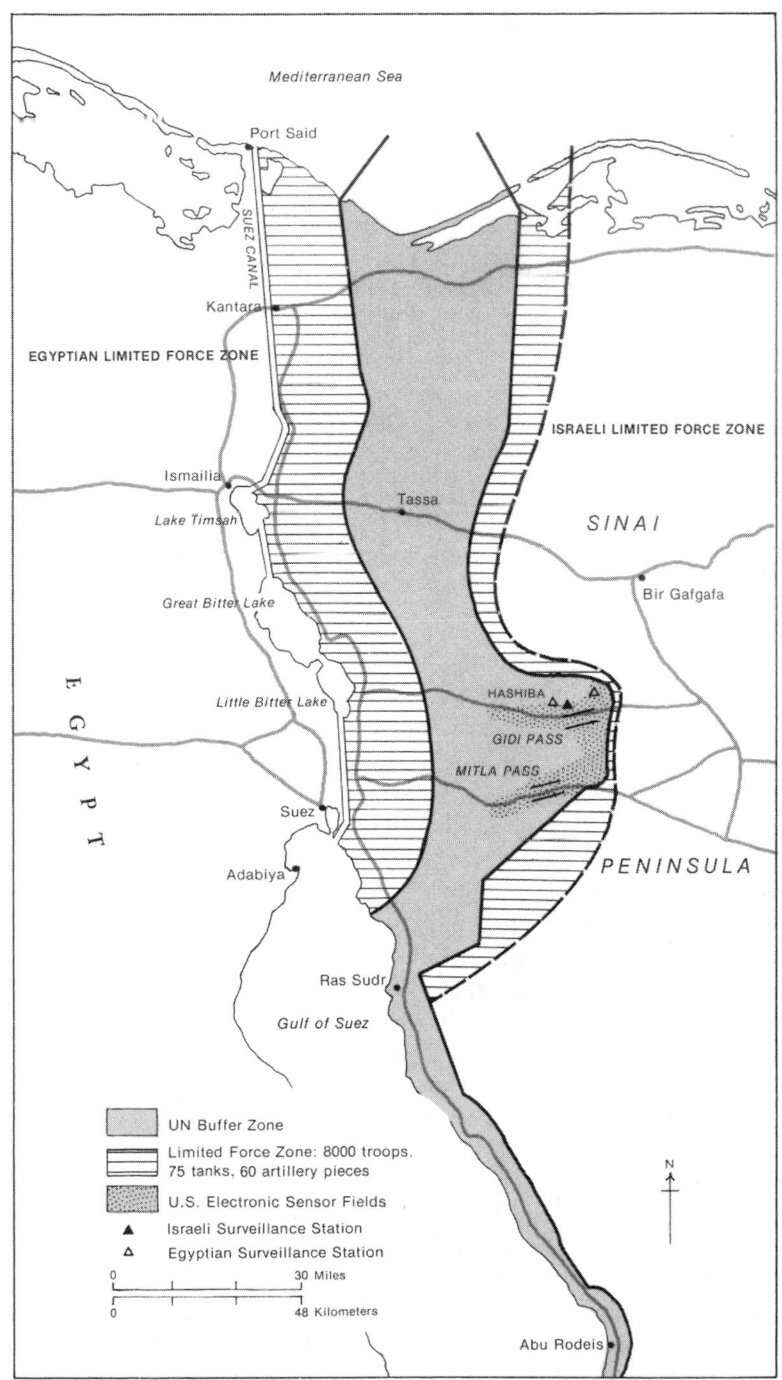

Second Israeli–Egyptian Sinai agreement, September 4, 1975. (Reprinted by permission of the publisher from *Israel, the Embattled Ally: The United States and Israel* by Nadav Safran. Cambridge, MA.: Belknap Press of Harvard University Press, 555. Copyright © 1978 by the president and fellows of Harvard College.)

agreed to several clauses, committing itself to nonbelligerency, a peaceful resolution of the Arab–Israeli conflict, and efforts to draw other Arab states, particularly Syria, into similar agreements.

The fact that Syria did not follow Egypt's lead at this time clearly indicated that Sadat was willing to stake out his own path apart from the rest of the Arab world despite the continued façade of commitment to the Palestinian issue. To Sadat and his supporters, Egypt had already bled too much for the cause of Arab nationalism. He saw how Nasser had become captive to Arab nationalist rhetoric, which eventually destroyed him. Egypt had always seen itself as apart in many ways from the rest of the Arab world, having its own long and glorious history that predated the arrival of the Arabs and Islam in the seventh century C.E. Indeed, Egypt really only became a player in the inter-Arab arena in the twentieth century, and it was actually a tenet of Arab nationalist ideologies that Egypt was, in fact, part of the Arab world, as if the Egyptians and the rest of the Arabs needed convincing. Maybe it was once again time for Egypt to look out for its own national interests first, and this meant retrieving the Sinai Peninsula and opening up the country to Western investment and American aid. And the latter would be forthcoming in droves. In order to facilitate the deal, the Ford administration increased U.S. military and economic aid to Israel and promised to assist Egypt in its economic development. Kissinger also agreed to an Israeli demand that the United States not recognize or negotiate with the PLO until it had recognized Israel, accepted UNSC Resolutions 242 and 338, and renounced terrorism. This demand, which appeared to Kissinger to be fairly innocuous at the time, was agreed to as an added enticement for Israel to sign on to Sinai II; but it eventually hampered Washington's ability to position itself as an honest broker in the Arab–Israeli arena. This clause was taken very seriously by Israel, however, and is seen as an important element that forced the PLO to recognize the Jewish state a decade later. Kissinger believed the alternative to an agreement could be war, which could result in enhanced Soviet influence and possibly another oil embargo. U.S. foreign policy in the Middle East rested on continuing to pull Egypt into the American orbit and supporting Sadat's pursuit of a peaceful resolution to the Arab–Israeli conflict, with the hope that it would draw in other moderate Arab states with which the United States enjoyed amicable relations, such as Saudi Arabia and Jordan.

Sinai II was immediately criticized and condemned by a number of groups in the United States—of course, it was roundly criticized in the Arab world. The basis for the criticism was as follows: if so much energy was expended, so many promises made, and so much money spent just to get the Israelis to withdraw some thirty kilometers in the Sinai, what in the world would it take to bring about a comprehensive peace accord that included Israeli withdrawal to something close to its June 4, 1967 borders? In addition, Kissinger's approach seemed only to be averting war by buying time rather than achieving real peace by addressing the problems at the root of the conflict. Indeed, the Brookings Institution, a left-of-center think tank in Washington, DC, issued a report in late 1975 that concluded that the step-by-step approach had exhausted itself, leaving too many issues unresolved, which could again lead to rising tensions and the outbreak of war in the region with all of its untold consequences. The time had apparently come for a new approach, one that would bring about that elusive comprehensive settlement.

CAMP DAVID AND THE 1979 EGYPTIAN–ISRAELI PEACE TREATY

Jimmy Carter became U.S. president after winning the 1976 election, and he came into office with the Middle East as a high priority within his foreign policy platform. Basing his approach to a significant degree upon the 1975 Brookings Institution report, several of the authors of which would serve in his administration (including National Security Advisor Zbigniew Brzezinski), Carter sought at first to convene an international conference in Geneva with the express purpose of seeking a comprehensive settlement. Unfortunately for the Carter administration, many of the same issues that prevented the convening of a conference under the Ford administration still existed. In addition, a window of opportunity may have been lost when, in May 1977, the former leader of the Irgun, Menachem Begin, became prime minister of Israel, the first time the right-wing Likud party had come to power in Israeli history. The Likud party had adopted a hard-line approach toward negotiations with the Arab states and was much more reluctant to return land for peace than their Labor party counterparts, wanting to keep most, if not all, of the Occupied Territories for strategic, nationalist, and/or religious reasons; indeed, the more nationalist and religious Jewish parties called the West Bank "Judea and Samaria," following the biblical reference to the area. Israel's negotiating position regarding the territories at the time can be summarized as follows: (1) direct negotiations with individual Arab states; (2) if some land should be returned, Israel must retain substantial portions of the Occupied Territories on all fronts for security reasons; (3) Jerusalem was the undivided, eternal capital of the state of Israel and was nonnegotiable; (4) the PLO was a terrorist organization and Israel would not negotiate with it; (5) Israel would not accept a Palestinian state in the West Bank and/or Gaza Strip because it would be a direct threat to Israel; and (6) full and immediate normalization of relations with any Arab state in a peace agreement based on the assumption that this was the only way the Arabs could prove that they really wanted peace. Begin also authorized more frequent preemptory and retaliatory strikes against Palestinian positions, especially in southern Lebanon, and began to support more vigorously right-wing Lebanese Christian forces in Lebanon against the Palestinians there. Of course, this led to an intensified cycle of violence as the PLO then would retaliate against the retaliations. All the while, Lebanon was drawn more and more into the teeth of the Arab–Israeli conflict.

The establishment of Jewish settlements in the Occupied Territories also accelerated under Begin. The settlement process had actually begun under the auspices of the Labor party, although, following the Allon plan, the Jewish settlements were akin to military outposts and away from Arab population centers, with the important exception of Gush Etzion, located southeast of Jerusalem, which was established on the grounds of a settlement lost by Israel in the 1948 war. The mid-1970s saw a 50% increase in the number of settlements, and they were more intermingled among the Arab towns and villages so as to make it that much more difficult for future governments to dismantle them and for any Palestinian entity to have geographical contiguity. By 1977 when Likud assumed power from Labor, there were thirty-six settlements in the West Bank (which had thirty-one) and Gaza Strip (which had five) populated by over 4,500 settlers. Jewish groups, such as the Gush Emunim (Bloc of the Faithful) created in 1974 (in part created after the partial withdrawal in the Sinai for fear that the same could happen eventually in the West Bank), started to agitate for more settlements and keep the territories in perpetuity much more aggressively, to the point where they became important political forces in the Israeli parliamentary system. The Sephardic or "Oriental" Jews in Israel as well as recent immigrants tended to vote more on economic grounds with Likud and were the backbone for Begin's victory in the 1977 elections, but on the whole they also adopted the Likud's rigid position on the territories.

But Sadat had been sending clear signals to Carter that he was anxious to move forward on peace negotiations with Israel. Israeli officials saw this "anxiety" as something that could be exploited to peel Egypt away from the Arab fold. In other words, they correctly sensed that Sadat might be willing to go off on his own and sign a separate peace with Israel in order to get the Sinai back with little more than lip service to the Arab cause and Palestinian rights. This became manifest when Egyptian officials secretly engaged in high-level talks with Israeli officials (one of whom was Yitzhak Rabin) in Morocco in September 1977. This was something that even Begin could not pass up, for this had been a primary Israeli foreign policy objective since the creation of the Jewish state. In addition, Carter was getting increasingly perturbed at Begin's policies, which ran totally counter to the president's efforts to convene an international conference. At one point Carter remarked that "we are financing their conquest and they simply defy us in an intransigent fashion and generally make a mockery of our advice and preferences."[21] In October 1977, the Carter administration even tried to work with the Soviet Union to arrange a Geneva conference with a joint statement calling for a comprehensive settlement, including an Israeli withdrawal from the territories occupied in the 1967 war and guaranteeing the "legitimate rights of the Palestinian people." Israel vociferously opposed the U.S.–Soviet statement, as did pro-Israeli supporters in the U.S. Congress and even elements within the Carter administration who ran afoul of reversing Kissinger's approach of excluding Moscow as much as possible. Carter was forced to back down. For domestic reasons, he was reluctant to apply the necessary pressure on Israel, promising Tel Aviv that he would not impose a peace settlement on the Jewish state. This episode tended to convince the Israelis that Carter would be malleable to domestic pressures and would not stand fast against Israel. The Arabs, on the other hand, particularly Sadat, concluded that the United States not only would not but also could not bring enough pressure to bear on Israel to force it to make significant concessions. This also proved counterproductive to the PLO position, which at the time gave indications of moderating its stance. But American pressure could not compel the PLO to accept Resolution 242 and recognize Israel because it was apparent to Arafat and other PLO officials that the United States under Carter could not even come close to pressuring Israel to withdraw from the West Bank and Gaza Strip. Without assurances that the United States would play this role, the PLO was not about to give up its main bargaining chips in the *hope* that Carter would come through for them.

As a result of all this, a stalemate ensued in the prospective Arab–Israeli peace process. As he had done in 1973 during another diplomatic lull, Anwar al-Sadat engineered another bold move in order to break the impasse. In 1973 he chose war; on November 19, 1977, he made the incredibly dramatic gesture of visiting Israel, the first official visit by an Arab head of state. With his visit and speech before the Israeli Knesset, Sadat implicitly recognized Israel, again, the first Arab head of state to do so; convinced skeptical Israelis that Egypt was serious about peace; and perforce restored momentum to the peace process. In his speech to the Knesset, Sadat said "I declare to the whole world that we accept to live with you in permanent peace based on justice." There was little progress on substantive issues in talks between Sadat and Begin at the time, but a very important psychological barrier had been breached. Knowing that hard negotiations lay ahead, both sides mapped out initial positions that were obviously unacceptable to the other, making sure that any concession would be considered significant enough to warrant something similar in return. The Egyptian president had grown impatient with a process that never seemed to get going—it needed a kick-start, and the dramatic way in which he did so was consistent with his own stylistic flair and heightened sense of his role in what was becoming history in the making.[22] Instead of dealing with Israel in conjunction with the other Arab states, Egypt would show the way, expecting that it would force countries such as Jordan, Saudi Arabia, and possibly even Syria to do the same, knowing full well that they could no longer confront Israel without Egypt. He had staked his position and his prestige on reacquiring the Sinai, and he had already gone far out on a limb—he could not fail, but this was also his diplomatic vulnerability.

Sadat's historic visit did not elicit the forthcoming response from Begin in the ensuing months that was hoped for by the Egyptian regime. Begin was certainly reluctant to enter into a process that might expand from bilateral Israeli–Egyptian issues to the Palestinian problem as well as the other Occupied Territories. The Israeli prime minister was careful and smart not to close the door completely, but his position was much stronger than Sadat's since his support base within Likud was also reluctant to give up any land—he could hold out for terms that were to his liking. He saw this as a possible unique opportunity to engage in direct, one-on-one negotiations with an Arab state, the type, as mentioned previously, Israelis preferred since it gave them more bargaining leverage and prevented a coalition of forces gathered at an international peace conference from pressuring Israel to make concessions it did not want to make or imposing a solution from the outside. Contrary to what one might think, Israel prefers that Washington is minimally involved, whereas the Arab states usually want more active American diplomatic intervention, because both sides understand that the United States is the only country on the planet that can pressure Israel—and, as Carter found out, even this is anything but a given. Yes, if the Sinai Peninsula was relinquished, Israel would lose that physical buffer it had long wanted and have to dismantle the settlements there and return the lucrative oil fields; but it was believed that this would be more than offset strategically by peace and economically by eliminating the costly state of constant military readiness it was forced to adopt vis-à-vis Egypt. Begin and his supporters also saw a possible return of the Sinai Peninsula, which was never part of Eretz Yisrael (the Land of Israel), as making it more likely that Israel could keep the rest of the Occupied Territories and deflect attention away from the Palestinian situation. On Begin's strategy, Israeli Defense Minister Ezer Weizman, who was the most fervent proponent for peace with Egypt in the Israeli Cabinet, commented that the Likud leader would "use every ruse to sabotage the peace efforts leading to Geneva and to promote Israel's longstanding goal of separating Egypt from the other Arab states as a means of weakening Arab bargaining power and making it easier for Israel to hold on to the remainder of the occupied territories and to ignore the Palestinian problem."[23]

Egyptian–Israeli progress stalled again, even though Sadat's forthcoming maneuvers had forced Begin to spell out Israel's position more specifically. In a meeting with Sadat at Ismailiyya, Egypt, in December 1977, he indicated that he was prepared conditionally to make a phased withdrawal from the Sinai Peninsula. Begin also presented a plan regarding the Palestinians in the West Bank and Gaza Strip that provided for limited administrative autonomy, with the possibility of municipal elections. However, he positively ruled out negotiating with the PLO or allowing the creation of a Palestinian state in the West Bank and Gaza Strip. With Begin digging his feet in, there was not much progress in the spring and summer of 1978. This was compounded by Israel's invasion of south Lebanon in June 1978 to clear out PLO positions in the area that had been the staging ground for attacks against Israel. This was something of an embarrassment to Sadat since many Arab officials had warned that if Egypt entered into a peace agreement with Israel, the IDF would be freed up to move with virtual impunity against Lebanon and/or Syria. This also further diminished the chances that any other Arab states, even if they were inclined to do so, would support Sadat's peace initiative. By the end of the summer of 1978, it was clear that any hope for an Egyptian–Israeli agreement would require outside intervention to break the many impasses that had developed between Begin and Sadat. President Carter, not wanting to see the process totally derailed, which might undermine Sadat's position in Egypt with untold consequences, inserted himself directly into the mix by inviting both Begin and Sadat to the presidential retreat located at Camp David, Maryland, in September 1978 to hash out a framework for peace. For thirteen tumultuous and dramatic days, the participants bargained extremely hard, with brinksmanship and threatened departures becoming more the order of the day as the days progressed. The talks came to the precipice of breaking down on numerous occasions; indeed, after initial meetings between the three leaders, Begin and Sadat did not meet face to face for the remainder of the Camp David talks, with President Carter carrying out his own bit of shuttle diplomacy from one cabin to another at the picturesque retreat.[24]

Sadat, however, came to Camp David in a weakened bargaining position. He had split the Arab world and therefore lost the bargaining power that a united Arab front might have provided. He also had relinquished his primary bargaining chip of recognition of Israel by traveling to Jerusalem in November 1977. In addition, everyone knew that he had committed his prestige, indeed his future, to the success of his initiative—he could not afford to come away with nothing from Camp David. Carter was also not in the strongest of negotiating positions. He had committed the prestige of the White House by inviting Begin and Sadat to Camp David. He needed to come away with something for his efforts. As such, Carter and, especially, Sadat were compelled to make concessions in order to ensure some level of success; indeed, as the days wore on at Camp David, Carter usually found himself pressuring, if not pleading with, Sadat to make the necessary concessions for peace because Begin hardly budged. To the contrary, Begin was in a very strong bargaining position because he was in a win–win scenario—he had much to gain and little to lose. If the talks broke down, he would have been seen by his Likud base as not having caved into pressure and valiantly maintained his hard-line position; if there was an agreement that was basically on his terms, then he would be viewed triumphantly as having made a killer of a deal. As is commonly known, the worst bargaining position to be in when buying a car is to be desperately in need of one; the best bargaining position is to be just as content to leave the car lot without buying one. Sadat and, to a lesser extent, Carter were in a desperate position—Begin was not. On the other hand, despite all the criticism directed at him in the Arab world, Sadat *did* get the Sinai back, which was ultimately his primary objective. This proved, however, to be too narrow for the tastes of most Egyptians and Arabs at the time.

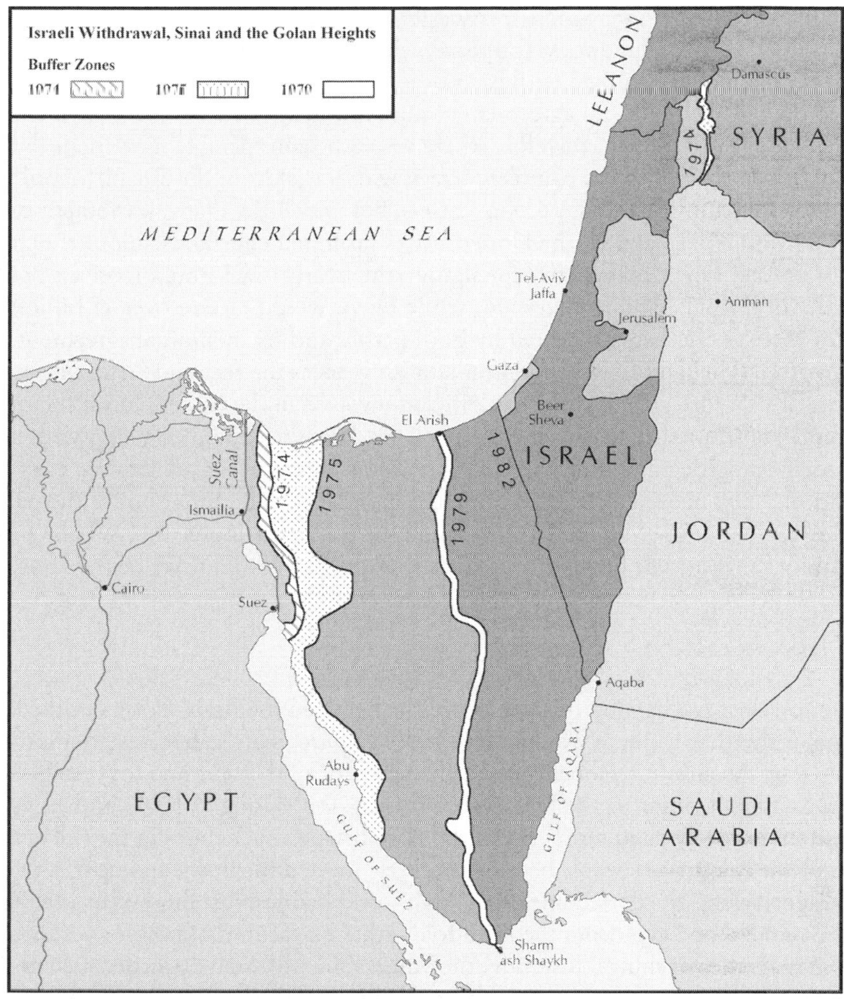

Israeli withdrawal, Sinai and the Golan Heights. (Middle East Studies Association, Justin McCarthy, University of Louisville, © 2003.)

On September 17, two frameworks for peace were signed, collectively known as the Camp David accords. One was entitled "A Framework for the Conclusion of a Peace Treaty between Egypt and Israel," which dealt primarily with bilateral Egyptian-Israeli issues, including a phased Israeli withdrawal from the remainder of the Sinai Peninsula in return for the establishment of full normal diplomatic, economic, and cultural relations between the two countries. The second framework was titled "A Framework for Peace in the Middle East," which was intended to provide the basis for a comprehensive settlement to the Arab–Israeli conflict based on UNSC Resolution 242 in all its parts, including progress on the Palestinian problem.

After several more months of haggling on all sides, including some more shuttle diplomacy by Carter, this time in the Middle East, the Egyptian–Israeli peace treaty, the first between Israel and an Arab state, was signed in Washington with President Carter presiding on March 26, 1979. The treaty essentially reflected the Camp David accords, consisting of the two frameworks for peace, which as the treaty's critics quickly pointed out, were not indelibly linked with each other. In other words, progress on one track, the Egyptian–Israeli bilateral agreement, would not necessarily have to be matched by progress on the other track; therefore, there would be considerable movement forward on the former, leading to the complete Israeli withdrawal from the Sinai by April 1982, including the removal of about 6,000 settlers, but very little, if any, movement on the latter. As with Sinai I and II, the United States promised enormous amounts of aid to both Israel and Egypt as incentive for signing the treaty. Israel would receive $3 billion annually of financial and military aid, while Egypt would receive over $2 billion, the ratio of three to two being accepted by both parties and set by mutual agreement with Washington. Israel and Egypt would remain for years as the first and second largest recipients of U.S. foreign aid. American officials involved in the process admit the treaty's inherent flaws, but they reasoned that it was the best they could come up with at the time considering Begin's strong bargaining position. In any event, something, even a less than ideal treaty, needed to be consummated in order to take the air out of the balloon of rising tension in the Middle East that could lead to a catastrophic war. Whatever one's opinion of the treaty, for better or worse, the Middle East would never be the same.

REPERCUSSIONS

In essence, the 1979 Egyptian–Israeli peace treaty ended the Arab–Israeli conflict in its original form; that is, there would be no more coalitions of Arab states attempting to defeat Israel. An all-out regional conflict characteristic of the 1967 and 1973 Arab–Israeli wars was a moot point in the foreseeable future—or as long as Israel and Egypt remained on relatively good terms. From the Arab perspective, achieving the full and just rights of the Palestinian people became infinitely more difficult the moment Anwar al-Sadat signed along the dotted line—the Arab world had just lost most of its leverage.

The removal of Egypt from the Arab fold created a vacuum of power and disturbed the regional order of things. Instantly, the vulnerability of Arab countries such as Syria and Iraq was, in their view, heightened considerably; and the Israeli regime of Menachem Begin began to think that it could act aggressively on a number of fronts with impunity, from accelerating the Jewish settlements in the Occupied Territories to Lebanon. It was not a surprise that Syria and Iraq, both officially ruled by the Ba'th party, cooperated for a short time following the signing of the peace treaty in an attempt to present a united front against Israel—there was even talk of union. The Iraqi–Syrian entente, however, would break apart shortly thereafter because of the inherent differences between the two countries. The respective regimes emerged from rival branches of the Ba'th party, and there were differences over a host of other issues, including water sharing regarding the downstream riparian status of the Euphrates River that flows through both countries.

With Egypt out of the picture for the time being, the Arab world began to disintegrate into regional blocs, whether willingly or unwillingly. As Ghassan Salame writes, "A North African (*maghribi*) or a Gulf Arab (*khaliji*) identity, which had once been an anathema, was no longer so, and the 'Egypt first' slogan that had once been held in check gradually became acceptable." He continues,

> The geographical disintegration of the regional system into local subsystems also had a legitimizing ideology but not a vocal one. Subsystems were ostensibly founded on realism,

> which is an ideology in itself. In fact, this ideology's discourse was produced after these internally integrated but loosely connected local subsystems were established. More often than not, local groupings were formed around a newly assertive local power.[25]

Critics of the peace treaty often point to the effects it had on Iraq and in Lebanon as examples of its tragically negative repercussions. Iraq—or, more to the point, the regime of Saddam Hussein—asserted itself in the inter-Arab arena much more aggressively now that Egypt had effectively been sidelined—or, again, maybe it would be better to say that it willingly removed itself from the inter-Arab arena. Historically, since World War II, Iraq believed it was the natural leader of the Arab world, especially when Egypt was distracted elsewhere. It was no different under Saddam Hussein. Emblematic of his attempt to fill the void in the Arab world, the two emergency Arab League summit meetings, one held in November following the Camp David accords and the other on March 31 after the signing of the Egyptian–Israeli peace treaty, were convened in Baghdad. Egypt was ostracized in the Arab world, with every Arab nation, save for Oman and the Sudan, breaking diplomatic relations with Cairo. The Arab League headquarters was transferred from Cairo to Tunis, Tunisia. It seems as if, rather than Egypt leading the way with other Arab states joining in, it became isolated—in a way, it was the reverse of what Egypt had done to Iraq with the Baghdad Pact. With Egypt's removal, there was no effective break at the regional level on Saddam Hussein's attempts to achieve his dual ambitions of attaining a hegemonic position in both the Arab–Israeli and Persian Gulf arenas, the latter opportunity availing itself to him with the culmination of the Iranian Revolution in February 1979, which resulted in the overthrow of the shah, who had been the dominant power in the Gulf. This made it much more easy for Saddam Hussein to invade in 1980 what was thought to be a vulnerable new Islamic Republic of Iran. Ostensibly, he did so for defensive reasons, fearing the exportation of the Islamist revolution next door; but his ambitious offensive reasons were always just below the surface. What ensued was a very destructive eight-year Iran–Iraq war, the results of which destabilized the Gulf for the next fifteen years, including two more Gulf wars that involved the United States.

For Lebanon, the Egyptian–Israeli treaty turned out to be a nightmare. Many of Sadat's Arab friends had been telling him that if he made peace with Israel, the Jewish state would then have a free pass to move against the PLO in Lebanon and manipulate Lebanese affairs, all in an attempt to weaken the predominant Syrian influence there. Indeed, because Israel and Syria were reluctant to directly confront each other, both chastened by the destructiveness of the 1973 war, Lebanon became the proxy battleground between the two. The culminating result was the 1982 Israeli invasion of Lebanon. This episode will be examined in more detail in Chapter 9, but suffice it to say at this point that the invasion intensified the Lebanese civil war and led to the virtual destruction of Beirut and much of the rest of the country, a bitter result for what had been called the "Paris of the Middle East."

Sadat was also vilified in the Arab world for essentially abandoning the Palestinian cause—not that any of the other Arab states had done much for it, but the Egyptian president's actions were much more obvious. As stated earlier, the two frameworks for peace were not organically linked. So while Begin and Sadat rushed to consummate the one, the other languished. Sadat at least wanted to make sure that he did not give the outward appearance of having downgraded the priority of the Palestinian people;

i.e., he wanted cover. Although Sadat would attempt, with U.S. support, to revive the Palestinian issue with Israel after signing the treaty, a truculent Begin was not about to negotiate away any more land. There were even severe differences between Begin and Carter regarding a moratorium for settlement expansion; whereas Carter assumed Begin had agreed to a moratorium over a five-year transition period, the Israeli prime minister believed he had only assented to a three-month respite—indeed, Begin approved over twenty more settlements in 1980–1981. In Begin's mind and in those of many Israelis, Resolution 242 had been met, and territories (and not *the* territories) had been returned; now his regime could go about consolidating Israel's position on the remaining Occupied Territories, especially in the West Bank—and there might even be less international pressure to do so, particularly with the searing images of Israeli soldiers having to use force to dismantle the Jewish settlements in the Sinai per the peace treaty. Obviously, the PLO rejected the treaty, and the status of the 800,000 Palestinians in the West Bank and the 500,000 in the Gaza Strip at the time remained indefinitely in the air, one that was growing thicker and thicker with Palestinian angst and frustration. For Sadat and Carter, the treaty was seen as a beginning—a model—with hopefully other Arab states getting on the bandwagon toward a comprehensive resolution to the Arab–Israeli conflict with similar arrangements. For Begin, the treaty was more of an end—Israel had done its part and satisfied UN resolutions. Because of Sadat's perceived abandonment of the Palestinian cause and, for Islamists, the abandonment of Islam's third holiest city, Jerusalem, to the Jews, the opposition to his rule in Egypt increased, especially as the promised economic takeoff buoyed by U.S. aid and Western investment did not take place. As a result, Sadat would actually not live to see the return of the final portion of the Sinai in April 1982. He was assassinated by Islamic extremists who were members of a more violent breakaway faction from the Muslim Brethren, called Islamic Jihad. Elements of Jihad had penetrated the army and rushed the viewing stand during the military parade on Egypt's National Day on October 6, 1981.

The final tally for the Egyptian–Israeli peace treaty is not all bad however. One positive thing can at least be said: the treaty has lasted all of these years despite many bumps on the road. Even though it has more often than not been a cold peace and possibly bought by American largesse, its continued existence has shown that there can be a long-lasting peace between Israel and its Arab neighbors. If the Arab world's most powerful country had done so, why not others? And it would be much easier for other Arab states to sign peace treaties with Israel because the leading light in the Arab world had already done so. By surviving, despite its acknowledged flaws, the treaty provided something of a template for succeeding Arab–Israeli agreements and destroyed psychological barriers along the way. This last point may be the most important long-term development: as Saad Eddin Ibrahim, the renowned Egyptian sociologist, stated,

> Most Egyptians may be disenchanted, disillusioned, or outraged at Israeli behavior. Some organized political forces have continuously called for the abrogation of Camp David and the treaty, and several have called for the severing of relations and an end to normalization. But none has reiterated the pre-1977 language of existential negation. None has suggested a declaration of war or a return to the state of war with the Jewish state. Camp David "normalized the feelings" of most Egyptians toward Israel across the spectrum—hate, anger, disapproval, acceptance, accommodation, and even disposition for cooperation—but no negation.[26]

The Egyptian–Israeli peace treaty has had enormous influence at the practical level as well. The ideas of phased withdrawals, interim agreements, and secluded settings for negotiations have all found their way into the lexicon and process of peace. The "modalities" of peace often became as important as the prospective peace agreement itself. Security arrangement, border demarcations, and early warning systems have all been a part of the peace negotiations in the thirty years since Sadat's landmark visit to Israel. In addition, the role of the United States in Middle East peace negotiations was inestimably enhanced for a time. It became clear that Washington was the only power capable of extracting even the tiniest of concessions from Israel, and its role as a broker in Arab–Israeli negotiations was established by the process that commenced after the 1973 war and culminated with the 1979 treaty. As William Quandt writes,

> Whatever one thought of the contents of the Camp David Accords, all saw that the United States had played an essential part. On his own, Sadat would probably have gotten far less from Israel, and indeed it is questionable whether a deal could have been struck at all. This realization raised the question of whether or not the United States could be brought back into the game to do for the Palestinians—and perhaps the Syrians as well—what it had done for Sadat.[27]

Enough history has yet to transpire to pass final judgment on the Egyptian–Israeli peace treaty. It had glaring shortcomings that directly and indirectly produced untold suffering for a great many people throughout the Middle East. However, we cannot test the counterfactual; in other words, if it had not come into being, would there have been another all-out Arab–Israeli conflict, and if so, would the level of resulting carnage have dwarfed what has occurred in reality?

NOTES

1. Yezid Sayigh, *Armed Struggle and the Search for a State: The Palestinian National Movement, 1949–1993* (Oxford: Clarendon Press, 1997), 220.

2. Along with Israel, Iran, also a non-Arab state in the Middle East then under Shah Muhammad Reza Pahlavi, became the other U.S. surrogate, particularly as the so-called gendarme of the Persian Gulf. Iran as well received hundreds of millions of dollars of U.S. weaponry. The reliance on both Israel and Iran to protect U.S. interests, i.e., prevent the expansion of Soviet influence, was a product of the Nixon doctrine, enunciated by the president in 1969, that at first was aimed toward the "vietnamization" of the war in southeast Asia to lessen the burden of deterrence for the United States. This philosophy for the increasingly economically and militarily pinched superpower was extended to the Middle East.

3. The fourth revenue producer was (and is) remittances from Egyptians working abroad, at the time primarily as laborers in the oil-rich countries of the Persian Gulf and in professional positions throughout the Arab world.

4. Abraham Rabinovich, *The Yom Kippur War: The Epic Encounter that Transformed the Middle East* (New York: Schocken Books, 2004), 7.

5. Quoted in ibid., 8.

6. Ibid.

7. Ibid., 27.

8. Robert O. Freedman, *Soviet Foreign Policy Toward the Middle East Since 1970* (New York: Praeger, 1982), 102.

9. Galia Golan, *Yom Kippur and After* (Cambridge: Cambridge University Press, 1977), 30. When Asad was defense minister under Salah Jadid in the late 1960s, there was a disagreement between the two over how close to draw to the Soviet Union. Asad favored a more limited relationship, enabling Syria to adopt a more independent posture. The Soviets actually supported Jadid in his struggles against Asad, something Asad probably did not forget. Even though Egypt and Iraq each signed a treaty of friendship and cooperation with Moscow in 1971 and 1972, respectively, Syria resisted doing so until 1980, when its strategic position in the Middle East was quite different and more desperate following the 1979 Egyptian–Israeli peace treaty.

10. In the December 1973 elections, Labor won fifty-one seats, down from fifty-six, and the newly formed Likud party, a coalition primarily of the Herut and Liberal parties engineered by Ariel Sharon, won thirty-nine seats. Ian J. Bickerton and Carla L. Klausner, *A Concise History of the Arab–Israeli Conflict* (Upper Saddle River, NJ: Prentice Hall, 1998), 189.

11. These military numbers from Rabinovich, *The Yom Kippur War,* 3–4.

12. John Westwood, *The History of the Middle East Wars* (North Dighton, MA: JG Press, 2002), 136.

13. Nadav Safran, *Israel, the Embattled Ally* (Cambridge, MA: Harvard University Press, 1982), 278.

14. Egyptian operations actually began earlier as commandos stealthily crossed the canal and plugged up pipes the Israelis had built to flood the canal with oil, which would be ignited in order to prevent any mass crossing by the enemy.

15. See Janice Gross Stein, "Flawed Strategies and Missed Signals: Crisis Bargaining Between the Superpowers, October 1973," in David W. Lesch, ed., *The Middle East and the United States: A Historical and Political Reassessment* (Boulder: Westview Press, 2003), 211–232.

16. In fact, Asad was informed of the exact timing of the attack personally by Egyptian Minister of War Ahmad Ismail on a visit to Damascus on October 3, 1973, which prompted Syrian anger over the short notice given. Mohammed Heikal, *The Road to Ramadan* (New York: Quadrangle, 1975), 244.

17. The first temple was built by King Solomon and destroyed later by Nebuchadnezzar's Babylonians in the sixth century B.C.E. The second temple was built shortly after the Babylonian captivity in 450 B.C.E., yet it was destroyed once again by the Romans in 70 C.E. Dayan's reference to the "third temple" was Israel itself.

18. Approximately 5,000 Egyptians were killed, 3,100 Syrians, and a few hundred Arabs from other countries, such as Iraq and Jordan, who participated in the fighting. There were 2,838 Israelis killed. Trevor N. Dupuy, *Elusive Victory: The Arab–Israeli Wars, 1947–1974* (New York: Harper & Row, 1978), 609.

19. Patrick Seale, *Asad of Syria: The Struggle for the Middle East* (London: I. B. Tauris, 1988), 244.

20. The resolution passed 72–35, with 32 abstentions. The resolution was revoked by UNGA 4686 on December 16, 1991.

21. Zbigniew Brzezinski, *Power and Principle: Memoirs of the National Security Adviser, 1977–1981* (New York: Farrar, Straus & Giroux, 1983), 105.

22. Apparently, Sadat was also upset at President Carter for trying to bring the Soviet Union back into the process through another proposed Geneva conference.

23. Brzezinski, *Power and Principle,* 108.

24. For a definitive account of the Camp David negotiations (as well as what went on beforehand and the aftermath), see William B. Quandt, *Camp David: Peacemaking and Politics* (Washington, DC: Brookings Institution, 1986). Quandt was a member of the National Security Council staff, reporting directly to Zbigniew Brzezinski, the national security advisor in the Carter administration. His primary area of responsibility was the Arab–Israeli conflict, and he participated in most discussions in and around Camp David and the Egyptian–Israeli peace treaty.

25. Ghassan Salame, "Inter-Arab Politics: The Return of Geography," in William B. Quandt, ed., *The Middle East: Ten Years after Camp David* (Washington, DC: Brookings Institution, 1988), 322–323. Salame adds that in addition to the Gulf Cooperation Council led by Saudi Arabia and formed in 1981 and the Levant trying to be led by Syria, the North African states had been relatively neutralized in inter-Arab affairs after displaying considerable influence, especially Morocco and Algeria, in the early to mid-1970s. In addition, in my opinion, Egypt acted as not only a geographical bridge between the Maghrib (the "western" Arab states, i.e., North Africa) and the Mashriq (or the Arab east, which may or may not include Egypt) but also a political one, something of a conduit into mainstream Arab affairs. One must remember that Nasser touted Egypt as the link or center of three concentric circles: the Arab world, Africa, and the Islamic world. After the peace treaty, the Egyptian link was severed.

26. Saad Eddin Ibrahim, "Domestic Developments in Egypt," in Quandt, *The Middle East,* 60.

27. Quandt, "Introduction," in ibid., 5

United Nations Security Council Resolution 338

The Security Council,

Calls upon all parties to present fighting to cease all firing and terminate all military activity immediately, no later than 12 hours after the moment of the adoption of this decision, in the positions after the moment of the adoption of this decision, in the positions they now occupy; Calls upon all parties concerned to start immediately after the cease-fire the implementation of Security Council Resolution 242 (1967) in all of its parts;

Decides that, immediately and concurrently with the cease-fire, negotiations start between the parties concerned under appropriate auspices aimed at establishing a just and durable peace in the Middle East.

---

http:www.yale.edu/lawweb/avalon/un/un338.htm (accessed February 1, 2006).

Rabat Arab Summit Resolutions (October 28, 1974)

The conference of the Arab Heads of State: 1. Affirms the right of the Palestinian people to return to their homeland and to self-determination. 2. Affirms the right of the Palestinian people to establish an independent national authority, under the leadership of the PLO in its capacity as the sole legitimate representative of the Palestine people, over all liberated territory. The Arab States are pledged to uphold this authority, when it is established, in all spheres and at all levels. 3. Supports the PLO in the exercise of its national and international responsibilities, within the context of the principle of Arab solidarity. 4. Invites the Kingdom of Jordan, Syria and Egypt to formalize their relations in the light of these decisions and in order that they may be implemented. 5. Affirms the obligation of all Arab States to preserve Palestinian unity and not to interfere in Palestinian internal affairs.

Bernard Reich, ed., *Arab–Israeli Conflict and Conciliation: A Documentary History* (Westport, CT: Praeger, 1995), 19–25.

President Anwar Sadat: Peace with Justice (November 20, 1977)

... I come to you today on solid ground to shape a new life and to establish peace. We all love this land, the land of God, we all, Moslems, Christians and Jews, all worship God.

Under God, God's teachings and commandments are: love, sincerity, security and peace.

I do not blame all those who received my decision when I announced it to the entire world before the Egyptian People's Assembly...with surprise and even with amazement....

Many months in which peace could have been brought about have been wasted over differences and fruitless discussions on the procedure of convening the Geneva conference. All have shared suspicion and absolute lack of confidence.

But to be absolutely frank with you, I took this decision after long thought, knowing that it constitutes a great risk, for God Almighty has made it my fate to assume responsibility on behalf of the Egyptian people, to share in the responsibility of the Arab nation, the main duty of which, dictated by responsibility, is to exploit all and every means in a bid to save my Egyptian Arab people and the pan-Arab nation from the horrors of new suffering and destructive wars, the dimensions of which are foreseen only by God Himself....

Those who like us are shouldering the same responsibilities entrusted to us are the first who should have the courage to make determining decisions that are consonant with the magnitude of the circumstances. We must all rise above all forms of obsolete theories of superiority, and the most important thing is never to forget that infallibility is the prerogative of God alone.

If I said that I wanted to avert from all the Arab people the horrors of shocking and destructive wars I must sincerely declare before you that I have the same feelings and bear the same responsibility toward all and every man on earth, and certainly toward the Israeli people.

Any life that is lost in war is a human life, be it that of an Arab or an Israeli. A wife who becomes a widow is a human being entitled to a happy family life, whether she be an Arab or an Israeli.

Innocent children who are deprived of the care and compassion of their parents are ours. They are ours, be they living on Arab or Israeli land.

They command our full responsibility to afford them a comfortable life today and tomorrow.

For the sake of them all, for the sake of the lives of all our sons and brothers, for the sake of affording our communities the opportunity to work for the progress and happiness of man, feeling secure and with the right to a dignified life, for the generations to come, for a smile on the face of every child born in our land—for all that I have taken my decision to come to you, despite all the hazards, to deliver my address.

I have shouldered the prerequisites of the historic responsibility and therefore I declared on Feb. 4, 1971, that I was willing to sign a peace agreement with Israel. This was the first declaration made by a responsible Arab official since the outbreak of the Arab–Israeli conflict. Motivated by all these factors dictated by the responsibilities of leadership on Oct. 16, 1973, before the Egyptian People's Assembly, I called for an international conference to establish permanent peace based on justice. I was not heard.

I was in the position of a man pleading for peace or asking for a cease-fire. Motivated by the duties of history and leadership, I signed the first disengagement agreement, followed by the second disengagement agreement in Sinai.

Then we proceeded, trying both open and closed doors in a bid to find a certain road leading to a durable and just peace. . . .

How can we achieve permanent peace based on justice? Well, I have come to you carrying my clear and frank answer to this big question, so that the people in Israel as well as the entire world may hear it. All those devoted prayers ring in my ears, pleading to God Almighty that this historic meeting may eventually lead to the result aspired to by millions.

Before I proclaim my answer, I wish to assure you that in my clear and frank answer I am availing myself of a number of facts which no one can deny.

The first fact is that no one can build his happiness at the expense of the misery of others.

The second fact: never have I spoken, nor will I ever speak, with two tongues; never have I adopted, nor will I ever adopt, two policies. I never deal with anyone except in one tongue, one policy and with one face.

The third fact: direct confrontation is the nearest and most successful method to reach a clear objective.

The fourth fact: the call for permanent and just peace based on respect for United Nations resolutions has now become the call of the entire world. It has become the expression of the will of the international community, whether in official capitals where policies are made and decisions taken, or at the level of world public opinion, which influences policymaking and decision-taking.

The fifth fact, and this is probably the clearest and most prominent, is that the Arab nation, in its drive for permanent peace based on justice, does not proceed from a position of weakness. On the contrary, it has the power and stability for a sincere will for peace.

The Arab declared intention stems from an awareness prompted by a heritage of civilization, that to avoid an inevitable disaster that will befall us, you and the whole world, there is no alternative to the establishment of permanent peace based on justice, peace that is not swayed by suspicion or jeopardized by ill intentions.

In the light of these facts which I meant to place before you the way I see them, I would also wish to warn you, in all sincerity I warn you, against some thoughts that could cross your minds. . . .

First, I have not come here for a separate agreement between Egypt and Israel. This is not part of the policy of Egypt. The problem is not that of Egypt and Israel.

An interim peace between Egypt and Israel, or between any Arab confrontation state and Israel, will not bring permanent peace based on justice in the entire region.

Rather, even if peace between all the confrontation states and Israel were achieved in the absence of a just solution of the Palestinian problem, never will there be that durable and just peace upon which the entire world insists.

Second, I have not come to you to seek a partial peace, namely to terminate the state of belligerency at this stage and put off the entire problem to a subsequent stage. This is not the radical solution that would steer us to permanent peace.

Equally, I have not come to you for a third disengagement agreement in Sinai or in Golan or the West Bank.

For this would mean that we are merely delaying the ignition of the fuse. It would also mean that we are lacking the courage to face peace, that we are too weak to shoulder the burdens and responsibilities of a durable peace based upon justice.

I have come to you so that together we should build a durable peace based on justice to avoid the shedding of one single drop of blood by both sides. It is for this reason that I have proclaimed my readiness to go to the farthest corner of the earth.

Here I would go back to the big question:

How can we achieve a durable peace based on justice? In my opinion, and I declare it to the whole world, from this forum, the answer is neither difficult nor is it impossible despite long years of feuds, blood, faction, strife, hatreds and deep-rooted animosity.

The answer is not difficult, nor is it impossible, if we sincerely and faithfully follow a straight line.

You want to live with us, part of the world.

In all sincerity I tell you we welcome you among us with full security and safety. This in itself is a tremendous turning point, one of the landmarks of a decisive historical change. We used to reject you. We had our reasons and our fears, yes.

We refused to meet with you, anywhere, yes.

We were together in international conferences and organizations and our representatives did not, and still do not, exchange greetings with you. Yes. This has happened and is still happening.

It is also true that we used to set as a precondition for any negotiations with you a mediator who would meet separately with each party.

Yes. Through this procedure, the talks of the first and second disengagement agreements took place.

Our delegates met in the first Geneva conference without exchanging direct word, yes, this has happened.

Yet today I tell you, and I declare it to the whole world, that we accept to live with you in permanent peace based on justice. We do not want to encircle you or be encircled ourselves by destructive missiles ready for launching, nor by the shells of grudges and hatreds.

I have announced on more than one occasion that Israel has become a fait accompli, recognized by the world, and that the two superpowers have undertaken the responsibility for its security and the defense of its existence. As we really and truly seek peace we really and truly welcome you to live among us in peace and security.

There was a huge wall between us which you tried to build up over a quarter of a century, but it was destroyed in 1973. It was the wall of an implacable and escalating psychological warfare.

It was a wall of the fear of the force that could sweep the entire Arab nation. It was a wall of propaganda that we were a nation reduced to immobility. Some of you had gone as far as to say that even for 50 years to come, the Arabs would not regain their strength. It was a wall that always threatened with a long arm that could reach and strike anywhere. It was a wall that warned us of extermination and annihilation if we tried to use our legitimate rights to liberate the occupied territories.

Together we have to admit that that wall fell and collapsed in 1973. Yet, there remains another wall. This wall constitutes a psychological barrier between us, a barrier of suspicion, a barrier of rejection; a barrier of fear, of deception, a barrier of hallucination without any action, deed or decision.

A barrier of distorted and eroded interpretation of every event and statement. It is this psychological barrier which I described in official statements as constituting 70 percent of the whole problem.

Today, through my visit to you, I ask you why don't we stretch out our hands with faith and sincerity so that together we might destroy this barrier? Why shouldn't our and your will meet with faith and sincerity so that together we might remove all suspicion of fear, betrayal and bad intentions?...

Ladies and gentlemen, to tell you the truth, peace cannot be worth its name unless it is based on justice and not on the occupation of the land of others. It would not be right for you to demand for yourselves what you deny to others. With all frankness and in the spirit that has prompted me to come to you today, I tell you you have to give up once and for all the dreams of conquest and give up the belief that force is the best method for dealing with the Arabs.

You should clearly understand the lesson of confrontation between you and us. Expansion does not pay. To speak frankly, our land does not yield itself to bargaining, it is not even open to argument. To us, the nation's soil is equal to the holy valley where God Almighty spoke to Moses. Peace be upon him.

We cannot accept any attempt to take away or accept to seek one inch of it nor can we accept the principle of debating or bargaining over it.

I sincerely tell you also that before us today lies the appropriate chance for peace. If we are really serious in our endeavor for peace, it is a chance that may never come again. It is a chance that if lost or wasted, the resulting slaughter would bear the curse of humanity and of history.

What is peace for Israel? It means that Israel lives in the region with her Arab neighbors in security and safety. Is that logical? I say yes. It means that Israel lives within its borders, secure against any aggression. Is that logical? And I say, yes. It means that Israel obtains all kinds of guarantees that will ensure these two factors. To this demand, I say yes.

Beyond that we declare that we accept all the international guarantees you envisage and accept. We declare that we accept all the guarantees you want from the two superpowers or from either of them or from the Big Five or from some of them.

Once again, I declare clearly and unequivocally that we agree to any guarantees you accept, because in return we shall receive the same guarantees.

In short then, when we ask what is peace for Israel, the answer would be that Israel lives within her borders, among her Arab neighbors in safety and security, within the framework of all the guarantees she accepts and which are offered to her.

But, how can this be achieved? How can we reach this conclusion which would lead us to permanent peace based on justice? There are facts that should be faced with courage and clarity. There are Arab territories which Israel has occupied and still occupies by force. We insist on complete withdrawal from these territories, including Arab Jerusalem.

I have come to Jerusalem, the city of peace, which will always remain as a living embodiment of coexistence among believers of the three religions. It is inadmissible that anyone should conceive the special status of the city of Jerusalem within the framework of annexation or expansionism. It should be a free and open city for all believers.

Above all, this city should not be severed from those who have made it their abode for centuries. Instead of reviving the precedent of the Crusades, we should revive the spirit of Orriar Emil Khtab and Saladin, namely the spirit of tolerance and respect for right.

The holy shrines of Islam and Christianity are not only places of worship but a living testimony of our interrupted presence here. Politically, spiritually and intellectually, here let us make no mistake about the importance and reverence we Christians and Moslems attach to Jerusalem.

Let me tell you without the slightest hesitation that I have not come to you under this roof to make a request that your troops evacuate the occupied territories. Complete withdrawal from the Arab territories occupied after 1967 is a logical and undisputed fact. Nobody should plead for that. Any talk about permanent peace based on justice and any move to ensure our coexistence in peace and security in this part of the world would become meaningless while you occupy Arab territories by force of arms.

For there is no peace that could be built on the occupation of the land of others, otherwise it would not be a serious peace. Yet this is a foregone conclusion which is not open to the passion of debate if intentions are sincere or if endeavors to establish a just and durable peace for our and for generations to come are genuine.

As for the Palestine cause—nobody could deny that it is the crux of the entire problem. Nobody in the world could accept today slogans propagated here in Israel, ignoring the existence of a Palestinian people and questioning even their whereabouts. Because the Palestine people and their legitimate rights are no longer denied today by anybody; that is nobody who has the ability of judgment can deny or ignore it.

It is an acknowledged fact, perceived by the world community, both in the East and in the West, with support and recognition in international documents and official statements. It is of no use to anybody to turn deaf ears to its resounding voice, which is being heard day and night, or to overlook its historical reality.

Even the United States of America, your first ally, which is absolutely committed to safeguard Israel's security and existence and which offered and still offers Israel every moral, material and military support—I say, even the United States has opted to face up to reality and admit that the Palestinian people are entitled to legitimate rights and that the Palestine problem is the cause and essence of the conflict and that so long as it continues to be unresolved, the conflict will continue to aggravate, reaching new dimension.

In all sincerity I tell you that there can be no peace without the Palestinians. It is a grave error of unpredictable consequences to overlook or brush aside this cause.

I shall not indulge in past events such as the Balfour Declaration 60 years ago. You are well acquainted with the relevant text. If you have found the moral and legal justification to set up a national home on a land that did not all belong to you, it is incumbent upon you to show understanding of the insistence of the people of Palestine for establishment once again of a state on their land. When some extremists ask the Palestinians to give up this sublime objective, this in fact means asking them to renounce their identity and every hope for the future.

I hail the Israeli voices that called for the recognition of the Palestinian people's right to achieve and safeguard peace.

Here I tell you, ladies and gentlemen, that it is no use to refrain from recognizing the Palestinian people and their right to statehood as their right of return. We, the Arabs, have faced this experience before, with you. And with the reality of the Israeli existence, the struggle which took us from war to war, from victims to more victims, until you and we have today reached the edge of a horrible abyss and a terrifying disaster unless, together, we seize this opportunity today of a durable peace based on justice.

You have to face reality bravely, as I have done. There can never be any solution to a problem by evading it or turning a deaf ear to it. Peace cannot last if attempts are made to impose fantasy concepts on which the world has turned its back and announced its unanimous call for the respect of rights and facts.

There is no need to enter a vicious circle as to Palestinian rights. It is useless to create obstacles, otherwise the march of peace will be impeded or peace will be blown up. As I have told you, there is no happiness [based on] the detriment of others.

Direct confrontation and straightforwardness are the short cuts and the most successful way to reach a clear objective. Direct confrontation concerning the Palestinian problem and tackling it in one single language with a view to achieving a durable and just peace lie in the establishment of that peace. With all the guarantees you demand, there should be no fear of a newly born state that needs the assistance of all countries of the world.

When the bells of peace ring there will be no hands to beat the drums of war. Even if they existed, they would be stilled. Conceive with me a peace agreement in Geneva that we would herald to a world thirsting for peace. A peace agreement based on the following points:

Ending the occupation of the Arab territories occupied in 1967.

Achievement of the fundamental rights of the Palestinian people and their right to self-determination, including their right to establish their own state.

The right of all states in the area to live in peace within their boundaries, their secure boundaries, which will be secured and guaranteed through procedures to be agreed upon, which will provide appropriate security to international boundaries in addition to appropriate international guarantees.

Commitment of all states in the region to administer the relations among them in accordance with the objectives and principles of the United Nations Charter. Particularly the principles concerning the nonuse of force and a solution of differences among them by peaceful means.

Ending the state of belligerence in the region.

Ladies and gentlemen, peace is not a mere endorsement of written lines. Rather it is a rewriting of history. Peace is not a game of calling for peace to defend certain whims or hide certain admissions. Peace in its essence is a dire struggle against all and every ambition and whim.

Perhaps the example taken and experienced, taken from ancient and modern history, teaches that missiles, warships and nuclear weapons cannot establish security. Instead they destroy what peace and security build.

For the sake of our peoples and for the sake of the civilization made by man, we have to defend man everywhere against rule by the force of arms so that we may endow the rule of humanity with all the power of the values and principles that further the sublime position of mankind.

Allow me to address my call from this rostrum to the people of Israel. I pledge myself with true and sincere words to every man, woman and child in Israel. I tell them, from the Egyptian people who bless this sacred mission of peace, I convey to you the message of peace of the Egyptian people, who do not harbor fanaticism and whose sons, Moslems, Christians and Jews, live together in a state of cordiality, love and tolerance.

This is Egypt, whose people have entrusted me with their sacred message. A message of security, safety and peace to every man, woman and child in Israel. I say, encourage your leadership to struggle for peace. Let all endeavors be channeled toward building a huge stronghold for peace instead of building destructive rockets.

Introduce to the entire world the image of the new man in this area so that he might set an example to the man of our age; the man of peace everywhere. Ring the bells for your sons. Tell them that those wars were the last of wars and the end of sorrows. Tell them that we are entering upon a new beginning, a new life, a life of love, prosperity, freedom and peace.

You, sorrowing mother, you, widowed wife, you, the son who lost a brother or a father, all the victims of wars, fill the air and space with recitals of peace, fill bosoms and hearts with the aspirations of peace. Make a reality that blossoms and lives. Make hope a code of conduct and endeavor. . . .

Excerpts from speech delivered by the Egyptian president before the Israeli Parliament. Walter Laqueur and Barry Rubin, eds., *The Israeli–Arab Reader: A Documentary History of the Middle East Conflict* (New York: Penguin, 1984), 592–601.

Menachem Begin's Reply to President Sadat

November 20, 1977

Mr. Speaker, Mr. President of the State of Israel, Mr. President of the Arab Republic of Egypt, Ladies and Gentlemen, members of the Knesset, we send our greetings to the President, to all the people of the Islamic religion in our country, and wherever they may be, on this the occasion of the Feast, the Festival of the Sacrifice, Id al-Adha. This feast reminds us of the binding of Isaac. This was the way in which the Creator of the World tested our forefather, Abraham—our common forefather—to test his faith, and Abraham passed this test.... Thus we contributed, the people of Israel and the Arab people, to the progress of mankind, and thus we are continuing to contribute to human culture to this day.

I greet and welcome the President of Egypt for coming to our country and on his participating in the Knesset session. The flight time between Cairo and Jerusalem is short, but the distance between Cairo and Jerusalem was until last night almost endless. President Sadat crossed this distance courageously. We, the Jews, know how to appreciate such courage, and we know how to appreciate it in our guest, because it is with courage that we are here and this is how we continue to exist, and we shall continue to exist.

Mr. Speaker, this small nation, the remaining refuge of the Jewish people which returned to its historic homeland has always wanted peace and, since the dawn of our independence, on 14 May 1948 5th Iyar Tashah, in the Declaration of Independence in the founding scroll of our national freedom, David Ben-Gurion said: We extend a hand of peace and good-neighbourliness to all the neighbouring countries and their peoples. We call upon them to cooperate, to help each other, with the Hebrew people independent in its own country....

But it is my bounden duty, Mr. Speaker, and not only my right, not to pass over the truth, that our hand outstretched for peace was not grasped and, one day after we had renewed our independence—as was our right, our eternal right, which cannot be disputed—we were attacked on three fronts and we stood almost without arms, the few against many, the weak against the strong, while an attempt was made, one day after the Declaration of Independence, to strangle it at birth, to put an end to the last hope of the Jewish people, the yearning renewed after the years of destruction and holocaust.

No, we do not believe in might and we have never based our attitude to the Arab people on might; quite the contrary, force was used against us. Over all the years of this generation we have never stopped being attacked by might, the might of the strong arm stretched out to exterminate our people, to destroy our independence, to deny our rights. We defended ourselves, it is true.... With the help of Almighty God, we overcame the forces of aggression, and we have guaranteed the existence of our nation, not only for this generation, but for the coming generations, too. We do not believe in might; we believe in right, only in right and therefore our aspiration, from the depth of our hearts, has always been, to this very day, for peace....

Therefore, permit me, today, to set out the peace programme as we understand it. We want full, real peace, with complete reconciliation between the Jewish and the Arab peoples....

I do not wish to dwell on memories of the past, although they are bitter memories. We shall bury them, we shall worry about the future.... For it is true indeed that we shall have to live in this area.... Therefore we must determine what peace means....

The first clause of a peace treaty is cessation of the state of war, for ever. We want to establish normal relations between us, as they exist between all nations, even after wars....

Let us sign a peace treaty and let us establish this situation forever, both in Jerusalem and in Cairo, and I hope the day will come when the Egyptian children wave the Israeli flag and the Egyptian flag just as the children of Israel waved both these flags in Jerusalem.

And you, Mr. President, will have a loyal ambassador in Jerusalem and we shall have an ambassador in Cairo. And even if differences of opinion arise between us, we shall clarify them, like civilized peoples, through our authorized envoys.

We are proposing economic cooperation for the development of our countries. There are wonderful countries in the Middle East, the Lord created it thus: oases in the desert, but we can make the deserts flourish as well. Let us cooperate in this field, let us develop our countries, let us eliminate poverty, hunger, homelessness....

As I pointed out, we want this in the south, in the north, in the east; so I am renewing my invitation to the President of Syria to follow in your footsteps, Mr. President, and come to us to open negotiations for a peace between Israel and Syria, so that we may sign a peace treaty between us.... I invite King Husayn to come to us to discuss all the problems which need to be discussed between us. And genuine representatives of the Arabs of Eretz Yisra'el, I invite them to come and hold clarification talks with us about our common future, about guaranteeing the freedom of man, social justice, peace, mutual respect. And if they invite us to come to their capitals, we shall accept their invitations. If they invite us to open negotiations in Damascus, in Amman or in Beirut, we shall go to those capitals in order to hold negotiations with them there....

Mr. Speaker, it is my duty today to tell our guest and the peoples watching us and listening to our words about the link between our people and this land. The President [of Egypt] recalled the Balfour Declaration. No, sir, we did not take over any strange land; we returned to our homeland. The link between our people and this land is eternal. It arose in the earliest days of the history of humanity and was never altered. In this country we developed our civilization. We had our prophets here and their sacred words stand to this day. Here the Kings of Judah and Israel knelt before their God. This is where we became a people, here we established our Kingdom. And when we were expelled from our land, when force was used against us, no matter how far we went from our land, we never forgot it for even one day. We prayed for it, we longed for it, we believed in our return to it from the day these words were spoken: When the Lord restores the fortunes of Zion, we shall be like dreamers. Our mouths will be filled with laughter, and our tongues will speak with shouts of joy. These verses apply to all our exiles and all our sufferings, giving us the consolation that the return to Zion would come.

This, our right, was recognised. The Balfour Declaration was included in the mandate laid down by the nations of the world, including the United States of America, and the preface to this recognised international document says: Whereas recognition has the bible given to the historical connection of the Jewish people with Palestine and to the grounds for reconstituting their national home in that country the historic connection between the Jewish people and Palestine or, in Hebrew, Eretz Yisra'el, was given reconfirmation—reconfirmation as the national homeland in that country, that is, in Eretz Yisra'el.

In 1919 we also won recognition of this right by the spokesman of the Arab people and the agreement of 3 January 1919, which was signed by Prince Faysal and Chaim Weizmann. It reads: Mindful of the racial kinship and ancient bonds existing between the Arabs and the Jewish people and realising that the surest means of working out the consummation of the national aspirations is the closest possible collaboration in the development of the Arab State and of Palestine. And afterwards come all the clauses about cooperation between the Arab state and Eretz Yisra'el. That is our right. The existence—truthful existence.

What happened to us when our homeland was taken from us? I accompanied you this morning, Mr. President, to Yad Vashem. With your own eyes you saw the fate of our people when this homeland was taken from it. It cannot be told. Both of us agreed, Mr. President, that anyone who has seen with his own eyes everything there is in Yad Vashem cannot understand what happened to this people when it was without a homeland, when its own homeland was taken from it. And both of us read a document dated 30 January 1939, where the word "vernichtung"—annihilation—appears....

And during those six years, too, when millions of our people, among them one and a half million of the little children of Israel who were burnt on all the strange beds, nobody came to save them, not from the East and not from the West. And because of this, we took a solemn oath, this entire generation—the generation of extermination and revival—that we would never again put our people in danger, that we would never again put our women and children, whom it is our duty to defend—if there is a need of this, even at the cost of our lives—in the Hell of the exterminating fire of an enemy. It is our duty for generations to come to remember that certain things said about our people must be taken with complete seriousness....

President Sadat knows and he knew from us before he came to Jerusalem that we have a different position from his with regard to the permanent borders between us and our neighbours. However, I say to the President of Egypt and to all our neighbours: Do not say there is not, there will not be negotiations about any particular issue. I propose, with the agreement of the decisive majority of this parliament, that everything be open to negotiation.... No side will say the contrary. No side will present prior conditions. We shall conduct the negotiations honourably. If there are differences of opinion between us, this is not unusual. Anyone who has studied the history of wars and the signing of peace treaties knows that all negotiations over a peace treaty began with differences of opinion between the sides. And in the course of the negotiations they came to an agreement which permitted the signing of peace treaties and agreements. And this is the road we propose to take.

T. G. Fraser, *The Middle East, 1914–1979* (London: Palgrave Macmillan, 1980), 163–69.

Peace Treaty Between Israel and Egypt

March 26, 1979 (excerpts)

The Government of the Arab Republic of Egypt and the Government of the State of Israel;

PREAMBLE

Convinced of the urgent necessity of the establishment of a just, comprehensive and lasting peace in the Middle East in accordance with Security Council Resolutions 242 and 338;

Reaffirming their adherence to the "Framework for Peace in the Middle East Agreed at Camp David," dated September 17, 1978;

Noting that the aforementioned Framework as appropriate is intended to constitute a basis for peace not only between Egypt and Israel but also between Israel and each of its other Arab neighbors which is prepared to negotiate peace with it on this basis;

Desiring to bring to an end the state of war between them and to establish a peace in which every state in the area can live in security;

Convinced that the conclusion of a Treaty of Peace between Egypt and Israel is an important step in the search for comprehensive peace in the area and for the attainment of settlement of the Arab–Israeli conflict in all its aspects;

Inviting the other Arab parties to this dispute to join the peace process with Israel guided by and based on the principles of the aforementioned Framework;

Desiring as well to develop friendly relations and cooperation between themselves in accordance with the United Nations Charter and the principles of international law governing international relations in times of peace;

Agree to the following provisions in the free exercise of their sovereignty, in order to implement the "Framework for the Conclusion of a Peace Treaty Between Egypt and Israel";

Article I The state of war between the Parties will be terminated and peace will be established between them upon the exchange of instruments of ratification of this Treaty. Israel will withdraw all its armed forces and civilians from the Sinai behind the international boundary between Egypt and mandated Palestine, as provided in the annexed protocol (Annex I), and Egypt will resume the exercise of its full sovereignty over the Sinai. Upon completion of the interim withdrawal provided for in Annex I, the parties will establish normal and friendly relations, in accordance with Article III (3).

Article II The permanent boundary between Egypt and Israel in the recognized international boundary between Egypt and the former mandated territory of Palestine, as shown on the map at Annex II, without prejudice to the issue of the status of the Gaza Strip. The Parties recognize this boundary as inviolable. Each will respect the territorial integrity of the other, including their territorial waters and airspace.

Article III The Parties will apply between them the provisions of the Charter of the United Nations and the principles of international law governing relations among states in times of peace. In particular: They recognize and will respect each other's sovereignty, territorial integrity and political independence; They recognize and will respect each other's right to live in peace within their secure and recognized boundaries; They will refrain from the threat or use of force, directly or indirectly, against each other and will settle all disputes between them by peaceful means. Each Party undertakes to ensure that acts or threats of belligerency, hostility, or violence do not originate from and are not committed from within its territory, or by any forces subject to its control or by any other forces stationed on its territory, against the population, citizens or property of the other Party. Each Party also undertakes to refrain from organizing, instigating, inciting, assisting or participating in acts or threats of belligerency, hostility, subversion or violence against the other Party, anywhere, and undertakes to ensure that perpetrators of such acts are brought to justice. The Parties agree that the normal relationship established between them will include full recognition, diplomatic, economic and cultural relations, termination of economic boycotts and discriminatory barriers to the free movement of people and goods, and will guarantee the mutual enjoyment by citizens of the due process of law. The process by which they undertake to achieve such a relationship parallel to the implementation of other provisions of this Treaty is set out in the annexed protocol (Annex III).

Article IV In order to provide maximum security for both Parties on the basis of reciprocity, agreed security arrangements will be established including limited force zones in Egyptian and Israeli territory, and United Nations forces and observers, described in detail as to nature and timing in Annex I, and other security arrangements the Parties may agree upon. The Parties agree to the stationing of United Nations personnel in areas described in Annex I. The Parties agree not to request withdrawal of the United Nations personnel and that these personnel will not be removed unless such removal is approved by the Security Council of the United Nations, with the affirmative vote of the five Permanent Members, unless the Parties otherwise agree. A Joint Commission will be established to facilitate the implementation of the Treaty, as provided for in Annex I. The security arrangements provided for in paragraphs 1 and 2 of this Article may at the request of either party be reviewed and amended by mutual agreement of the Parties.

Article V Ships of Israel, and cargoes destined for or coming from Israel, shall enjoy the right of free passage through the Suez Canal and its approaches through the Gulf of Suez and the Mediterranean Sea on the basis of the Constantinople Convention of 1888, applying to all nations, Israeli nationals, vessels and cargoes, as well as persons, vessels and cargoes destined for or coming from Israel, shall be accorded non-discriminatory treatment in all matters connected with usage of the canal. The Parties consider the Strait of Tiran and the Gulf of Aqaba to be international waterways open to all nations for unimpeded and non-suspendable freedom of navigation and overflight. The parties will respect each other's right to navigation and overflight for access to either country through the Strait of Tiran and the Gulf of Aqaba.

ANNEX I PROTOCOL CONCERNING ISRAELI WITHDRAWAL AND SECURITY AGREEMENTS

Article I Concept of Withdrawal Israel will complete withdrawal of all its armed forces and civilians from the Sinai not later than three years from the date of exchange of instruments of ratification of this Treaty. To ensure the mutual security of the Parties, the implementation of phased withdrawal will be accompanied by the military measures and establishment of zones set out in this Annex and in Map 1, hereinafter referred to as "the Zones." The withdrawal from the Sinai will be accomplished in two phases: The interim withdrawal behind the line from east of El-Arish to Ras Mohammed as delineated on Map 2 within nine months from the date of exchange of instruments of ratification of this Treaty. The final withdrawal from the Sinai behind the international boundary not later than three years from the date of exchange of instruments of ratification of this Treaty. A Joint Commission will be formed immediately after the exchange of instruments of ratification of this Treaty in order to supervise and coordinate movements and schedules during the withdrawal, and to adjust plans and timetables as necessary within the limits established by paragraph 3, above. Details relating to the Joint Commission are set out in Article IV of the attached Appendix. The Joint Commission will be dissolved upon completion of final Israeli withdrawal from the Sinai.

Article II Determination of Final Lines and Zones In order to provide maximum security for both Parties after the final withdrawal, the lines and the Zones delineated on Map 1 are to be established and organized as follows: Zone A Zone A is bounded on the east by line A (red line) and on the west by the Suez Canal and the east coast of the Gulf of Suez, as shown on Map 1. An Egyptian armed force of one mechanized infantry division and its military installations, and field fortifications, will be in this Zone. The main elements of that Division will consist of: Three mechanized infantry brigades. One armed brigade. Seven field artillery battalions including up to 126 artillery pieces. Seven anti-aircraft artillery battalions including individual surface-to-air missiles and up to 126 anti-aircraft guns of 37 mm and above. Up to 230 tanks. Up to 480 armored personnel vehicles of all types. Up to a total of twenty-two thousand personnel. Zone B Zone B is bounded by line B (green line) on the east and by line A (red line) on the west, as shown on Map 1. Egyptian border units of four battalions equipped with light weapons and wheeled vehicles will provide security and supplement the civil police in maintaining order in Zone B. The main elements in the four Border Battalions will consist of up to a total of four thousand personnel. Land based, short range, low power, coastal warning points of the border patrol units may be established on the coast of this Zone. There will be in Zone B field fortifications and military installations for the four border battalions. Zone C Zone C is bounded by line B (green line) on the west and the International Boundary and the Gulf of Aqaba on the east, as shown on Map 1. Only United Nations forces and Egyptian civil police will be stationed in Zone C. The Egyptian civil police armed with light weapons will perform normal police functions within this Zone. The United Nations Force will be deployed within Zone C and perform its functions as defined in Article VI of this annex. The United Nations Force will be stationed mainly in camps located within the following stationing areas shown on Map 1, and will establish its precise locations after consultations with Egypt: In that part of the area in the Sinai lying within about 20 Km. of the Mediterranean Sea and adjacent to the International Boundary. In the Sharm el Sheikh area. Zone D Zone D is bounded by line D (blue line) on the east and the international boundary on the west, as shown on Map 1. In this Zone there will be an Israeli limited force of four infantry battalions, their military installations, and field fortifications, and United Nations observers. The Israeli forces in Zone D will not include tanks, artillery and anti-aircraft missiles except individual surface-to-air missiles. The main elements of the four Israeli infantry battalions will consist of up to 180 armored personnel vehicles of all types and up to a total of four thousand personnel. Access across the international boundary shall only be permitted through entry check points designated by each Party and under its control. Such access shall be in accordance with laws and regulations of each country. Only those field fortifications, military installations, forces, and weapons specifically permitted by this Annex shall be in the Zones.

Article V Early Warning Systems Egypt and Israel may establish and operate early warning systems only in Zones A and D respectively.

Article VI United Nations Operations The Parties will request the United Nations to provide forces and observers to supervise the implementation of this Annex and employ their best efforts to prevent any violation of its terms. With respect to these United Nations forces and observers, as appropriate, the Parties agree to request the following arrangements: Operation of check points, reconnaissance patrols, and observation posts along the international boundary and line B, and within Zone C. Periodic verification of the implementation of the provisions of this Annex will be carried out not less than twice a month unless otherwise aqreed by the Parties. Additional verifications within 48 hours after the receipt of a request from either Party. Ensuring the freedom of navigation through the Strait of Tiran in accordance with Article V of the Treaty of Peace. The arrangements described in this article for each zone will be implemented in ones A, B, and C by the United Nations Force and in Zone D by the United Nations Observers. United Nations verification teams shall be accompanied by liaison officers of the respective Party. The United Nations Force and observers will report their findings to both Parties. The United Nations Force and Observers operating in the Zones will enjoy freedom of movement and other facilities necessary for the performance of their tasks. The United Nations Force and Observers are not empowered to authorize the crossing of the international boundary. The Parties shall agree on the nations from which the United Nations Force and Observers will be drawn. They "ill be drawn from nations other than those which are permanent members of the United Nations Security Council. The Parties agree that the United Nations should make those command arrangements that will best assure the effective implementation of its responsibilities.

APPENDIX TO ANNEX I ORGANIZATION OF MOVEMENTS IN THE SINAI

Article III United Nations Forces The Parties shall request that United Nations forces be deployed as necessary to perform the functions described in the Appendix up to the time of completion of final Israeli withdrawal. For that purpose, the Parties agree to the redeployment of the United Nations Emergency Force. United Nations forces will supervise the implementation of this Appendix and will employ their best efforts to prevent any violation of its terms. When United Nations forces deploy in accordance with the provisions of Article and II of this Appendix, they will perform the functions of verification in limited force zones in accordance with Article VI of Annex I, and will establish check points, reconnaissance patrols, and observation posts in the temporary buffer zones described in Article II above. Other functions of the United Nations forces which concern the interim buffer zone are described in Article V of this Appendix.

Article VIII Exercise of Egyptian Sovereignty Egypt will resume the exercise of its full sovereignty over evacuated parts of the Sinai upon Israeli withdrawal as provided for in Article I of this Treaty.

ANNEX III PROTOCOL CONCERNING RELATIONS OF THE PARTIES

Article 1 Diplomatic and Consular Relations The Parties agree to establish diplomatic and consular relations and to exchange ambassadors upon completion of the interim withdrawal.

Article 2 Economic and Trade Relations The Parties agree to remove all discriminatory barriers to normal economic relations and to terminate economic boycotts of each other upon completion of the interim withdrawal. As soon as possible, and not later than six months after the completion of the interim withdrawal, the Parties will enter negotiations with a view to concluding an agreement on trade and commerce for the purpose of promoting beneficial economic relations.

Article 3 Cultural Relations The Parties agree to establish normal cultural relations following completion of the interim withdrawal. They agree on the desirability of cultural exchanges in all fields, and shall, as soon as possible and not later than six months after completion of the interim withdrawal, enter into negotiations with a view to concluding a cultural agreement for this purpose.

Article 4 Freedom of Movement Upon completion of the interim withdrawal, each Party will permit the free movement of the nationals and vehicles of the other into and within its territory according to the general rules applicable to nationals and vehicles of other states. Neither Party will impose discriminatory restrictions on the free movement of persons and ve icles from its territory to the territory of the other. Mutual unimpeded access to places of religious and historical significance will be provided on a non-discriminatory basis.

Article 5 Cooperation for Development and Good Neighborly Relations The Parties recognize a mutuality of interest in good neighbourly relations and agree to consider means to promote such relations. The Parties will cooperate in promoting peace, stability and development in their region. Each agrees to consider proposals the other may wish to make to this end. The Parties shall seek to foster mutual understanding and tolerance and will, accordingly, abstain from hostile propaganda against each other.

For the Government of Israel For the Government of the Arab Republic of Egypt
Witnessed by: Jimmy Carter President of the United States of America

---

http:www.yale.edu/lawweb/avalon/mideast/isregypt.htm (accessed February 1, 2006).

Arab League Summit Communique, Baghdad, Iraq

March 31, 1979

As the Government of the Arab Republic of Egypt has ignored the Arab summit conferences' resolutions, especially those of the sixth and seventh conferences held in Algiers and Rabat; as it has at the same time ignored the ninth Arab summit conference resolutions—especially the call made by the Arab kings, presidents and princes to avoid signing the peace treaty with the Zionist enemy—and signed the peace treaty on 26 March 1979;

It has thus deviated from the Arab ranks and has chosen, in collusion with the United States, to stand by the side of the Zionist enemy in one trench; has behaved unilaterally in the Arab–Zionist struggle affairs; has violated the Arab nation's rights; has exposed the nation's destiny, its struggle and aims to dangers and challenges; has relinquished its pan-Arab duty of liberating the occupied Arab territories, particularly Jerusalem, and of restoring the Palestinian Arab people's inalienable national rights, including their right to repatriation, self-determination and establishment of the independent Palestinian state on their national soil.

The Arab League Council, on the level of Arab foreign ministers, has decided the following:

1. A. To withdraw the ambassadors of the Arab states from Egypt immediately.
   B. To recommend the severance of political and diplomatic relations with the Egyptian Government. The Arab governments will adopt the necessary measures to apply this recommendation within a maximum period of one month from the date of issuance of this decision, in accordance with the constitutional measures in force in each country.
2. To consider the suspension of the Egyptian Government's membership in the Arab League as operative from the date of the Egyptian Government's signing of the peace treaty with the Zionist enemy. This means depriving it of all rights resulting from this membership.
3. To make the city of Tunis, capital of the Tunisian Republic, the temporary headquarters of the Arab League....

Walter Laqueur and Barry Rubin, eds., *The Israel–Arab Reader: A Documentary History of the Middle East Conflict* (New York: Penguin Books, 1984), 6–11.

Nine

MUTUAL FALLOUTS

Lebanon and the Arab–Israeli Conflict

This is a sad story. Describing what would become the virtual destruction of a city and much of a country is never easy. It is especially difficult when juxtaposed next to the political and economic environment that had preceded it. Beirut was popularly known as the "Paris of the Middle East," with its fashionable corniche astride Mediterranean beaches, its open atmosphere beguiling to tourists from across the Arab world and Europe alike, and its reputation as a financial center and cultural beacon in the region. While certainly far from perfect, Lebanon was a functioning democracy, albeit a perpetually precarious one, in the midst of Arab authoritarianism.[1] The inherent factionalism in Lebanon that would become a gaping weakness, one exploited by a train of external powers, also provided a melting pot of religious and cultural diversity that was one of the alluring aspects of this small nation. As noted Middle East scholar Albert Hourani wrote in the 1960s, "[Lebanon is] a country which had achieved an almost miraculous balance between different communities and interests and which was enjoying political stability and peace, a comparative neutrality in the conflicts of the region, and a prosperity which seemed to be self-perpetuating."[2]

Lebanon had some serious problems long before the Arab–Israeli conflict intruded, but in fits and spurts the country found a way to persevere. But its main problem was something it was powerless to change: its location. Lebanon had hoped to be something like the Switzerland of the Middle East, a small, prosperous country that remained neutral amid a region awash in conflict. It proved to be an impossible task. Located between Israel and Syria, it seemed, in retrospect, inevitable that the Arab–Israeli conflict would spill across the borders into Lebanon at some point. And when it happened, it did so with a fury that still is being felt to this day.

THE PROBLEM OF LEBANON

Lebanon emerged, as did Syria, as an independent country following World War II after having been a French mandate territory since World War I. It had been effectively carved out of the Syrian hinterland by the French in order to protect the Francophile Lebanese Christian community and as part of France's divide-and-rule colonial tactics. The French did implement a unified economic policy in the Lebanese and Syrian mandates in terms of customs, currency, and taxation; and they maintained open borders between the two for travelers and trade. The National Pact of 1943 defined the political system under which Lebanon would operate. It would be a confessional democratic system of political apportionment based on a specious 1932 census possibly rigged by the French that counted the Maronite Christians as the largest religious sect in Lebanon, followed in order by the Sunnis, Shiites, and Druze. As such, according to the pact, a Maronite Christian would be president, a Sunni Muslim would be prime minister, and a Shiite Muslim would be speaker of the parliament—and on down the line in the staffing of the government. The size of the political blocs in parliament would also be apportioned in a ratio of six Christians for every five Muslims.

The basic problem in Lebanon since independence has always been one revolving around political representation and, within this paradigm, its orientation toward the West or toward the Arab world. Since the 1932 census, the demographics have shifted considerably. Probably by the 1970s the Shiites (poorer and correspondingly with higher birth rates) constituted the largest sect in the country (today approximately 33%), followed roughly equally by Sunnis and Maronites (today about 20% each)—altogether Muslims currently account for about 60% of the overall population of 3.7 million and Christians about 40%.[3] There is also a significant Palestinian refugee population in Lebanon dating back to the Palestinian exodus in the 1947–1949 war. The Palestinians lived for the most part in United Nations (UN)–administered refugee camps and were not granted citizenship. But the Maronites as well as other established interests, both Christian and Muslim, did not want to relinquish power, which would most certainly have occurred under a confessional system if a new census were held. The Maronites forcefully resisted this, not only to stay in power politically but also to maintain their loftier economic and social status that accrued from political power. This "status" became all the more evident with the influx of oil wealth via tourism, commercial transactions, and financial services that flowed into Lebanon following the oil boom after the 1973 Arab–Israeli war. This, however, only made the economic disparities between rich and poor all the more visible, a divide that more often than not was also based on Christian and Muslim affiliation.

As the demographic shifts became obvious, there would be political crises from time to time in Lebanon, such as that which occurred in 1958 that involved the landing of U.S. Marines in Beirut to maintain stability. The confessional system of government tends to give the impression that the political disputes in Lebanon are religiously based, i.e., Christian versus Muslim. While this view is not entirely incorrect, it is, however, much more complicated than that, with Christian groups and individuals vying with other Christians, and Muslim groups vying with other Muslims or even allying with certain Christian groups with shared objectives. It has generally been a political maze of labyrinthine proportions, and in acute situations it invites external dabbling in internal Lebanese affairs. Overall, however, the Lebanese experiment worked fairly well as most parties to the equation were able to compromise or at least paper over the differences.

Left on their own, the Lebanese may have been able to resolve these political problems eventually without resort to civil war. But being caught geographically between Syria and Israel seemed to fate Lebanon toward entanglement in the Arab–Israeli conflict, especially when the destructive power of the 1973 Arab–Israeli war informed Syria and Israel that they might be better off fighting each other through proxies rather than head-on.

Tensions started to rise domestically once again by the late 1960s as Muslim groups called for the "deconfessionalization" of Lebanon, but the situation started to spiral out of control upon the entrance of the Palestine Liberation Organization (PLO) into the country by 1971 following its expulsion from Jordan. The Palestinian population in Lebanon was already developing into a state within a state, with about 300,000 Palestinian refugees joined by 15,000 PLO officials and guerilla fighters. Even though the Cairo agreement of 1969, as delineated in Chapter 7, limited the area in southern Lebanon in which the PLO could operate (often called "Fatahland"), Palestinians still began to dominate certain villages, towns, and cities, replete with checkpoints and a pseudogovernment that was often seen as oppressive by the indigenous—mostly Shiite—population in the south. Now, with the entrance of the PLO, not only did this reinforce and embolden the Palestinian position in the country, which became manifest in the heightened level of attacks against northern Israeli targets after the 1967 war, but it also automatically placed Lebanon in the crosshairs of the Arab–Israeli conflict. This became apparent when Israel launched a daring raid on Beirut International Airport in 1968, destroying over a dozen civilian aircraft in retaliation against PLO attacks. This would become the Israeli modus operandi in Lebanon against the PLO and later Hizbollah, i.e., not only strike directly against enemy targets but also hit state facilities in order to compel the Lebanese government to take action on its own to restrain or expel the PLO. Although the Lebanese government tried to degrade the PLO's ability to launch raids through such vehicles as the Arab League, one such occasion leading to the 1969 Cairo agreement, there was little more the weak central authority and armed forces could do against an organization with well-trained guerilla fighters who enjoyed the sympathy of the masses in the Arab world.

The fissiparous environment in Lebanon became a microcosm of conflicts regional and international that played themselves out: the Arab–Israeli conflict, the Iran–Iraq war, inter-Arab rivalries, and the superpower cold war. Lebanon might have blown apart eventually anyhow under the weight of its own political contradictions, but it did not stand a chance amid the voracious appetite of bigger powers near and far.

CIVIL WAR

When I began taking Middle East courses in college in the late 1970s and early 1980s, the "Lebanese civil war" referred to a finite bloc of time: April 1975–October 1976. There was certainly discord that followed upon this, but other than an Israeli sweep of southern Lebanon in 1978, it seemed as if it was business as usual until the more robust Israeli invasion in 1982. Only after the tragic results of the 1982 invasion became apparent as the years went by toward the end of the decade did scholars begin to see the Lebanese civil war as a fifteen-year-long conflict, the initial phase occurring in 1975–1976. History was being recategorized before our very eyes as there was a general recognition that the various stages of the violence in Lebanon were intimately related and continuous at least to some degree since its outbreak in 1975.

The initial phase of the civil war that began in April 1975 generally pitted right-wing Christian Phalange militias against what was called the Lebanese National Movement (LNM), an amalgam of mostly Muslim Lebanese parties founded by Druze leader Kamal Jumblatt and supported by the Palestinians. The LNM opposed the apportionment of power in Lebanon's confessional system of government and began to agitate more forcefully its call for reform and a more equal distribution of power. The Phalange was a Maronite party formed in the 1930s and led by Pierre Gemayel. It had taken the lead in opposition to the PLO presence in Lebanon, and as such, it developed close ties with Israel, itself interested in eliminating the PLO from its northern environs. The Maronites and the Israelis to some degree considered themselves products of and/or inexorably tied to the West, and therefore, they were threatened minorities in a Muslim-dominated landscape. There was a natural convergence of interests that blossomed into a strategic partnership in Lebanon, with Israel giving an extensive amount of military aid to the Maronites during the entire length of the civil war.

Tensions in the early 1970s were on the rise, especially with the weak central government of President Sulayman Franjieh (1970–1976) unable to assert its authority. In this vacuum of power, both the Phalange and its Christian allies, on the one hand, and the LNM on the other began to prepare for conflict, arming themselves for what would become a perpetual nightmare of sectional rivalry for fifteen years. The civil war officially ignited in April 1975, when a Phalange paramilitary group attacked a bus carrying Palestinians, killing twenty-seven of them. The PLO and Maronite militias engaged in two months of fighting in and around Beirut before the PLO agreed to a cease-fire in June. However, in August, street battles erupted between Christian and Muslim militias, turning downtown Beirut into ravaged ruins. It seemed as though the initial round of fighting removed the gloves of sectarian conflict, and once the civil strife began, it created a momentum of it own, drawing in other disaffected parties toward all-out civil war. The sectarian lines in Beirut became more distinct by the end of the year as rival groups began sequestering themselves in certain quarters of the city and expelling those who did not belong.

For Syria's part, Hafiz al-Asad simply wanted stability in Lebanon so as not to create troubled waters in which the Israelis could fish at Syria's expense or generate sectarian strife that could spill over into his own country. Lebanon had been a haven for a variety of Syrian opposition groups over the years, many of them funded by other Arab states and/or Western powers; therefore, extension of Syrian military–security influence, if not control, in Lebanon was viewed as something of a strategic necessity, especially as Israel developed a relationship with the Maronites. With Sadat heading out in his own direction, Asad saw the situation in Lebanon as an opportunity to gain more control over Lebanese politics as well as the PLO to utilize them as arrows in an increasingly bare quiver against Israel and in the inter-Arab arena. He also wanted to prevent these same elements from unwarrantedly precipitating an unwanted conflict with Israel. With this in mind, Asad initially supported the PLO's Rejection Front of groups opposed to the Egyptian–Israeli peace process and Jumblatt's LNM forces against the Maronites.

In response, the Phalange and other Maronite groups formed in January 1976 the Lebanese Front in an attempt to coalesce its forces. The military arm of the Lebanese Front, the Lebanese Forces, went on the offensive against Palestinian refugee camps in a more concerted effort to knock out the PLO. This brought the PLO back into the fray, after having withdrawn from the conflict the previous June. By early 1976, then, the tide seemed to be turning against the Maronites. It is at this point that Asad abruptly switched sides in the conflict and began to support the Maronites. He feared that if the Maronites were in danger of losing their position in Lebanon, the Israelis might intervene—after all, Asad was most interested in a stable balance of power subject to Syrian designs and keeping the Israelis out as much as possible. In addition, if the Muslim forces emerged victorious, it would result in a strengthened PLO that would be less malleable to Syrian influence. This type of strategic shift on the part of Asad, contrary to what was expected, would be repeated by the Syrian president in coming years, so in retrospect it was not as unorthodox as it seemed at the time on the surface. On the other hand, the fractious situation in Lebanon was so chaotic and confusing that it was difficult to delineate who was on which side of the conflict—alliances seemed to shift as quickly as the wind. Emblematic of this is a passage from Charles Smith's *Palestine and the Arab–Israeli Conflict*: "The Maronites used money from the Saudis and conservative Arab states, such as Kuwait, to buy arms from Czechoslovakia and Bulgaria, communist regimes whose master, the Soviet Union, was arming Syria, and through it, the PLO."[4] If this wasn't enough, by the summer of 1976 both Syria and Israel were supporting the Maronites, support that received the tacit acquiescence of the United States.

Finally, in October 1976, the PLO and Syria accepted a cease-fire that had been arranged by the Arab League. With its new found political power accruing from its oil wealth and position within the Organization of Petroleum Exporting Countries (OPEC), Saudi Arabia took the lead in mediating an end to the conflict. According to the agreement, an Arab League–mandated Arab Deterrent Force was stationed in Lebanon to maintain stability. The force numbered some 40,000 troops and, as it turned out, would be composed mostly of Syrian troops, through which Damascus was able to deepen its involvement in Lebanon. The PLO, per Syrian sanction, was allowed to maintain and even build up its presence in south Lebanon below the so-called red line (taken to be the Litani River) that unofficially separated Syrian- and Israeli-backed forces. U.S. mediation helped establish this red line, which Syrian forces would not be allowed to cross without an Israeli response. One gets the impression that this was something of a gentleman's agreement for the partitioning of Lebanon. Israel maintained a presence in southern Lebanon by supporting and arming an allied Christian militia called the South Lebanon Forces, led by Major Saad Haddad, a Greek Catholic.

The consequences of this initial phase of the Lebanese civil war were many. It weakened the military and political bargaining positions of the Arabs, including that of the PLO, at a time when relative quiescence on the Arab front could have combined with the added international weight of the Arab oil-producing countries and an Israel that seemed more vulnerable and was experiencing domestic political turmoil following the 1973 war, to produce more comprehensive bargaining leverage vis-à-vis Israel. As it was, the Lebanese conflict distracted attentions in the Arab world, particularly that of Syria's, allowing Sadat to pursue his more unilateral approach. The environment in the Middle East with the civil war also contributed to the Ford administration's decision to suspend its efforts on the peace front following the signing of Sinai II, while the Labor party was still in power in Israel, i.e., before the more hard-line Likud party came to power in 1977. As one might expect, the civil war also exacerbated tensions between the various factions in Lebanon, leaving a polity more fragile and subject to external interference than ever before as the country became cordoned off into sectional boundaries and antagonisms. There was no legitimate central authority that could lead Lebanon in the direction of political reform that might redirect the rising sectional animosities. It seemed to be a country teetering on the balance and more susceptible to a resuscitation of civil strife. Finally, the civil war brought Lebanon squarely into the middle of the Arab–Israeli conflict, with Israel and Syria becoming more deeply involved militarily and politically in the fractured state. Lebanon would become the proxy battleground between Syria and Israel, with all the inherent dangers of a direct confrontation resulting from it.

THE 1982 ISRAELI INVASION

When coming to power in May 1977, Menachem Begin adopted a more muscular foreign policy, harking back to the days of David Ben-Gurion. Begin was particularly interested in eliminating terrorist attacks as well as securing the borders of the Israeli state. Since the PLO increased its activities against Israel in the hope of derailing the Egyptian–Israeli peace process under way and since the PLO headquarters was now located in West Beirut, Lebanon naturally became a target for Begin to achieve the former. The latter, securing the borders, included accelerated Jewish settlement activity in the Occupied Territories. Other manifestations of Israel's more assertive foreign policy under Begin would be the extension of Israeli law to the Golan Heights in 1981—in essence, annexation. Also in 1981, Israel destroyed in a daring air raid a suspected nuclear power plant capable of developing nuclear weapons in Iraq. These events also displayed the growing weakness in the collective Arab position as Egypt ventured out on its own away from the Arab fold with its peace treaty with Israel.

Begin's more assertive approach toward Lebanon began with a major military operation (Operation Litani) in June 1978 aimed at clearing out PLO positions in southern Lebanon. It was, in part, a direct response to rising domestic pressures upon the government to take action following a bloody PLO attack along the Israeli coast that killed twenty-eight Israelis. With the weakness of the Lebanese government in the aftermath of the hostilities in 1975–1976, the PLO was able to reinforce its position in the country ranging from its headquarters in West Beirut all the way to the Israeli border. Israel sent some 25,000 troops into Lebanon as far north as the Litani River, which acted as the so-called red line between Israel and Syria. The timing of the invasion was embarrassing to Sadat, coming as it did when he was hoping for progress on Egyptian–Israeli negotiations following his visit to Jerusalem in November 1977. This contributed to the stalled environment on the negotiating front in the summer of 1978 that compelled President Jimmy Carter to invite the Egyptian and Israeli leaders to Camp David in September. For the Israelis, the operation was neither a complete success nor a complete failure. The Israel Defense Forces (IDF) was, in coordination with Saad Haddad's Christian South Lebanese Forces, able to establish a nine-mile-wide security belt north of the border after Israeli forces withdrew following a three-month presence. It was anything but airtight, but it certainly complicated PLO capabilities with regard to raiding northern Israeli towns and, with Syrian connivance, did not stop them. In addition, as part of a resolution of this miniwar, the UN agreed to send in peacekeeping units, UN Interim Forces in Lebanon (UNIFIL), to act as a buffer between Israeli and PLO forces. UNIFIL, as well, was unable to control PLO activities and, in any event, was an obvious testament to the inability of the Lebanese government to extend its authority anywhere outside of portions of Beirut. It was an inconclusive outcome from Begin's perspective, and it turned out to be only a prelude for a much larger invasion in 1982 that the Israeli prime minister believed was necessary in order to deal with the problems in Lebanon once and for all.

In the three years following Operation Litani, the frequency of PLO raids and Israeli reprisals did not abate, with the Israeli response going deeper into Lebanon all the way to Beirut. In April 1981, two Syrian helicopters were shot down in the Bekaa Valley by Israeli aircraft while in support of Maronite militias; in response, the Syrians began to position SAM-6 sites in the Bekaa Valley, temporarily deterring further Israeli incursions via the sky.[5] As usual, it would be Lebanese civilians who suffered the most, thousands of them streaming away from the fighting toward Beirut, which altered the demographic makeup of Lebanon. It reached a point in 1981 where a U.S. mediator, Philip Habib, was inserted into the mix to arrange a UN cease-fire that held up into 1982. All of this tit-for-tat violence seemed to be a rehearsal for what lay ahead. With the traumatic withdrawal from the final portion of the Sinai Peninsula in April 1982, thus meeting the final requirements of the Egyptian–Israeli peace treaty, the stage appeared to be set for Begin to lash out in a manner that showed one and all that Israel was as strong as ever despite the evacuation while protecting northern Israel from PLO incursions. It was classic Ben-Gurionism: hitting the enemy first and hitting them hard. In any event, he did not have to worry about Egypt if he turned his country's attentions northward.

This he did with the launching of Operation Peace for Galilee on June 6, 1982. About 90,000 Israeli soldiers began a three-pronged advance into Lebanon, but this time it would be much more than a sweep of the south. The ostensible reason for the Israeli invasion was the attempted assassination of the Israeli ambassador to London, Shlomo Argov, by Palestinian elements on June 3. The irony is that the assailants were members not of the PLO but of the anti-Arafat breakaway Abu Nidal group, which usually undertook actions designed to undermine Arafat and the mainstream PLO. Arafat publicly disavowed the assassination attempt in London, but a convenient immediate pretext had been provided nonetheless. The dye had been cast much earlier as Begin and his defense minister Ariel Sharon were determined to get rid of the PLO raids emanating from Lebanon.

The professed aim of the operation was similar to that of 1978's, i.e., to eliminate PLO strongholds in south Lebanon, this time extending the cordon sanitaire to twenty-five miles rather than just nine. In the process, it was hoped that the weakening of the PLO would allow Israel to negotiate directly with Palestinians in the West Bank and Gaza Strip, who were known on the whole to be more moderate; in any event, it would show them that the PLO could no longer adequately represent their interests,

Smoke rising from West Beirut on June 7, 1982, as the city was being bombed by Israeli forces. (Bettmann/CORBIS, BE024049.)

thus compelling them to accept an Israeli fait accompli, even though it would be less than the independent state for which they were hoping. But there was another agenda held by Begin and Sharon that went far beyond this, and in the end, it was this that led to what many believe was Israel's "Vietnam," i.e., a self-induced quagmire from which there was little, if any, hope of victory—only escape.

Israel tried to play kingmaker in the classic imperialist sense of the term, and it met with the typically calamitous results encountered by those classic imperialists from the past. The Israeli prime minister and his defense minister secretly prepared a plan to extend their military forces all the way to Beirut if necessary. In the process, Israel would get the PLO and Syria entirely out of Lebanon, making it almost an Israeli client-state. Israel could then place in power a Maronite ally, in this case Bashir Gemayel, a son of the founder of the Phalange, who was at the time the head of the Lebanese Forces. He had long-established contacts with Israel, and he had developed a personal relationship with Ariel Sharon. Gemayel was a charismatic, popular, and commanding figure in the Maronite community, someone who was vociferously against the PLO and Syrian presence in Lebanon. With Gemayel elected as president in the scheduled

August election, Israel would have a friendly government on its northern border that would be expected to sign a peace treaty with the Jewish state. In one fell swoop, Israel would weaken, indeed outflank, Syria, isolating it more than it already was in the region, especially as Damascus adopted the rather unpopular position in the Arab world of supporting non-Arab Iran against its Ba'thist rival, Iraq, in the Iran–Iraq war that commenced in September 1980. And this is exactly how Syrian President Hafiz al-Asad viewed the Israeli invasion: a flanking operation that would place Syria at an irretrievable strategic disadvantage, making it almost impossible for it to regain the Golan Heights from such a weak bargaining position. As such, Asad saw the invasion as a life-and-death struggle for survival for the regime; and he would, and did, do everything he could to prevent Israel from achieving its objectives.

The IDF would easily move deep into Lebanon. The 40,000 Syrian forces stationed in the country as the Arab Deterrent Force were no match for the Israelis. Neither was the Syrian air force. Some sixty Syrian fighter jets were shot down in the first few days of the invasion with the loss of just one Israeli aircraft. Soon thereafter, the Syrian SAM-6 sites were taken out by the Israelis after pilotless drones revealed their locations for precision Israeli air strikes. By mid-June the Israelis, now clearly signaling their full intent by going well beyond the Litani River, had reached the outskirts of Beirut and engaged in a bombardment of the city, especially West Beirut, where PLO guerillas and Syrian troops had retreated and hunkered down. The Israelis were hesitant to enter the city to root out the enemy forces directly for fear of the high casualties that would likely result from urban warfare characterized by street-by-street advances and house-to-house searches. Finally, with the carnage resulting from the barrage turning Beirut into, as one commentator remarked at the time, "hell on earth," with extensive civilian casualties visible to the whole world over the airwaves, the international community began to mobilize to bring an end to the bloodbath. Opposition to Israeli tactics mounted not just outside of Israel but also domestically. On August 18, the United States and France took the lead in establishing a multinational force (MNF) composed of American, French, and Italian soldiers to intercede in the conflict. Notice that this was not a UN force. The administration of Ronald Reagan now in power in the United States harkened back to the zero-sum cold war struggle of the 1950s. The Soviet Union was viewed as the "evil empire," and it needed to be excluded and contained at all costs. Indeed, the superpower cold war had reignited in earnest with the Soviet invasion of Afghanistan in December 1979, the repercussions of which in the United States contributed to the election of an inveterate cold warrior as president. A UN force might never have gotten off the ground with a potential Soviet veto in the Security Council; in any event, an MNF outside the purview of the UN effectively excluded the Soviets from shaping the postconflict environment.

The objective of the MNF was to escort the remaining PLO fighters, including Arafat, and Syrian soldiers out of Beirut, thus removing one side of antagonists from the war equation. In addition, the MNF committed to safeguarding the Palestinian refugee camps left vulnerable by the departure of the PLO guerillas. In the meantime and with Israeli forces sitting in the catbird seat, Bashir Gemayel was elected as Lebanese president on August 23. By September 1, the exodus was completed, and the MNF withdrew to their ships moored in the Mediterranean within view of Beirut. From Begin's and Sharon's perspectives, things seemed to be going according to plan. Although Israel did not personally eliminate the PLO or its chair, it had been effectively eliminated from the Lebanese landscape and its Maronite ally had become the officially sanctioned strongman in the country. But, as often happens in the Middle East, the best-laid plans can unravel completely due to unforeseen and unpredictable circumstances.

A conflict, by its very definition, can frequently elicit movement toward peace. The Reagan administration tried to take advantage of what it thought was a favorable position with the withdrawal of the PLO to present a new peace plan, the so-called Reagan plan. The Reagan administration was a strong supporter of Israel, and it shared the Israeli interest in marginalizing the PLO. The Reagan plan was designed to reinvigorate the Camp David process by circumventing the PLO and drawing into a strategic consensus the Arab moderate states such as Jordan and Saudi Arabia. The plan called for full Palestinian self-government (not statehood) in the West Bank and Gaza Strip in confederation with Jordan, and negotiations were to be carried out with Palestinians from the territories who were not members of the PLO. This coincided with Israeli interests; however, the Reagan plan also called for a freeze on Jewish settlements and for full Palestinian autonomy, on neither of which the Begin government was willing to compromise. In the end, the Israelis rejected the plan, as did the Arab states (with the exception of Jordan), because they could not accept the exclusion of the PLO—remember, the 1974 Arab League summit meeting declared the PLO the sole legitimate representative of the Palestinian people. The Arabs, in turn, hurriedly gathered in Fez, Morocco, and issued on September 9 their riposte, what became known as the Fez plan. It called for an Israeli withdrawal from the territories occupied in the 1967 war, including East Jerusalem; the removal of Jewish settlements in the territories; and the establishment of an independent Palestinian state led by the PLO. This plan was actually a revamped version of the Fahd peace plan, named after Saudi Crown Prince Fahd ibn ʿAbd al-Aziz Al Saʿud, that had been proffered almost a year earlier.[6] In light of Egypt's isolation in the Arab world in the wake of its peace treaty with Israel as well as its enhanced oil wealth and accompanying political power, Saudi Arabia was in a position to fill the perceived vacuum of power in the inter-Arab arena (Iraq and Syria had ambitions to do the same). In addition, Riyadh was interested in presenting a positive face to the U.S. Congress in light of the Reagan administration's intent to sell the Saudis five AWAC (airborne warning and control) planes and F-15 equipment. The plan was based on UN Security Council Resolution 242, stating that "all states in the region should be able to live in peace," which was an implicit recognition of Israel. The Steadfastness and Rejection Front states (Syria, Libya, South Yemen, and Algeria) opposed the plan, especially Syria, which had its own eyes on filling the inter-Arab void. The Reagan administration, at first, was not particularly enamored of it either, preferring not to abandon the Camp David model established between Egypt and Israel. Israel vehemently rejected it, and Begin, who was reelected to office in June 1981, also did not want an alternative process to Camp David developing. The Israelis did not trust the Saudis at the time, and many voiced concerns that the Fahd plan was simply a ploy to destroy the Jewish state. The United States became a bit more interested in the plan after Sadat's assassination in early October 1981, seeing that an alternative route to peace might be necessary; however, continuing Arab opposition at a Fez Arab League summit meeting later in October effectively shelved the plan for the time being. The Saudis dusted off the plan following the Israeli invasion of Lebanon since the inter-Arab political environment seemed to be more receptive: Syria, which had led the way in opposition to the plan the preceding October, had been weakened in its confrontation with Israel, as had the PLO. As such, at the Fez Arab League summit meeting in September, a modified version of the Fahd plan was adopted.[7] Obviously, with the Reagan plan having been put forward (itself opposed by Tel Aviv), both Israel and the United States found the Fez plan unacceptable. Whatever peace plans were floating around at the time, they would soon be overtaken by events in Lebanon.

On September 14, 1982, Bashir Gemayel was assassinated at his headquarters in Beirut, most likely by Syrian or Palestinian elements. Israel sent its forces back into Beirut, ostensibly to maintain stability in the wake of the assassination; however, quite the opposite occurred. Gemayel's Phalangist paramilitary units were out for revenge, and they found an easy target for it in the Palestinian refugee camps, which had been denuded of able-bodied fighters. Over the next couple of days they went on a killing spree in two Palestinian refugee camps in south Beirut, Sabra and Shatila. Depending upon the source, anywhere from several hundred to over a thousand largely defenseless women, children, and elderly men were slaughtered. It was an area that was under the control of the Israelis, and it was later concluded by an Israeli investigating body, the Kahan commission, that both military and civilian Israeli officials were indirectly responsible for the massacres, having essentially cast a blind eye toward the marauding, avenging Christian militia; indeed, Sharon was forced to resign his defense portfolio in the government, and this tragic episode became a permanent blot on Begin's record that presaged the looming disaster of the Lebanese imbroglio. The prime minister would resign in August 1983.[8]

Shortly after the massacres, the MNF, still anchored offshore, felt obliged to return to Beirut, albeit this time with the nebulous and ill-defined task of restoring order to an increasingly chaotic situation and somehow engaging in state-building. Amin Gemayel, Bashir's older and less charismatic brother, assumed the presidency; but the central government was powerless. The longer the MNF stayed in Lebanon, the more it began to be seen, certainly from Syria's perspective, as a pro-Maronite—and thus Israeli—prop, attempting to solidify Gemayel's position. The successful attempt by the Reagan administration to broker an Israeli–Lebanese security accord in May 1983 that arranged for the withdrawal of Israeli forces, without Syrian or Soviet participation, seemed to be a case of the United States trying to do through diplomacy what the Israelis had failed to do militarily. This, along with the Reagan plan, appeared to Damascus to be a flanking operation against Syria through diplomatic means, this time via Lebanon and Jordan.

From this desperate position, Syria lashed out against the diplomatic pincer movement any way it could. Fortunately for Damascus, the MNF presence and extended Israeli stay had alienated a panoply of factions, including the Druze, Sunni parties, and Shiites, thus producing a coincidence of interests that Syria could employ to its advantage. It is in this context that one should read the April 1983 bombing of the U.S. embassy in Beirut, with over ninety people killed, including a number of important Central Intelligence Agency (CIA) operatives, in an attempt to derail the negotiations leading up to the May accord. This environment also resulted in the tragic bombing in October 1983 of the U.S. Marine barracks at Beirut International Airport, killing 241 U.S. personnel. There were countless other attacks against U.S. and French forces in the MNF, who were perceived as being just another hostile and tendentious group among the multitude of factions vying for position in the gaping political void so exacerbated by the Israeli invasion. A number of high-profile Westerners would be taken and held hostage by various factions in Lebanon as well throughout most of the rest of the decade, fanning the flames of sectional and great power rivalry in a country torn asunder. Under continuous barrage with no hope in site, the MNF meekly withdrew in February 1984. Increasing opposition to the Israeli occupation in both Lebanon and Israel (and within the Jewish community in the United States) compelled Tel Aviv to withdraw its force in early 1985 to its security zone in the south. Israel would unilaterally and completely withdraw from Lebanon in May 2000.

For the first time in its brief history, many Israelis themselves perceived the invasion of Lebanon to be offensive in orientation, even imperialist, rather than defensive. Israeli society had been split wide open as it had never been before regarding Israeli military action. Operation Litani in 1978 produced the dovish Peace Now in Israel, which only gained steam with Operation Peace for Galilee. Begin and Sharon played kingmaker, and they got burned. The PLO and Arafat, although weakened, were not dealt a death blow, and they would live to see another day. In fact, Arafat and many of his cohorts would return to Lebanon a short time after their escorted exit from Beirut by the MNF, only to be expelled from Tripoli in northern Lebanon in 1983 by Syrian forces, Amal, and an anti-Arafat group within al-Fatah led by Abu Musa. Arafat would then establish his official PLO headquarters in Tunis, far removed geographically from the Arab–Israeli conflict but certainly not out of it; indeed, by 1990 there were again many PLO fighters in Lebanon, although the Lebanese government had scuttled the 1969 Cairo agreement, thus officially degrading the PLO's status in the country.

But maybe the single most important repercussion of the war was the alienation of the Shiite community in south Lebanon, who generally welcomed the Israeli invasion initially because it liberated them from the clenches of and the dangerous environment created by the PLO. But the Israelis stayed on, in what may be Israel's single biggest foreign policy mistake. The Israelis were soon seen not as liberators but as occupiers, and they became a target. In the process, the disruption and subsequent radicalization of the Shiite community allowed for the entrance of the Shiite Islamic Republic of Iran into the fray, anxious to portray itself following the 1979 Iranian Revolution as a pan-Islamic force rather than just a Persian Gulf power. What was born from this volatile mix was Hizbollah (Party of God), a militant Shiite Islamist party that eventually forced Israel to leave Lebanon after a fifteen-year guerilla war against Israeli and Israeli-supported forces. Israel would slowly wilt under the pressure of this sustained low-level warfare; in effect, it was another War of Attrition, one that did, indeed, sap the level of public support in Israel as well as the morale of the armed forces. The Shiite community in Lebanon became empowered with organizations such as Hizbollah and Amal. The latter had been the primary Shiite political party, having been formed in the mid-1970s by the popular Shiite religious leader Imam Musa al-Sadr, who disappeared in Libya in 1978 under mysterious circumstances. The movement lived on, however, seeking political, economic, and social justice for the long downtrodden Shiite community in Lebanon. These groups allied themselves with Syria, and Asad would use them to secure his position in Lebanon and as bargaining leverage vis-à-vis Israel. The Syrian–Iranian alliance that emerged out of the Iran–Iraq war merged with Hizbollah's political program to make the latter that much more lethal and difficult to ignore.

Asad had won. Through his strategic use of various Lebanese factions, rearming by the Soviet Union, and the commitment born by being pressed against the wall, Syria reemerged as the dominant power in Lebanon, its western flank secure. After having its Arab nationalist image tarnished with its actions against the PLO in 1976 and its support for Iran in the Iran–Iraq war, Syria's Arab credentials were somewhat restored for taking on Israel and the United States and not just surviving but winning. Syria was the only player that could have provided some semblance of stability in Lebanon, and essentially the playing field was laid open for Damascus to try to do so. Amin Gemayel abrogated the May 1983 Israeli–Lebanese agreement, and by the end of 1984 he was traveling to Damascus at Asad's behest. The October 22, 1989, Taif accord brokered by the Saudis was an important turning point in ending the civil war as most of the Lebanese factions finally realized that the National Pact had to be amended, even though it still did not take into equal account the prevalence of Shiites in the country. In theory, the president, prime minister, and speaker of the parliament were placed on equal footing, with a rough parity in parliament between Christian and Muslim representatives. The Taif accord also called on Syria to withdraw its troops from Beirut to at least the Bekaa Valley within two years and for the disarming of the militia. In addition, in accordance with UN Security Council Resolution 425, passed in 1978 following the Israeli incursion into Lebanon, the agreement called on Israel to withdraw its troops from the country. The 1991 Brotherhood treaty between Beirut and Damascus was, in essence, the cementing of Syria's position in Lebanon, the exact opposite of the intended Israeli plan.

Syria had kicked Arafat out of Lebanon in 1983, in the process of which it brought together traditional radical factions of the PLO, such as the Popular Front for the Liberation of Palestine (PFLP) and Democratic Front for the Liberation of Palestine (DFLP), to establish the Damascus-controlled Palestine National Salvation Front. In the end, however, it was Arafat's popularity, or maybe it would be more appropriate to say his

Brothers Confrontation in Syria

In the midst of the crisis in Lebanon in November 1983 precipitated by the 1982 Israeli invasion, Syrian President Hafiz al-Asad became very ill, inaugurating a chain of events that would soon pit the president against his brother, Rifaat, in a confrontation in Damascus that came perilously close to civil war. It was popularly thought that Asad suffered a heart attack since he was rumored to have heart problems. He did, indeed, suffer from diabetes and live a very sedentary yet hard-working and stressful lifestyle. However, according to Patrick Seale, Asad's preeminent biographer, the Syrian president was simply exhausted from the stress surrounding the Lebanese situation—the fact that this crisis came on the heels of the Muslim Brethren (MB) uprising in Syria gave Asad literally no time to catch his breath.

Rifaat was one of the most powerful figures in Syria. He was charismatic and outgoing, almost the complete opposite in many ways from this brother. He had built up the formidable Defense Companies, something of a praetorian guard for the regime; and it was primarily he who protected the regime during the MB revolt, leading the notorious onslaught on the suspected MB center in the city of Hama in February 1982 that killed anywhere from 10,000 to 20,000 people. The Defense Companies were probably the best-trained, -paid, and -equipped of any single unit in the Syrian military. Because Asad's condition was unknown even to the higher echelons of leadership in Syria, many began to fear the worst. As such, a number of powerful figures in the country, particularly in the military, began to back Rifaat as the best alternative who would maintain the status quo in terms of political and economic privilege and position. But Asad recovered only to become furious that many of his orders had been ignored and superseded by Rifaat's.

The whole crisis came at a time of potential threat to Syria, especially as the United States rumbled away at Syrian positions in Lebanon with artillery and air force sorties in response to the marine barracks bombing in October. Although Asad was on the verge of victory in Lebanon, with the new Lebanese president Amin Gemayel (brother of the assassinated Bashir) planning to pay homage to Damascus (something he would formally do in February 1984 with the abrogation of the May 1983 Israeli–Lebanese agreement), there was still a very real possibility in the view of the ever-suspicious Syrian president that the United States could still orchestrate his overthrow. As a result, Rifaat's actions, particularly as he was somewhat enamored with the United States and enjoyed close relations with U.S. allies in the region, seemed all too coincidental. Hafiz continued to recover in December 1983, and he systematically tried to pull the noose around Rifaat's neck, hoping to contain and thwart any ambitions he might be seduced to entertain.

Finally, military units supporting each brother went out into the streets of Damascus in late March 1984. They faced off against one another, with periodic and sporadic minor encounters for days. Ultimately, in quite dramatic fashion, Hafiz, in full dress military uniform, along with his eldest son, Basil, walked alone past Rifaat's lines of defense to his home in the Mezzeh district of Damascus. There, with their mother as a witness, Hafiz basically demanded Rifaat stand down and heed his elder brother, which he did.

The crisis had passed, and Rifaat would be systematically torn down to vestigial status by a combination of demotions and exiles, with his Defense Companies significantly reduced in size and strength. But as Seale astutely noted, "Asad had triumphed, but in the crisis the institutions of his state had made a poor showing. In the end it was his personal authority and that alone which held the country together. He was the only pole holding up the tent. It was not a good augury for the future."*

*Patrick Seale, *Asad of Syria: The Struggle for the Middle East* (London: I. B. Tauris, 1988), 440.

institutionalization within the PLO as a whole, that prevented Asad's own outflanking attempt from succeeding. Syria's intervention against Arafat meant it lost many of the points in the Arab world it had gained in Lebanon—the self-professed standard-bearer of the Arab cause does not foment intra-Palestinian discord that undermines the movement as a whole. Even though the Jordanian option would fizzle out within a few years, by the end of the decade Arafat had clearly chosen a diplomatic resolution to the Palestinian problem and situated himself within the moderate Arab camp. Much to Syria's consternation, the PLO had been added to the growing list of Arab entities that seemed to be striking out on their own toward potential peace agreements with Israel. Asad had helped prevent, for the time being, a Camp David consensus from emerging in the Arab world, yet because of the regional effects of such events as the Iran–Iraq war, a moderate Arab consensus did indeed develop, one that had rehabilitated Egypt back into the Arab fold, naturally resulting in the swinging of the power pendulum in the Arab interstate system toward Cairo and away from Damascus, bringing Jordan and the PLO along for the ride.

FALLOUT FROM LEBANON: PALESTINIAN INTIFADA AND ISRAELI POLITICS

Although Lebanon paid the price as fallout from the Arab–Israeli conflict, there was plenty of money to go around following the debacle of the Israeli invasion. This time, however, the turmoil in Lebanon would reverberate in Israeli and Palestinian politics, dramatically altering the negotiating landscape by the end of the 1980s.

The Likud party had been damaged by the Lebanese quagmire, including the findings of the Kahan commission and the resignation of Begin. It would be unable to form a government on its own, i.e., produce a majority within the Knesset. Indeed, the Israeli polity fragmented, preventing either Labor or Likud from forming a majority in the Knesset without alliances with new and traditional smaller parties representing the full range of the political spectrum. As such, out of the tight Israeli elections in July 1984 emerged a "national unity" government between the Labor and Likud parties, each taking two-year turns as the governing authority as prime minister, the Cabinet sprinkled with members of both parties. In this rotation, Labor's Shimon Peres was prime minister until October 1986, whereupon Likud's Yitzhak Shamir, a leading figure in Lehi during the mandate period, assumed the position. Peres and Shamir each served as foreign minister when the other was prime minister during the national unity government from 1984 to 1988. With this type of divided government, and even divisions among leading figures in the parties themselves, such as the antagonism between Peres and Defense Minister Yitzhak Rabin, there would be very little forward progress on the Arab–Israeli negotiating front. Peres wanted to continue to explore the Jordanian option with King Hussein, but Shamir, Ariel Sharon (now minister of commerce and industry, which obviously showed that in Israeli politics one can rebound quickly from disgrace and censure), and even Rabin opposed negotiations with the Jordanian monarch. This opposition continued despite the determination of the Reagan administration to keep the Jordanian option alive; in any case, dealing directly with the PLO was still anathema to both countries, something Hussein had been hoping for by coming full circle since Black September and forming a joint policy with Arafat to jump-start negotiations—but Arafat appeared to be successfully marginalized in Tunis. Certainly, when Likud was in power the settlement process was accelerated with an eye toward annexation of the West Bank and Gaza Strip. Despite the lack of progress on the foreign policy front, the national unity government did make some progress on the economic front, which was one of the main objectives of its formation. Israel's foreign debt had doubled during the Begin era, fueled by the costs of the wars in Lebanon (one-third of the budget was earmarked for defense) and the expanding settlement process. The inflation rate trebled during this span of time as well. It seemed as if the Israeli economy was only being kept afloat by American largesse, which had risen from $1.5 billion per year after the 1973 war to over $3 billion annually by 1990.[9] The national unity government adopted measures to cut government expenditures and began to implement steps that would shift Israel more toward a market-oriented economy.

As was common during periods of entrenched intransigence, extremists within the PLO began to assert themselves, claiming Arafat was wasting his time by adopting a more moderate approach in league with King Hussein. Israel retaliated after three Israelis were killed by al-Fatah's Squad 17 group in September 1985 by bombing the PLO headquarters in Tunis. Throughout 1985 there were hijackings, attacks in the airport lounges in Vienna and Rome, and the taking of the passenger ship *Achille Lauro* in the Mediterranean by Abu al-Abbas' Palestine National Front group. A lone passenger, an American Jew confined to a wheelchair, Leon Klinghoffer, was killed by the Palestinian terrorists. The image of the PLO, whether or not the acts were sanctioned directly by Arafat, suffered even more so than in the past as nothing more than a terrorist organization, which only served the purpose of those who tried to exclude it from any negotiations. This is where the hydra-headed PLO structure began to disintegrate into its many constituent parts amid a weakened Arafat, with small, extremist factions carrying out acts of terror based on their own narrow agendas.

Things did not get any better for the Palestinians in the West Bank and Gaza Strip either. Likud was able to assemble a majority coalition (without Labor this time) in the Knesset in the 1988 Israeli elections, and Shamir was thus able to extend his stay as prime minister to 1992. While the Labor party was amenable to trading land for peace, the Likud party dug in its heels, insisting on retaining all of the territories and increasing the number of Jewish settlements in them. The hard-line government of Shamir accelerated property confiscation of Palestinian land, arrested and deported suspected Palestinian activists and malcontents by the thousands, and set up more security checkpoints that made the free flow of Palestinian people and goods in and out of the West Bank and Gaza Strip that much more difficult. In general, Palestinian life was degraded by Israeli government action, even down to complicating the task of obtaining business permits and basic licenses. The Palestinians appeared to be isolated and alienated by a deliberate Israeli policy that seemed to be paving the way for eventual annexation. Commenting on the effects of Israel's policy, one Palestinian academic commented in the following manner:

> The denial of natural rights and more harsh treatment caused eventually an awareness that "we are occupied." Everyone felt threatened. Your national existence was targeted. This realization finally sunk into the consciousness of Palestinians, so the occupation was resisted.[10]

And resist they did. The result was the launching of the Palestinian *intifada,* or uprising, in late 1987.[11]

As is usually the case with sustained periods of unrest, a single incident served as the ignition. On December 9, 1987, in Gaza, an Israeli military vehicle was involved in a road accident that killed four Palestinians and wounded several others. Palestinians then demonstrated to protest the incident. In an attempt to control the demonstrations, Israeli soldiers shot and killed several Palestinian protesters. This was all that was needed to unleash the seething resentment against the occupation brewing just underneath the surface of Palestinian society. The West Bank and Gaza Strip were within days in the throes of an intifada.

It is clear that the outbreak and initial stages of the intifada were a spontaneous combustion of Palestinian frustration over the Israeli occupation, especially the harsher measures adopted by Shamir's government. It was also an expression of frustration at the relative impotence of the PLO. This was driven home to Palestinians in the West Bank and Gaza Strip when at the Arab League summit meeting in November 1987, convened in Amman, Jordan, the Palestinian issue was not a top priority. Grabbing the lion's share of the attention among the Arab leaders was the Iran–Iraq war, which was still raging, by that time with the United States militarily involved in a direct fashion in the conflict in the Persian Gulf. The low priority accorded the Palestinian issue was a first in Arab circles since the creation of the state of Israel, which informed those Palestinians in the Occupied Territories that they were essentially on their own. The PLO was marginalized, with Arafat and his cronies living in luxurious exile in Tunis, and the Arab states, whose commitment to the Palestinian cause had always been in question, seemed to be following Egypt's lead with more concern directed at their own national, rather than pan-Arab, interests.

Life in the West Bank and Gaza Strip was brought to a standstill by a combination of Israeli attempts to snuff out the uprising and Palestinian efforts to keep it going in order to hurt Israel as much as possible, making Israelis realize that the occupation cost more than it was worth. Schools and universities were closed, businesses ceased operating, curfews were imposed, houses were bulldozed, additional security checkpoints were set up, and Palestinians and Israelis continued to be killed and wounded. In a way, it was a cathartic expression of Palestinian angst as well as an unintentional call to the outside world to sit up and take notice of their suffering, strangely similar to what Anwar al-Sadat had intentionally done in 1973 to reactivate diplomacy. As the uprising spread throughout the West Bank and Gaza Strip across sectional, religious, and class lines, an underground Palestinian leadership developed to coordinate Palestinian activities, maintain the momentum that spontaneously emerged in late 1987 and early 1988, and establish a common set of objectives. The Unified National Leadership of the Uprising (UNLU), made up of various leaders representing the spectrum of Palestinian parties in the territories, was formed to issue instructions regarding such things as the timing of demonstrations and general strikes, which, on the whole, were generally followed to the letter by the Palestinians. It was during this uprising that most of the younger generation of Palestinian leaders who emerged in the intifada that began in September 2000 cut their teeth, adding a new dimension to the leadership struggles that followed the symbolic passing of the older, original generation of leading Palestinian figures with the death of Yasser Arafat in November 2004.

Again, the UNLU program was designed to make the occupation as much of a burden on Israel as possible. It demanded that Israel freeze its settlement expansion and its confiscation of Palestinian property as well as the special taxes and restrictions that were required only of Palestinians. In addition, Palestinians boycotted Israeli goods and attempted to become as self-sufficient as possible in the territories themselves. The UNLU determined that a campaign of civil disobedience would be more prudent at this point as well as play on the international stage better than outright violence employing guns and knives against Israeli interests. This, indeed, for the first time in the history of the movement, began to shift public opinion even in the United States toward a more positive—and sympathetic—view of the Palestinians. Just coming off the fiasco of the Lebanese imbroglio, Israelis themselves began to question the tactics of the army and government. Scenes were splashed across television sets the world over of Palestinian teens throwing rocks at well-armed Israeli soldiers and armored vehicles. With the Shamir government determined to crush the uprising, Israel looked the part of the aggressor and not the

Palestinians, the latter, for the first time in the United States at least, being viewed as the victim. Shamir's iron fist policy only emboldened the uprising and led to more and more Palestinians participating in it. In the first three years of the intifada, over 1,000 Palestinians were killed, about a quarter at the hands of Palestinians themselves for allegedly being Israeli collaborators, and fifty-six Israelis died; several tens of thousands of Palestinians had been wounded and arrested, many of the latter being deported.[12]

THE PLO RESUSCITATED

Yasser Arafat and the PLO were given another life by the intifada. Even though it was the marginalization of the PLO following its expulsion from Lebanon that contributed to the uprising, the organization and its inveterate leader had so institutionalized themselves within the Palestinian consciousness and in the regional and international arenas that the West Bankers and Gazans really had no alternative when gazing around for ultimate leadership. Arafat found another life, due in large measure to the considerable effort of one of his lieutenants, Khalid al-Wazir (Abu Jihad), who was later assassinated in Tunis by Israel. The PLO was out to take organizational control of the intifada. This was clear in the UNLU's fourteen-point program, one point of which was the creation of an independent Palestinian state led by the PLO. Since it was obvious that the achievement of this objective would involve high-level negotiations not only with Israel but also with the international powers, there was really no substitute for the supposedly hardened PLO leadership. It had the political clout, experience, overall support of the Palestinian diaspora, and money. But rather than the Palestinians in the Occupied Territories moving closer to the PLO's official positions, it would be the other way around. The intifada was driving Palestinian dynamics at the moment, and it would be the more moderate political program of the Palestinians in the West Bank and Gaza Strip, one that revolved around a two-state solution (an independent Palestinian state living side-by-side with Israel), that would dictate the future course of events regarding statehood, not the PLO.

Arafat had generally understood the need for a two-state solution for at least a decade, but now he could bring onboard a good portion of the rest of the PLO and take the steps necessary to begin serious negotiations. For anything to happen, he knew at this point that he had to meet the U.S. conditions that would allow Washington to negotiate directly with the PLO; he also knew the United States was the only country that could possibly pressure Israel to make the necessary concessions, primarily the withdrawal to the borders that existed prior to the 1967 Arab–Israeli war.

In the fall of 1988, Arafat finally met these conditions, even though he did so in a somewhat strained manner. There was already some momentum building by the summer of 1988. With the Reagan administration seeking to end its tenure in power with some success in the Middle East, as opposed to what it had encountered earlier in the decade in Lebanon and perhaps to recover from the embarrassment of the Iran–Contra affair, Secretary of State George Schulz engaged in his own brand of shuttle diplomacy. Other than trying to reactivate the Jordanian option, he had very little to show for his efforts. The Jordanian option was removed from the table, however, in July 1988 when King Hussein renounced his claim to the West Bank. Jordan continued to administer affairs in the territory, but the Palestinians increasingly began to assume many of these duties. Hussein had finally realized that the Palestinians would never accept Jordanian suzerainty and that almost a decade of pursuing the so-called Jordanian option had not produced the expected results. In essence, Hussein had cleared the way for the PLO to move in and fulfill its self-proclaimed role of leading the way toward an independent Palestinian state. The stage was set for Arafat.

He did not disappoint. This was his last chance at relevance before events could leave him in the dustbowl of history. In November 1988, Arafat somewhat ambiguously announced that the PLO recognized Israel's right to exist, condemned the use of terrorism, and accepted UN Resolutions 242 and 338 as the basis to convene an international conference. These were the conditions that the United States had set before it would agree to negotiate with the PLO. In this declaration, the PLO also proclaimed an independent Palestinian state in the West Bank and Gaza Strip with Jerusalem as its capital, therefore publicly accepting the two-state solution. For once, the PLO was pressing the diplomatic advantage. On November 3, the UN General Assembly voted 130 to 2 (the two being Israel and the United States) to censure Israeli activities in the Occupied Territories and violations of Palestinian human rights during the course of its attempts to repress the uprising. At the Arab League summit meeting in Algiers later in November, the Palestine National Council (the PLO's parliament in exile) voted 253 to 46 with 10 abstentions for the establishment of an independent Palestinian state. While the United States and Israel dismissed the declaration, most Arab states as well as the Soviet Union recognized the Palestinian state. There were still some ambiguities surrounding Arafat's pronouncement in November, particularly from the U.S. and Israeli points of view, which compelled the PLO chair to further stipulate in more specific terms the PLO position in mid-December in Geneva. He was in Switzerland because the United State refused to issue him a visa to attend a UN General Assembly meeting, so the UN, to accommodate Arafat, took the extraordinary step of convening in Geneva to allow Arafat the opportunity to speak. There, he was more explicit about recognizing Israel, accepting UN resolutions, and "renouncing"—not just "condemning"—terrorism. After this nearly two-month ordeal, Arafat exclaimed that "enough is enough." The United States shortly thereafter announced that the way was finally clear to begin negotiating with the PLO.

The U.S. embassy in Tunis then sponsored a series of meetings between American and PLO officials. Nothing could come of this unless Israel was willing to play along, and it was clear that the Shamir government would not do so. In a rebuke of the wishes of the administration of President George H. W. Bush, the Shamir government actually accelerated the construction of new settlements in the Occupied Territories after the United States had pressed for a freeze. Shamir offered up his own plan (the so-called Shamir plan) in response to Arafat's new diplomatic posture in late 1988; however, it called for nothing more than Palestinian autonomy under Israeli rule as well as municipal elections that would choose Palestinian representatives with whom the Israelis could negotiate the future disposition of the West Bank and Gaza Strip; i.e., it excluded the PLO. As expected, the PLO rejected the Shamir plan; indeed, it saw it as a slap in the face in light of the circumstances generated by the intifada as well as the PLO's declarations of late 1988. Bush's secretary of state, James Baker, attempted in May 1989 to bring the two sides closer together, calling on Israel to accept the PLO as a negotiating partner as well as consider territorial compromise. Baker admonished Israel to "lay aside once and for all the unrealistic vision of a greater Israel" and to "reach out to Palestinians as neighbors who deserve political rights." In addition, the secretary of state called on the Palestinians to "translate the dialogue of violence... into a dialogue of politics and diplomacy," in the process of which they would "convince" the Israelis of the seriousness of their intent. As he did with the efforts of the secretary of state who immediately preceded Baker, Shamir rejected the plan. It presaged later difficulties between the Bush administration and the Shamir government in the early 1990s.

Akin to 1977, all the pieces were not quite in place for sustained progress on the primary Arab–Israeli issues of the day. In 1977, while there were energized and willing partners for peace in Washington and Cairo, there was a hard-line government in Tel Aviv. A strained process then did produce the Egyptian–Israeli peace treaty, but it was much less than what had been hoped for at the beginning of the process, eliciting in the end as much on the negative side of the ledger as on the positive. In 1988–1989, the PLO had perforce come around to the more moderate stance of the Palestinians in the Occupied Territories, accepting the conditions long laid out by the United States to begin a dialogue with Washington toward progress on the Palestinian issue. In Washington, at the end of the Reagan administration and especially the beginning of the Bush administration, there was a willingness to insert the United States directly into the Arab–Israeli environment to bring about progress on the Palestinian front. But in Tel Aviv there was anything but a willing partner. Although it has been said, with a good deal of legitimacy, that only a Likud government in Israel can make peace with the Arabs, due to the apparent fact that only a right-of-center coalition can garner the necessary domestic support across the political spectrum in Israel to pursue peace, the Shamir government seemed to be beyond the pale and was committed to maintaining the territories at all costs. By 1990, there was very little progress. As such, when a splinter group within the PLO, the Libyan-backed Palestine Liberation Front, was foiled in May 1990 by the Israelis in an attempt to carry out an attack along the Israeli coast and when Arafat failed to denounce it, the Bush administration, under pressure from pro-Israeli groups in the United States, suspended negotiations with the PLO.

The intifada had failed. Although it would officially continue until the 1993 Oslo accords, by the summer of 1990 it was clear that it had lost a lot of steam. The result was a great deal of Palestinian frustration, which became apparent in the increasingly violent acts perpetrated against Israelis—the days of civil disobedience alone had passed. This frustration compelled Arafat to seek support in the Arab world to buffet his position vis-à-vis Israel as well as within the Palestinian movement, and it would fatefully lead to an alliance of sorts with Saddam Hussein's Iraq. As it turned out, Arafat's timing in this regard would again be considered less than stellar. The intifada did indeed resuscitate the PLO and gave Arafat renewed life and centrality, but in order to get it he felt compelled to give away what few bargaining chips he had, primarily his recognition of Israel, without getting very much in return. The Palestinian image in the United States improved to a measurable degree, with a commensurate strain in relations emerging between the Bush administration and the Shamir government that would become manifest within a couple of years, when the Bush team openly sided with the Labor alignment in the 1992 Israeli election, contributing to the fall of Shamir and the rise to power of Yitzhak Rabin as prime minister. As we shall see, with momentous regional and international events occurring in the interim, this would establish a new dynamic that again brought Arafat and the PLO front and center in peace negotiations with Israel.

The intifada also had an important effect at the macro level. It tended to confirm a trend in the Arab–Israeli equation that had essentially been in motion since the

1979 Egyptian–Israeli peace treaty: the Arab–Israeli conflict had become more of an Israeli–Palestinian dispute. Middle East peace efforts by the late 1980s and early 1990s had focused more narrowly upon the Israeli–Palestinian dynamic as the Arab countries pursued their own national interests more vigorously, more often than not giving lip service rather than real support to the Palestinian cause. The full repercussions of Egypt's peace with Israel were manifesting themselves. As a result, Palestinian leverage was significantly depleted at the regional level, convincing Arafat that he had to take his leap of faith in late 1988. The only apparent leverage the Palestinians seemed to have was the very act of intifada, but Israel's repressive apparatus proved to be too much to overcome—as well as Israel's support base in the United States. It was this weakened position that led Arafat to drift toward Saddam Hussein, searching hopelessly for the leverage that he had lost. Although there would be Arab–Israeli peace tracks in the 1990s other than the Palestinian one, the idea of a comprehensive Arab–Israeli peace had effectively gone by the wayside. The fact that there were separate tracks is testament to the fragmentation of the Arab–Israeli conflict, which was definitely to Israel's liking.

One of the more important repercussions of the intifada in the territories themselves was the emergence of the Islamist Palestinian organization Hamas (the word itself means "zeal" or "efforts," but it is also an acronym for *Harakat al-maqawama al-islamiyya*, the Islamic Resistance Movement). Islamic resistance to Israeli occupation had grown in the territories prior to the intifada. The relatively small Islamist organization Palestinian Islamic Jihad had formed in late 1970s and was inspired by the 1979 Iranian Revolution. It was a branch of the Islamic Jihad of Egypt, the group that had carried out the assassination of Anwar Sadat in 1981 and from which Osama bin Laden's right-hand man, Ayman al-Zawahiri, emerged to form the Islamic extremist transnational terrorist group al-Qa'ida. Islamic Jihad developed out of the environment of secular repression in Egypt in the 1950s through the 1970s, whether carried out by Nasser or by Sadat. It was an offshoot of the Muslim Brethren, the parent Islamist organization in the twentieth-century Middle East founded by Hassan al-Banna in Egypt in 1928. Islamic Jihad was inspired by the writings of Sayyid Qutb (d. 1966), who is generally considered to be the godfather of the more virulently anti-Western manifestation of Islamic fundamentalism in the last half-century, as well as the success of the Islamic revolution in Iran in 1979. It had grown weary of what it believed to be the more moderate posture adopted by the Muslim Brethren, accusing it of foregoing its activist past.

Hamas, on the other hand, was founded in February 1988 in the midst of the intifada by former Palestinian Muslim Brothers, most notably Shaykh Ahmad Yasin. Its formation was in direct response to the outbreak of the uprising as well as the emergence within Palestinian circles of the two-state solution. Both Islamic Jihad and Hamas reject the two-state solution, still clinging to the hope of eliminating Israel, in its place arising a Palestinian Islamic republic. Although their ultimate objectives differed, there was loose cooperation between the UNLU, the PLO, and the two Palestinian Islamist groups during the intifada because of the methodological coincidence of interests; after all, resistance was the sine qua non for Hamas and Islamic Jihad. But as the PLO lost influence due to the perceived lack of progress in the uprising, Islamic Jihad and especially Hamas gained by default, although in absolute numbers they were still small when compared to al-Fatah. Hamas was particularly popular in the Gaza Strip, which is not surprising considering the miserable overall conditions there, even when compared to the West Bank. The Gaza Strip had (and still has) perhaps the highest population density in the world in what in essence was an extended refugee camp. Palestinian life under Egyptian rule deteriorated, and after 1967, while some services improved, the Israeli occupation overall made life even more unbearable. In such conditions, the Islamist alternative gained more of a foothold here than in the West Bank. As Sara Roy stated, "One camp, Jabalya, is home to sixty thousand people living on one-half square mile of land, giving the camp a population density... double the density of Manhattan. The Strip's population is very young, with nearly 50 percent comprised of children 14 years of age and younger."[13] At the time there were about 2,500 Israeli settlers living in sixteen Jewish settlements strategically spread out across the Gaza Strip amid almost 1 million Palestinians, the latter having approximately 70% of the land despite making up 99% of the population. Out of Hamas grew a more militant response to the occupation, evident in the formation of a military wing of Hamas called the Izz al-Din al-Qassam Brigade, named after Shaykh Izz al-Din al-Qassam, who was killed (or "martyred") by British troops in 1935 during the mandate period.

One thing that is interesting about the emergence of Hamas and Islamic Jihad is that the Israelis were not terribly unnerved by (and may have encouraged) this development at first as they saw these Islamist organizations as a necessary counter to the secular, leftist PLO. This was not unusual at the time, however, as the United States during the 1980s also supported Islamist groups, particularly the *mujahideen* fighting the Soviets in Afghanistan, in order to thwart the spread of communist, pro-Soviet influence. Both Hamas and Islamic Jihad, as Islamist groups did elsewhere in the Muslim world, would establish charitable services and carry out civil society functions for everyday Palestinians who could not receive them from the Israelis or mainstream Palestinian organizations. This only enhanced their popularity and, especially in the case of the former, would help prepare the foundation for the development of a political role within the Palestinian movement.

NOTES

1. See Michael Hudson, *The Precarious Republic: Political Modernization in Lebanon* (Boulder: Westview Press, 1985).

2. Quoted in Dale F. Eickelman, *The Middle East: An Anthropological Approach* (Upper Saddle River, NJ: Prentice Hall, 1989.).

3. Estimates place the Greek Orthodox at a little over 8%, the Druze at 8%, the Greek Catholics at 6%, and the Armenian Orthodox at 4%.

4. Charles D. Smith, *Palestine and the Arab–Israeli Conflict: A History with Documents* (New York: Bedford/St. Martin's, 2004), 344.

5. John Westwood, *The History of the Middle East Wars* (North Dighton, MA: JG Press, 2002), 162.

6. Saudi initiatives are often issued in the name of the crown prince rather than the king (Khalid ibn 'Abd al-Aziz Al Sa'ud) to preserve the king's standing just in case the initiative fails. Fahd would replace Khalid as king upon the latter's death in 1982.

7. On the Fahd plan, see Elie Podeh, *From Fahd to 'Abdullah: The Origins of the Saudi Peace Initiatives and Their Impact on the Arab System and Israel* (Jerusalem: Harry S. Truman Research Institute for the Advancement of Peace, 2003), 3–18.

8. Begin's wife unexpectedly died shortly before this as well, which obviously had a tremendous effect upon him and contributed to his decision to leave the government.

9. Ian J. Bickerton and Carla L. Klausner, *A Concise History of the Arab–Israeli Conflict* (Upper Saddle River, NJ: Prentice Hall, 1998), 222–224.

10. Quoted in F. Robert Hunter, *The Palestinian Uprising: A War by Other Means* (Berkeley: University of California Press, 1993), 47.

11. Although taken to mean "uprising," the term "intifada" more accurately is translated as "shaking off."

12. William L. Cleveland, *A History of the Modern Middle East* (Boulder: Westview Press, 1994), 426.

13. Sara Roy, "From Hardship to Hunger: The Economic Impact of the Intifada on the Gaza Strip," *Arab–American Affairs* (Fall 1990): 109–110, as quoted in Smith, *Palestine and the Arab–Israeli Conflict,* 404.

United Nations Security Council Resolution 425

The Security Council,

Taking note of the letters of the Permanent Representative of Lebanon (S/12600 and S/12606) and the Permanent Representative of Israel (S/12607),

Having heard the statements of the Permanent Representatives of Lebanon and Israel,

Gravely concerned at the deterioration of the situation in the Middle East, and its consequences to the maintenance of international peace,

Convinced that the present situation impedes the achievement of a just peace in the Middle East, Calls for strict respect for the territorial integrity, sovereignty and political independence of Lebanon within its internationally recognized boundaries;

Calls upon Israel immediately to cease its military action against Lebanese territorial integrity and withdraw forthwith its forces from all Lebanese territory;

Decides, in the light of the request of the Government of Lebanon, to establish immediately under its authority a United Nations interim force for southern Lebanon for the purpose of confirming the withdrawal of Israeli forces, restoring international peace and security and assisting the Government of Lebanon in ensuring the return of its effective authority in the area, the force to be composed of personnel drawn from States Members of the United Nations.

Requests the Secretary-General to report to the Council within twenty-four hours on the implementation of this resolution.

---

http://www.yale.edu/lawweb/avalon/un/un425.htm (accessed February 1, 2006).

The Fahd Plan

August 7, 1981

...There are a number of principles which may be taken as guidelines toward a just settlement; they are principles which the United Nations has taken and reiterated many times in the last few years. They are:

First, that Israel should withdraw from all Arab territory occupied in 1967, including Arab Jerusalem.
Second, that Israeli settlements built on Arab land after 1967 should be dismantled.
Third, a guarantee of freedom of worship for all religions in the holy places.
Fourth, an affirmation of the right of the Palestinian people to return to their homes and to compensate those who do not wish to return.
Fifth, that the West Bank and the Gaza Strip should have a transitional period, under the auspices of the United Nations, for a period not exceeding several months.
Sixth, that an independent Palestinian state should be set up with Jerusalem as its capital.
Seventh, that all states in the region should be able to live in peace.
Eight, that the United Nations or member states of the United Nations should guarantee to execute these principles....

I wish to reaffirm that the principles of a just and comprehensive solution have become familiar and do not require great effort:

1. An end to unlimited American support for Israel.
2. An end to Israeli arrogance, whose ugliest facet is embodied in Begin's government. This condition will be automatically fulfilled if the first condition is fulfilled.
3. A recognition that, as Yasir Arafat says, the Palestinian figure is the basic figure in the Middle Eastern equation.

Walter Laqueur and Barry Rubin, eds., *The Israel–Arab Reader: A Documentary History of the Middle East Conflict* (New York: Penguin Books, 1984), 623–624.

Reagan Fresh Start Initiative (Reagan Peace Plan)

September 1, 1982

My fellow Americans, today has been a day that should make us proud. It marked the end of the successful evacuation of the Palestine Liberation Organization (PLO) from Beirut, Lebanon. This peaceful step could never have been taken without the good offices of the United States and, especially, the truly heroic work of a great American diplomat, Ambassador Philip Habib. Thanks to his efforts, I am happy to announce that the U.S. Marine contingent helping to supervise the evacuation has accomplished its mission. Our young men should be out of Lebanon within 2 weeks. They, too, have served the cause of peace with distinction, and we can all be very proud of them.

But the situation in Lebanon is only part of the overall problem of conflict in the Middle East. So, over the past 2 weeks, while events in Beirut dominated the front page, America was engaged in a quiet, behind-the-scenes effort to lay the groundwork for a broader peace in the region....

It seemed to me that, with the agreement in Lebanon, we had an opportunity for a more far-reaching peace effort in the region, and I was determined to seize that moment. In the words of the scripture, the time had come to "follow after the things which make for peace."

Tonight, I want to report to you on the steps we have taken, and the prospects they can open up for a just and lasting peace in the Middle East. America has long been committed to bringing peace to this troubled region. For more than a generation, successive U.S. administrations have endeavored to develop a fair and workable process that could lead to a true and lasting Arab–Israeli peace....

The Lebanon war, tragic as it was, has left us with a new opportunity for Middle East peace. We must seize it now and bring peace to this troubled area so vital to world stability while there is still time. It was with this strong conviction that over a month ago, before the present negotiations in Beirut had been completed, I directed Secretary of State Shultz to again review our policy and to consult a wide range of outstanding Americans on the best ways to strengthen chances for peace in the Middle East. We have consulted with many of the officials who were historically involved in the process, with members of the Congress, and with individuals from the private sector, and I have held extensive consultations with my own advisers on the principles I will outline to you tonight....

But the opportunities for peace in the Middle East do not begin and end in Lebanon. As we help Lebanon rebuild, we must also move to resolve the root causes of conflict between Arabs and Israelis. The war in Lebanon has demonstrated many things, but two consequences are key to the peace process:

First, the military losses of the PLO have not diminished the yearning of the Palestinian people for a just solution of their claims; and

Second, while Israel's military successes in Lebanon have demonstrated that its armed forces are second to none in the region, they alone cannot bring just and lasting peace to Israel and her neighbors.

The question now is how to reconcile Israel's legitimate security concerns with the legitimate rights of the Palestinians. And that answer can only come at the negotiating table. Each party must recognize that the outcome must be acceptable to all and that true peace will require compromises by all.

So, tonight I am calling for a fresh start. This is the moment for all those directly concerned to get involved—or lend their support—to a workable basis for peace. The Camp David agreement remains the foundation of our policy. Its language provides all parties with the leeway they need for successful negotiations.

I call on Israel to make clear that the security for which she yearns can only be achieved through genuine peace, a peace requiring magnanimity, vision, and courage.

I call on the Palestinian people to recognize that their own political aspirations are inextricably bound to recognition of Israel's right to a secure future.

And I call on the Arab states to accept the reality of Israel and the reality that peace and justice are to be gained only through hard, fair, direct negotiation.

In making these calls upon others, I recognize that the United States has a special responsibility. No other nation is in a position to deal with the key parties to the conflict on the basis of trust and reliability.

The time has come for a new realism on the part of all the peoples of the Middle East. The State of Israel is an accomplished fact; it deserves unchallenged legitimacy within the community of nations. But Israel's legitimacy has thus far been recognized by too few countries and has been denied by every Arab state except Egypt. Israel exists; it has a right to exist in peace behind secure and defensible borders; and it has a right to demand of its neighbors that they recognize those facts.

I have personally followed and supported Israel's heroic struggle for survival ever since the founding of the State of Israel 34 years ago. In the pre-1967 borders, Israel was barely 10 miles wide at its narrowest point. The bulk of Israel's population lived within artillery range of hostile Arab armies. I am not about to ask Israel to live that way again.

The war in Lebanon has demonstrated another reality in the region. The departure of the Palestinians from Beirut dramatizes more than ever the homelessness of the Palestinian people. Palestinians feel strongly that their cause is more than a question of refugees. I agree. The Camp David agreement recognized that fact when it spoke of the legitimate rights of the Palestinian people and their just requirements. For peace to endure, it must involve all those who have been most deeply affected by the conflict. Only through broader participation in the peace process—most immediately by Jordan and by the Palestinians—will Israel be able to rest confident in the knowledge that its security and integrity will be respected by its neighbors. Only through the process of negotiation can all the nations of the Middle East achieve a secure peace.

These then are our general goals. What are the specific new American positions, and why are we taking them?

In the Camp David talks thus far, both Israel and Egypt have felt free to express openly their views as to what the outcome should be. Understandably, their views have differed on many points.

The United States has thus far sought to play the role of mediator; we have avoided public comment on the key issues. We have always recognized—and continue to recognize—that only the voluntary agreement of those parties most directly involved in the conflict can provide an enduring solution. But it has become evident to me that some clearer sense of America's position on the key issues is necessary to encourage wider support for the peace process.

First, as outlined in the Camp David accords, there must be a period of time during which the Palestinian inhabitants of the West Bank and Gaza will have full autonomy over their own affairs. Due consideration must be given to the principle of self-government by the inhabitants of the territories and to the legitimate security concerns of the parties involved.

The purpose of the 5-year period of transition, which would begin after free elections for a self-governing Palestinian authority, is to prove to the Palestinians that they can run their own affairs and that such Palestinian autonomy poses no threat to Israel's security.

The United States will not support the use of any additional land for the purpose of settlements during the transition period. Indeed, the immediate adoption of a settlement freeze by Israel, more than any other action, could create the confidence needed for wider participation in these talks. Further settlement activity is in no way necessary for the security of Israel and only diminishes the confidence of the Arabs that a final outcome can be freely and fairly negotiated.

I want to make the American position well understood: The purpose of this transition period is the peaceful and orderly transfer of authority from Israel to the Palestinian inhabitants of the West Bank and Gaza. At the same time, such a transfer must not interfere with Israel's security requirements.

Beyond the transition period, as we look to the future of the West Bank and Gaza, it is clear to me that peace cannot be achieved by the formation of an independent Palestinian state in those territories. Nor is it achievable on the basis of Israeli sovereignty or permanent control over the West Bank and Gaza.

So the United States will not support the establishment of an independent Palestinian state in the West Bank and Gaza, and we will not support annexation or permanent control by Israel.

There is, however, another way to peace. The final status of these lands must, of course, be reached through the give-and-take of negotiations. But it is the firm view of the United States that self-government by the Palestinians of the West Bank and Gaza in association with Jordan offers the best chance for a durable, just and lasting peace.

We base our approach squarely on the principle that the Arab–Israeli conflict should be resolved through negotiations involving an exchange of territory for peace. This exchange is enshrined in U.N. Security Council Resolution 242 which is, in turn, incorporated in all its parts in the Camp David agreements. U.N. Resolution 242 remains wholly valid as the foundation stone of America's Middle East peace effort.

It is the United States' position that—in return for peace—the withdrawal provision of Resolution 242 applies to all fronts, including the West Bank and Gaza.

When the border is negotiated between Jordan and Israel, our view on the extent to which Israel should be asked to give up territory will be heavily affected by the extent of true peace and normalization and the security arrangements offered in return.

Finally, we remain convinced that Jerusalem must remain undivided, but its final status should be decided through negotiations.

In the course of the negotiations to come, the United States will support positions that seem to us fair and reasonable compromises and likely to promote a sound agreement. We will also put forward our own detailed proposals when we believe they can be helpful. And, make no mistake, the United States will oppose any proposal—from any party and at any point in the negotiating process—that threatens the security of Israel. America's commitment to the security of Israel is ironclad. And, I might add, so is mine.

During the past few days, our ambassadors in Israel, Egypt, Jordan, and Saudi Arabia have presented to their host governments the proposals in full detail that I have outlined here today. Now I am convinced that these proposals can bring justice, bring security, and bring durability to an Arab–Israeli peace. The United States will stand by these principles with total dedication. They are fully consistent with Israel's security requirements and the aspirations of the Palestinians. We will work hard to broaden participation at the peace table as envisaged by the Camp David accords. And I fervently hope that the Palestinians and Jordan, with the support of their Arab colleagues, will accept this opportunity. . . .

These, then, are the principles upon which American policy toward the Arab–Israeli conflict will be based. I have made a personal commitment to see that they endure and, God willing, that they will come to be seen by all reasonable, compassionate people as fair, achievable, and in the interests of all who wish to see peace in the Middle East.

Tonight, on the eve of what can be a dawning of new hope for the people of the troubled Middle East—and for all the world's people who dream of a just and peaceful future—I ask you, my fellow Americans, for your support and your prayers in this great undertaking.

Bernard Reich, *Arab–Israeli Conflict and Conciliation: A Documentary History* (Westport, CT: Praeger, 1995), 175–179.

Yasir Arafat, Press Conference Statement

Geneva, 14 December 1988

Let me highlight my views before you. Our desire for peace is a strategy and not an interim tactic. We are bent on peace come what may, come what may.

Our statehood provides salvation to the Palestinians and peace to both Palestinians and Israelis.

Self-determination means survival for the Palestinians and our survival does not destroy the survival of the Israelis, as their rulers claim. Yesterday in my speech I made reference to United Nations Resolution 181 [on the partition of Palestine] as the basis for Palestinian independence. I also made reference to our acceptance of resolutions 242 and 338 as the basis for negotiations with Israel within the framework of the international conference. These three resolutions were endorsed by our Palestine National Council session in Algiers.

In my speech also yesterday, it was clear that we mean our people's rights to freedom and national independence, according to Resolution 181, and the right of all parties concerned in the Middle East conflict to exist in peace and security, and, as I have mentioned, including the State of Palestine, Israel, and other neighbors, according to resolutions 242 and 338.

As for terrorism, I announced it yesterday in no uncertain terms, and yet, I repeat for the record. I repeat for the record that we totally and absolutely renounce all forms of terrorism, including individual, group, and state terrorism.

Between Geneva and Algiers, we have made our position crystal clear. Any more talk such as "The Palestinians should give more"—you remember this slogan?—or "It is not enough" or "The Palestinians are engaging in propaganda games and public relations exercises" will be damaging and counterproductive.

Enough is enough. Enough is enough. Enough is enough. All remaining matters should be discussed around the table and within the international conference.

Let it be absolutely clear that neither Arafat, nor any [one else] for that matter, can stop the intifadah, the uprising. The intifadah will come to an end only when practical and tangible steps have been taken toward the achievement of our national aims and establishment of our independent Palestinian state.

In this context, I expect the EEC [European Economic Community] to play a more effective role in promoting peace in our region. They have a political responsibility, they have a moral responsibility, and they can deal with it.

Finally, I declare before you and I ask you to kindly quote me on that: We want peace. We want peace. We are committed to peace. We are committed to peace. We want to live in our Palestinian state, and let live. Thank you.

William B. Quandt, *Peace Process: American Diplomacy and the Arab–Israeli Conflict Since 1967* (Washington, DC: Brookings Institution, 1993), 493–494.

Shamir Plan, May 14, 1989

GENERAL: 1. This document presents the principles of a political initiative of the Government of Israel which deals with the continuation of the peace process; the termination of the state of war with the Arab states; a solution for the Arabs of Judea, Samaria and the Gaza district; peace with Jordan; and a resolution of the problem of the residents of the refugee camps in Judea, Samaria and the Gaza district....

BASIC PREMISES: 3. The initiative is founded upon the assumption that there is a national consensus for it on the basis of the basic guidelines of the Government of Israel, including the following points: a) Israel yearns for peace and the continuation of the political process by means of direct negotiations based on the principles of the Camp David Accords. b) Israel opposes the establishment of an additional Palestinian state in the Gaza district and in the area between Israel and Jordan. c) Israel will not conduct negotiations with the PLO. d) There will be no change in the status of Judea, Samaria and Gaza other than in accordance with the basic guidelines of the Government.

SUBJECTS TO BE DEALT WITH IN THE PEACE PROCESS: 4. a) Israel views as important that the peace between Israel and Egypt, based on the Camp David Accords, will serve as a cornerstone for enlarging the circle of peace in the region, and calls for a common endeavor for the strengthening of the peace and its extension, through continued consultation. b) Israel calls for the establishment of peaceful relations between it and those Arab states which still maintain a state of war with it for the purpose of promoting a comprehensive settlement for the Arab–Israel conflict, including recognition, direct negotiation, ending the boycott, diplomatic relations, cessation of hostile activity in international institutions or forums and regional and bilateral cooperation. c) Israel calls for an international endeavour to resolve the problem of the residents of the Arab refugee camps in Judea., Samaria and the Gaza district in order to improve their living conditions and to rehabilitate them. Israel is prepared to be a partner in this endeavour. d) In order to advance the political negotiation process leading to peace, Israel proposes free and democratic elections among the Palestinian Arab inhabitants of Judea, Samaria and the Gaza district in an atmosphere devoid of violence, threats and terror. In these elections a representative will be chosen to conduct negotiations for a transitional period of self-rule. This period will constitute a test for co-existence and cooperation. At a later stage, negotiations will be conducted for a permanent solution during which all the proposed options for an agreed settlement will be examined, and peace between Israel and Jordan will be achieved. e) All the above-mentioned steps should be dealt with simultaneously....

THE PRINCIPLES CONSTITUTING THE INITIATIVE: STAGES: 5. The initiative is based on two stages. a) Stage A—A transitional period for an interim agreement. b) Stage B—Permanent Solution. 6. The interlock between the stages is a timetable on which the Plan is built: the peace process delineated by the initiative is based on Resolutions 242 and 338 upon which the Camp David Accords are founded. TIMETABLE: 7. The transitional period will continue for 5 years. 8. As soon as possible, but not later than the third year after the beginning of the transitional period, negotiations for achieving a permanent solution will begin.

PARTIES PARTICIPATING IN THE NEGOTIATIONS IN BOTH STAGES: 9. The parties participating in the negotiations for the First Stage (the interim agreement) shall include Israel and the elected representation of the Palestinian Arab inhabitants of Judea, Samaria and the Gaza district. Jordan and Egypt will be invited to participate in these negotiations if they so desire. 10. The parties participating in the negotiations for the Second Stage (Permanent Solution) shall include Israel and the elected representation of the Palestinian Arab inhabitants of Judea, Samaria and the Gaza district, as well as Jordan; furthermore, Egypt may participate in these negotiations. In negotiations between Israel and Jordan, in which the elected representation of the Palestinian Arab inhabitants of Judea, Samaria and the Gaza district will participate, the peace treaty between Israel and Jordan will be concluded.

SUBSTANCE OF TRANSITIONAL PERIOD: 11. During the transitional period the Palestinian Arab inhabitants of Judea, Samaria and the Gaza district will be accorded self-rule by means of which they will, themselves, conduct their affairs of daily life. Israel will continue to be responsible for security, foreign affairs and all matters concerning Israeli citizens in Judea, Samaria and the Gaza district. Topics involving the implementation of the plan for self-rule will be considered and decided within the framework of the negotiations for an interim agreement.

SUBSTANCE OF PERMANENT SOLUTION: 12. In the negotiations for a permanent solution every party shall be entitled to present for discussion all the subjects it may wish to raise. 13. The aim of the negotiations should be: a) The achievement of a permanent solution acceptable to the negotiating parties. b) The arrangements for peace and borders between Israel and Jordan.

DETAILS OF THE PROCESS FOR THE IMPLEMENTATION OF THE INITIATIVE: 14. First and foremost dialogue and basic agreement by the Palestinian Arab inhabitants of Judea, Samaria and the Gaza district, as well as Egypt and Jordan if they wish to take part, as above-mentioned, in the negotiations, on the principles constituting the initiative. 15. a) Immediately afterwards will follow the stage of preparations and implementation of the election process in which a representation of the Palestinian Arab inhabitants of Judea, Samaria and Gaza will be elected. This representation: I) Shall be a partner to the conduct of negotiations for the transitional period (interim agreement). II) Shall constitute the self-governing authority in the course of the transitional period. III) Shall be the central Palestinian component, subject to agreement after three years, in the negotiations for the permanent solution. b) In the period of the preparation and implementation there shall be a calming of the violence in Judea, Samaria and the Gaza district. 16. As to the substance of the elections, it is recommended that a proposal of regional elections be adopted, the details of which shall be determined in further discussions. 17. Every Palestinian Arab residing in Judea, Samaria and the Gaza district, who shall be elected by the inhabitants to represent them—after having submitted his candidacy in accordance with the detailed document which shall determine the subject of the elections—may be a legitimate participant in the conduct of negotiations with Israel. 18. The elections shall be free, democratic and secret. 19. Immediately after the election of the Palestinian representation, negotiations shall be conducted with it on an interim agreement for a transitional period which shall continue for 5 years, as mentioned above. In these negotiations the parties shall determine all the subjects relating to the substance of the self-rule and the arrangements necessary for its implementation. 20. As soon as possible, but not later than the third year after the establishment of the self-rule, negotiations for a permanent solution shall begin. During the whole period of these negotiations until the signing of the agreement for a permanent solution, the self-rule shall continue in effect as determined in the negotiations for an interim agreement.

Bernard Reich, *Arab–Israeli Conflict and Conciliation: A Documentry History* (Westport, CT: Praeger, 1995), 220–223.

Ten
A DECADE OF HOPE

On August 2, 1990, Saddam Hussein's Iraq invaded and occupied Kuwait. The administration of President George H. W. Bush then meticulously pieced together a wide-ranging U.S.-led United Nations (UN) coalition that would militarily evict Iraq from Kuwait in January and February 1991. The entire episode from start to finish is often called the 1990–1991 Gulf War. In the region itself, however, the Iraqi invasion and subsequent eviction is often referred to as the Second Gulf War, clearly betraying the links with the Iran–Iraq war (or the "first" Gulf War) and the regional instability initiated by the 1979 Iranian Revolution.

The Iran–Iraq war set the stage for the Iraqi invasion of Kuwait. Iraq's somewhat pyrrhic victory in its war with Iran was more a matter of Teheran relenting first and accepting a UN ceasefire than a result of Iraq's military success. But Saddam Hussein claimed victory nonetheless, and he therefore created heightened expectations within the military and among the populace, who anticipated some sort of victory dividend. The problem was that Iraq was severely in debt, having gone from a more than $60 billion surplus before the outbreak of the war in 1980 to a $40 billion debt—and dictators need money. As such, Saddam Hussein saw what was essentially a bank to the south called Kuwait, with its lucrative oil fields, which in combination with its own hefty reserves would have given Iraq control of 21% of the world's known oil reserves, placing it on a par with Saudi Arabia's 25% share, the largest in the world. One could say that Saddam Hussein attempted his own merger and acquisition. A significant portion of that debt was owed to Kuwait, which, unlike the Saudis, both of whom supported Iraq during the Iran–Iraq war with financial grants and loans, was unwilling to erase it. The Iraqis argued that they had, in essence, protected Kuwait with their blood and the physical destruction of a good part of Iraq—surely that was worth more than what they owed Kuwait.

In addition, Iraq had some outstanding territorial issues with the Kuwaitis that had not been satisfactorily put to rest, including the Rumaylah oil field that sat astride the border (claiming, apparently accurately, that the Kuwaitis were slant-drilling into the Iraqi side) and the Bubiyan and Warba islands belonging to Kuwait just off its northern coast. The Iranian conquest of the Fao (Faw) peninsula, which geographically makes Iraq a Persian Gulf country, had indicated to Baghdad just how easily it could be cut off from the gulf. Iraqi control of the islands would provide it with better access to the gulf; indeed, the taking of Kuwait entirely would expand the Iraqi coastline, thus making it less vulnerable in the future to any Iranian thrust across the Shatt al-Arab waterway, the confluence of the Tigris and Euphrates rivers in southern Iraq that lets into the Persian Gulf.

Perhaps the main reason Saddam Hussein invaded Kuwait is that he thought he could get away with it—possibly not unlike the feeling Gamal 'Abd al-Nasser had in late May–early June 1967. In fact, he came very close to getting away with it. Why he believed he could stems from the Iran–Iraq war, particularly the strong strategic and commercial relationship Baghdad had built up with the United States during the course of the war, brought together by the mutual desire of preventing an Iranian victory. Washington and Baghdad had reestablished diplomatic relations in 1984, having been broken ever since the 1967 Arab–Israeli war. Both the Reagan and Bush administrations believed Iraq could be a very useful surrogate in both the Persian Gulf and Arab–Israeli arenas, filling the empty shoes of both the shah of Iran and Anwar al-Sadat. Fittingly, Iraq moderated its position on a number of issues in order to appeal for support from the United States, Europe, and moderate Arab states, especially Egypt. The Bush administration tended to overlook the excesses of Saddam Hussein's actions in the latter portion and immediate aftermath of the war with Iran, such as the use of poison gas against the Kurds at the village of Halabja. Indeed, President Bush and Secretary of State James Baker admitted in the aftermath of the 1991 Gulf War that they had "stayed" with Saddam Hussein too long, hoping to moderate his policies and mold him into a positive force in the region. In doing so, they failed to appreciate signals that in fact indicated he had not changed his colors from prior to his invasion of Iran in 1980: he was an expansionist, repressive dictator determined to achieve his national and regional ambitions. Saddam Hussein concluded long before Washington that his ambitions could only be achieved at the cost of his relationship with the United States.[1]

The Iraqi president, on the other hand, in a case of possibly hearing only what he wanted to hear, also failed to read Washington's signals indicating its opposition to his policies, preferring instead the ambiguous statements from U.S. officials during the Iraqi military buildup along the Kuwaiti border during the summer of 1990, which on the surface seemed to portray American disinterest in the affair—as long as the oil continued to flow at reasonable prices, something that Saddam Hussein had made clear he would do. The U.S. reaction, or apparent lack thereof, tended to confirm that at least from the American point of view, the strategic relationship was still intact, making a forceful U.S. response unlikely. Baghdad appeared to conclude that the United States was also still hamstrung by the Vietnam syndrome, which would add to Washington's reluctance to become involved militarily in a far-flung region of the world, especially as, with the end of the superpower cold war, the Iraqi incursion was clearly not directed by Moscow or communist forces, which had been the only occasions since World War II that the United States sent hundreds of thousands of troops halfway across the world—Korea and Vietnam. Washington would have no stomach and little domestic and congressional support for military intervention to protect a nondemocratic regime with which it had not had a particularly close relationship.

Saddam Hussein obviously miscalculated. The Bush administration led the charge to liberate Kuwait for a variety of reasons: (1) it did not want Iraq controlling 21% of the world's known oil reserves, which would shake the oil market with a possible precipitous rise in the price per barrel of oil—among a number of negative economic repercussions, this would have a deleterious effect on the Eastern European countries just emerging out of the Soviet embrace and communist framework in the immediate aftermath of the end of the cold war, with the possibility that they could regress backward away from democratic and market-oriented reforms—(2) Iraq directly threatened Saudi Arabia, an American ally whose borders are the reddest of all red lines in the Middle East from the perspective of Washington—in fact, the decision to move Iraqi troops to the Saudi–Kuwaiti border may have been Saddam Hussein's biggest strategic error—(3) the Bush administration realized as the crisis wore on that it would be a strategic nightmare for the United States to have Iraq's million-man army and weapons of mass destruction capability as a perpetual menace in one of the most vital areas of national interest; (4) unfortunately for Saddam Hussein, President Bush's strategic thinking was not shaped by the Vietnam syndrome (although the Powell doctrine strategy in terms of the application of military force utilized in the war was) but by the Munich mentality that emerged out of World War II, in which Bush fought and was decorated—this experience taught Bush and others of his generation not to appease aggressors, as the Europeans had appeased Hitler at the Munich conference in 1938 that allowed Germany to appropriate the Sudetenland in Czechoslovakia, and aggression of this order must not be allowed to stand; and (5) Bush wanted to implement his New World Order, a new era in the wake of the end of the cold war that would usher in a cooperative international paradigm to rein in or prevent acts of "naked aggression," such as the one perpetrated by Saddam Hussein. Many in the administration believed that an assertive response in this situation would reinforce the leadership role of the United States—one that was being questioned internationally following the end of the cold war—since it was the only country capable of such large-scale military action.

As is well known, Operation Desert Storm, as the U.S.-led UN coalition military operation was termed, was launched in January 1991 with an intense aerial bombardment campaign, with the ground war commencing in February, a 100-hour thrust that successfully expelled Iraqi forces from Kuwait.

In the aftermath of the war, a Pax Americana had been clearly established in the Persian Gulf region, formally (and finally) supplanting the Pax Britannia that had enveloped the area for over a century until Britain's evacuation in 1971. From the Nixon Doctrine to the Carter Doctrine to the Kuwaiti reflagging operation during the Iran–Iraq war, the United States incrementally enhanced its position in the Persian Gulf until the climactic interlude of 1990–1991 inserted American might straight into the mix. It spelled the end of balance-of-power politics; the United States would no longer rely on either Iran or Iraq to be its gendarme of the gulf. In its place developed a policy of dual containment. It was hoped that containment of both Iraq and Iran, through economic, political, and military pressure, would bring about regime change or at least a change in behavior toward a more compliant, cooperative, and internationally accepted status.

The 1991 Gulf War had a salutary effect upon the Arab–Israeli arena. When the Bush administration began to recruit countries into the UN coalition arrayed against Iraq, it was to be expected that the Gulf Arab states as well as Washington's traditional allies in the Arab world, such as Egypt and Morocco, would join. With the end of the cold war and a Soviet Union on its last legs desperately needing economic assistance from the West, it was also not surprising that Moscow supported the formation of the coalition by not utilizing its veto in the UN Security Council. Syria, however, was most important of all the Arab states in the coalition. Its inclusion made it seem like it was almost the entire Arab world against Iraq rather than the usual pro-West suspects, especially since Damascus had traditionally been at the vanguard of the anti-Israeli front for decades.

In 1989, Syria's position seemed to take a turn for the worse. Iraq had emerged victorious in the Iran–Iraq war, and it was an Iraq that wanted to reexert its influence in the Middle East. Saddam Hussein remembered Syrian support for his enemy in the war and would make life as difficult as possible for Syria in Lebanon by supporting anti-Syrian groups such as the Christian militia led by Michel Aoun. Iraq would also draw Jordan deeper and deeper into its orbit through economic integration and dependence—similar to the Palestine Liberation Organization (PLO) through financial and political assistance. In the latter case, this led to Yasser Arafat's monumental mistake of tacitly supporting Saddam Hussein upon the outbreak of the 1990 Gulf crisis. Almost overnight the Palestinians lost what international goodwill they had garnered during the first years of the *intifada*. More importantly, the PLO lost crucial financial and political support from the Arab Gulf states which were angered at Arafat's stance. What emerged was, again, a weakened PLO and an intifada that seemed to be going nowhere.

Furthermore, for Syria (and the PLO), the pillar of Soviet support that had braced the regime for most of the decade virtually crumbled with the ascension to power of Mikhail Gorbachev in 1985 and the Red Army exit from Afghanistan by early 1989, both of which led to a dramatic reassessment of Soviet foreign policy that emphasized a drawing down of Soviet commitments abroad, more concentration on domestic restructuring, and improving ties with the United States. This did not bode well for Syria as Moscow first urged and then backed the PLO's decision to pursue a negotiated solution—in the process of all this, the Kremlin improved its relations with Israel. Gorbachev made it clear to Hafiz al-Asad upon the Syrian president's visit to Moscow in April 1987 that Syria's "reliance on military force in settling the Arab–Israeli conflict has completely lost its credibility," and he went on to suggest that Damascus abandon its doctrine of trying to attain strategic parity with Israel and seek to establish a "balance of interests" toward a political settlement in the Middle East.[2] In addition to these problems in the foreign policy arena, Syria's economy continued to deteriorate, owing in large measure to the concentration of economic resources in the military as well as the inherent frailties of its public sector–dominated state capitalist economy. Therefore, Syria joined the coalition. Not only was it participating in an alliance whose objective was to weaken, if not destroy, the war-making capacity of its archenemy in the Arab arena, Syria was also clearly situating itself in the Arab world's moderate camp and opening up the economic doors of investment and aid from the West and grateful Arab Gulf states.

Israel was not a member of the U.S.-led UN coalition, despite Saddam Hussein's attempts to draw it into the fray by lobbing Scud missiles into Israel proper, hoping to turn a Persian Gulf conflict into an Arab–Israeli one, thus prying away at least the Arab members of the coalition; therefore, the Arab states and Israel were de facto on the same side in the war, with similar objectives. For Israel, the destruction of the Iraqi war machine diminished any serious threat emanating from the Arab east, which had been a strategic concern for some time; indeed, this was behind the strategic relationship that Israel had established with the shah of Iran, both parties interested in containing and/or weakening Iraq.[3] Even though there was relatively little death and destruction caused by the forty or so Iraqi Scud missile attacks in Israel, the Bush administration had to apply a tremendous amount of pressure on Tel Aviv to restrain it from lashing out on its own, something to which it was accustomed to doing—sitting tight, waiting, and relying on someone else was not in Yitzhak Shamir's character, in addition to the prevalent view that not retaliating would damage Israel's deterrence posture. The United States even deployed batteries of Patriot antimissile defense systems to Israel to help defend the Jewish state, even though they proved to be much less efficient at shooting down the missiles than was anticipated. The Bush administration also committed to providing $13 billion in aid, $3 billion in immediate support to cover the damages caused by the missile attacks, and $10 billion in loan guarantees to assist in the settlement of Soviet Jews immigrating to Israel, provided that they were not settled in the Occupied Territories, which would complicate the administration's efforts to organize and engage in the peace process. The latter would become a major bone of contention between Shamir and Bush as many of the Soviet Jews were, in fact, settled in the Occupied Territories.

Soviet/Russian Jews to Israel

As we know from earlier in the book, Jewish immigration to Palestine/Israel has been one of the primary pillars of the Zionist program for creating and maintaining a Jewish state. Following the influx of Jews from Europe and the Middle East in the years immediately after the creation of the state of Israel, there were very few pockets of Jews in any numbers elsewhere in the world that might be inclined to emigrate to the new Jewish homeland—except for the areas that comprised the Soviet Union, which of course had been the source of many Jews immigrating to Palestine in the first few aliyahs.

During the superpower cold war, the Soviet Union aligned itself with a number of Arab states. As such, it was on the opposite side of Israel as the cold war was defined and fought in the Middle East; therefore, the Kremlin was hesitant, to say the least, to allow Soviet Jewish emigration to Israel, for it would upset its Arab friends in the region. In any event, Moscow did not want to see any more of a brain drain of Soviet Jewish and non-Jewish elements of the intelligentsia if the floodgates of immigration were opened. Along these lines, Soviet Premier Leonid

Brezhnev imposed what was called a "diploma tax" in 1972 on would-be emigrants who received higher education in the Soviet Union, thus acting as an economic deterrent to emigration. The diploma tax in many cases was extraordinarily high and far out of reach for most of those who contemplated leaving.

International protests escalated in the United States and elsewhere over the Soviet Union's restrictive immigration policies. The groundswell in Congress culminated with the passage of the so-called Jackson-Vanik Amendment to the 1974 Trade Act. Named after its cosponsors, Senator Henry "Scoop" Jackson (D-WA) and Representative Charles Vanik (D-OH), the amendment denied normal trade relations (then called "most favored nation" status) to countries with nonmarket economies that restricted emigration rights, although the president could grant yearly waivers to the provisions of the amendment (which has often been done, most notably with the People's Republic of China). President Gerald Ford signed the amendment into law on January 3, 1975, after it was approved unanimously by both houses of Congress.

Although it has been applied to a number of different countries, the amendment was primarily aimed at the Soviet Union and specifically related to the emigration of Soviet Jews. The Kremlin, with its increasingly moribund economy, was desperate to maintain normal trade relations with the United States, and it therefore reluctantly abided by the Jackson-Vanik Amendment. Although the Soviet Union dissolved in 1991, the amendment is still in force and applies to Russia and other former Soviet republics. Since the passage of the amendment, over 1 million Soviet/Russian Jews have immigrated to Israel. As noted in the text, this was vitally important to Israel in demographic terms in order to maintain the Jewish nature of the state, especially following the capture of the territories (and hundreds of thousands of more Palestinians) in the 1967 Arab–Israeli war, the higher birth rate among the Palestinians, and the over 1 million Israeli Arab population.

Soviet Jewish immigration to Israel again picked up some steam in 1989–1990 as Soviet leader Mikhail Gorbachev modified the Soviet Union's foreign policy across the board, attempting to improve Moscow's relations with the West, especially in terms of attracting much needed Western investment, and to be taken seriously as a partner to Washington with the launching of the Madrid peace process as a cosponsor in October 1991 following the Gulf War. To the Israelis, the Soviet wave of immigrants since the mid-1970s represented in itself another much needed aliyah, including the arrival of Jews from elsewhere, such as the 15,000 Ethiopian Jews brought to Israel in the Operation Solomon airlift in May 1991. To the Palestinians, the influx of Soviet Jews was yet another in a string of disasters, especially as Israeli leader Yitzhak Shamir publicly spoke of settling the incoming Jews in the Occupied Territories, a policy that ran afoul of the Bush administration's attempts to position itself as an honest broker on the eve of the Gulf crisis and war and the Madrid peace process and ultimately contributed to the Israeli prime minister's defeat in the 1992 election.

This political and strategic reorganization in the Middle East brought about by the UN coalition's victory in the Gulf War combined with the end of the superpower cold war to alter the regional balance of power, with Washington far and away the dominant outside force. Maybe even more importantly, many Arab–Israeli psychological barriers had been broken, opening the door to new possibilities for a comprehensive peace. The outcome was a meeting in Madrid in October 1991 that launched a peace process.

THE MADRID PEACE PROCESS

The end of the superpower cold war and the Gulf War compelled Hafiz al-Asad by circumstance and opportunity to engage in what became known as the Madrid peace process, launched by a plenary session of the participant countries and sponsors in the Spanish capital on October 30, 1991. Asad commented that he had made a "strategic choice for peace" with Israel, brought about by the new regional and international environment. He had already begun to reposition Syria toward the end of the 1980s, seeing the writing on the wall as far as continued support from the Soviet Union was concerned. He was, indeed, taking Gorbachev's advice. In December 1988, Asad "acknowledged the importance of Egypt in the Arab arena," the first time he had publicly praised Egypt since the 1979 Egyptian–Israeli peace treaty.[4] By the end of 1989 Damascus had reestablished full diplomatic relations with Cairo as Egypt became fully rehabilitated back into the Arab fold. And with an eye toward isolating Iraq as well as building bridges with the United States, Syria also began to improve its relationship with Saudi Arabia. Asad and other Arab leaders in the Gulf War coalition had stressed to the Bush administration that the United States must address the Arab–Israeli situation after evicting Saddam Hussein from Kuwait. It was an unspoken quid pro quo on which the Bush team made good by organizing the conference in Madrid.[5] As the U.S. Middle East envoy Dennis Ross noted, "Asad's choice [to attend the conference] put him in the center of post-Gulf War diplomacy," while Yasser Arafat's tacit support of Iraq sidelined the PLO leader.[6] For Syria, the roads to regaining the Golan Heights, to economic growth, and to protection from an Israel that was getting stronger as it grew weaker all went through Washington. Paradoxically, the road to Washington went through Israel. Ultimately, this is why Syria made some important concessions to launch the Madrid process; and without Syria's participation, it would not have happened.

The Bush administration worked diligently to organize the initial conference and establish parameters acceptable to the pertinent parties—a tall task indeed. Secretary of State Baker made numerous visits to the region during the summer and early fall of 1991 to push the respective leaders of the countries involved to the negotiating table. It was important to the Arab states, especially Syria, to at least have the opening session appear to be an international conference. As stated in previous chapters, the Arab states much preferred an international setting in which the United States, the Soviet Union, the UN, and multiple Arab parties would participate in order to maximize Arab leverage. Israel, on the other hand, traditionally preferred one-on-one negotiations with individual Arab states, in which Tel Aviv believed it had a clear bargaining advantage. This was the obstacle that had to be overcome in order to get the proceedings under way. It was successfully bridged by holding an opening plenary session that had all of the participants seated at the table, with the two superpowers as cosponsors of the meeting presiding. This was to be the "international conference" the Arab states had demanded, yet, following this opening session, the parties would break off into separate bilateral negotiating tracks, an Israeli–Jordanian track (including a Palestinian delegation) and an Israeli–Syrian/Lebanese one. The Arab participants were the remaining countries bordering Israel that were still officially at war with the Jewish state. Egyptian and Saudi Arabian representatives were also present in the background and working the corridors, so to speak, when necessary. Egypt would utilize its political muscle in the inter-Arab arena as the only Arab country at the time which had signed a peace treaty with Israel, and the Saudis would employ the power of the purse—for any agreements would most certainly require enormous amounts of financial aid to multiple parties as added inducement and incentive to remain at the negotiating table and consummate agreements.

Israeli Prime Minister Shamir, however, would be a tough nut to crack, for he was visibly unenthusiastic about the convening of such a conference, especially as the Arab front had been weakened with the end of the cold war and the defeat of Iraq in the Gulf War; furthermore, the PLO had been ostracized and marginalized by its tacit support of Iraq in the war.[7] Then again, maybe this was the time to strike a great deal from the Israeli perspective. The PLO was desperate to—in any way, shape, or form—get involved in the game again, much as it was following its expulsion from Lebanon. Jordan was desperate to get back in the good graces of the United States after King Hussein also tacitly supported Saddam Hussein, mostly because over half his population was Palestinian in addition to the fact that his country had become so economically dependent upon Iraq. And Syria, of course, was in no position to play hardball at the time. Still, Shamir would play hard just to set his country up for some attractive inducements from the West. The inducements did come: the Soviet Union resumed full diplomatic relations with Israel on October 18, thus continuing to facilitate the arrival of Soviet Jewish immigrants;[8] the United States worked for the repeal of the "Zionism is Racism" UN resolution passed in 1975, which was revoked in the UN in December; and in bending to Shamir's demand not to have official PLO members take part in the negotiations, a joint Jordanian–Palestinian delegation was constructed to represent Palestinian interests, composed of Palestinians from the Occupied Territories (but not East Jerusalem, which in Shamir's view may have given sanction to Palestinian claims to the Holy City) and led by Dr. Haidar Abd al-Shafi, a physician from Gaza. The Palestinian delegation, which also included Faisal al-Husseini and Hanan Ashrawi, both of whom became leading spokespersons for the Palestinian position, remained, however, in close contact with the PLO. But there was also heavy U.S. pressure. The Bush administration correctly saw this as a unique opportunity to finally make significant progress toward a comprehensive Arab–Israeli peace—the regional and international alignment of forces seemed to be working in its favor. As such, Bush indicated a willingness to hold the loan guarantees hostage to progress on the peace front in addition to Israel's commitment not to use the money to house settlers in the territories, especially those Jewish immigrants arriving from the Soviet Union.

The "Framework for Peace in the Middle East" that emerged from the Camp David accords thirteen years earlier provided the parameters for discussion. This was ironically appropriate since it was the framework that was not implemented in any meaningful way following the Egyptian–Israeli peace treaty, but it did indicate the acceptance of the idea of interim measures leading to broader agreements. The bilateral negotiations focused on the nature of any peace treaties that may be signed, border issues between Israel and the Arab participants, and the Palestinian issue, including the disposition of the Occupied Territories. In addition, a series of multilateral talks were established that included an international cast of participants in and outside of the Middle East to discuss a variety of important issues. These multilateral discussions, which were boycotted by Syria and Lebanon (and on one occasion Israel), were convened in a variety of locales in Europe, Asia, and North America, establishing five working groups to discuss regional economic development, arms control and regional security, refugees, water sharing, and environmental issues.

As might have been expected, with such enmity existing between the negotiating parties for two generations, the talks progressed in fits and spurts on both the Palestinian and Syrian tracks, often getting bogged down on seemingly trivial procedural matters but also subject to violent acts perpetrated by elements opposed to peace or seeking some sort of real or imagined leverage in the talks. The opening session itself in Madrid was acrimonious, with Israeli and Arab officials trading accusations of obstinacy, aggression, and terrorist policies.[9] It was clear that positions were being articulated in the extreme to satisfy nervous populations back home and to establish starting points for negotiations. Shamir, however, was sticking to his guns. He essentially did not offer up anything more than what the Shamir plan had laid out several years earlier, i.e., nothing more than Palestinian autonomy with limited self-rule but no Israeli withdrawal from the land. The Israeli premier also had to look toward the next Israeli general elections scheduled for June 1992, so he was not going to ruffle his base of support in and outside of Likud by making concessions in the Madrid process. This may have been politically astute in a domestic sense, but his perceived obstinacy angered the Bush administration, which had expended a tremendous amount of political capital to get the whole thing started. As a result, in February 1992, the Bush administration announced that it was holding up the $10 billion in loan guarantees until there was a cessation in Israeli settlement activity, implicitly accusing the Shamir government of using already appropriated funds to settle Jews in the territories in contradistinction of the peace process, which, from the U.S. and Arab points of view, demanded at least a temporary freeze in settlement activity as an act of good faith and to not prejudice any negotiations over the same lands. The Bush administration was not the first to protest Israeli settlement activity; after all, it had been official U.S. policy for administration after administration. But his was the first that actively adopted a stance against Israeli settlement activity and utilized its financial leverage to curtail it.[10]

In a way, the Bush administration was taking sides in the upcoming elections, hoping that the Labor party would emerge victorious, as it was willing to engage in land-for-peace negotiations more willingly. Israelis would take note of how Shamir seemed to alienate the country's single most important ally, and this contributed, along with continuing economic difficulties and the failure to adequately integrate Soviet Jews into Israeli society, to the defeat of the Shamir government in the election. The Labor party would indeed come to power, this time led by former prime minister and military chief of staff Yitzhak Rabin, who appointed his longtime rival within the Labor party, Shimon Peres, as his foreign minister. The loan guarantees subsequently went through with presidential approval by October 1992. The stage seemed to be set for some real progress in the Madrid process.

OSLO BY WAY OF SYRIA

In many ways, Yitzhak Rabin was the perfect choice under the circumstances. He had been the military chief of staff during the 1967 Arab–Israeli war, former ambassador to the United States, and former prime minister from 1974 to 1977. In addition, he was charged with crushing the Palestinian intifada, adopting an iron-fist policy, especially as the Palestinian attacks took on a more violent form. Rabin therefore was someone who had had good relations with the United States, a relationship that badly needed repairing by mid-1992, and he certainly had the security credentials. He was, indeed, the best of both worlds to the Israeli electorate at the time. He had the requisite military background to ensure Israelis that he would not sacrifice security for peace, yet he adhered to a Labor platform that was much more willing to explore peace options. On the other hand, Shimon Peres, even though he had been an architect of Israel's defense establishment as well as its nuclear program—and a former defense minister himself—did not bring with him the cachet of a military hero along the lines of Rabin, Moshe Dayan, Ariel Sharon, or later Ehud Barak. He was seen as an unmitigated dove who sought peace for the sake of peace itself, and thus he was perceived as more willing to risk Israeli security prerogatives. Peres could not carry enough of the center and right in the Israeli electorate to be a viable prime minister; indeed, even though Peres would serve a couple of turns as prime minister, it was never as the direct result of an election.

Rabin and new U.S. President Bill Clinton actually preferred the Syrian track over the Palestinian one because the former consisted of a much more direct set of circumstances revolving around a straight land-for-peace exchange—it was, in a word, easier.[11] To the Israelis, Syria was a more dangerous threat than the Palestinians, the latter being seen more as a nuisance than something that could inflict severe damage upon the country. In addition, gaining ground in Washington was the idea that Syria was the key to an overall Middle East peace. If Syria would sign along the dotted line, so would Lebanon and Jordan in an immediate sense. All of this would open the door for Saudi Arabia and the rest of the Arab Gulf states to enter into peace agreements with Israel. At the same time, Saddam Hussein's Iraq would be isolated and the PLO, with little Arab leverage behind it, would be compelled to seek a more rapid and conciliatory peace with Israel.

This is not to say that a Syrian–Israeli peace agreement would be easy to consummate—history would soon enough show this to be the case. But there were—and still are—some important differences with the situation in the West Bank compared to that of the Golan Heights. There are considerably fewer Israeli settlements and settlers in the Golan Heights compared with the West Bank. Today, there are currently thirty-three Jewish settlements on the Golan Heights, numbering in total about 18,000 people. There are a similar number of Syrian Druze in four villages in the Golan Heights who were "caught," so to speak, on the Golan during the Israeli capture of the territory in 1967, although most have become naturalized Israeli citizens since that time. Compare this with the West Bank, where there are approximately 230,000 Israeli settlers in over 150 settlements, not to speak of another 200,000 Jews in East Jerusalem.[12] In contrast, there are over 2 million Palestinians in the West Bank. There is also much less geographic intermingling between Jewish settlements and Arab villages in the Golan Heights, while it is quite the opposite in the West Bank. There is less religious significance attached by Israelis to the Golan Heights than the

West Bank (or Judea and Samaria, as the more nationalistic Jews are apt to call it). In addition, an agreement on the Golan Heights rests primarily on issues concerning border demarcation, security arrangements, and the pace and nature of normalizing relations, i.e., all things that can be negotiated in a tractable fashion. In the West Bank, on the other hand, there are the much more intractable issues of what to do with the numerous Israeli settlements, the status of Jerusalem, and the question of the return of Palestinian refugees within the pre-1967 borders of Israel. It is little wonder, then, that American and Israeli officials consistently sought to explore the prospects of a Syrian–Israeli peace before a Palestinian–Israeli one.

Rabin was prepared to focus on the Syrian track for all the reasons just mentioned in addition to the fact that he was skeptical that Yasser Arafat could "deliver in the end."[13] As opposed to his hardline predecessor, Rabin agreed that UN Security Council Resolution 242 applied to the Golan Heights. But as with most Israeli leaders, Rabin felt the Israeli public could absorb only so much at one time, i.e., a peace agreement on one track but not on the other until sufficient time had passed—it would be diplomatic overload to heavily engage in both at the same time. Rabin's initial explorations regarding peace negotiations with Syria through American intermediaries, however, did not proceed fast enough.

Hafiz al-Asad was renowned for his methodical and incremental negotiating approach, born as much by suspicion as by style and strategy. Some progress was made in terms of both sides signaling willingness to enter into peace negotiations, and there was an Israeli willingness to discuss withdrawal from the Golan Heights, which is what really caught Asad's eye. But things bogged down over the definition of "full withdrawal" from the Golan Heights and the extent of "normalization" of relations between the two states. Asad insisted that full Israeli withdrawal meant to the border as it existed on June 4, 1967, the day before the 1967 war began. Israel preferred a return to the 1923 international border demarcation between mandatory British Palestine and mandatory French Syria. The June 4 line would, at least in theory, provide Syria with direct access to the Sea of Galilee, whereas the 1923 line is, at its closest point, some ten meters off the shore of the Sea of Galilee. The June 4 line represents Syrian advances during the 1947–1949 Arab–Israeli war and thereafter up to 1967. It is popularly suspected that one of the reasons for Asad's insistence on the June 4 line was so that Syria would appear to have more territory returned than that which Anwar Sadat received in the 1979 Egyptian–Israeli peace treaty, which itself was based on a 1923 demarcation by the European powers. Since Asad held out so much longer than Sadat, so it goes, he should expect at least a little bit more for his steadfastness. Additionally, the 1923 border, from the Syrian perspective, was the colonial border drawn arbitrarily by the European mandate powers; therefore, it was really not legitimate to begin with. All of these issues, however, would be negotiable, as time would tell; but for the moment, Rabin was disappointed in Asad's hesitancy and gave the green light to proceed with what became known as the "Oslo channel" with the Palestinians, all of which placed the Syrian–Israeli track on the back burner for the time being.

In August 1993 it was revealed that Israeli and PLO officials had been meeting secretly since January in Norway outside of the Madrid framework. Terje Rod Larsen, who would become an important UN Middle East envoy in the next decade, at the time was head of a Norwegian research institute that was examining living conditions in the Occupied Territories. During the course of his research in 1992, Larsen came into contact with Israeli and PLO officials who showed an interest in meeting with their counterparts to explore possible negotiations. Labor party Deputy Foreign Minister Yossi Beilin, who was in the mold of Shimon Peres regarding the pursuit of peace, along with Yair Hirschfeld, a professor of Middle East history at Haifa University, were put in touch with PLO officials Ahmed Qureia (whose nom de guerre was Abu Ala), the head of the finance department, and Mahmoud Abbas (Abu Mazen), head of the international section and a close confidante of Yasser Arafat. The Norwegians became mediators between the two sides, with foreign minister Johan Joergan Holst playing a key role. The Norwegians were also able to successfully suppress any news about the talks until that August. Interestingly, what in retrospect seems to fit the model, the Israeli Knesset repealed a law in January 1993 that forbade contact with PLO members, thus opening the door for further meetings—and at higher levels as time progressed and interest grew, with Beilin informing Peres and then the Israeli foreign minister informing Rabin in April 1993.

There are a number of reasons that converged to make the Oslo process happen. Both sides obviously believed it was in their interest to pursue this hidden track or else it would not have occurred. For Yasser Arafat and the mainstream PLO, this was perceived to be an opportunity to regain some relevance following the repercussions of its tacit backing of Saddam Hussein in the Gulf War. They also probably felt that this might be this aging generation of PLO leaders' last chance to bring about a Palestinian state. In addition, PLO leaders saw that the new Clinton administration was much more pro-Israeli in orientation—at least at first—than the Bush administration had been. Clinton also seemed to be much more interested in domestic, rather than foreign, affairs, which was the emphasis of his political platform that defeated Bush in the 1992 presidential election. The Madrid process had also bogged down by then on both tracks. If the PLO did not act now, building on the stalled momentum of Madrid before the whole process became a memory, then its negotiating position—its relevance—might continue to dissipate. Besides, nothing else had worked to this point: rejectionism, militancy, guerilla warfare, terrorism, distant diplomacy—none of it had produced the long-sought-after Palestinian state. Finally, as the intifada continued and as the PLO became marginalized again in the aftermath of the Gulf War, Hamas was gaining in popularity by leaps and bounds, especially in the Gaza Strip. Hamas was able to take aggressive action against Israel, while the PLO seemed impotent; and its charitable organizations were providing civil society functions that won plaudits and converts in the territories. Arafat believed that unless the PLO reinforced its centrality as the heart of the Palestinian movement, his vision of a secular Palestinian state living side by side with Israel would give way to a movement that called for the destruction of Israel and replacing it with a Palestinian Islamic republic, one in which Islamic law, *shari'a*, served as the constitution of the state.

It was also seen as a propitious time to act from Rabin's perspective as well. The Israelis also began to see Hamas as a distinct threat that might replace the secular PLO in terms of leadership in at least the Gaza Strip but also possibly even the West Bank. Even though the Israelis at first saw Hamas as an effective counter to the leftist, Soviet-supported PLO, it was growing too big for its britches—and for Israeli peace of mind, marginalizing Hamas and Islamic Jihad was an attractive option, especially as they had stepped up their terrorist attacks against Israeli civilians and armed forces. There were also concerns in Tel Aviv about increasing interconnectedness between Islamic extremist groups in the region, particularly the prospects of Hizbollah support for Palestinian Islamist groups. As such, Israel switched gears and all of a sudden began to see Arafat's PLO as an effective break against the rising appeal of Hamas. The PLO's involvement in a peace process could effectively marginalize Hamas while building up, this time intentionally, Yasser Arafat as the preferred alternative. The Israelis were also becoming frustrated with the lack of progress in the Madrid process. The whole idea of non-PLO members as part of a joint Jordanian–Palestinian delegation seemed to be counterproductive (at least from Rabin's and Peres' point of view—it is probably exactly what Shamir would have wanted). The Palestinian delegates could not make significant decisions on their own, having always to consult with PLO officials in Tunis first, in itself a procedural impediment to the proceedings. Finally, the PLO was weak, and Rabin knew it. With such a distinct bargaining advantage, it made sense to try to strike a deal knowing the PLO would be compelled to make the lion's share of concessions. So with all of these considerations, in addition to the fact that it followed the more forward peace platform on which the Labor party had campaigned, the Israeli prime minister decided to authorize official meetings in Norway by May 1993.

There would be eleven rounds of meetings between PLO and Israeli officials over the late spring and summer of 1993. Finally, on August 20, Israeli representative Uri Savir and Ahmed Qureia signed, with Shimon Peres witnessing, the Declaration of Principles between Israel and the PLO—the Oslo accords. Generally speaking, the accords provided for mutual recognition and established the parameters and timetable for negotiations regarding the nature and extent of Palestinian autonomy in the West Bank and Gaza Strip. The Americans were finally brought into the loop officially when Peres and Holst met with Secretary of State Warren Christopher on August 27 in California and briefed him on the accords. The Clinton administration then publicly announced its support for the Oslo accords—the Madrid process, for the moment, had been relegated to the background.

Reminiscent of Camp David, there were two documents comprising the Oslo accords. One dealt with Israeli–Palestinian mutual recognition, which was signed by Arafat in Tunis on September 9, in which the PLO recognized Israel's right to exist in peace and security with its neighbors, renounced terrorism, and committed itself to removing clauses in the PLO charter that called for the elimination of Israel. Holst then brought the document to Jerusalem, where Rabin then signed it, recognizing the PLO as the legitimate representative of the Palestinian people and accepting it as a negotiating partner. The second agreement was formally known as the Declaration of Principles on Palestinian Self-Rule, most often just referred to as the Declaration of Principles. This was the historic document that was signed on September 13, 1993, on the White House lawn.

The Declaration of Principles outlined a phased approach comprised of interim arrangements that dealt with Palestinian autonomy as well as the parameters for negotiating what have been called the final status issues toward a permanent resolution of the Israeli–Palestinian problem. The Palestinians hoped and expected this would all lead to the creation of a viable, independent Palestinian state in the West Bank and Gaza Strip to the June 4, 1967, lines, with East Jerusalem as its capital—a two-state solution. It was unclear, perhaps intentionally so, what the Israelis envisioned as the endgame of the Oslo process. Rabin was categorically ruling out sovereign statehood for the Palestinians as well as reiterating the Israeli chorus that Jerusalem would remain the undivided "eternal capital" of Israel. Even on the issue of the Jewish settlements Rabin did not implement the total freeze that was demanded by the Bush administration, allowing thousands of units under construction to be completed. What *was* clear was that any final resolution would be the result of hard negotiations. Until a final agreement was signed, Israel would retain ultimate sovereignty over the territories. A phased negotiating period was delineated in the accord in which the Palestinians would undertake more and more administrative responsibility. The first stage of the agreement, the so-called Gaza–Jericho first phase, called for the withdrawal of Israeli troops from the Gaza Strip and the West Bank town of Jericho. To be completed by July 1994, the next phase would encompass the election of a Palestinian legislative council that would take over a variety of civic and administrative responsibilities in the territories now under its nominal control, including that of collecting taxes, health, education, welfare, and tourism. Israeli forces would continue to redeploy (not "withdraw") outside of Palestinian towns and villages in the West Bank, although they would still be responsible for the security of Israeli settlements. The last phase revolved around negotiations that would begin by December 1995 and last no more than three years (December 1998). During this phase, final status issues would be discussed, such as Jerusalem, Jewish settlements, delineating final borders, and the right of return for Palestinian refugees. The idea was that if the Oslo process began with these final status issues, negotiations would be stillborn, whereas if they were left to the end, maybe the interim agreements, combined with the expected heightened trust between the two parties and public confidence produced by them, would create a more propitious environment to resolve these most difficult problems.

There was certainly a great deal of hope on that day in September on the White House lawn. With President Clinton, Yasser Arafat, and Yitzhak Rabin looking on, Shimon Peres and Mahmoud Abbas signed the Declaration of Principles, with Warren Christopher and Russian Foreign Minister Andrei Kosyrev signing as witnesses. The fact that the United States and Russia were present, despite being left completely out of the Oslo channel, indicated that the Israelis and Palestinians could only bring the process so far—they needed the superpowers, especially the United States, to broker, cajole, pressure, persuade, and guarantee elements of what was to come. It was a very emotional day. The principals then made speeches, capturing the apparent moment in history. Rabin exclaimed that there had been "enough of blood and tears. Enough!" Clinton proudly stated that "a peace of the brave is within our reach." Arafat also gave a speech, in front of the White House no less, only about five years after he first recognized Israel in Geneva because the United States would not allow him a visa to enter the country to speak at the UN—the guerilla fighter and revolutionary had become an accepted statesman. Then Arafat reached out to shake Rabin's hand, and the old Israeli warrior, with visible discomfort—and with a nudge from Clinton whose outstretched arms behind the leaders seemed to be culling the two together—relented and grasped Arafat's hand with his own. The "discomfort" apparent in Rabin was, in retrospect, perhaps an indication of the immense challenges that still lay ahead.

A TALE OF TWO TRACKS

The Oslo accords did not appear without criticism from a variety of circles. Arafat came under the most intense criticism, mostly from Palestinian and other Arab sources who believed he gave up, à la Anwar al-Sadat, what little leverage he had—final recognition of Israel—without any guarantee that the process would lead to an independent Palestinian state. This was a fair critique. It captured the relative weakness of the PLO's bargaining position vis-à-vis Israel, but Arafat was in a desperate situation and accepted a great deal on hope and trust, especially toward the United States to sufficiently pressure Israel to make the necessary concessions—it may have been wishful thinking. Hamas viewed Arafat's actions as treasonous and included in its charter vociferous opposition to the Oslo accords, much less the existence of Israel altogether. Rabin also encountered vehement opposition from Israel's own brand of extremists: the ultranationalist and religious groups who called the Israeli prime minister a traitor for entering a process that portended at least a partial relinquishment of the Occupied Territories and set the stage for possibly more land-for-peace transactions. Settler movements such as the Gush Emunim (Bloc of the Faithful) organized rallies and demonstrations against any hint of withdrawal from occupied lands. The opposition from the orthodox Jewish parties bordered on the apocalyptic, i.e., that Rabin had severed a covenant with God by giving up portions of Judea and Samaria. Emblematic of this more violent tone in the Israeli politic was the February 25, 1994, massacre of twenty-nine Muslims at the Mosque of Abraham (Ibrahim) in the Tomb of the Patriarchs in Hebron by a Jewish zealot by the name of Baruch Goldstein. Goldstein was a Jewish settler who belonged to Meir Kahane's ultra-right-wing and militant Kach party, which in itself exemplified the increasing polarization of Israeli society over the question of whether or not to trade land for peace. The Israeli government immediately denounced the killings and ordered an investigation, but the continuing actions of extremists in both the Israeli and Palestinian camps tended to erode popular support for the peace process as a self-fulfilling prophecy; i.e., one terrorist act begot another one (Hamas in April carried out two suicide bombings, killing fifteen Israeli civilians ostensibly in revenge for the Hebron massacre), which led to more Israeli crackdowns and subsequent Palestinian violence, all of which made progress on peace more and more difficult when weighed down by the anchor of extremism. And both sets of extremists could not be ignored or forcibly silenced without negative political repercussions. The respective Israeli and Palestinian ruling authorities were in a "catch-22," which is exactly what the extremists wanted.

Despite this opposition, there was noticeable progress made on the Oslo accords over the next couple of years. The Israeli Knesset as well as the Palestine National Council quickly ratified the Declaration of Principles. It seems that peace was indeed being given a chance. An international conference of some forty donor countries organized by the United States pledged in October 1993 over $2 billion of aid for the envisioned Palestinian entity as laid out in the accords: $600 million coming from the European Union, $500 million from the United States, and a healthy portion of the remainder coming from Israel, Saudi Arabia, and the United Arab Emirates. Financial aid and its efficient application were crucial to the success of Palestinian self-government. Arafat had to show tangible economic progress for the Palestinian population, that engagement in the peace process bought economic development and a general improvement in the lot of everyday Palestinian lives. Unless this occurred, the peace process would be seen to be hollow by most Palestinians, who then might be drawn more to support the rejectionist viewpoint of groups such as Hamas, Islamic Jihad, and the secular Popular Front for the Liberation of Palestine (PFLP), all of which opposed the Oslo accords.

In fact, in many ways, 1994 could be considered the high point of both the Madrid and Oslo peace processes. Per the Gaza–Jericho plan, the Palestinians were to establish a governing authority over the territories over which they had administrative control. This would be called the Palestinian Interim Self-Government Authority, most often just referred to as the Palestinian National Authority or simply the Palestinian Authority (PA). The first of many target dates during the course of the 1990s (this one in April 1994) would pass in terms of the Israeli withdrawal, but by early May the final arrangements were signed and the Israelis completed their withdrawal by May 18.[14] Arafat then triumphantly entered Gaza City on July 1 amid raucous celebrations by the Palestinians. Four days later in Jericho, which would become Arafat's headquarters, the PA was established and the members sworn in. In the areas under the PA's purview, the Palestinians were permitted "their own postage stamps and international dialing code, control of exports and imports, and the right to issue travel documents; but they were denied their own currency and the right to station Palestinian police on the Allenby Bridge [connecting the West Bank with Jordan across the Jordan River]."[15] The Israelis were also ultimately responsible for security as well as access to and from the West Bank and Gaza Strip. The PA assumed more responsibilities in the ensuing months in the areas of health, education, taxation, tourism, and health services.

While the Israeli-Palestinian track progressed, the Israeli–Syrian track also saw some important movement in 1994–1995. Asad was at first furious with Arafat for striking out on his own with Israel. From Syria's perspective, the sine qua non for effectively bargaining with Israel was strength in numbers—in other words, stick together. Once the PLO went in its own direction, it was much easier for other Arab countries to soften their positions vis-à-vis Israel because the Palestinian problem had been the single most important issue that united the Arab world. By default then, the Oslo accords weakened Syria's bargaining position. On the other hand, now that the PLO had, indeed, abandoned the "all-together" approach in pursuit of its objectives vis-à-vis negotiations with Israel, Asad was much less beholden to maintaining the pretense of sticking to the Arab nationalist line. He could now pursue Syria's own national objectives regarding the Golan Heights with less concern about the Palestinian problem. Until this time Syria had been at the head of the line in the Arab world by stating that it would not sign an agreement with Israel until the Palestinian issue had been satisfactorily addressed. This no longer held true.

As a result, Syrian–Israeli negotiations within the context of the Madrid process began to pick up steam in late 1994 and lasted in earnest until early 1996, with each country's respective ambassador to the United States leading the negotiating teams in Washington: for Israel, Itamar Rabinovich, a scholar who specialized on Syria and Lebanon, and for Syria, Walid Mou'allem—both of these individuals were capable negotiators and, more importantly, were moderate and reasonable diplomats.[16] The Israelis seemed to be juggling both tracks, to the point where both Palestinian and Syrian negotiators accused Tel Aviv of purposely playing one track off against the other in order to extract more concessions on each. Perhaps, however, the continuing commitment on the part of Israel to engage in the Syrian track while ostensibly still negotiating with the Palestinians betrayed the Israeli preference for an agreement with Syria for reasons outlined earlier. As such, during this period, the basic parameters for a Syrian–Israeli peace were laid, and serious progress was made on a host of important issues; indeed, if a Syrian–Israeli peace should materialize in the foreseeable future, it would no doubt be based in large measure on the progress made at a series of discussions between the two sides brokered by the United States during this time frame. The timing and extent of a withdrawal of Syrian and Israeli forces after a return of the Golan Heights was a crucial obstacle to overcome.

Since Israel is much smaller than Syria, the former wanted an asymmetrical withdrawal—Syria keeping forces and certain types of weapons systems farther away from the new negotiated border than Israel—in a longer, more phased approach. Syria, while eventually agreeing to asymmetrical demilitarization, wanted a more rapid, total withdrawal. Security measures in the form of early-warning stations were negotiated—where they would be located and who would man them. Also discussed was the exact nature of a peace, in that Israel wanted full normalization with an exchange of embassies as well as trade and cultural interaction as part of the process of withdrawal (as it had done with Egypt) in order to build up a level of trust with Damascus and to measure the extent to which Syria really wanted peace. Syria, on the other hand, spoke of "normal" relations, something falling short of an integrative relationship, stating that full normalization could occur over time, after an agreement was reached. In this regard, critics would accuse Asad of simply trying to create what was essentially a non-belligerency pact in his attempt to improve his relationship with the United States and use the peace process itself as protection against what Damascus viewed as Israeli aggression and expansionism. There were the matters concerning adequate water sharing, water protection procedures, and mechanisms for the tributaries traversing the Golan Heights, an issue that was central to Israeli concerns. Finally, of course, there was the question of where exactly the new Syrian–Israeli border would be drawn. While Asad stuck to his June 4, 1967, line, the Israelis sought to amend the border somewhat to keep Syria from the shores of the Sea of Galilee, possibly in exchange for some other territory adjacent to the Golan Heights (such as the al-Hamma area that juts out like a finger from the Golan toward Jordan). As was pointed out in later negotiations in 1999, however, the shoreline of the Sea of Galilee had actually receded significantly since the 1967 Arab–Israeli war, thus offering the possibility of Syria getting the June 4 line and Israel keeping the Syrians away from the valuable body of water that fed the Jordan River, the lifeblood of Israel.[17] Complicating the issue, according to U.S. Middle East envoy Dennis Ross, is that there does not exist a map delineating the actual disposition of forces on the day of June 4, 1967.[18] In addition, it appears that the Israelis under Rabin made a commitment through American intermediaries (so that it could plausibly be denied if negotiations broke down) that was passed on to the Syrians that Israel would be willing to implement a full withdrawal from the Golan Heights, although, again, the definition of a "full withdrawal" in terms of a new border was still left ambiguous. Regardless, the two sides were *really* talking and negotiating over substantive issues.

Adding even more impetus to Syrian concerns that they could be left behind in the pursuit of peace was the rapid progress on the Israeli–Jordanian front. This was not surprising however. Of all the Arab countries since the creation of the state of Israel, including Egypt, Jordan had been the most ready and willing to make peace with its neighbor. Because of its relative weakness in the inter-Arab arena and, more importantly, the fact that over half the population of Jordan is Palestinian, King Hussein had to first await tangible progress on the Israeli–Palestinian front before anything concerning Jordan could happen. After the Oslo accords and the successful implementation of the first stage per the Gaza–Jericho plan, it was only a matter of time before Amman and Tel Aviv would agree to a peace treaty. With a Pax Americana in the region as well as Syria itself engaged in peace negotiations, Jordan had little to fear in terms of retributive actions by any disenchanted parties. And this was the quickest way to get back in the good graces of the United States—after having chosen to tacitly back Saddam Hussein in the 1990–1991 Gulf War—and help rebuild the country economically, especially in terms of tourism once a peace accord was signed.

There had been reports that King Hussein and Yitzhak Rabin met privately in Washington as early as June 1994, agreeing to restart negotiations after they had broken off following the Hebron massacre the previous February. In July, Warren Christopher met in Jordan with Shimon Peres and Jordanian Prime Minister 'Abd al-Salam al-Majali. Negotiations just picked up speed from there. On July 25, Rabin and Hussein officially declared an end to the state of war between the two countries upon a visit to Washington in another ceremony on the White House lawn (appropriately called the Washington Declaration), both later appearing before a joint session of Congress proclaiming their mutual commitment to a peace treaty. It was a strategically planned address as Congress responded in kind by promising debt relief to the debt-ridden Jordanian economy in return for the expenditure of efforts on the part of Amman to end the Arab economic boycott against Israel and full support of the international sanctions regime that had been established by the UN against Iraq following the Gulf War. King Hussein had, indeed, ingratiated himself with Washington and became a central figure in the overall peace process during his remaining years.

Considering the rapid chain of events on the Israeli–Jordanian front since early summer, it was almost anticlimactic when on October 26, 1994, Yitzhak Rabin and King Hussein formally signed a peace treaty near the Jordanian city of Aqaba, establishing full diplomatic relations in late November. President Clinton was a cosigner to the agreement, after which he visited with Syrian President Hafiz al-Asad in Damascus on his way back to the United States. This was the first visit by a U.S. president to Syria since Nixon made the trip in 1974, and it was obviously designed to ensure Asad and the Israelis of the importance of the Israeli–Syrian track and the Clinton administration's commitment to it. Among other things, the peace treaty provided for new border crossing points, the sharing of water resources, direct telephone service between the two countries, plans for economic cooperation (which would reach its fruition in the tourist sector), air flights between Amman and Tel Aviv, and continued Israeli recognition of Jordan's "special role" in administering the Muslim holy places located on the Haram al-Sharif in the Old City of Jerusalem, something with which the Palestinians were not particularly pleased since they ultimately held that function to be their own responsibility. In addition, King Hussein promised that his country would not allow other foreign Arab armies to enter the kingdom (which had occurred in prior Arab–Israeli wars), while Israel committed itself to not expelling Palestinians to Jordan.

Contributing to the positive peace environment that seemed to be breaking out all over the region was the incremental dropping by many Arab countries of the secondary and tertiary economic boycott against Israel—and some Arab countries (and corporations) even quietly dealt directly with Israeli entities, thus undermining the primary Arab boycott.[19] The lifting of the Arab economic boycott was a primary policy objective of Israel. Not only would this lead to the country's peaceful integration into the region, but also, since Israel's economy dwarfed those of the Arab countries, it could immediately establish itself as a regional economic power—which, of course, generated a good bit of concern among a number of Arab parties. Morocco, Tunisia, and the Gulf Cooperation Council countries were among the first Arab states to at least partially lift the economic boycott. Syria, Lebanon, Iraq, and Libya did not.

Dovetailing these developments were a series of three annual regional economic conferences held in the Middle East (Casablanca in 1994, Amman in 1995, and Doha in 1996) that turned out to be inclusive global business conferences that convened leading political and business figures from around the world to mingle with Arabs and Israelis to discuss ways of promoting regional economic growth. This was part and parcel of Shimon Peres' dream of a Middle East common market in which he envisioned an Israeli economic juggernaut lifting all ships in the region. Economic integration would further generate indigenous growth as well as attract foreign investment, all of which would contribute to the painful process of transforming all of the states in the area, including Israel, into more market-oriented economies.[20] The seriousness with which the participants engaged in their discussion groups and offered ideas and the enthusiasm emerging from the Casablanca meeting in particular was quite palpable. The Middle East on the whole seemed to be turning the corner away from decades of conflict toward a lasting comprehensive peace.

To cap off a frenetic year, on December 10, 1994, Yitzhak Rabin, Shimon Peres, and Yasser Arafat received the Nobel Prize for Peace in Oslo, recognizing their historic achievements toward peace in the Middle East.

OSLO II AND THE ASSASSINATION OF RABIN

There were still a number of issues to be decided regarding the relationship between Israel and the territories under the jurisdiction of the PA. Such issues as security arrangements, police powers, agriculture, labor movement, trade, water usage, etc., were slowly but surely tackled by Palestinian and Israeli negotiators throughout much of 1995. A final agreement on these and other issues was signed in Washington on September 28, 1995, in what became known as the Israeli–Palestinian Interim Agreement or, more popularly, as Oslo II, which was negotiated between the parties in the Red Sea resort of Taba in Egypt, where Husni Mubarak played a key mediating role. Despite the presence of Rabin, Peres, Arafat, King Hussein, and Mubarak, observers point to the noticeable lack of jubilation and hope that had accompanied the signing of the Declaration of Principles (Oslo I) two years earlier. It seemed as if the weight of all of the issues still left unresolved was beginning to sink in. According to the Interim Agreement, final status negotiations were set to begin by May 1996. More importantly, it spelled out in specific detail in a lengthy document (over 350 pages) the stages of redeployment of the Israel Defense Forces (IDF) from areas in the West Bank that would to varying degrees be turned over to Palestinian civil authority. The Israeli redeployment would be phased and the extent of PA control would vary according to three types of zones set out in the document. To say that Oslo II was complicated is a gross understatement.

The three zones were delineated as follows: land designated as Area A would be under the direct control of the PA, which amounted to 3% of the West Bank and contained, with the exception of Hebron, the major Palestinian population centers; in Area B, comprising 24% of the West Bank, Israel and the Palestinians would have joint control (Palestinian civil control and Israeli security control); finally, in Area C, which accounted for the remaining 73% of the territory, Israel would retain total civil and security control. It was in Area C that the approximately 150 Jewish settlements in the West Bank were located in addition to so-called military areas reserved for security purposes, largely along the border with Jordan. Most of the Palestinian population resided in Areas A and B. According to the agreement, the IDF would redeploy (again, not "withdraw") from major Palestinian population centers such as Ramallah, Bethlehem, Nablus, Jenin, and Tulkarm, as well as several hundred smaller Palestinian villages. Following the redeployment of the IDF, the Palestinians would hold elections for a legislative council as well as the head of the PA.

Palestinian criticism began to mount because any cursory examination of the Oslo II map of the West Bank would suggest that it would be practically impossible to create a contiguous Palestinian state out of it. It appeared that the so-called Palestinian state would be no more than a series of "Bantustans" separated from each other and crisscrossed by Israeli-controlled highways, checkpoints, and settlements. The final status issues, including the possibility of a Palestinian state and its ultimate composition and borders, were still left to be negotiated; but after several years of talks, it appeared to many Palestinians that all Arafat had achieved to date was a measly 3% of the West Bank and a Gaza Strip that most Israelis wanted nothing to do with anyhow. The incremental and gradual nature of the redeployment as spelled out in the Interim Agreement was of great concern to many Palestinians who believed that Israel would ultimately renege on the deal, especially if terrorist acts by Palestinian extremists during the course of the phased redeployment slowed the process to a halt. To the Israelis, the phased approach allowed for a more stable and secure transfer of authority while providing a period of time in which to test the sincerity of Palestinians to live in peace side by side with Israel and the ability of the PA to be successfully self-governing. The Israeli government had to play to multiple constituencies domestically. As we already know, the religious and ultranationalist groups were vociferously opposed to the Oslo process from the beginning and saw Oslo II as a reaffirmation of Rabin's willingness to abandon tracts of biblical Israel. The discourse against Rabin among these elements grew increasingly violent, many calling the Israeli prime minister a traitor, with some rabbis even sanctioning his death. Many of these same rabbis also issued decrees calling on Israeli soldiers to disobey their superiors and not evacuate their positions in the West Bank. As Hamas attacks continued, even centrist Israelis who had supported the Oslo process began to question the wisdom of it.

The intense political atmosphere culminated on November 4, 1995, when Yitzhak Rabin was assassinated by a Jewish zealot. The assassination was without precedent in modern Israel, and many Israelis were compelled to look inward and question how the political atmosphere had deteriorated so much. Rabin was murdered by an Israeli citizen named Yigal Amir, who believed he was acting on a mandate from God. He was a law student at Bar-Ilan University and from the town of Herziliya. Rabin had just completed a speech to about 100,000 of his supporters in Kings of Israel Square in Tel Aviv to galvanize support for the peace process. As he headed down the stage toward his car, he was gunned down. The man known affectionately as "Mr. Security" apparently lacked a sufficient amount of it that evening, and he died at the hands of an

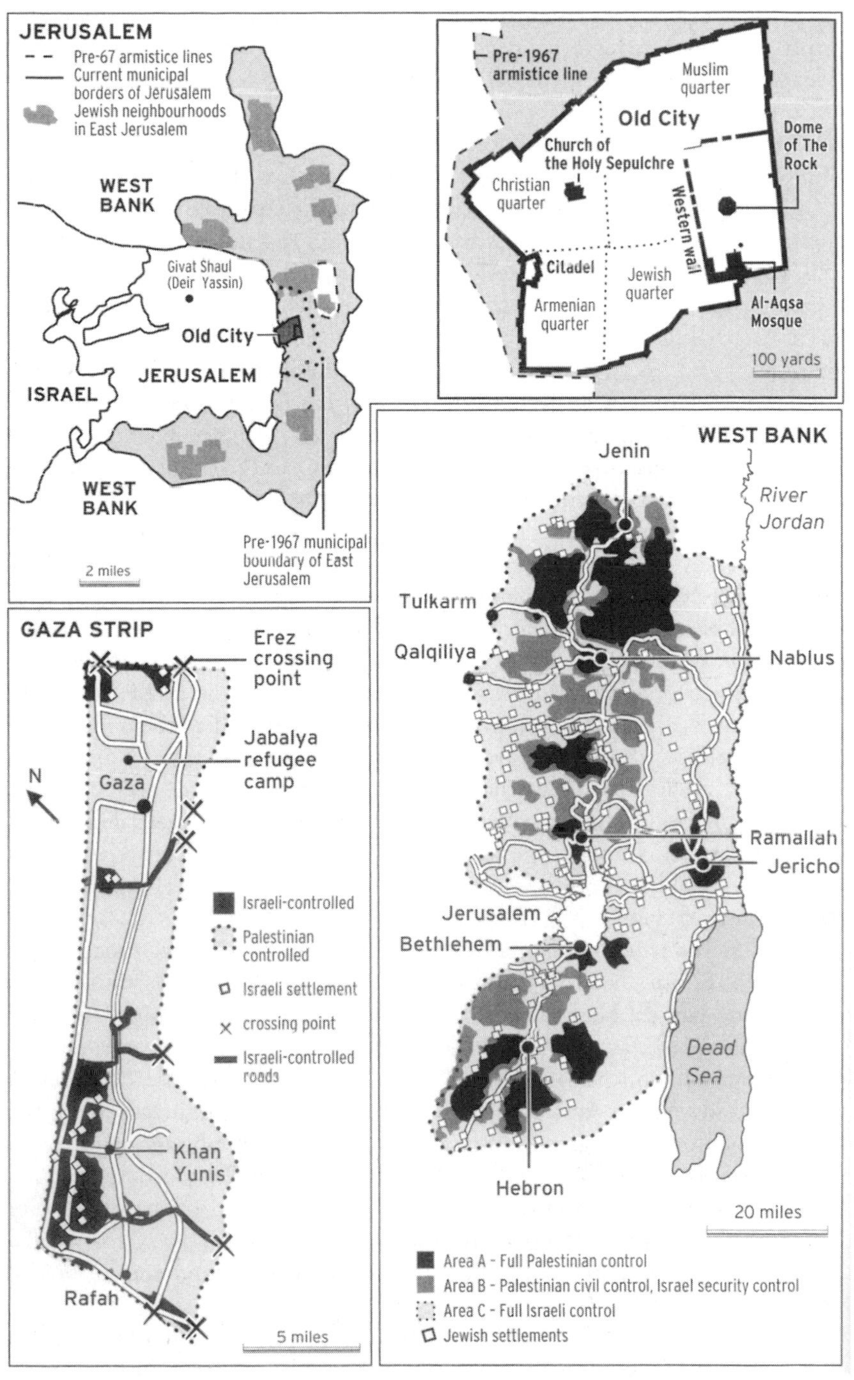

The Occupied Territories prior to the 2005 Israeli withdrawal from the Gaza Strip. (*War without End: Israelis, Palestinians, and the Struggle for a Promised Land* by Anton LaGuardia. New York: St. Martin's Press, 2003, xxiv.)

extremist. Once again, the extremists on both sides seemed to have a veto on progress by simply carrying out terrorist attacks. Rabin's funeral was attended by a slew of world leaders, including President Clinton, King Hussein, and Husni Mubarak. Arafat did not attend the funeral as a security precaution, but he called upon Leah Rabin, Yitzhak's widow, to express his condolences.

Shimon Peres was asked to form a new government; with the outpouring of sympathy in Israel following the assassination, he had little trouble in doing so, and he became the next Israeli prime minister. Even though the vast majority of Israelis expressed support for the peace process in the wake of Rabin's assassination, many of these same people had certain qualms about Peres, who did not have the perceived security credentials and often appeared too eager to trade land for peace. Peres committed himself and his government to taking up the mantle of Rabin and continue the peace process—in fact, he even accelerated it, hoping to utilize the favorable post-Rabin political environment as a base of support.

The Palestinian legislative elections as outlined in Oslo II took place on January 20, 1996. There was high voter turnout, clearly displaying the desire among most Palestinians for a participatory political process that could form the foundation for a functioning democracy—73% of eligible voters in the West Bank and 85% in the Gaza Strip. There were only two candidates for the office of president of the PA, a virtual nobody and Yasser Arafat. The latter garnered 88% of the vote and became the first president of the PA. For the eighty-eight-seat legislature, over 700 candidates ran for office, although Hamas and radical secular groups such as the PFLP boycotted the elections. Arafat's al-Fatah dominated the legislature as well as the composition of his government, but it was an impressive showing that gave Arafat—and the peace process—some much needed legitimacy for the time being. Things seemed to be proceeding fairly smoothly. On the Syrian track, Peres redoubled Israel's efforts to come to an agreement with Damascus, and two rounds of talks between Syrian and Israeli negotiators were held at the Wye Plantation in Maryland, one in December 1995 and the other in January 1996.

But just as a Jewish extremist had potentially blunted the peace process with the assassination of Rabin, in early 1996 it was the turn of Palestinian Islamic extremists. In February and March, Hamas carried out a series of suicide bombings in Israel that killed fifty-nine Israelis and wounded hundreds more. The attacks were ostensibly in response to Israel's assassination of Fathi Shqaqi, an Islamic Jihad leader, in Malta in October 1995, and Yahya Ayyash, otherwise known as the "engineer" for his ability to organize suicide bombings, in January 1996 when his cell phone, rigged by Israeli intelligence agents, exploded in his ear. It is believed that Peres ordered the Ayyash assassination to bolster his security credibility as well as that of the Israeli General Security Services following the perceived failure to protect Rabin. As is usually the case, violence begot violence, and it ultimately ended up costing Peres his position as prime minister.

Despite Arafat's condemnation of the terrorist acts, peace negotiations on all fronts were suspended by Peres. Since Hamas locates its political offices in Damascus, Tel Aviv expected Hafiz al-Asad to publicly condemn the attacks, which he chose not to do, this coming on top of his noticeable silence following the assassination of Rabin. Indeed, quite to the opposite, exhortations over Syrian radio tacitly supported the suicide bombings. This was a major diplomatic faux pas on the part of Asad. Scheduled meetings between Syria and Israel at the Wye Plantation were subsequently called off. This episode certainly paints in stark relief the totally different wavelengths of Syria and Israel with regard to public diplomacy. Asad was always someone who played his cards close to the vest, never giving up any of them until he absolutely had to do so. The pace of Peres' march toward a Syrian–Israeli agreement was already uncomfortably fast for the methodical Syrian president. The Israelis, who had in mind the overtly dramatic public gestures of Anwar al-Sadat that jump-started the Egyptian-Israeli peace process, expected Asad also to do something in the public arena that might reassure the Israelis about his sincere desire for peace.

Asad was a notoriously private man. He was consciously devoid of the dramatic flare of Sadat, who he felt relinquished his most expensive bargaining chips by de facto recognizing Israel before an agreement. The Israelis may have expected too much from Asad in this regard and never really appreciated the fact that even though he was at the apex of an authoritarian structure, he also had a constituency to play to among the Syrian elite, the Syrian population, and the wider Arab world. Beyond that, various elements in the Syrian regime were not shy about firing some warning shots across the bow through state controlled media outlets to send subtle and not so subtle signals to Asad that he needed to slow down a bit in his march toward a peace agreement with Israel, for many of these same elements could be deleteriously affected by an Israeli–Syrian peace treaty. He could not go too far out in front of them, just as Rabin, Peres, and later Ehud Barak could not be seen to be too far out in front of their own respective domestic constituencies. But Asad's hesitancy, including Syria's failure to participate in the multilateral talks or at the Casablanca and Amman economic summit conferences, fed into the claims of those Israelis who from the beginning doubted the sincerity of Syria's interest in peace. This is where Syria's traditional role at the vanguard of Arab nationalism and the rejectionist anti-Israeli front and its oft-stated commitment to the Palestinian cause possibly hampered its ability to break out from this self-professed paradigm and embrace the ameliorating opportunities such as that which presented itself following the suicide attacks. Unfortunately, Hafiz al-Asad probably did not even know what the term "public diplomacy" really meant—and he was never too much interested in finding out.

With the Israeli–Syrian track off-track for the moment, Hizbollah began to launch Katyusha rocket attacks against towns and villages in northern Israel, coupled with intensified operations against Israeli forces in the south Lebanon security zone. Although Hizbollah acts with more independence from Syria than most perceive, it has been utilized as necessary leverage by Damascus in an indirect fashion against Israel. Asad considered Hizbollah to be the other side of the peace negotiations coin, to be cashed when necessary to pressure Israel in the few remaining ways it could do so. This showed—or at least was supposed to show—Israel that there was something to be gained—i.e., quelling the Hizbollah threat—by returning the Golan Heights and something to be lost by not doing so. Hizbollah as well as its other state sponsor, Iran, provide Damascus with some strategic depth in case of war with Israel, a military consideration that was a central feature of Hafiz al-Asad's overall strategic conception vis-à-vis Tel Aviv. Syria was also at the time very wary of improving Israeli–Turkish relations, the two countries having signed extensive defense agreements and engaged in joint military exercises. Damascus tended to see the evolving Israeli–Turkish relationship as a pincer movement designed to weaken Syria, especially at a time when Istanbul was heavily pressuring the Asad regime to cease and desist its support of Kurkish separatist elements (the Kurdistan Workers' Party [PKK], particularly its leader, Abdullah Ocalan) residing in Syria. Hizbollah's attacks could also, then, have been a Syrian response to what it perceived to be a more threatening environment.[21] Israel, however, tends to see Syrian influence over Hizbollah as a threat that must be met with force in order to convince Damascus to de-link itself from the Shiite Islamist group or compel it to stand down.

Unfortunately for Peres, in February, before the Hamas suicide bombings, he had called for early elections to take place in May 1996 that were originally scheduled the following October. At the time it seemed to be a politically astute move, taking advantage of the post-Rabin sentiments that favored the Peres government. But with the Hamas bombings followed so closely by the Hizbollah attacks, the Israeli populace began to see the peace process as unraveling before their very eyes and adopted a more belligerent attitude. This was exactly the type of political atmosphere that was uncomfortable for Peres, perceived as more of a peacenik, whereas it indelibly improved Likud's position as the party that placed security before anything else. Peres could not just sit back and do nothing in response to these attacks in the midst of what was in effect an election campaign against Likud party leader Benjamin (Binyamin) Netanyahu.

The Hizbollah attacks into Israeli proper had violated an unwritten agreement brokered by Warren Christopher in 1993 following another round of Hizbollah and Israeli military exchanges. After Israel's Operation Accountability in 1993, consisting mostly of air attacks and artillery barrages in Lebanon, a cease-fire agreement was reached in which Hizbollah committed itself to only launching attacks against Israeli positions in the security zone and not into Israel itself. Peres' response this time was to launch Operation Grapes of Wrath on April 11 in Lebanon as punishment for the Hizbollah attacks.[22] The military campaign was directed not only against Hizbollah positions but also against various manifestations of the Lebanese government, such as power grids, to convince Beirut that it would suffer too by casting a blind eye toward what Hizbollah was doing in the south. There was also the hope that the general Lebanese population would then turn against Hizbollah even more for bringing the "wrath" of Israel down upon them. It turned out to be a public relations nightmare as the operation led to the displacement of over 400,000 Lebanese civilians and the deaths of over 100 noncombatants due to an Israeli artillery barrage that mistakenly hit a refugee camp in the village of Qana on April 19—of course, all of this destruction and suffering was instantly shown to the world through the global media. By April 27, Christopher again intervened to broker an agreement that temporarily led to a cessation of hostilities—and this time the agreement to confine attacks to the security zone was written down accompanied by a monitoring committee composed of the pertinent parties (Israel, Lebanon, Syria, France, and the United States).

While Peres may have sanctioned Operation Grapes of Wrath in part to toughen up his image to the Israeli electorate prior to the election, because of the international uproar associated with the civilian casualties and displacement in Lebanon in a military campaign that seemed disproportionate to the act that precipitated it, the Israeli prime minister's gamble actually had quite the opposite effect. If anything, it raised doubt among Israeli voters about the ability of Shimon Peres to navigate Israel through an increasingly more hostile regional and domestic environment. This was just enough to allow Benjamin Netanyahu to eke out a victory in the May election, becoming the next Israeli prime minister. Significantly, Israeli actions in Lebanon angered a great many Israeli Arabs, who make up almost one-fifth of the population in Israel and 12% of the electorate. Many of them had relatives in Lebanon. They certainly did not vote for Netanyahu, but they stayed at home in droves, depriving Peres of much needed votes. Netanyahu was a hard-line Likudnik and proponent of Vladimir Jabotinsky's revisionist program who preached "peace with security" instead of "land for peace," and he had vociferously opposed the Oslo process.

RETRENCHMENT

Netanyahu's victory was less than overwhelming, winning by a very narrow margin over Peres. As such, the new prime minister had a difficult time patching together a coalition of parties that would provide him with at least sixty-one votes in the 120-member Israeli Knesset. To be expected, Netanyahu relied heavily on nationalist and religious parties to form a governing coalition, which resulted in their enhanced influence despite their small numbers in the Knesset. In return for joining a coalition, these smaller parties would gain a desired portfolio in the Cabinet or other concessions, usually ones revolving around financial assistance for various pet projects. Because he had to rely on elements opposed to the peace process to form the coalition, Netanyahu adopted in many ways a more critical view of Oslo and Madrid than was envisioned. He did not want just to "slow down" the process but to effectively terminate it.

In the process of trying to do so, while promising peaceful coexistence with the Palestinians, he accelerated once again the settlement process and land confiscation in the West Bank, with approximately 5,000 new housing units under construction in 1997 alone. The government continued to subsidize housing in the Occupied Territories to attract settlers, essentially continuing the traditional prosettler policy of creating facts on the ground that would make it even more difficult for a viable Palestinian state to come into being. Despite the apparent commitments made in the Oslo accords, the continuing Israeli settlement policy was a direct affront to the PA, and it emerged as the biggest threat to Palestinian statehood. The Palestinians viewed it as a sustained and systematic land-creep that obviated their national aspirations and, from their perspective, made a mockery of the peace process. Arafat could and would complain loudly but was powerless to stop it, especially with a U.S. administration that was reluctant to do more than advise against such Israeli activity. Palestinian Islamist groups reacted by carrying out more attacks, with the Israelis not only responding in force but also pressuring Arafat to do more to police his own in order to prevent such attacks. Arafat, as a result, was placed in the unenviable position of something of a security guard hired by Israel to do a job the Israelis would rather not do themselves—essentially doing Israel's dirty work. As Raja Shehadeh somberly put it:

> With the Arab markets open to them now that the Palestinians have signed an agreement with Israel, and, in the words of Shimon Peres, with "Arafat taking care of terror," Israel achieved what it had for years worked for: relieving itself from the administration and governance over the Palestinians living in the Occupied Areas while retaining full control over the settlements and Israelis living in them. At the same time it left all options open especially the very real option of eventual annexation of large areas of the settlement blocs to Israel.[23]

For his part, Arafat was unable and unwilling to crack down on Palestinian militants in the fashion that Israel wanted; to the Palestinian leader, to do so would be suicidal in addition to the fact that, à la Asad, he probably saw groups such as Hamas as indirect forms of pressure on Israel and he would not come down hard on them unless he received something substantial in return. He began to realize that much of what his critics said with regard to his giving up too much when he signed the Oslo accords was most likely correct.

What remained of Oslo seemed in danger of unraveling altogether. This became readily apparent in September 1996 when Netanyahu gave the green light to the opening of a second entrance to the archeological site known as the Hasmonean Tunnel. This entrance was close to the Dome of the Rock, and the Palestinians as well as the Jordanians and Egyptians had not been consulted prior to the opening. While seemingly trivial in and of itself, in such a hotly contested area as the Temple Mount/Haram al-Sharif where archeological evidence could potentially be used in a proprietary manner, any slight alteration could be explosive. It was. Ensuing riots gave the appearance of a mini-intifada in the midst of the Oslo process, with eighty-six Palestinians and fifteen Israeli troops being killed. It also at a very early stage of Netanyahu's term in office severely circumscribed the possibility of a positive working relationship with Arafat.

In an attempt to rescue the Oslo process, Israel and the PA negotiated a settlement regarding the city of Hebron. The city of Hebron in the West Bank is holy to both Jews and Muslims as it is the location of the Mosque of Ibrahim (Abraham) that also happens to be the Jewish Tomb of the Patriarchs. Until Baruch Goldstein went on his rampage in 1994, Jews and Muslims had prayed at the same site in separate prayer areas. Through the efforts primarily of Gush Emunim, about 450 militant Jewish settlers (most of whom belonged to Meir Kahane's Kach party) established fortified compounds in Hebron amid 200,000 Palestinians. The Israeli army went to great efforts to protect the Jews in the city. From the Palestinian viewpoint, it was a potent symbol of disproportion in their overall predicament under occupation. The Hebron agreement essentially divided the city into a Jewish area and a much larger Arab zone, with the Palestinians assuming governance in their area. In the agreement, Israel also committed itself to three further withdrawals, although it did not stipulate the nature of the withdrawals, while the PA promised to intensify its efforts to curb terrorism and to cooperate with Israeli forces in terms of enhancing overall security. Many hailed the Hebron accord as revivifying the Oslo process, but it was an ominous sign that so much political capital had to be expended for apparently so little; from the Palestinians' perspective, it also proved to be very worrisome that the Israeli government could not (or would not) remove 450 settlers in a city that was clearly demarcated as Palestinian—and that the United States seemed unwilling or unable to insert itself in the mix in a more assertive fashion.

President Clinton finally decided to intervene more directly in the peace process by 1998. With Netanyahu in power, the Clinton administration had been hesitant to commit the prestige of the office of the president when there was very little hope of progress to begin with. Dennis Ross, who continued as U.S. Middle East envoy during the Clinton years, made numerous trips to Damascus, for instance, before and after the three years Netanyahu was in office but none during his tenure in power.[24] Clinton officials, however, began to realize that the lack of progress on the Israeli–Palestinian front was detrimental to the U.S. policy of containing Iraq and maintaining the UN inspection teams that had been placed there searching for weapons of mass destruction in the aftermath of the Gulf War. Saddam Hussein was emboldened by the breakdown of the peace processes, championing the Palestinian cause (and eventually even offering financial aid to the families of Palestinian suicide bombers) and improving low-level relations with Syria, the latter badly needing the economic boost that enhanced trade with Iraq could provide. There were multiple showdowns between the United States and Iraq during 1998 over the continued presence of the UN inspection teams, ultimately leading toward the end of the year to another U.S. air bombing and cruise missile campaign against selected Iraqi sites—the UN inspectors were withdrawn, not to return again until early 2003. In order to help garner more regional and international support for his policy vis-à-vis Iraq, Clinton needed to make progress on the Israeli–Palestinian front.

Clinton's intervention succeeded in bringing Arafat and Netanyahu to the Wye Plantation in Maryland for talks in October 1998. Only after some acrimonious discussions, in which Clinton often sided with Arafat, did the two leaders sign what came to be known as the Wye memorandum or Wye accords. Essentially, the agreement only provided for an additional Israeli withdrawal from 13% of the West Bank, while restating the land-for-peace principle delineated in the Oslo agreements. While seemingly minor, Netanyahu's reaffirming the land-for-peace formula split his Likud party as well as alienated some of the smaller nationalist and religious parties in the coalition, all of whom were steadfastly against the long-established land-for-peace framework. Due to the opposition, which could have caused his governing coalition to break apart, thus necessitating new elections, Netanyahu suspended any planned withdrawal from that 13% of the West Bank agreed to at the Wye Plantation. Netanyahu was now between a rock and a hard place: in an attempt to placate different constituencies, he placated no one. This was not an enviable position during the run-up to the 1999 elections. In such circumstances, Netanyahu naturally tacked toward his support base in Likud and cozied up further to orthodox Jewish parties such as Shas with financial subsidies. He seemed to many in the Israeli electorate to be beholden to Israeli special interests at the expense of pursuing peace; as with Shamir, his frosty relationship with Clinton did not enhance his "electability."

The result was the decisive victory (56% to 44% of the votes) of the new Labor party leader, Ehud Barak, in the election on May 17, 1999.

A LAST PUSH

Even with Barak's decisive victory for the presidency, the Knesset was still composed of a variety of smaller parties, with neither Labor nor Likud able to assemble a ruling coalition by itself. This was largely the result of a change in the election laws in Israel that began in the 1996 election that brought Netanyahu to power. Israeli voters cast two ballots, one for the prime minister and the other for the party list; therefore, there was an explosion of parties represented in the Knesset that received a certain minimum of votes, especially as many voters split the two ballots—e.g., voting for Barak on the prime minister ballot but then voting for non-Labor parties on the party list ballot. There were thirty-three parties that put forth candidates in the 1999 election, with fifteen of them gaining seats in the Knesset, a number of them representing the narrowest of interests—e.g., one party that fielded candidates represented taxi drivers. As such, despite his landslide victory, in such a factionalized political environment Barak was compelled to form a coalition in which he had to include parties that at times inhibited his ability to pursue peace negotiations in the manner he had wanted. The Jewish orthodox party Shas became the third largest bloc behind Labor and Likud in the Knesset. Although Shas did not necessarily oppose the peace process, it was able to win concessions from Barak in the sociocultural arena in pursuit of its objective of a state ruled by strict Jewish law.

In the person of Barak, however, Israel elected a prime minister in the mold of Yitzhak Rabin; indeed, Barak was something of a protégé of Rabin. The new prime minister was a military man as a former chief of staff of the IDF and the most decorated soldier in Israeli history. Israelis could be more trustful, then, of Barak's efforts to reignite peace talks on both tracks without sacrificing Israeli security, as was the case with Rabin. He was a "dovish hawk."[25] Again, similar to Rabin, although he reengaged with the Palestinians, Barak tended to prefer the Syrian track, if anything, to help facilitate one of his primary foreign policy objectives: the withdrawal of Israeli troops from Lebanon. Barak also had some Anwar al-Sadat in him, prone to the dramatic, bold move to secure a peace agreement—and his place in history. But, as discussed earlier, this was the antithesis of Hafiz al-Asad's negotiating style, to which a succession of U.S. negotiators can attest. Dennis Ross notes that "Asad did not like to rush under any circumstances; it was not his style. He was never in a hurry lest it appear that he needed an agreement more than the other side. And that, of course, was the very message Barak would be sending—he was anxious, and if so, why would Asad concede anything?"[26] The differences in negotiating style would prove to be fatal under the bright lights of international attention and expectations by early 2000.

Lebanon had long become a quagmire for Israeli troops due to the effective guerilla campaign carried out by Hizbollah. With Israeli deaths incrementally mounting in south Lebanon, the Israeli public had grown quite tired of the whole ordeal. Barak wanted a withdrawal from Lebanon to be part of an overall settlement with Syria. In this way, Israel would not be seen as cutting and running, and Hizbollah would not be perceived as having won. In addition, Syria could be brought on board as a guarantor of security along the Israeli–Lebanese border. If there was an Israeli–Syrian peace agreement, what need then would Damascus have for Hizbollah vis-à-vis Israel? Also, Barak seemed to prefer dealing with Asad rather than Arafat, whom no Israeli leader ever really trusted. Asad was, from the Israeli perspective, difficult to deal with as well. The Syrian president once commented that "Our stance in the battle for peace will not be less courageous than our stances on the battlefield."[27] Or as Shimon Peres once observed, Asad was "conducting the peace process just as one conducts a military campaign—slowly, patiently, directed by strategic and tactical considerations."[28] Given this, however, Asad could be trusted to comply with any agreement reached, and he was more straight-forward with regard to the issues that needed to be discussed. As Ross states, Barak "knew that what mattered to the Syrians was the land, and that what most mattered to Israelis was security and water."[29] In addition, Asad's son Bashar, the putative heir to his father, had praised Barak following the election, which many Israelis believe was a signal sent by Damascus, thus encouraging even more attention to this track.

Syrian–Israeli negotiations heated up with behind-the-scenes contacts during the summer and fall of 1999, especially as the second-term Clinton administration was eager to broker a comprehensive Arab–Israeli peace before it left office in January 2001. This would be the capstone to Clinton's presidency, creating a legacy apart from the scandals and impeachment that rocked his administration in the second term. In addition, Asad may well have wanted to make a deal with a willing Israeli prime minister while he could so that Bashar could inherit a more congenial regional environment when the time came. Asad's deteriorating health, which outside observers had been commenting on for years, appeared also to become an issue of increasing concern. American negotiators could see for themselves that Asad was becoming more gaunt and frail in late 1999 and into 2000. They had also heard reports from other Arab state officials that his ability to engage in everyday affairs was limited and that even his lucidity was called into question at times. One sensed that the momentum building toward direct Syrian–Israeli negotiations in late 1999 was a race against time, a last-ditch attempt to orchestrate an agreement before being overtaken by events, namely the death of Asad.

The climax came in January 2000, when Barak and his support staff met with Syrian Foreign Minister Farouk al-Shar'a and his staff at a retreat in Shepherdstown, West Virginia, about an hour and fifteen minutes from Washington by car. Camp David was specifically not chosen because the Syrians in no way, shape, or form wanted to be associated with Sadat and the Egyptians at Camp David in 1978; and the Wye Plantation was no longer a viable option since it had been the locale used by Arafat and Barak to produce the Wye accords in October 1998. Shepherdstown was still close enough to Washington for Clinton to fly back and forth via helicopter to help mediate the talks when necessary. A good deal of progress was made at Shepherdstown, building upon the Syrian–Israeli talks of 1994–1996. Ross, who was present at the meetings, was very impressed with the flexibility on the part of the Syrians, which to him showed the seriousness with which they were pursuing a peace agreement; indeed, while acknowledging that there was enough blame to go around for the failure of a definitive agreement emerging out of the talks at Shepherdstown, Ross explicitly states that "Barak was more at fault than the Syrians."[30] Even so, the process was not dead after Shepherdstown, especially with a U.S. president who was willing to take some risks in the pursuit of an agreement. Syrian officials commented that at the time an agreement was 80% of the way there.

An ill-timed leak of a draft agreement between Syria and Israel crafted by the Americans at Shepherdstown soon after the parties adjourned inestimably complicated the progress that had taken place. It is highly likely that the draft was intentionally leaked by someone in the Barak government as a trial balloon, for Barak was very concerned about public support for his position. It could also have been designed to drum up domestic support for Barak in the negotiations as well as an Israeli public referendum promised by Barak on any Syrian–Israeli accord. The leak, which confirmed some significant concessions by Damascus, embarrassed, if not infuriated, Asad, who would receive indirect criticism in Syria for having gone too far without the requisite guaranteed returns. It certainly compelled him to lurch backward from the negotiating table.

Despite this, contacts continued at the insistence of the United States, and President Clinton threw the full weight of his office into the fray by meeting personally with

Hafiz al-Asad in Geneva, Switzerland, in March 2000 in what appeared to be a last-gasp attempt to salvage an accord. The fact that Asad met him in Geneva created a great deal of public anticipation that an agreement was at hand. They would be disappointed.

NOTES

1. For an excellent essay on this subject see Amatzia Baram, "U.S. Input into Iraqi Decisionmaking, 1988–1990," in David W. Lesch, editor, *The Middle East and the United States: A Historical and Political Reassessment*, 3rd ed. (Boulder: Westview Press, 2003), 328–356.

2. Quoted in Moshe Maoz, "Changes in Syria's Regional Strategic Position vis-à-vis Israel," in Moshe Maoz, Joseph Ginat, and Onn Winckler, eds., *Modern Syria: From Ottoman Rule to Pivotal Role in the Middle East* (Brighton: Sussex Academic Press, 1999), 266. Also see David W. Lesch, *The New Lion of Damascus: Bashar al-Asad and Modern Syria* (New Haven: Yale University Press, 2005), 52–56. For an illuminating treatment of the transformation of Soviet policy toward the Middle East under Gorbachev, see Georgiy Mirsky, "The Soviet Perception of the U.S. Threat," in Lesch, *The Middle East and the United States,* 397–405.

3. This also contributed to Israeli and Iranian support of separatist Kurdish movements in Iraq to tie down the Iraqi military. The Algiers accord between Iraq and Iran in 1975, which, among other things, resulted in the end of formal Iranian support for the Kurds in Iraq, was not looked upon too kindly by the Israelis.

4. Quoted in Maoz, "Changes in Syria's Regional Strategic Position," 267.

5. For Syria, another quid pro quo was the Bush administration's looking the other way in late 1990 when Syrian troops helped to force out Christian militia leader General Michel Aoun, thus securing Damascus' dominant position in Lebanon. Aoun had actually been receiving support, mostly financial, from Saddam Hussein as something of a payback for Syria's backing of Iran during the Iran–Iraq war.

6. Dennis Ross, *The Missing Peace: The Inside Story of the Fight for Middle East Peace* (New York: Farrar, Straus and Giroux, 2004), 48–49.

7. For example, before the Gulf War the PLO received on average about $250 million annually from the Arab Gulf states, most of it coming from Saudi Arabia and Kuwait. Only $40 million made its way from the Gulf to the PLO in 1992.

8. Moscow established a consular office in Israel in 1987, with Israel doing the same in Moscow in 1988. Facilitating the resumption of diplomatic relations was the ouster of hardliners in the Kremlin who were opposed to the move in the abortive coup in September 2001.

9. In one classic piece of irony, after Shamir had finished his opening speech in which he accused Syria of sponsoring terrorism, Syria's Minister of Foreign Affairs Farouk al-Shar'a (Hafiz al-Asad did not attend) in his opening remarks pulled out an old photo of a young Yitzhak Shamir as a "most wanted" terrorist on Interpol's list following the assassination of Count Folke Bernadotte in 1948. In effect, Shar'a was saying, "how dare *you* call *us* terrorists." This is one of the few occasions when the Syrians would have the upper hand vis-à-vis the Israelis in any negotiations, if only for a brief moment bordering on a publicity stunt.

10. In this, the Bush administration was supported by some Jewish American organizations, such as Americans for Peace Now.

11. On this discussion, see Lesch, *The New Lion of Damascus*, 146–148.

12. At the time of the September 1993 signing of the Declaration of Principles, there were approximately 120,000 Israeli settlers in the West Bank, 4,500 in the Gaza Strip, and 160,000 in East Jerusalem. At the same time there were approximately 1.5 million Palestinians in the West Bank, 830,000 in the Gaza Strip, and 180,000 in East Jerusalem.

13. Ross, *The Missing Peace,* 111.

14. In yet another sign of the challenges to the interim process, at the final agreement detailing the Gaza–Jericho plan in Cairo on May 4, Arafat actually bolted out of the proceedings after examining one of the documents that included a map of Jericho. The PLO chair wanted more square mileage attached to the Jericho area. Finally, Rabin agreed to attach an amendment to the agreement stating that the map was not the final word, and the Israelis later assented to twenty-five extra square miles to the Jericho area under PA control.

15. Ian J. Bickerton and Carla L. Klausner, *A Concise History of the Arab–Israeli Conflict* (Upper Saddle River, NJ: Prentice Hall, 2002), 282.

16. For a firsthand account of this stage of the Israeli–Syrian negotiations, see Itamar Rabinovich, *The Brink of Peace* (Princeton: Princeton University Press, 1998).

17. Ross, *The Missing Peace,* 574.

18. Ibid., 525.

19. The secondary boycott entailed not conducting business with companies that did business with Israel; the tertiary boycott was not doing business with companies that do business with companies that do business with Israel. The primary boycott was pretty much followed by the Arab states (when they were not at peace with Israel), whereas the secondary and tertiary boycotts were unevenly applied.

20. Israel had already received something of a peace dividend from the peace process. Foreign investment in Israel increased from $72 million in 1990 to $197 million in 1995. Raja Shehadeh, *From Occupation to Interim Accords: Israel and the Palestinian Territories* (London: Kluwer Law International, 1997), 28–29.

21. Turkey had come to understand that supporting Israel inestimably helped its position in Washington (particularly vis-à-vis Greek lobbyists), especially as pro-Israeli groups often lobbied on behalf of Turkish causes that were not inimical to Israeli interests. On this dynamic, see Efraim Anbar, *The Resilience of Israeli–Turkish Relations* (Ramat Gan, Israel: Begin-Sadat Center for Strategic Studies, 2005).

22. And just days after former President George H. W. Bush visited with Hafiz al-Asad in Damascus during a Middle East trip to several countries.

23. Shehadeh, *From Occupation to Interim Accords,* 29.

24. The failure of the 1997 Doha economic summit, especially when compared to its predecessors in Casablanca and Amman, also indicated to Clinton administration officials that the peace process was breaking down.

25. William L. Cleveland, *A History of the Modern Middle East* (Boulder: Westview Press, 2004), 514.

26. Ross, *The Missing Peace,* 523.

27. Quoted in Patrick Seale and Linda Butler, "Assad's Regional Strategy and the Challenge from Netanyahu," *Journal of Palestine Studies* 26, no. 1 (1996): 36–37.

28. Quoted in Raymond Hinnebusch, "Does Syria Want Peace: Syrian Policy in the Syrian–Israeli Negotiations," *Journal of Palestine Studies* 26, no. 1 (1996): 44–45.

29. Ross, *The Missing Peace,* 517.

30. Ibid., 569. The Syrians, for instance, agreed for the first time to an American presence at an early-warning station in Mount Hermon for five years after the Israeli withdrawal from the Golan Heights, which had been a major hurdle to that point. Along these lines, Ross also states the following: "Amnon Shahak [former deputy chief of staff of the IDF, minister of tourism under Barak who was involved in the Syrian negotiations] was to tell me in the summer of 2002 that the Middle East changed the day in Shepherdstown when, unbeknownst to us, Barak received the results of a poll that made doing the deal with Syria more problematic than he had thought. It was at that time that Barak decided to hold fast in Shepherdstown regardless of the Syrian moves. It was then that a deal was probably lost" (p. 589).

Madrid Peace Conference Letter of Invitation

October 18, 1991

After extensive consultations with Arab states, Israel and the Palestinians, the United States and the Soviet Union believe that an historic opportunity exists to advance the prospects for genuine peace throughout the region. The United States and the Soviet Union are prepared to assist the parties to achieve a just, lasting and comprehensive peace settlement, through direct negotiations along two tracks, between Israel and the Arab states, and between Israel and the Palestinians, based on United Nations Security Council Resolutions 242 and 338. The objective of this process is real peace.

Toward that end, the president of the U.S. and the president of the USSR invite you to a peace conference, which their countries will co-sponsor, followed immediately by direct negotiations. The conference will be convened in Madrid on October 30, 1991.

President Bush and President Gorbachev request your acceptance of this invitation no later than 6 P.M. Washington time, October 23, 1991, in order to ensure proper organization and preparation of the conference.

Direct bilateral negotiations will begin four days after the opening of the conference. Those parties who wish to attend multilateral negotiations will convene two weeks after the opening of the conference to organize those negotiations. The co-sponsors believe that those negotiations should focus on region-wide issues of water, refugee issues, environment, economic development, and other subjects of mutual interest.

The co-sponsors will chair the conference which will be held at the ministerial level. Governments to be invited include Israel, Syria, Lebanon and Jordan. Palestinians will be invited and attend as part of a joint Jordanian–Palestinian delegation. Egypt will be invited to the conference as a participant. The European Community will be a participant in the conference, alongside the United States and the Soviet Union and will be represented by its presidency. The Gulf Cooperation Council will be invited to send its Secretary-general to the conference as an observer, and GCC member states will be invited to participate in organizing the negotiations on multilateral issues. The United Nations will be invited to send an observer, representing the secretary-general.

The conference will have no power to impose solutions on the parties or veto agreements reached by them. It will have no authority to make decisions for the parties and no ability to vote on issues of results. The conference can reconvene only with the consent of all the parties.

With respect to negotiations between Israel and Palestinians who are part of the joint Jordanian–Palestinian delegation, negotiations will be conducted in phases, beginning with talks on interim self-government arrangements. These talks will be conducted with the objective of reaching agreement within one year. Once agreed, the interim self-government arrangements will last for a period of five years; beginning the third year of the period of interim self-government arrangements, negotiations will take place on permanent status. These permanent status negotiations, and the negotiations between Israel and the Arab states, will take place on the basis of Resolutions 242 and 338.

It is understood that the co-sponsors are committed to making this process succeed. It is their intention to convene the conference and negotiations with those parties who agree to attend.

The co-sponsors believe that this process offers the promise of ending decades of confrontation and conflict and the hope of a lasting peace. Thus, the co-sponsors hope that the parties will approach these negotiations in a spirit of good will and mutual respect. In this way, the peace process can begin to break down the mutual suspicions and mistrust that perpetuate the conflict and allow the parties to begin to resolve their differences. Indeed, only through such a process can real peace and reconciliation among the Arab states, Israel and the Palestinians be achieved. And only through this process can the peoples of the Middle East attain the peace and security they richly deserve.

Bernard Reich, *Arab–Israeli Conflict and Conciliation: A Documentary History* (Westport, CT: Praeger, 1995), 226–228.

Israel–PLO Recognition

September 9, 1993

LETTER FROM ARAFAT TO RABIN:

The signing of the Declaration of Principles marks a new era in the history of the Middle East. In firm conviction thereof, I would like to confirm the following PLO commitments:

The PLO recognizes the right of the State of Israel to exist in peace and security.

The PLO accepts United Nations Security Council Resolutions 242 and 338.

The PLO commits itself to the Middle East peace process, and to a peaceful resolution of the conflict between the two sides and declares that all outstanding issues relating to permanent status will be resolved through negotiations.

The PLO considers that the signing of the Declaration of Principles constitutes a historic event, inaugurating a new epoch of peaceful coexistence, free from violence and all other acts which endanger peace and stability, Accordingly, the PLO renounces the use of terrorism and other acts of violence and will assume responsibility over all PLO elements and personnel in order to assure their compliance, prevent violations and discipline violators.

In view of the promise of a new era and the signing of the Declaration of Principles and based on Palestinian acceptance of Security Council Resolutions 242 and 338, the PLO affirms that those articles of the Palestinian Covenant which deny Israel's right to exist, and the provisions of the Covenant which are inconsistent with the commitments of this letter are now inoperative and no longer valid. Consequently, the PLO undertakes to submit to the Palestinian National Council for formal approval the necessary changes in regard to the Palestinian Covenant.

LETTER FROM ARAFAT TO NORWEGIAN FOREIGN MINISTER:

I would like to confirm to you that, upon the signing of the Declaration of Principles, the PLO encourages and calls upon the Palestinian people in the West Bank and Gaza Strip to take part in the steps leading to the normalization of life, rejecting violence and terrorism, contributing to peace and stability and participating actively in shaping reconstruction, economic development and cooperation.

LETTER FROM RABIN TO ARAFAT:

In response to your letter of September 9, 1993, I wish to confirm to you that, in light of the PLO commitments included in your letter, the Government of Israel has decided to recognize the PLO as the representative of the Palestinian people and commence negotiations with the PLO within the Middle East peace process.

Bernard Reich, *Arab–Israeli Conflict and Conciliation: A Documentary History* (Westport, CT: Praeger, 1995), 229–230.

Israel–Palestine Liberation Organization Agreement: 1993

The Government of the State of Israel and the Palestinian team representing the Palestinian people agree that it is time to put an end to decades of confrontation and conflict, recognize their mutual legitimate and political rights, and strive to live in peaceful coexistence and mutual dignity and security to achieve a just, lasting and comprehensive peace settlement and historic reconciliation through the agreed political process. Accordingly, the two sides agree to the following principles.

ARTICLE I AIM OF THE NEGOTIATIONS

The aim of the Israeli Palestinian negotiations within the current Middle East peace process is, among other things, to establish a Palestinian Interim Self-Government Authority, the elected Council (the "Council"), for the Palestinian people in the West Bank and the Gaza Strip, for a transitional period not exceeding five years, leading to a permanent settlement based on Security Council Resolutions 242 and 338.

It is understood that the interim arrangements are an integral part of the whole peace process and that the negotiations on the permanent status will lead to implementation of Security Council Resolutions 242 and 338.

ARTICLE II FRAMEWORK FOR THE INTERIM PERIOD

The agreed framework for the interim period is set in this declaration of principles.

ARTICLE III ELECTIONS

1. In order that the Palestinian people in the West Bank and Gaza Strip may govern themselves according to democratic principles, direct, free and general political

elections will be held for the Council under agreed supervision and international observation, while Palestinian police will insure public order.

2. An agreement will be concluded on the exact mode and conditions of the elections in accordance with the protocol attached as Annex I, with the goal of holding the elections not later than nine months after the entry into force of this Declaration of Principles.

3. The elections will constitute a significant interim preparatory step toward the realization of the legitimate rights of the Palestinian people and their just requirements.

ARTICLE IV JURISDICTION

Jurisdiction of the Council will cover West Bank and Gaza territory, except for issues that will be negotiated in the permanent status negotiations. The two sides view the West Bank and Gaza Strip as a single territorial unit, whose integrity will be preserved during the interim period.

ARTICLE V TRANSITIONAL PERIOD AND PERMANENT STATUS NEGOTIATIONS

1. The five-year transitional period will begin upon the withdrawal from the Gaza Strip and Jericho area.

2. Permanent status negotiations will commence as soon as possible, but not later than the beginning of the third year of the interim period between the Government of Israel and the Palestinian peoples representatives.

3. It is understood that these negotiations shall cover remaining issues, including: Jerusalem, refugees, settlements, security arrangements, border, relations and cooperation with their neighbors, and other issues of common interest.

4. The two parties agreed that the outcome of the permanent status negotiations should not be prejudiced or preempted by agreements reached for the interim period.

ARTICLE VI PREPARATORY TRANSFER OF POWERS AND RESPONSIBILITIES

1. Upon the entry into force of this Declaration of Principles and withdrawal from the Gaza and Jericho area, a transfer of authority from Israeli military government and its Civil Administration to the authorized Palestinians for this task, as detailed herein, will commence. This transfer of authority will be of preparatory nature until the inauguration of the Council.

2. Immediately after the entry into force of this Declaration of Principles and the withdrawal from the Gaza Strip and the Jericho area, with the view of promoting economic development in the West Bank and Gaza Strip, authority will be transferred to the Palestinians on the following spheres: education and culture, health, social welfare, direct taxation, and tourism, the Palestinian side will commence in building the Palestinian police, as agreed upon. Pending the inauguration of the Council, the

two parties may negotiate the transfer of additional powers and responsibilities, as agreed upon.

ARTICLE VII INTERIM AGREEMENT

1. The Israeli and Palestinian delegations will negotiate an agreement on the interim period (the "Interim Agreement").

2. The Interim Agreement shall specify, among other things, the structure of the Council, the number of its members, and the transfer of powers and responsibilities from the Israeli military government and its Civil Administration to the Council. The Interim Agreement shall also specify the Council's executive authority, legislative authority in accordance with Article IX below, and the independent Palestinian judicial organs.

3. The Interim Agreement shall include arrangements, to be implemented upon the inauguration of the Council, for the assumption by the Council of all of the powers and responsibilities transferred previously in accordance with Article VI above.

4. In order to enable the Council to promote economic growth, upon its inauguration, the Council will establish, among other things, a Palestinian Electricity Authority, a Gaza Sea Port Authority, a Palestinian Development Bank, a Palestinian Export Promotion Board, a Palestinian Environmental Authority, a Palestinian Land Authority and a Palestinian Water Administration Authority, and any other authorities agreed upon, in accordance with the Interim Agreement that will specify their powers and responsibilities.

5. After the inauguration of the Council, the Civil Administration will be dissolved, and the Israeli military government will be withdrawn.

ARTICLE VIII PUBLIC ORDER AND SECURITY

In order to guarantee public order and internal security for the Palestinians of the West Bank and Gaza Strip, the Council will establish a strong police force, while Israel will continue to carry the responsibility for defending against external threats, as well as the responsibility for overall security of Israelis for the purpose of safeguarding their internal security and public order.

ARTICLE IX LAWS AND MILITARY ORDERS

1. The Council will be empowered to legislate, in accordance with the Interim Agreement, within all authorities transferred to it.

2. Both parties will review jointly laws and military orders presently in force in remaining spheres.

ARTICLE X JOINT ISRAELI–PALESTINIAN LIAISON COMMITTEE

In order to provide for a smooth implementation of this Declaration of Principles and any subsequent agreements pertaining to the interim period, upon the entry into force of this Declaration of Principles, a Joint Israeli-Palestinian Liaison Committee will be established in order to deal with issues requiring coordination, other issues of common interest, and disputes.

ARTICLE XI ISRAELI–PALESTINIAN COOPERATION IN ECONOMIC FIELDS

Recognizing the mutual benefit of cooperation in promoting the development of the West Bank, the Gaza Strip and Israel, upon the entry into force of this Declaration of Principles, an Israeli– Palestinian Economic Cooperation Committee will be established in order to develop and implement in a cooperative manner the programs identified in the protocols attached as Annex III and Annex IV.

ARTICLE XII LIAISON AND COOPERATION WITH JORDAN AND EGYPT

The two parties will invite the Governments of Jordan and Egypt to participate in establishing further liaison and cooperation arrangements between the Government of Israel and the Palestinian representatives on one hand, and the Governments of Jordan and Egypt, on the other hand, to promote cooperation between them. These arrangements will include the constitution of a Continuing Committee that will decide by agreement on the modalities of admission of persons displaced from the West Bank and Gaza Strip in 1967, together with necessary measures to prevent disruption and disorder. Other matters of common concern will be dealt with by the Committee.

ARTICLE XIII REDEPLOYMENT OF ISRAELI FORCES

1. After the entry into force of this Declaration of Principles, and not later than the eve of elections for the Council, a redeployment of Israeli military forces in the West Bank and the Gaza Strip will take place, in addition to withdrawal of Israeli forces carried out in accordance with Article XIV.
2. In redeploying its military forces, Israel will be guided by the principle that its military forces should be redeployed outside populated areas.
3. Further redeployments to specified locations will be gradually implemented commensurate with the assumption of responsibility for public order and internal security by the Palestinian police force pursuant to Article VIII above.

ARTICLE XIV ISRAELI WITHDRAWAL FROM THE GAZA STRIP AND JERICHO AREA

Israel will withdraw from the Gaza Strip and Jericho area, as detailed in the protocol attached as Annex II.

ARTICLE XV RESOLUTION OF DISPUTES

1. Disputes arising out of the application or interpretation of the Declaration of Principles, or any subsequent agreements pertaining to the interim period, shall be resolved by negotiations through the Joint Liaison Committee to be established pursuant to Article X above.

2. Disputes which cannot be settled by negotiations may be solved by a mechanism of conciliation to be agreed upon by the parties.

3. The parties may agree to submit to arbitration disputes relating to the interim period, which cannot be settled through reconciliation. To this end, upon the agreement of both parties, the parties will establish an Arbitration Committee.

ARTICLE XVI ISRAELI–PALESTINIAN COOPERATION CONCERNING REGIONAL PROGRAMS

Both parties view the multilateral working groups as an appropriate instrument for promoting a "Marshall Plan" for the West Bank and Gaza Strip as indicated in the protocol attached as Annex IV.

ARTICLE XVII MISCELLANEOUS PROVISIONS

1. This Declaration of Principles will enter into force one month after its signing.

2. All protocols annexed to this Declaration of Principles and Agreed Minutes pertaining thereto shall be regarded as an integral part hereof.

---

http://www.yale.edu/lawweb/avalon/mideast/isrplo.htm (accessed February 1, 2006).

The Israeli–Palestinian Interim Agreement on the West Bank and the Gaza Strip, Washington, D.C. (September 28, 1995)

The Government of the State of Israel and the Palestine Liberation Organization (hereinafter "the PLO"), the representative of the Palestinian people;

PREAMBLE

WITHIN the framework of the Middle East peace process initiated at Madrid in October 1991;

REAFFIRMING their determination to put an end to decades of confrontation and to live in peaceful coexistence, mutual dignity and security, while recognizing their mutual legitimate and political rights;

REAFFIRMING their desire to achieve a just, lasting and comprehensive peace settlement and historic reconciliation through the agreed political process;

RECOGNIZING that the peace process and the new era that it has created, as well as the new relationship established between the two Parties as described above, are irreversible, and the determination of the two Parties to maintain, sustain and continue the peace process;

RECOGNIZING that the aim of the Israeli–Palestinian negotiations within the current Middle East peace process is, among other things, to establish a Palestinian Interim Self-Government Authority, i.e. the elected Council (hereinafter "the Council" or "the Palestinian Council"), and the elected Ra'ees of the Executive Authority, for the Palestinian people in the West Bank and the Gaza Strip, for a transitional period not exceeding five years from the date of signing the Agreement on the Gaza Strip and the Jericho Area (hereinafter "the Gaza-Jericho Agreement") on May 4, 1994, leading to a permanent settlement based on Security Council Resolutions 242 and 338;

REAFFIRMING their understanding that the interim self-government arrangements contained in this Agreement are an integral part of the whole peace process, that the negotiations on the permanent status, that will start as soon as possible but not later than May 4, 1996, will lead to the implementation of Security Council Resolutions 242 and 338, and that the Interim Agreement shall settle all the issues of the interim period and that no such issues will be deferred to the agenda of the permanent status negotiations;

REAFFIRMING their adherence to the mutual recognition and commitments expressed in the letters dated September 9, 1993, signed by and exchanged between the Prime Minister of Israel and the Chairman of the PLO;

DESIROUS of putting into effect the Declaration of Principles on Interim Self-Government Arrangements signed at Washington, DC on September 13, 1993, and the Agreed Minutes thereto (hereinafter "the DOP") and in particular Article III and Annex I concerning the holding of direct, free and general political elections for the Council and the Ra'ees of the Executive Authority in order that the Palestinian people in the West Bank, Jerusalem and the Gaza Strip may democratically elect accountable representatives;

RECOGNIZING that these elections will constitute a significant interim preparatory step toward the realization of the legitimate rights of the Palestinian people and their just requirements and will provide a democratic basis for the establishment of Palestinian institutions;

REAFFIRMING their mutual commitment to act, in accordance with this Agreement, immediately, efficiently and effectively against acts or threats of terrorism, violence or incitement, whether committed by Palestinians or Israelis;

FOLLOWING the Gaza–Jericho Agreement; the Agreement on Preparatory Transfer of Powers and Responsibilities signed at Erez on August 29, 1994 (hereinafter "the Preparatory Transfer Agreement"); and the Protocol on Further Transfer of Powers and Responsibilities signed at Cairo on August 27, 1995 (hereinafter "the Further Transfer Protocol"); which three agreements will be superseded by this Agreement;
HEREBY AGREE as follows:

CHAPTER 1—THE COUNCIL

Article I

Transfer of Authority

1. Israel shall transfer powers and responsibilities as specified in this Agreement from the Israeli military government and its Civil Administration to the Council

in accordance with this Agreement. Israel shall continue to exercise powers and responsibilities not so transfer.

2. Pending the inauguration of the Council, the powers and responsibilities transferred to the Council shall be exercised by the Palestinian Authority established in accordance with the Gaza–Jericho Agreement, which shall also have all the rights, liabilities and obligations to be assumed by the Council in this regard. Accordingly, the term "Council" throughout this Agreement shall, pending the inauguration of the Council, be construed as meaning the Palestinian Authority.
3. The transfer of powers and responsibilities to the police force established by the Palestinian Council in accordance with Article XIV below (hereinafter "the Palestinian Police") shall be accomplished in a phased manner, as detailed in this Agreement and in the Protocol concerning Redeployment and Security Arrangements attached as Annex I to this Agreement (hereinafter "Annex I").
4. As regards the transfer and assumption of authority in civil spheres, powers and responsibilities shall be transferred and assumed as set out in the Protocol Concerning Civil Affairs attached as Annex III to this Agreement (hereinafter "Annex III").
5. After the inauguration of the Council, the Civil Administration in the West Bank will be dissolved, and the Israeli military government shall be withdrawn. The withdrawal of the military government shall not prevent it from exercising the powers and responsibilities not transferred to the Council.
6. A Joint Civil Affairs Coordination and Cooperation Committee (hereinafter "the CAC"), Joint Regional Civil Affairs Subcommittees, one for the Gaza Strip and the other for the West Bank, and District Civil Liaison Offices in the West Bank shall be established in order to provide for coordination and cooperation in civil affairs between the Council and Israel, as detailed in Annex III.
7. The offices of the Council, and the offices of its Ra'ees and its Executive Authority and other committees, shall be located in areas under Palestinian territorial jurisdiction in the West Bank and the Gaza Strip.

Article II

Elections

1. In order that the Palestinian people of the West Bank and the Gaza Strip may govern themselves according to democratic principles, direct, free and general political elections will be held for the Council and the Ra'ees of the Executive Authority of the Council in accordance with the provisions set out in the Protocol concerning Elections attached as Annex II to this Agreement (hereinafter "Annex II").
2. These elections will constitute a significant interim preparatory step towards the realization of the legitimate rights of the Palestinian people and their just requirements and will provide a democratic basis for the establishment of Palestinian institutions.
3. Palestinians of Jerusalem who live there may participate in the election process in accordance with the provisions contained in this Article and in Article VI of Annex II (Election Arrangements concerning Jerusalem).

4. The elections shall be called by the Chairman of the Palestinian Authority immediately following the signing of this Agreement to take place at the earliest practicable date following the redeployment of Israeli forces in accordance with Annex I, and consistent with the requirements of the election timetable as provided in Annex II, the Election Law and the Election Regulations, as defined in Article I of Annex II.

Article III

Structure of the Palestinian Council

1. The Palestinian Council and the Ra'ees of the Executive Authority of the Council constitute the Palestinian Interim Self-Government Authority, which will be elected by the Palestinian people of the West Bank, Jerusalem and the Gaza Strip for the transitional period agreed in Article I of the DOP.
2. The Council shall possess both legislative power and executive power, in accordance with Articles VII and IX of the DOP. The Council shall carry out and be responsible for all the legislative and executive powers and responsibilities transferred to it under this Agreement. The exercise of legislative powers shall be in accordance with Article XVIII of this Agreement (Legislative Powers of the Council).
3. The Council and the Ra'ees of the Executive Authority of the Council shall be directly and simultaneously elected by the Palestinian people of the West Bank, Jerusalem and the Gaza Strip, in accordance with the provisions of this Agreement and the Election Law and Regulations, which shall not be contrary to the provisions of this Agreement.
4. The Council and the Ra'ees of the Executive Authority of the Council shall be elected for a transitional period not exceeding five years from the signing of the Gaza–Jericho Agreement on May 4, 1994.
5. Immediately upon its inauguration, the Council will elect from among its members a Speaker. The Speaker will preside over the meetings of the Council, administer the Council and its committees, decide on the agenda of each meeting, and lay before the Council proposals for voting and declare their results.
6. The jurisdiction of the Council shall be as determined in Article XVII of this Agreement (Jurisdiction).
7. The organization, structure and functioning of the Council shall be in accordance with this Agreement and the Basic Law for the Palestinian Interim Self-Government Authority, which Law shall be adopted by the Council. The Basic Law and any regulations made under it shall not be contrary to the provisions of this Agreement.
8. The Council shall be responsible under its executive powers for the offices, services and departments transferred to it and may establish, within its jurisdiction, ministries and subordinate bodies, as necessary for the fulfillment of its responsibilities.
9. The Speaker will present for the Council's approval proposed internal procedures that will regulate, among other things, the decision-making processes of the Council.

Article IV

Size of the Council The Palestinian Council shall be composed of 82 representatives and the Ra'ees of the Executive Authority, who will be directly and simultaneously elected by the Palestinian people of the West Bank, Jerusalem and the Gaza Strip.

Article V

The Executive Authority of the Council

1. The Council will have a committee that will exercise the executive authority of the Council, formed in accordance with paragraph 4 below (hereinafter "the Executive Authority").
2. The Executive Authority shall be bestowed with the executive authority of the Council and will exercise it on behalf of the Council. It shall determine its own internal procedures and decision making processes.
3. The Council will publish the names of the members of the Executive Authority immediately upon their initial appointment and subsequent to any changes.
4.
   a. The Ra'ees of the Executive Authority shall be an ex officio member of the Executive Authority.
   b. All of the other members of the Executive Authority, except as provided in subparagraph c. below, shall be members of the Council, chosen and proposed to the Council by the Ra'ees of the Executive Authority and approved by the Council.
   c. The Ra'ees of the Executive Authority shall have the right to appoint some persons, in number not exceeding twenty percent of the total membership of the Executive Authority, who are not members of the Council, to exercise executive authority and participate in government tasks. Such appointed members may not vote in meetings of the Council.
   d. Non-elected members of the Executive Authority must have a valid address in an area under the jurisdiction of the Council.

CHAPTER 2—REDEPLOYMENT AND SECURITY ARRANGEMENTS

Article X

Redeployment of Israeli Military Forces

1. The first phase of the Israeli military forces redeployment will cover populated areas in the West Bank—cities, towns, villages, refugee camps and hamlets—as set out in Annex I, and will be completed prior to the eve of the Palestinian elections, i.e., 22 days before the day of the elections.
2. Further redeployments of Israeli military forces to specified military locations will commence after the inauguration of the Council and will be gradually implemented commensurate with the assumption of responsibility for public order and internal security by the Palestinian Police, to be completed within 18 months from

the date of the inauguration of the Council as detailed in Articles XI (Land) and XIII (Security), below and in Annex I.

3. The Palestinian Police shall be deployed and shall assume responsibility for public order and internal security for Palestinians in a phased manner in accordance with Article XIII (Security) below and Annex I.
4. Israel shall continue to carry the responsibility for external security, as well as the responsibility for overall security of Israelis for the purpose of safeguarding their internal security and public order.
5. For the purpose of this Agreement, "Israeli military forces" includes Israeli Police and other Israeli security forces.

Article XI

Land

1. The two sides view the West Bank and the Gaza Strip as a single territorial unit, the integrity and status of which will be preserved during the interim period.
2. The two sides agree that West Bank and Gaza Strip territory, except for issues that will be negotiated in the permanent status negotiations, will come under the jurisdiction of the Palestinian Council in a phased manner, to be completed within 18 months from the date of the inauguration of the Council, as specified below:
   a. Land in populated areas (Areas A and B), including government and Al Waqf land, will come under the jurisdiction of the Council during the first phase of redeployment.
   b. All civil powers and responsibilities, including planning and zoning, in Areas A and B, set out in Annex III, will be transferred to and assumed by the Council during the first phase of redeployment.
   c. In Area C, during the first phase of redeployment Israel will transfer to the Council civil powers and responsibilities not relating to territory, as set out in Annex III.
   d. The further redeployments of Israeli military forces to specified military locations will be gradually implemented in accordance with the DOP in three phases, each to take place after an interval of six months, after the inauguration of the Council, to be completed within 18 months from the date of the inauguration of the Council.
   e. During the further redeployment phases to be completed within 18 months from the date of the inauguration of the Council, powers and responsibilities relating to territory will be transferred gradually to Palestinian jurisdiction that will cover West Bank and Gaza Strip territory, except for the issues that will be negotiated in the permanent status negotiations.
   f. The specified military locations referred to in Article X, paragraph 2 above will be determined in the further redeployment phases, within the specified time-frame ending not later than 18 months from the date of the inauguration of the Council, and will be negotiated in the permanent status negotiations.
3. For the purpose of this Agreement and until the completion of the first phase of the further redeployments:

   "Area A" means the populated areas delineated by a red line and shaded in brown on attached map No. 1;

a. "Area B" means the populated areas delineated by a red line and shaded in yellow on attached map No. 1, and the built-up area of the hamlets listed in Appendix 6 to Annex I; and
b. "Area C" means areas of the West Bank outside Areas A and B, which, except for the issues that will be negotiated in the permanent status negotiations, will be gradually transferred to Palestinian jurisdiction in accordance with this Agreement.

Article XIV

The Palestinian Police

1. The Council shall establish a strong police force. The duties, functions, structure, deployment and composition of the Palestinian Police, together with provisions regarding its equipment and operation, as well as rules of conduct, are set out in Annex I.
2. The Palestinian police force established under the Gaza–Jericho Agreement will be fully integrated into the Palestinian Police and will be subject to the provisions of this Agreement.
3. Except for the Palestinian Police and the Israeli military forces, no other armed forces shall be established or operate in the West Bank and the Gaza Strip.
4. Except for the arms, ammunition and equipment of the Palestinian Police described in Annex I, and those of the Israeli military forces, no organization, group or individual in the West Bank and the Gaza Strip shall manufacture, sell, acquire, possess, import or otherwise introduce into the West Bank or the Gaza Strip any firearms, ammunition, weapons, explosives, gunpowder or any related equipment, unless otherwise provided for in Annex I.

Article XV

Prevention of Hostile Acts

1. Both sides shall take all measures necessary in order to prevent acts of terrorism, crime and hostilities directed against each other, against individuals falling under the other's authority and against their property, and shall take legal measures against offenders.
2. Specific provisions for the implementation of this Article are set out in Annex I.

Article XVI

Confidence Building Measures With a view to fostering a positive and supportive public atmosphere to accompany the implementation of this Agreement, to establish a solid basis of mutual trust and good faith, and in order to facilitate the anticipated cooperation and new relations between the two peoples, both Parties agree to carry out confidence building measures as detailed herewith:

1. Israel will release or turn over to the Palestinian side, Palestinian detainees and prisoners, residents of the West Bank and the Gaza Strip. The first stage of release

of these prisoners and detainees will take place on the signing of this Agreement and the second stage will take place prior to the date of the elections. There will be a third stage of release of detainees and prisoners. Detainees and prisoners will be released from among categories detailed in Annex VII (Release of Palestinian Prisoners and Detainees). Those released will be free to return to their homes in the West Bank and the Gaza Strip.

2. Palestinians who have maintained contact with the Israeli authorities will not be subjected to acts of harassment, violence, retribution or prosecution. Appropriate ongoing measures will be taken, in coordination with Israel, in order to ensure their protection.
3. Palestinians from abroad whose entry into the West Bank and the Gaza Strip is approved pursuant to this Agreement, and to whom the provisions of this Article are applicable, will not be prosecuted for offenses committed prior to September 13, 1993.

Article XXXI

Final Clauses

1. This Agreement shall enter into force on the date of its signing
2. The Gaza–Jericho Agreement, the Preparatory Transfer Agreement and the Further Transfer Protocol will be superseded by this Agreement.
3. The Council, upon its inauguration, shall replace the Palestinian Authority and shall assume all the undertakings and obligations of the Palestinian Authority under the Gaza–Jericho Agreement, the Preparatory Transfer Agreement, and the Further Transfer Protocol.
4. The two sides shall pass all necessary legislation to implement this Agreement.
5. Permanent status negotiations will commence as soon as possible, but not later than May 4, 1996, between the Parties. It is understood that these negotiations shall cover remaining issues, including: Jerusalem, refugees, settlements, security arrangements, borders, relations and cooperation with other neighbors, and other issues of common interest.
6. Nothing in this Agreement shall prejudice or preempt the outcome of the negotiations on the permanent status to be conducted pursuant to the DOP. Neither Party shall be deemed, by virtue of having entered into this Agreement, to have renounced or waived any of its existing rights, claims or positions.
7. Neither side shall initiate or take any step that will change the status of the West Bank and the Gaza Strip pending the outcome of the permanent status negotiations.
8. The two Parties view the West Bank and the Gaza Strip as a single territorial unit, the integrity and status of which will be preserved during the interim period.
9. The PLO undertakes that, within two months of the date of the inauguration of the Council, the Palestinian National Council will convene and formally approve the necessary changes in regard to the Palestinian Covenant, as undertaken in the letters signed by the Chairman of the PLO and addressed to the Prime Minister of Israel, dated September 9, 1993 and May 4, 1994.
10. Pursuant to Annex I, Article IX of this Agreement, Israel confirms that the permanent checkpoints on the roads leading to and from the Jericho Area (except those

related to the access road leading from Mousa Alami to the Allenby Bridge) will be removed upon the completion of the first phase of redeployment.

11. Prisoners who, pursuant to the Gaza–Jericho Agreement, were turned over to the Palestinian Authority on the condition that they remain in the Jericho Area for the remainder of their sentence, will be free to return to their homes in the West Bank and the Gaza Strip upon the completion of the first phase of redeployment.
12. As regards relations between Israel and the PLO, and without derogating from the commitments contained in the letters signed by and exchanged between the Prime Minister of Israel and the Chairman of the PLO, dated September 9, 1993 and May 4, 1994, the two sides will apply between them the provisions contained in Article XXII, paragraph 1, with the necessary changes.
13.
   a. The Preamble to this Agreement, and all Annexes, Appendices and maps attached hereto, shall constitute an integral part hereof.
   b. The Parties agree that the maps attached to the Gaza–Jericho Agreement as:
      a. map No. 1 (The Gaza Strip), an exact copy of which is attached to this Agreement as map No. 2 (in this Agreement "map No. 2");
      b. map No. 4 (Deployment of Palestinian Police in the Gaza Strip), an exact copy of which is attached to this Agreement as map No. 5 (in this Agreement "map No. 5"); and
      c. map No. 6 (Maritime Activity Zones), an exact copy of which is attached to this Agreement as map No. 8 (in this Agreement "map No. 8");

   are an integral part hereof and will remain in effect for the duration of this Agreement.
14. While the Jeftlik area will come under the functional and personal jurisdiction of the Council in the first phase of redeployment, the area's transfer to the territorial jurisdiction of the Council will be considered by the Israeli side in the first phase of the further redeployment phases.

Done at Washington DC, this 28th day of September, 1995.

____

For the Government of the State of Israel

____

For the PLO

Witnessed by:

____

The United States of America

____

The Russian Federation

____

The Arab Republic of Egypt

____

The Hashemite Kingdom of Jordan

____

The Kingdom of Norway

____

The European Union

http://www.public.asu.edu/~itayim2/palestine/peace/interim.htm (accessed February 3, 2006).

The Wye River Memorandum

October 23, 1998

THE WHITE HOUSE

Office of the Press Secretary

The following are steps to facilitate implementation of the Interim Agreement on the West Bank and Gaza Strip of September 28, 1995 (the "Interim Agreement") and other related agreements including the Note for the Record of January 17, 1997 (hereinafter referred to as "the prior agreements") so that the Israeli and Palestinian sides can more effectively carry out their reciprocal responsibilities, including those relating to further redeployments and security respectively. These steps are to be carried out in a parallel phased approach in accordance with this Memorandum and the attached time line. They are subject to the relevant terms and conditions of the prior agreements and do not supersede their other requirements.

I. FURTHER REDEPLOYMENTS

A. Phase One and Two Further Redeployments

1. Pursuant to the Interim Agreement and subsequent agreements, the Israeli side's implementation of the first and second F.R.D. will consist of the transfer to the Palestinian side of 13% from Area C as follows:

1% to Area (A) 12% to Area (B)

The Palestinian side has informed that it will allocate an area/areas amounting to 3% from the above Area (B) to be designated as Green Areas and/or Nature Reserves. The Palestinian side has further informed that they will act according to the established scientific standards, and that therefore there will be no changes in the status of these areas, without prejudice to the rights of the existing inhabitants in these areas including Bedouins; while these standards do not allow new construction in these areas, existing roads and buildings may be maintained.

The Israeli side will retain in these Green Areas/Nature Reserves the overriding security responsibility for the purpose of protecting Israelis and confronting the threat of terrorism. Activities and movements of the Palestinian Police forces may be carried out after coordination and confirmation; the Israeli side will respond to such requests expeditiously.

2. As part of the foregoing implementation of the first and second F.R.D., 14.2% from Area (B) will become Area (A).

2. PLO Charter

The Executive Committee of the Palestine Liberation Organization and the Palestinian Central Council will reaffirm the letter of 22 January 1998 from PLO Chairman Yasir Arafat to President Clinton concerning the nullification of the Palestinian National

Charter provisions that are inconsistent with the letters exchanged between the PLO and the Government of Israel on 9–10 September 1993. PLO Chairman Arafat, the Speaker of the Palestine National Council, and the Speaker of the Palestinian Council will invite the members of the PNC, as well as the members of the Central Council, the Council, and the Palestinian Heads of Ministries to a meeting to be addressed by President Clinton to reaffirm their support for the peace process and the aforementioned decisions of the Executive Committee and the Central Council.

IV. PERMANENT STATUS NEGOTIATIONS

The two sides will immediately resume permanent status negotiations on an accelerated basis and will make a determined effort to achieve the mutual goal of reaching an agreement by May 4, 1999. The negotiations will be continuous and without interruption. The United States has expressed its willingness to facilitate these negotiations.

V. UNILATERAL ACTIONS

Recognizing the necessity to create a positive environment for the negotiations, neither side shall initiate or take any step that will change the status of the West Bank and the Gaza Strip in accordance with the Interim Agreement.

ATTACHMENT: Time Line

This Memorandum will enter into force ten days from the date of signature.
Done at Washington, DC this 23rd day of October 1998.
For the Government of the State of Israel
For the PLO
Witnessed by: The United States of America

---

http://www.yale.edu/lawweb/avalon/mideast/wyeriv.htm (accessed February 1, 2006).

Eleven
BREAKDOWN . . .

Despite growing pessimism about the peace process among Israelis, Palestinians, and Syrians by early 2000, there remained some positive signs that all was not lost. Indeed, an air of desperation seemed to be setting in as Bill Clinton was in his last year in office wanting to stake out a legacy apart from the scandals that occupied his second term, as Ehud Barak's governing coalition teetered on the edge of collapse, as Yasser Arafat's position suffered in comparison with the more active radical Palestinian groups amid overall Palestinian frustration, and as Hafiz al-Asad's health continued to deteriorate.

With yet one more accord, this time at the Egyptian resort town of Sharm al-Shaykh in the Sinai Peninsula on September 4, 1999, it was agreed that the parameters for a settlement of the final status issues would be determined by February 13, 2000, with a final agreement by September 13, 2000, the seven-year anniversary of the signing of the Declaration of Principles. Following the accord at Sharm al-Shaykh, there was an Israeli release of 199 Palestinian prisoners and a further 7% transfer of land in the West Bank to the Palestinian Authority (PA) per the 1998 Wye River memorandum (this land was transferred from Area C to Area B control, which was in addition to the 2% of the 13% agreed to in the Wye accord that had be transferred to the PA before Netanyahu ended the process). Both Arafat and Barak were coming under domestic fire from those who had opposed the peace process. Both were trying to maintain a critical mass of support to hopefully carry on toward a mutually acceptable resolution. In the process, both were compelled to give in at times to radical elements within their constituencies in order to essentially buy off opposition, not completely understanding that in doing so they had weakened their power base and limited their flexibility. Talks stalled, however, in November over many of the same issues that had proven so difficult for so long: borders, Jerusalem, and Israeli settlements. February 13, 2000, would pass with nary anyone noticing. With American prodding, however, Israeli–Palestinian talks resumed in April with a renewed sense of urgency as the September deadline approached. The White House would soon commit its considerable prestige for one last push toward peace.

THE END OF THE SYRIAN TRACK

While the Israeli–Palestinian talks stalled in late 1999 and proceeded in fits and spurts in early 2000, the Israeli–Syrian track acquired some unexpected momentum.[1] In what had become something of a pattern, when one track slowed down, the other gained some speed. As examined in Chapter 10, although a good deal of progress was made between Syrian and Israeli negotiators at Shepherdstown in early 2000, an ill-timed leak of the concessions offered at the meetings caused both parties, particularly the Syrians, to back down from the more forward positions put forth in West Virginia.[2] Again, Washington would intervene to reenergize the talks. President Clinton invited Hafiz al-Asad to Geneva, Switzerland, in March 2000 to hopefully bridge the remaining differences between Syria and Israel and set the stage for a Syrian-Israeli peace treaty. Stories differ on all sides as to what happened at Geneva that resulted in a failed summit. The Syrians believe they were promised an agreement that confirmed Israel's withdrawal from the Golan to the June 4, 1967, line; and when something less than this was offered by Clinton, they backed away. Jeremy Pressman argues that it appears that the offer the United States presented to Syria in Geneva was a withdrawal to the June 4 line in name only since the map Dennis Ross was showing the Syrians moved the June 4 line even farther back to the east of the 1923 line, thus farther away from the Sea of Galilee. According to this view, perhaps the United States and Israel were trying to get Syria to agree to the demarcation, calling it the June 4 line while knowing that it probably was not. If this is true, then it follows that Barak probably in the end did not agree to withdraw to the June 4 border that was more consistent with Syria's idea of where it was. As such, it is little wonder that Asad "cried foul," leading to the stark failure of the summit.[3] In an interview I conducted with Syrian President Bashar al-Asad in May 2004, who at the time of the Geneva summit was thoroughly integrated into the regime and, by most accounts, was being systematically groomed to succeed his father, he recounted the Geneva meeting in the following manner:

> The last time my father met with Clinton in April 2000, Clinton called my father, and [Saudi Crown] Prince Abdullah was involved. There were good relations between my father and Clinton. My father asked Clinton what he wanted to discuss, why a summit, as my father did not think it was appropriate. But then Clinton called him to meet with him because he was on his way back from Asia, Pakistan I think, and he stopped in Oman, then he went on to Geneva. He called my father and told him he was on his way to Geneva and that he would like to meet there because he had good news, that Barak accepted the June 4th on line. However, at Geneva my father was told that Barak accepted to withdraw from 95 percent of the land, so my father was angry and he wanted to leave. He was surprised and Clinton was surprised; Clinton was surprised he [Hafiz al-Asad] refused, so somebody told him that we would accept this offer. When he stopped in

> Oman, Clinton met with some Omani officials along with [U.S. national security adviser] Sandy Berger and [U.S. ambassador to Syria] Chris Ross—they told Clinton at the time that since my father was sick he wants to have a peace before he dies so that he can help his son be president . . . so he [Hafiz al-Asad] will accept anything. And they hinted to Clinton that they had asked my father and that he had said OK. So Clinton presumed that my father had agreed to the proposal. What happened was that Barak was a little bit weak in Israel, and he wanted to play two cards, one for peace and one not for peace. For those who wanted peace he would tell the world he is a peacemaker, for the extremists in Israel he would say he would take peace but not give all the land back, so this is how it failed. It was not Clinton's fault or the Syrians, but then the Israelis said my father was not interested in peace. In this way Barak could say my father only wanted peace on his conditions, and therefore the Arabs are responsible [for the breakdown].[4]

Others believe that Asad, his health having deteriorated even more, was not really interested at all in peace negotiations at that moment because he was concentrating more specifically on preparing the way for Bashar to come to office with cabinet and military personnel reshuffling. Domestic politics was the immediate priority, and he could not be locked into another protracted round of negotiations with the Israelis. He attended the summit meeting with Clinton, according to this view, as a show of strength to those who had been criticizing him at home. As Dennis Ross stated, he would "stand up to the President of the United States and not compromise vital Syrian–interests," thus shoring up the support of powerful elements within Syria that would help ensure Bashar's succession.[5] Regardless of which view is more accurate, the Syrian–Israeli track was effectively moribund. This became an even more concrete reality when Hafiz al-Asad died in June, ending his long 30-year reign. His son, Bashar, did indeed succeed to the presidency in a relatively smooth transition. The way had been well prepared, but for the foreseeable future the new Syrian president, while recommitting to Syria's "strategic choice for peace" with Israel in his inaugural speech in July, would concentrate on consolidating his power base and dealing more so with domestic issues, particularly the deteriorating Syrian economic situation.[6] After witnessing what had happened on the Syrian-Israeli front over the previous six months, Bashar was reluctant to enter into the diplomatic fray so soon.

With the Syrian track dead, Barak moved forward with what had been one of his primary objectives as prime minister: getting out of south Lebanon. Even before the failed Asad–Clinton summit meeting in Geneva, the Israeli cabinet had agreed in early March 2000 to withdraw from Lebanon by July. Since it was apparent that a withdrawal would not be linked to a Syrian-Israeli peace agreement, Barak decided to unilaterally do so in May. The fact that it was a unilateral decision attests to the breakdown by that time of the Madrid peace process on the Syrian–Lebanese front. The rapidity of the withdrawal, over a month in advance of the deadline set by the Israeli cabinet, caught many by surprise, which may have been the intent for strategic reasons. The Israelis wanted the withdrawal to look as if it was of their own accord and that the Israel Defense Forces (IDF) were not being chased out by Hizbollah. At first, Israeli units turned over their positions to elements of the allied South Lebanon Army (SLA), now under the command of Antoine Lahad. Fearing reprisals from a variety of Lebanese groups, however, SLA members began to defect in droves, being forced out by or abandoning their posts to Hizbollah. About a quarter of the 2,500-man SLA defected to Israel by the time the IDF had fully withdrawn (a number that ballooned to about 6,000 to include family members and others who had helped the Israelis). Many of those who elected to stay behind were imprisoned after surrendering to Lebanese authorities, although some of the SLA leaders had managed to escape into exile. By May 24, Israel had completely withdrawn its forces from Lebanon, and a very divisive and dark chapter in Israeli history had apparently been put to rest. Syria stood on the sidelines, in part satisfied that a threat to its position in Lebanon had been reduced but also in part concerned that it would have less leverage to use against Israel (by supporting Hizbollah attacks against the Israeli occupation) vis-à-vis a return of the Golan Heights.

Hizbollah, on the other hand, was jubilant. The Shiite Islamist group became widely perceived in the Arab and Muslim worlds as the only combatant to ever defeat Israel. It would parlay this added popularity in Lebanon into enhancing its role in the country as a legitimate political party and increasing its representation in the Lebanese parliament. It would slowly but surely position itself as a Lebanese national entity rather than as a supranational Islamist party. This became evident when Hizbollah's leader, Shaykh Hassan Nasrallah, spoke of the "victory" with the Lebanese flag—in addition to Hizbollah's traditional yellow flags—in the background. Just as important, however, the Israeli withdrawal from Lebanon outside of the auspices of an agreement gave rise in the Arab world to the effectiveness of the Hizbollah "model," i.e., that steady, consistent low-level resistance and guerilla warfare is the only way to inflict enough pain on Israel, without confronting it directly en masse, in a way that compels the small Jewish state, one so sensitive to the loss of each and every Israeli soldier, to give up territory. Palestinians took notice.

United Nations (UN) Secretary-General Kofi Annan visited the Israeli–Lebanese border and verified on June 16 that Israeli forces had fully withdrawn in accordance with UN Security Council Resolution 425, which was passed in June 1978 in reaction to the Israeli sweep of south Lebanon. It called on Israel at the time to "withdraw forthwith its forces from all Lebanese territory" and to monitor and confirm such a withdrawal it established the UN Interim Force in Lebanon (UNIFIL). Despite this, there remained some disputed area along the Syrian–Lebanese–Israeli border called the Shebaa Farms. The Shebaa Farms is an area measuring about twenty-five square kilometers and consists of fourteen farms located just south of Shebaa, a Lebanese village on the western slope of Mt. Hermon astride the borders of the three countries. When Israel withdrew its forces in May, it did not do so from the Shebaa Farms, which it claims was part of the Golan Heights taken from Syria in 1967 and thus subject to negotiations with Damascus. Lebanon, particularly Hizbollah, and Syria claim that it is a part of Lebanon and, as such, Israel has therefore not fully withdrawn. Since the withdrawal, Hizbollah carried out periodic attacks against Israeli positions in the Shebaa Farms area. The Israelis believe Syria manufactured the Shebaa Farms case to maintain at least some level of Israeli–Lebanese friction that legitimated Syria's military position in Lebanon as well as retain at least a tad of negotiating quid pro quo with Israel over the Golan. Accordingly, continuing tension with Israel at least at some level might help the new regime of Bashar al-Asad drown out the increasing rancor in Lebanon, especially from within the Lebanese Christian community, calling for a Syrian withdrawal from the country since the raison d'etre for its presence had been removed.

The inability of the Syrians and the Israelis to consummate a peace treaty may well be one of the great missed opportunities in the Middle East in the modern era. A peace treaty *should* have materialized given the tractability of the issues dividing the two states and the tangible progress made on most of these issues in the discussions throughout the 1990s. History could have been quite different in that event. Upon a Syrian–Israeli peace treaty, Lebanon would have certainly signed along the dotted line soon thereafter, with the Arab Gulf states not too far behind (and North African members of the Arab League, with the exception of Libya, most likely would have joined the chorus). Although many believe the "Syrian option" and its regional repercussions would have weakened the Palestinian negotiating position due to the lack of collective Arab support, it is also possible that Israel, feeling more safe than ever before following peace treaties with its Arab neighbors, might have felt more comfortable with making certain concessions than it would otherwise not make in an environment still characterized by an official state of war with most of the Arab countries. In this scenario, then, the Palestinians might still have received a viable, independent state. The holdouts to peace with Israel, such as Iraq, would have become more isolated. Saddam Hussein's resuscitation in the Arab world due in part to the breakdown of the Arab–Israeli peace process by the end of the decade would not have occurred, with potentially important results for his ability to maintain power as well as the subsequent U.S.-led war against Iraq in 2003. In addition, there is no telling how a comprehensive Arab–Israeli peace might have deleteriously affected al-Qa'ida and other Islamic extremist groups, especially in terms of recruitment. Even though their existence was not predicated upon Arab–Israeli hostility or the plight of the Palestinians, these issues have played a prominent role in their propaganda. But what would history be without these tantalizing "what ifs."

CAMP DAVID II

With the Israelis out of Lebanon and the Syrian–Israeli track dead, attention shifted back to the Palestinian–Israeli track in the summer of 2000. Yasser Arafat began to renew his not-so-subtle threats that he would unilaterally declare Palestinian statehood if there continued to be little or no progress on the negotiating front, even arranging for the PLO Central Council to declare that September 13, 2000, would be the de facto deadline. While it might reenergize the peace process, it also threatened to increase the violence on both sides along with an Israeli public and government becoming less enamored of peace talks with the Palestinians. In the face of this, Barak's coalition, built with the support of religious parties such as Shas and the National Religious Party (NRP) as well as Soviet immigrant Natan Sharansky's Yisrael B'Aliyah party (created in 1995 to assist in the assimilation of Soviet Jews immigrating to Israel), was beginning to fracture. These parties vehemently opposed the Israeli prime minister's engagement in peace talks with either the Syrians or Palestinians, threatening to bolt the coalition, forcing a call for new elections while also demanding concessions on sociocultural issues important to them in terms of attempting to shape Israeli society toward a stricter adherence to Jewish law. While meeting some of these demands, Barak risked alienating other small Israeli parties that comprised his secular base, especially Israeli Arab parties and Meretz. Barak seemed to be constantly rallying his troops to defeat no-confidence motions in the Knesset.

With the Oslo process on the brink of unraveling, Barak rolled the dice in what seemed to be a desperate gamble that had the potential for a fabulous payoff. Barak suggested to the Americans a summit meeting between himself, Arafat, and Clinton to iron out the remaining final status issues and once and for all settle the Israeli–Palestinian conflict. Barak had long had his doubts about the Oslo process, and he actually abstained in the Knesset vote on the Interim Agreement. He wanted to take the "interim" out of any arrangements with the Palestinians because he felt that continued Israeli redeployment would erode Israel's bargaining position when it came to discuss the final status issues. He wanted to move right to negotiations on a comprehensive accord, waiving the remaining elements of what was scheduled to be implemented under the Wye River memorandum.[7] Arafat's instincts informed him not to go with Barak's approach at first, sensing that it was important to complete the steps that were outlined in prior agreements instead of going for broke and possibly getting nothing. But the Clinton administration, a bit perplexed itself on how to respond to Barak's demarches, tended to pressure Arafat to give the Israeli prime minister a chance since Barak was perceived in Washington as having the gravitas and moxy to make it all happen. Arafat usually relented, the first manifestation of this being the September 1999 Sharm al-Shaykh agreement. The Palestinians became immediately wary when not so long after this agreement Barak switched back to the Syrian track toward the end of 1999. But with Israel out of Lebanon and the Syrian track dead, Barak turned once again toward the Palestinians.

Barak certainly was independent-minded, and he tended to have an exaggerated view of his own political skills, which most in retrospect would say were not particularly well honed. Clinton, also desperate to establish a legacy apart from his dalliance with Monica Lewinsky, invited on July 5 Barak and Arafat to Camp David. Although the Camp David accords negotiated almost twenty-two years prior to this had largely been viewed with disdain throughout most of the Arab world, the Clinton administration hoped to re-create the "magic" again at the Maryland presidential retreat, even repeating to the letter some of the details of the first go-around. Arafat, understanding the questionable legacy of the first Camp David in the Arab mind-set, arrived in the United States already with a very guarded attitude, knowing full well what had happened to Anwar Sadat when he was perceived as giving up far too much with so little in return and for essentially selling the Palestinian, Arab, and Muslim causes down the river.

With Barak's formal acceptance of the invitation, Shas (seventeen seats in the Knesset), Yisrael b'Aliyah (four seats), and the NRP (five seats) left the prime minister's coalition, leaving him with forty-two seats in a minority government. Barak was banking on the expectation that a final Palestinian–Israeli agreement would be enough to restore his position in the government. The three leaders began their two weeks of meetings at Camp David on July 11. After many long nights of discussions, threatened and actual departures toward the airport, and a plethora of interesting ideas regarding the final status issues floating about, the summit broke up on July 25 with no agreement and an exceptional amount of exasperation and frustration that could clearly be seen on the faces of the participants.

The blame game commenced almost immediately following the failed summit meeting, with most of the fingers, including those of President Clinton, pointing directly at Arafat. This despite Arafat's hesitancy in going to Camp David and his apparent plea to Clinton that he would not be blamed if the talks broke down.[8] While Clinton did not specifically blame Arafat in the closing communiqué, the tenor of the administration certainly tacked in this direction soon in the summit's aftermath, which meshed with the dominant Israeli position. According to this view, the Palestinians,

(*Left* to *right*) Israeli Prime Minister Ehud Barak, President Bill Clinton, and Palestinian Authority President Yasser Arafat at Camp David peace talks in Maryland, July 11, 2000. (Reuters/CORBIS, UT0035288.)

by not accepting Barak's generous offer, committed a historic mistake on par with that which occurred in 1947 when the partition plan was rejected. Barak apparently was a one-man show entering the talks, offering some concessions that, according to one high-placed U.S. official present at the talks, caught both Arafat and the Americans off-guard. As such, Arafat almost reflexively jerked backward, suspecting perfidy and fearing the consequences back home if he was judged to have been taken advantage of, à la Sadat. Israel offered to return 92% of the West Bank and all of the Gaza Strip toward the creation of a Palestinian state, heretofore the most any Israeli government had put on the table. In addition, there were discussions concerning East Jerusalem that might have allowed a more liberal interpretation of the borders of the city that could act as the foundation for a Palestinian capital called "Jerusalem."[9] To many Israelis, Arafat's refusal of this offer, as well as the lack of a counteroffer following the summit, proved that he was never really interested in peace, which reinforced the Israeli critique of the Oslo process from the very beginning in right-of-center circles.

From the Palestinian perspective, Barak did not even meet the minimum requirements of the Palestinian delegation. Yes, the 92% figure was attractive, but sections of the Jordan Valley would remain under Israeli control for as long as twelve years for strategic reasons. In addition, Arafat held tight to the idea of a complete Israeli withdrawal to the June 4, 1967, borders as set by UN Security Council Resolution 242, including all of East Jerusalem. From the Palestinian perspective, accepting the 1967 lines as the borders for an independent state was a huge concession in its own right, considering the fact that it only constituted 22% of all of mandatory Palestine. In their view, they had already given up 78% of the land. Another problem was the issue of

Palestinian refugees. Arafat would not budge on this issue, wanting the right of return of all UN-registered refugees and their descendants along with an Israeli admission of responsibility for creating the refugee problem. At the time there were approximately 3.7 million registered Palestinian refugees, most of them living in Lebanon, Syria, Jordan, and, of course, the West Bank and Gaza Strip.[10] To Israel, of course, the Palestinian refugee problem is nonnegotiable. The refugees can return to a Palestinian state but not en masse within the 1967 borders of Israel. At most, Israel might allow 10,000 or so refugees to return within the framework of family repatriation and only as a humanitarian gesture, not setting a precedent. Israel would not admit any guilt, but it would certainly, along with the United States, the Arab world, and the international community, work on a formula for financial compensation for the Palestinian refugees. This issue, I think to the surprise of the Israeli and American negotiators, was not as easy to transcend as anticipated. Since it seems on the surface to be such an unreasonable Palestinian demand, especially considering the fact that hell would freeze over before the Israelis agreed to it, American and Israeli officials possibly took it for granted that this one final status issue could be settled with relative ease. To the Palestinians, however, the refugee issue cuts to the core of the Palestinian national identity, superceding even that which was sanctioned by UN General Assembly Resolution 194 calling on the return to their homes of those displaced by the first Arab–Israeli war. It is a matter of delineating what they view as a correct version of history and their almost innate right to return to their homes. Perhaps Clinton and Barak did not realize how wedded Arafat was compelled to be to the right of return, knowing that the Palestine Liberation Organization's (PLO's) support base also rested in the refugee camps throughout the region.

The different wavelengths upon which the parties were operating and what the Israelis and Americans determined was Palestinian intransigence were on full display when Arafat returned to the West Bank amid a hero's welcome for not caving in to U.S.–Israeli pressure. To the Palestinians, Israel's less than expected concessions confirmed suspicions that it really wanted to keep the territories under its control in perpetuity—perhaps, as many thought, a more militant alternative should now be adopted. Despite the very public failure of the summit, there was some progress made on substantive final status issues that would become manifest in about six months and, no doubt, in any future Israeli–Palestinian agreement—it was not a total loss. However, the widely held international perception that Arafat was to blame for the summit breakdown severely hurt his standing, especially with European nations that had been traditionally much more favorably disposed toward him and his cause than the United States. In addition, Arafat's claim that the Jewish Temple was never located in Jerusalem further eroded his standing in the eyes of the outside world, and it further convinced many in Israel that he was uninterested in peace. As Barak wrote, "At Camp David, Mr. Arafat well understood that the moment of truth had come and that painful decisions needed to be made by both sides. He failed this challenge."[11]

The Camp David summit probably should have never happened. It was premature. There was very little preparation on any of the hard issues that needed to be discussed. Neither the Israelis nor the Palestinians did anything to condition their respective constituencies for the concessions that needed to be made for a final status agreement; instead, they only mapped out extremist positions to meet the chorus of those who opposed a summit meeting as well as to establish a tough bargaining stance. Prior to the 1978 Camp David accords there was a slew of meetings preparing the ground for the talks, yet an agreement was still difficult to consummate and required the personal intervention of the U.S. president in the months following the summit. There was little, if any, preparation apparent in July 2000. As Yoram Meital points out,

> Discussion of the complex issues involved—refugees, Jerusalem, the holy sites, an end to the conflict, and all the subtopics that these issues entail—made precise preparation mandatory. Deliberations on Jerusalem required far more knowledge than the parties displayed, as well as creative thinking on territory, security, border crossings, sovereignty, and religious services for multiple groups. Jerusalem's division and some sort of decision about arrangements for the Temple Mount are not unfamiliar notions. Yet few people seemed to appreciate exactly what compromise meant. The nuts and bolts should have been worked out in advance. A summit is hardly the place and time to start grappling with them.[12]

The Arab heads of state had not been consulted or brought on board ahead of time to give Arafat some political cover, and the Clinton administration is largely to blame for this. Essentially, there were two political leaders desperate for a political milestone that would re-define their political careers and a third (Arafat) who believed that not attending a summit would be worse than going because he would then be portrayed as being not really interested in peace—it was almost a no-win scenario for Arafat since he did not expect summit success to begin with, which is also why he was so insistent on not being blamed if Camp David failed. Barak's negotiating inexperience, even brusqueness, was also on display at the Maryland retreat. He avoided directly discussing matters with Arafat, and he often made proposals without consulting the rest of the Israeli delegation. In addition, as in 1978 with Carter and Sadat, the American president in July 2000 placed more pressure on the Arab party to make concessions than on Israel, usually in terms of trying to explain the vulnerable domestic situation of the Israeli prime minister without taking into adequate account the very real and equally vulnerable political arena in which the Arab leader had to participate. This conformed to the misplaced assumption on the part of American negotiators that since Israel is a working democracy, domestic politics need to be taken into account, whereas since Arab political systems are largely authoritarian, Arab leaders have to worry much less about their domestic constituencies. One would have thought that the assassination of Sadat by elements from his domestic constituency would have dispelled U.S. officials of this notion long ago.

Most importantly, though, the failure of Camp David II seemed to embolden radical elements in both the Israeli and Palestinian populations who had been opposed to the Oslo process from the very beginning. The years of seemingly fruitless negotiations that only appeared to be accompanied by increasing violence and despair legitimated the more confrontational view that the ultimate answer lies in only militancy, repression, and separation. A decade of hope had been replaced with frustration on both sides. The Oslo process was effectively over. An air of rising tension was filling a balloon that was ready to burst—and burst it did with the so-called al-Aqsa *intifada* in September 2000.

THE PROBLEMS OF THE OSLO PROCESS

The Oslo process was not fated to its inglorious end, but there were significant problems from the very beginning that made ultimate success that much more difficult.

Maybe the most important of these was the asymmetry between the two parties: Israel and the PLO. Israel was by far the more powerful of the two. It retained its qualitative military advantage over any combination of Arab states and had just seen its primary Arab threat, Iraq, significantly degraded in the 1991 Gulf War. Israel's economy also dwarfed that of the Arab states, and it was continuing to grow, led by a very dynamic high-tech sector. Furthermore, a number of Arab states seemed almost eager to deal with the Israelis in the aftermath of the Gulf War as well as the end of the superpower cold war in a regional diplomatic environment that was now dominated by Israel's best friend, the United States, which itself was grateful to Tel Aviv for not responding to Saddam Hussein's Scud missile attacks. The PLO, on the other hand, had been severely weakened politically and economically in the regional and international arenas for its tacit support of Saddam Hussein during the Gulf War. Even at the height of its popularity, strength, and unity the PLO was no match for Israel, much less in 1992–1993 when it was at its weakest point to date. Arafat had very little bargaining leverage to bring to the table, and this became manifest when he met Israel's most basic preconditions without any guarantee of a Palestinian state in return. And signing the Declaration of Principles in 1993 freed up the other Arab states, such as Jordan and Syria, to pursue peace with Israel on their own terms, while Tel Aviv was able to pursue relations with the Arab states without making any major concessions to the Palestinians. In order to survive, therefore, the PLO agreed to a structure that placed it at almost a permanent disadvantage, which proved to be fatal to achieving its objectives. Israel, understandably, would seek to exploit its bargaining advantage at the negotiating table to strike the most favorable deal it could. As Glenn Robinson notes, "The temptation for the hegemonic party to dictate terms is too great under such circumstances, and the resulting resentment and rage in the weaker party too powerful to lead to a healthy peace."[13]

This power disparity between Israel and the PLO led to a fundamental problem: Arafat was compelled to accept an interim approach, in effect the step-by-step approach once again, replete with confidence-building measures without a defined final outcome—and no consequences for failing to meet stated deadlines. As many critics of the Oslo accords point out, contrary to popular belief, it did not specifically delineate the creation of a Palestinian state at the end, although it was assumed with the inclusion of a discussion of borders as part of the final status issues—i.e. what "borders" were to be discussed if not those pertaining to the establishment of an independent Palestinian state? But with the Israelis adopting a very legalistic approach to the accords, assumptions do not count for much. Again, as Robinson comments,

> Arafat was willing to accept an interim arrangement as opposed to a comprehensive settlement, was willing to accept Jerusalem's exclusion from the interim arrangements, and was willing to leave the settlements and refugee issues to a later date. These far-reaching concessions came out of the PLO's weakness, and Rabin, the old warrior, wisely seized them. But the very weakness of the PLO that led to such short-term advantage for Israel also helped guarantee the ultimate failure of Oslo.[14]

It is this fundamental weakness that, perhaps, compelled Arafat to refrain from doing everything he could—as demanded by the United States and Israel—to clamp down on Palestinian militant groups attacking Israeli soldiers and civilians; in other words, without any other leverage to call his own, he, like Hafiz al-Asad, saw the ability to unleash or restrain terrorism as one remaining bargaining chip. For the Israelis, however, it only sowed distrust, anger, and reprisals, which, of course, only led to more Palestinian attacks in a seemingly unending cycle of violence.

Perhaps nowhere was the power imbalance more noticeable than in the continued building and expansion of Israeli settlements in the midst of the Oslo process.[15] During the 1990s, the number of West Bank settlers almost trebled, from 78,000 to nearly 200,000, and ironically much of it occurred under Labor governments.[16] The fact that this continued, indeed accelerated, during the Oslo process was an indication to many Palestinians that the Israelis were ultimately not interested in relinquishing the land and were using the negotiations as a way to buy time to create more facts on the ground to make it virtually politically impossible for any Israeli government in the future to remove the settlements. The fact that much of this transpired under Labor convinced many Palestinians that the Israeli government was not only unwilling but also unable to confront the small but politically powerful settler movement in Israel. Even though Labor was prepared to trade land for peace, it is apparent that both Rabin and Barak wanted to avoid a confrontation with the settler movement until it absolutely had to—why precipitate a domestic political crisis until the prospects of a final deal are in place? In addition, a number of small religious nationalist parties in the Knesset formed part of the ruling coalitions, so to freeze or even substantially restrict the settlement process risked bringing about a fall of the government and calls for new elections with a no-confidence vote. As Mnookin and Eiran wrote, "By avoiding conflict, the government traded long term negotiating flexibility for short term political stability."[16a] From the Palestinian point of view, this may have been the single most important factor that threatened and ultimately destined the Oslo process to failure.

In addition, the Labor government under Rabin created "semantic loopholes" by using terms such as "natural growth," suggesting that no new settlements would be created but that the only construction undertaken would be to accommodate the children of settlers who wanted to live on their own away from their parents. In this way, thousands of new housing units could be built without drawing the ire of the United States.[17] There were also exceptions to settlement construction in the "Greater Jerusalem" (itself liberally defined) and Jordan Valley areas, in the latter case strategic reasons always serving as the rationale.[18] "New neighborhoods" of already existing settlements were constructed as well as an emphasis in certain settlements on vertical, rather than horizontal, growth. Israel also confiscated chunks of Palestinian land to build hundreds of kilometers of bypass roads that allowed Israelis to travel from settlement to settlement while bypassing Palestinian villages and towns; of course, this only further fragmented Palestinian-controlled areas.

It is ironic that the Israelis seemed hamstrung by the settler movement considering the fact that less than 5% of the Jewish population actually live in settlements and, of these, only about 25% are considered national religious settlers, the most ideologically committed of the lot. Yet this group has had a disproportionate amount of influence in Israeli politics, contributing to the making and breaking of several governments. Israeli politicians over the years have been loath to even mention withdrawal from the territories and evacuation of the settlements, deeming it to be political suicide to do so. Paraphrasing Amos Oz, one of Israel's foremost authors and a founder of the Peace Now movement, from the caboose of the Zionist train, national religious Israelis moved to the front car and seized control of the locomotive. Perhaps this is why only someone such as Ariel Sharon, with the credentials of being a hard-line Likudnik and one of the architects of the settlement process following the 1967 war, had the political wherewithal to dismantle settlements in the Gaza Strip upon the Israeli withdrawal in 2005—and even *he* did so only with great difficulty and unorthodox political alignments. Mnookin and Eiran list a number of reasons that the national religious settlers, epitomized by organizations such as Gush Emunim and the Yeshu Council, have such inordinate political power in Israel, which are summarized below.

1. *The settler movement's ability to sound themes that have religious and ideological resonance with broad appeal within Israel.* To Israelis, the West Bank (or Judea and Samaria) included the ancient Jewish kingdoms of Yehuda and Yisrael and, together with Jerusalem, is part of what is called the Promised Land in Old Testament stories, i.e., the cradle of Jewish civilization; therefore, resettling on biblical land has great appeal to even the more secular Israelis. Even though Zionism is a secular, nationalist movement, its core Jewish identity by definition has a strong religious basis. There are also a small portion of the religious settlers who are messianic, believing (ironically as do evangelical Christians in the United States, who for similar reasons are avid supporters of the settler movement and vehemently against Israel withdrawing from the West Bank) that the settling of the biblical land is a necessary prelude for the coming of the long-awaited messiah.[19] Settling the land allowed them to play a vital role in their eschatological story. In the eyes of religious settlers, the settling of the land would also revive Zionism, which in their view had long been in decline—the territories were the only remaining "new frontier." Gush Emunim's set of principles articulated in 1975 states in the beginning "we have to make it unequivocally clear to ourselves and the nations of the world that the people of Israel are fully committed to opposing any attempt to force upon them a withdrawal, through political or military means, from parts of Eretz-Yisrael." Even to secular Israeli Jews, the state of Israel was in large part established by the pioneering spirit of the earliest settlers. Their struggles, tragedies, and triumphs form a powerful narrative in modern Jewish history. In this vein, the *kibbutzim*, while declining in numbers over the years, are seen as the foundation of the early settlers' survival and ultimate success. Thus, it is almost innately distasteful to oppose those who are the last representatives of the pioneering spirit in what in effect is the last frontier. As one religious settler commented, "The people of Gush Emunim embarked on the settlement project out of complete Zionist consciousness . . . they saw their project as a natural continuation of the Zionist movement. In their dress, they had copied the original pioneers of Labor Zionism: the hair style, a shirt outside of their pants, sandals to their feet, weapon on their shoulder."[20]

2. *The institutional structure of the governmental entities representing the settlers combined with the inordinate influence of small, minority parties in the Israeli political system.* Through the entrance of small parties in the Knesset, many of which are needed to form coalition governments, the settlers are substantially overrepresented. In 2003, eleven of the 120 members were settlers, accounting for 9% of the Knesset even though settlers only make up 3% of the electorate. Governmental functions in both the Occupied Territories, such as sewage and water treatment, land planning and zoning, and social and educational services, are primarily administered by local and not the central government. City councils administer communities with a population of over

20,000; local councils administer communities of 3,000–20,000; and regional councils have local responsibility for small Jewish communities of fewer than 3,000. One-hundred twenty-five out of the 140 recognized settlements in the West Bank and Gaza Strip are—or were in the case of Gaza—governed by one of seven regional councils (one in the Gaza Strip and six in the West Bank). Local councils administer fourteen larger settlements, and three of the largest settlements have a city council government. Therefore, as Mnookin and Eiran observe, "local and regional councils have used their budgetary control to expand settlements and outposts, [and] to finance campaigns against settler relocation during the Oslo process. . . ."[21] And because the ideologically committed national religious settlers tend to live in smaller communities, the regional and local councils are dominated by them, whereas the more nonideological Jews in Israel (regarding the settlement process) tend to live in more urbanized areas that have a city council form of local government.

3. *The settlers' threat of hard-bargaining tactics and even violence to achieve their objectives has made the Israeli government hesitant and even reluctant to take them on, fearing even the outbreak of civil war.* The settlers, of course, have done everything they can to propagate these fears; even the majority of law-abiding ones often point out they would have difficulty controlling the most militant elements, which, ironically, is the same argument Arafat used in the years following the Oslo accords with regard to his own radical factions. And these are not seen as empty threats, as the massacre of Muslim worshippers in Hebron in February 1994 and the assassination of Yitzhak Rabin in November 1995 clearly displayed. Israeli government authorities have constantly worried about how the armed forces would react to religious decrees and calls by national religious settler leaders to not take part in the evacuation of settlers, especially as it is thought that settlers and other religious nationalists are overrepresented in the junior officer corps and in combat units.[22] Despite the fact that intra-Jewish violence is culturally and historically anathema, the almost apocalyptic perceived repercussions of giving up the land raised the stakes—and the tension—in Israeli society ever since the 1993 Declaration of Principles.

4. *Finally, there are national security arguments that have been accepted by both religious and secular Jews in Israel.* The settlements, in this view, help provide control of territories that give Israel much needed strategic depth. Even the Labor party's Yigal Allon, in the so-called Allon plan, envisioned settlements as a strategic necessity. Former Israeli foreign minister Abba Eban, who was considered a dove on the peace front, called the slim ten-mile-wide neck of Israel in its pre-1967 form the "Auschwitz Border," because the state could be easily cut in two and lead to the "extermination" of the country. The national religious settlers have, therefore, portrayed themselves in the role of protecting Israel. The lack of any organized Palestinian oppositional movement for two decades after the territories were taken in 1967 created a political vacuum in the Occupied Territories that was freely exploited by Israeli settlers with direct and indirect government and popular support.

Of course, to many of these arguments the Israeli Left would respond in the manner of Dror Etkes of Peace Now:

> [the] settlements in the occupied territories threaten our existence as a Jewish, democratic state, weaken the security of Israel, drain our economic resources, undermine our society's

> moral fiber, and serve to perpetuate Israeli rule over another people in a way that prevents Israel from reaching peace with the Palestinians. The settlements today pose an existential threat to the future of Israel. Let me be very clear: it is in Israel's own best interests to separate itself from settlements and the occupied territories that the settlers would have us bind to the state.[23]

There were a host of problems concerning the Palestinian leadership that also hindered progress in the Oslo process. Yasser Arafat never made the necessary transition from a revolutionary and guerilla fighter to the political head of state. The monopolization of power and use of bribery, militancy, and cronyism that worked for him as chair of the PLO did not work nearly as well as president of the PA. Arafat brought with him into the PA leadership structure many of what the indigenous Palestinians in the West Bank and Gaza Strip disdainfully called the "Tunisians," i.e., Palestinian exiles who had lived a comparatively luxurious existence in Tunis and elsewhere while they suffered under Israeli occupation. The late Edward Sa'id, the prominent Palestinian scholar at Columbia University who became the most articulate Palestinian voice in Western circles, famously stated that the PLO leadership was a group of "fat, cigar-chomping bureaucrats who want their business deals preserved and their VIP passes renewed, and who have lost all trace of decency or credibility."[24] A younger generation of Palestinians who grew up in the territories and rose to prominence during the 1987–1993 intifada wanted political space commensurate with their efforts that did so much to rehabilitate Arafat and the PLO. But they were generally excluded from power, as evidenced in the 1996 elections to the Palestinian Legislative Council. Arafat's supporters dominated the council, and he himself was elected president; then, he "simply ignored the new council and proceeded to set up an authoritarian regime buttressed by an elaborate hierarchy of security forces."[25] Indeed, Arafat went on to establish some dozen or so security services, numbering over 40,000 men, many of them overlapping and becoming sinecures of power in and of themselves, over time fragmenting the PA's overall ability to rule yet maintaining Arafat's dominant position.

The sine qua non for Palestinian support for the peace process would be if they would generally see an improvement in their economic well-being. This did not happen. The Israelis did not help matters much with their frequent closures of the territories in response to Palestinian attacks, prohibiting thousands of Palestinians from going to work inside Israel as well as inhibiting the free flow of goods. The PA also became a sieve in which there was very little, if any, accountability, rule of law, or transparency—and there was a great deal of corruption. Foreign aid allotted for infrastructure projects and economic development often was redirected by Arafat toward the security services and the bureaucracy in order to maintain their loyalty by paying their salaries (and then some, in many cases). As such, a number of countries that had committed millions of dollars in foreign aid to the PA refused to disburse it until there was more accountability and they were certain the money went to productive use. The corruption became rampant: profiteering, black market, artificial monopolies, and business nepotism. The outsiders, the "Tunisians," seemed to be enriching themselves, while those who had toiled under the Israeli occupation for a generation and suffered during the intifada were becoming more destitute and politically impotent. Despite some showy projects, such as the building of a Palestinian airport at Gaza, and some tourism-related activities, per capita income for the Palestinians steadily declined during the 1990s. The low opinion that many Palestinians adopted toward Arafat and the PA was inversely proportional to the higher opinion they had toward groups such as Hamas or younger secular firebrands who cut their teeth during the intifada such as Marwan Barghouti, Jibril Rajoub, and Muhammad Dahlan.

The Palestinians were also fighting a rear-guard battle against the Israelis at the negotiating table that placed them at a disadvantage—in short, they were outclassed. Raja Shehadeh ably charts how this occurred.[26] First of all, there was a lacuna of trained Palestinian lawyers and diplomats; indeed, there was no school of law in either the West Bank or Gaza Strip between 1948 and 1967.[27] While Palestinian delegations consisted of professors and politicians, Israeli delegations included experienced and hardened lawyers and diplomats. Second, the PLO exiles guarded their turf ferociously against the encroachment in the negotiations by Palestinians in the Occupied Territories. This was one reason that Arafat chose the Oslo channel: to regain PLO control of the Palestinian negotiating process. As Shehadeh comments,

> Numerous articles, pamphlets and books were written on every legal aspect of the occupation and its activities. Several conferences were held over the years inside and outside Palestine on the legal and human rights aspect of the occupation. The support for Palestinian rights and the conviction that Israeli settlements were illegal extended to a significant sector of Israeli society, who joined in many common actions against these illegalities. And yet when it came to the negotiations with Israel very little of this preparation was used. The Palestinian political establishment outside [i.e. Arafat and the "Tunisians"] showed little interest in these initiatives even when they had clearly made a significant contribution to fostering a better international understanding about the Palestinian legal case.... We also saw that, in the course of proceeding in the alternative secret talks in Oslo, none of the preparation and experience gained from the two years of negotiating with Israel [during the Madrid process] were used. The political objective of winning recognition for the PLO overrode all other considerations. The political battle was all and everything; there was little room to appreciate the legal angle.[28]

As a result, as Israeli scholar Meron Benvenisti notes, "Israeli authorities, in their quest to take possession of land in the territories, have been using every legal and quasi-legal means in the book and are inventing new ones to attain their objectives."[29] The Palestinians were ill-prepared for this legal and diplomatic onslaught. Along this line, Shehadeh further states,

> Israel ... had been preparing its legal case for many years. Its success in negotiating an agreement that enables it to realize its goals in the final status through an interim agreement did not come from a void. Astute as the Israeli negotiators may have been, they had the advantage of years of preparation and a political structure behind them which understood the significance of legal arrangements and had developed the language and concepts that were able to translate political objectives into legal norms and positions.[30]

A major problem with the Oslo process was also Arafat's inability and unwillingness to rein in Palestinian attacks by both secular (e.g., the Popular Front for the Liberation of Palestine) and especially Islamist (Hamas and Islamic Jihad) groups.

Arafat's claim was that the degradation of the PA structure, including its security and police forces, caused by Israeli actions, from freezing PA funds to military incursions, inhibited his ability to clamp down on Palestinian attacks against Israel. The Israelis believed that Arafat willingly decided not to restrain or disarm the militant groups, and on the rare occasion when he did arrest militants, they were often freed soon thereafter. According to this view, as mentioned previously, Arafat exploited the militants' attacks rather than confronting them in an attempt to gain leverage in the ongoing negotiations with the Israelis.[31] In any event, there was some fear among Palestinians that as Hamas grew in popularity any sustained crackdown could incite a Palestinian civil war. Arafat did not want to be perceived as Israel's policeman in the territories, doing the dirty work that Israel was no longer willing to do. In a way, as Cleveland states, "Israel encouraged Arafat to become the authoritarian ruler he was already inclined to be. Yet in complying with Israeli demands and conducting raids against Hamas organizations and jailing hundreds of suspected activists, Arafat undermined his credibility and turned Palestinians against his administration."[32] The PA president was, indeed, in a very difficult position, and as a result he did just enough to anger many Palestinians but not nearly enough to satisfy the Israelis. It is clear, however, that groups such as Hamas and Islamic Jihad were committed to at least disrupting, if not destroying, the Oslo process regardless of what Arafat could or could not do. And just as the continued expansion of Jewish settlements in the territories soured Palestinians on the peace process, so did the continued Palestinian attacks for many Israelis. Most Israelis had very little trust in Arafat, and the PLO chair did little to build a level of trust with the Israeli public, much less skeptical government officials. Israelis would often comment on how different Arafat's speeches were before Israeli and Western cameras from those that he gave in other venues. They point to Arafat's speech in Johannesburg, South

Water

Water is obviously vital for human survival. It is important not only for daily consumption but also in terms of agricultural and industrial productivity and growth. The Commission on the Sustainable Development noted in 1997 that by 2025 two-thirds of the world's population will suffer from moderate to severe water stress resulting from overdemand and pollution. Today, 3.5 billion people live on less than 50 liters per day, only one-seventh of the quantity used by the average American. The Middle East is experiencing severe water stress in many areas; indeed, despite the fact that some countries, such as Turkey and Lebanon, enjoy relatively plentiful water supplies, the region as a whole entered a water-deficit phase by 1970. In fact, the Middle East and North Africa (MENA) is the most water-scarce region in the world, comprising about 6.3% of the world's population yet containing only 1.4% of the world's renewable fresh water.

The combination of water scarcity (limited surface and subsurface resources) with territorial disputes, historical antagonisms, refugee and immigration flows, and rapid population growth has produced a potentially volatile situation in the region, to the point where the phrase *water wars* has entered the lexicon of possible characterizations of the future for the Middle East. Water, in fact, has already entered into the calculations of combatants in the region. As noted in the text, Israel's diversion of the headwaters of the Jordan River in the early 1960s (and Arab attempts at preventing it) raised the level of tension in the Arab–Israeli arena leading up to the 1967 Arab–Israeli war, and in that war the Israeli takeover of the Golan Heights was driven as much by the desire to control the tributaries feeding into the Jordan River as by strategic necessity. In addition, questions concerning water ownership and management have exacerbated relations among a host of riparian states associated with the Tigris–Euphrates river system, the Nile River, and the Jordan River basin, all three of which cross international borders and demand diplomatic cooperation and resolution of competing claims. The issue of adequate water sharing and water ownership greatly complicates a resolution to the Israeli–Palestinian conflict as vital underground aquifers that feed into Israel's National Water Carrier are located in the West Bank, together providing about 50% of Israel's total water consumption. A water-stressed country is one defined as having less than 1,700 cubic meters of water per capita, while a water-scarce country is one with less than 1,000 cubic meters per capita, which cannot for long meet even the basic needs of an organized society on its own. In 1945, Bahrain, Jordan, and Kuwait were considered to be water-scarce countries. By 1990, eight more joined the list (Algeria, Qatar, Saudi Arabia, Somalia, Tunisia, the United Arab Emirates, Yemen, and the Occupied Territories/Palestine). UN studies estimate that by the year 2025 Egypt, Ethiopia, Iran, Libya, Morocco, Oman, and Syria will join the ranks of water-scarce nations. Studies indicate that by 2025 the per capita water availability in the MENA region will be 700 cubic meters, half of what it was in the 1990s. By contrast, the United States has almost 9,000 cubic meters of water per capita.

It is not only the quantity of water that is at issue but also the quality in terms of whether downstream riparian states receive enough sweet, as opposed to salinated, water for productive agricultural utilization. To deal with these water shortages, countries in the region have attempted a variety of short-term expedients and long-term plans from water-sharing agreements, high-yield agriculture, and conservation to high-cost alternatives such as desalinization plants and water transport—or simply fixing leaky pipes (in Damascus, e.g., it is estimated that 30% of the water is lost due to leaky pipes, whereas in Israel the figure is 12%, about what it is in most states in the United States). Whatever may come of the water situation in the Middle East, it is a tremendously complex problem that involves economics, geography, ecology, politics, and international relations—and maybe most importantly, flexibility and imagination.

Africa, in May 1994 when he stated that the Oslo accords were akin to the Treaty of Hudaybiyya in 628 C.E. negotiated between the prophet Muhammad's fledgling Islamic community in Medina and the city of Mecca, which opposed him at the time. It was supposed to be a ten-year peace accord, but only two years later, in 630, the Muslims successfully conquered Mecca. These types of Janus-faced statements by Arafat fed right into the Israeli fear that the PLO was only using the peace process as a way to create a foundation from which it could take over all of Israel. Reflecting this, the level of vitriol and belittling, if not racist, rhetoric adopted by officials on each side toward the other—with either side doing little, if anything, to temper or disavow it—only reinforced preconceived and rapidly developing notions that violence was the only answer. To many Israelis, the Oslo process was supposed to make their lives more, not less, secure. If Israeli security continued to be in question, then maybe the right-wing critique of Oslo was correct, i.e., that it would actually result in more insecurity for Israelis.[33] And if this was the case, then maybe the talks with the Palestinians should end and other alternatives to deal with the situation should be explored. As Yoram Meital states, "more than a decade after the breakthrough of Oslo, it is all too clear that the sides managed to put in place a 'process' reflecting numerous agreements and arrangements but very little 'peace.'"[34]

Most of the leaders on all sides during the Oslo (and Madrid) peace process made bold—if not always wise—moves at considerable risk to themselves. No leader is perfect. It is easy for most of us to cast aspersions from afar and criticize leaders for doing this or not doing that. We are not the ones facing the crush of history, emotions, and sentiments. And as the Rabin assassination made clear, we are not the ones putting our lives on the line. Having said this, however, there were also a number of moments at critical junctures when prudent leadership was lacking: Rabin's acquiescence to expanding settlements; Peres' Grapes of Wrath operation; Netanyahu's rejectionist approach; Barak's arrogance combined with political naivete; Arafat's diplomatic lethargy and unwillingness to do more to rein in the radicals; and, finally, Clinton's belated involvement in the Israeli–Palestinian process and his inability to comprehend the ill-preparedness for Camp David, masked in part as it was by political opportunism.

THE "AL-AQSA" INTIFADA[35]

On September 28, 2000, Ariel Sharon, one of the architects of the settler movement, Israeli war hero, hard-line Likudnik, and someone the Palestinians loathed because of his indirect role in the Sabra and Shatilla massacres in Lebanon in 1982 and direct role in raids against Palestinians in the 1950s at Qibya and Qalqiyya, provocatively visited the Temple Mount/Haram al-Sharif (Noble Sanctuary) accompanied by about 1,000 Israeli police officers. While not actually entering the Dome of the Rock or the al-Aqsa Mosque, the presence of such a controversial figure at Islam's third holiest site at such a volatile time in Israeli–Palestinian relations following the failure at Camp David was bound to produce a convulsive Palestinian response. There were immediate Palestinian demonstrations, and over the next two days eighteen Palestinians died at the hands of Israeli security forces attempting to quell the protests. By the end of the year, this new and more violent intifada was being painted by observers as nothing less than a mini-civil war. As one might expect, there are different Israeli and Palestinian narratives as to the causes of the uprising that ensued almost immediately after Sharon's visit. Regardless of who is more to blame, it is clear that what became known as the al-Aqsa intifada in most circles took on a life of its own and had important repercussions beyond what was envisioned by either side.

For most Israelis, Arafat is to blame.[36] According to this view, because of the failure at Camp David, the Palestinians consciously adopted a policy of violence to force the Israelis to make the concessions they did not make in July. Sharon's visit only provided the Palestinians with a convenient excuse to begin the uprising. Devoid of any leverage throughout the Oslo process, the intifada would provide Arafat some needed bargaining chips—it would show the Israelis what he could unleash if necessary. While it is fairly clear that Arafat exploited the intifada for political purposes once it was launched, most agree that he did not plan it ahead of time. The U.S.-sponsored Mitchell committee, sent to Israel in late 2000 to investigate the situation and recommend a resolution to the crisis, rejected the idea that Arafat or the PA was behind the outbreak of the intifada. A number of Israeli officials and academics agreed. The former head of Israel's Shin Bet (the domestic General Security Service, akin to the FBI in the United States), Ami Ayalon, commented that "Yasser Arafat neither prepared nor triggered the Intifada."[37] Israeli scholar Menachem Klein stated that "there is no evidence whatsoever that there was any such pre-planned decision by the Palestinian Authority."[38] On the contrary, there is a good deal of evidence to suggest that the PA took measures to prevent an outbreak of violence; indeed, in the nine months preceding the intifada, only one Israeli died from Palestinian terrorism. According to a number of reports, including the Mitchell report, Palestinian and U.S. officials strongly urged the Israeli government to stop the Sharon visit to the Haram al-Sharif, fearing it could ignite the incendiary environment. In the days preceding the planned visit, many on both sides were predicting violence if Sharon followed through with it.

It is unknown exactly why Sharon made what he surely knew would be a provocative visit. Most believe he did it for domestic political reasons. At the time he was in a struggle with Benjamin Netanyahu for leadership of the Likud party. Sharon's visit would then be a vivid indication of his commitment to the tenets of the Likud party's position on retention of the territories, most especially an undivided Jerusalem as the eternal capital of the state of Israel. Netanyahu was trying to make a comeback from his tenure in power and the financial scandals that became associated with his government; indeed, he was cleared of a political scandal on September 27, one day before Sharon's visit. Sharon's move was thus an attempt to trump Netanyahu's potential rise back to power within Likud. As a possible added inducement, Sharon, who had, of course, been an outspoken critic of the Oslo process, might have envisioned the visit as a way to scuttle it once and for all. The balanced Mitchell report, however, concluded that "the Sharon visit did not cause the Al-Aqsa Intifada. But it was poorly timed and the provocative effect should have been foreseen; indeed it was foreseen by those who urged that the visit be prohibited."[38a]

The most basic cause of the intifada, in my opinion, was pent-up frustration on both sides of the equation. For the Palestinians, the hope of a viable, independent state had receded far into the background, even before the last hurrah at Camp David. Their lives did not improve in a measurable way; indeed, for most Palestinians during the Oslo period, life became more difficult and desperate. With the continuing expansion of Jewish settlements, the Oslo peace process became a farce, nothing more than a cover for Israeli attempts to control the land. As Muhammad Dahlan, a Fatah leader in charge of security in the Gaza Strip, stated, the intifada "did not occur because of planning or ill intentions but due to Palestinian desperation after seven years without arriving at a final agreement. . . . The intifada happened because of the loss of hope in the peace process."[39]

The intifada was also the result of frustration in the younger generation of Palestinians who came of age during the first intifada against what they saw as the corrupt and anachronistic leadership of Arafat and his cronies. This younger generation, both its Islamist and secular representations, saw the futility of diplomacy and wanted to adopt more aggressive tactics to undo the Israeli occupation—or, at least for the nationalist secular groups, improve their bargaining position should talks resume at some point in the future; in other words, it was not a complete rejection by all Palestinians of diplomacy of any kind.[40] The release of Palestinian prisoners from Israeli jails was an issue that divided Palestinians as many believed the process was much too slow during the Oslo period. The PA would negotiate with Israeli authorities, the latter granting partial releases here and there, usually as a gesture of goodwill in return for Palestinian concessions or as incentive to more vigorously arrest militants. There was even a split within Fatah between those who had lived their entire lives under occupation, such as Muhammad Dahlan, Marwan Barghouti (the head of the Tanzim militia within Fatah), and Jibril Rajoub (one of the heads of Palestinian security in the West Bank), all of whom made their mark during the first intifada. As opposed to the Islamist Palestinian factions such as Hamas and Islamic Jihad, which rejected any peace with Israel and were committed to the return of all of Palestine, the new generation of secular leaders generally supported the two-state solution—they just differed in tactics from the official PA position. Beyond these, many younger Fatah members had been elected to various committees within Fatah in an attempt to wrest control of the organization away from the older generation of Palestinian leaders. A Fatah offshoot militia, the al-Aqsa Martyrs Brigade, formed in the midst of the new intifada, became another manifestation of the internal generational struggle within the Palestinian movement. Some young Palestinians were members of a security service during the day and Tanzim or the al-Aqsa Martyrs Brigade (or both) at night. With the breakdown of PA control as the al-Aqsa intifada waged on, lawlessness in the Palestinian territories increased as bands of territorial gangs emerged to compete with the militias and the PA itself. In fact, intra-Palestinian clashes between armed militias, including the plethora of overlapping security services nominally under the control of Arafat, marked this intifada as much as Israeli–Palestinian confrontations. It led some to conclude that the al-Aqsa intifada was as much an intergenerational Palestinian struggle as a war against Israel. Of course, this just complicated attempts to quell the uprising from within and without, especially as the popularized violence against Israelis placed Arafat in a dilemma: should he do what the Israelis and the United States were demanding, i.e., clamp down on the militants, thus being seen as selling out and undercutting his base, or should he tacitly support the militants, thus maintaining his position within the Palestinian movement as well as providing him with what he thought would be leverage whenever the peace process resumed? In the end, Arafat did not do either, thus pleasing no one, but if anything, he tended to gravitate toward casting a blind eye toward the militants for fear of unleashing the dreaded Palestinian civil war if he cracked down on them.[41] The inability of the PA to develop political institutions, due to its own authoritarian tendencies and corruption, in addition to Israel's inhibiting actions had come home to roost, thus escalating the violent political culture emerging in the territories. As Jeremy Pressman stated "In the absence of democratic governance for Palestinians, being armed was the major currency of political power. One's ability to defend one's political strength turned, in part, on one's ability to show or use force.... the commitment to the use of force was the default position... or they risked looking like an American–Israeli accomplice."[42]

Frustration also contributed to the intensity of the Israeli response to the uprising, in both military and political terms. As with many Palestinians, many Israelis concluded that diplomacy was not the answer. The fact that Arafat did not come up with any serious counterproposals following Camp David further indicated that he was not interested in peace to begin with. The PA president would always be the revolutionary guerilla fighter, never a statesman. Echoing Palestinian sentiments about the use of force, a number of Israelis were saying the same thing in reverse; i.e., the Palestinians only understand force. The IDF was prepared to use massive force to nip the intifada in the bud, and it had been taking steps along this line for several years in preparation for such a day. Yoram Peri noted that "IDF planners were convinced that a real show of strength immediately following the outbreak of violence would make the rioters understand the heavy price they would have to pay for the continued violence, and that would cool their ardor at once."[43] This time around a Palestinian intifada was not going to linger year after year—or so it was thought. Unfortunately, it only led to a spiraling cycle of violence. Barak even hinted at Israel's determination to crush any uprising in a July 26, 2000, statement following the failed summit meeting at Camp David: "To our neighbors, the Palestinians, I say today: We do not seek conflict. But if any of you should dare to put us to the test, we will stand together, strong and determined, convinced in the justness of our cause in the face of any challenge, and we shall triumph."[44] But bloodshed on one side led to vengeful calls for bloodshed on the other. The Mitchell report identified as one of the most significant elements of the outbreak of the intifada "the decision of the Israeli police on 29 September to use lethal means against the Palestinian demonstrators; and the subsequent failure . . . of either party to exercise restraint."[44a]

Unfortunately, both sides often viewed the violence perpetrated as intentional in terms of attempting to eliminate the other rather than as a cathartic expression of frustration and betrayal. The latter would require steps taken to rebuild a level of trust and slowly eliminate the causes of that frustration; all the former required was force.

LAST GASP FOR PEACE

When it became apparent that the events of September 28–29 were much more enduring than the typical spasmodic outbreak of violence, various parties attempted to reel in the uprising before it got out of hand and totally eliminated any hope for peace. President Clinton convened a summit meeting at Sharm al-Shaykh with Barak and Arafat on October 16, 2000, winning what would turn out to be hollow pledges to curtail the violence. Clinton subsequently ordered a commission of inquiry to investigate and analyze the causes of the intifada. It was led by former U.S. senator George Mitchell, who had gained invaluable experience in such trying circumstances as Clinton's special envoy to Northern Ireland, where he helped broker what became known as the "Good Friday" agreement between Protestants and Catholics (the commission's findings were issued the following year as the "Mitchell report").

The Arab world was outraged over Israel's heavy-handed response to the intifada, this time the images being sent via the Arab satellite news agency al-Jazeera into the home of anyone with a satellite dish. The lasting image for Arabs in the early part of the intifada was the death from Israeli–Palestinian crossfire of 12-year-old Muhammad al-Dureh in the arms of his father at Netzarim Junction. An emergency Arab League summit meeting was convened in Cairo on October 21–22. The anti-Israeli rhetoric

A child stands in front of a billboard placed by Hizbollah alongside a road in Sidon, Lebanon, in October 2000 depicting the Dome of the Rock in Jerusalem above and beside pictures of one of the more famous scenes captured on film in the early part of the al-Aqsa intifada, when a young Palestinian boy was killed in the arms of his father by gunshots after they were caught in the crossfire of the Israeli troops and Palestians. (Reuters/Corbis, UT0050196.)

spewing forth from one Arab leader after another harkened back to the heyday of the Arab–Israeli conflict. Some Arab leaders bombastically—and unrealistically—called for a military response, while also demanding the reimposition of the full Arab boycott of Israel. Egypt and Jordan did everything they could do among the Arab moderates to maintain the hope for a diplomatic resolution in the summit communiqué, which ended up calling on the international community to actively intervene to bring the crisis to an end. The Egyptian–Israeli peace treaty had weathered many storms over the years, but Husni Mubarak had long decided its maintenance was a sine qua non for stability in the region, which better served Egyptian (and Jordanian) interests. Even so, Egypt did recall its ambassador as a sign of displeasure with Israeli tactics; Jordan, as well, kept its new ambassador to Israel at home instead of replacing the outgoing one on schedule. Other moderate Arab states, such as Morocco, Oman, Tunisia, and Qatar, downgraded or severed the unofficial (mostly economic) ties they had established with Tel Aviv in the 1990s. With the Arab public integrated into the information age by this time, the daily repetition over the airwaves of Israeli "brutality" and Palestinian "suffering" began to be reflected across the sociocultural spectrum in the Arab world, not unlike that which occurred in the aftermath of the 1967 Arab–Israeli war. As Meital comments,

> The intifada, as an expression of the legitimate struggle of the Palestinian people, was upheld by the broader Arab public and lauded by writers, poets, artists, and intellectuals. Television and radio, the Internet, newspapers, and magazines all revolved around it. Literature, poetry, theater, documentaries, and feature films served as rich, unique sources, conveying how different Arab publics perceived, embedded, and accepted the intifada from September 2000 on.[45]

All of this, of course, tended to restrict the flexibility of moderate Arab leaders, compelling them to at least be seen to be doing as much as possible to assist the Palestinians. On the other hand, the vitriolic anti-Israeli rhetoric just resuscitated the latent fears among Israelis of their country's isolated location in a hostile environment, again feeding into a growing sentiment in Israel that security, rather than any sort of peace process, was the priority in such a climate.

President Clinton, building upon some of the ideas put forth at Camp David, directly reentered the fray in December, offering up an Israeli–Palestinian final status peace plan that appeared to be another attempt to resolve the conflict and establish his legacy in the Middle East before he left office in January. For Barak, it was also a last-gasp attempt, but in his case it was to somehow miraculously forge a final agreement with the Palestinians that might win him another term as prime minister in the elections scheduled for February 2001. He needed something, for he was lagging far behind Likud party leader Ariel Sharon in the polls. Even Arafat, who continued to be hesitant under such circumstances, at least played along in order to counter the perception that grew out of Camp David that he was an out-an-out rejectionist. On December 23, 2000, Clinton presented his new initiative. It was bold and creative, and it was much closer to the Palestinian position than what Barak had offered at Camp David. It is just a shame it was not presented at Camp David rather than at the end of two of the three leaders' terms in office, in itself practically consigning the venture to failure since there would be no guarantee, especially from Arafat's point of view, that the new administration in Washington and the expected new prime minister in Tel Aviv would honor any understandings that had been reached or continue the negotiations, although there was some feeling in the PA that they might be able to get more concessions at the bargaining table under President George W. Bush, anticipating that he might be as even-handed on the Israeli–Palestinian issue as his father had been.

Under Clinton's plan, Israel would withdraw from about 95% of the West Bank and Gaza Strip, with the Palestinians being partially compensated for the land that would remain under Israeli control with 1–3% of existing Israeli territory, most likely in the adjacent Negev. Israel would withdraw over a three-year period, with its security outposts in the Jordan Valley vacated over an additional three-year time frame, being replaced by early warning stations. An international presence would assist in the transition, and most of the Jewish settlers would concentrate in settlement blocs astride the June 4, 1967, line, comprising that 5% of the West Bank remaining in Israeli hands. The Palestinian state would have security forces but would be nonmilitarized, with an international force deployed for border security and deterrence. On the question of Jerusalem, East Jerusalem (or "al-Quds," the Arabic/Muslim name for Jerusalem) would become the capital of the Palestinian state, dividing the Haram al-Sharif/Temple Mount area between the two parties: the Palestinians would receive the Haram al-Sharif itself with its Islamic shrines, while Israel would retain sovereignty over the Jewish quarter in the Old City and the Western Wall. There would be special arrangements concerning excavations beneath the Haram al-Sharif/Temple Mount as well as international monitoring concerning a host of issues, including open travel in and out of the holy places.

Utilizing Clinton's initiative as a basis for discussion, Israeli and Palestinian representatives met at the Egyptian resort city of Taba, just across the Israeli border in the Sinai, beginning on January 21, 2001. There was apparently a good deal of progress made during their week-long sojourn in Taba, many of the participants describing the discussions as never having been so close to a final agreement. The final communiqué was very close to the Clinton plan, but no breakthrough occurred.[46] For one thing, neither Barak nor Arafat attended the talks, and there were no American representatives present. This was to be expected after the fiasco of Camp David, but it also hamstrung any chance for a dramatic breakthrough simply because they were fast running out of time before the February 7 Israeli election. The timing was ill-conceived and smacked of desperation. Even though what was agreed to at Taba was the closest any discussions have come to the minimal position of the Palestinians, Arafat was again slow to respond; and when he did, he added a number of conditions that almost rendered the Clinton plan moot. It was yet another mistake in public diplomacy for Arafat as again he was perceived as being at least a hindrance to peace if not an outright opponent of it. To one of the lead Palestinian negotiators, however, if Camp David "was too little, Taba was too late."[47] In any event, the constituencies for both Arafat and Barak had long been radicalized over the preceding six months, making public support for a new peace initiative lukewarm at best. The most immediate manifestation of this was the landslide victory for Ariel Sharon in the February election, bringing Likud back to power and for the first time as prime minister a man who was considered one of the prime architects of the settler movement, a vociferous opponent of the Oslo process, and someone who had tremendous personal animosity for Arafat.

NOTES

1. Some have suggested that Barak's focus on the Syrian track at this time might have squandered the opportunity to advance Israeli–Palestinian discussions during a period of relative calm. See Jeremy Pressman, "From Madrid to Oslo," in David W. Lesch, *The Middle East and the United States: A Historical and Political Reassessment*, 4th ed. (Boulder: Westview Press, 2007).

2. "Ill-timed," of course, only if one was supportive of the talks.

3. Jeremy Pressman, "Lost Opportunities," *Boston Review* 29 (December 2004/January 2005): 44–45.

4. David W. Lesch, *The New Lion of Damascus: Bashar al-Asad and Modern Syria* (New Haven: Yale University Press, 2005), 259.

5. Dennis Ross, *The Missing Peace: The Inside Story of the Fight for Middle East Peace* (New York: Farrar, Straus and Giroux, 2004), 589.

6. For the small portion of Bashar's inaugural speech devoted to Israel, see Lesch, *The New Lion of Damascus*, 156–157.

7. Yoram Meital, *Peace in Tatters: Israel, Palestine, and the Middle East* (Boulder: Lynne Rienner, 2006), 57.

8. According to Charles Enderlin, in a meeting with President Clinton at the White House on June 15, 2000, regarding the possibility of a summit meeting with Barak, Arafat

stated "I think Barak has decided to put us in the position of the guilty party, and I need your promise that, wherever we go with the negotiations, you won't shift the blame for failure onto us and won't back us into a corner." Clinton reportedly responded by saying "I promise you that under no circumstances will I place the blame for the failure on you." Charles Enderlin, *Shattered Dreams: The Failure of the Peace Process in the Middle East, 1995–2002* (New York: Other Press, 2003), 162–165.

9. Abu Dis, a Palestinian suburb of East Jerusalem, would be given over to the PA as a possible site for the capital. In addition, parts of East Jerusalem, particularly in the Old City, would be under Palestinian municipal jurisdiction, with the Palestinian flag allowed to fly over Christian and Muslim holy places; but ultimate sovereignty still rested with Israel.

10. More than 1 million of these live in fifty-nine UN-operated refugee camps, twenty-seven of which are in the West Bank and Gaza Strip. About half of the over 3 million Palestinians in the West Bank and Gaza Strip are registered refugees, with more than 600,000 living in camps. Jordan has about 1.6 million registered refugees, Lebanon 376,000, and Syria 383,000. Al-Awda, the Palestinian Right of Return Coalition, estimates that there are 2 million more refugees who are not registered living in other countries (www.cnn.com/SPECIALS/2001/mideast/stories/issues.refugees/index.html).

11. Ehud Barak, "Israel Needs a True Partner for Peace," *New York Times*, July 30, 2001.

12. Meital, *Peace in Tatters*, 81.

13. Glenn E. Robinson, "The Oslo Accords Were a Failure," in David W. Lesch, ed., *History in Dispute: The Middle East Since 1945*, 2nd series, vol. 15 (New York: St. James Press, 2004), 190.

14. Ibid, 187.

15. To many, the Jewish settlements in the Occupied Territories are illegal under international law according to the Fourth Geneva Convention of 1949. The Geneva Convention prohibits an occupying power from transferring its own civilian population to the occupied territory. Numerous UN resolutions have confirmed the illegality of the settlements, which is also in accordance with the official U.S. position over the years. For opposing views on the legality of the settlements, see the point-counterpoint essays by Yitzhak Klein and Jeremy Pressman in Lesch, *History in Dispute*, 1st series, vol. 14, 151–158.

16. Robert H. Mnookin and Ehud Eiran, "Discord 'Behind the Table': The Internal Conflict Among Israeli Jews Concerning the Future of Settlements in the West Bank and Gaza," *Journal of Dispute Resolution* (Fall 2005): 23. This is an outstanding essay on the history of the Israeli settlements, the various domestic forces supporting and opposing the settlement process, and the relationship between the settler movement and Israeli politics. Unless otherwise noted, much of the information in this section is drawn from this essay.

16a. Quoted in ibid, 24.

17. From 1993 to 2001, there was a 54% increase in the number of housing units in the West Bank (excluding East Jerusalem) and the Gaza Strip—20,400 to 31,400. The most significant portion of this increase took place in 2000 under Ehud Barak's government. Ibid., 24. Under Yitzhak Rabin's tenure in the 1990s, the settlement expansion largely occurred in the existing major settlements of the West Bank ("thickening" as it was called) of Gush Etzion, Ma'ale Adumim, and Ariel, three large blocs that under Ariel Sharon's unilateral withdrawal plan by 2004 would fall within new Israeli borders in the West Bank behind the security fence.

18. Including the quite large Jewish settlement at Har Homa amidst the Palestinian neighborhoods of East Jerusalem (the Palestinians call this land Jabal Abu Ghanim).

19. Rabbi Avram Isaac Kook (1864–1935) and his son Rabbi Tzvi Yehuda Kook (1890–1981) are the two leading ideologues behind this line of thought that forms one of the bases for Gush Emunim, whose members, for the most part, had belonged to the NRP but became dissatisfied with their muted activism. The Kooks saw the secular state as the beginning of Jewish redemption, reflecting a "fusion of religious and Zionist ideologies." Mnookin and Eiran, "Discord,"

20–21. Indeed, religious Zionists, based on the Kook ideology, argued that returning any territory captured in 1967 "would be a reversal of the messianic process and . . . a sin against God." The establishment of Israel was the first stage of the messianic redemptive period and the capture of the West Bank (Judea and Samaria), of such biblical importance in Jewish eschatology, was the second stage. Robert O. Freedman, "Disengagement and Its Aftermath: Challenges to the Future of Israel and the Peace Process," *Israel Horizons* (Autumn 2005). Gush Emunim had established a "settlement department" called Amana (Covenant), and even though the "bloc of the faithful" had dissipated as a political movement by the early 1980s, Amana maintained its active role in expanding settlements.

20. Quoted in Mnookin and Eiran, "Discord," 29.

21. Ibid., 31.

22. Ibid., 33.

23. Quoted in ibid., 16.

24. Edward Said, *The End of the Peace Process* (London: Granta Books, 2002), 368.

25. William L. Cleveland, *A History of the Modern Middle East* (Boulder: Westview Press, 2004), 508.

26. Raja Shehadeh, *From Occupation to Interim Accords: Israel and the Palestinian Territories* (London: Kluwer Law International, 1997).

27. Ibid., 161.

28. Ibid., 160–161.

29. Meron Benvenisti, *The West Bank Data Project: A Survey of Israel's Policies* (Washington, DC: American Enterprise Institute for Public Policy Research, 1984), 30.

30. Shehadeh, *From Occupation to Interim Accords*, 72.

31. The Mitchell report found that there was "no evidence on which to conclude that the PA made a consistent effort to contain the demonstrators and control the violence once it began."

32. Cleveland, *A History*, 599.

33. For a list of actual and suspected Palestinian attacks on Israelis in the period between the signing of the Declaration of Principles in September 1993 and the outbreak of the al-Aqsa intifada in Septmber 2000, see the Israeli Ministry of Foreign Affairs website at www.mfa.gov.il/MFA and click "Terrorism."

34. Meital, *Peace in Tatters,* 2.

35. For Israelis, the so-called al-Aqsa intifada was variously termed *Homat Maggen* ("defensive shield"), *Derekh Nehusha* ("resolve"), or *Milhement Kiyum* ("a war for survival"). Many in Israeli officialdom called it simply the "intifada" minus the "al-Aqsa," depriving it of its symbolism yet clearly denoting which side started the violence.

36. For an excellent discussion of the Israeli and Palestinian narratives on who (and what) is to blame for the outbreak of the intifada, on which much of the information on this section is based, see Jeremy Pressman, "The Second Intifada: Background and Causes of the Israeli-Palestinian Conflict," *Journal of Conflict Studies* 22, no. 2 (2003): 114–141.

37. Quoted in ibid., 116.

38. Ibid.

38a. Quoted in ibid, 118.

39. Quoted in ibid, 122.

40. As Palestinian leader Marwan Barghouti stated, "The only thing the Israelis understand is force. . . . You [Israel] don't want to end the occupation and you don't want to stop the settlements, so the only way to convince you is by force. This is the Intifada of peace." Quoted in ibid., 128.

41. As Meital notes, however, "despite the divisions of Palestinian society, there are also attenuating influences against armed flare-up, namely the sociopolitical situation that finds members of the same families belonging to different factions. In Gaza, for example, where Hamas enjoys the widest support, many of the movement's activists are close kin of members of the PA's regular security forces. This is the dam against Palestinian civil war." Meital, *Peace in Tatters*, 205.

42. Ibid., 126.

43. Yoram Peri, "The Israeli Military and Israel's Palestinian Policy: From Oslo to the al-Aqsa Intifada" (United States Institute of Peace), *Peaceworks* 47 (November 2002): 31.

44. Quoted in Pressman, "The Second Intifada," 124.

45. Meital, *Peace in Tatters*, 103.

46. In the final communiqué was the following statement: "The sides declare that they have never been closer to reaching an agreement and it is thus our shared belief that the remaining gaps could be bridged with the resumption of negotiations following the Israeli elections." (www.mideastweb.org/tuba.htm)

47. Nabil Sha'th, quoted in Meital, *Peace in Tatters*, 89.

President William J. Clinton Statement on the Middle East Peace Talks at Camp David

July 25, 2000

President, William J. Clinton
Statement on the Middle East Peace Talks at Camp David
The White House, The James S. Brady Press Briefing Room
Washington, DC, July 25, 2000
Released by The White House Office of the Press Secretary

12:07 P.M. EDT

The President: First of all, let me say, like all of you I just heard the news of the crash of the Concorde outside Paris, and I wanted to extend the deepest condolences of the American people to the families of those who were lost.

After 14 days of intensive negotiations between Israelis and Palestinians, I have concluded with regret that they will not be able to reach an agreement at this time. As I explained on the eve of the summit, success was far from guaranteed—given the historical, religious, political and emotional dimensions of the conflict.

Still, because the parties were not making progress on their own and the September deadline they set for themselves was fast approaching, I thought we had no choice. We can't afford to leave a single stone unturned in the search for a just, lasting and comprehensive peace.

Now, at Camp David, both sides engaged in comprehensive discussions that were really unprecedented because they dealt with the most sensitive issues dividing them; profound and complex questions that long had been considered off limits.

Under the operating rules that nothing is agreed until everything is agreed, they are, of course, not bound by any proposal discussed at the summit. However, while we did not get an agreement here, significant progress was made on the core issues. I want to express my appreciation to Prime Minister Barak, Chairman Arafat and their delegations for the efforts they undertook to reach an agreement.

Prime Minister Barak showed particular courage, vision, and an understanding of the historical importance of this moment. Chairman Arafat made it clear that he, too, remains committed to the path of peace. The trilateral statement we issued affirms both leaders' commitment to avoid violence or unilateral actions which will make peace more difficult and to keep the peace process going until it reaches a successful conclusion.

At the end of this summit, I am fully aware of the deep disappointment that will be felt on both sides. But it was essential for Israelis and Palestinians, finally, to begin to deal with the toughest decisions in the peace process. Only they can make those decisions, and they both pledged to make them, I say again, by mid-September.

Now, it's essential that they not lose hope, that they keep working for peace, that they avoid any unilateral actions that would only make the hard task ahead more difficult. The statement the leaders have made today is encouraging in that regard.

Israelis and Palestinians are destined to live side by side, destined to have a common future. They have to decide what kind of future it will be. Though the differences that remain are deep, they have come a long way in the last seven years, and, notwithstanding the failure to reach an agreement, they made real headway in the last two weeks.

Now, the two parties must go home and reflect, both on what happened at Camp David and on what did not happen. For the sake of their children, they must rededicate themselves to the path of peace and find a way to resume their negotiations in the next few weeks. They've asked us to continue to help, and as always, we'll do our best. But the parties themselves, both of them, must be prepared to resolve profound questions of history, identity and national faith—as well as the future of sites that are holy to religious people all over the world who are part of the Islamic, Christian and Judaic traditions.

The children of Abraham, the descendants of Isaac and Ishmael can only be reconciled through courageous compromise. In the spirit of those who have already given their lives for peace and all Israelis, Palestinians, friends of peace in the Middle East and across the world, we long for peace and deserve a Holy Land that lives for the values of Judaism, Islam and Christianity.

Thank you.

---

http://www.yale.edu/lawweb/avalon/mideast/mid027.htm (accessed February 3, 2006).

Twelve

. . . AND RECONSTRUCTION?

9/11 AND U.S. FOREIGN POLICY

President George W. Bush assumed office on January 20, 2001. In the early months of his term in office, his administration was not much inclined to turn its attentions to the Middle East, particularly the Israeli–Palestinian situation. This was certainly understandable at first, having just witnessed his predecessor engage directly in the Israeli–Palestinian process and commit the prestige of the office of the president of the United States in an attempt to seek a final status agreement, with little to nothing to show for it; indeed, the Clinton administration's efforts unintentionally contributed to the outbreak of the al-Aqsa *intifada* that was now raging in full force. There did not seem to be anything to gain by involving the administration in intensive diplomacy, especially since President Bush's domestic situation was less than ideal, having won the presidency by only a razor-thin (and controversial) margin, presiding over an economic downturn, and with the Republican edge in the Senate whittled down to a mere one as a result of the fall 2000 election (a margin it would lose several months later when a liberal Republican became an Independent who voted with the Democrats).[1] In addition, there was no longer a willing partner in peace in Israel with Ariel Sharon becoming prime minister in the February 2001 election. For all intents and purposes, the Oslo process was dead. Finally, the partisan bitterness that had come to characterize Washington politics found its way into foreign policy as well, with the new administration embracing what was amusingly called the "ABC" approach—i.e., "Anything But Clinton." Republican pundits gleefully exclaimed that "grown-ups" were now directing U.S. foreign policy, with Colin Powell as secretary of state, Donald Rumsfeld as defense secretary, Condoleezza Rice as national security adviser, and Vice President Dick Cheney assuming an active role in the foreign policymaking apparatus. Gone were the perceived chaotic Clintonian diplomatic adventures as well as the nation-building exercises of the type that the Clinton administration implemented in Bosnia and Kosovo.

Representative of this relative disinterest in Middle East affairs at the time was the fact that a new assistant secretary of state for Near Eastern affairs was not appointed until late May 2001.[2] The U.S. special envoy to the Middle East, Dennis Ross, who had served the two previous administrations, retired in January 2001, yet no replacement was named until May. Colin Powell stated succinctly the bent of the administration in December 2000 before taking office: "We will facilitate, but at the end of the day, it will have to be the parties in the region who will have to find the solution."[3] In addition, the Bush administration supported Sharon's position regarding the Camp David and Taba talks, i.e., that they were "off the table" once his new government was formed. Powell in March would comment in more specific terms that "the U.S. stands ready to assist, not insist. Peace arrived at voluntarily by the partners themselves is likely to prove more robust... than peace widely viewed as developed by others, worse yet, imposed."[4] This was very close to the Israeli view of dealing with Arab parties directly and not in an international setting in which there was a greater likelihood of a peace agreement being imposed upon the Jewish state. And in what would become a mantra of the administration throughout the intifada, Bush, clearly placing more of the blame for the violence on the Palestinians, stated "The Palestinian Authority should speak out publicly and forcibly in a language that the Palestinian people [understand] to condemn violence and terrorism.... The signal I am sending to the Palestinians is stop the violence and I can't make it any more clear."[5] All of this was despite a great deal of optimism in the Arab world (and in the Arab–American community in the United States) that George W. Bush, would be as impartial an arbiter on the Arab–Israeli conflict as his father, George H. W. Bush, had been. They would be bitterly disappointed. Instead, the United States remained an aloof observer, casting a virtual blind eye toward Sharon's settlement expansion activities and the use of targeted assassinations of suspected Palestinian militants and employing some verbal prestidigitation, as when Sharon claimed that the West Bank and Gaza Strip were not "occupied" but "disputed" territories; thus, their disposition was subject to negotiation (although the State Department did issue a forceful rebuke of Sharon's use of words; however, nothing was heard from the White House).[6]

This was the general predisposition of the Bush administration toward the Middle East on the eve of the most lethal terrorist attack in history on September 11, 2001, or what has simply become known as "9/11."

As is well known, soon after the workday had begun on the morning of September 11, passenger planes hijacked by terrorists slammed into the World Trade Center's "Twin Towers" in New York City and the Pentagon in Washington, killing almost 3,000 people. The attacks were organized and carried out by the transnational terrorist network called al-Qa'ida ("the base"), led by Osama bin Laden. Bin Laden and many al-Qa'ida leaders had taken refuge in and were operating from Afghanistan under the protection of the puritanical Sunni Islamist Taliban regime. The global repercussions of 9/11 would be enormous, with distinct reverberations in the Arab–Israeli arena.

For Americans, the world definitely changed. The distance traveled from the secure, if not invincible, feeling Americans had prior to 9/11 to the sense of vulnerability following the attacks was enormous. The world was a different place—it *had* to be. Outside of the United States, there was worldwide sympathy expressed in the immediate aftermath of that horrid day. As Gerald Baker stated, "when Iranian mullahs, French editorialists, and Chinese Communist party officials rush to express support for Americans, you know something large has happened in international relations."[7] To many in the outside world, though, the event in and of itself was not as earth-shattering as the Bush administration was making it out to be. Many countries had been dealing with terrorism for decades, although nowhere had it been more dramatically perpetrated in what was essentially a single act. The problem, though, is that when the single most powerful country in the world, in what many began to call the unipolar international environment in the wake of the bipolar superpower cold war, believes the world has changed and adopts certain dramatic policies in response, the event *becomes* earth-shattering whether one believes it actually was or not.

Generally speaking, the post-9/11 foreign policy of the Bush administration has been frequently compared with the era of Manifest Destiny in the 1840s. Most often offered for comparison is the religiously laced rhetoric that accompanied U.S. policies. In coining the term, New York lawyer and journalist John L. O'Sullivan proclaimed in 1845 that it is "the right of our manifest destiny to overspread and to possess the whole of the continent which Providence has given us for the development of the great experiment of liberty and federated self-government entrusted to us." Manifest Destiny was almost a mystical religious belief in a divinely mandated mission to humankind for U.S. expansion in the name of liberty. It was, indeed, a crusade to civilize more primitive peoples and societies. While critics point to Manifest Destiny as an arrogant rationalization of real-life territorial aggression, it seems to have provided a veneer of idealism, which the American traditional exceptionalist view of self demands, that masked, intentionally and unintentionally, policies based on strategic and economic necessity. The twentieth century produced a liberal, capitalist world order in which the United States thrived; and any attempts to subvert that prosperous order had to be countered with all due urgency and force. As George W. Bush stated in a speech during his presidential campaign on November 19, 1999, "Some have tried to pose a choice between American ideals and American interests, between who we are and how we act. But the choice is false. America, by decision and destiny, promotes political freedom and gains the most when democracy advances... to turn this time of American influence into generations of democratic peace."[7a] The basic objective of U.S. foreign policy over the decades has been to produce and maintain a stable world order where U.S. trade and investment could increase and U.S. institutions could be implanted. Instability interfered with trade and offered disruptive external forces opportunities to advance their interests at the expense of U.S. interests. Nazism and communism challenged U.S. supremacy, and both were beaten back. After 9/11, the perception in the United States was that there is a new force, most often identified as Islamic extremism, attempting to undermine the economic, political, and cultural hegemony of a United States whose power was reinforced and enhanced by a decade of breakout globalization in the 1990s. This new threat must be defeated, and the terminology employed by Bush administration officials was framed within this paradigm.[8] As Bush announced in a speech shortly after 9/11: "We have seen their kind before. They are the heirs of all the murderous ideologies of the twentieth century. By sacrificing human life to serve their radical visions, by abandoning every value except the will to power, they follow in the path of fascism, and Nazism, and totalitarianism."[8a]

The initial U.S. riposte to 9/11 came in the form of invading Afghanistan in October 2001 to rid the country of the Taliban and al-Qa'ida presence. With the considerable assistance of local Afghani factions that had opposed the Taliban regime for years, the United States did just that by early December. Article V of the North Atlantic Treaty Organization (NATO) charter was invoked, legitimizing the U.S.-led military response as an act of collective self-defense. Throughout the Middle East, even from traditional foes of the United States such as Iran and Libya, the 9/11 attacks were roundly condemned. While the cynic may doubt the sincerity of such pronouncements, seeing them as more of a convulsive gesture just to let Washington know they had nothing to do with the terrorist acts (and, therefore, would not be subjected to the expected U.S. military response), there was an outpouring of grief at the grassroots level. Religious figures across the Islamic world condemned the attacks, stating that they were totally inconsistent with the teachings of Islam. Shaykh Yusuf al-Qaradawi, who is a very influential figure in the Islamic community and hosts a popular religious program on Arab satellite news network al-Jazeera, condemned all suicide attacks. Yasser Arafat, not wanting to repeat his mistake during the Gulf crisis and war of 1990–1991 when he tacitly aligned the PLO with Iraq, was filmed giving blood for the victims of the tragedy and later supported the U.S. war in Afghanistan. Unfortunately, this show of goodwill was overwhelmed by shots of some Palestinians celebrating the 9/11 attacks. Most Palestinians, though, reflecting a duality of emotions, would probably comment as one Palestinian did in the following manner:

> [9/11] was an awful thing, a tragedy, and since we live a continuous tragedy, we felt like this touched us. But when we see something like this in Israel or the US, we feel a contradiction. We see it's a tragedy, but we remember that these are the people behind our tragedy. Even small children know that Israel is nothing without America. And here America means F-16, M-16, Apache helicopters, the tools Israelis use to kill us and destroy our homes.[9]

President Bush went out of his way to make sure that the Islamic world understood that Washington was not castigating an entire religion or culture, just the extremists who perverted the true meaning of Islam. Saudi Arabia, from which fifteen of the nineteen hijackers originated (not to speak of Osama bin Laden himself), quietly increased its supply of oil to the United States to soften the anticipated economic blow following the attacks.

For a short while in the aftermath of 9/11, the Bush administration actively courted the Arab world as an ally against the new terrorist threat and in its Afghani campaign, attempting to construct a broad coalition not unlike what his father did in the 1991 Gulf War.[10] Indeed, Ariel Sharon was getting a bit nervous about the repercussions that this new American bent might have on Israel's policies vis-à-vis the Palestinians. In fact, Bush began to pressure Sharon to agree to a cease-fire in the intifada in order to facilitate the U.S. attempt to attract allies in the Arab and Muslim world against the Taliban. In a terse statement that he would later soften, Sharon shot back that "Israel would not be sacrificed as part of the West's appeasement of the Arab world."[11] This, of course, had been a fear with both Labor and Likud governments in Israel ever since the end of the cold war and the breakup of the Soviet Union: that the reduced strategic utility of Israel in the wake of the end of the cold war, combined with soaring government deficits and calls by members of Congress to cut back on foreign aid, would degrade the U.S.–Israeli relationship and lead to a significant reduction in the $3 billion dollars of annual assistance the United States provided Israel.[12] By the mid-1990s, Israeli leaders were warning the United States of the brewing threat of Islamic extremism, hoping to position Israel once again as a key U.S. ally in the fight against a global menace arising in the wake of the fall of communism. As we shall see, Sharon's fears, while understandable at that specific moment, would turn out to be very much unfounded.

The goodwill the United States garnered following 9/11, however, began to dissipate toward the end of the year. European states began to question whether or not Article V of the NATO charter was too hastily invoked. Media coverage, especially over al-Jazeera, of civilian casualties in Afghanistan as well as questions over the legality and morality of the treatment of Afghani and al-Qa'ida prisoners taken to the American naval base at Guantánamo Bay in Cuba began to erode the international support for U.S. policies. To many in the Muslim world, it was indeed becoming a war against Islam. Across the Atlantic, the Europeans began to see the United States exploit the new international environment as an imprimatur to act unilaterally, building on the unilateralist trend of the Bush administration before 9/11, manifest in its refusal to sign the Kyoto treaty on global warming, its opposition to the International Criminal Court, and its tariff policies. The United States seemed to be sending its troops all over the world to find al-Qa'ida operatives. President Bush stated in a speech in June 2002 at the military academy at West Point that the United States would take the battle to the enemy and would root out terrorist forces "in any dark corner of the world."[12a] While acknowledging the "unorthodox methods" that may be needed to confront the new threat of transnational terrorism, Sir Michael Howard, commented that "to hostile skeptics they look like the assertion of a hunter license for American armed forces to operate anywhere in the world without concern for the constraints imposed by national sovereignty or international law."[13] Fears began to arise that, with the unprecedented military and economic power in the possession of the United States, the world had entered a new era of imperialism orchestrated from Washington. Nowhere was this more apparent than in the Arab world, which in a way felt targeted because of its centrality in the Islamic world and the Arab origins of al-Qa'ida. In the Arab world, there already existed a level of disgust at U.S. policy over the years, what Arabs believed was the almost unconditional support Washington has given Israeli economically, militarily, and politically. They see multiple double standards in U.S. foreign policy that elicit frustration and generate distrust. How could the United States insist on Iraqi compliance with U.N. resolutions when at the same time it allows Israel to snub its nose at them? How can the self-professed beacon of liberty and freedom in the world extol the virtues of democracy while it supports quite nondemocratic authoritarian regimes in countries such as Saudi Arabia and Egypt? It seems to many that U.S. policy is case-specific, based on its own perceived interests at any given moment. As much as Washington tries to portray itself as preaching a consistent ethical code in the foreign policy arena, this seems to be more of a peculiar American trait that emerged out of its own historical experience of exceptionalism since the beginning of the republic rather than an intuitive set of principles applied with equilibrium around the globe.

The war in Afghanistan elevated the influence of the Pentagon at the White House. As the war turned into such a rousing military success story, the so-called neo-conservatives, who formed an important ideological base for the administration, especially at the Pentagon and in the White House, trumpeted the advantages and utility of power to achieve foreign policy objectives. Strategic power was seen as an asset, and in this sense Israel was always viewed with admiration by the "neo-cons." As such, the old wound and unfinished business of Iraq vaulted to the top of the policy priority list even before the overthrow of the Taliban had been completed. Iraq suddenly became part and parcel of the global war against terror as it became linked by (what is now known to be very questionable) intelligence to al-Qa'ida (and even 9/11) as well as developing weapons of mass destruction in abeyance of United Nations (UN) resolutions. President Bush's state of the union address in January 2002 appeared to be the capstone of this policy shift, when he teamed Iraq up with Iran and North Korea as the "axis of evil." As Rashid Khalidi noted, the neo-cons had moved from the conservative think tanks in the 1990s to the policymaking corridors in

What is a Neo-Con?

The "neo-cons," short for "neo-conservative," became quite prominent during the administration of President George W. Bush, especially during his first term. So-called neo-cons populated a number of foreign policy positions in the higher echelons of the White House, Pentagon, and State Department. Known for advocating a more hawkish foreign policy, the neo-cons are seen as having provided the ideological foundation for the Bush administration's reaction to the terrorist attacks of 9/11 as articulated in the National Security Strategy announced in September 2002, otherwise known as the "Bush Doctrine." The most spectacular applications of the neo-con foreign policy were the initiation of the war against Iraq in 2003 as well as the related attempts to promote democracy throughout the Middle East in order to eliminate the rampant authoritarianism viewed as one of the primary causes for creating the facilitating environment of despair and repression that gives rise to Islamic extremism. In their view, democracies do not go to war against one another, so a world populated with them will be a more stable and prosperous one that will help perpetuate American dominance.

One of the founders of neo-conservativism was social commentator Irving Kristol, who as a student was a Trotskyite, then a liberal, then eventually a self-professed neo-con. He was part of an influential group of Jewish intellectuals who attended the City College of New York in the 1930s and 1940s and became the brain trust of the neo-conservative ideology. He coined the term "neo-conservative" in the early 1970s, although by the mid-1990s he felt the term was no longer useful since in his view neo-conservatism, especially after the Reagan years, had become part of mainstream America. Kristol's son, William, and Robert Kagan helped revive the term in the 1990s as part of the Project for a New American Century, a foreign policy "ginger group." Neo-conservative philosophy was at first primarily focused on domestic issues. The neo-cons promoted the value of local government, parent–teacher associations, and faith-based initiatives and opposed the "social engineering" exemplified by affirmative action, welfare, and busing, which tended to require massive government intervention that caused societal disruptions and often backfired with unintended negative repercussions.

The neo-cons are firm believers in American democracy, and this enthusiastic belief filtered its way into the foreign policy arena. Power is seen to be a strategic asset to be used in order to attain foreign policy objectives. In this sense, preemptive warfare and regime change are necessary tools in order to bring about the rise of democracies. All that authoritarian and totalitarian regimes need is a push from the outside that will force them to crumble. The experience of the end of the cold war, especially with the fall of communist and the rise of democratic regimes in Eastern Europe, become something of a template to the new generation of neo-cons. As some critics have pointed out, it is almost as if the neo-cons expect democracy to be the default condition in states that rid themselves of authoritarianism rather than the result of a long-term process of institutional and political evolution. It is a highly interventionist and aggressive foreign policy posture, but neo-cons believe that the United States will morally exercise this power in a relatively restrained and benevolent fashion. In many ways, it is positively Wilsonian in the sense of "making the world safe for democracy" but, in the neo-con case, without the association with international institutions (such as the United Nations) that President Woodrow Wilson promoted after World War I. Critics of the neo-con foreign policy, especially in its application in the Middle East, point to the fact that it is avowedly biased in favor of Israel, ergo the Bush administration's strong support for Israel under Ariel Sharon. Neo-con supporters would counter that the support for Israel is primarily based on the fact that it is the only working democracy in a sea of tyranny, and therefore, it is a natural ally of the United States—and an especially powerful one at that. The problems the United States encountered in Iraq following the acute phase of the war in 2003 have taken some of the wind out of the neo-con sails, particularly as some of the leading neo-cons in the administration, such as Paul Wolfowitz, have left to pursue jobs in other venues. Some of the underlying foundations of neo-con foreign policy thought and practice are still present in Washington, however, and all of this has added to the already existing foreign policy paradigms that future presidential administrations will be compelled to consider.*

*For an excellent explanation of the neo-con philosophy, especially in its foreign policy application, as well as a critique, see Francis Fukuyama, "After Neoconservatism," *New York Times Magazine*, February 19, 2006.

Washington when the Bush administration came to power. What they brought with them were some very interesting ideas regarding U.S. Middle East policy.

A chorus along these lines rang out from within a strain of the Republican party in the mid-1990s. The turning point was the 1994 midterm congressional elections that brought the Republicans a majority in both the House and the Senate. Most remember this Republican "revolution" led by, among others, Newt Gingrich for its domestic policy repercussions, especially over welfare reform and the budget, including the shutting down of the government in late 1995. However, it also established the foundation for important shifts in foreign policy if and when there arose a sympathetic administration in the White House and/or a more propitious environment, both of which occurred with Bush coming to power, followed swiftly by the repercussions of 9/11. As James Zogby, president of the Arab American Institute, wrote in 1997, "This new Republican leadership is not from the traditional pro-business moderate wing of the Party once represented by Texans like George Bush [George H. W. Bush], James Baker, and John Connally. The new Republican leadership in Congress is an alliance between ideological neo-conservatives and the Christian fundamentalist movement."[13a]

A seminal representation of this emerging viewpoint was a six-page report prepared by the Jerusalem-based Institute for Advanced Strategic and Political Studies in 1996, entitled "A Clean Break: A New Strategy for Securing the Realm."[14] As the report states, it was compiled from discussions among the Study Group on a New Israeli Strategy Toward 2000, consisting of, among others, Richard Perle, Douglas Feith, David Wurmser, and Meyrav Wurmser. All of these people have or had important positions either in the Bush administration itself or in entities that are closely aligned to various elements within the administration. The report was constructed for Likud party leader Benjamin Netanyahu in the immediate aftermath of his election victory as Israeli prime minister in 1996, offering recommendations regarding Middle East policy; indeed, the report even has passages in bold print marked "TEXT" to highlight what are suggestions for a "possible speech" by the new Israeli premier. In many ways, this report became something of a blueprint for the Bush administration's Middle East policy. Although others have focused on aspects of the report that center on Saddam Hussein's regime in Iraq, the primary target for "securing the realm" for Israel was Syria, the removal of Saddam Hussein being a necessary precursor for isolating Damascus.

The report contends that "efforts to salvage Israel's socialist institutions—which include pursuing supranational over national sovereignty and pursuing a peace process that embraces the slogan, 'New Middle East'—undermine the legitimacy of the nation and lead Israel into strategic paralysis under the previous government's [that of Yitzhak Rabin and Shimon Peres] 'peace process.'" In order to "secure the nation's streets and borders in the immediate future," the authors of the report suggest Israel do the following:

"1. Work closely with Turkey and Jordan to contain, destabilize, and roll-back some of its most dangerous threats [clearly Syria and Iraq]. This implies a clean break from the slogan 'comprehensive peace' to a traditional concept of strategy based on balance of power.

2. Change the nature of its relations with the Palestinians, including upholding the right of hot pursuit for self-defense into all Palestinian areas and nurturing alternatives to Arafat's exclusive grip on Palestinian society.

3. Forge a new basis for relations with the United States—stressing self-reliance, maturity, strategic cooperation on areas of mutual concern, and furthering values inherent to the West. This can only be done if Israel takes serious steps to terminate aid, which prevents economic reform."

The report also suggests that:

> Israel can shape its strategic environment, in cooperation with Turkey and Jordan, by weakening, containing, and even rolling back Syria. This effort can focus on removing Saddam Hussein from power in Iraq—an important Israeli strategic objective in

> its own right—as a means of foiling Syria's regional ambitions. . . . Most important, it is understandable that Israel has an interest supporting diplomatically, militarily and operationally Turkey's and Jordan's actions against Syria, such as securing tribal alliances with Arab tribes that cross into Syrian territory and are hostile to the Syrian ruling elite.

The report closes with the following ominous bold print "TEXT" admonition: "Israel will not only contain its foes; it will transcend them." Interestingly, Netanyahu visited Washington in 1996 advocating a policy of "triple containment," i.e., the containment of Iraq, Iran, and Syria.

If this type of foreign policy paradigm was lurking in the policymaking corridors of Washington at the beginning of the Bush administration, 9/11 brought it front and center in the Pentagon and at the White House. The shock of 9/11 merged two ideological factions in the Republican foreign policymaking apparatus: the neo-cons (or what some have also called the "democratic imperialists," among whom Richard Perle, Paul Wolfowitz, and William Kristol are counted as some of the leading lights) and the so-called assertive nationalists, among whom Secretary of Defense Donald Rumsfeld and even Vice President Cheney are included. A realist or internationalist wing of the Republican party was present primarily in the State Department, led by Secretary of State Colin Powell, who, for the most part, was outflanked by Rumsfeld and Cheney and marginalized in the run-up to the war in Iraq in 2003 and in the immediate postwar reconstruction period. Both the neo-cons and the assertive nationalists had a unilateralist bent in terms of utilizing (or not utilizing) international institutions such as the UN. The assertive nationalists employed their unilateralism as a protective shield to guard the United States from various threats, and they were absolutely opposed to nation-building—they would deal with the threat, diminish or get rid of it, and then pull out. The neo-cons, on the other hand, were Wilsonian, viewing a unilateralist approach as the most efficient way to remake the world or, as Wilson famously stated, "make the world safe for democracy," although without the support and involvement of the international institutions that Wilson envisioned. The neo-cons saw this as the best antidote to Islamic extremism, i.e., eliminating the facilitating environments of authoritarianism, corruption, and socioeconomic distress that spawn it. These two factions shared similar ideas about the nature of the new threat against the United States in the post-9/11 environment as well as the need to go to war in Iraq in 2003, but they differed dramatically on determining the ultimate objectives and how best to achieve them—which, in my view, was one of the main problems in developing a coherent and workable postwar reconstruction plan in Iraq.

As a result, the United States shifted its strategic modus operandi in the post-9/11 era to that of preventive war as articulated in the administration's National Security Strategy of September 2002, or what has become known as the "Bush Doctrine." It is a strategy that advocates when necessary a preventive war through preemptive military action against what are determined to be imminent threats to U.S. security—there would be no more 9/11's. The use by al-Qa'ida of the failed-state environment in Afghanistan to build up its terrorist network convinced policymakers that the United States could no longer wait for a threat to become manifest. It was now compelled to deal with countries that from the viewpoint of Washington facilitated terrorism before the actual threat emerged. The war in Afghanistan was retributive. The war in Iraq was the first real application of the Bush Doctrine, although some would say it was still part and parcel of a cathartic American response to 9/11, especially as Iraq was "low-hanging fruit"; i.e., it was doable. Iraq was a relatively easy foe to defeat. Even before the war began in March 2003, two-thirds of the country had been overflown by U.S., British, and French aircraft on a daily basis ever since the end of the 1991 Gulf War; it had been debilitated by severe, if imperfect, UN sanctions for a dozen years; and its military had been ravaged by war, purges, and neglect.

More importantly for the Arab–Israeli equation, the shifting sands in Washington by the end of 2001 also served to align the Bush administration with Ariel Sharon's view of the Palestinians, that, indeed, what Israel was doing was no different from what the United States was attempting to do in Afghanistan: rooting out terror. Yasser Arafat and the Palestine Liberation Organization (PLO), therefore, were nothing more than another version of Osama bin Laden and al-Qa'ida. Slowly but surely the Bush administration began to see Arafat and the PLO in a similar fashion. As National Security Adviser Condoleezza Rice stated in reference to Arafat in November 2001, "You cannot help us with al-Qa'ida and hug Hezbollah or Hamas. And so the President makes that clear to Mr. Arafat."[15] The Palestinians, of course, did little to help their cause by stepping up attacks against Israeli civilians (and the assassination of Israeli Cabinet minister Rehavam Zeevi in October 2001 in a Jerusalem hotel) and getting caught receiving arms from Iran when Israeli forces captured the ship *Karine-A* in January 2002, carrying fifty tons of weapons including Katyusha rockets and C-4 explosives. Arafat's denial of the latter in the face of clear evidence of guilt continued to undermine his credibility in the eyes of the Bush administration and the Israeli public. As one Israeli official commented,

> If they [Palestinians] had played their cards right and joined the forces against terror, the intifada would have been over by now and we would be back to the negotiating table. If the Palestinians had stopped using terror it would have been different. Ordinary Americans make the terror connection and, if the Palestinians had wanted to be hated by the Americans, they couldn't have done better.[16]

Thus, the Israeli–Palestinian conflict became a function of the U.S. global war on terror, despite attempts by a number of Arab and European states to convince the Bush administration to delink the two and treat the Arab–Israeli arena on its own terms.

TENTATIVE U.S. REENGAGEMENT AND AN ARAB PEACE PLAN

Despite the apparent wall being created between the United States and the Palestinian Authority (PA), or more specifically Yasser Arafat, President Bush would come out with statements from time to time that offered some hope for a reconstruction of the peace process. In November 2001 at the UN, Bush stated that "we are working for the day when two states, Israel and Palestine, live peacefully together within secure and recognized boundaries," although he added that "peace will come when all have sworn off forever incitement, violence, and terror. There is no such thing as a good terrorist."[17] These mixed signals sent from Washington would come to characterize the U.S. approach. On the one hand, U.S. officials would say all the right things that seemed to portend possible openings toward a resumption of Israeli–Palestinian negotiations, yet, on the other hand, these statements were often associated with conditions that were easily breached, left open to a wide latitude of interpretation, or hard-pressed to meet, especially by the Palestinians. For example, Colin Powell would reiterate in a major speech on November 19 U.S. support for a two-state solution as well as call for a freeze on Israeli settlement activity, yet he called on the Palestinians to make a 100% effort to stop terrorism, leaving undetermined what is considered to be a 100% effort and who would make that determination. This reflected the ambiguity of the situation with regard to U.S. plolicy. The Bush administration definitely had abandoned its hands-off approach toward the Israeli–Palestinian conflict, but it had yet to develop a clear idea on how to go about doing it. In addition, in what would come to characterize U.S. policy toward Syria and Iraq, there were different factions in the Bush administration's foreign policymaking apparatus that were pushing and pulling U.S. policy (and making statements) in competing directions at times. Because of these mixed signals, regimes in the Middle East were left to interpret which ones were more reflective of where the United States actually stood. More often than not, however, these regimes would choose to believe those statements that were more in alignment with their own positions; unfortunately, they frequently chose the wrong ones (usually the marginalized State Department), which as a result tended to reinforce competing arguments emanating from the Pentagon and the White House.

In November, as a reflection of Powell's renewed engagement, former Marine General Anthony Zinni was dispatched to the region to work for an Israeli–Palestinian cease-fire that would then allow for the application of the Mitchell report. In what would become a pattern over the next few years, the Zinni mission failed miserably, primarily due to a slew of Palestinian terrorist attacks, capped off by a suicide bombing on December 1 in the Ben Yehudah pedestrian mall in Jerusalem that killed ten Israeli teenagers. The next day, fifteen Israelis were killed by a suicide bomber on an Israeli bus in Haifa, an attack claimed by Hamas. Despite denunciations of the attacks by Arafat, Washington and Tel Aviv were quickly losing their patience. Sharon started to attack symbols of Arafat's position directly, destroying the PA president's helicopters at the Gaza airport and attacking PA security headquarters in the West Bank and Gaza. The United States tacitly stood behind Sharon's actions. White House spokesperson Ari Fleischer commented that "obviously Israel has the right to defend herself, and the president understands that clearly," while adding that "the president thinks it is very important that Palestinian jails not only have bars on the front, but no longer have revolving doors at the back."[18] With yet another spate of suicide bombings the next week, Israel decided to break off all contact with Arafat, declaring him to be "irrelevant." To reinforce the point, Israeli tanks surrounded Arafat's compound at Ramallah, isolating the Palestinian leader even more. The *Karine-A* episode in January brought the Bush administration in line with the Sharon government's disgust with and isolation of Arafat.

The tensions were mounting on the Israeli–Palestinian front yet there was no movement toward restarting negotiations. On March 12, 2002, the Israel Defense Forces (IDF) launched a raid inside Palestinian territory that killed thirty-one Palestinians. That same day, the United States introduced UN Security Council Resolution 1397, which was unanimously passed (with Syria abstaining). The resolution reiterated the vision that "two States, Israel and Palestine, live side by side within secure and recognized borders," the first time such a proclamation had been officially accepted on the international stage. The resolution also called for an end of violence, incitement, and terrorism. The U.S. push for peace at this time may have been less than altruistic. Recall that the Bush administration was quickly turning its focus toward regime change in Iraq, stamped by the president's inclusion of Iraq in his January state of the union address. Vice President Dick Cheney shortly thereafter met with a host of Arab leaders in the Middle East, ostensibly to deal with the rapidly escalating situation in Israel but actually sounding out U.S. allies in the Arab world regarding Iraq. It was made clear to Cheney that Arab support for the U.S. position vis-à-vis Iraq was hamstrung by the deteriorating Israeli–Palestinian front. With the deaths of Palestinians at the hands of Israeli forces beamed into the Arab world via satellite television on an almost daily basis, Arab leaders were compelled to distance themselves from the United States.

It was in this dynamic diplomatic environment that the Arab world took the lead in offering a plan to reinvigorate the peace process. Saudi Arabia, with Crown Prince Abdullah as its de facto ruler (with King Fahd increasingly incapacitated by the stroke he suffered in the mid-1990s), laid out for the first time in Arab quarters a set of principles for a permanent Arab–Israeli peace.[19] He introduced the plan at an Arab League summit meeting in Beirut in late March.[20] The Saudis were concerned about the dangerous drift of events in the al-Aqsa intifada that could undermine regional stability; in addition, it was not a bad propaganda move to play the part of peace brokers following the bad press Saudi Arabia received in the United States after 9/11, in which, as stated earlier, fifteen of the nineteen hijackers were Saudi.[21] It called for the Israeli withdrawal from all Arab territories Israel acquired in the June 1967 war; the establishment of an independent Palestinian state, with East Jerusalem (al-Quds) as its capital; an end to the Arab–Israeli conflict, with peace treaties signed between Israel and the Arab states; and a just resolution to the Palestinian refugee problem based on UN Resolution 194. In the summit's closing statement, the Arab League reiterated the "suspension of establishing any relations with Israel in view of the setback to the peace process and the reactivation of the Bureau of the Arab Boycott of Israel until Israel responds by implementing the resolutions of international legitimacy."

It was not a detailed peace plan "but a common Arab statement of principles for a political settlement of the Israeli–Arab conflict" that would entail complex negotiations emerging from this "Arab vision for achieving peace in the Middle East."[22] The Sharon government was not very responsive, revealing its own consciously adopted lack of vision at the time regarding any sort of a peace process. As Henry Siegman commented, the Saudi peace plan "seems to have been greeted with a yawn by the Israeli government."[23] In any event, even if Israel had been more forthcoming, it most certainly would have been derailed by another round of lethal Palestinian suicide attacks that would, once again, reverse any momentum toward peace. Since an end of the violence was a precondition for resuming negotiations, it automatically gave extremists on both sides virtual veto power over the peace process. This time, on March 27, the first day of the Jewish Passover holiday, twenty-nine Jews were killed in a suicide bombing in the Israeli coastal resort town of Netanya. Over the next three days, seventeen Israelis were killed in a series of suicide bombings in Tel Aviv, Haifa, and Jerusalem.

Sharon had had enough. The IDF launched Operation Defensive Shield in early April, which entailed a military sweep of major Palestinian cities in the West Bank, essentially reoccupying a good portion of the territory that had fallen under PA administrative control during the Oslo process. The IDF continued to bombard Arafat's compound at Ramallah, with probably only U.S. insistence that prevented Israel from killing the Palestinian leader. The Bush administration tacitly supported Sharon's actions, but with demonstrations throughout the Arab world amid U.S. attempts to win Arab support for the more aggressive American stance toward Iraq, Bush called on

Israel to withdraw from the territories it had reoccupied and sent Colin Powell to the region to work for a cease-fire. This revealed, however, the political dilemma of the Bush administration vis-à-vis the growing Israeli–Palestinian conflict. Two mainstays of the Bush domestic base, the neo conservatives and evangelical Christians, were, for different reasons, adamantly against any U.S. pressure on Israel to withdraw. As a clear expression of this opposition, American Jewish organizations along with a number of Christian evangelical groups staged a huge demonstration in support of Israel on the Mall astride the Washington Monument in the nation's capital, numbering some 250,000 people and including as speakers a variety of Jewish and evangelical notables as well as pro-Israeli members of Congress.

In the face of this domestic pressure, Bush announced a major shift in U.S. policy toward the Palestinians. In a speech in June 2002, while emphasizing his "vision" of two states "living side by side in peace and security," Bush called for "a new and different Palestinian leadership."[24] In a direct rebuff of Arafat, the president called on the Palestinian people to "elect new leaders, leaders not compromised by terror. I call upon them to build a practicing democracy, based on tolerance and liberty. If the Palestinian people pursue these goals, America and the world will actively support their efforts."[25] The American president was strongly urging not only a change of Palestinian leadership before progress could be made but also that the Palestinians must demonstratively move forward on the road to creating a working democracy. This certainly added to the pre-conditions for reengaging in the peace process, but it also fit in with the dominant neo-con foreign policy paradigm developing in the administration of supporting the growth of democracy in the Middle East as a whole so as to drain the facilitating swamp of terrorism bred by decades of authoritarianism that had been tolerated, if not supported, by previous U.S. administrations. As such, the Bush administration began looking around for a suitable replacement for Arafat, the latter partially complying a year later by appointing Mahmoud Abbas (Abu Mazen) to the newly created position of PA prime minister in summer 2003. Ostensibly, the position was accorded enough power to begin to shift the Palestinian position, particularly with regard to cracking down on Palestinian terrorism. Abbas seemed to be a good choice, even though he was considered one of the old-guard Fatah leaders; however, he had been one of the lead Palestinian negotiators in the Oslo process and had voiced his reservations about the utility of the intifada. Any authority he had, however, was illusory, as Arafat still clung to the mantle of power and at the very least passively worked to undermine Abbas' position, the diminution of which would thus make him less threatening to Arafat's own stranglehold over the PA. Arafat's whole existence since the early 1980s revolved around fighting off attempts to make him irrelevant and maintaining his central position within the Palestinian movement—and thus a central position in international diplomacy aimed at resolving the Israeli–Palestinian conflict. He would not be easy to cast aside despite his confinement in what remained of his compound in Ramallah.

ROAD MAPS, WAR IN IRAQ, AND ITS AFTERMATH

Building on President Bush's June 24, 2002, speech, the United States supported what was in effect a discussion group beginning in July designed to produce ideas on how best to get the peace process going again and draw up a blueprint for a resolution to the Israeli–Palestinian conflict. The group came to be called the Quartet, and it included representatives from the United States, the European Union, Russia, and the UN. By December 20, the Quartet had completed a draft proposal called "A Performance-Based Roadmap to a Permanent Two-State Solution to the Israeli–Palestinian Conflict," most often just referred to as the "Roadmap." It would be officially announced and presented to the Israelis and Palestinians on April 30, 2003. The plan outlined a three-phase process, the ultimate goal or "destination" being "a final and comprehensive settlement of the Israeli–Palestinian conflict by 2005, as presented in President Bush's speech of 24 June. . . .[25a]" In the preamble, the basic requirements, more specifically discussed later in the document, are spelled out in a general fashion:

> A two-state solution to the Israeli–Palestinian conflict will only be achieved through an end to violence and terrorism, when the Palestinian people have a leadership acting decisively against terror and willing and able to build a practicing democracy based on tolerance and liberty, and through Israel's readiness to do what is necessary for a democratic Palestinian state to be established, and a clear, unambiguous acceptance by both parties of the goal of a negotiated settlement. . . .

Phase I was entitled "Ending Terror and Violence, Normalizing Palestinian Life, and Building Palestinian Institutions"—a tall order to say the least, yet according to the plan all of this was to occur in a mere six months. During this phase, among other things, the Palestinians were to "immediately undertake an unconditional cessation of violence . . . accompanied by supportive measures undertaken by Israel," including resuming "security cooperation based on the Tenet work plan [named after CIA Director George Tenet] to end violence, terrorism, and incitement through restructured and effective Palestinian security forces."[26] In addition, in Phase I, Palestinian political reforms were supposed to be implemented: "Palestinians undertake comprehensive political reform in preparation for statehood, including drafting a Palestinian constitution, and free, fair, and open elections. . . ." Mahmoud Abbas' appointment as prime minister was part of Arafat's attempt to meet these standards. Echoing Bush's June 24 speech, Israel was also supposed to withdraw from Palestinian areas occupied since September 28, 2000 (the day before the outbreak of the intifada), and freeze all settlement activity, including the dismantling of settlement outposts erected since March 2001 (when Sharon formally assumed power).

Phase II was intended to be a "transition" period, and it was also allotted a mere six months. Efforts during this phase were to be "focused on the option of creating an independent Palestinian state with provisional borders and attributes of sovereignty, based on the new constitution, as a way station to a permanent settlement." Emphasizing again that this could only be achieved with Arafat gone and the PA on the road to democracy, the document stated in this section that "with such leadership, reformed civil institutions and security structures, the Palestinians will have the active support of the Quartet and the broader international community in establishing an independent, viable state." Through Phase II, while the Roadmap calls on Israel to undertake a number of measures, many of them ill-defined, the onus for progress on this front clearly lay with the Palestinians.

The final status issues were the focus of Phase III. As with the Oslo process, these commonly accepted "intractable" problems were put off until the end. Two years of negotiations were allowed to settle the issues of borders, settlements, Palestinian refugees, and Jerusalem, with a permanent status agreement no later than the end of 2005. At that time as well, it was envisioned that progress would be made on an overall Arab–Israeli settlement, primarily targeting an Israeli agreement with Syria and Lebanon. Most of the elements and objectives articulated in Phase I have yet to be implemented or accomplished.

There were many skeptics at the time regarding the Roadmap, seeing it as a not-so-altruistic attempt by the Bush administration to win European and Arab support for its emerging plans vis à vis Iraq. This is not surprising as the attentions of the Bush administration by fall 2002 were definitely focused more upon building the case for war against Iraq in the United States and in the UN.

The construction of the Roadmap did, however, indicate to Sharon that the United States wanted a political resolution to the Israeli–Palestinian problem, not just a military solution.[27] But this is something that the Israeli prime minister was beginning to realize himself, especially as it had become apparent that the intifada was exacting a heavy economic as well as human toll on the country. Israel was in a deep recession, unemployment was at an all-time high, while the gross national product growth rate was at an all-time low. Foreign investment and tourism had dwindled to a trickle of what they had been in the high-tech boom of the 1990s.

A turning point in this regard for Sharon became apparent with the carefully orchestrated speech he gave at a conference in Herzliya on December 4, 2002. While laden with criticism of Arafat, calling again for the "replacement of the Palestinian leadership which has lied and disappointed" and emphasizing that nothing can move forward without a cessation of violence, Sharon accepted "in principle" Bush's vision as articulated in the Roadmap. Most importantly, however, the man who had been a staunch advocate of the mantra of the Israeli right, "Jordan is Palestine," and who had significantly contributed to slowing down, if not ending, the Oslo process while at the same time marginalizing Arafat, reiterated that Israel would permit the creation of a Palestinian state "with borders yet to be finalized" and was "prepared to make painful concessions for a true peace." The latter phrase was taken to mean that Sharon, was now prepared to at least consider withdrawal from occupied land. Essentially, Sharon was acknowledging that Israel could not go on indefinitely as an economically viable and politically democratic state by continuing its rule over the Palestinians.

There arose a vocal chorus of opposition to Sharon's shifting position among those elements in Israeli society who had traditionally been his strongest supporters. From this moment until Sharon's decision to leave Likud to form a new, more centrist party called Kadima ("forward" in Hebrew) in November 2005, his appearances before the Knesset and in the Likud Central Committee discussing issues related to the Israeli–Palestinian situation were often drowned out by vitriolic rhetoric from those opposed to withdrawing from the territories. Signs, billboards, and graffiti started appearing all over Israel with such choice phrases as "map of illusions," "document of surrender," and "Roadmap to Auschwitz."[28] Sharon's responses to his detractors elicited even more concern regarding his intentions, particularly as he emphasized the need for a "political settlement" and famously stated "the idea that it is possible to keep three and a half million Palestinians under occupation is wrong for Israel, for the Palestinians and for the Israeli economy."[29]

Amid this growing turmoil in the Israeli domestic political scene, the Bush administration launched Operation Iraqi Freedom on March 19, 2003. Bush had successfully gained the support of Congress the previous fall for the use of military force against Iraq, and the administration won unanimous approval on November 8, 2002, for UN Security Council Resolution 1441, which cited Iraq as remaining in "material breach" of its obligations and authorized the return of UN inspectors to search for weapons of mass destruction (WMD). Despite little support from the international community (including the UN) for the use of military force against Iraq, U.S. forces within a few weeks led a small coalition (mostly British) toward Baghdad and engineered the removal of Saddam Hussein's regime. Even though it was initially a military triumph, bad omens of the quagmire the United States was entering began to appear in short notice. Be that as it may, for the time being the Bush administration certainly seemed to be moving in the right direction toward achieving its hoped-for transformation of the Middle East, with the implantation of democracy in Iraq engendering a democracy domino effect in the Arab world that would eliminate the authoritarianism that was rampant in the region.

With the United States apparently perched on the edge of another Pax Americana in the Middle East with the Roadmap (officially introduced on April 30) leading the diplomatic way, along with Sharon's subtle shifts in his position, Arafat was compelled to play along. It is during this time that Arafat created the post of prime minister, with Mahmoud Abbas taking up the mantle of presumed power and Muhammad Dahlan in charge of security. Abbas and Dahlan made bold statements regarding the disarming of Palestinian militias, but immediately Hamas, Islamic Jihad, and the al-Aqsa Martyrs Brigade pledged that they would not do so. With Arafat conveniently aloof along with continuing Israeli actions that undermined the PA's ability to extend its control, Abbas believed he could do nothing but attempt to negotiate a cease-fire with the militant groups, fearing the possibility of open civil war and the PA being cast as Israel's dupe in doing the dirty work for Sharon.

Still awash in victory in Iraq and probably hoping (with considerable encouragement from British Prime Minister Tony Blair) to utilize the postwar environment and regional balance of power to orchestrate a peace process much in the way his father had, Bush attended a conference at Sharm al-Shaykh in early June, meeting with Egyptian President Husni Mubarak, King Abdullah of Jordan, Saudi Crown Prince Abdullah, PA Prime Minister Mahmoud Abbas, and the emir of Bahrain, Shaykh Hamad bin Isa Al Khalifa. The next day (June 4), Bush traveled to Aqaba, Jordan, to meet with Abbas and Ariel Sharon. He again met with Abbas and Sharon in July in Washington. Bush was certainly investing his considerable prestige in trying to get Phase I of the Roadmap off and running.

Abbas continued his negotiations with Palestinian groups (with considerable mediation and pressure exerted by the Egyptians) and arranged by the end of June a 90-day *hudna*, an Islamic term that calls for a pause or suspension of fighting while peace talks proceed. It was only partially successful as Hamas, Tanzim, and Islamic Jihad agreed to honor the hudna, while the al-Aqsa Martyrs Brigade did not. Many Israelis were wary of the pause, suspecting that the Palestinian factions intended to use the truce to rearm and regroup. Although at a lesser rate, attacks continued during the hudna, with Arafat impeding Abbas' ability to clamp down on the militants. Abbas tried to convince anyone who was willing to listen to allow him the time and give him the support necessary to negotiate a permanent truce with the militant factions. By late August, however, his time had run out. A Palestinian terrorist attack on August 19 in

Jerusalem killed twenty-one Israelis, including a number of children. Sharon ordered the IDF to step up efforts against the Palestinian militants, including a resumption of targeted assassinations. Hamas subsequently declared an end to the hudna. More Palestinian attacks and Israeli reprisals (or Israeli attacks and Palestinian reprisals—it all depends on to whom one talks) in September seemed to bring the situation back to square one. Abbas resigned on September 6, 2003, with a just as ineffective Ahmad Qureia (Abu Ala), another "old guard" PLO member who was also a leading figure in the Oslo talks, taking his place as prime minister.

WHAT HAPPENED TO SYRIA?[30]

As mentioned previously, despite Bashar al-Asad's reiteration that his country continued to make a "strategic choice of peace" with Israel, the Syrian–Israeli track was already moribund before he even assumed office in July 2000. With the tensions rising in the region following the outbreak of the al-Aqsa intifada as well as American policies in the aftermath of 9/11, there was little hope for a resumption of negotiations on this front, especially as Asad needed time to consolidate his power base in Damascus and try to map out his domestic political program. But soon enough there were ominous signs that not only would there be little, if any, effort exerted to reconstitute a Syrian–Israeli track but also there were powerful currents in Washington that would place Syria increasingly in the crosshairs of the United States, which in and of itself allowed Israel under Sharon to adopt a more aggressive policy vis-à-vis Damascus.

Despite Syria's intelligence cooperation with the United States following 9/11, voices began to be heard in Congress regarding Syrian support for terrorism, viewing groups such as Hizbollah and Hamas as no different from al-Qa'ida.[31] By the end of 2002, there was movement in Congress toward slapping economic sanctions against Syria (the Syrian Accountability Act) as well as elements in the Pentagon that were becoming more vociferous in their complaints about Syria and pressure groups, including Christian Lebanese agitating for the withdrawal of Syrian troops from Lebanon, Syrian prodemocracy exiles, and pro-Israeli Christian evangelicals and neo-conservatives, that heightened their anti-Syrian rhetoric while trying to convince the Bush administration that Syria belonged with Iran, Iraq, and North Korea in the "axis of evil." All of this would reach a crescendo with the war in Iraq in March–April 2003.

But Damascus was still receiving mixed signals from Washington. The State Department, Central Intelligence Agency (CIA), and the Bush administration (at least for a time) still believed that engagement with Syria was important, not so much for Syrian participation in any sort of a peace process but for Bashar al-Asad's assistance in destroying al-Qa'ida, especially as Lebanon was seen as a possible locale where al-Qa'ida might attempt to regroup, and in drumming up support in the Arab world for (or at least not being an obstacle to) a possible U.S.-led war in Iraq—especially as Syria held a seat on the UN Security Council at the time. As such, the Syrian regime believed that U.S.–Syrian relations would remain status quo and that the policy of engaging Syria would remain intact.

Damascus may have grown a bit too complacent, secure in the knowledge that the State Department mantra that Syria had helped save American lives with its intelligence assistance—would insulate the country from the more forward U.S. policy under the Bush Doctrine. Essentially, Asad and his foreign policy advisers did not adequately adjust to the changes in American foreign policy as a result of 9/11. Damascus thought the old rules of the game were still in place—the traditional "honey and vinegar" relationship—and State Department and other administration officials led it to believe that such was the case. But at the same time the new rules of the game were being written in Washington in the corridors of Congress, the Pentagon, and influential conservative think tanks by those who saw Syria as part of the problem rather than the solution. Because of this, Asad's continued vitriol against Israel focusing on the al-Aqsa intifada played right into the hands of the ascending group of American foreign policy ideologues whose positions seemed to mirror the security concerns and methodology of Ariel Sharon. Little did Asad know that with each and every passing day he and his regime were becoming more of a target. Syria had been one of the few countries in the Arab world that could play on both sides of the fence, so to speak. It could adopt a radical anti-Israeli, anti-imperialist posture when the regional environment dictated it because of its traditional Arab nationalist leadership role, yet it could also, when necessary, follow a more conciliatory and cooperative foreign policy and participate in peace processes—it seemed to benefit from the best of both worlds. Now, however, it failed to appreciate how much the Bush administration was emphasizing the fact that Damascus had to choose which side of the fence it wanted to be on and that, if it was not 100% on the cooperative side, it would be treated as an enemy in the war on terror.

Even though Asad expressed lukewarm support for the Beirut Arab League summit peace plan, Syria still tried to maintain its distance from any new peace process with Israel that might emerge. Syrian officials successfully watered down some aspects of the Saudi plan, particularly replacing the term "normalization" in the phrase "normalization of relations" with the word "normal," which entails something less than full integrative relations with Israel, essentially just a state of nonbelligerency. Asad's father believed that one should begin with "normal relations," the bare minimum of diplomatic interaction, and build up over time toward "normalization." To the Israelis, this seemed to confirm the contention that Syria did not necessarily want true peace, i.e., that a virtual state of war with Israel justifies Syria's authoritarian structure, heavily dependent as it is on the bloated military–security apparatus as well as the perceived necessity of remaining in Lebanon. Given the heightened regional tensions at the time along with the unsettled domestic political environment, Asad most likely believed that he had very little room to maneuver vis-à-vis Israel and more to gain domestically and regionally by adopting a more hard-line position.[32]

The 2003 war in Iraq severely strained U.S.–Syrian relations, due mainly to U.S. accusations that the Syrian government was either actively or passively supporting groups in Iraq fighting against the American-led military presence. As such, the regime of Asad became increasingly marginalized in the eyes of the Bush administration as not-so-subtle threats were hurled in Syria's direction by top U.S. officials during and after the initial phase of the conflict in March and April. Syria was now being accused of *costing,* not saving, American lives. This provided momentum for the Syrian Accountability Act and grease for the gears for those elements in Washington who had been advocating regime change in Damascus. No longer was it the case, as had long been the argument of the State Department, that the differences separating the United States and Syria (e.g., Syrian support for what Washington termed "terrorist groups,"

Syria's troop presence in Lebanon, and its development of WMD) could be resolved *after* an Israeli–Syrian peace treaty. Syria now had to meet all of these concerns *before* negotiations could even begin with Israel. This was a fundamental shift in U.S. policy toward Syria with regard to the Arab–Israeli arena, one that seemed to catch Damascus off-guard.

Syria's marginalization was confirmed in the Roadmap proffered by the Quartet, in which Syria was barely mentioned—as almost an afterthought. The Syrian track seemed no longer to exist in the eyes of Washington. Asad was not invited to the Sharm al-Shaykh meeting with Bush and a number of Arab leaders in June 2003. It almost seemed as though Asad had been relegated to pariah status and isolated, à la Arafat in his Ramallah compound. It was a very dangerous period for Asad, now excluded from the Middle East peace process and with over 100,000 American troops next door in Iraq. And things would get worse.

On October 5, 2003, Israel launched an air strike against what it claimed was a Palestinian terrorist training camp at 'Ain Saheb just northwest of Damascus. It was the first Israeli strike in Syria itself in almost thirty years. The camp was apparently abandoned, although some sources claim it was being renovated for future use by the Popular Front for the Liberation of Palestine—General Command, one of the Palestinian groups allegedly supported by Syria. The attack was in retaliation for a Palestinian suicide bombing in Haifa that killed twenty people the previous day. Dore Gold, one of Ariel Sharon's foreign policy advisers, declared after the attack that "no one can strike Israel with impunity."[33] The Israeli attack was a symbolic, albeit a strong and direct, message to Asad to desist in Syrian support for Palestinian groups engaged in suicide bombings against Israelis. The Bush administration was conspicuously mute in its response, saying only that Israel "must not feel constrained" in defending itself; indeed, the general anti-Syrian tone adopted by a Congress that was soon to pass the Syrian Accountability Act (December 2003) as well as an administration that had been consistently warning Syria regarding its behavior no doubt emboldened the Israelis to believe that they could get away with the raid without American censure or opprobrium.[34]

It was under these circumstances that Asad tacked in a different direction by openly advocating a resumption of peace negotiations with Israel—the regime finally and completely understood that, rather than the United States protecting Syria from Israel, it was now at least casting a blind eye toward, if not sanctioning, a more assertive Israeli policy. In a *New York Times* interview on November 30, 2003, Asad offered the following regarding negotiations with Israel and the issue of the Golan Heights:

> Some people say there are Syrian conditions, and my answer is no; we don't have Syrian conditions. What Syria says is this: negotiations should be resumed from the point at which they had stopped [during the Madrid peace process into early 2000] simply because we have achieved a great deal in these negotiations. If we don't say this, it means we want to go back to point zero in the peace process. This would also mean wasting a lot more time, and every day we waste more people are being killed and more violence erupts in the region.[35]

Asad's response from the United States came in the form of the Bush administration's signing of the Syrian Accountability Act into law in December, although it would not be activated until May 2004. Israeli officials also responded coolly to Syria's peace overture, believing that it was only prompted by U.S. pressure as well as the fall of the fellow Ba'thist regime in Baghdad. Ariel Sharon was certainly on the more cautious side, especially as he was always someone who preferred to keep the high ground strategically; but some Israeli officials began to wonder whether or not it might be a mistake to rebuff Asad at a time when Syria was in a relatively weak position, thus allowing Israel to strike a deal to its own advantage (akin to the PLO in 1993).[36] But Sharon reportedly told a U.S. senator on his way from Israel to Damascus to meet with Asad to inform the Syrian president that Israel was not interested in being Syria's "springboard to the White House."[37] In addition, while the Sharon government was dealing with its announced intention to unilaterally withdraw from the Gaza Strip, it would be overloading the Israeli public by simultaneously engaging in the Syrian track again. Besides, many Israelis felt that they should just stay put and ride the new American posture vis-à-vis Syria to pressure Damascus to abandon its policies that are inimical to Israeli interests—why short-circuit U.S. pressure before it had run its course?

Asad would continue to indicate publicly that he was ready to renew peace talks with Israel well into the summer of 2004. There were a few positive signs. The Israeli army chief of staff, Lt. General Moshe Yaalon, commented in August that Israel would be prepared to give up the Golan Heights in return for peace with Syria and that the IDF could defend Israel without the Golan. In October 2004, Israeli Foreign Minister Silvan Shalom stated "I think that peace with Syria is a strategic goal for the State of Israel . . . it would mean that all the countries we share a border with would be at peace with us and of course that would also make future negotiations with the Palestinians easier."[38]

Any subtle movement along these lines, however, soon took a back seat to events in Lebanon, particularly Syria's disastrous meddling in Lebanese affairs once again in August and September 2004. Pressure had been building on Syria to withdraw its troops and intelligence agents from Lebanon ever since Israel's evacuation in May 2000 and Hafiz al-Asad's death the following June. In response to a growing and more vocal Lebanese opposition to the Syrian presence, Bashar al-Asad had actually reduced and re-positioned the number of Syrian troops in Lebanon from 40,000 to about 14,000 by summer 2004. But this did not mean that Damascus was prepared to relinquish its position and influence in Lebanon entirely. Lebanon was too important economically and strategically to Syria; besides, Syrians believed that they helped right the ship in Lebanon in the 1980s and 1990s when no one else wanted to or could.

Things came to a head in August 2004 when, with Syria manipulating the political process behind the scenes, Lebanese President Emile Lahoud orchestrated an extraconstitutional extension of his term in office. It was widely condemned by the international community, leading to the passage of UN Security Council Resolution 1559, which, among other things, called for the withdrawal of "foreign forces" from Lebanon (read: Syria) and for the "disbanding and disarmament of all Lebanese and non-Lebanese militias," which most agree primarily targeted Hizbollah. Asad claims that France had been working on just such a UN resolution as early as May 2004, so in his estimation UN Security Council (UNSC) Resolution 1559 had nothing to do with the extension of Lahoud's term in office—it was just a convenient pretext.[39] Apparently, according to the Syrians, French President Jacques Chirac had become disenchanted with Lahoud (and probably even Asad) and may have been using the situation in Lebanon to patch up relations with the United States that were soured by French opposition to the U.S. war in Iraq. Regardless, certainly at least in retrospect, Syria's arranging Lahoud's extension was a diplomatic blunder of major proportions. This mistake internationalized the issue of Lebanon, gave ammunition to anti-Syrian hawks in the Bush administration, galvanized the Lebanese opposition, further alienated a traditional friend in Europe (France), and maybe most importantly, alienated Rafiq Hariri, the powerful Sunni prime minister of Lebanon.

To this point, Hariri had a working, if not always a smooth, relationship with Damascus. According to a number of reports, Hariri was summoned to Damascus and told in no uncertain terms to support the extension of Lahoud. Hariri complied, but then he resigned from office in protest. Subsequently, he reportedly encouraged the United States and France to push through the UN resolution, and he began to cooperate more with opposition leaders in Lebanon, including Druze patriarch Walid Jumblatt and Lebanese Christian factions. It appeared that Hariri was also angling to return to government in elections scheduled for Spring 2005.

It was under these circumstances that Rafiq Hariri was assassinated in a massive car bomb explosion in Beirut on February 14, 2005. Immediately, cries rang out in Lebanon and throughout most of the international community holding Syria responsible, either directly or indirectly. Vociferous demonstrations spontaneously erupted in Beirut and other Lebanese cities accusing Damascus and its pro-Syrian allies in Lebanon. It was unprecedented open criticism accompanied by calls for Syrian troops and intelligence agents to leave the country. The Bush administration was careful not to accuse Damascus directly for the incident, preferring to not pass judgment until a UN investigation into the killing ran its course. However, administration officials did publicly hold Syria responsible in a general sense since it was the powerbroker in Lebanon, ostensibly there to provide stability and security. The Bush administration did recall its ambassador to Syria on February 15. Both Washington and Paris strongly renewed their calls to implement UNSC 1559.

While condemning the murder of Hariri and vehemently claiming to be innocent, the Syrian regime was compelled by the mounting international pressure to finally withdraw from Lebanon, the last troops leaving by the end of April after an almost thirty-year presence. New Lebanese elections beginning in May brought to power the first parliament in many a year not dominated by pro-Syrian elements, with the party of Hariri's son, Sa'd, gaining the largest bloc of seats. Meanwhile, the UN investigation continued. In October, Detlev Mehlis, the UN representative in charge of investigating the Hariri assassination, produced his preliminary report to the UN Security Council. The detailed report in effect basically concluded that the assassination could not have occurred without Syrian connivance, the trail of evidence in the report leading all the way to the heart of the regime in Damascus, including the powerful head of Syrian intelligence Asef Shawkat (who also happens to be Asad's brother-in-law) and Asad's younger brother, Maher al-Asad. While it is doubtful that Asad was directly involved in the assassination, his reputation was further smeared because if he was not associated with it, then this was a troubling indication of the lack of power he really wields in the country.[40] Upon hearing the Mehlis report, the UN Security Council unanimously passed another resolution (UNSC 1636) calling on Syria to fully cooperate with the UN investigation or possibly face further measures, probably entailing more widespread sanctions, this time including Europe, which would really hurt Syria since most of its trade is with the European Union. Syria cooperated to a minimal extent with the UN investigation, the mandate for the latter extended well into 2006. In any event, UN Security Council members such as Russia, China, and Algeria were opposed to expanding the breadth of the investigation as well as the imposition of a tougher sanctions regime against Syria. And by early 2006 the focus of the Bush administration seemed to shift more toward concerns regarding Iran's alleged attempts to pursue nuclear weapons capability. With the United States ensconced in Iraq and dumbing-down its definition of success in order to begin the politically palatable withdrawal of U.S. forces, the threat environment from the perspective of Damascus had receded somewhat. Syria seemed to have weathered the storm for the time being.

While calls in the United States for regime change in Damascus intensified, reports out of Israel indicated that Tel Aviv was against this, preferring to have someone it knows remain in power rather than deal with the unknown potential chaos in Syria if the regime was precipitously removed. Regardless of this, Asad was almost literally fighting for his life for a time, and he has been consolidating his domestic position in the wake of the fissures created by the enhanced international pressure. In the process of doing so, he has become much more Syrian nationalist (rather than pan-Arabist), which is not a bad thing; but he has resorted to anti-American and anti-Israeli slogans that are popular in the Arab street and tightened regime control in the country in order to solidify his power base. Besides, Washington is not particularly interested in engaging the Asad regime, and the Israelis were in a state of political uncertainty well into 2006. Asad astutely utilized the nationalistic response against UN and U.S. pressure and funneled it toward support for his regime. His cabinet reshuffling of February 2006 and contemporaneous moves in the military–security apparatus suggest a leader who has most of the people he wants in positions of power. The cabinet has been given more authority than any other in recent memory, representing the sense of security and confidence (perhaps overconfidence) that Asad has accrued over the year or so. Whether this can be leveraged into a resumption of a peace process with Israel still depends on a variety of factors, although the regime itself has sent out no shortage of signals that it wants to resume negotiations with Israel within the framework of a regional accord.

CHARTING HIS OWN PATH

By fall 2003, the Palestinian hudna had ended and the Roadmap was going nowhere. Sharon could now, with little hesitation, do what he had always intended to do: unilaterally resolve the Israeli–Palestinian conflict. But for Sharon this really never entailed a negotiated solution but a series of unilateral moves that would establish the borders of the state of Israel—and, by default, what was left over would become the independent Palestinian state. After all, it had become an accepted opinion among a large segment of the Israeli population emanating from the top that there was "no partner" for peace—this was the result of the continuing violence of the intifada as well as the ostracizing and marginalizing of Yasser Arafat. In this way, then, Sharon could ensure a permanent Jewish majority in Israel (especially considering the 3.3% Palestinian growth rate per annum versus less than 1% for Israel—not to even speak of the over 1 million Israeli Arabs who are citizens of Israel living within the pre-1967 borders), an undivided Jerusalem, and security for Israelis via separation from the Palestinians. He would attempt to do all of this in primarily two ways: (1) the construction of a "barrier" or "security fence" in the West Bank separating the Palestinians from most Israelis (the Israeli government officially calls it an "antiterrorist fence") and (2) unilateral withdraw from the Gaza Strip, therefore ridding Israel of the burden of responsibility for 1.3 million Palestinians.

A barrier in the West Bank had been discussed in both Labor and Likud circles throughout the Oslo process. Indeed, it was Ehud Barak who ordered a feasibility study of the construction of such a security fence, the results of which were submitted to Sharon in 2002.[41] The idea of an artificial barrier, intended to protect Israelis from Palestinian terrorism, was generally supported by the Israeli public and security establishment. The plan was to build a barrier approximately 360 miles in length roughly along the Green Line, i.e., the June 4, 1967, border, at a cost of some $1.5 billion. However, the barrier would be built east of that line, in some cases jutting considerably into the West Bank, based on security rationale but mostly to envelope the largest Jewish settlements in the territory. By the end of 2005 about half of the barrier had been constructed. In most places, it was really just a high fence with barbed wire and other impediments; in other, mostly urban, areas, the barrier was a series of tall concrete sections placed side by side.

As noted, most Israelis enthusiastically supported the barrier since the diplomatic route obviously did not provide the security they expected. The settler groups generally opposed the barrier because they thought it would impede, if not entirely prevent, continued settlement growth in the West Bank. The United States and the Palestinians opposed the barrier because they saw it as establishing de facto borders between Israel and a Palestinian state devoid of negotiations. From the Palestinian perspective, the barrier ate away at significant chunks of what they expected to be their new state, containing some of the most fertile land as well as water resources in underground aquifers. At a more practical level, the barrier sometimes divided Palestinians from other Palestinians and, in many spots, greatly inhibited the movement of people and goods since there were proscribed entry and exit points between de facto Israeli and Palestinian areas. The Israeli government emphasized that the barrier would not prejudice negotiations and could be adjusted or even torn down if necessary, which seemed to be enough to satisfy the Bush administration, which ultimately acquiesced in its continued construction. The International Court of Justice at the Hague ruled in an advisory opinion that the wall went against the Fourth Geneva Convention and called for Israel to cease construction and dismantle the portions of it that deviated from the Green Line.[42] With Israel's traditional wariness of international organizations, the ruling was summarily dismissed; however, an Israeli Supreme Court decision could not be. While the Supreme Court defended the construction of the barrier, it stated that the route had to be adjusted so as not to "injure" the Palestinian population, and in several areas the location of the fence was adjusted accordingly; indeed, it cut by half the amount of land between the Green Line and the barrier. Now, 8% of the West Bank would fall between the Green Line and the security fence, which, as some Israelis point out, is close to the 5% that the Clinton administration put forward in 2000. With this adjustment, 99.5% of the Palestinians in the West Bank will live outside of the barrier in 92% of West Bank land. Less than 10,000 of the 2 million Palestinians in the West Bank would be "caught," so to speak, on the Israeli side, not including the 195,000 Palestinians living in East Jerusalem along with 175,000 Israelis.

Seventy-four percent of the Israeli settlers, some 177,000 living for the most part in the large settlements, would live on the Israeli side of the barrier, with the other 26%, some 63,000, fated to live among the Palestinians outside of the barrier (or leave, as I am sure many would do). As one Israeli scholar noted, "People associate Sharon with being Mr. Settlement and react with a certain churlishness, saying he's trying to trade Gaza for the West Bank. But the real story is how Mr. Settlement, who wanted to build on 100 percent of the West Bank, is down to 8 percent. If we're talking about Maale Adumim, it means that Sharon sees this as the main battleground, not Elon Moreh or the Jordan Valley."[43] Palestinians, of course, claim that all Israeli settlements beyond the Green Line are illegal and reject the 1967 annexation of East Jerusalem. They add that even that adjusted 8% of the West Bank behind the barrier is some of the best land for agriculture and housing—unilateralism, say the Palestinians, is no substitute for negotiations. And they point to the fact that Israel has yet to freeze settlement growth as called upon in the first phase of the Roadmap, but Israeli officials retort that since the Palestinians have not dismantled the militant organizations as also called for in the first phase, they should not be held to it either. Indeed, as further indication of Sharon's de facto redrawing of the West Bank demographic and political map, settlement "thickening" continued in places such as Maale Adumim, adjacent to East Jerusalem. As with many settlement municipalities, the boundaries are huge, leaving room for future growth without technically expanding beyond existing settlements. In fact, the official municipal boundaries of Maale Adumim are larger than Tel Aviv's, and they practically stretch all the way to Jericho. By the end of 2005, housing and other associated structures have only been built on about 15% of its official area.[44]

The second objective in Sharon's policy vis-à-vis the Palestinians was the unilateral disengagement from the Gaza Strip. Again, this was something that the great majority of Israelis favored. To them, the Gaza Strip had become a cesspool of Palestinian militancy amid a 45% Palestinian unemployment rate, with most Gazan families living on less than $2 per day. Sentiments among Israelis for withdrawal had been present for a number of years. Many Israelis believed that the cost in terms of human, monetary, and military resources of protecting some 7,500–8,000 Jewish settlers living in settlements comprising 33% of the 140 square miles of the twenty-five-mile long, six-mile wide Gaza Strip, surrounded by 1.3 million Palestinians (with one of the highest population densities in the world at 14,000 per square mile) far outweighed any benefits. In any event, one of the original security arguments for settling the Gaza Strip—defense against Egypt—was an invalid one since Israel and Egypt had been at peace since 1979. In addition, Gaza was never a part of the Jewish state intended by the 1948 UN partition plan. More importantly, perhaps, it appears that the Gaza Strip (and most of the coastal area of what is now the state of Israel) was never under Israelite or Judean control during their heyday from about 1250 B.C.E. to 135 C.E.; therefore, unlike the West Bank, it does not comprise the land of biblical Israel.[45] Finally, disengagemet would reduce the level of international pressure against Israel regarding the Palestinian issue, especially from the direction of Europe and the United States.

Again it was a speech at a security forum in Herzliya (sponsored by the Institute for Policy and Strategy), this one on December 18, 2003, at which Sharon announced his intention to unilaterally disengage from the Gaza Strip.[46] Sharon commented in his announcement that it was a "security measure, not a political one," a mantra that would be often repeated by Israeli officials. There were a number of skeptics regarding the plan, anticipating that what came to be called "Gaza first" might be "Gaza last" in terms of Israeli withdrawal from the Occupied Territories. Similar to what Begin's rationale had been in withdrawing from the Sinai Peninsula, the skeptics figured that a withdrawal from the Gaza Strip would strengthen Israel's hold of the West Bank. These fears were enhanced when one of Sharon's close advisors, Dov Weisglass, in an interview with an Israeli newspaper published on October 8, 2004, stated the following regarding the disengagement from the Gaza Strip:

> The significance is the freezing of the political process. And when you freeze that process you prevent the establishment of a Palestinian state and you prevent the discussion about the refugees, the borders and Jerusalem. Effectively, this whole package that is called the Palestinian state, with all that it entails, has been removed from our agenda indefinitely.... All with a [U.S.] presidential blessing and the ratification of both houses of Congress....[47]

Sharon made an attempt to repudiate Weisglass' statement, but the muted way in which he did so only reinforced the doubts. But Sharon had more to worry about within his own coalition. Certainly the national religious settler groups and parties opposed the disengagement plan, as did many within Likud. The settlers, of course, did not want to see any sort of precedent set that might lead to similar action in the West Bank. In addition, opponents worried that a unilateral withdrawal without getting anything concrete in return from the Palestinians would be to repeat what Barak had done in evacuating south Lebanon, enabling a terrorist group—Hizbollah—to claim victory and reinforce its political position in Lebanon's political system. The same thing could transpire with Hamas and Islamic Jihad; in other words, it would be a victory for the terrorists, which would only encourage more and not less terrorism perpetrated against Israel and enhance the popularity and position of the militant Palestinian groups at the expense of the PA.

The Bush administration, for its part, grasping at straws to depict progress in the moribund Roadmap, especially in a presidential election year, attempted to portray the Gaza disengagement plan as something of a first step in the process—and Sharon would dutifully declare his commitment to the Roadmap from time to time. This mutual support hid the fundamentally different wavelengths the United States and Israel were on regarding the Palestinian issue. While the Bush administration saw what was happening in terms of being part of a negotiated peace process, Sharon was less concerned with negotiations with the Palestinians and much more focused on the security of Israel through undertaking a series of unilateral measures, ones that the Bush administration had no choice but to sign onto because at least at a superficial level, if properly packaged and presented, the United States would be seen as remaining diplomatically engaged.

This simultaneous convergence and divergence between Israel and the United States became manifest in an important meeting between Bush and Sharon in Washington on April 14, 2004. For Bush, the main objective of the meeting was a show of support for Sharon that would help the Israeli prime minister win over his Likud party and Israeli electorate for the Gaza withdrawal plan. A secondary objective was, in an election year, to win more Jewish support in the United States, especially in important swing states such as Florida that, as in the 2000 presidential election, was forecasted to be a very close race. As such, in a letter from Bush to Sharon following the meeting, the U.S. president called for the settling of Palestinian refugees in a future Palestinian state rather than in Israel. Importantly, in a clear shift of U.S. policy of past administrations, Bush declared "In light of new realities on the ground, including already existing major Israeli population centers, it is unrealistic to expect that the outcome of final status negotiations will be a full and complete return to the armistice lines of 1949." Bush did add, however, that "the United States supports the establishment of a Palestinian state that is viable, sovereign, and independent" and reiterated that "the barrier being erected by Israel should be a security rather than a political barrier, should be temporary, and therefore not prejudice any final status issues including final borders. . . ." And as part of the negotiations with the Israelis, the Bush administration won a commitment from Sharon that, in addition to the Gaza Strip, Israel would also withdraw from four Jewish settlements in the northern West Bank. While even many Palestinians might acknowledge the likely reality that they are not going to receive 100% of the West Bank or be allowed to return anything more than a trickle of refugees to pre-1967 war Israel, they were aghast at Bush's letter simply because, from their point of view, once again a solution was being imposed on them rather than resulting from negotiations.

In a hurry to leverage his meeting with Bush for domestic political points, Sharon raced home triumphantly with the letter in hand, boldly declaring to the Knesset on April 22 that "the political support we won on my visit to the US is an unprecedented gain for Israel. Political support of the scope and force expressed in the President's letter has not been given us since the establishment of the state of Israel. . . . The Palestinians regard the President's letter as their hardest blow since the War of Independence."[48]

Despite this open support from the United States, the disengagement plan was defeated by a count of 60–40 in a Likud Central Committee meeting, with former Israeli prime minister Benjamin Netanyahu, who was Sharon's finance minister, leading the calls to abandon the Gaza plan. But Sharon rode the popularity among the Israeli populace at large for disengagement from the Gaza Strip. In addition, he acquired support from some rather unexpected directions as the Labor and Meretz (Yahad) parties voiced their approval, opening the door for a realignment of the ruling coalition in order to obtain Knesset approval. In fact, for the remainder of 2004 and much of 2005, until the withdrawal from Gaza actually took place in August and September 2005, Sharon consistently fought off attempts from the Israeli right wing, mostly within his own party, to undermine the disengagement plan.

The Palestinians, for their part, were in something of a quandary regarding the Israeli withdrawal. On the one hand, how could they not support at least in principle the concept of an Israeli withdrawal from land the Palestinians had earmarked for their independent state? On the other hand, they attempted to portray the disengagement as a harbinger of renewed peace talks and as a first step toward Israel's complete withdrawal from the West Bank. The Quartet also attempted to maintain the fiction that it was part and parcel of the Roadmap. Hamas was eager to portray the Israeli disengagement from Gaza as the result of the military attacks that it and others had perpetrated against Israel. Just as emphatically, Sharon wanted to make sure that Hamas could not make such a boast and over the course of the next year and a half would authorize IDF operations in Gaza to make clear that Israel was withdrawing from a position of strength and not being forced out.

DEATH OF ARAFAT AND SHARON'S UNILATERALISM

On November 11, 2004, Yasser Arafat, the venerable president of the PA and the iconic PLO revolutionary, died of undisclosed causes at the age of seventy-five in a Paris hospital following his emergency evacuation from Ramallah. It is interesting to note that the death of such an important historical figure in modern Middle East history was greeted with a good deal of relief, even among some Palestinians, in that a popularly perceived implacable impediment to a resumption of Israeli–Palestinian negotiations had been eliminated. It seemed that only death was able to remove this ultimate survivor from the Middle East equation. He certainly became the symbol of Palestinian nationalism in the post-World War II period, and he established the PLO as a force to be reckoned with. But to many, he had become an anachronism. He had outlived his usefulness, if not his ability to manipulate Palestinian politics. As Harvey Sicherman noted in what in effect was his obituary on Arafat:

> The Rais [Arafat] was not interested in good government or economic development. He quickly established a "cronycracy," equal parts corruption and incompetence. The Old Guard from Tunis exploited the flow of foreign assistance, ran monopolies and local extortions.... Among all the national liberation icons of his era, Arafat was most expert in working the interstices of the international system, his movement more than a conspiracy but less than a government. In the end he was never able to escape that limbo, to move from terrorism aimed at destroying Israel, the work of war, to the building of a real Palestinian state, the work of peace. Perhaps, he became too comfortable with the struggle, for achieving his end meant also the end of him. The rest of his life would be spent in a strange limbo of simultaneous relevance and irrelevance. Nothing could happen without him, but nothing could happen with him.[49]

There was immediate concern that without Arafat there could be a breakdown of structure in the PA, with chaos ensuing and potentially even civil war, especially if groups such as Hamas attempted to assertively fill the perceived political vacuum. These fears, however, proved to be overblown in the near term as most Palestinians were prudently cognizant of the possibility of a breakdown of political and social order and worked to keep what was left of the system running. Mahmoud Abbas won the election in January 2005 to replace Arafat as the PA president. In an amazing feat considering the deteriorating conditions and as a testament to the potential of a democratic Palestinian state, international observers overwhelmingly determined that the elections were conducted in a fair and transparent manner. Abbas was not tied to terrorism as Arafat had been, and the Bush administration heartily welcomed the change. The new PA president committed himself to democratization and fighting terror, two subjects dear to the Bush administration's core foreign policy themes. As a result, in a clear distinction with Arafat, who was persona non grata with the Bush administration, Abbas visited the White House in May 2005. The Bush administration subsequently became engaged on the Israeli–Palestinian front in a more assertive fashion than it had been in some time, sending General William Ward to help rebuild and reorganize the beaten-down labyrinth of Palestinian security forces. It also sent former World Bank head James Wolfenson to assist in the difficult plans for economic development in the Gaza Strip in the wake of the anticipated Israeli withdrawal.[50]

With Arafat gone, replaced by a Palestinian president who publicly disavowed terrorism (in English *and* Arabic) and enjoyed the strong support of the Bush administration, Sharon was compelled to reengage in negotiations. With the momentum produced by the Palestinian elections, Sharon met with Abbas, Husni Mubarak, and Jordan's King Abdullah at Sharm al-Shaykh on February 8, 2005. At the meeting, Abbas and Sharon agreed to a mutual cease-fire, one that held up fairly well for the remainder of the year despite (less frequent) incidences of attacks and reprisals. Again, however, Abbas stuck to his plan to reduce the incidence of Palestinian attacks by negotiating with groups such as Hamas and the al-Aqsa Martyrs Brigade and co-opting them through participation in the political process, while Israel continued to press him to take more direct action to disarm the militants. Abbas constructed an agreement (the Cairo Declaration) with Hamas and other Palestinian organizations on March 19 that called for a period of calm as long as Israel displayed a more restrained policy as well—despite the occurrence of sporadic violence, it more or less held up for the remainder of 2005 and into 2006. The meeting and cease-fire agreement were significant for legitimizing Abbas' position, which the United States was keen on doing in order to provide the foundation for what it hoped would be continued progress on the Roadmap following the Israeli withdrawal from the Gaza Strip. Indeed, even after an Islamic Jihad (which did not agree to the cease-fire) suicide bombing in Tel Aviv on February 26 that killed four and wounded scores of Israelis, both the Bush administration and Sharon's government deflected blame for this away from Abbas toward Syria, which was accused again of supporting radical Palestinian groups that have offices in Damascus. As Deputy Defense Minister Zeev Boim stated, "There is no doubt that Syria is a center of terrorist activity, this time against Israel, but also regionally. Operations by us against Syria are certainly possible. We have done it in the past. If Asad needs another message from us, then he will certainly get it."[51] This chimed in with the Bush administration's policy of ratcheting up the pressure on Damascus vis-à-vis its alleged support for the Iraqi insurgency. The White House press secretary added that "We do have firm evidence that the bombing in Tel Aviv was not only authorized by Palestinian Islamic Jihad leaders in Damascus, but that Islamic Jihad leaders in Damascus participated in the planning."[52]

For Sharon, the cease-fire lessened the tension in Israel prior to the Gaza withdrawal, and it was a key to convincing some skeptical Israelis that it would not lead to an increase in terrorism nor was Israel retreating in the face of terrorism. It also was a boon to the centrist and left-of-center parties, particularly Labor, that had joined Sharon's coalition in January 2005 in something of a national unity government in order to have the necessary votes in the Knesset to carry through with the withdrawal (with Shimon Peres as vice premier). As a result, on February 16, the Knesset finalized and approved the Gaza withdrawal plan by a vote of 59 in favor, 40 opposed, and five abstaining.[53] The cease-fire, and at least the appearance of a resumption of Israeli–Palestinian contacts, raised confidence in the economy as well, and it responded with healthy growth figures (4% by most estimates) for the remainder of 2005, especially in the tourist sector. In addition, there was a general feeling in Israel that if the peace process did not move forward, there was the possibility of what in effect would be a third intifada, with, among other things, deleterious repercussions for the recovering Israeli economy.[54] The danger here would be that polls indicated that two-thirds of Israelis believed they won the second intifada and would be willing to "pay the price" for a third one as well, whereas two-thirds of Palestinians felt that it was the violence of the intifada that compelled Israel to withdraw from the Gaza Strip, and they equally were committed to a full-fledged re-activation of the uprising if necessary.[55] This is something that both Israel and the PA have a mutual interest in avoiding.

In the remaining months before the planned withdrawal in August, Sharon continued to fend off attempts to undermine the plan by elements within his own party as well as a campaign of protest and demonstrations orchestrated by the religious nationalist parties, messianic Zionists, and settler groups. Netanyahu resigned on August 7 just prior to Cabinet ratification (17 to 5) of the first phase of the disengagement. Reflecting the concern of a number of Israelis, especially on the Right, he stated that "I don't know when terrorism will erupt in full force—my hope is that it won't ever. But I am convinced today that the disengagement will eventually aggravate terrorism instead of reducing it. The security establishment also expects an increase in terrorism. The withdrawal endangers Israel's security, divides its people and sets the standards of the withdrawal to the '67 border."[56] Sharon reiterated on August 15 that "It is out of strength and not weakness that we are taking this step," and it has given Israel the "diplomatic initiative."[57]

The evacuation of the twenty-one civilian settlements in the Gaza Strip was completed by August 15, with the IDF leaving the territory by September 12. Ten days later, the four outpost settlements in the northern West Bank were evacuated. Although it was a gut-wrenching exercise for Israeli society, with difficult scenes of Israeli settlers being pulled out of their homes, the evacuation in both the Gaza and West Bank went much more smoothly and without incident than many had thought possible. On August 31, the Knesset voted to withdraw from the Gaza–Egyptian border, allowing Egyptian border police along the demilitarized Egyptian side of the border; and by November 2005 Palestinians, in a detailed, technical agreement brokered at the eleventh hour by Secretary of State Condoleezza Rice, gained control of their side of the border with Egypt, including customs and passport control.[58] The Israeli civil war did not occur. Many Israelis rejoiced in the fact that the state exerted its control—that the government could face down the settler groups and messianic Zionists and follow through with the withdrawal. It was a devastating defeat for the settler movement, as Ari Shavit, a historian with the Israeli daily *Haaretz,* commented,

> It was a blow, in the sense that they failed to frighten off the government, and it was proven that it could be done. They are also facing a deep theological crisis, because their rabbinical leadership made very messianic and irresponsible promises how it would not happen and were proven wrong. They've had a really lethal clash with reality. We've known for a while that at least 70 percent of Israelis are politically sane. We've discovered now that even on the political right, 70 percent are also sane. They want a greater Israel and the settlements, but when faced with the power of the Israeli majority, they finally accepted it.[59]

But there are still many challenges that lie ahead as a result of the Gaza withdrawal. As prominent Israeli author Shlomo Avineri notes, practical Zionism accepted the partition of Palestine in 1947 as "a real refuge for real Jews in real time," but the magnitude of the victory in 1967 was a tremendous boost to the "messianic and maximalist" Zionists.[59a] He points out, then, that there is a difference between those who remember the pre-1967 borders, which were "dangerous and ideologically meaningful, with

Masked Hamas members pray before their march in Jabaliya refugee camp outside Gaza City, August 26, 2005. (DAMIR SAGOLJ/Reuters/Corbis, 42-15716889.)

the Wailing Wall on the other side" and "people 20 to 30 years old, who don't think about them or feel them, let alone recognize them." This portends an even more traumatic societal jolt if and when a withdrawal from West Bank territory is envisioned. As Israeli writer Amos Oz notes,

> Hundreds of thousands of Israelis are convinced, intellectually and emotionally, that if Israel keeps hold of the occupied territories it will cease to exist—nothing less than that. Hundreds of thousands of other Israelis are convinced that if Israel pulls out, it will cease to exist—nothing less than that. Both sides are armed with precedents and expert opinions, indications that appear to them infallible. Both sides sense an imminent catastrophe. Both sides share a sense of emergency.[60]

For the Palestinians, the Gaza Strip has become a test case as to whether or not they can govern and produce a viable, peaceable state. But they will need time because of its dilapidated condition following decades of occupation and mismanagement. The Gaza Strip is practically lawless and an economic disaster. The PA will need considerable foreign assistance to make it work, creating more jobs, more security, and the promise of a better future for Palestinians in order to wean them away from the radicalism of Hamas, which has claimed credit for forcing the Israelis out. But the PA will also need to transform itself into a much more efficient and transparent body in order to attract the necessary foreign assistance. Muhammad Dahlan is saying all the right things regarding development in the Gaza Strip when he comments that "These projects won't be done in the dark, or behind the backs of citizens. It will be as clear as daylight."[61] Ten-year plans envision two main cities—Khan Yunis in the south and Gaza City in the north—with four east–west green corridors for agriculture. There are plans for free-trade zones near the proposed airport and seaport, along with industrial estates along the border with Israel.[62] But after the withdrawal, there was still much left to be done, with a rising number of complaints that the PA was conducting business as usual, i.e., in a nepotistic, corrupt, and authoritarian fashion.

In Israel, however, there occurred in the months following the disengagement a political earthquake of enormous proportions that redrew the political map of the Jewish state. It began with the surprising victory of Amir Peretz over Shimon Peres (42% to 40%) in the Labor party primary on November 10. Born in Morocco in 1952 and arriving in Israel four years later, the new leader of Labor is the first Sephardic head of the party. He is a long-standing member of the Peace Now movement in Israel. Peretz first made his mark as mayor of Sderot; then he was elected to the Knesset in 1988, where he switched back and forth as leader of the Histadrut union federation. He has a limited military background, however; to address this, he has brought on board former Shin Bet head Ami Ayalon to boost his security credentials. With his leftist credentials, his critics decry him as a "Bolshevik," wanting to return the economy to state control. Peretz responded to this by gaining the support of some important entrepreneurs and economists, with his supporters claiming he is more Blairite (after British Prime Minister Tony Blair) than Bolshevik. He would, however, be the first Israeli leader to come to power with a platform that emphasized social and economic issues over security. As one writer comments,

> He [Peretz] has identified an anomaly in Israeli politics whereby people are categorized as leftwing or rightwing not, as elsewhere, according to their views on welfare or public ownership but rather on whether they are hawks or doves in their attitudes to the Israeli–Palestinian conflict. He blames this distortion on the occupation of Palestinian territories. He wants to break the current pattern in which poor people vote for the rightwing that promises to hold on to occupied land but appears to show little concern for their welfare.[63]

Even though the Israeli economy measurably grew in 2005, Peretz hoped to tap into those who had been hurt by the accompanying unequal distribution of wealth and benefits.

The earthquake began when, reflecting his wing of the Labor party, Peretz believed Labor had done enough for Sharon in helping to push through the Gaza disengagement scheme. It was now time for a return to politics, and he convinced the party leadership to pull out of the almost one-year coalition government. This decision sealed the fate of Sharon's government. On November 21, the Israeli prime minister asked President Moshe Katsav to dissolve parliament, paving the way for a general election in March 2006. But Sharon was not done.

On the same day, Sharon announced he was leaving the party he had helped create over thirty years earlier to form a new, centrist party called Kadima ("forward"). In forming the Kadima as a new "liberal movement for Israel," Sharon stated that Likud in its present format was "unable to lead Israel to its national goals." Reflecting polls in Israel that showed that two-thirds of the Israeli electorate favored a peace settlement with the

Palestinians leading to the creation of a Palestinian state, he reiterated that he would pursue peace with the Palestinians toward a two-state solution according to the parameters established by the Roadmap, but he emphasized the responsibility of the PA to dismantle the terrorist organizations for there to be progress.[64] In addition to himself, thirteen other Likud Knesset members bolted the party to join Kadima, and even Shimon Peres announced his intention to join Sharon. Initials polls indicated that Kadima would win the largest bloc in the Knesset in the election.[65]

THE UNEXPECTED IN THE MIDDLE EAST

It is almost an axiom in the Middle East that just when a pattern seems to be taking shape or a new historical trend seems to be developing, something happens that brings almost everything back to square one. This occurred on January 4, 2006, when 77-year-old Prime Minister Ariel Sharon suffered a massive stroke that left him in a coma.[66] It became clear that he would be physically and mentally incapacitated. He would be difficult to replace, especially as he had so dominated Israeli politics in the preceding years as he moved closer to the center of the Israeli political spectrum, attracting a broad swath of the Israeli electorate on the left and the right.

Becoming acting prime minister was Ehud Olmert, who was deputy prime minister in the Sharon government. Olmert joined Sharon in the new Kadima party, becoming the natural choice for party leader in the aftermath of Sharon's incapacitation.[67] Olmert is quite a different breed in many ways from Sharon, the former being the cosmopolitan 60-year-old lawyer who loves a good cigar and who married an avowedly dovish artist, while the latter, of course, presented the image of the gruff, no-nonsense military man. The acting prime minister served in the Israeli military in the Golani Brigade and as a correspondent for a military newspaper, generally fulfilling his military commitment, as with most Israelis, in a nondescript fashion, whereas Sharon had been an experienced and heroic military figure of the first order. Olmert first was elected to the Knesset in 1973 on the Likud ticket. He actually opposed the 1978 Camp David accords and the subsequent Egyptian–Israeli peace treaty, although before the Gaza withdrawal in 2005 he stated he owed Menachem Begin an apology.[68] In 1993 Olmert unseated the Labor party icon Teddy Kollek as mayor of Jerusalem, and he proceeded to consolidate Israel's hold of East Jerusalem; indeed, it was Olmert who oversaw the opening of the second entrance to the Hasmonean Tunnel in 1996. However, in January 2006, prior to the Palestinian legislative elections, Olmert, under U.S. pressure, reversed Sharon's prohibition of Palestinians residing in East Jerusalem from voting. It seems as though Olmert, for many of the same reasons, had undergone a similar transformation as Sharon had and was prepared to continue the unilateralist policy vis-à-vis the Occupied Territories. As David Makovsky states: "After forty years of occupying the territories, people are sick and tired of it. They don't want to have anything to do with Palestinians. They were going to give Sharon a big victory in the [March 28] elections. If he plays his cards right, Olmert may win a smaller but still significant victory, too, because unilateral disengagement is what the public wants."[69]

This unilateralism became all the more likely following the surprising results of the January 25, 2006, Palestinian legislative elections. Prior to the election, most analysts figured that Hamas, not boycotting the election this time as it did in 1996, would have a good showing and win a considerable number of seats in the 132-seat legislature but definitely remain in the minority. The Bush administration through the Agency for International Development even funded a $2 million program of civic activities in the West Bank (e.g., street-cleaning, distributing free food and water at border crossings, donating computers, and sponsoring a national youth soccer tournament) in the months preceding the election to improve the image of Fatah and other secular Palestinian candidates.[70] Despite all this, Hamas candidates won 74 of the 132 seats, a majority. The victory seemed to catch off-guard not only the United States and other countries but even Hamas, whose leaders commented on the election result in an uncoordinated and unexpected manner, not quite knowing whether to take a more or less conciliatory tone.

Hamas' victory was not a total shock, however, given the disrepute the PA had fallen into in recent years. Many Palestinians who voted for the Islamist group stated that it was not so much a vote for Hamas but a vote against Fatah and the PA. Growing lawlessness, especially in the Gaza Strip, a deteriorating economy, and widespread corruption among the senior PA leaders compelled many Palestinians to vote for Hamas candidates. Despite their militancy that often brought more hardship to Palestinians from Israeli reprisals, Hamas was known and admired for its civic functions not provided by the PA, its discipline, and its reputation for integrity when compared to the corrupt Palestinian old guard. As Mustafa Barghouti of the Palestinian National Initiative party stated, "Mostly, they were voting for opposition and voting against Fatah—against corruption, against nepotism, against the failure of the peace process, and against the lack the leadership."[71] In addition, since the peace process was moribund, particularly in light of Sharon's unilateralism, Palestinian voters tended to compare Fatah and Hamas on other matters, many of which favored the latter. As Palestinian pollster Khalil Shikaki stated, "There is a great deal of disappointment over where the peace process is. . . . The question is whether they believe achieving an agreement is possible at all. And when people don't think it matters one way or another, they will look at Hamas and Fatah on other issues."[72]

Washington and Tel Aviv were taken aback by the Hamas victory. For the Bush administration it presented quite the dilemma. As noted earlier, one of the primary objectives of the Bush foreign policy by 2005 was the promotion of democracy through free and fair elections in the Middle East. Yet in Iraq it produced a Shiite majority largely controlled by Shiite Islamist parties, many of which have close ties to Iran. In Egypt in fall 2005 it produced historic gains by the Muslim Brethren (its members running as independents) in the National Assembly, although Husni Mubarak's National Democratic Party still held a clear majority. Then there were the results in January, in what was widely considered by internal and external observers to be a fair and legitimate election. These were not exactly the optimal results the Bush administration was looking for, but it also felt compelled to honor the electoral process and its outcome. While agreeing with many analysts that it was a rejection of the failure of the PA to provide the basic necessities of life, it did not push for a negation of the election; rather, Bush administration officials hoped that Hamas would become a responsible government authority that would recognize Israel, renounce violence, and honor prior agreements between the PA and Israel. This gets to the core debate revolving around the issue of whether or not to allow Islamist groups to run in democratic elections; it is a debate that goes back to the nullified outcome of the Algerian elections in the early 1990s by the Algerian military when the Islamic Salvation Front won a majority in the parliament, the result of which was a bloody civil war that has killed over 150,000 Algerians to date. In other words, even if Islamist parties win in democratic elections (as in Kuwait and Jordan in the 1990s), they will be less likely to want to overthrow or inflict violence upon a government of which they are now part. In this sense, Islamists will increasingly be co-opted into the idea of peaceful change from the inside without disrupting government and society—at the very least it will separate the moderate Islamists from the more radical ones, thus weakening the whole. The more pessimistic view, however, is that Islamist groups will utilize the democratic process to come to power and then impose an Islamic state—i.e., one person, one vote, one time.

It was thought that Hamas could also be pressured by withholding Israeli tax payments of some $55 million per month to an already beleaguered PA (an act made official on February 19) as well as getting international donors to stop their payments. This could economically squeeze the Palestinians into calling for new elections. Behind this lies the idea that Fatah lost because it fielded too many candidates in the same voting districts, thus splitting the vote and allowing Hamas candidates to win; in addition, rivalries between younger and older Fatah groups and candidates prevented the secular parties from running a coordinated and organized campaign. Rectifying these issues along with pressuring Hamas might produce a more acceptable result, or so this line of thought goes.

It is clear, however, that Hamas entered into an internal debate of its own over what direction it should pursue once it acquired the office of PA prime minister and formed a new government. At the urging of Palestinian secular elements as well as Israel and the United States, Mahmoud Abbas continued as president, although, as one writer commented, Abbas "carries all the weight of Mr. Arafat's failures without any credit for his successes."[73] The exiled political head of Hamas, Khalid Mishal, stated from Damascus in the aftermath of the elections that Hamas would not "submit to pressure to recognize Israel, because the occupation is illegitimate and we will not abandon our rights."[74] He also stated that Hamas would not disarm and insisted that "resistance is a legitimate right that we will practice and protect," while also saying that Hamas was "ready to work with Europe and even the United States if they wish."[75] Yet other, more moderate Hamas officials, particularly those who won seats in the legislature, talked of extending the cease-fire agreed to in early 2005 or declaring a long-term truce as long as Israel pulled back to the 1967 lines.

There are those who believe that Hamas will, perforce, moderate its position much as the PLO did by the late 1980s. It will have to work with the Israelis at some level, even if it is only coordinating municipal functions; and this could build a level of trust and interaction that might evolve into more significant contact. It will also have to answer to the Palestinian population—it is no longer in the opposition where from a safe distance it can throw stones at the ruling authority; it must now provide a viable program to correct the many ills in Palestinian society that go beyond the question of occupation. On the other hand, there are those who believe that Hamas will not change colors. It is a religious movement, where the struggle for Palestine is a religious obligation. In the Hamas charter, written in 1988, it states that it "believes that the land of Palestine has been an Islamic waqf [religious endowment] throughout the generations and until the Day of Resurrection, no one can renounce it or part of it, or abandon it or part of it." It describes Hamas as a "distinct Palestinian movement which owes its loyalty to Allah, derives from Islam its way of life and strives to raise the banner of Allah over every inch of Palestine." The charter is also full of anti-Semitic and stereotypical references to the Jews, and it explicitly calls for the elimination of Israel.[76]

But the PLO changed its charter once it moderated its position vis-à-vis Israel, adopting the two-state solution. Many believe that Hamas already moderated its position, exemplified by its running in the election to begin with and adopting a platform of committing itself to improving the lives of Palestinians. Even Hamas' founder, Shaykh Ahmad Yassin, years ago stated that there were pragmatists and hardliners in the organization. Maybe the pragmatists will become dominant. A number of countries seemed to agree. In early February, Russia invited Hamas leaders to visit Moscow, breaking with what the United States hoped would be a unified stance in the Quartet to isolate Hamas until it met certain conditions. Turkey, whose ruling party is Islamist, met with Hamas officials, symbolically showing how an Islamist party could rule a secular state that has good relations with the West (and Israel). The European countries also adopted a wait-and-see approach to Hamas before deciding on any punitive measures. There were a bevy of plans being discussed on how to get allocated funds to the PA in a way that circumvented Hamas (even going directly to Abbas) so that Palestinian society did not break down altogether.[77]

On the other hand, Ehud Olmert toughened his stance toward Hamas in the run-up to the March 28 election. He actively tried to organize an international boycott of Hamas, cut off Israeli taxes to the PA, and reiterated plans for unilaterally determining the borderlines of Israel in the West Bank (encompassing withdrawal from West Bank territory except for the large settlement blocs, security zones, and all of Jerusalem), particularly as the possibility of negotiations with Hamas in power were off the table.[78] Olmert did not want to be outflanked on the right by Benjamin Netanyahu, who took over the leadership of Likud following Sharon's defection. As some of his critics have said, Netanyahu lives and dies by Hamas, a reference to the Hamas attacks in early 1996 that helped turn the election tide in his favor versus Shimon Peres a few months later. Despite Kadima's victory in the election and its formation of a coalition government, events soon turned in the direction of those Israelis opposing unilateral withdrawal, or what Olmert refers to as "realignment."

SPRING AND SUMMER 2006 AND BEYOND

Kadima won the most seats in the Knesset in the March 28 election, although fewer than preelection polls had predicted. Twenty-nine seats in the Israeli parliament went to Kadima, nineteen to Labor, and twelve each to Shas, the ultraorthodox religious party, and to the right-wing Russian-oriented Yisrael Beiteinu party led by Avignor Lieberman, an obvious beneficiary of the Likud party's problems, which itself garnered only eleven seats. By early May Prime Minister Olmert won formal parliamentary approval for his four-party coalition government with 67 of the 120 Knesset seats (Kadima = 29, Labor = 19, Shas = 12, Pensioners party = 7). The fact that Kadima and Labor won the most seats was a clear electoral affirmation of Olmert's platform of continuing Sharon's unilateral withdrawal policy in the West Bank. That Hamas secured the formation of a government with Ismail Haniyeh as prime minister of the PA reinforced the notion among most Israelis that there was no viable Palestinian negotiating partner; by default, then, Israel had to take it upon itself to define the nature of withdrawal and redraw its borders in a way that was not subject to Palestinian or international interference or obstruction. With American encouragement, Olmert continued to withhold the transfer of $55 million in monthly tax and customs revenues that Israel collects on behalf of the PA as well as to squeeze foreign financial contributions to the PA. Israel also closed the main cargo crossing into the Gaza Strip in an attempt to further isolate Hamas through economic pressure, hoping along with Washington that it might fall from power for lack of funds, thus clearing the way for the return of the more amenable Fatah faction. It was a determined strategy, for nearly half of the PA's $2 billion annual budget comes from foreign aid and half of the PA's monthly payroll comes from the frozen tax and customs receipts. Minus the ability to pay basic government salaries, along with a few well-timed strikes and demonstrations by Palestinian civil servants protesting against the lack of pay (which started to occur with more frequency in June, no doubt organized to some degree by Fatah), the Hamas-led government might be compelled to moderate its policies vis-à-vis Israel or fall completely from power.

Mahmoud Abbas maintained the pressure on Hamas by calling for a public referendum on recognizing Israel if Hamas did not at least implicitly do so. He also endorsed the so-called prisoners plan drawn up by a broad spectrum of Palestinians held in Israeli jails. The plan called for a Palestinian state in the West Bank, Gaza Strip, and East Jerusalem; the release of all Palestinian political prisoners in Israeli jails; the right of return for Palestinian refugees; and certain security and political reforms in the PA. While radical Hamas leaders rejected the plan, Prime Minister Haniyeh called it a positive sign, with an overwhelming number of Palestinians supporting it according to polls.

There seemed, then, to be some positive movement, if ever so slight. Maybe Abbas and Haniyeh could piece together something that might restart negotiations with the Israelis before Olmert made a West Bank withdrawal a fait accompli. But on June 25, 2006, eight Palestinian militants, mostly affiliated with Hamas, killed two Israeli soldiers and captured a third, Corporal Gilad Shalit, after emerging from a tunnel dug some 300 yards into Israel from the Gaza Strip. Some say the Palestinian attack was a function of an intra-Hamas struggle between moderate factions led by Haniyeh and more radical ones led by Khalid Mishal and his Syrian backers in Damascus. Elements of the latter, according to this view, carried out the attack to scuttle any progress by moderate Hamas leaders that might marginalize Mishal and his supporters as well as the Syrians and even the Iranians. Others contend that it was simply a case of Hamas fighting back against Israel's policy of attempting to eliminate them from the PA—it was seen as a natural riposte to what Hamas viewed as heightened Israeli aggression in recent weeks, including the targeted assassination of a Popular Resistance Committee figure on June 8 and Israeli military reprisals in northern Gaza (with the deaths of a number of Palestinian civilians) to rid the area of Qassem rockets that were being fired indiscriminately into Israel proper.

Whatever the motivation for the Palestinian raid, any momentum toward moderation was lost for the time. Israel, after allowing for a few days of fruitless diplomacy centering around proposed prisoner exchanges that Olmert flatly rejected, started a strategic bombing campaign and sent troops into the Gaza Strip seeking to pressure Hamas into releasing the Israeli soldier. The Gaza Strip was essentially closed off and shut down in a military reversal of the Israeli settler withdrawal that had occurred nearly a year earlier. Palestinians and other critics of Israel claim Tel Aviv was using the Shalit kidnapping as an excuse to enter Gaza militarily and further degrade Hamas as a political entity and military threat. Still others point to Israel's action as classic Ben-Gurionism, i.e., hitting back hard in order to establish or reinforce Israel's deterrent power.

Three weeks into the Gaza operation, without obtaining the release of Corporal Shalit and amid rising internal criticism of Olmert and his inexperienced defense minister, Labor party head Amir Peretz, Israel was unexpectedly hit again, this time in the north. On July 12, Hizbollah carried out a daring daylight raid into Israel just across the border, killing eight Israeli soldiers and capturing two. In an almost cathartic response of a country feeling itself under siege, Israel launched punitive air strikes into Lebanon against Hizbollah positions as well as transit routes, including Beirut International Airport, to prevent the transfer of the two soldiers out of the country. Hizbollah responded by firing scores of Katyusha rockets into northern Israel, launching a 34-day conflict that saw several thousand more Katyushas fired indiscriminately into Israel as far south as Haifa, an intensive Israeli air campaign over most of Lebanon, especially in south Beirut and south Lebanon against Hizbollah strongholds, and eventually a ground campaign to root out Hizbollah positions in southern Lebanon. During the conflict, 159 Israelis (118 soldiers and 41 civilians) and some 1,070 Lebanese were killed, with hundreds of thousands of Lebanese and Israelis fleeing the warfare to safer environs.[79] The level of destruction in Lebanon itself reminded many of 1982; and the destruction in northern Israel, and perhaps even more importantly the fears generated, informed Israelis that they are not yet safe in the Middle East despite their overwhelming conventional military strength.

As in the case of the Hamas raid, it is unclear as to exactly why Hizbollah carried it out. Perhaps it was simply, as Hizbollah leader Shaykh Hassan Nasrallah said, to help the Palestinians under attack in Gaza by diverting Israel's attentions—he is widely known to say what he means and to do what he says. This allowed Hizbollah the opportunity to transcend its Lebanese Shiite roots to the broader the Arab–Islamic arena, amply displaying that it alone in the region had the temerity to take on Israel and fight on behalf of the Palestinians. Others claim it was either ordered by Hizbollah's patron, Iran, or carried out independently by Hizbollah on behalf of Teheran in order to show the West that Iran has lethal means it can employ if the international pressure on its nuclear enrichment program escalates into military action. The fact that Hizbollah launched the attack on the same day as an important UN deadline for receiving a response from Teheran regarding its nuclear enrichment activities lends some credence to this view. In addition, ever since the passage of UNSC Resolution 1559 and the subsequent Syrian withdrawal from Lebanon, Hizbollah saw its position in the country being undermined. It was resisting attempts, as ordained in 1559, for the Lebanese government to disarm it. Stirring up trouble with Israel, this line of thought proceeds, would confirm Hizbollah's role as a legitimate resistance organization; thus, it would be able to retain its arms as well as position itself more favorably in the constellation of political forces that make up the Lebanese polity.[80] Syria, which also supports Hizbollah, namely with logistical assistance in terms of transferring Iranian arms and funds, might also, by default, enhance its influence in Lebanon and gain a seat at the diplomatic table in any sort of resolution to the conflict and postconflict attempts to restart Arab–Israeli peace negotiations. Hizbollah's rationale may have been one or all of the above.

There was widespread support in Israel for Olmert's military response in Lebanon, although many outside of Israel saw it as wildly disproportionate to the act itself. It was a response that definitely caught Hizbollah by surprise, although it was effectively prepared to resist it. It appeared that the Bush administration delayed inserting itself actively into the mix to arrange a cease-fire, as previous administrations had done when

Israeli–Hizbollah violence flared up and threatened to escalate beyond Lebanon—this despite the desperate pleas for help from the pro-U.S. government of Lebanese Prime Minister Fuad Siniora. The United States clearly was allowing Israel the opportunity to deal Hizbollah a decisive blow. This would not only allow the Lebanese government to extend its control but also damage Syrian and Iranian interests; indeed, in Washington it seemed the Arab–Israeli conflict was being folded neatly into a U.S.-vs.-Iran dynamic, despite the fact that the root causes of the problems in the Arab–Israeli arena in general, and in Lebanon specifically, long predated the 1979 Iranian revolution and had unique dynamics of their own that needed to be addressed directly. But the Bush administration believed that the events of the summer of 2006 could weaken both Hamas and Hizbollah, and the Israelis were poised to inflict irreversible damage.

But Israel was unable to "defeat" Hizbollah. As Robert Malley stated, Olmert, "who claimed that Hizbollah would be destroyed, defined victory in terms that ensured a loss. Hizbollah's leader, Hassan Nasrallah, whose stated goal was to withstand the onslaught, characterized success in a way that ruled out defeat. A war waged to reassert Israel's power of deterrence and to spoil Hizbollah's image has significantly eroded the former while unintentionally improving the latter."[81] Hizbollah military preparations (including underground tunnels and bunkers) and stockpiles of weapons were much more extensive than Israeli intelligence had anticipated. In addition, Olmert and Peretz came under heavy internal criticism for not carrying out the war in an effective fashion, i.e., depending too much on airpower and not enough on a ground campaign that in any event came too little, too late.

With both Israel and Hizbollah appearing to seek a way out as civilian casualties mounted and a military solution appeared fleeting, U.S. and UN diplomacy engaged toward arranging a cease-fire. By August 14, UNSC Resolution 1701 (passed by the Security Council on August 11) was accepted and implemented by the governments of Lebanon (which included Hizbollah representation) and Israel.[82]

Both sides, of course, claimed victory. But it was also clear that the Olmert government had been rattled and weakened, with the right-wing parties empowered as they had consistently opposed unilateral withdrawal, fearing what on the surface actually came to pass, i.e., that it opened the door for groups such as Hamas and Hizbollah to operate freely and build up their military capabilities to launch attacks against Israel. The survival of the Olmert coalition was certainly in doubt. As a result, any talk of further withdrawal (or realignment) from the West Bank was put on hold indefinitely. It was also equally clear that the failure to carry out withdrawal within the framework of a negotiated settlement that would hold a legitimate party such as the PA in Gaza or Syria in Lebanon (in 2000) responsible for extending and maintaining the terms of the agreement had come home to roost. Although unilateral withdrawal is off the table for the time being, perhaps a negotiated withdrawal along the lines of the Egyptian–Israeli peace treaty will eventually gain some traction.

For Hizbollah, the conflict was a mixed bag. Hizbollah and Nasrallah became in the span of a month the most popular group and leader in the Arab and Muslim worlds. By winning the reconstruction efforts in Lebanon through its already existing and pervasive social welfare networks and institutions—along with copious amounts of Iranian money pouring in—Hizbollah seemed to have improved its political position in Lebanon and solidified its claim as a resistance group, able to keep its weapons. On the other hand, the damage to Lebanon, especially in the Shiite-dominated south, was extensive, so much so that Nasrallah pointed out in a refreshingly honest manner after the conflagration that had he known beforehand the extent of the damage that Israel would inflict he absolutely would not have ordered the July 12 raid. In the early stages of the conflict, some Arab leaders (notably Sunni countries such as Saudi Arabia and Egypt) and a number of Lebanese openly pinned the blame for initiating the war on Hizbollah. While these sentiments disappeared under the weight of Arab solidarity as the death and destruction in Lebanon grew, some level of opprobrium is likely to return, especially inside the country, once the postconflict dust settles down.

As has been seen often in the Arab–Israeli conflict, a crisis can create opportunities for peace, with many wanting to build on the momentum of whatever brought the conflagration to a close. It was no different in the late summer and early fall of 2006.

With the perception that Iran was on the ascendant in the region as Hizbollah gained ground in Lebanon and as the United States position in Iraq deteriorated, there seemed to be a general recognition in policy circles in Washington that the Arab–Israeli peace process needed a jumpstart before Teheran consolidated its gains. Israeli military power did not subdue Hizbollah or Hamas; maybe diplomacy could. There was a swirl of calls for the Bush administration to engage in a dialogue with Syria, since it was apparent that any real solution to the situation in Lebanon would require the involvement of Damascus.[83] This could also have serendipitous repercussions elsewhere for the United States and Israel. Perhaps, as the thinking went, if an Israeli–Syrian peace process commenced, Damascus might lessen its support for Hamas and Hizbollah as a quid pro quo for the return of the Golan Heights. This could, in turn, help Mahmoud Abbas and Fatah gain the upper hand in intra-Palestinian politics and allow him to reengage Tel Aviv in a meaningful Israeli–Palestinian peace process. In addition, Syria could assist the United States regarding a political solution in Iraq, as well as more energetically stem the flow of support for the Iraqi insurgency crossing its border. Finally, it might be possible to then split Syria from Iran, by default weakening the latter's influence in the region and emboldening an anti-Iranian moderate Arab consensus that would be prepared to arrive at a comprehensive resolution to the Arab–Israeli conflict.

Syria felt empowered. As a result, Damascus sent out clear signals that it was ready to talk peace with Israel, and a number of U.S. congresspersons met with President Bashar, capped off by Speaker of the House Nancy Pelosi's visit to Damascus in April 2007. This generated debate in and outside the Israeli government over whether or not to accept Bashar al-Asad's olive branch, or at the very least to explore the possibility.[84] These feelings gathered momentum in late 2006 following the November midterm Congressional elections in the United States, when the Democrats won back control of both Houses of Congress in what appeared to be a resounding public repudiation of the Bush administration's policy in Iraq, and by implication, its overall foreign policy in the Middle East. A month later, the high-powered, bipartisan Iraq Study Group, led by former secretary of state, James Baker, and former congressman, Lee Hamilton, published its final report.[85] Along with a number of suggestions regarding how to improve the U.S. position in Iraq, one of the report's strongest recommendations was for the Bush administration to embark upon a region-wide diplomatic initiative with the primary objective being a resolution to the Arab–Israeli dispute. In doing so, the authors recommended that the United States establish a dialogue with and diplomatically engage Syria (and even Iran).

Optimism in this regard, however, began to fade almost as quickly as it had risen. Hamas and Fatah failed repeatedly in the fall and winter of 2006 to form a national unity government that would meet the conditions laid out by the Quartet powers (Hamas recognition of Israel, renunciation of violence against Israel, and abiding by already existing Israeli–Palestinian agreements) that would lift the international boycott of the Hamas-led PA government and facilitate a resumption of Israeli–Palestinian peace talks. Worse still, Fatah and Hamas security forces engaged in what was a virtual Palestinian civil war in the Occupied Territories in late 2006 and into early 2007, all of which made peace talks seem even more remote. In addition, the Bush administration made it clear in December 2006 that it was not going to enter into a dialogue with Syria—the policy of isolation of Damascus, if not support for regime change, would continue virtually unabated. Ehud Olmert seemed to concur, and in any event, it was widely assumed that Washington was pressuring Israel to forgo any inclination it might have to open up a serious peace channel to Damascus, especially if Tel Aviv wanted continued U.S. support against Israel's primary strategic regional challenge, i.e. preventing Iran from developing a nuclear capability. In lieu of this, the Bush administration began to rely more and more on regional Sunni Arab allies such as Saudi Arabia, Egypt, and Jordan to help create a more favorable environment for Israeli–Palestinian negotiations as well as confront what was perceived to be an emerging Shiite-led axis composed of Hizbollah, Iran, Syria, and (Sunni) Hamas, or what some commentators were calling the "HISH" alliance.[86] Saudi King Abdullah even hosted Palestinian leaders in Mecca (Mahmoud Abbas, exiled Hamas leader Khalid Mishal, and PA Prime Minister Ismail Haniya) in early February 2007, a meeting that produced a tentative agreement between the two sides to form a national unity government, although the conditions for doing so fell far short of the Quartet requirements for lifting the international boycott. It seemed that ending the cycle of intra-Palestinian violence was the immediate priority. It remains to be seen whether this agreement will be a stepping-stone toward something more grand in terms of a peace process. Importantly, Syria did support what in effect was the reissuance of the 2002 Beirut Arab peace plan at the March 2007 Arab League summit in Riyadh, with the 2008 meeting to be held in Damascus. Saudi–Syrian relations, so damaged after the Hariri assassination, seem to be on the mend, with potential significant repercussions for realigning Syria within a moderate Arab front, resolving the politically unstable situation in Lebanon, and, ultimately, restarting Israeli–Syrian negotiations.

The powers at be perpetuate the absence of peace at their own peril. Historians are keen to point out those "what-ifs" connected with perceived missed opportunities in history. If conditions deteriorate in the Middle East, no doubt future historians will point to the failure to consummate an Israeli–Palestinian final peace accord and/or an Israeli–Syrian peace agreement in the late 1990s and in 2000 as two of them. Historians also like to ponder the counterfactual in history, i.e., what would have happened had the subject under discussion *not* happened. This is difficult, to say the least, because it is totally hypothetical. As noted earlier in the book, the 1979 Egyptian–Israeli peace treaty has been roundly criticized over the years. But one can speculate that although it did not stop Arab–Israeli conflict in its absolute sense, which since 1982 usually occurred by proxy in Lebanon, it did prevent the eruption of another all-out Arab–Israeli war.

In some important ways, we have seen in recent years the counterfactual to peace, or what *should* have been the counterfactual to the Arab–Israeli peace that *should* have occurred by 2000. Quite probably, the al-Aqsa intifada, the 2003 war in Iraq, the Israeli–Hizbollah conflict in 2006, and maybe even 9/11 (or at least the extremism that caused it) are all the counterfactual turned reality to that should-have-been comprehensive peace. Hopefully, historians in the near future will not conclude that another opportunity for peace was missed.

NOTES

1. Robert O. Freedman, "The Bush Administration and the Arab–Israeli Conflict: The First Term and Beyond," in David W. Lesch, ed., *The Middle East and the United States: A Historical and Political Reassessment*, 4th ed. (Boulder: Westview Press, 2007), p. 280.

2. Ibid.

3. *Washington Post*, December 17, 2000.

4. *Financial Times*, March 20, 2001.

5. *Washington Post*, March 30, 2001, as quoted in Freedman, "The Bush Administration."

6. Again, while the State Department condemned the use of targeted assassinations, Vice President Cheney stated in a Fox TV interview in August 2001 that "if you've got an organization that had plotted or is plotting some kind of suicide bomber attack, for example, and they have hard evidence of who it is and where they're located, I think there's some justification in their trying to protect themselves by preempting." And it was very clear to the Israelis that Cheney spoke with much more authority than the State Department at the time. Cheney's statement also foreshadows what would become known as the Bush Doctrine, which sanctioned preemptive U.S. military action in order to protect the country from terrorism. It also hints at the ideological framework, pushed by Cheney's office, behind the more liberal rules regarding U.S. interrogation of terrorist suspects that many claimed went beyond the pale of internationally sanctioned behavior.

7. *Financial Times*, September 9, 2002.

7a. www.mtholyoke.edu/acad/intrel/bush/wspeech.htm

8. Bush administration officials often spoke in apocalyptic terms, describing the battle as one of good versus evil or the forces of good versus the "evil-doers." This reflected President Bush's own evangelical background as well as a direct appeal to the evangelical Christian base of the Republican party that so avidly supported the Bush campaign. This *weltanschauung* led to the unfortunate use of the term "crusade" by Bush in one of his post-9/11 speeches to rally the American public to the U.S. response, a word that for obvious reasons in the Muslim Middle East resonated very badly.

8a. www.whitehouse.gov/news/releases/2001/09/20010920-8.html

9. *Christian Science Monitor*, September 27, 2001.

10. In fact, on October 8, 2001, the UN General Assembly elected Syria to a nonpermanent rotating two-year seat on the Security Council. The fact that the United States did not lobby against the choice of Syria was a clear indication that Washington was courting the Arab world at the time in the new war against terror and the war in Afghanistan. Syria would actually cooperate with U.S. intelligence and provide valuable information regarding al-Qa'ida in the months ahead.

11. *Financial Times*, September 5, 2002.

12. For an interesting essay on this dynamic, see Scott Lasensky, "Paying for Peace: The Oslo Process and the Limits of American Foreign Aid," *Middle East Journal* 58, no. 2 (2004): 210–234.

12a. www.whitehouse.gov/news/releases/2002/06/20020601–3.html

13. *Financial Times*, September 7–8, 2002.

13a. James Zogby, "Why Congress Is Out of Control," *Washington Watch*, August 11, 1997, as quoted in David W. Lesch, *The New Lion of Damascus*, 106.

14. The full text of the report can be found at www.israeleconomy.org/strat1.htm.

15. Quoted in Freedman, "The Bush Administration," 287.

16. *Financial Times*, September 5, 2002. Of course, the Palestinian response to this is that taking a more moderate course and cracking down on the militants would not have mattered since U.S. support for Israel is so unequivocal. The intifada had been raging for over a year, and the Bush administration had shown little interest in the plight of the Palestinians. See also David W. Lesch, "Changed or Just Revealed?: The Arab Middle East After 9/11," in Lenard Cohen, Brian Job, and Alexander Moens, eds., *Foreign Policy Realignment in the Age of Terror* (Toronto: Canadian Institute of Strategic Studies, 2003), 60–77.

17. *New York Times*, November 12, 2001 (full text of speech).

18. Quoted in Freedman, "The Bush Administration," 289.

19. Interestingly, according to a *Washington Post* report, Crown Prince Abdullah was absolutely furious upon hearing President Bush's televised comments on August 24, 2001, when he stated that "the Israelis will not negotiate under terrorist threat, simple as that...and if the Palestinians are interested in a dialogue, then I strongly urge Mr. Arafat to put 100 percent effort into...stopping the terrorist activity." Believing Bush to be totally partial in favor of Israel, Abdullah apparently immediately fired off a very strongly worded message to the American president through Prince Bandar bin Sultan, the Saudi ambassador to the United States. In the note to Bush, Abdullah basically threatened that Saudi Arabia would be compelled to go its own way from now on, essentially ending its unique relationship with the United States. This letter reportedly "shocked" the Bush administration, which scrambled to patch things up with the Saudi crown prince. Bush sent an ameliorating letter back to Abdullah professing his impartiality as well as endorsing the idea of a viable Palestinian state in the West Bank and Gaza Strip, along with an invitation to Abdullah to visit with Bush at his ranch in Crawford, Texas. Abdullah was mollified and assiduously began to work as an intermediary between Bush and Arafat, hoping to set up a meeting between the two at the upcoming UN General Assembly meeting in late September. U.S. and Saudi officials on September 8 and 9 were reportedly discussing the possibility of a major speech by Bush or Colin Powell that would jump-start the peace process and end the intifada, and it appeared that the Bush administration was eager to comply. Of course, then came the events of September 11, 2001, and all bets were off. Robert G. Kaiser and David B. Ottaway, "Saudi Leader's Anger Revealed Shaky Ties," *Washington Post*, February 10, 2002.

20. Apparently, *New York Times* columnist Thomas Friedman helped Abdullah come forward with his plan in a meeting he had with the Saudi crown prince in February 2002. See Friedman's essay "An Intriguing Signal from the Saudi Crown Prine," *New York Times*, February 17, 2002.

21. Elie Podeh, *From Fahd to 'Abdallah: The Origins of the Saudi Peace Initiatives and Their Impact on the Arab System and Israel* (Jerusalem: Harry S. Truman Research Institute for the Advancement of Peace, 2003), 19. Podeh asserts that the Saudi initiative was also an attempt to strengthen the moderate faction within the Saudi elite against Islamic radicals in the country as well as assert Saudi primacy over Egypt regarding the Palestinian issue; indeed, Mubarak did not attend the Arab League summit in Beirut, although he quietly supported the summit communiqué.

22. Yoram Meital, *Peace in Tatters: Israel, Palestine, and the Middle East* (Boulder: Lynne Rienner, 2006), 150.

23. *New York Times*, February 21, 2002.

24. President Bush also called on Israel to "withdraw fully to positions they held prior to September 28, 2000 [i.e., the day before the intifada broke out with Ariel Sharon's visit to the Temple Mount/Haram al-Sharif]. And consistent with the recommendation of the Mitchell Committee, Israeli settlement activity in the Occupied Territories must stop...[and] freedom of movement should be restored."

25. *New York Times*, June 25, 2002.

25a. www.state.gov/r/pa/pss/ps/2003/20062.htm

26. The Tenet plan was essentially the security accompaniment to the Mitchell report. Proposed in June 2001, the plan reaffirmed existing security arrangements between the Israelis and the PA and outlined a series of "realistic security steps immediately to reestablish security cooperation. . . ." In addition to delineating steps toward better communication between Israeli and Palestinian security services, the plan also involved U.S. technical and training assistance, mainly to the PA security forces.

27. Meital, *Peace in Tatters*, 150.

28. Ibid., 166.

29. *New York Times*, May 27, 2003.

30. This section is drawn from David W. Lesch, *The New Lion of Damascus*, 161–175.

31. For an extensive sampling of comments by congresspersons in 2001 and 2002, see ibid., 98–101.

32. For instance, in his speech at the opening plenary session at the Beirut summit meeting, Asad termed the intifada a "movement for independence" and called on Arab nations to sever relations with Israel. He pointed out that "the Palestinian intifada was legitimate resistance against occupation," and he closed by saying that "for us, terrorism comes from Israel." Ibid., 164.

33. *Washington Post*, October 6, 2003.

34. The U.S. Senate passed the act in November 2003 by a vote of 89–4; in October the House passed it by a vote of 398–4. The act was signed into law by President Bush on December 12, 2003. The act directs the president to block the export to Syria of items on the U.S. Munitions List or Commerce Control List of dual-use items. In addition, it requires the president to impose at least two of the following sanctions on Syria: (1) prohibit export of U.S. products (other than food or medicine); (2) prohibit U.S. businesses from investing or operating in Syria; (3) restrict the movement of Syrian officials in Washington, DC, and New York; (4) prohibit aircraft of any Syrian carrier from using U.S. airspace or from taking off or landing in the United States; (5) reduce U.S. diplomatic presence in Syria; and (6) block property transactions in which the government of Syria has an interest or is subject to U.S. jurisdiction. In May 2004 Bush activated numbers one and four, both of which are mostly symbolic considering the fact that there were no Syrian carriers in the United States to begin with and that trade between the two countries was minimal, less than $300 million in exports and less than $200 million in imports in 2002.

35. *New York Times*, December 1, 2003.

36. In fact, Israeli President Moshe Katsav publicly offered to meet with Asad in a place of Asad's choosing in order to assess the prospects for peace. Asad was not about to accept the invitation given the fact that Sadat was so roundly criticized for his visit to Israel in 1977 before negotiations actually began. Regarding the proposed meeting, Asad stated that "It was like a maneuver. . . . But why go? Just to shake hands, have dinner? If you want peace, we have criteria, and you start by saying the Golan should be returned to Syria and you start negotiating." Interview with the author in Damascus, May 27, 2004, in Lesch, *The New Lion of Damascus*, 168–169. It is interesting that Katsav also offered on February 25, 2002, to meet with Saudi Crown Prince Abdullah to discuss his peace initiative (see Podeh, *From Fahd to 'Abdallah*, 24). Katsav's offer was similarly dismissed, but it almost seems as if the Israeli president was utilized as something of a trial balloon to feel out and discern the sincerity of Arab intent.

37. *Financial Times*, January 10–11, 2004.

38. www.haaretz.com (accessed October 10, 2004). Shalom did add, however, that Syria must first stop aiding Palestinian militants and end its logistical assistance to Hizbollah, saying that "President Asad can't hold a stick from both sides . . . the seriousness of intentions will be proven if he acts on these issues." Ibid.

39. See Lesch, *The New Lion of Damascus*, 128–129. Asad told me in an interview in Damascus on May 3, 2005, that "We didn't have any other choice but to support Lahoud [in the face of French pressure]. He has always supported Syria—he never changed. He is a strong person, and I know him well as a person. If we did not have him there, we thought we would

have a lot of problems. The UN resolution really had nothing to do with the extension of Lahoud. It was coming anyway."

40. Intelligence reports in Israel seemed to agree that Syrian security elements were behind the assassination, without Asad's knowledge.

41. Meital, *Peace in Tatters*, 178.

42. Ibid., 183.

43. David Makovsky, quoted in *New York Times*, April 19, 2005.

44. *New York Times*, April 19, 2005.

45. Benny Morris, "Palestinians on the Right Side of History," *New York Times*, August 24, 2005.

46. An interesting note on this is that the Labor party under Amran Mitzna ran on the idea of unilateral withdrawal in the January 2003 election, something that Sharon at the time opposed. Coming around full circle by the end of the year in his Herzliya speech helps explain the general consensus in the Israeli electorate for Sharon's later unilateral withdrawal from the Gaza Strip.

47. *Haaretz*, October 8, 2004.

48. Quoted in Meital, *Peace in Tatters*, 193.

49. Harvey Sicherman, "Arafat, the Man Who Wanted Too Much, " *Peacefacts: A Briefing on the Middle East Peace Process*, Foreign Policy Research Institute, 11, no. 1 (2004), www.fpri.org.

50. Robert O. Freedman, "Disengagement and Its Aftermath: Challenges to the Future of Israel and the Peace Process," *Israel Horizons* (Autumn 2005). Wolfenson used his contacts and experience (and some of his own money) to obtain pledges from the G-8 countries of $9 billion to help rehabilitate the Gaza Strip; however, as Freedman points out, the lack of security in Palestinian-controlled territories, which has always been a problem in terms of translating monetary pledges into actual investment, if anything, is now less in the Gaza Strip in the immediate aftermath of the Israeli withdrawal. For an essay on the challenges confronting economic development in the Gaza Strip, see Harvey Morris, "Palestinians Grow Frustrated Waiting for the Expected Economic Recovery," *Financial Times*, November 29, 2005.

51. www.baltimoresun.com, February 28, 2005.

52. Associated Press Report, "U.S.: Terrorists in Syria Bombed Tel Aviv," www.yahoo.com/news, March 2, 2005. This accusation ran counter to reports from Arab sources that Syrian President Bashar al-Asad had actually been cooperative with Egypt and Jordan prior to the Sharm al-Shaykh meeting to do what he could to pressure Palestinian radical groups to accept the cease-fire.

53. A proposed amendment to submit the withdrawal plan to a public referendum was voted down 72–29. In any event, polls consistently showed that about 60% of the Israeli population approved of the Gaza disengagement plan, although that number dipped as the date of withdrawal actually approached and as the divisions in Israeli society became more vociferous. It is likely, however, that the number went down because a number of Israelis, while still supporting the withdrawal in principle, feared the societal repercussions—even civil war—of the disengagement, especially as the vitriolic rhetoric and protest demonstrations increased among the religious nationalists, messianic Zionists, and settlers in the summer of 2005.

54. Robert O. Freedman, "Disengagement and Its Aftermath."

55. Ibid.

56. www.arutzsheva.com/news.php3?id=87263, from wikipedia.com.

57. www.jpost.com/servlet/Satellite?pagename=Jpost/Jparticle/ShowFull&cid=1123986011043.

58. See "For Rice, a Risky Dive into the Mideast Storm," *New York Times*, November 16, 2005.

59. *New York Times*, August 22, 2005.

59a. Quoted in ibid, in the International Herald Tribune (www.iht.com/articles/2005/08/21/news/mideast.php).

60. Amos Oz, *Israel, Palestine, and Peace: Essays* (New York: Harcourt Brace, 1995), 78.
61. *New York Times*, August 27, 2005.
62. Ibid.
63. Harvey Morris, "Israel's Challenger Within," *Financial Times*, November 26/27, 2005.
64. *Financial Times*, November 22, 2005.
65. The distribution of Knesset seats prior to Sharon's announcement went as follows: Likud = 40, Labor = 22, Shinui = 15, Shas = 11, National Union = 7, Meretz = 6, National Religious Party = 6, United Torah Judaism = 5, Hadash = 3, Balad (Arab) = 3, United Arab List = 2.
66. In what in retrospect was a sign of things to come, Sharon suffered a minor stroke on December 18, 2005, and stayed in the hospital for a few days, returning to work soon thereafter.
67. Apparently Shimon Peres even contemplated taking over Kadima but quickly realized Olmert was in a much better position to lead the new party.
68. Scott Wilson, "The Heir of Israel's Troubles," *Washington Post*, February 2, 2006.
69. Quoted in Joe Klein, "Israel's Quiet Crisis," *Time*, January 23, 2006, 37.
70. *Washington Post*, January 22, 2006.
71. www.cnn.com, January 26, 2006.
72. Quoted in the *Washington Post*, January 14, 2006. It is interesting that Hamas traditionally does well in the urban landscape, where corruption, insecurity, and militancy amid a worsening economy give it a natural base, whereas Fatah remains stronger in rural areas where clan relations and party history play a more important role. *Washington Post*, January 22, 2006.
73. Steven Erlanger, "In Era After Arafat, Islamic Militants Are Edging into Power," *New York Times*, December 18, 2005.
74. *New York Times*, January 29, 2006.
75. Ibid.
76. Ibid.
77. This is ironic given the fact that the donor countries went to so much trouble to make sure that money did not go directly to the PA president under Arafat's tenure in power because of rampant corruption and lack of accountability and transparency.
78. See *Financial Times*, January 30, 2006; also *Financial Times*, February 8, 2006.
79. Over 4,000 Lebanese and over 1,000 Israelis were wounded.
80. Especially, as Hizbollah has done in the past (even when Sharon was in power), if it could arrange for a prisoner exchange.
81. Robert Malley, "A New Middle East," *New York Review of Books* 53, no. 14 (September 21, 2006): 10–15.
82. The resolution actually called for a "cessation of hostilities" and not a formal cease-fire, with a combination of the Lebanese army and a beefed up UNIFIL moving into the south to act as a buffer to take up positions that were vacated by Israeli forces as the international troops took up their positions.
83. For instance, see David W. Lesch, "Try Talking to Syria," *The Washington Post*, July 27, 2006. Also see, David W. Lesch, "The More Things Seem to Change the More They Remain the Same," Center for International Relations, International Affairs Forum, Global Perspectives 2007, Syria, January 9, 2007, www.ia-forum.org/Content/ForumContent.cfm?ForumTopicID=9.
84. Although President Asad was very clear that he did not want another Oslo-type secret channel. He wanted any sort of resumption of negotiations with Israel to be public, and he wanted the United States to be officially involved. Author's interview with President Bashar-al-Asad in Damascus, Syria, July 23, 2006.
85. For a copy of *The Iraq Study Group Report: The Way Forward-A New Approach*, see www.usip.org/isg/index.html, published on December 6, 2006.
86. For example, see Barry Rubin, "Why Syria Matters," *The Middle East Review of International Affairs*, Vol. 10, No. 4, article 2/7, December 2006.

President George W. Bush's State of the Union Speech, January 2002 (excerpt)

Thanks to the work of our law enforcement officials and coalition partners, hundreds of terrorists have been arrested. Yet, tens of thousands of trained terrorists are still at large. These enemies view the entire world as a battlefield, and we must pursue them wherever they are. (Applause.) So long as training camps operate, so long as nations harbor terrorists, freedom is at risk. And America and our allies must not, and will not, allow it. (Applause.)

Our nation will continue to be steadfast and patient and persistent in the pursuit of two great objectives. First, we will shut down terrorist camps, disrupt terrorist plans, and bring terrorists to justice. And, second, we must prevent the terrorists and regimes who seek chemical, biological or nuclear weapons from threatening the United States and the world. (Applause.)

Our military has put the terror training camps of Afghanistan out of business, yet camps still exist in at least a dozen countries. A terrorist underworld—including groups like Hamas, Hezbollah, Islamic Jihad, Jaish-i-Mohammed—operates in remote jungles and deserts, and hides in the centers of large cities.

While the most visible military action is in Afghanistan, America is acting elsewhere. We now have troops in the Philippines, helping to train that country's armed forces to go after terrorist cells that have executed an American, and still hold hostages. Our soldiers, working with the Bosnian government, seized terrorists who were plotting to bomb our embassy. Our Navy is patrolling the coast of Africa to block the shipment of weapons and the establishment of terrorist camps in Somalia.

My hope is that all nations will heed our call, and eliminate the terrorist parasites who threaten their countries and our own. Many nations are acting forcefully. Pakistan is now cracking down on terror, and I admire the strong leadership of President Musharraf. (Applause.)

But some governments will be timid in the face of terror. And make no mistake about it: If they do not act, America will. (Applause.)

Our second goal is to prevent regimes that sponsor terror from threatening America or our friends and allies with weapons of mass destruction. Some of these regimes have been pretty quiet since September the 11th. But we know their true nature. North Korea is a regime arming with missiles and weapons of mass destruction, while starving its citizens.

Iran aggressively pursues these weapons and exports terror, while an unelected few repress the Iranian people's hope for freedom.

Iraq continues to flaunt its hostility toward America and to support terror. The Iraqi regime has plotted to develop anthrax, and nerve gas, and nuclear weapons for over a decade. This is a regime that has already used poison gas to murder thousands of its own citizens—leaving the bodies of mothers huddled over their dead children. This is a regime that agreed to international inspections—then kicked out the inspectors. This is a regime that has something to hide from the civilized world.

States like these, and their terrorist allies, constitute an axis of evil, arming to threaten the peace of the world. By seeking weapons of mass destruction, these regimes pose a grave and growing danger. They could provide these arms to terrorists, giving them the means to match their hatred. They could attack our allies or attempt to blackmail the United States. In any of these cases, the price of indifference would be catastrophic.

We will work closely with our coalition to deny terrorists and their state sponsors the materials, technology, and expertise to make and deliver weapons of mass destruction. We will develop and deploy effective missile defenses to protect America and our allies from sudden attack. (Applause.) And all nations should know: America will do what is necessary to ensure our nation's security.

We'll be deliberate, yet time is not on our side. I will not wait on events, while dangers gather. I will not stand by, as peril draws closer and closer. The United States of America will not permit the world's most dangerous regimes to threaten us with the world's most destructive weapons. (Applause.)

Our war on terror is well begun, but it is only begun. This campaign may not be finished on our watch—yet it must be and it will be waged on our watch.

---

http://www.whitehouse.gov/news/releases/2002/01/20020129-11.html (accessed February 1, 2006).

President Bush Calls for New Palestinian Leadership

The Rose Garden

3:47 p.m., June 24, 2002

THE PRESIDENT: For too long, the citizens of the Middle East have lived in the midst of death and fear. The hatred of a few holds the hopes of many hostage. The forces of extremism and terror are attempting to kill progress and peace by killing the innocent. And this casts a dark shadow over an entire region. For the sake of all humanity, things must change in the Middle East.

It is untenable for Israeli citizens to live in terror. It is untenable for Palestinians to live in squalor and occupation. And the current situation offers no prospect that life will improve. Israeli citizens will continue to be victimized by terrorists, and so Israel will continue to defend herself.

In this situation the Palestinian people will grow more and more miserable. My vision is two states, living side by side in peace and security. There is simply no way to achieve that peace until all parties fight terror. Yet, at this critical moment, if all parties will break with the past and set out on a new path, we can overcome the darkness with the light of hope. Peace requires a new and different Palestinian leadership, so that a Palestinian state can be born.

I call on the Palestinian people to elect new leaders, leaders not compromised by terror. I call upon them to build a practicing democracy, based on tolerance and liberty. If the Palestinian people actively pursue these goals, America and the world will actively support their efforts. If the Palestinian people meet these goals, they will be able to reach agreement with Israel and Egypt and Jordan on security and other arrangements for independence.

And when the Palestinian people have new leaders, new institutions and new security arrangements with their neighbors, the United States of America will support the creation of a Palestinian state whose borders and certain aspects of its sovereignty will be provisional until resolved as part of a final settlement in the Middle East.

In the work ahead, we all have responsibilities. The Palestinian people are gifted and capable, and I am confident they can achieve a new birth for their nation. A Palestinian state will never be created by terror—it will be built through reform. And reform must be more than cosmetic change, or veiled attempts to preserve the status quo. True reform will require entirely new political and economic institutions, based on democracy, market economics and action against terrorism.

Today, the elected Palestinian legislature has no authority, and power is concentrated in the hands of an unaccountable few. A Palestinian state can only serve its citizens with a new constitution which separates the powers of government. The Palestinian parliament should have the full authority of a legislative body. Local officials and government ministers need authority of their own and the independence to govern effectively.

The United States, along with the European Union and Arab states, will work with Palestinian leaders to create a new constitutional framework, and a working democracy for the Palestinian people. And the United States, along with others in the international community will help the Palestinians organize and monitor fair, multi-party local elections by the end of the year, with national elections to follow.

Today, the Palestinian people live in economic stagnation, made worse by official corruption. A Palestinian state will require a vibrant economy, where honest enterprise is encouraged by honest government. The United States, the international donor community and the World Bank stand ready to work with Palestinians on a major project of economic reform and development. The United States, the EU, the World Bank, the International Monetary Fund are willing to oversee reforms in Palestinian finances, encouraging transparency and independent auditing.

And the United States, along with our partners in the developed world, will increase our humanitarian assistance to relieve Palestinian suffering. Today, the Palestinian people lack effective courts of law and have no means to defend and vindicate their rights. A Palestinian state will require a system of reliable justice to punish those who prey on the innocent. The United States and members of the international community stand ready to work with Palestinian leaders to establish finance—establish finance and monitor a truly independent judiciary.

Today, Palestinian authorities are encouraging, not opposing, terrorism. This is unacceptable. And the United States will not support the establishment of a Palestinian state until its leaders engage in a sustained fight against the terrorists and dismantle their infrastructure. This will require an externally supervised effort to rebuild and reform the Palestinian security services. The security system must have clear lines of authority and accountability and a unified chain of command.

America is pursuing this reform along with key regional states. The world is prepared to help, yet ultimately these steps toward statehood depend on the Palestinian people and their leaders. If they energetically take the path of reform, the rewards can come quickly. If Palestinians embrace democracy, confront corruption and firmly reject terror, they can count on American support for the creation of a provisional state of Palestine.

With a dedicated effort, this state could rise rapidly, as it comes to terms with Israel, Egypt and Jordan on practical issues, such as security. The final borders, the capital and other aspects of this state's sovereignty will be negotiated between the parties, as part of a final settlement. Arab states have offered their help in this process, and their help is needed.

I've said in the past that nations are either with us or against us in the war on terror. To be counted on the side of peace, nations must act. Every leader actually committed to peace will end incitement to violence in official media, and publicly denounce homicide bombings. Every nation actually committed to peace will stop the flow of money, equipment and recruits to terrorist groups seeking the destruction of Israel—including Hamas, Islamic Jihad, and Hezbollah. Every nation actually committed to peace must block the shipment of Iranian supplies to these groups, and oppose regimes that promote terror, like Iraq. And Syria must choose the right side in the war on terror by closing terrorist camps and expelling terrorist organizations. Leaders who want to be included in the peace process must show by their deeds an undivided support for peace. And as we move toward a peaceful solution, Arab states will be expected to build closer ties of diplomacy and commerce with Israel, leading to full normalization of relations between Israel and the entire Arab world.

Israel also has a large stake in the success of a democratic Palestine. Permanent occupation threatens Israel's identity and democracy. A stable, peaceful Palestinian state is necessary to achieve the security that Israel longs for. So I challenge Israel to take concrete steps to support the emergence of a viable, credible Palestinian state.

As we make progress towards security, Israeli forces need to withdraw fully to positions they held prior to September 28, 2000. And consistent with the recommendations of the Mitchell Committee, Israeli settlement activity in the occupied territories must stop.

The Palestinian economy must be allowed to develop. As violence subsides, freedom of movement should be restored, permitting innocent Palestinians to resume work and normal life. Palestinian legislators and officials, humanitarian and international workers, must be allowed to go about the business of building a better future. And Israel should release frozen Palestinian revenues into honest, accountable hands.

I've asked Secretary Powell to work intensively with Middle Eastern and international leaders to realize the vision of a Palestinian state, focusing them on a comprehensive plan to support Palestinian reform and institution building.

Ultimately, Israelis and Palestinians must address the core issues that divide them if there is to be a real peace, resolving all claims and ending the conflict between them. This means that the Israeli occupation that began in 1967 will be ended through a settlement negotiated between the parties, based on U.N. Resolutions 242 and 338, with Israeli withdrawal to secure and recognize borders.

We must also resolve questions concerning Jerusalem, the plight and future of Palestinian refugees, and a final peace between Israel and Lebanon, and Israel and a Syria that supports peace and fights terror.

All who are familiar with the history of the Middle East realize that there may be setbacks in this process. Trained and determined killers, as we have seen, want to stop it. Yet the Egyptian and Jordanian peace treaties with Israel remind us that with determined and responsible leadership progress can come quickly.

As new Palestinian institutions and new leaders emerge, demonstrating real performance on security and reform, I expect Israel to respond and work toward a final status agreement. With intensive effort by all, this agreement could be reached within three years from now. And I and my country will actively lead toward that goal.

I can understand the deep anger and anguish of the Israeli people. You've lived too long with fear and funerals, having to avoid markets and public transportation, and forced to put armed guards in kindergarten classrooms. The Palestinian Authority has rejected your offer at hand, and trafficked with terrorists. You have a right to a normal life; you have a right to security; and I deeply believe that you need a reformed, responsible Palestinian partner to achieve that security.

I can understand the deep anger and despair of the Palestinian people. For decades you've been treated as pawns in the Middle East conflict. Your interests have been held hostage to a comprehensive peace agreement that never seems to come, as your lives get worse year by year. You deserve democracy and the rule of law. You deserve an open society and a thriving economy. You deserve a life of hope for your children. An end to occupation and a peaceful democratic Palestinian state may seem distant, but America and our partners throughout the world stand ready to help, help you make them possible as soon as possible.

If liberty can blossom in the rocky soil of the West Bank and Gaza, it will inspire millions of men and women around the globe who are equally weary of poverty and oppression, equally entitled to the benefits of democratic government.

I have a hope for the people of Muslim countries. Your commitments to morality, and learning, and tolerance led to great historical achievements. And those values are alive in the Islamic world today. You have a rich culture, and you share the aspirations of men and women in every culture. Prosperity and freedom and dignity are not just American hopes, or Western hopes. They are universal, human hopes. And even in the violence and turmoil of the Middle East, America believes those hopes have the power to transform lives and nations.

This moment is both an opportunity and a test for all parties in the Middle East: an opportunity to lay the foundations for future peace; a test to show who is serious about peace and who is not. The choice here is stark and simple. The Bible says, "I have set before you life and death; therefore, choose life." The time has arrived for everyone in this conflict to choose peace, and hope, and life.

---

http://www.whitehouse.gov/news/releases/2002/06/20020624-3.html (accessed February 3, 2006).

Prime Minister Ariel Sharon's Speech at the Herzliya Conference, December 2002

Twenty-seven months ago the Palestinian Authority commenced a campaign of terror against the State of Israel. Since then, we have been confronting a ferocious battle against a culture of bloodshed and murder, which has targeted Jews and Israelis everywhere. This campaign of terror was not coincidental; it was meticulously planned and prepared by the Chairman of the Palestinian Authority who misconstrued the high regard for human life in Israeli society as a way to compel us to capitulate to terrorism and coerce us into additional political concessions, concessions with nothing in return.

The past two years have been a difficult and painful test for Israel's national strength. The callousness and brutality of the terrorists was aimed first and foremost at undermining the sense of justness of the people of Zion. This is not the place to ask what led the PA Chairman to question the inner strength and determination which has always characterized the citizens of Israel, but it is clear that the terror has not defeated and will never defeat the State of Israel. They tried to break our spirit and failed. This failure has resulted in scathing Palestinian criticism of Arafat, his path of terrorism and ongoing strategy of violence against Israel.

Today, most of the weight of the global leadership is in the United States. From the first days of the establishment of the State of Israel, our bond with the United States has been a supreme strategic asset. My Government has further consolidated our relations with the United States and formed a special closeness with the U.S. Administration and Congress. These special relations, the understanding of Israel's needs, and the cooperation with President Bush and his administration are unprecedented. Israel has in the United States true friends who genuinely and honestly care for our security.

Our political understandings with the United States and the Administration's understanding of our security needs have provided us with the required leeway in our ongoing war on terrorism. The war on terror has been accompanied by exorbitant costs and harsh financial damage, and I hope and believe that in the coming months we will receive special aid, to support us in our economic campaign.

On June 24th this year, President Bush presented his plan for a true solution to our conflict with the Palestinians. The peace plan outlined in the President's speech is a reasonable, pragmatic and practicable one, which offers a real opportunity to achieve an agreement. We have accepted in principle the President's plan and the sequence presented therein. Our agreements with the Palestinians are based on the lessons the Americans learned from the Clinton–Barak plan, and my experience as one who has, for many years, participated in the security and political campaign in the Palestinian arena.

After concerted efforts, the U.S. Administration has understood and agreed that the only way to achieve a true peace agreement with the Palestinians is progress in phases, with the first phase being a complete cessation of terror. President Bush's speech is a fatal blow to Arafat's policy of terrorism and serves as proof of the failure of his attempt to achieve political gains by means of violence and terrorism. Only after a cessation of terror—and this is already agreed by most world leaders—will the commencement of peace negotiations between the parties be possible.

The American plan defines the parties' progress according to phases. The transition from one phase to the next will not be on the basis of a pre-determined timetable which would have resulted in a buildup of heavy pressure on Israel towards the end of one phase and approaching the next phase. Rather, progress is determined on the basis of performance—only once a specific phase has been implemented, will progress into the next phase be possible.

On the basis of lessons learned from past agreements, it is clear to all that Israel can no longer be expected to make political concessions until there is proven calm and Palestinian governmental reforms.

In this context, it is important to remember that political concessions which will be made in the future—as those made in the past—are irreversible. Even the current security reality, with the IDF operating freely inside Palestinian cities, arises from security needs and has not changed the political situation of two years ago. Israel will not re-control territories from which it withdrew as a result of political agreements.

Therefore, the achievement of true and genuine coexistence must be a pre-condition to any discussion on political arrangements.

The Jewish people seek peace. Israel's desire is to live in security and in true and genuine coexistence, based, first and foremost, on the recognition of our natural and historic right to exist as a Jewish state in the land of Israel, while maintaining genuine peace.

The achievement of true coexistence must be carried out, first and foremost, by the replacement of the Palestinian leadership which has lied and disappointed, with different leadership which can—and more importantly—is willing to achieve real peace with the State of Israel. Unfortunately, there remain a few in Israel who believe that Arafat is still relevant. However, the U.S. Administration—with the world following in its footsteps—has already accepted our unequivocal position that no progress will be possible with Arafat as the Chairman of the Palestinian Authority. This man is not—and never will be—a partner to peace. He does not want peace.

The reconstruction of a Palestinian government should commence with governmental reforms which will ultimately lead to the establishment of a new, honest peace-seeking administration, the removal of Arafat from his command of power and sources of financing, and from the decision-making process, and his relegation to a symbolic role. In concordance with the sequence presented by President Bush, a Chief Executive Officer for Reforms will be appointed to the Palestinian Authority, and will constitute the head of the executive authority and the source of administrative authority. The provisional Palestinian government will administer a more efficient governmental system, fight the prevailing corruption in the PA and adhere to regulations of proper management. That government will lead a comprehensive process of reforms, maintain coexistence and prepare the general elections. The elections in the Palestinian Authority should be held only at the conclusion of the reform process and after proper governmental regulations have been internalized. The goal is that these will be true elections—free, liberated and democratic.

Parallel with, and perhaps even prior to, the governmental reforms, a security reform will be carried out, consisting of three principal parts:

1. Dismantling all existing security (terrorist) bodies, the majority of which are, in fact, involved in terror; these organizations, which are directly subordinate to Arafat, are essentially corrupt, and responsible for the deaths of hundreds of Israelis. These bodies will be replaced by two or three new organizations which will consist of a police force and security services; these new organizations will have a uniform command, which will be responsible for dismantling the current complex web of militias and armed gangs.
2. A Minister of the Interior will be appointed, and will be responsible for collecting illegal weapons and transferring them to a third party which will remove them from the PA territories and destroy them, and outlawing terrorist organizations.
3. In addition, cooperation on security issues between the PA and Israel will be renewed immediately.

The security reform must accompany a sincere and real effort to stop terrorism, while applying the "chain of preventive measures" outlined by the Americans: intelligence gathering, arrest, interrogation, prosecution and punishment.

Another important matter is the international demand for honest, effective, noncorrupt and transparent administration of the PA financial system; it is of great importance that the PA manage its financial affairs in concordance with the rules of proper government which will obligate the Palestinian Authority, interalia, to produce a detailed budget, under a budgetary control system. This budgetary auditing system will ensure a balance between income and expenditure, and will verify that budget spending only serves appropriate economic purposes for the benefit and welfare of the Palestinian people. Such a supervising mechanism will also prevent the transfer of money for the financing of organizations or individuals involved in terror. Taking the financial system out of Arafat's hands, and appointing a strong Minister of Finance with authority, constitutes an important factor for stopping the terrorist system operated by the Palestinian Authority. We are hopeful that the newly appointed PA Minister of Finance will operate a body to oversee and handle foreign aid funds received by the PA, and channel those funds to clearly defined projects which will benefit the Palestinian people and which are not contaminated by terror and corruption.

Peace and coexistence cannot be achieved without reform in the fields of education, media and information; the virulent incitement mechanism instigated by the PA against Israel must be stopped immediately; there can be no peace while the Palestinian education system instills in their young generation a culture of hatred, violence and terror.

Today, there is an increasing understanding in the world that stopping the phenomenon of suicide terrorism is dependent on: the cessation of incitement, ending the religious ratification of terrorism by radical elements in the Muslim world—with the encouragement and support of various Arab states.

The Palestinian justice system and law-enforcement must also undergo significant reforms. It is unheard of that in a law-abiding country, one hour after being arrested for theft, a suspect is sentenced and hanged, while on the other hand those involved in terror enter and leave prison in the "revolving door" principle. As long as those who commit crimes against the State of Israel are not severely punished, no progress will be made in President Bush's sequence.

The two sides will advance to the next phase of President Bush's sequence when a new, different, responsible and non-corrupt Palestinian leadership emerges. Terror will cease, and the Palestinian leadership will not allow it to be renewed. Civil and economic cooperation will be established. Incitement will be stopped and education towards peace will be fostered. At the same time, Israel will act to lift military pressure, create territorial continuity between Palestinian population centers, and ease daily life for the Palestinian population.

The second phase of President Bush's sequence proposes the establishment of a Palestinian state with borders yet to be finalized, and which will overlap with territories A and B, except for essential security zones. This Palestinian state will be completely demilitarized. It will be allowed to maintain lightly armed police and interior forces to ensure civil order. Israel will continue to control all entries and exits to the Palestinian state, will command its airspace, and not allow it to form alliances with Israel's enemies.

As I have promised in the past, President Bush's sequence will be discussed and approved by the National Unity Government which I intend to establish after the elections, and I will do my utmost to establish as broad a National Unity Government as possible.

In the final phase of President Bush's sequence negotiations will be opened to determine the final status of the Palestinian state and fix its permanent borders. As I emphasized, no progress will be made from one phase to the next until such time as quiet has been restored, Palestinian rule has undergone fundamental changes, and coexistence is ensured.

We all want peace. It is not a competition over who wants peace more. We also know that entering into political negotiations for peace is the true path which will bring about acceleration of economic growth and prosperity. I have said it before, and will say it again today: Israel is prepared to make painful concessions for a true peace. However, the government under my leadership will not be seduced into believing false promises which will endanger the security of the State of Israel.

My ideological and political path is well-known to you from the many functions I was privileged to fill during my decades of public service. These decisions are not easy for me, and I cannot deny that I have doubts, reservations and fears; however, I have come to the conclusion that in the present regional and international reality Israel must act with courage to accept the political plan which I described. There are risks involved, but also enormous opportunities.

I know that there are many who will attack the political outline I have just detailed. During the last few years many of us were tempted to believe in lightning-quick solutions which would lead to the security and peace we have longed for, and that this long-lasting conflict between our two peoples could be solved by the "blade of a sword"—I am familiar with these voices from both sides of the political spectrum.

Regrettably, this is not the way things are. These methods have failed—the solution to the conflict must be gradual and controlled. We must, in all stages, act with prudence and determination, exercise judgment, and make very sure that all commitments and agreements are implemented by both sides.

It is true that this is not a shining path which will lead us to instant, magical solutions, but I am certain that only by going forward in this direction, step by step, will we be able to achieve security for the Israeli people, and reach the peace we all yearn for.

Thank you, and happy holiday.

State of Israel, Prime Minister's Office, 4 December 2002, http://www.pmo-gov.il/english/ts.exe?tsurl=0.41.6842.0.0.

03/27/2002 Speech by Deputy Prime Minister and Commander of the National Guard Crown Prince Abdullah bin Abdulaziz at the 14th Arab Summit in Beirut, Lebanon

In the Name of God, the Most Merciful and the Most Compassionate

Praise be to God Almighty, the knower of the unseen and the unknown who revealed the following in the Holy Qur'an: "Dispute not one with another lest ye falter and your strength depart from you." Peace and prayer be upon the prophet of mercy, who urged that ranks and objectives be unified by stating that "the believers in their amicability, compassion and warmth are like the human body; if an organ feels an ailment, the rest of the body will react with pain and sleeplessness."

My brethren, the leaders of the Arab nation:
My brethren, the people of our Arab and Islamic nation:
God's peace and mercy be upon you.

I greet all of you with the greeting of Islam. And I thank the fraternal country of Lebanon; the Lebanon of pride and national unity; the Lebanon of all Arabs, with all its religious and sectarian affiliations, for hosting this Summit at this critical and turbulent juncture in history in which events are unfolding, and whose ultimate outcome is known only to God Almighty.

In spite of all that has happened—and what still may happen—the primary issue in the heart and mind of every person in our Arab and Islamic nation is the restoration of legitimate rights in Palestine, Syria and Lebanon. These rights, which are bound to the cherished occupied lands, cannot be erased from memory, nor will the passage of time diminish their importance. No right is lost that has an advocate behind it.

Those who follow the Intifadah of our brothers in Palestine, which has the support of all Arabs and Muslims, realize that steadfastness will not wither, that bravery will not retreat, and that justice will prevail. Every person in Palestine—young and old—understands that the way to the liberation of his land and soil is either through steadfastness and struggle, or a just and comprehensive peace. It is therefore incumbent on the Israeli government to realize and understand this and deal with it by embarking on a new path, and that is the path of peace.

My Dear Brethren:
The Noble People of the Arab and Islamic Nation:

When the Arabs opted for peace as a strategic choice, they did not do so out of crippling desperation or debilitating weakness, and Israel is mistaken if it believes that it can impose an unjust peace by force. We embarked upon the peace process with open eyes and clear minds, and we have not accepted then, nor will we accept now, that this process is transformed into a non-binding obligation imposed by one party on the other.

Peace is a free and voluntary choice made by two equal parties, and it cannot survive if it is based on oppression and humiliation. The peace process is based on a clear principle: land for peace. This principle is accepted by the international community as a whole, and is embodied in U. N. Security Council resolutions 242 and 338, and was adopted by the Madrid Conference in 1991. It was confirmed by the resolutions of the European Community and other regional organizations, and reemphasized once more this month, by U.N. Security Council Resolution 1397.

My Esteemed Brethren:

It is clear in our minds, and in the minds of our brethren in Palestine, Syria and Lebanon, that the only acceptable objective of the peace process is the full Israeli withdrawal from all the occupied Arab territories, the establishment of an independent Palestinian state with al-Quds al-Shareef (East Jerusalem) as its capital, and the return of refugees. Without moving towards this objective, the peace process is an exercise in futility and a play on words and a squandering of time which perpetuates the cycle of violence.

The return to the negotiating table is a meaningless endeavor, if the negotiations do not produce tangible and positive results, as has been the case for the past ten years.

Allow me at this point to directly address the Israeli people, to say to them that the use of violence, for more than fifty years, has only resulted in more violence and destruction, and that the Israeli people are as far as they have ever been from security and peace, notwithstanding military superiority and despite efforts to subdue and oppress.

Peace emanates from the heart and mind, and not from the barrel of a cannon, or the exploding warhead of a missile. The time has come for Israel to put its trust in peace after it has gambled on war for decades without success. Israel, and the world, must understand that peace and the retention of the occupied Arab territories are incompatible and impossible to reconcile or achieve.

I would further say to the Israeli people that if their government abandons the policy of force and oppression and embraces true peace, we will not hesitate to accept the right of the Israeli people to live in security with the people of the region.

We believe in taking up arms in self-defense and to deter aggression. But we also believe in peace when it is based on justice and equity, and when it brings an end to conflict. Only within the context of true peace can normal relations flourish between the people of the region and allow the region to pursue development rather than war and destruction.

Dear Brethren:

In light of the above, and in this place with you and amongst you, and with your backing and that of the Almighty, I propose that the Arab Summit put forward a clear and unanimous initiative addressed to the United Nations Security Council based on two basic issues: normal relations and security for Israel in exchange for full withdrawal from all occupied Arab territories, recognition of an independent Palestinian state with al-Quds al-Shareef (East Jerusalem) as its capital, and the return of refugees. At the same time, I appeal to all friendly countries throughout the world to support this noble humanitarian proposal which seeks to remove the danger of destructive wars and the establishment of peace for all the inhabitants of the region, without exception.

I ask God Almighty to guide us to the correct decision, and to provide us with the determination of the believer, for He is our Lord and ultimate benefactor.

God's peace and blessing be upon you.

---

http://saudiembassy.net/2002News/Statements/SpeechDetail.asp?cIndex=141 (accessed February 3, 2006).

President Bush's Aqaba Speech

Released by Office of the White House Press Secretary
Aqaba, Jordan
June 4, 2003

King Abdullah, thank you for hosting this event. Your Majesty, thank you for your hospitality. It is fitting that we gather today in Jordan. King Abdullah is a leader on behalf of peace and is carrying forward the tradition of his father, King Hussein.

I'm pleased to be here with Prime Minister Sharon. The friendship between our countries began at the time of Israel's creation. Today, America is strongly committed, and I am strongly committed, to Israel's security as a vibrant Jewish state.

I'm also pleased to be with Prime Minister Abbas. He represents the cause of freedom and statehood for the Palestinian people. I strongly support that cause, as well. Each of us is here because we understand that all people have the right to live in peace. We believe that with hard work and good faith and courage, it is possible to bring peace to the Middle East. And today we mark important progress toward that goal.

Great and hopeful change is coming to the Middle East. In Iraq, a dictator who funded terror and sowed conflict has been removed, and a more just and democratic society is emerging. Prime Minister Abbas now leads the Palestinian Cabinet. By his strong leadership, by building the institutions of Palestinian democracy and by rejecting terror, he is serving the deepest hopes of his people.

All here today now share a goal: the Holy Land must be shared between the state of Palestine and the state of Israel, living at peace with each other and with every nation of the Middle East.

All sides will benefit from this achievement and all sides have responsibilities to meet. As the road map accepted by the party makes clear, both must make tangible immediate steps toward this two-state vision.

I welcome Prime Minister Sharon's pledge to improve the humanitarian situation in the Palestinian areas and to begin removing unauthorized outposts immediately. I appreciate his gestures of reconciliation on behalf of prisoners and their families, and his frank statements about the need for the territorial contiguity.

As I said yesterday, the issue of settlements must be addressed for peace to be achieved. In addition, Prime Minister Sharon has stated that no unilateral actions by either side can or should prejudge the outcome of future negotiations. The Prime Minister also recognizes that it is in Israel's own interest for Palestinians to govern themselves in their own state. These are meaningful signs of respect for the rights of the Palestinians and their hopes for a viable, democratic, peaceful, Palestinian state.

Prime Minister Abbas recognizes that terrorist crimes are a dangerous obstacle to the independent state his people seek. He agrees that the process for achieving that state is through peaceful negotiations. He has pledged to consolidate Palestinian institutions, including the security forces and to make them more accountable and more democratic. He has promised his full efforts and resources to end the armed intifada. He has promised to work without compromise for a complete end of violence and terror. In all these efforts, the Prime Minister is demonstrating his leadership and commitment to building a better future for the Palestinian people.

Both Prime Ministers here agree that progress toward peace also requires an end to violence and the elimination of all forms of hatred and prejudice and official incitement—in school books, in broadcasts, and in the words used by political leaders. Both leaders understand that a future of peace cannot be founded on hatred and falsehood and bitterness.

Yet, these two leaders cannot bring about peace if they must act alone. True peace requires the support of other nations in the region. Yesterday, in Sharm el-Sheikh, we made a strong beginning. Arab leaders stated that they share our goal of two states, Israel and Palestine, and living side-by-side in peace and in security. And they have promised to cut off assistance and the flow of money and weapons to terrorist groups, and to help Prime Minister Abbas rid Palestinian areas of terrorism.

All sides have made important commitments, and the United States will strive to see these commitments fulfilled. My government will provide training and support for a new, restructured Palestinian security service. And we'll place a mission on the ground, led by Ambassador John Wolf. This mission will be charged with helping the parties to move towards peace, monitoring their progress and stating clearly who was fulfilling their responsibilities. And we expect both parties to keep their promises.

I've also asked Secretary of State Colin Powell, and National Security Advisor Condoleezza Rice to make this cause a matter of the highest priority. Secretary Powell and Dr. Rice, as my personal representative, will work closely with the parties, helping them move toward true peace as quickly as possible.

The journey we're taking is difficult, but there is no other choice. No leader of conscience can accept more months and years of humiliation, killing and mourning. And these leaders of conscience have made their declarations today in the cause of peace.

The United States is committed to that cause. If all sides fulfill their obligation, I know that peace can finally come.

Thank you very much, and may God bless our work.

---

http://www.state.gov/p/nea/rls/rm/21193.htm (accessed October 18, 2006).

Resolution 1559 (2004): Adopted by the Security Council at its 5028th Meeting, on 2 September 2004

The Security Council,

Recalling all its previous resolutions on Lebanon, in particular resolutions 425 (1978) and 426 (1978) of 19 March 1978, resolution 520 (1982) of 17 September 1982, and resolution 1553 (2004) of 29 July 2004 as well as the statements of its President on the situation in Lebanon, in particular the statement of 18 June 2000 (S/PRST/2000/21),

Reiterating its strong support for the territorial integrity, sovereignty and political independence of Lebanon within its internationally recognized borders,

Noting the determination of Lebanon to ensure the withdrawal of all non-Lebanese forces from Lebanon,

Gravely concerned at the continued presence of armed militias in Lebanon, which prevent the Lebanese Government from exercising its full sovereignty over all Lebanese territory,

Reaffirming the importance of the extension of the control of the Government of Lebanon over all Lebanese territory,

Mindful of the upcoming Lebanese presidential elections and underlining the importance of free and fair elections according to Lebanese constitutional rules devised without foreign interference or influence,

1. *Reaffirms* its call for the strict respect of the sovereignty, territorial integrity, unity, and political independence of Lebanon under the sole and exclusive authority of the Government of Lebanon throughout Lebanon;

2. *Calls upon* all remaining foreign forces to withdraw from Lebanon,

3. *Calls* for the disbanding and disarmament of all Lebanese and non-Lebanese militias;

4. *Supports* the extension of the control of the Government of Lebanon over all Lebanese territory;

5. *Declares* its support for a free and fair electoral process in Lebanon's upcoming presidential election conducted according to Lebanese constitutional rules devised without foreign interference or influence;

6. *Calls upon* all parties concerned to cooperate fully and urgently with the Security Council for the full implementation of this and all relevant resolutions concerning the restoration of the territorial integrity, full sovereignty, and political independence of Lebanon;

7. *Requests* that the Secretary-General report to the Security Council within thirty days on the implementation by the parties of this resolution and decides to remain actively seized of the matter.

---

http://domino.un.org/UNISPAL.NSF/d744b47860e5c97e85256c40005d01 d6/764dc777bfc. . . (accessed January 1, 2006).

A Performance-Based Roadmap to a Permanent Two-State Solution to the Israeli–Palestinian Conflict

April 30, 2003

Press Statement
Office of the Spokesman
Washington, DC
April 30, 2003

The following is a performance-based and goal-driven roadmap, with clear phases, timelines, target dates, and benchmarks aiming at progress through reciprocal steps by the two parties in the political, security, economic, humanitarian, and institution-building fields, under the auspices of the Quartet [the United States, European Union, United Nations, and Russia]. The destination is a final and comprehensive settlement of the Israeli–Palestinian conflict by 2005, as presented in President Bush's speech of 24 June, and welcomed by the EU, Russia and the UN in the 16 July and 17 September Quartet Ministerial statements.

A two-state solution to the Israeli–Palestinian conflict will only be achieved through an end to violence and terrorism, when the Palestinian people have a leadership acting decisively against terror and willing and able to build a practicing democracy based on tolerance and liberty, and through Israel's readiness to do what is necessary for a democratic Palestinian state to be established, and a clear, unambiguous acceptance by both parties of the goal of a negotiated settlement as described below. The Quartet will assist and facilitate implementation of the plan, starting in Phase I, including direct discussions between the parties as required. The plan establishes a realistic timeline for implementation. However, as a performance-based plan, progress will require and depend upon the good faith efforts of the parties, and their compliance with each of the obligations outlined below. Should the parties perform their obligations rapidly, progress within and through the phases may come sooner than indicated in the plan. Non-compliance with obligations will impede progress.

A settlement, negotiated between the parties, will result in the emergence of an independent, democratic, and viable Palestinian state living side by side in peace and security with Israel and its other neighbors. The settlement will resolve the Israeli–Palestinian conflict, and end the occupation that began in 1967, based on the foundations of the Madrid Conference, the principle of land for peace, UNSCRs 242, 338 and 1397, agreements previously reached by the parties, and the initiative of Saudi Crown Prince Abdullah—endorsed by the Beirut Arab League Summit—calling for acceptance of Israel as a neighbor living in peace and security, in the context of a comprehensive settlement. This initiative is a vital element of international efforts to promote a comprehensive peace on all tracks, including the Syrian–Israeli and Lebanese–Israeli tracks.

The Quartet will meet regularly at senior levels to evaluate the parties' performance on implementation of the plan. In each phase, the parties are expected to perform their obligations in parallel, unless otherwise indicated.

PHASE I: ENDING TERROR AND VIOLENCE, NORMALIZING PALESTINIAN LIFE, AND BUILDING PALESTINIAN INSTITUTIONS—PRESENT TO MAY 2003

In Phase I, the Palestinians immediately undertake an unconditional cessation of violence according to the steps outlined below; such action should be accompanied by supportive measures undertaken by Israel. Palestinians and Israelis resume security cooperation based on the Tenet work plan to end violence, terrorism, and incitement through restructured and effective Palestinian security services. Palestinians undertake comprehensive political reform in preparation for statehood, including drafting a Palestinian constitution, and free, fair and open elections upon the basis of those measures. Israel takes all necessary steps to help normalize Palestinian life. Israel withdraws from Palestinian areas occupied from September 28, 2000, and the two sides restore the status quo that existed at that time, as security performance and cooperation progress. Israel also freezes all settlement activity, consistent with the Mitchell report.

At the outset of Phase I:

Palestinian leadership issues unequivocal statement reiterating Israel's right to exist in peace and security and calling for an immediate and unconditional cease-fire to end armed activity and all acts of violence against Israelis anywhere. All official Palestinian institutions end incitement against Israel.

Israeli leadership issues unequivocal statement affirming its commitment to the two-state vision of an independent, viable, sovereign Palestinian state living in peace and security alongside Israel, as expressed by President Bush, and calling for an immediate end to violence against Palestinians everywhere. All official Israeli institutions end incitement against Palestinians.

Security

Palestinians declare an unequivocal end to violence and terrorism and undertake visible efforts on the ground to arrest, disrupt, and restrain individuals and groups conducting and planning violent attacks on Israelis anywhere.

Rebuilt and refocused Palestinian Authority security apparatus begins sustained, targeted, and effective operations aimed at confronting all those engaged in terror and dismantlement of terrorist capabilities and infrastructure. This includes commencing confiscation of illegal weapons and consolidation of security authority, free of association with terror and corruption.

GOI takes no actions undermining trust, including deportations, attacks on civilians; confiscation and/or demolition of Palestinian homes and property, as a punitive measure or to facilitate Israeli construction; destruction of Palestinian institutions and infrastructure; and other measures specified in the Tenet work plan.

Relying on existing mechanisms and on-the-ground resources, Quartet representatives begin informal monitoring and consult with the parties on establishment of a formal monitoring mechanism and its implementation.

Implementation, as previously agreed, of U.S. rebuilding, training and resumed security cooperation plan in collaboration with outside oversight board (U.S.–Egypt–Jordan). Quartet support for efforts to achieve a lasting, comprehensive cease-fire.

All Palestinian security organizations are consolidated into three services reporting to an empowered Interior Minister.

Restructured/retrained Palestinian security forces and IDF counterparts progressively resume security cooperation and other undertakings in implementation of the Tenet work plan, including regular senior-level meetings, with the participation of U.S. security officials.

Arab states cut off public and private funding and all other forms of support for groups supporting and engaging in violence and terror.

All donors providing budgetary support for the Palestinians channel these funds through the Palestinian Ministry of Finance's Single Treasury Account.

As comprehensive security performance moves forward, IDF withdraws progressively from areas occupied since September 28, 2000, and the two sides restore the status quo that existed prior to September 28, 2000. Palestinian security forces redeploy to areas vacated by IDF.

Palestinian Institution-Building

Immediate action on credible process to produce draft constitution for Palestinian statehood. As rapidly as possible, constitutional committee circulates draft Palestinian constitution, based on strong parliamentary democracy and cabinet with empowered prime minister, for public comment/debate. Constitutional committee proposes draft document for submission after elections for approval by appropriate Palestinian institutions.

Appointment of interim prime minister or cabinet with empowered executive authority/decision-making body.

GOI fully facilitates travel of Palestinian officials for PLC and Cabinet sessions, internationally supervised security retraining, electoral and other reform activity, and other supportive measures related to the reform efforts.

Continued appointment of Palestinian ministers empowered to undertake fundamental reform. Completion of further steps to achieve genuine separation of powers, including any necessary Palestinian legal reforms for this purpose.

Establishment of independent Palestinian election commission. PLC reviews and revises election law.

Palestinian performance on judicial, administrative, and economic benchmarks, as established by the International Task Force on Palestinian Reform.

As early as possible, and based upon the above measures and in the context of open debate and transparent candidate selection/electoral campaign based on a free, multi-party process, Palestinians hold free, open, and fair elections.

GOI facilitates Task Force election assistance, registration of voters, movement of candidates and voting officials. Support for NGOs involved in the election process.

GOI reopens Palestinian Chamber of Commerce and other closed Palestinian institutions in East Jerusalem based on a commitment that these institutions operate strictly in accordance with prior agreements between the parties.

Humanitarian Response

Israel takes measures to improve the humanitarian situation. Israel and Palestinians implement in full all recommendations of the Bertini report to improve humanitarian conditions, lifting curfews and easing restrictions on movement of persons and goods, and allowing full, safe, and unfettered access of international and humanitarian personnel.

AHLC reviews the humanitarian situation and prospects for economic development in the West Bank and Gaza and launches a major donor assistance effort, including to the reform effort.

GOI and PA continue revenue clearance process and transfer of funds, including arrears, in accordance with agreed, transparent monitoring mechanism.

Civil Society

Continued donor support, including increased funding through PVOs/NGOs, for people to people programs, private sector development and civil society initiatives.

Settlements

GOI immediately dismantles settlement outposts erected since March 2001.

Consistent with the Mitchell Report, GOI freezes all settlement activity (including natural growth of settlements).

PHASE II: TRANSITION—JUNE 2003–DECEMBER 2003

In the second phase, efforts are focused on the option of creating an independent Palestinian state with provisional borders and attributes of sovereignty, based on the new constitution, as a way station to a permanent status settlement. As has been noted, this goal can be achieved when the Palestinian people have a leadership acting decisively against terror, willing and able to build a practicing democracy based on tolerance and liberty. With such a leadership, reformed civil institutions and security structures, the Palestinians will have the active support of the Quartet and the broader international community in establishing an independent, viable state.

Progress into Phase II will be based upon the consensus judgment of the Quartet of whether conditions are appropriate to proceed, taking into account performance of both parties. Furthering and sustaining efforts to normalize Palestinian lives and build Palestinian institutions, Phase II starts after Palestinian elections and ends with possible creation of an independent Palestinian state with provisional borders in 2003. Its primary goals are continued comprehensive security performance and effective security cooperation, continued normalization of Palestinian life and institution-building, further building on and sustaining of the goals outlined in Phase I, ratification of a democratic Palestinian constitution, formal establishment of office of prime minister, consolidation of political reform, and the creation of a Palestinian state with provisional borders.

International Conference: Convened by the Quartet, in consultation with the parties, immediately after the successful conclusion of Palestinian elections, to support Palestinian economic recovery and launch a process, leading to establishment of an independent Palestinian state with provisional borders.

Such a meeting would be inclusive, based on the goal of a comprehensive Middle East peace (including between Israel and Syria, and Israel and Lebanon), and based on the principles described in the preamble to this document.

Arab states restore pre-intifada links to Israel (trade offices, etc.).

Revival of multilateral engagement on issues including regional water resources, environment, economic development, refugees, and arms control issues.

New constitution for democratic, independent Palestinian state is finalized and approved by appropriate Palestinian institutions. Further elections, if required, should follow approval of the new constitution.

Empowered reform cabinet with office of prime minister formally established, consistent with draft constitution.

Continued comprehensive security performance, including effective security cooperation on the bases laid out in Phase I.

Creation of an independent Palestinian state with provisional borders through a process of Israeli–Palestinian engagement, launched by the international conference. As part of this process, implementation of prior agreements, to enhance maximum territorial contiguity, including further action on settlements in conjunction with establishment of a Palestinian state with provisional borders.

Enhanced international role in monitoring transition, with the active, sustained, and operational support of the Quartet.

Quartet members promote international recognition of Palestinian state, including possible UN membership.

PHASE III: PERMANENT STATUS AGREEMENT AND END OF THE ISRAELI–PALESTINIAN CONFLICT—2004–2005

Progress into Phase III, based on consensus judgment of Quartet, and taking into account actions of both parties and Quartet monitoring. Phase III objectives are consolidation of reform and stabilization of Palestinian institutions, sustained, effective Palestinian security performance, and Israeli–Palestinian negotiations aimed at a permanent status agreement in 2005.

Second International Conference: Convened by Quartet, in consultation with the parties, at beginning of 2004 to endorse agreement reached on an independent Palestinian state with provisional borders and formally to launch a process with the active, sustained, and operational support of the Quartet, leading to a final, permanent status resolution in 2005, including on borders, Jerusalem, refugees, settlements; and, to support progress toward a comprehensive Middle East settlement between Israel and Lebanon and Israel and Syria, to be achieved as soon as possible.

Continued comprehensive, effective progress on the reform agenda laid out by the Task Force in preparation for final status agreement.

Continued sustained and effective security performance, and sustained, effective security cooperation on the bases laid out in Phase I.

International efforts to facilitate reform and stabilize Palestinian institutions and the Palestinian economy, in preparation for final status agreement.

Parties reach final and comprehensive permanent status agreement that ends the Israeli–Palestinian conflict in 2005, through a settlement negotiated between the parties based on UNSCR 242, 338, and 1397, that ends the occupation that began in 1967, and includes an agreed, just, fair, and realistic solution to the refugee issue, and a negotiated resolution on the status of Jerusalem that takes into account the political and religious concerns of both sides, and protects the religious interests of Jews, Christians, and Muslims worldwide, and fulfills the vision of two states, Israel and sovereign, independent, democratic and viable Palestine, living side-by-side in peace and security.

Arab state acceptance of full normal relations with Israel and security for all the states of the region in the context of a comprehensive Arab–Israeli peace.

[End]

Released on April 30, 2003

---

http://www.yale.edu/lawweb/avalon/mideast/roadmap.htm (accessed February 1, 2006).

UN Security Council Resolution 1701: Adopted Unanimously by the Security Council on August 11, 2006

The full text of Security Council resolution 1701 (2006) reads as follows:

The Security Council,

Recalling all its previous resolutions on Lebanon, in particular resolutions 425 (1978), 426 (1978), 520 (1982), 1559 (2004), 1655 (2006) 1680 (2006) and 1697 (2006), as well as the statements of its President on the situation in Lebanon, in particular the statements of 18 June 2000 (S/PRST/2000/21), of 19 October 2004 (S/PRST/2004/36), of 4 May 2005 (S/PRST/2005/17), of 23 January 2006 (S/PRST/2006/3) and of 30 July 2006 (S/PRST/2006/35),

Expressing its utmost concern at the continuing escalation of hostilities in Lebanon and in Israel since Hizbollah's attack on Israel on 12 July 2006, which has already caused hundreds of deaths and injuries on both sides, extensive damage to civilian infrastructure and hundreds of thousands of internally displaced persons,

Emphasizing the need for an end of violence, but at the same time *emphasizing* the need to address urgently the causes that have given rise to the current crisis, including by the unconditional release of the abducted Israeli soldiers,

Mindful of the sensitivity of the issue of prisoners and *encouraging* the efforts aimed at urgently settling the issue of the Lebanese prisoners detained in Israel,

Welcoming the efforts of the Lebanese Prime Minister and the commitment of the Government of Lebanon, in its seven-point plan, to extend its authority over its territory, through its own legitimate armed forces, such that there will be no weapons without the consent of the Government of Lebanon and no authority other than that of the Government of Lebanon, *welcoming also* its commitment to a United Nations force that is supplemented and enhanced in numbers, equipment, mandate and scope of operation, and *bearing in mind* its request in this plan for an immediate withdrawal of the Israeli forces from southern Lebanon,

Determined to act for this withdrawal to happen at the earliest,

Taking due note of the proposals made in the seven-point plan regarding the Shebaa farms area,

Welcoming the unanimous decision by the Government of Lebanon on 7 August 2006 to deploy a Lebanese armed force of 15,000 troops in South Lebanon as the Israeli army withdraws behind the Blue Line and to request the assistance of additional forces from UNIFIL as needed, to facilitate the entry of the Lebanese armed forces into the region and to restate its intention to strengthen the Lebanese armed forces with material as needed to enable it to perform its duties,

Aware of its responsibilities to help secure a permanent ceasefire and a long-term solution to the conflict,

Determining that the situation in Lebanon constitutes a threat to international peace and security,

1. *Calls for* a full cessation of hostilities based upon, in particular, the immediate cessation by Hizbollah of all attacks and the immediate cessation by Israel of all offensive military operations;
2. Upon full cessation of hostilities, *calls upon* the Government of Lebanon and UNIFIL as authorized by paragraph 11 to deploy their forces together throughout the South and *calls upon* the Government of Israel, as that deployment begins, to withdraw all of its forces from southern Lebanon in parallel;
3. *Emphasizes* the importance of the extension of the control of the Government of Lebanon over all Lebanese territory in accordance with the provisions of resolution 1559 (2004) and resolution 1680 (2006), and of the relevant provisions of the Taif Accords, for it to exercise its full sovereignty, so that there will be no weapons without the consent of the Government of Lebanon and no authority other than that of the Government of Lebanon;

4. *Reiterates* its strong support for full respect for the Blue Line;
5. *Also reiterates* its strong support, as recalled in all its previous relevant resolutions, for the territorial integrity, sovereignty and political independence of Lebanon within its internationally recognized borders, as contemplated by the Israeli–Lebanese General Armistice Agreement of 23 March 1949;
6. *Calls on* the international community to take immediate steps to extend its financial and humanitarian assistance to the Lebanese people, including through facilitating the safe return of displaced persons and, under the authority of the Government of Lebanon, reopening airports and harbours, consistent with paragraphs 14 and 15, and *calls on* it also to consider further assistance in the future to contribute to the reconstruction and development of Lebanon;
7. *Affirms* that all parties are responsible for ensuring that no action is taken contrary to paragraph 1 that might adversely affect the search for a long-term solution, humanitarian access to civilian populations, including safe passage for humanitarian convoys, or the voluntary and safe return of displaced persons, and *calls on* all parties to comply with this responsibility and to cooperate with the Security Council;
8. *Calls for* Israel and Lebanon to support a permanent ceasefire and a long-term solution based on the following principles and elements:
   — full respect for the Blue Line by both parties;
   — security arrangements to prevent the resumption of hostilities, including the establishment between the Blue Line and the Litani river of an area free of any armed personnel, assets and weapons other than those of the Government of Lebanon and of UNIFIL as authorized in paragraph 11, deployed in this area;
   — full implementation of the relevant provisions of the Taif Accords, and of resolutions 1559 (2004) and 1680 (2006), that require the disarmament of all armed groups in Lebanon, so that, pursuant to the Lebanese cabinet decision of 27 July 2006, there will be no weapons or authority in Lebanon other than that of the Lebanese State;
   — no foreign forces in Lebanon without the consent of its Government;
   — no sales or supply of arms and related material to Lebanon except as authorized by its Government;
   — provision to the United Nations of all remaining maps of land mines in Lebanon in Israel's possession;
9. *Invites* the Secretary-General to support efforts to secure as soon as possible agreements in principle from the Government of Lebanon and the Government of Israel to the principles and elements for a long-term solution as set forth in paragraph 8, and *expresses* its intention to be actively involved;
10. *Requests* the Secretary-General to develop, in liaison with relevant international actors and the concerned parties, proposals to implement the relevant provisions of the Taif Accords, and resolutions 1559 (2004) and 1680 (2006), including disarmament, and for delineation of the international borders of Lebanon, especially in those areas where the border is disputed or uncertain, including by dealing with the Shebaa farms area, and to present to the Security Council those proposals within thirty days;
11. *Decides*, in order to supplement and enhance the force in numbers, equipment, mandate and scope of operations, to authorize an increase in the force strength

of UNIFIL to a maximum of 15,000 troops, and that the force shall, in addition to carrying out its mandate under resolutions 425 and 426 (1978):

(a) Monitor the cessation of hostilities;

(b) Accompany and support the Lebanese armed forces as they deploy throughout the South, including along the Blue Line, as Israel withdraws its armed forces from Lebanon as provided in paragraph 2;

(c) Coordinate its activities related to paragraph 11 (b) with the Government of Lebanon and the Government of Israel;

(d) Extend its assistance to help ensure humanitarian access to civilian populations and the voluntary and safe return of displaced persons;

(e) Assist the Lebanese armed forces in taking steps towards the establishment of the area as referred to in paragraph 8;

(f) Assist the Government of Lebanon, at its request, to implement paragraph 14;

12. Acting in support of a request from the Government of Lebanon to deploy an international force to assist it to exercise its authority throughout the territory, *authorizes* UNIFIL to take all necessary action in areas of deployment of its forces and as it deems within its capabilities, to ensure that its area of operations is not utilized for hostile activities of any kind, to resist attempts by forceful means to prevent it from discharging its duties under the mandate of the Security Council, and to protect United Nations personnel, facilities, installations and equipment, ensure the security and freedom of movement of United Nations personnel, humanitarian workers and, without prejudice to the responsibility of the Government of Lebanon, to protect civilians under imminent threat of physical violence;

13. *Requests* the Secretary-General urgently to put in place measures to ensure UNIFIL is able to carry out the functions envisaged in this resolution, *urges* Member States to consider making appropriate contributions to UNIFIL and to respond positively to requests for assistance from the Force, and *expresses* its strong appreciation to those who have contributed to UNIFIL in the past;

14. *Calls upon* the Government of Lebanon to secure its borders and other entry points to prevent the entry in Lebanon without its consent of arms or related material and *requests* UNIFIL as authorized in paragraph 11 to assist the Government of Lebanon at its request;

15. *Decides* further that all States shall take the necessary measures to prevent, by their nationals or from their territories or using their flag vessels or aircraft:

(a) The sale or supply to any entity or individual in Lebanon of arms and related material of all types, including weapons and ammunition, military vehicles and equipment, paramilitary equipment, and spare parts for the aforementioned, whether or not originating in their territories; and

(b) The provision to any entity or individual in Lebanon of any technical training or assistance related to the provision, manufacture, maintenance or use of the items listed in subparagraph (a) above;

except that these prohibitions shall not apply to arms, related material, training or assistance authorized by the Government of Lebanon or by UNIFIL as authorized in paragraph 11;

16. *Decides* to extend the mandate of UNIFIL until 31 August 2007, and *expresses its intention* to consider in a later resolution further enhancements to the mandate

and other steps to contribute to the implementation of a permanent ceasefire and a long-term solution;

17. *Requests* the Secretary-General to report to the Council within one week on the implementation of this resolution and subsequently on a regular basis;
18. *Stresses* the importance of, and the need to achieve, a comprehensive, just and lasting peace in the Middle East, based on all its relevant resolutions including its resolutions 242 (1967) of 22 November 1967, 338 (1973) of 22 October 1973 and 1515 (2003) of 18 November 2003;
19. *Decides* to remain actively seized of the matter.

---

www.un.org/News/Press/docs/2006/sc8808.doc.htm

GLOSSARY

Alawite (Alawi): Shiite Muslim offshoot, the name refers to "those who follow Ali," the son-in-law and cousin to the prophet Muhammad (also the fourth caliph or successor to the Prophet during the Rashidun period). Also known as "Nusayris," a name derived from a ninth-century Muslim prophet, Muhammad ibn Nusayr al-Namiri, the Alawites integrate some Christian and even Persian Zoroastrian rituals and holidays into their fairly obscure faith. As such, most Muslims over the centuries considered the Alawites to be heretical, and it has therefore been a persecuted Islamic sect throughout most of its history.

Aliyah (Hebrew: ascent): Zionist term for the waves of Jewish immigration to Palestine and then Israel.

Aliyah Bet: Organization sponsoring illegal Jewish immigration to Palestine.

Al-Qa'ida (Arabic: the base): Transnational militant Islamic terrorist organization led by Osama bin Laden.

Amal (Arabic: hope): Shiite movement in Lebanon founded by Imam Musa al-Sadr in 1974. Since the imam's mysterious disappearance in 1978, Amal has been led by Nabih Berri.

Arab Higher Committee: Palestinian Arab political leadership committee formed in 1936 and led by Hajj Amin al-Husayni. It was disbanded in October 1937 for its role in fomenting the 1936 Arab revolt.

Arab League (League of Arab States): Formed in 1945 and headquartered in Cairo, Egypt, the founding Arab members were Egypt, Iraq, Lebanon, Saudi Arabia, Syria, Transjordan, and Yemen. Modeled along the lines of the United Nations, it was intended to provide the Arab states with more political clout in the regional and international arenas via Arab cooperation and coordination of policies.

Arab Legion: Small but elite fighting force formed in Transjordan in 1920 by the British. Under the guidance of General Sir John Bagot Glubb, the Arab Legion, from the Israeli perspective, became the most formidable military force in the Arab world.

Ashkenazim: Jews of eastern European and German descent. Also has been used as a reference to Jews from any part of Europe.

Ba'th (Arabic: renaissance or rebirth): Name of the pan-Arab party founded in the 1930s primarily by Syrians. The Ba'th advocated, according to its slogan, freedom, unity, and socialism. It became the ruling party in both Syria and Iraq in 1963 and has small branches in a number of other Arab countries. As of this writing, it remains the ruling party in Syria; however, it was eliminated in Iraq with the removal of the regime of Saddam Hussein in the 2003 Iraq War.

Black September: Palestinian reference to the Jordanian civil war that occurred in September 1970 between the PLO and the Jordanian government. Also the name of the Palestinian terrorist group that captured and killed eleven members of the Israeli Olympic delegation at the 1972 Summer Olympiad in Munich, Germany.

Capitulations: Provisions in treaties between European powers, on the one hand, and states and empires over whom they had influence, on the other. These clauses stipulated a number of advantages in trade (such as lower or nonexistent tariffs) and diplomatic immunity for the Europeans.

DFLP: Democratic Front for the Liberation of Palestine.

Diaspora: Term for the "dispersion" of Jews or other groups throughout the world.

DOP: Declaration of Principles signed between Israel and the PLO in September 1993.

Druze: Obscure offshoot of Isma'ili Shiite Islam that draws its name from an eleventh-century man by the name of al-Darazi, who had apotheosized the Fatimid caliph al-Hakim in Cairo. Most of the Druze today live in Lebanon, Syria, and Israel.

Eretz Yisrael: "Land of Israel" in Hebrew.

Fatah (Arabic: conquest): Name of the largest and most politically powerful faction within the PLO. It is also the reverse acronym of *harakat al-tahrir al-filisteen*, the Palestine Liberation Movement.

Fedayeen, singular **fida'i** (Arabic: self-sacrificers): Name given to Palestinian guerillas/commandos.

Green Line: Armistice lines between Israel and the Arab states it bordered between 1948 and 1967.

Gush Emunim (Hebrew: Bloc of the Faithful): Religious nationalist movement established in 1974 to advance the settlement process of Jews in and even the annexation of the Occupied Territories.

Haganah (Hebrew: defense): Formed in 1920 as a defense organization in the Yishuv, it is the precursor to the Israel Defense Forces (IDF).

Hamas (Arabic: efforts or zeal): Also the Arabic acronym for Islamic Resistance Movement, it is a non-PLO Islamist Palestinian group founded in 1988 during the first Palestinian intifada. Traditionally calling for the elimination of Israel and against the Oslo peace process, it advocates an Islamist Palestinian state in which Islamic law, *shari'a*, acts as the law of the land and the basis for a constitution.

Haram al-Sharif (Arabic: Noble Sanctuary): Muslim reference to what Jews call the Temple Mount in the Old City of Jerusalem. The platform consists of the al-Aqsa Mosque and the Dome of the Rock, which is the primary reason most Muslims consider Jerusalem to be the third holiest site in Islam after Mecca (the *ka'ba* in the Grand Mosque is the center of Islam and direction or *qibla* for prayer) and Medina (the first capital of the Islamic state during and immediately after Muhammad's lifetime as well as the site for the Prophet's tomb).

Hashemites: The family of the prophet Muhammad. Today, the monarchies in Jordan (through the Sharif Husayn) and Morocco claim descent from the family of the Prophet and therefore are considered Hashemite kingdoms.

Hashomer (Hebrew: the watchman): Defense organization during the second aliyah.

Haskallah: Reference to the Jewish "Enlightenment," a movement for spreading modern European culture among Jews in Europe.

Herut (Hebrew: freedom): Israeli party established in 1948 by former Irgun members and led by Menachim Begin. Adopted an extreme right-wing platform, calling for the establishment or expansion of the Jewish state on both sides of the Jordan River. It merged with the Liberal party to become the Gahal party in 1965, which later morphed into the Likud party in 1973.

Hibbat Zion or Hovevi Zion (Hebrew: Lovers of Zion): Society formed primarily in Russia that organized the first aliyah to Palestine.

Histadrut: General Federation of Workers, founded in 1920 in the Yishuv. A kind of labor union, it is generally considered to be Israel's most powerful organization.

Hizbullah (Arabic: Party of God): Formed in the aftermath of the Israeli invasion of Lebanon in 1982 (formally founded in 1988), it is a Shiite Islamist group originally established as a resistance paramilitary organization to Israeli occupation of south Lebanon that has since also become a legitimate political party holding seats in the Lebanese parliament.

IBRD: International Bank of Reconstruction and Development, more commonly known as the World Bank.

IDF: Israel Defense Forces.

Infitah (Arabic: opening up): Program of economic liberalization, associated most famously with the policies pursued by Egyptian President Anwar al-Sadat in the 1970s.

Intifada (Arabic: shaking off or uprising): Name used by Palestinians to refer to their uprising against Israeli occupation that began in late 1987. Also used in reference to another uprising (the al-Aqsa intifada) that began in September 2000.

Irgun Zevai Leumi (Hebrew: National Military Organization): Founded in 1937 and led by Menachem Begin in 1941. Often considered a terrorist organization, it was committed to taking almost any action that brought about the creation of the state of Israel. The Irgun particularly viewed the British as the major impediment to Jewish statehood, and it carried out a series of attacks against British interests, most spectacularly the blowing up of the British military headquarters in the King David Hotel in Jerusalem in 1946, as well as against Palestinians. It was dissolved by the Israeli government in 1948.

Islamic Jihad (Palestine): Non-PLO Palestinian militant Islamist group in the Occupied Territories that split off from the Muslim Brethren in 1986, adopting a more activist and violent struggle against Israeli occupation.

Izz al-Din al-Qassam Brigades: Military wing of Hamas, its namesake (1895–1935) was born in Syria and moved to Haifa in the mid-1920s, where he actively preached for the removal of British forces and Zionists from Palestine. He promoted armed resistance, and practicing what he preached, he died in a clash with the British in 1935.

Jewish Agency: Established in 1929, it was the primary Zionist organization that organized and facilitated Jewish immigration to Palestine, purchased land in Palestine, promoted the adoption of the Hebrew language and culture, and developed Jewish settlements and agricultural collectives. In essence, it acted as a precursor to the Israeli government. It originally was formed to act as a liaison between the British Mandate authorities and the Yishuv.

Jihad (Arabic: struggle): Often translated in the West as "holy war," it has come to refer to those who fight in the way of Islam, or *mujahideen* (holy warriors). In traditional Islam, it refers as much to an inner struggle to become a better Muslim.

Kach: Militant religious nationalist Israeli party that promoted the expulsion of Arabs from Israel. It was founded in 1971 and led by Meir Kahane (1932–1990), an extremist who in 1969 founded in the United States the Jewish Defense League. Kahane was assassinated by an Arab in New York City in 1990, after which the movement split into Kach and Kahane Chai (Kahane lives).

Kadima (Hebrew: forward): Centrist Israeli political party formed in late 2005 by then prime minister Ariel Sharon—who broke away from the Likud bloc—and joined by other figures from the left and right of the political spectrum.

Kibbutz, plural **kibbutzim** (Hebrew: gathering or together): Collective agricultural settlement with common ownership of the land in the Yishuv/Israel.

Knesset (Hebrew: assembly): Israeli parliament, first convened in January 1949 and consisting of 120 seats.

Labor Alignment: Left-of-center alliance of the Labor party and the socialist Mapam party formed in 1969. Mapam is the Hebrew acronym for the United Workers Party.

Lehi: Hebrew acronym for "Fighters for the Freedom of Israel," also known as the Stern Gang after its founder Abraham Stern, who formed the extremist militant (many would say terrorist) group in 1939 and who himself was killed by the British in 1942. It was responsible for the assassination of UN mediator Count Folke Bernadotte, and one of its leaders was Yitzhak Shamir, a future Israeli prime minister.

Likud (Hebrew: unity or cohesion): Formed in 1973, it is a parliamentary bloc composed of right-wing parties. First came to power in the 1977 election with Menachem Begin becoming prime minister.

MACs: Mixed Armistice Commissions, formed following the 1947–1949 Arab–Israeli war.

Majlis (Arabic: assembly): Term often used to refer to anything from local councils to consultative assemblies and parliaments in the Arab world.

Mandate: System of trusteeships established by the League of Nations for the administration of former Ottoman territories following World War I.

Maronite: Named after St. Maron, who lived in the early fifth century, the Maronites are the largest and most influential Christian party in Lebanon. It is an Eastern Catholic sect in full communion with the pope in Rome. The president of Lebanon is traditionally a Maronite.

Moshav, plural **Moshavim** (Hebrew: settlement or village): Cooperative agricultural settlement in which individuals can hold land and income is permitted.

Mossad (Hebrew: institute): Intelligence directorate in Israel formed in 1951. Often compared to the CIA in the United States, its full name is the Institute for Intelligence and Special Missions.

Mukhabarat: Arabic reference to intelligence/security agencies and departments in Arab countries.

Muslim Brethren, Muslim Brotherhood, or Muslim Brothers (Ikhwan al-Muslimun): Islamist party founded by Hasan al-Banna in Egypt in 1928. It became the largest and most influential Islamist (or Islamic fundamentalist) party in the Arab world, with branches established in almost every Arab state.

Nakba (Arabic: disaster): What Arabs/Palestinians often call the 1947–1949 Arab–Israeli war.

National Religious Party (Hebrew acronym is **Mafdal**): Aimed at restoring more religious values in the state of Israel as well as the Torah in the Israeli constitution, it was formed in 1956 when the Ha-Poel HaMizrahi and HaMizrahi movements merged.

OPEC: Organization of Petroleum Exporting Countries, founded in September 1960.

OAPEC: Organization of Arab Petroleum Exporting Countries.

PA or PNA: Palestinian Authority or Palestine National Authority.

PFLP: Popular Front for the Liberation of Palestine.

PFLP-GC: Popular Front for the Liberation of Palestine—General Command.

PLA: Palestine Liberation Army.

PLO: Palestine Liberation Organization.

PNC: Palestine National Council, the PLO's parliament, composed of some 400 members representing various Palestinian factions.

Palmach: Hebrew acronym for "striking platoons," it was the name of the commando units in the Haganah.

Peace Now: Israeli peace movement founded in 1977. Although it is nonpartisan, it is generally considered to be left of center on the political spectrum based on its advocacy of peace with Israel's Arab neighbors and general opposition to the Israeli settlement process in the Occupied Territories.

Pogrom: Outbreaks of violence against Jews and Jewish interests, particularly in czarist Russia.

Ramadan: The name of the ninth month in the Islamic calendar, it is also the holy month of fasting (*sawm*), one of the five pillars of Islam, the basic duties of a Muslim. The four other pillars are *shahada*, bearing witness to God (Allah) by saying "There is no God but God, and Muhammad is His Messenger"; *salat*, prayers five time a day; *zakat*, alms to the poor; and *hajj*, the pilgrimage to Mecca at least once in a Muslim's lifetime if able to do so.

RCC: Revolutionary Command Council, the ruling body that led the Egyptian Revolution in 1952 that brought the Free Officers to power, including Gamal 'Abd al-Nasser, the leader of the RCC.

Salafiyya/Salafism (Arabic: ancestors): Reference derived from the first generation of Muslims, called *al-salif al-salih* (the "pious ancestors"), this is an Islamic intellectual movement that called for a return to the purity of the first Muslims and their foundational texts, namely the Qur'an and Hadith (a collection of the sayings and actions of the prophet Muhammad).

Sephardim: Hebrew reference to Jews from the Iberian Peninsula, particularly those who were exiled during the Spanish Inquisition in the late 1400s and into the 1500s. Most settled in Arab lands in North Africa. As such, it is often used to refer to "Oriental" or "Eastern" Jews, i.e., not Ashkenazim.

Shari'a (Arabic: the way or path): Islamic law.

Shas: Hebrew abbreviation of "Guardian of the Torah." It is an ultraorthodox Jewish party that broke away from Agudat Israel (Hebrew: Union of Israel), the main ultra-orthodox party in Israel. Founded by Mizrahi Jews, it has called for the creation of a Jewish theocracy in Israel and is led by Rabbi Ovadia Yossef. Shas has held as many as seventeen seats in the Israeli parliament and has become a significant power broker in the formation of ruling coalitions.

Shinui (Hebrew: change): Centrist Israeli political party formed in 1974.

SLA: South Lebanese Army.

Supreme Muslim Council: Founded in 1922, it ran Muslim affairs during the British Mandate in Palestine until it was disbanded during the 1936 Arab revolt. Its leader was Hajj Amin al-Husayni.

Tanzimat (Turkish: regulations): Ottoman reform movement in the nineteenth century, officially launched in 1839.

UAR: United Arab Republic.

'ulama, singular **'alim:** Muslim religious scholars.

UNDOF: United Nations Disengagement Observer Force (Golan Heights).

UNEF: United Nations Emergency Force (Sinai Peninsula).

UNGA: United Nations General Assembly.

UNIFIL: United Nations Interim Forces in Lebanon.

UNSC: United Nations Security Council.

UNRWA: United Nations Relief and Works Agency.

UNSCOP: United Nations Special Committee on Palestine.

Vaad Leumi (Hebrew: National Committee): National assembly in the Yishuv that was the precursor to the Israeli Knesset.

WMD: Weapons of mass destruction—usually taken to mean nuclear, biological, and/or chemical weapons.

Yishuv (Hebrew: settlement): Term used to refer to the Jewish community in Palestine before the creation of the state of Israel.

CHRONOLOGY

1789–1807	Sultanate of Selim III (Ottoman Empire)
1790–1791	Russian law passed restricting Jews to the Pale of Settlement
1798–1801	French forces under the command of Napoleon Bonaparte control Egypt
1805	Muhammad Ali takes control of Egypt (personal rule lasts until 1848, dynasty lasts until 1952)
1808–1839	Sultanate of Mahmud II (Ottoman Empire)
1831–1840	Muhammad Ali's Egypt rules Syria and Palestine
1839	Khatt-i Sharif of Gulkhane issued—beginning of Tanzimat period
1839–1861	Sultanate of Abd al-Majid II (Ottoman Empire)
1840	Treaty of London ends Egyptian rule in Syria and Palestine
1854–1856	Crimean War
1858	Ottoman land reform law
1869	Opening of Suez Canal
1875	Ottoman bankruptcy
1876–1908	Sultanate of Abd al-Hamid II (Ottoman Empire)
1880	'Urabi revolt in Egypt
1881	Leo Pinker's *Autoemancipation* published
1882	British occupation of Egypt; founding of Hibbat Zion and BILU; beginning of first Aliyah
1896	Theodore Herzl's *Der Judenstaat* (*The Jewish State*) published
1897	First World Zionist Organization congress held in Basle, Switzerland
1901	Jewish National Fund created
1904–1914	Second aliyah
1905	Naguib Azoury's *Le Reveil de la Nation Arabe* published
1908	Young Turk revolution (Ottoman Empire); Sharif Hussein appointed the guardian of the Two Holy Places (Mecca and Medina)

1913 Enver, Jamal, and Talat Pasha (the triumvirate) take over Ottoman Empire

1914 World War I begins; Ottoman Empire enters the war on the side of Germany; Britain declares Egypt a protectorate

1915 Gallipoli campaign begins; Constantinople Agreement; de Bunsen committee report issued in London; Hussein–McMahon correspondence begins (through January 1916)

1916 Sykes-Picot Agreement; launching of the Arab revolt (sharifian revolt) in the Hijaz

1917 Balfour Declaration; Bolshevik Revolution in Russia; British forces take Jerusalem

1918 Woodrow Wilson enunciates his "Fourteen Points"; Declaration to the Seven; Arab forces enter Damascus; Ottoman Empire surrenders, Armistice of Mudros signed, Anglo–French Declaration; World War I ends

1919 Paris peace conference convenes; King-Crane commission tours Syria and Palestine

1920 Kingdom of Syria under Faisal bin Husayn declared by Syrian National Congress; San Remo conference approves the mandate system; French forces enter Damascus, end of Hashemite Kingdom of Syria; Haganah founded in the Yishuv

1921 Cairo Conference convened by Winston Churchill; Hajj Amin al-Husayni appointed Mufti of Jerusalem

1922 Churchill White Paper; League of Nations ratifies mandates

1929 Western (Wailing) Wall riots in Palestine

1930 Shaw Report, Passfield White Paper

1933 Hitler comes to power in Germany

1936–1939 Arab revolt in Palestine

1937 Peel Commission report; Irgun founded; Hajj Amin al-Husayni leaves Palestine

1939 White Paper; World War II begins

1940 Lehi (Stern Gang) established

1942 Biltmore program announced at conference in New York City

1944 Alexandria Protocol

1945 League of Arab States created; President Franklin D. Roosevelt dies and is succeeded by Harry S. Truman; World War II ends

1946 Anglo–American Committee of Inquiry report is issued

1947	Truman Doctrine announced; UN General Assembly Resolution 181 passed, partitioning Palestine; beginning of first Arab–Israeli war
1948	State of Israel proclaimed by David Ben-Gurion, Israel's first prime minister—Arab states go to war with Israel the next day; Lehi assassinates Count Folke Bernadotte
1949	First Arab–Israeli war ends with signing of armistice agreements
1950	Tripartite Declaration
1951	Jordan's King Abdullah assassinated
1952	Egyptian Revolution (Free Officers coup)
1953	Dwight D. Eisenhower becomes U.S. president
1954	Moshe Sharett becomes Israeli prime minister; Lavon affair; Anglo–Egyptian accord
1955	Gaza raid; Baghdad Pact formed; Czech (Soviet)–Egyptian arms deal; David Ben-Gurion returns as Israeli prime minister; United States and Great Britain agree to fund Aswan High Dam project in Egypt
1956	Egypt's Gamal 'Abd al-Nasser nationalizes Suez Canal Company; Suez war
1957	Eisenhower Doctrine announced and passed by Congress; Jordanian crisis; American–Syrian crisis
1958	United Arab Republic (UAR) forms with merger of Egypt and Syria; Iraqi Revolution; Lebanese crisis, NSC 5820 passed
1961	Syria secedes from the UAR
1962	Beginning of Yemeni civil war
1963	U.S. President John F. Kennedy assassinated, succeeded by Lyndon B. Johnson; Levi Eshkol becomes Israeli prime minister upon Ben-Gurion's retirement; Ba'th party comes to power separately in Iraq and Syria
1964	Arab League summit meeting in Cairo considers reaction to Israeli diversion of headwaters of Jordan River; Palestine Liberation Organization (PLO) created
1966	Intra-Ba'th coup in Syria brings radical wing to power; Egyptian–Syrian mutual defense pact
1967	June Arab–Israeli war; Arab League summit meeting in Khartoum, UN Security Council Resolution 242 passed
1968	Labor party formed in Israel
1969	War of Attrition (March 1969–August 1970); Golda Meir becomes Israeli prime minister after death of Levi Eshkol; Richard M. Nixon becomes U.S. president; Rogers plan unveiled

1970 Rogers initiative leads to Egyptian–Israeli cease-fire in War of Attrition; Jordanian civil war (Black September); Egyptian President Gamal 'Abd al-Nasser dies, succeeded by Anwar al-Sadat; Hafiz al-Asad takes power in Syria, formally assumes presidency in March 1971

1971 PLO relocates headquarters to Beirut; Lebanon

1972 Egypt expels Soviet advisers; Black September takes eleven members of Israeli Olympic delegation hostage at Munich Olympics—all eleven die in rescue attempt by West German authorities

1973 Likud party established in Israel; October Arab–Israeli War; UN Security Council Resolution 338 passed; OAPEC announces oil embargo

1974 Sinai I agreement between Egypt and Israel; Golda Meir resigns, Yitzhak Rabin becomes prime minister of Israel; Syrian-Israeli disengagement agreement; Rabat Arab League summit meeting proclaims the PLO to be the "sole legitimaterepresentative of the Palestinian people"; PLO Chair Yasser Arafat addresses UN General Assembly

1975 Sinai II accord signed between Egypt and Israel; beginning of Lebanese civil war

1977 Jimmy Carter becomes U.S. president; Menachem Begin becomes Israeli prime minister; Anwar al-Sadat visits Israel

1978 Israeli "sweep" of south Lebanon; establishment of security zone; Camp David accords

1979 Iranian Revolution brings Ayatollah Khomeini to power; Egyptian–Israeli peace treaty; Saddam Hussein formally becomes president of Iraq; U.S. embassy personnel taken hostage in Teheran, Iran; taking of Grand Mosque in Mecca by Islamic militants; Soviet invasion of Afghanistan

1980 Iraq invades Iran; beginning Iran–Iraq war—lasts into 1988

1981 Ronald Reagan becomes U.S. president; Israel destroys suspected nuclear reactor in Iraq; Anwar al-Sadat assassinated in Cairo by Islamic militants; Husni Mubarak succeeds as Egyptian president

1982 Israeli invasion of Lebanon; Reagan peace plan announced, Lebanese president-elect Bashir Gemayel assassinated in Beirut; Sabra and Shatila massacres in Beirut; Multinational Force (MNF) enters Lebanon

1983 Menachem Begin resigns; Yitzhak Shamir succeeds as Israeli prime minister; suicide bombing of U.S. Marine barracks at Beirut International Airport

1984 MNF withdraws from Lebanon

1985 Israeli forces withdraw to security zone in south Lebanon

1987 Palestinian intifada begins

1988 Hamas founded; Jordan's King Hussein renounces claims to Palestine; PLO announces acceptance of UNSC Resolution 242, renounces the use of terrorism, and recognizes Israel (U.S. officials begin negotiations with PLO officials in Tunis)

1989 George H. W. Bush becomes U.S. president; al-Ta'if accord revises Lebanese political system; fall of Berlin Wall, symbolizing end of superpower cold war

1990 Iraq invades and occupies Kuwait

1991 Desert Storm begins, the U.S.-led UN coalition expels Iraq from Kuwait; Madrid peace conference held, launching Madrid peace process; dissolution of Soviet Union

1992 Bill Clinton assumes power as U.S. president; Labor party's Yitzhak Rabin becomes Israeli prime minister

1993 Israeli–Palestinian Declaration of Principles signed on White House lawn

1994 Palestinian self-rule begins in Jericho (West Bank) and the Gaza Strip; Jordan–Israel peace treaty signed

1995 Interim Agreement (Oslo II) signed by Rabin and Arafat; Yitzhak Rabin assassinated, Shimon Peres becomes interim prime minister

1996 Israel launches "Grapes of Wrath" military operation in Lebanon following rocket attacks by Hizbollah; Benjamin Netanyahu elected Israeli prime minister

1998 Wye memorandum signed by Netanyahu and Arafat

1999 Jordan's King Hussein dies, succeeded by his son, King Abdullah II; Ehud Barak elected Israeli prime minister

2000 Israel unilaterally withdraws from Lebanon; Syrian President Hafiz al-Asad dies, succeeded by his son, Bashar al-Asad; Camp David summit between Bill Clinton, Ehud Barak, and Yasser Arafat; Al-Aqsa intifada begins

2001 George W. Bush becomes U.S. president; Ariel Sharon is elected Israeli prime minister; 9/11 attacks against World Trade Center in New York City and the Pentagon in Washington, DC—carried out by al-Qa'ida; United States invades Afghanistan and removes Taliban from power in response to 9/11

2002 President Bush's "axis of evil" state of the union address; Saudi peace initiative at Beirut Arab League summit meeting; Bush Doctrine (National Security Strategy) announced

2003 U.S.-led invasion of Iraq begins; Roadmap to peace from "Quartet" officially unveiled

2004 Yasser Arafat dies, Mahmoud Abbas (Abu Mazen) succeeds as president of Palestinian Authority; UNSC Resolution 1559 passed

2005 Former Lebanese prime minister Rafiq Hariri is assassinated in Beirut; Syria withdraws military forces from Lebanon; Israel unilaterally withdraws from Gaza Strip (and four Jewish settlements in West Bank); Prime Minister Ariel Sharon breaks away from Likud to form Kadima party

2006 Israeli Prime Minister Ariel Sharon suffers incapacitating stroke, Ehud Olmert becomes acting prime minister (Olmert officially becomes prime minister after March elections); Palestinian legislative elections (January) brings Hamas to power; Israel–Hizbollah conflict in Lebanon (UNSC 1701 passed)

2006 Democrats take control of both houses of Congress in midterm elections; Iraq Study Group Report Published

2007 Hamas–Fatah violence/conflict in occupied territories

2007 Saudi Arabia playing mediating role between Hamas and Fatah, Mecca agreement in February; Arab League summit meeting in Riyadh in March reissues Arab League peace plan

FOR FURTHER READING

Chapter One

Abu-Lughod, Ibrahim, ed. *The Transformation of Palestine: Essays on the Origin and Development of the Arab–Israeli Conflict.* Evanston, IL: Northwestern University Press, 1971.

Divine, Donna Robinson. *Politics and Society in Ottoman Palestine: The Arab Struggle for Survival and Power.* Boulder: Lynne Rienner, 1994.

Gorny, Yosef. *Zionism and the Arabs, 1882–1948: A Study of Ideology.* London: Oxford University Press, 1987.

Muslih, Muhammad. *The Origins of Palestinian Nationalism.* New York: Columbia University Press, 1989.

Owen, Roger, ed. *Studies in the Economic and Social History of Palestine in the Nineteenth and Twentieth Centuries.* Carbondale: Southern Illinois University Press, 1982.

Owen, Roger. *The Middle East in the World Economy, 1800–1914.* London: I. B. Tauris, 1993.

Smith, Pamela Ann. *Palestine and the Palestinians, 1876–1983.* New York: St. Martin's Press, 1984.

Yapp, M. E. *The Making of the Modern Near East, 1792–1923.* London: Longman, 1990.

Chapter Two

Antonius, George. *The Arab Awakening: The Story of the Arab National Movement.* New York: Capricorn Books, 1965.

Avishai, Bernard. *The Tragedy of Zionism: Revolution and Democracy in the Land of Israel.* New York: Farrar, Straus, & Giroux, 1985.

Dawn, C. Ernest. *From Ottomanism to Arabism: Essays on the Origins of Arab Nationalism.* Urbana: University of Illinois Press, 1973.

Gelvin, James L. *The Modern Middle East: A History.* New York: Oxford University Press, 2005.

Geshoni, Israel and James Jankowski, eds. *Rethinking Nationalism in the Arab Middle East.* New York: Columbia University Press, 1997.

Gilbert, Martin. *Israel: A History.* New York: William Morrow and Company, 1998.

Haim, Sylvia, ed. *Arab Nationalism: An Anthology.* Berkeley: University of California Press, 1964.

Hertzberg, Arthur. *The Zionist Idea: Historical Analysis and Reader.* New York: Atheneum, 1979.

Hourani, Albert. *Arabic Thought in the Liberal Age, 1798–1939.* Cambridge: Cambridge University Press, 1983.

Kayali, Hasan. *Arabs and Young Turks: Ottomanism, Arabism, and Islamism in the Ottoman Empire, 1908–1918.* Berkeley: University of California Press, 1997.

Khalidi, Rashid, Lisa Anderson, Muhammad Muslih, Reeva S. Simon, et al., eds. *The Origins of Arab Nationalism.* New York: Columbia University Press, 1991.

Khoury, Philip S. *Urban Notables and Arab Nationalism: The Politics of Damascus, 1860–1920.* Cambridge: Cambridge University Press, 1983.

Luz, Ehud. *Parallels Meet: Religion and Nationalism in the Early Zionist Movement, 1882–1904.* New York: Jewish Publication Society, 1988.
Mandel, Neville. *The Arabs and Zionism Before World War I.* Berkeley: University of California Press, 1976.
Nafi, Basheer M. *Arabism, Islamism and the Palestine Question, 1908–1941: A Political History.* Reading, UK: Ithaca Press, 1998.
Shafir, Gershon. *Land, Labor and the Origins of the Israeli–Palestinian Conflict 1882–1914.* Cambridge: Cambridge University Press, 1989.
Stein, Leslie. *The Hope Fulfilled: The Rise of Modern Israel.* Westport, CT: Praeger, 2003.

Chapter Three

Cohen, Michael J. *The Origins and Evolution of the Arab–Zionist Conflict.* Berkeley: University of California Press, 1987.
Friedman, Isaiah. *The Question of Palestine, 1914–1918: British–Jewish–Arab Relations.* New Brunswick, NJ: Transaction Books, 1992.
Fromkin, David. *A Peace to End All Peace.* New York: Henry Holt and Company, 1989.
Goldstein, Erik. *Winning the Peace: British Diplomatic Strategy, Peace Planning, and the Paris Peace Conference, 1916–1920.* London: Oxford University Press, 1991.
Kedourie, Elie. *England and the Middle East: The Destruction of the Ottoman Empire, 1914–1921.* London: Cassell, 1987.
Kent, Marian. *Moguls and Mandarins: Oil, Imperialism, and the Middle East in British Foreign Policy.* Portland, OR: Frank Cass Publishers, 1993.
Ovendale, Ritchie. *The Origins of the Arab–Israeli Wars.* London: Longman, 1999.
Sanders, Ronald. *The High Walls of Jerusalem: A History of the Balfour Declaration and the Birth of the British Mandate for Palestine.* New York: Holt, Rinehart & Winston, 1983.
Smith, Charles D. *Palestine and the Arab–Israeli Conflict: A History with Documents.* New York: Bedford/St. Martin's, 2004.
Stein, Leonard. *The Balfour Declaration.* London: Magnes Press, 1983.
Yapp, M. E. *The Making of the Modern Near East, 1792–1923.* London: Longman, 1990.

Chapter Four

Cleveland, William L. *A History of the Modern Middle East.* Boulder: Westview Press, 2005.
Heller, Joseph. *The Stern Gang: Ideology, Politics, and Terror, 1940–1949.* Portland, OR: Frank Cass Publishers, 1995.
Kolinsky, Martin. *Law, Order, and Riots in Mandatory Palestine, 1928–1935.* New York: St. Martin's Press, 1993.
Lesch, Ann M. *Arab Politics in Palestine 1917–1939: The Frustration of a Nationalist Movement.* Ithaca: Cornell University Press, 1979.
Lockman, Zachary. *Comrades and Enemies: Arab and Jewish Workers in Palestine.* Berkeley: University of California Press, 1996.
Mattar, Philip. *The Mufti of Jerusalem: Al-Hajj Amin al-Husayni and the Palestinian National Movement.* New York: Diane Publishing, 1988.
McCarthy, Justin. *The Population of Palestine: Population History and Statistics of the Late Ottoman Period and the Mandate.* New York: Columbia University Press, 1990.
Pappe, Ilan. *A History of Modern Palestine: One Land, Two Peoples.* Cambridge: Cambridge University Press, 2004.
Segev, Tom. *One Palestine Complete: Jews and Arabs Under the British Mandate.* New York: Henry Holt and Company, 2000.

Stein, Kenneth. *The Land Question in Palestine, 1917–1939*. Chapel Hill: University of North Carolina Press, 1984.
Stein, Leslie. *The Hope Fulfilled: The Rise of Modern Israel*. Westport, CT: Praeger, 2003.

Chapter Five

Benson, Michael. *Harry S. Truman and the Founding of Israel*. Westport, CT: Praeger, 1997.
Cohen, Michael J. *Palestine and the Great Powers, 1945–1948*. Princeton: Princeton University Press, 1982.
Cohen, Michael J. *The Origins and Evolution of the Arab–Zionist Conflict*. Berkeley: University of California Press, 1987.
Cohen, Michael J. *Truman and Israel*. Berkeley: University of California Press, 1990.
Ganin, Zvi. *Truman, American Jewry, and Israel, 1945–1948*. New York: Holmes & Meier Publishers, 1979.
Herzog, Chaim. *The Arab–Israeli Wars: War and Peace in the Middle East*. New York: Random House, 1982.
Karsh, Efraim. *The Arab–Israeli Conflict: The Palestine War 1948*. Oxford: Osprey Publishing, 2002.
Louis, W. Roger. *The British Empire in the Middle East, 1945–1951: Arab Nationalism, the United States and Postwar Imperialism*. Oxford: Oxford University Press, 1984.
Morris, Benny. *The Birth of the Palestinian Refugee Problem, 1947–1949*. Cambridge: Cambridge University Press, 1988.
Morris, Benny. *Righteous Victims: A History of the Zionist-Arab Conflict*. New York: Alfred A. Knopf, 1999.
Ovendale, Ritchie. *The Arab–Israeli Wars*. London: Longman, 1999.
Pappe, Ilan. *The Making of the Arab–Israeli Conflict, 1947–1951*. London: I. B. Tauris, 1994.
Rogan, Eugene L. and Avi, Shlaim, eds. *The War for Palestine: Rewriting the History of 1948*. Cambridge: Cambridge University Press, 2001.
Rubenberg, Cheryl A. *Israel and the American National Interest*. Urbana: University of Illinois Press, 1986.
Shadid, Mohammed K. *The United States and the Palestinians*. New York: St. Martin's Press, 1981.
Shlaim, Avi. *Collusion Across the Jordan: King Abdullah, the Zionist Movement, and the Partition of Palestine*. New York: Columbia University Press, 1988.
Snetsinger, John. *Truman, the Jewish Vote and the Creation of Israel*. Stanford, CA: Hoover Institution Press, 1974.
Sternhell, Zeev. *The Founding Myths of Israel: Nationalism, Socialism and the Making of the Jewish State*. Princeton: Princeton University Press, 1999.
Tessler, Mark. *A History of the Israeli-Palestinian Conflict*. Bloomington: Indiana University Press, 1994.
Wilson, Evan M. *Decision on Palestine: How the U.S. Came to Recognize Israel*. Stanford, CA: Hoover Institution Press, 1979.

Chapter Six

Alteras, Isaac. *United States–Israel Relations, 1953–1960*. Gainesville: University Press of Florida, 1995.
Beattie, Kirk J. *Egypt During the Nasser Years: Ideology, Politics, and Civil Society*. Boulder: Westview Press, 1994.
Campbell, John C. *Defense of the Middle East: Problems of American Policy*. New York: Harper & Brothers, 1960.

Cooper, Chester L. *The Lion's Last Roar: Suez, 1956*. New York: Harper & Row, 1978.
Copeland, Miles. *The Game of Nations: The Amorality of Power Politics*. New York: Simon and Schuster, 1969.
Divine, Robert A. *Eisenhower and the Cold War*. London: Oxford University Press, 1981.
Gerges, Fawaz A. *The Superpowers and the Middle East: Regional and International Politics, 1955–1967*. Boulder: Westview Press, 1994.
Gordon, Joel. *Nasser's Blessed Movement: Egypt's Free Officers and the July Revolution*. New York: Oxford University Press, 1992.
Hahn, Peter L. *The United States, Great Britain, and Egypt, 1945–1956: Strategy and Diplomacy in the Early Cold War*. Chapel Hill: University of North Carolina Press, 1991.
Hahn, Peter L. *Caught in the Middle East: U.S. Policy toward the Arab–Israeli Conflict, 1945–1961*. Chapel Hill: University of North Carolina Press, 2006.
Heikel, Mohamed. *Cutting the Lion's Tail: Suez Through Egyptian Eyes*. New York: William Morrow & Company, 1987.
Hoopes, Townsend. *The Devil and John Foster Dulles*. Boston: Little, Brown & Company, 1973.
Kaufman, Burton I. *Trade and Aid: Eisenhower's Foreign Economic Policy 1953–1961*. Baltimore: Johns Hopkins University Press, 1982.
Kerr, Malcolm H. *The Arab Cold War: Gamal 'Abd al-Nasir and His Rivals, 1958–1970*. London: Oxford University Press, 1971.
Lesch, David W. *Syria and the United States: Eisenhower's Cold War in the Middle East*. Boulder: Westview Press, 1992.
Lesch, David W., ed. *The Middle East and the United States: A Historical and Political Reassessment*, 4th ed. Boulder: Westview Press, 2007.
Love, Kenneth. *Suez: The Twice-Fought War*. New York: McGraw-Hill, 1969.
Monroe, Elizabeth. *Britain's Moment in the Middle East 1914–1956*. London: Chatto & Windus, 1963.
Morris, Benny. *Israel's Border Wars, 1949–1956: Arab Infiltration, Israeli Retaliation, and the Countdown to the Suez War*. Oxford: Clarendon Press, 1993.
Neff, Donald. *Warriors at Suez*. Brattleboro, VT: Amana Books, 1988.
Nutting, Anthony. *Nasser*. London: Constable, 1972.
Podeh, Elie. *The Quest for Hegemony in the Arab World: The Struggle over the Baghdad Pact*. Leiden: E. J. Brill, 1995.
Rabinovich, Itamar. *The Road Not Taken: Early Arab–Israeli Negotiations*. London: Oxford University Press, 1991.
Seale, Patrick. *The Struggle for Syria: A Study of Post-War Arab Politics, 1945–1958*. New Haven: Yale University Press, 1986.
Smolansky, Oles M. *The Soviet Union and the Arab East Under Khrushchev*. Lewisburg, PA: Bucknell University Press, 1974.
Spiegel, Steven L. *The Other Arab–Israeli Conflict: Making America's Middle East Policy, from Truman to Reagan*. Chicago: University of Chicago Press, 1985.
Yodfat, Aryeh. *Arab Politics in the Soviet Mirror*. New York: Halsted Press, 1973.

Chapter Seven

Abu-Lughod, Ibrahim, ed. *The Arab–Israeli Confrontation of 1967: An Arab Perspective*. Evanston, IL: Northwestern University Press, 1970.
Bar-Siman-Tov, Yaacov. *The Israeli–Egyptian War of Attrition, 1969–1970*. New York: Columbia University Press, 1980.
Bass, Warren. *Support Any Friend: Kennedy's Middle East and the Making of the U.S.–Israeli Alliance*. London: Oxford University Press, 2003.

Heikal, Mohamed. *The Sphinx and the Commissar: The Rise and Fall of Soviet Influence in the Middle East*. New York: Harper & Row, 1978.

Heikal, Mohamed Hassanein. *The Cairo Documents*. Garden City: Doubleday, 1973.

Kaufman, Burton I. *The Arab Middle East and the United States: Inter-Arab Rivalry and Superpower Diplomacy*. New York: Twayne, 1996.

Kerr, Malcolm H. *The Arab Cold War: Gamal 'Abd al-Nasir and His Rivals, 1958–1970*. Oxford: Oxford University Press, 1971.

Korn, David A. *Stalemate: The War of Attrition and Great Power Diplomacy in the Middle East, 1967–1970*. Boulder: Westview Press, 1992.

Mufti, Malik. *Sovereign Creations: Pan-Arabism and Political Order in Syria and Iraq*. Ithaca: Cornell University Press, 1996.

Neff, Donald. *Warriors for Jerusalem: The Six Days that Changed the Middle East*. New York: Simon and Schuster, 1984.

Oren, Michael B. *Six Days of War: June 1967 and the Making of the Modern Middle East*. New York: Ballantine Books, 2003.

Parker, Richard B. *The Politics of Miscalculation*. Bloomington: Indiana University Press, 1993.

Parker, Richard B., ed. *The Six-Day War: A Retrospective*. Gainesville: University Press of Florida, 1996.

Paterson, Thomas G., ed. *Kennedy's Quest for Victory: American Foreign Policy, 196[illegible] 1963*. London: Oxford University Press, 1989.

Quandt, William B. *Peace Process: American Diplomacy and the Arab–Israeli Conflict Since 1967*. Berkeley: University of California Press, 2001.

Safran, Nadav. *Israel, the Embattled Ally*. Cambridge, MA: Harvard University Press, 1981.

Spiegel, Steven L. *The Other Arab–Israeli Conflict: Making America's Middle East Policy, from Truman to Reagan*. Chicago: University of Chicago Press, 1985.

Chapter Eight

Dupuy, Trevor N. *Elusive Victory: The Arab–Israeli Wars, 1947–1974*. New York: Harper & Row, 1978.

Freedman, Robert O. *Soviet Foreign Policy Toward the Middle East Since 1970*. New York: Praeger, 1982.

Golan, Galia. *Yom Kippur and After*. Cambridge: Cambridge University Press, 1977.

Heikal, Mohammed. *The Road to Ramadan*. New York: Quadrangle, 1975.

Lesch, David W. *1979: The Year that Shaped the Modern Middle East*. Boulder: Westview Press, 2001.

Quandt, William B. *Camp David: Peacemaking and Politics*. Washington, DC: Brookings Institution, 1986.

Quandt, William B., ed. *The Middle East: Ten Years After Camp David*. Washington, DC: Brookings Institution, 1988.

Quandt, William B. *Peace Process: American Diplomacy and the Arab–Israeli Conflict Since 1967*. Berkeley: University of California Press, 2001.

Rabinovich, Abraham. *The Yom Kippur War: The Epic Encounter that Transformed the Middle East*. New York: Schocken Books, 2004.

Safran, Nadav. *Israel, the Embattled Ally*. Cambridge, MA: Harvard University Press, 1982.

Sayigh, Yezid. *Armed Struggle and the Search for a State: The Palestinian National Movement, 1949–1993*. London: Oxford University Press, 2000.

Seale, Patrick. *Asad of Syria: The Struggle for the Middle East*. London: I. B. Tauris, 1988.

Shawdran, Benjamin. *Middle Eastern Oil Crises Since 1973*. Boulder: Westview Press, 1986.

Spiegel, Steven L. *The Other Arab–Israeli Conflict: Making America's Middle East Policy, from Truman to Reagan*. Chicago: University of Chicago Press, 1985.

Stein, Kenneth W. *Heroic Diplomacy: Sadat, Kissinger, Carter, Begin, and the Quest for Arab–Israeli Peace*. New York: Routledge, 1999.

Westwood, John. *The History of the Middle East Wars*. North Dighton, MA: JG Press, 2002.

Chapter Nine

Abu-Amr, Ziad. *Islamic Fundamentalism in the West Bank and Gaza: Muslim Brotherhood and Islamic Jihad*. Bloomington: Indiana University Press, 1994.

Ajami, Fouad. *The Vanished Imam: Musa al-Sadr and the Shi'a of Lebanon*. Ithaca: Cornell University Press, 1986.

Hunter, F. Robert. *The Palestinian Uprising: A War by Other Means*. Berkeley: University of California Press, 1993.

Khalidi, Rashid. *Under Siege: PLO Decisionmaking During the 1982 War*. New York: Columbia University Press, 1986.

Khalidi, Walid. *Conflict and Violence in Lebanon: Confrontation in the Middle East*. Cambridge, MA: Harvard University Center for International Affairs, 1984.

Lesch, Ann Mosely, and Mark Tessler. *Israel, Egypt, and the Palestinians from Camp David to Intifada*. Bloomington: Indiana University Press, 1989.

Lesch, David W. *The New Lion of Damascus: Bashar al-Asad and Modern Syria*. New Haven: Yale University Press, 2005.

Norton, Augustus Richard. *Amal and the Shi'a: Struggle for the Soul of Lebanon*. Austin: University of Texas Press, 1987.

Norton, Augustus Richard. *Hizbollah of Lebanon: Extremist Ideas vs. Mundane Politics*. New York: Council on Foreign Relations, 1999.

Peretz, Don. *Intifada: The Palestinian Uprising*. Boulder: Westview Press, 1990.

Podeh, Elie. *From Fahd to 'Abdullah: The Origins of the Saudi Peace Initiatives and Their Impact on the Arab System and Israel*. Jerusalem: Harry S. Truman Research Institute for the Advancement of Peace, 2003.

Quandt, William B. *Peace Process: American Diplomacy and the Arab–Israeli Conflict Since 1967*. Berkeley: University of California Press, 2001.

Rabinovich, Itamar. *The War for Lebanon: 1970–1985*. Ithaca: Cornell University Press, 1985.

Salibi, Kamal. *A House of Many Mansions: The History of Lebanon Reconsidered*. Berkeley: University of California Press, 1988.

Sayigh, Yezid. *Armed Struggle and the Search for State: The Palestinian National Movement, 1949–1993*. London: Oxford University Press, 2000.

Schiff, Ze'ev, and Ehud Ya'ari. *Intifada: The Palestinian Uprising: Israel's Third Front*. New York: Simon and Schuster, 1990.

Chapter Ten

Amery, Hussein A., and Chilibi Mallet, eds. *Water in the Middle East: A Geography of Peace*. Austin: University of Texas Press, 2000.

Aronson, Geoffrey. *Settlements and the Israeli–Palestinian Negotiations: An Overview*. Washington, DC: Institute for Palestine Studies, 1996.

Beilin, Yossi. *Touching Peace: From the Oslo Accord to a Final Settlement*. London: Weidenfeld & Nicolson, 1999.

Bickerton, Ian J., and Carla L. Klausner. *A Concise History of the Arab–Israeli Conflict*. Upper Saddle River, NJ: Prentice Hall, 2002.

Bregman, Ahron and Jihan El-Tahri. *Israel and the Arabs: An Eyewitness Account of War and Peace in the Middle East*. New York: TV Books, 2000.

Dumper, Michael. *The Politics of Jerusalem Since 1967*. New York: Columbia University Press, 1997.
Harub, Khalid. *Hamas: Political Thought and Practice*. Washington, DC: Institute for Palestine Studies, 2000.
Heller, Mark and Sara Nusseibeh. *No Trumpets, No Drums: A Two-State Solution to the Israeli–Palestinian Conflict*. New York: Hill and Wang, 1999.
Lesch, David W. *The Middle East and the United States: A Historical and Political Reassessment*, 4th ed. Boulder: Westview Press, 2007.
Lesch, David W. *The New Lion of Damascus: Bashar al-Asad and Modern Syria*. New Haven: Yale University Press, 2005.
Makovsky, David. *Making Peace with the PLO: The Rabin Government's Road to Oslo*. Boulder: Westview Press, 1996.
Maoz, Moshe. *Syria and Israel: From War to Peacemaking*. Oxford: Oxford University Press, 1995.
Mazen, Abu (Mahmoud Abbas). *Through Secret Channels: The Road to Oslo: Senior PLO Leader Abu Mazen's Revealing Story of the Negotiations with Israel*. Concord, MA: Paul and Company Publishers, 1995.
Mishal, Shaul, and Avraham Sela. *The Palestinian Hamas: Vision, Violence, and Coexistence*. New York: Columbia University Press, 2006.
Rabinovich, Itamar. *The Brink of Peace*. Princeton: Princeton University Press, 1998.
Rabinovich, Itamar. *Waging Peace: Israel and the Arabs at the End of the Century*. New York: Farrar, Straus and Giroux, 1999.
Robinson, Glenn. *Building a Palestinian State: The Incomplete Revolution*. Bloomington: Indiana University Press, 1997.
Ross, Dennis. *The Missing Peace: The Inside Story of the Fight for Middle East Peace*. New York: Farrar, Straus and Giroux, 2004.
Rouyer, Alwyn R. *Turning Water into Politics: The Water Issue in the Palestinian–Israeli Conflict*. New York: St. Martin's Press, 2000.
Savir, Uri. *The Process: 1,000 Days that Changed the Middle East*. New York: Random House, 1998.
Shehadeh, Raja. *From Occupation to Interim Accords: Israel and the Palestinian Territories*. London: Kluwer Law International, 1997.
Watson, Geoffrey R. *The Oslo Accords: International Law and the Israeli–Palestinian Peace Agreements*. Oxford: Oxford University Press, 2000.

Chapter Eleven

Aruri, Naseer H. *Dishonest Broker: The U.S. Role in Israel and Palestine*. Cambridge, MA: South End Press, 2003.
Dumper, Michael. *The Old City of Jerusalem in the Middle East Conflict*. Boulder: Lynne Rienner, 2002.
Enderlin, Charles. *Shattered Dreams: The Failure of the Peace Process in the Middle East, 1995–2002*. New York: Other Press, 2003.
Lesch David W. *The New Lion of Damascus: Bashar al-Asad and Modern Syria*. New Haven: Yale University Press, 2005.
Lesch, David W., ed. *The Middle East and the United States: A Historical and Political Reassessment*, 4th ed. Boulder: Westview Press, 2007.
Meital, Yoram. *Peace in Tatters: Israel, Palestine, and the Middle East*. Boulder: Lynne Rienner, 2006.
Ross, Dennis. *The Missing Peace: The Inside Story of the Fight for Middle East Peace*. New York: Farrar, Straus and Giroux, 2004.

Rubenberg, Cheryl A. *The Palestinians: In Search of a Just Peace*. Boulder: Lynne Rienner, 2003.

Said, Edward. *The End of the Peace Process*. London: Granta Books, 2002.

Swisher, Clayton E. *The Truth About Camp David: The Untold Story About the Collapse of the Middle East Peace Process*. New York: Nations Books, 2004.

Wright, J. W., ed. *Structural Flaws in the Middle East Peace Process: Historical Contexts*. New York: Palgrave, 2002.

Chapter Twelve

Cohen, Lenard, Brian Job and Alexander Moens, eds. *Foreign Policy Realignment in the Age of Terror*. Toronto: Canadian Institute of Strategic Studies, 2003.

Esposito, John L. *Unholy War: Terror in the Name of Islam*. New York: Oxford University Press, 2002.

Halliday, Fred. *Two Hours that Shook the World, September 11, 2001: Causes and Consequences*. London: Saqi, 2002.

Lesch, David W., ed. *The Middle East and the United States: A Historical and Political Reassessment*, 4th ed. Boulder: Westview Press, 2007.

Meital, Yoram. *Peace in Tatters: Israel, Palestine, and the Middle East*. Boulder: Lynne Rienner, 2006.

Podeh, Elie. *From Fahd to ʿAbdallah: The Origins of the Saudi Peace Initiatives and Their Impact on the Arab System and Israel*. Jerusalem: Harry S. Truman Institute for the Advancement of Peace, 2003.

Ruthven, Malise. *A Fury for God: The Islamist Attack on America*. New York: Granta, 2002.

INDEX